OverSuccess

Healing the American Obsession with Wealth, Fame, Power, and Perfection

Jim Rubens

GREENLEAF
BOOK GROUP PRESS

Published by Greenleaf Book Group Press, LLC
4425 Mo Pac South, Suite 600
Longhorn Building, 3rd Floor
Austin, TX 78735

Distributed by Greenleaf Book Group LLC

For ordering information or special discounts for bulk purchases, please contact Greenleaf Book Group LLC at 4425 Mo Pac South, Suite 600, Longhorn Building, 3rd Floor, Austin, TX 78735, (512) 891-6100.

Design and composition by Greenleaf Book Group LLC
Cover design by Greenleaf Book Group LLC

Publisher's Cataloging-In-Publication Data
(Prepared by The Donohue Group, Inc.)

Rubens, Jim (James M.)
  OverSuccess : healing the American obsession with wealth, fame, power, and perfection / Jim Rubens. -- 1st ed.

    p. ; cm.

  Includes bibliographical references.
  ISBN: 978-1-929774-76-0

1. Success--Psychological aspects--United States--21st century. 2. Success--Social aspects--United States--21st century. 3. Self-esteem--United States--21st century. 4. Motivation (Psychology)--United States--21st century. 5. United States--Social conditions--21st century. I. Title. II. Title: Over success.

BF637.S8 R82 2009
158/.2   2008931124

Printed in the United States of America on acid-free paper

12 11 10 09 08   10 9 8 7 6 5 4 3 2 1

First Edition

Like political campaigns, writing is far tougher on the spouse. So, this is dedicated to my wife, Susan, for putting up with date-night conversations about debt and dopamine receptors and for tolerating the self-imprisonment I require to fashion an intelligible paragraph, and to my son, Matthew, who grew out of his sandbox into a generous and thoughtful boy while I fashioned these 1,600 paragraphs.

CONTENTS

THE INCUBATION OF MY OBSESSION

If you desire glory, you may envy Napoleon. But Napoleon envied Caesar, Caesar envied Alexander, and Alexander, I daresay, envied Hercules, who never existed.[1]
—Bertrand Russell, 1930

MY SECOND EPIPHANY STRUCK me in 1973 as I stood hitchhiking home in a bone-chilling November drizzle. I had finished my last day at work at the recycling center that I had just sold for the tiny sum of $3,200, the proceeds going to charity anyway. To me, my woolen ski hat and grease-stained Goodwill clothing were proud badges of anti-consumerism. To the stream of Thanksgiving holiday traffic that passed me by, I looked like a homeless alcoholic. No one would risk a dirty car seat or a deranged conversation. The leaden clouds, the cold and barren pavement, and my crumbling dignity merged into a bleak, gray soup.

As I watched the shiny new cars pass by with their clean seats and working heaters, I resolved at that moment to abandon my two-year experiment with hippie communes and voluntary simplicity. There were no brownie points for small-time do-gooders. I would dress in new clothes and drive a new car with a working heater. I would mark my place in the world, as do most Americans, with visible achievement. It was there in the November gloom, at the bottom of America's status hierarchy and unable to get a ride, that I decided to achieve success the way most of us define it.

Thirty years later, my wife and I are sitting on our deck in the company of a couple of close friends, sipping from our fat goblets of red wine. It is one of those two or three warm and perfect June evenings that occur each year in New England. Sunset over the mountains has faded to shades of salmon and soft azure. We watch a few thousand fireflies dance over the unmowed meadow, early in their six-week mating season. The males cruise a few yards of airspace above the meadow, blinking for female attention. The outnumbered females can afford to be choosy. If the male blinks are bright and long enough—an unfakeable indicator of his genetic fitness and the size of the food gift he will offer to nourish the female and her eggs—a receptive female will blink back from her perch. Back and forth go the blinks and responses, as multiple males converge on the female. The pile-on decides which are the nimblest and strongest males, the ones who deliver their gifts and successfully consummate the sexual encounter. Later in the season, after many males have died off, females outnumber males, and the males become choosier. They will reject females, likely by smell, that are often infected by an internal parasite rendering them barren.[2]

Fireflies are different from us humans because their battles for success, status, and survival are bounded by natural limits. Spent from his first mating, a male firefly is thereafter limited to smaller food gifts. Outlandishly bright blinks are a waste of bioluminescence, because brightness as perceived by a potential mate falls off quickly with distance. Fireflies who blink too frequently, too long, or too promptly are simply ignored as those of an irrelevant, alien species.

We humans inherited our ambition from the fireflies and reptiles. Like all animals, we are hardwired not only to eat, sleep, explore, and have sex but to strive to achieve a high and secure place in our species' hierarchy. We pursue success through status and social visibility, using varied, sophisticated, and unbounded markers of wealth, fame, beauty, and power as indicators of our reproductive and survival prowess. Like the fireflies, we are equipped with neurotransmitters and receptors that make us exquisitely sensitive even to the most nuanced of these markers. At any moment, we know exactly where we stand. Moreover, we start knowing it early: by age six, children can accurately identify the social rank of all members of their group.[3] Within one-tenth of a second after meeting a stranger, we subconsciously measure our relative status, making snap judgments about that person's attractiveness, likeability, trustworthiness, competence, aggressiveness, and power. Our conscious minds pick up from there, tricking us into thinking that these powerful and automatic intuitions are under our rational control.

Unalterably embedded in the psychology of the human animal is the drive to achieve—and display—as much status as we can. We will spend days in hot pursuit of a cell phone number ending in two zeros; we will work for a lifetime on a masterpiece no one will comprehend for two generations; we will kill over a smudged sneaker. Embedded into our brains and behavior by evolution, our pursuit of success, and the status it confers is the central motivator of humankind's most horrific excrescences and celestial achievements.

But today in America, our natural pursuit of success has turned into an obsession, one that too many of us pursue mindlessly and without satisfaction. I call this OverSuccess, an unslaked obsession with winners and with the markers of winning. This book explains how—and why—our innate ambition has become unhinged from reasonableness, our healthy and necessary status-seeking turned into a pathology.

The individual and collective disease of OverSuccess is depriving us of satisfying and meaningful lives. It will continue to dispossess us from our authentic selves until we take the big and small steps required to restore the primacy of healthy success.

AMERICAN SUCCESS: BLESSING BECOMES AFFLICTION

The pursuit of success has made humans the earth's most successful species ever. In our quest to be top dog, we create not only ephemeral little monuments to our egos but also lasting material and cultural progress. Our globe's go-getters have brought us not just subprime mortgages, purses the size of duffel bags with gold hardware, and college admissions consultants who cost as much as our grandparents' houses did; they have also given us musical polyphony, constitutional government, clothespins, calculus, and one-size coffee cup lids.

And nowhere has success succeeded as it has in America. Our nation's founders launched a political, economic, and social system that is the world's most compatible with inborn human motivation; they unleashed individual ambition and restrained it only where history had proven it harmful to the whole. The founders' experiment is a stunning achievement. Ambition's sweet fruits have concentrated in contemporary America as in no other place and time. In our short existence as a nation, we have enjoyed greater material quality-of-life gains than in all of prior human existence. The great good in the American system of success is far too valuable to discard with its flaws.

We are, first of all, living longer—and better. Since just 1776, we have more than doubled our lifespans from 30 to 78 years—an additional life and a half in which to become wise or to nurture grandchildren. When our nation was founded, death limited the length of the average marriage to twelve years, and forty percent of children had lost a parent before they turned 21.[4] Fewer than one hundred years ago, medical knowledge was so rudimentary that epidemics were considered immutable features of life, and Congress appropriated no research funding to combat the flu, a disease that claimed the lives of 675,000 Americans in 1918 and 1919.[5] Since then, we have achieved a remarkable victory over many deadly infectious diseases. Over the past century, accidental death rates have been cut by over half, infant mortality has decreased by 93 percent, and maternal mortality in childbirth has fallen by 99 percent. Since 1950, heart disease has declined by over half, and since 1960, five-year cancer survival has increased by over 60 percent.

We now live in the safest society in recorded history. Since just 1970, age-standardized death rates from all causes have decreased by 32 percent.[6] While environmental pollution continues to exact large health costs, even as science discloses new problems such as global climate change, American air and water have become much cleaner. Since 1970, air pollution is down 48 percent; twice the numbers of lakes and rivers are now safe for swimming and fishing.[7] The fraction of our population perishing in war and violence has dropped in the past few decades to tiny levels. "Today we are probably living in the most peaceful moment of our species' time on earth," says Harvard cognitive scientist Steven Pinker.[8]

And we prosper, at least by the blunt measures we now use to track economic progress. Poverty rates have declined sharply from the 60- to 70-percent range one hundred years ago to 11 to 15 percent since 1990.[9] While progress on reducing poverty has stagnated since 1970, an American family at the poverty line now has a living standard higher than 80 percent of the world population. Eighty percent of all episodes of poverty end in one year or less.[10] Fifty percent of Americans living below the federal poverty line have air-conditioning, 60 percent have microwave ovens and VCRs, 70 percent possess at least one car, 77 percent have a phone, 93 percent own at least one color TV, and 98 percent have a refrigerator. Of all American households, no more than one in 150 experience hunger on any single day because of inability to afford enough food.[11] Our public and private safety nets, even with their intolerable gaps in housing and healthcare, have almost banished involuntary hunger.

We have more money, time, and space. In 1900, Americans worked for most of their waking hours, starting full time during their teens. Today, we work about half our waking hours, but now we begin our full-time working lives in our early twenties and anticipate the likelihood of fifteen to twenty years of healthy retirement. Favorable economic trends have indeed slowed and even reversed for some of us since the mid-1970s, but over the last century, inflation-adjusted wages for the average American have increased four times.[12] Household income for African Americans is up by ten times in that period. Since 1950, the average floor space per occupant in the new American home has tripled.[13] We use all this space to contain a battery of material possessions whose number and conveniences would astound a time-traveler from just 1940.

Comfort has become wealth, for many. As of about 1980, America became the first society in history to support mass affluence. Over eight percent of U.S. households are now millionaires. After adjusting for inflation, this is twelve times the proportion of 1900.[14] As of 2006, one in five households earned a pre-tax income of at least $97,000. Five percent of all households, almost six million, earned an annual income of at least $174,000.[15]

We are better educated: high school completion is up fourfold since 1900 and college attendance has moved from rare to typical.[16] We have access to more information than ever; today's fourth grader with a $15 scientific pocket calculator has more computing power than all of the world's greatest mathematicians possessed a century ago and hundreds of terabytes of detailed, accurate information about nearly all subjects are free and instantly available on the Internet to almost every American. The incremental cost of instantaneous communication with one or more people anywhere in the world has dropped to zero. We take technological progress so for granted that we are blasé about this astonishing accomplishment.

In our daily lives we have ever-greater conveniences and creature comforts, at lower cost. Most Americans never lack for precisely the food and drink we desire. Our homes remain at a comfortable temperature year-round. We can take a long, hot shower daily, free of any physical effort but turning a control knob, chosen from among hundreds available in any price range or finish and whose pleasant design is the product of three thousand years' aesthetic refinement. We can summon at will the most sublime music of the past five centuries, flawlessly performed by the world's most gifted artists. Most of us can travel almost anywhere we wish. Levels of health, wealth, safety, nutrition, affordability, and features of consumer goods and services have all shown spectacular gains.

Our ambition has led to a greater measure of justice. We have increased social equality for many of us who were disenfranchised, such as racial and ethnic minorities, women, and disabled people. Our personal freedoms and material abundance have inspired half the world's people to establish democracies like our own.

So why are sixty million American adults—one in three of us—pervasively dissatisfied with our lives? Why do so many of us feel overwhelmed, intimidated, discouraged, isolated? Compared with those born before World War II, why is major depression seven times more likely than among those born after 1970? Why are one in four of us addicted to at least one substance or behavior? Why is America drowning in record personal and public debt? Why did over 100,000 people humiliate themselves with a desperate and hopeless fifteen seconds in the spotlight auditioning for Fox's *American Idol*?[17] Why are eighty percent of women unhappy with their bodies?[18] Why does America consume eighty percent of the world's Ritalin-class drugs and produce eighty percent of its serial killers?[19]

What is it about contemporary America—more so than any other time and place—that connects such a constellation of personal and social pathologies, from the swelling prevalence of depression, behavioral addictions, eating disorders, debt, materialism, sleep deprivation, and family breakdown, to rudeness, fame fixation, ethical collapse, mistrust, and monstrous acts of personal violence?

LOSING OUR PLACE: OVERSUCCESS AND THE AMERICAN OBSESSION

Not long ago, Americans knew where we belonged. We lived in small towns and neighborhoods. We knew our neighbors well enough to entrust them with the discipline of our own kids. We were valued members of churches, social clubs, sororities, fraternal orders, and extended families living close enough to share Sunday dinners. Our dreams were big, but not beyond our capacities to achieve them.

During times still in our elders' memories, most Americans compared themselves to the varied and generally average people with whom we lived in small, geographically bound groups. Almost everyone could earn recognition and status for some valued role. We might not be the richest guy in town, but we baked the best bread. We might not be as smart as the schoolmaster, but we could tie knots better than anyone else. We might not be a princess, but people applauded our 12-figure dance on Saturday night at the Grange hall. Most of us could find a place among our tribe: the good mother, the singer who could always hold pitch for the national anthem, the teller of campfire stories, the gardener who knew all the local insects, the prettiest girl at the prom, the shepherd who rarely lost a lamb during birthing. We knew the members and dimensions of our tribe; we knew where we belonged. Even if one's contribution was modest, almost everyone was needed to ensure survival in a life where large institutions were non-existent or too slow moving or distant to help.

Global social space is a phenomenon new to human history. Until the invention of agriculture about 10,500 years ago, social groups were not typically larger than the 100 to 200 people we can know personally. But since about the mid-1960s, we have increasingly focused outward on the global social space created by America and inward on our struggle to find recognition among its anonymous billions. But these have not replaced the close bonds of small society we have abandoned. Where we once found our place in local community, we now yearn for visibility in the world. We grab for material status markers and fixate on celebrities to dampen the frustration and fill the emotional emptiness.

Small society is also being eclipsed by ubiquitous, 24-7, mass communication media. Over the past six centuries, from Renaissance art to polyphonic music, printing and literacy, photography, film, and television, media have become more emotionally compelling, immediate, and everywhere. I trace this progression in Chapter 5 of *OverSuccess*. Americans now fill almost half our waking lives with content from these media, content dominated by those successful enough to hold our attention. So almost half our waking lives are occupied with vivid, intimate, but one-way relationships with the world's most wealthy, brilliant, beautiful, powerful, famous, and fascinating people. Consider the celebrities who define our appearance aspirations; they never appear without SWAT teams of plastic surgeons, clothing engineers, makeup artists, and digital retouchers. Those at the top of every other realm of human endeavor are equally scrupulous at managing their images and status. But we are generally not conscious of this reality when we compare our digitally unretouched selves to the globe's most successful people. Media ownership is also concentrated in an increasingly small number of hands. The result is larger audiences for the successful, but fewer places that allow ordinary people to gain sustaining recognition.

You may be the top bicyclist at Peru State College in Nebraska, but you're no Lance Armstrong. You may run a thoroughly competent computer repair business, but you are a peasant compared to Bill Gates. You may be the smoothest jazz trumpeter in Fairbanks, but hearing Wynton Marsalis makes you cringe at your clichés. As I show in Chapter 4, the competitive benchmarks of success have skyrocketed, and top prizes have become toweringly desirable—but unattainable for most. The world's successful people are more gifted, better prepared, and more highly motivated than ever before, not to mention streamlined for success by parents and mentors starting inside the womb—and we know it. The lavish attention and gargantuan winnings at the top of the global meritocracy have intensified competition and lured tens of millions of us contestants away from the small, invisible vineyards of kin and local place. America stands alone in history in promoting and rewarding individual success—and making psychological and status defeat a mass phenomenon.

I log on to AOL, one of America's top four most-visited websites, to process the morning email. I can slightly customize my initial welcome screen, but I cannot bypass the daily flux of iconic images. Oprah Winfrey, Donald Trump, Albert Einstein, Bill Gates, Bono, Princess Diana. Simultaneously fascinated and intimidated, I go on to read exactingly descriptive profiles of America's twenty-five most envied people, who tell me that they are smarter, richer, more famous, and have better hair and sex than I do. Next up on my homepage, further roughing up my bruised ego, are lures enticing me to spring for the top ten most expensive homes, cars, or vacations.

The media make us desperately want what we can't have. *Architectural Digest* and *People* broadcast the new wealth and sophistication benchmarks in mega-pixel detail, implying their accessibility to ordinary people. These false messages of accessibility have tricked almost half of us into thinking that we are now or will someday be wealthy. Three in ten of us think we will someday be famous. Even the highbrow *New York Times Magazine* engages in this same trickery, but while aiming at a readership already within America's top five percent of earners. In 2005, the magazine ran a style-section photo feature with the tagline "Beyond the celebrity sightings is a private Aspen outsiders rarely get to see."[20] But thanks to the *Times*, we do see these celebrities at play, in excruciating Technicolor. We become at once insiders and more outsiders than ever. My own modest personal successes are mocked by the *Times'* lurid, double-page spreads of flawless real estate, global power couples, and their Stanford-bound progeny whose cheekbones are secured only through three generations of rigorously class-selective breeding.

The more sensitive among us are starved for social recognition and obsessed by success because both have become so much more valuable and difficult to get. Progress and material comfort have ceased to make us happier. We are trapped on a hamster treadmill of ever more rapidly rising measures of success that we can never attain. The gold ring we think we've grabbed turns into a trinket in a Cracker Jack box as soon as we see that it's standard issue in our new, higher-reference group. This pointless pursuit turns into self-absorption, frustration, and a sense of personal failure.

As I'll show, success benchmarks are accelerating upward in every realm of endeavor and along every barometer of status. If you build your own small but growing fair-trade cookie company, your efforts and invention feel dwarfed by Newman's Own. Your hybrid Lexus shrinks in significance when your neighbor gets a limited edition Tesla all-electric. You publish a novel that gets a nice review in *Time* and optioned for a movie; someone else's face from your college yearbook gets the magazine's cover. Your cool new cabin cruiser becomes an embarrassing cipher in the wake of the world's largest private yacht, which is now longer than a World War II battleship. You endow a local homeless shelter; Bill Gates' foundation cures malaria. Your thousand-dollar-a-night vacation and million-dollar home have become uselessly middle class. It's no wonder that people with half-million-dollar incomes (the bottom third of the top one percent) look enviously at the aspiration group above themselves and describe American society as "unfair."[21]

These escalating benchmarks both juice up and frustrate our innate success drive. The result is a perfect storm that has turned the healthy pursuit of worthy goals into the American obsession that is OverSuccess.

OverSuccess is an acute problem for every ambitious and status-conscious person in America, which is to say most of us. It especially afflicts the nearly 80 million in my baby boomer generation. Reared in a time of endlessly rising expectations, we are now confronted by age discrimination, the topping-out of our careers, the bankruptcy of federal retirement programs, and our impending mortality. Unless we change our attitudes and actions—unless we change our nation's culture—we will die alone and unhappy with our basalt countertops, Sub-Zero wine storage, and massive credit card debt. As I explore in Chapter 9, males in all age groups bear the greater burden of the obsession. Men are soon to become the new economic underclass. Because of his greater biological sensitivity to status contests, the rise of the collaboration economy, and the offshoring of manufacturing jobs not requiring advanced education, the typical American male absorbs well more than his fair share of the psychological injury of status defeat. This is not to shortchange concern about OverSuccess and females, 80 percent of whom are bludgeoned by magazine covers into disliking their own bodies, and who are torn more than men in the conflict between work and family.[22]

OverSuccess promises to become more toxic unless we confront our allegiance to impossible status yardsticks. The soon-to-arrive, next generation of major technological breakthroughs further jack-up success pressures. Mediated reality—think of it as the thought-controlled, hardware-free version of SecondLife—will soon replace television and film as our medium of choice. The commercial avatars with whom we will relate, virtual creatures unbounded by reality and cleansed of unwanted flaws, will make "normal" people boring. Within a generation, walk-in clinics will offer cut & paste repairs to our own genes. As I show in Chapter 3, just as plastic surgery, Paxil, and Provigil have become accepted tools for personal advancement, so will embryo selection for intelligence and social dominance be considered as necessary as SAT test-prep so as to ensure that our children can compete in an OverSuccessed world. Serious moral cautions will tame but not stop the intensification of these forces.

It's time to confront OverSuccess—and to do it without confining our assessment of the problem to the standard rubrics of either left- or right-wing ideology. The right decries our deteriorated traditional values, but it dismisses concerns about American success culture as whining victimology or neo-Luddism. To the left, America's problems are irredeemably linked to the shortcomings of competition and economic progress. Neither political construct provides a sufficient or practical framework for solutions to the syndrome of OverSuccess. The proposals I offer in this book will, I believe, transcend that divide, working as they do from practical optimism about America's ability to invent new ways to make success more compatible with more widespread satisfaction with life.

Unlike most treatments of our excesses, my prescription does not look to the European social democracies for cures. Nor do I suggest dialing down American ambition, individuality, and our pursuit of excellence and achievement. Suiting up in hemp and Birkenstocks, choking on teargas at anti-globalism rallies, and rejecting the earthly delights may be an answer for some people, but not for me, not for most of us. Instead, I show how America and Americans can tame OverSuccess while continuing our quest for recognition and excellence. I offer twenty specific and workable strategies to heal our success obsession, from cleaning up our open sewer of bad manners in public (starting with ourselves), to curing status defeat with gene therapy, to grafting millions of new, small social groups onto global society. The intention of this book is to free me and tens of millions like me from the hamster's treadmill.

FROM FAST TRACK TO COUNTERCULTURE: MY INITIAL FLIGHT FROM SUCCESS

Painful firsthand experience had led to my commitment to helping us all overcome OverSuccess. I tell my story here because it is a cautionary tale and because I could not have written this book without having lived through OverSuccess myself.

I'll start on a warm Saturday afternoon in 1971. I had nearly completed the degree requirements for my chemistry major at Dartmouth College. Taking a break from a loud outdoor party, I took a walk deep into the woods for some quiet contemplation, but instead was blindsided by my life's first epiphany. I was suddenly overwhelmed by an awareness of the exquisite delicacy in the relationships between the patterns of plant growth and sun, wind, slope, soil type, and moisture. I had of course seen all these things before, but I had never felt the awe I was experiencing at this moment. I sat down on a log to absorb what I was seeing and noticed my boots, manufactured in Korea of plastic, leather, and steel. I was horrified to realize how the subtle perfection of the natural environment was utterly incompatible with the modern human world, with the waste and destruction associated with everything I wore and ate. Over the next few days, I tortured myself with images of Ohio's Cuyahoga River, so polluted it caught fire, and of the news photograph I had seen of nine-year-old Kim Phuc running naked and screaming, half her skin burned off in a Vietnam napalm attack.[23] I had wanted to be a research chemist, but my aspirations were crushed by my new sensitivity to the uses to which this science had been put. Within a few weeks, I dropped out of college.

When I left Dartmouth, I purged myself of every conventional notion of success. I abandoned all but the most basic material possessions and the ambition my father had worked so hard to instill in me. My father was an orphan, driven by his need to prove himself to the world. He left home in Connecticut's affluent Fairfield County each morning to commute to Manhattan's Madison Avenue, departing too early to speak with his children, and returning in mid-evening, bone tired and stressed beyond his capacity by the adman-eat-adman corporate politics of the 1960s advertising business. On weekends, he cocooned himself in headphones, his jazz blotting out family life. Before the age of the remote control, he was scrupulous about killing the audio as he watched advertisements on TV—even his own. He survived on and despised commercialism. I learned irony early.

My mother, laconic, tender, self-absorbed, often forgot to prepare meals, caught up as she was in her own psychological struggles. My siblings and I would scrounge the barren refrigerator, foraging past the moldy ricotta and partially consumed cans of frozen orange juice opened months before. By the time I entered prep school (courtesy of my grandfather's education trust fund), my teenaged sisters had learned to shop and cook for themselves. When my parents announced their divorce, my sister eased the tension by expressing our shared relief that their arguing would no longer keep us awake in fear many nights.

The high spot of my prep-school years was academics, where adult influence was greatest. But all-boy residential life was a lab rodent's nightmare of twisted pubescent sexuality, a psychic concentration camp of acne flares and the boys' merciless taunting of any visible sensitivity. Sometimes, I was the perpetrator—for example, visiting the dorm room of our class's obsessive-compulsive and rotating by ten degrees his exactingly positioned desktop accessory. Sometimes, I was the victim, my milky skin and peach fuzz firing the barely concealed aggression of the football team captain, consummation from whom I narrowly escaped. My troubled family life, as well as these brutal prep-school experiences, hardened into my adolescent decision to get rich fast and so escape society's stifling norms and authorities. I imagined myself inventing something like the Polaroid camera and collecting royalty checks fat enough so that I could say and do whatever I wanted for as long as I lived.

Instead, I dropped out of college. I have often asked myself: who in hell authorized an adolescent to decide that the adult me would be a college dropout? Like many of my peers, maybe I was given too much. We attacked or rejected everything we received. At college, one clique of over-indulged kids would shuffle slackjawed, eyes bloodshot, into the dining hall on Sunday mornings, making a conspicuous show of how wrecked they were from their weekend's psychedelic and barbiturate binge. Many in my class would boast that we had the highest dropout rate in College history. Like draft card burners, we made a big show of repudiating our meal tickets. Most of us would crawl back into investment banking a few years later.

After dropping out, I became as poor as a middle-class kid could be in the wealthiest nation in human history. I gave away all my scrupulously accumulated summer earnings to the Cambodian refugees, and went straight to work as close to the bottom of society as I could—collecting scrap metal from New Hampshire dumps. In the years before they were turned into lined landfills, garbage dumps stank of smoldering mattresses and maggoty meat that fed rats the size of small cats. But the dumps were also treasure chests of industrial raw material, courtesy of America's bulimic consumer economy. I learned the junkie's trade from a white-haired, five-foot-three Irishman with hands stained as black as used crankcase oil. He showed me how to harvest copper from dead refrigerators. I used twelve-inch bolt cutters to snip the tubing. Don't waste time fussing for the last half-inch. Quickly pull your head aside to avoid breathing in the acrid almond smell of the escaping Freon. We had no idea that we were helping to double the size of the earth's ozone hole.

I cashed out my copper every few days at Roger Henry's nearby scrapyard, making the equivalent of about thirty dollars an hour—a bonanza compared with the going $1.60 minimum wage. Roger took a liking to me and hired me to sort brass and copper and weigh up the deliveries of the incoming customers. This allowed Roger to retire to his kitchen to play poker in his pajamas for most of the day. After a few months, he invited me to join these smoky bull sessions around his chrome-legged Formica table. I never played, but I got to know people as alien to the Fairfield County social classes of my childhood as you could get. They had bad grammar and worse teeth, but they were wise and cagey and tender and knew several times more than I did about life.

The owner of a larger scrap operation spotted my junkyard talents and hired me to cut steel in Barre, Vermont. This job required me to spend eight hours a day stooping over auto rear ends and grader blades with an acetylene cutting torch that I had to keep aimed as steady as a shotgun tracking a flying clay. I would ignore the flakes of molten rust that popped off the cut line into my hair or inside my stiff leather gloves. Hot rust sandwiched by a glove onto the back of my hand felt like about two hornet stings. The welts took about two weeks to heal.

At the more interesting offsite jobs, I would convert a train wreck or an obsolete factory into the maximum five-by-one-foot dimensions that made #1-grade scrap steel. For one sweltering, mid-summer week, I dismembered the metal guts of a mothballed chicken-processing plant. No one else would tolerate the stench. To cut the steel, I first had to burn through the half inch of chicken fat that had congealed over every inch of the equipment. The fat did not actually burn; it evaporated in a cologne of rancid barbecue, permeating into my clothes, hair, and lungs. That week confirmed my nascent vegetarianism for life.

Back pain forced me to quit after six months. My days were spent on my feet, my torso bent at my lower spine, my hands about a foot from the ground. A few minutes after I assumed this position, the pain would numb out. After work or when I was in other body positions, the pain became intolerable. My co-workers, French-Canadians with few other opportunities in this dying mill town, stayed on. I had other options.

I returned to New Hampshire and, along with some other back-to-the-land types, opened a free summer camp to accommodate the Day-Glo pilgrimage of teens fleeing orthodonture and suburban barrenness for northern New England's promised land of cheap drugs and free love. What these disappointed teens found instead was a bunch of earnest, clean-living nature lovers who only looked like hippies. Our campers feigned little interest in my lessons on how build water wells and stonewalls. I lived on a bucolic hilltop in a wood-heated, one-room cabin with a rain-barrel water supply, trading free rent in return for work building a woodshed. My abundant leisure hours were filled with my studies of obscure, Russian soil-science texts, organic gardening, hiking, and playing washtub bass at potluck dinners and music parties that were spontaneously organized most nights. I was blissfully unconcerned about my prospects for return to a conventional career track. For me, this happy, healthy life among friends was success, a word I never even thought to employ at the time.

Maybe subconsciously putting a stake through the heart of my father's vicarious hope for his elder son, and in a final act of wholesale rejection of American economic and cultural values, in 1972 I joined the Wooden Shoe, one of the period's first rural communes. *Life* magazine had just run a two-page photo spread on commune life, which to horrified parents must have looked like an Appalachian poverty scene. There were indeed sex and drugs, but rather less than *Life* promised. We spent our days weeding carrots, boiling dirty diapers, and erecting barns and sheds with salvaged building materials. I insulated the house walls with layers of scrap lumber and cardboard refrigerator boxes. We had no electricity or phone. Naked children played in the dirt. Stew pots of bloody animal entrails simmered in the kitchen. Scruffy chickens milled around the front door. When a Long Island couple ginned up the nerve to see what had befallen their once-fast-tracked, Ivy-educated son, they were forced to bolt to their motel after an hour because they would not dare squat on the open-air latrine.

The locals, with their gun racks and chewing tobacco, were said to hate hippies, but we became fast friends. They taught us how to make head cheese from hog brains. We taught them how not to gawk at bare-chested women splitting firewood. We helped our neighbors through births and deaths; they helped us recover from a burned barn. Bonds like these had never developed in the suburbia we had fled. More than anything, the Wooden Shoe was an experiment in creating family and community around shared values of equality and respect for the land. Even child rearing was equally shared, with biological mothers and fathers yielding all responsibility for their offspring until their own childcare day came up on the calendar. All group decisions and disputes were resolved by consensus at Sunday meeting. One holdout on any matter would leave all ten or twenty of us watching the wood stove go twice from blaze to embers, as we sat knitting or chainsaw-sharpening on the scavenged but well-tended upholstery of our common room. One endless discussion resolved in agreement that Oliver (not his real name), jealous of a budding romance between his wife and a newcomer, would purge his feelings by watching the new couple engage in their maiden copulation immediately following the meeting.

After eighteen months I left the Wooden Shoe, as would everyone else within a few years, all of us returning to single-family housing and the nuclear family structure we once scorned. For most of us, try as we might, the submission of our individuality to pure egalitarianism and small-scale socialism was not sustainable. I returned to my volunteer work at the combination natural food store and counter-culture community center, where I ran the basement recycling operation. My job was to smash empty Bordeaux bottles contributed by the local academics who were torn between their love of the grape and their discomfort with the capitalist system that brought its wine at such low cost to warm conversation over their Danish-modern coffee tables. Our fifty-gallon drums filled with glass shards were then hand-carried to a waiting pickup truck by four R. Crumb characters, who were always hanging out ready to be drafted into whatever project needing doing: unloading wheat germ, picking up a visiting spiritual healer at the bus station, or guinea-pigging for someone's Rolfing apprenticeship.

To navigate the marginally operable community pickup truck over the 150 miles to the glass recycling factory required three males, one each for mechanical repairs, slide guitar, and bookkeeping. The truck, named something like Fred or Sweetwater, was fashionably vintage enough to blur its origins in the military-industrial complex. Its iconoclasm was worth far more than the days spent bloodying our knuckles on its rusted bolts and doing the endless brake, clutch, and front-end work that squeaked it through state inspections. More gasoline, granola, and wheatgrass cleansers were consumed along the way than the four barrels of broken glass were ever worth even at the peak of the market.

My budding business instincts told me that the viability of this approach to recycling was gravely doubtful. I phoned an expert at the Environmental Protection Agency, who told me that recycling could not be profitably done where I lived, so far from industrial markets. Not even slightly deterred, within a few months, I negotiated a lease on a plot of land near the Lebanon city landfill, where I organized the building of several huge, paved outdoor bins and the rental of a few trailer bodies to store glass, cans, paper, and cardboard for bulk shipment. Within weeks of opening for business, I was profitably recycling five percent of the entire residential solid waste from the surrounding twenty-town region. I got an out-of-the-blue offer for the operation and sold it, contributing the proceeds to an area nonprofit. The buyer was a freshly minted B-school grad, lured, no doubt, by an industry consolidation study, his eye on a corner CEO suite atop a glass tower far, far from this little town. During his first weekend as owner, he demonstrated his 20/60 corporate vision, backing one of his brand-new, highly leveraged diesel compactor trucks with its boorishly huge recycling logo into the front door of someone's Volvo. Before year-end, the budding conglomerator went Chapter 11.

FROM SUCCESS TO OVERSUCCESS

Having decided to become successful as I hitchhiked home in the drizzle from my last day at the recycling center, I assessed my portfolio: no credentials or contacts, $3,500 in savings, a new chainsaw, and common sense inherited from my Yankee grandfather. Within a month, I finagled some seller financing and purchased a three-family apartment house on the wrong side of the tracks in White River Junction, Vermont. I bought a used but newly painted pickup truck with a working heater and started my second business, as a tree surgeon. Initially, I had to take the jobs my competitors did not want. But within three years, I had learned my craft, hired employees, purchased new trucks and equipment, and developed a variety of new techniques, publishing scientific papers on two of them. I was now naming my price and had supplanted my two leading competitors to dominate the quality end of the regional market. The work was emotionally gratifying and financially rewarding, and it put me at the top of a field I had mastered. I often found myself in what psychologist Mihaly Csikszentmihalyi calls flow state—so immersed in my craft during many days that I lost awareness of time and self.

I spent the next fifteen years as a serial entrepreneur, starting, running, and selling businesses. I renovated that apartment house, increased its cash flow, leveraged it twice, and began to speculate in land and invest in and develop commercial real estate, far surpassing my rainy November financial goals. I became a millionaire a few times over and retired from business in my early forties.

I jumped directly into my truest passion, politics. In my first run for office, I was elected a (Republican) state senator, a job I thoroughly enjoyed, in spite of the bone-crushing blows of modern election campaigns. As a legislator, I selected and framed issues, mobilized constituencies, and navigated person-alities and bureaucracies to get good ideas made into law. During this rising trajectory of my public career, I bathed in camera light during press confer-ences, my opponents skulking in the rear of ballrooms, forced to tolerate my applause lines, sycophants and well-wishers beaming and waiting in line to shake my hand or offer their help.

Flash forward to today. By all external yardsticks, I am successful. In the financial top one percent, I could pose for the cover shot of a junk-mail come-on promising the American dream in return for a $10,000 franchise invest-ment. For the photo, I could smile in front of my million-dollar hilltop home in an exclusive exurb of meticulously restored brick federals, fitted with nickel hardware and granite countertops by the acre. Ten steps take me outdoors for a walk in my personal twenty-acre park, which I tend myself, enjoying the hard physical exercise and the resulting organized beauty, nature spilling containably back through our domestic boundaries. A recent family vacation involved private charter flights, organic meals on white linen, and a private bungalow set between wilderness rainforest and Pacific beach sand.

I've engaged in many worthwhile endeavors. I've served in elected office. I chair multiple volunteer organizations. I co-host a TV show and editorial-ize on controversial subjects of my choice. I do venture capital and real estate deals. Like millions of my generation, I am endowed with a pampered and stimulating life. My toughest challenges arise when I ask myself what creative, fulfilling, and meaningful things I should choose to do next. With my physi-cal needs and wishes thoroughly satisfied, I am the grateful beneficiary of the staggeringly immense gift of human material progress and the American culture that has so well fostered it.

But too gradually for me to notice, I traded the thoroughly satisfying, attainable goals of my youth for a reckless quest for relevance and purpose on a larger stage. From the foothills of serial entrepreneur and state senator, the peak of the next higher mountain appeared tantalizingly but deceptively close. The success I had earned in the form of money and, particularly, visibility and power were intoxicating; they increased rather than satisfied my appetites. My goals soared from reasonable next steps into the grandiose. I wanted to lead at the live edge of transformational change. So I left my safe senate seat, ran for governor.

Then came defeat and failure. It didn't matter that I had lost my primary race for governor by only 2,700 votes. At a post-election public hearing on the issue that weeks earlier had been my ticket to the front page, a vengeful committee chair forced me to wait until last to speak. All the media were gone, my press releases were irrelevant and unread, and my remaining aide too young, underpaid, and naïve to tell me that I was stone dead.

So I tried my hand again in entrepreneurship, but scaled up to my new aspirational benchmarks. I recruited Jim Fishkin, inventor of the deliberative poll, to launch an online democracy website which was to feature online deliberative polling.[24] Two rivals beat me to venture capital funding by two months. I dusted myself off and formed another company which would make personal financial, medical, and web surfing anonymous, allowing users to rent their personal data on a per-use basis to marketers without disclosing their identity. This startup foundered on impossibly overreaching negotiations involving IBM and Experian.

While my education-funding platform lived on to become state policy six years later, online deliberative polling is now being used in research settings, and I have used my experience to advocate worthy causes, these accomplishments provided me no visibility. I took failure hard. Rather than finding joy in the simple pleasures of a stone wall well built or my son's delight in learning to ride his bike, I mooned over the National Press Club speech I would never give. Rather than taking pride in organizing a movement that would defeat the legalization of casinos in my state or in signing a new commercial tenant for one of my properties—jobs I do well—I instead lusted after Morgan Stanley's advice on an industry consolidation I would never undertake. After I pulled the plug on my Internet startups, just seeing the cover of the bubble bible the *Industry Standard* would land me in a swamp of regret and self-criticism. My efforts at sustained introspection, my pleasure in friendships and in the deliciously contrapuntal fragrances of warm forest air—nothing could dull the stab I felt in my gut when I saw a politician basking in the camera lights while discussing my signature issues, or when I read about an inventor whose business vision became a life-enhancing new product with an eighty-percent world market share.

There are no second prizes for losers in America. Rather than sustaining me, my modest successes became the yardsticks of my failure. My million-dollar house, investment accounts, and political achievements were pointless and microscopic by comparison. Rather than finding comfort in material wealth and personal freedom, I wallowed in wants, obsessed by things beyond my reach, by what I did not have and what I could not be. Though I had far exceeded my original goals, I was psychologically no better off than the bedraggled hitchhiker I once was, who had thought success meant decent clothes and a warm car. Why, after so much success, did craving crowd my consciousness? Was there a defect in my faith, philosophy, or neurochemistry? Or is there something poisonous in the American success story?

After four years of difficult introspection and a very deep dive into the relevant sciences that might explain my feelings and the excesses of our era, I realized I was not alone in suffering from success obsession, from status defeat—from OverSuccess.

OVERSUCCESS: ITS DEFINITIONS, AND SOME CAVEATS

Before we go further, let me define more precisely what I mean by OverSuccess and its related terms. First, OverSuccess is different from genuine success. For the purposes of this book, *healthy success* is the process of attaining a personal goal—one for which we are motivated by some combination of altruism and love of mastery, accompanied by the natural desire for recognition that is in reasonable balance with the value of the goal itself. *OverSuccess* is an obsession with, a sustained effort to reach, or the attainment of a lofty goal—but an effort motivated largely by status concerns.

A success obsession can manifest itself as chronic and disproportionate goal-seeking, or consuming fixation upon a success object without expectation of gain, for example, celebrity worship. To fall into the OverSuccess trap, you can be an actor or an observer, an aspiring rock star with a tin ear, or a groupie. Generally in this book, failure means defeat in a social or status contest, rather than simply not accomplishing a goal.

When I use the term "success obsession," I am not implying a precise psychological diagnosis. While there is no one best word for a persistent and consuming behavior or motivation that does far more harm than good, "obsession" fits better than addiction or compulsion. As a part of its definition of Obsessive-Compulsive Disorder, the American Psychiatric Association's *Diagnostic and Statistical Manual of Mental Disorders* (DSM-IV) uses the term "obsession" to refer to ideas, images, or impulses that repeat themselves, interfere significantly with normal life, and cannot be stopped voluntarily. Obsessions are not cured by pursuing them. A compulsion is a repetitive behavior in response to an obsession. Addiction refers more specifically to a dependency upon a behavior or substance. In any case, recent neuroscience is showing that obsessions, compulsions, and addictions are surprisingly close biological siblings.

When I use the word "depression," I mean Major Depressive Disorder, as defined in the DSM-IV. The symptoms include: depressed mood most of the day and nearly every day, loss of interest or pleasure in most activities, significant weight loss or gain, difficulty sleeping or staying awake, constant fatigue or loss of energy, feelings of worthlessness, diminished ability to think or concentrate, recurrent thoughts about death or suicide, and impairment of ability to function in normal daily roles, with five or more of these symptoms simultaneously present during a minimum 2-week period.[25]

The obsessive pursuit of or fixation upon high status is central to OverSuccess. Status-seeking can manifest itself in many ways: we can chase attention, celebrity, notoriety, fame, respect, power, dominance, rank, title, education, knowledge, recognized achievement, wealth, possessions, or beauty. Common to all these is increased personal visibility. I call these types of status displays "visible success." Status display can be subtle, even undetectable to the average observer, or it can be as crudely obvious as a chromed-up Hummer. Status can be measured by who returns your phone calls or by how long you can speak without being interrupted. Before the Concorde was mothballed, high status for its routine passengers (who paid $6,000 for a 3.3-hour flight between New York and London) took the form of arriving latest at the gate with the least luggage. Status is always about showing off to some audience.

Critiquing the pursuit of status can be taken too far. The recognition of status is a healthy and necessary feature of properly functioning social organizations. Without status rankings, group action becomes mired in inefficient process and wasteful, sometimes physically dangerous power contests. We are often motivated to engage in status-yielding accomplishments by their inherent worth, by the pleasure of personal mastery, or by altruism, with our place in the pecking order of little or secondary concern. OverSuccess overvalues status, estranging it from its natural role as a motivator of cooperative human behavior, making status the only real goal. It confuses the laurel wreath of victory with victory itself.

OverSuccess takes form among individuals in different ways. Because of our diverse capacities and tolerances, what might be a success obsession for me might not be for you. The generalizations I make about humans and Americans fit only the aggregate population. We each have different personality traits, behaviors, and motivations that vary along a spectrum. There is no bright line between healthy determination and harmful obsession, between genius and schizophrenia, between talented comedian and attention addict. According to evolutionary theorists, schizophrenia, obsessive-compulsive disorder, and ADHD appear in such a high proportion of us (one, two, and four percent, respectively) that they must have had an adaptive purpose—enhancing human survival and reproductive fitness. For example, those with mild to moderate ADHD are more alert and responsive to random stimuli. The hunters who found and killed the food that carried our species through droughts and ice ages would be the medicated fidgeters in today's classrooms. Schizophrenics are strikingly adept at ignoring context and thereby seeing accurately through optical illusions, which has led Harvard psychologist Shelly Carson to say, "I have no doubt that the genes for schizophrenia are associated with the genes for creativity," while warning about medicalizing moderate differences in our psychologies.[26] Wherever the demarcation point, the line between giftedness and mental disorder is different for each individual and life stage. We must therefore be careful not to label the next Thomas Edison as OverSuccessed when he tests the thousandth design for his new light bulb.

To rely on any single explanation for America's success obsession is to grossly oversimplify. The syndrome has become pervasive in the U.S. not only because we are hardwired for success in a country whose citizens often succeed. We are just beginning to understand the relationships among genetic, psychological, physiological, socioeconomic, political, and cultural forces that shape our characters, motivations, and behaviors. Changes in cultural and social values can redefine the unacceptable and make it normal. America would not become ideal if all television were PBS instead of *American Idol* and all our free time were spent on family hikes instead of shopping. So take the explanations I offer in the coming pages as among the likely contributors to OverSuccess, each one significant but none a necessary and sufficient cause.

To provide support for this book's argument, I draw from, and make associations among, abundant new research in several still-too-segregated fields, including neuroscience, genetics, evolutionary psychology, economics, public opinion, and social epidemiology. Over the past decade, the quality of scientific research and statistical tools has improved markedly. Social science, still the under-appreciated bastard child of the sciences, is now better integrated with the "hard" sciences, its conclusions supported by far more rigorous techniques and large bodies of reliable, longitudinal data. Social science is not just for liberals anymore.

Unfortunately, it is not possible to fully explore human motivation and behavior without moving from established fact to theory and reasonable speculation. However levelheaded our conjectures, we must watch our backs. What we do not yet know about human behavior is far greater than what we know. Until embarrassingly few years ago, psychologists were probing ids for Oedipal complexes and penis envy. As a non-scientist, I can reach across knowledge gaps without wrecking my grant-getting ability the way professionals would, but I will distinguish fact from speculation so that you can draw your own conclusions. I have also attempted to avoid use of data driven by cyclical effects (i.e., recessions) rather than by the multi-decade trend to OverSuccess that began during the 1960s. If unattributed or uncited, claims made are my own.

The concept of OverSuccess is my own synthesis of research into the causes and symptoms of America's current social and psychological recession. My hope is that scientists, political and business leaders, and ordinary readers will be better able to understand OverSuccess and use the tools I offer to turn it back into healthy success.

Here, then, is the ground that I will cover in the pages to follow:

- I'll introduce the science that explains our urge to seek success (Chapter 2) and why that drive is amplified by American culture and technological progress (Chapters 3 and 4) and by contemporary media (Chapter 5).
- I will show how commercial culture is both a product of and a key contributor to OverSuccess (Chapter 6).
- I'll go on to document the impact of OverSuccess on our individual and social well-being, our behavior, the economy (Chapters 7 and 8), and the American male (Chapter 9).
- I'll suggest twenty voluntary and institutional cures for OverSuccess that will not compromise our personal freedom or dampen the ambitions of the talented that drive America's invention engine (Chapter 10).

2

THE SCIENCE OF OVERSUCCESS

Life is a continued struggle to be what we are not, and to do what we cannot.[27]
—William Hazlitt, 1820

WHAT IS THE ROOT CAUSE of OverSuccess? Over the past two million years, humans have adapted to life in small, relatively stable, and face-to-face social groups. But our social world has changed rapidly over the past few centuries, with these changes accelerating as of the mid-1960s. Today, the groups in which we live and work are in constant flux, and they number in the thousands to billions, from the 2,000-student high school to the 200,000-employee company to the two billion around the globe who share Hollywood's cultural products. The evolution of our brains has not kept pace. Our automatic psychological mechanisms are poorly suited to the contemporary social environment. To an unnaturally great degree, we are now forced to compare ourselves—and to compete against—an unnaturally large number of people, many of whom are inevitably better endowed and higher ranked than we are at whatever skills and qualities our group fosters.

With no respite from continuous exposure to our status superiors, we have damaged our psychological and physical health. In OverSuccess we are facing an evolutionary novelty—just as we are in the American obesity epidemic, arguably the result of the fact that humans are not evolutionarily engineered to resist eating the tasty, high-calorie foods that are suddenly within reach at almost every moment. So too, our unnaturally frequent experiences of social isolation and defeat in status contests are unprecedented from an evolutionary standpoint. The result is an epidemic of depression in post-1960s America— and the futile attempt at compensation that is OverSuccess.

In Chapter 1, I talked about OverSuccess as the result of an obsession with status. While "obsession" remains the best overall word to describe the Over-Success syndrome, in this chapter I will show the scientific parallels between OverSuccess and addiction. Sex, food, addictive drugs, and social attention are all measured by our brain's "reward system." When we discover something good for us, our reward system automatically adjusts our expectations and priorities, instructing us to seek more. But for those of us with genes predisposing us to addiction, our reward systems can be hijacked by unnaturally powerful stimulants. For some of us, the possibility of outsized success can be just as addictive as cocaine or pornography. OverSuccess also "cross-sensitizes" us to other addictions. A gambling addict and a status-contest loser are both more likely to become smokers or alcoholics. Cross-sensitization by OverSuccess helps explain why about one in four Americans are clinically addicted to a substance or behavior.

In this chapter I will show the links among social defeat, depression, and addictions and how they can damage our brain's reward and learning systems and cause physical illness. I will explore the emerging scientific basis for viewing OverSuccess as America's most costly social disease.

DOES STATUS COMPETITION EXPLAIN HUMAN PROGRESS?

To answer this question, I will ask two more. Why did the brains of *homo sapiens* and our nearest ancestors almost double relative to body weight in just two million years?[28] How did humans advance from being a biological flyspeck to dominating the entire planet in just the past 60,000 years, when the first symbol-wielders left Africa to girdle the globe?

More than any other benefit, our large brains gave us the ability to manage complex group social relationships. Our social groups, in turn, gave us collective survival and reproductive advantages far more potent than any we could wield individually and than any evolution had yet invented. Within the entire history of life on earth, our new facility within social groups is a "major transition," in the words of evolutionary biologist David Sloan Wilson and renowned sociobiologist Edward O. Wilson, as rare and momentous as the evolution of multi-cellular organisms or social insects. Each of these major transitions made cooperation within groups suddenly and sharply more advantageous, generating new forms of life that came to dominate the groups' ecosystems. "Our ability to function as team players in coordinated groups enabled our species to achieve worldwide dominance, replacing other hominids and many other species along the way," write the two Wilsons.[29]

The notion that evolution can act upon competing groups—even though only individuals have genes they can pass on—is known as "group selection theory," which until recently was discredited as scientific heresy. Group selection theory holds that individual fitness is determined at both the level of the individual competing within the group and at the level of the individual's group competing against other groups. Because humans can sustain beneficial cooperation among unrelated individuals in groups larger than a few dozen, we are unique (along with marmoset monkeys) in being subject to group selection. The fact that groups can provide survival and reproduction advantages to individuals gives us the first satisfying explanation for why, over the history of our species and in all known cultures, humans have been willing to make anonymous sacrifices to help non-kin group members. Bees and bacteria pull off sustained cooperation, but only because all group members share a familial genetic resemblance. Worker bees will forsake breeding to care for their colony because their selfish genes are better able to replicate via the survival of their close relatives. When myxobacteria, a highly social soil bacteria, confront food shortages, they will cluster in groups of 100,000, with a minority of individuals morphing into balls of hardy spores to wait out the bad times, the rest committing suicide and so forming a stalk to support the spores and aid in their future dispersal.

Human cooperative behaviors among non-kin include food sharing, caring for the sick and elderly, reproductive monogamy, adherence to moral restraints, and voluntary policing of anti-group behavior by others. I call this suite of self-sacrificing behaviors extended cooperation. There are no specific genes for extended cooperation. Instead, it was made possible by a toolkit of newly evolved human genes governing nuanced facial expression, speech and language, and acute sensitivity to fairness and status. Scientists have recently documented the rapid and recent evolution of specific brain regions associated with these social skills.[30] This toolkit enabled humans to manage a larger number of dramatically more intricate and varied social relationships than any other species.

But the killer app was not our genes for sophisticated social relations. Instead, it was that our social facility gave us the ability to invent and quickly establish group cultures and efficient behavioral customs. Whereas an advantageous gene can take thousands of years to spread among humans, advantageous cultural and behavioral norms can be adopted by mutual agreement within a group within a single generation. The adopted cultural and behavioral norms can either greatly foster or inhibit extended cooperation. Groups establishing cultures fostering extended cooperation could gain decisive fitness and competitive advantage over rival groups with less cooperative cultures. For example, extended cooperation allowed skills specialization and the painstaking accumulation of knowledge about medicinal plants, food locations, and climate patterns, knowledge that could be quickly transmitted at very low cost through teaching and learning. Equipped with the capacity for extended cooperation, humans could invent, refine, and pass on limitless types of advantageous group behavior. This competitive strategy was so successful that the enabling genes spread quickly among all humans.

But how did groups adopting cultures fostering extended cooperation so quickly prevail over and replace groups that did not? Samuel Bowles, a behavioral scientist and economist at the Santa Fe Institute, has built a theoretical model providing a plausible explanation.[31] Bowles' argument begins with natural climate change. Data from ice core samples taken from glaciers and ice caps have allowed scientists to provide fairly precise global average temperature estimates going back several hundred thousand years. These data show that the stability of Earth's climate over the past 10,000 years is highly atypical. Most of human and hominid history over the past two million years is punctuated by sharp swings in climate and by more than twenty ice ages. In mere decades, average temperature sometimes changed by half the difference between today's conditions and an ice age, with some continental shelf coastlines invading by miles.[32] Such changes would have devastated habitats and human food supplies, forcing group migrations and, often, territorial warfare over land and food.

Climate change therefore made our hunter-gatherer past a world of frequent and lethal conflict between groups. Reasonably sound and conservative data show that about fifteen percent of all hunter-gatherer deaths resulted from warfare. Wars were at least an annual event in one-third of societies, and rare in only one in five. Groups lacking the kind of extended cooperation that produced warriors willing to sacrifice their lives for the good of the group were defeated and quickly lost population. Ironically, frequent wars may have made us the exquisitely social, uniquely cooperative species we are today. Fortunately, as Bowles points out, our social facility genes give us the ability to quickly establish and transmit a cultural norm of tolerance and even cooperation with outsiders.[33] The dramatically declining rate of death by warfare over the past few hundred years shows that we have succeeded at teaching peace.

The upshot of our two-million-year history of evolution, ice ages, and warfare is that individual social facility within groups quickly became the distinct human advantage. The centrality of social organization to our species' extraordinary success explains the immense importance we attach to social relationships. Later in this chapter, I will discuss the more ancient part of our brain that rewards us for achieving high social status within our group. Reptiles win status by providing superior displays of brute force. But how, if not through brute force, do humans achieve high status where fairness, altruism, and cooperation are genetic and cultural imperatives? How did status-seeking change as we moved from small, more egalitarian hunter-gatherer groups to larger, hierarchical societies? How did we display status when there were few consumer products, no currency to accumulate, and no media to magnify our image? If it didn't happen through competitive accumulation, perhaps status was first earned through competitive giving.

Canadian cultural anthropologist Brian Hayden has amassed solid substantiation for the idea that status competition drove humans to form complex, non-egalitarian hunter-gatherer societies—and then to abandon these for trade, agriculture, and cities. He upends the more obvious theory that climate shift or population pressure forced the rapid and widespread adoption of agriculture. Simple hunter-gatherers lived lives of relative leisure, typically working less than 20 hours per week. Agricultural society, rather than being a technological blessing, seems to have made life worse for most making the transition. The stored foods of agriculture were less nutritional than fresh kills or pickings. Skeletal records of the earliest farmers show more tooth crowding and decay and more disease and malnutrition than among hunter-gatherers living at the same time.

Food abundance, Hayden believes, was more about status than sustenance. He finds evidence in the archaeological record of hunter-gatherers and in existing, non-agricultural societies for what he calls "competitive feasting." Hunter-gatherer power-seekers put on costly feasts to create political debts, cement social bonds, obtain favors and desirable mates, and display their power. But feasting required the accumulation of food surpluses, which meant that socially dominant individuals had to use domesticated crops and animals to bank food—and thus provide more elaborate feasts and accrue greater social benefits and debts.[34] Some farmed products, such as the earliest known Central American crops of chilies and gourds, provided little nutritional value but were used to display wealth and power at competitive feasts. Similarly, the first traded commodities and city-like building clusters appear to have had ceremonial and social rather than economic purposes.[35]

Abundance as an aggrandizer of status in pre-modern societies was not just a matter of serving rich and flashy food. Even as recently as the 1940s, north Pacific coast Native American tribal leaders held potlatches, showering lavish gifts on guests to display their wealth and increase their prestige. For the largest potlatches, the hosts required up to ten years to accumulate a sufficiently impressive supply of food and gifts. Gift-giving among hosts and guests would itself become competitive: Boys at a potlatch would vie with their peers in a grueling gift-exchange ritual. A challenger would select a rival boy to receive a gift; the recipient could either double the gift in return or refuse the gift and admit defeat.[36]

Indeed, recent experimental evidence confirms the existence of "competitive altruism" as an embedded human trait. In modern society, the most visibly generous group members earn the highest status in that group and are more frequently picked as team members for new tasks.[37] From feasting hunter-gatherers to the power contest between the Medicis and the Borgias to today's billionaire space race, an essential evolutionary truth has emerged: the status economy has been the major prod for human progress from our earliest days.

OVERSUCCESS AS EVOLUTIONARY MISMATCH

But OverSuccess has allowed the reach of the human brain to exceed its grasp. We no longer live in the world of local potlatches. There is evidence that our brains may simply not be evolved for healthy psychological life in the large, fluid social groups of our contemporary world—a mismatch compounded by our heavy and persistent exposure via the media to highly successful status superiors.

The British researcher Robin Dunbar—another anthropologist who has provided evidence suggesting that the chief advantage of our large frontal lobes is our capacity for more complex social relationships—wanted to know more about the "natural" size of human social groups. Dunbar compared the size of the typical social group of thirty-six species of social primate with the dimensions of their neocortexes. He found a highly consistent mathematical relationship: the larger the species' neocortex (relative to total brain volume), the larger the social group. Dunbar then applied his formula to the human brain, yielding the number 150—the largest social-group size among all primates.[38]

Direct evidence provides confirmation for Dunbar's number. Over the past century, anthropologists have documented group size among surviving hunter-gatherer societies in Australia, the South Pacific, Africa, and North and South America. The globe's most stable social units, the permanent villages and defined clans, range from 100 to 200 people. Anthropologist Lewis Binford has exhaustively compiled known group size for 185 hunter-gatherer societies: the median number is 162.[39] In an indication of the smallness of society even in pre-Renaissance Europe, people historically knew each other by a single name; surnames did not come into common use until the twelfth century.[40] Our everyday experience reinforces the idea that effective human groups top out at about 150 individuals. In corporate and military organizations, the operating cohesion of a unit begins to fragment somewhere above 150 members. Test yourself: count the number of people you would feel comfortable asking a personal favor. Few of us can make such a list beyond one hundred. Our larger cognitive capacity is finite; we are limited in the number of people with whom we can maintain a personal, predictable relationship. For sizes much beyond the small group, it is not possible to recall who is competent or trustworthy. The glue of social cohesion fails when it is spread too thinly.

The limits to our capacity to maintain personal connections suited us just fine for most of our species' existence. Then, just 10,500 years ago, we invented agriculture and food surpluses, for the first time supporting far larger, more complex societies. Until the invention of agriculture, all humans probably lived in clans limited in size to the number Dunbar posits. Food plenty and scarcity were shared about equally. Most personal relationships were lifelong. Clans were intimate, stable, and relatively closed and hostile to outsiders. All communication was person-to-person, not mediated by third parties. Anonymity was impossible, reputations known firsthand; liars, cheaters, and freeriders could not conceal themselves. This is not to say that, pre-agriculture, there was no interaction among members of different groups. Evidence from anthropological research and surviving hunter-gatherer societies—such as the existence of seasonal resource shortages, severe environmental shocks, trading, warfare, mate-seeking, and the presence language shared by ten thousand or more people—shows that we were not completely insulated from interactions with outsiders. But these interactions were probably exceptions to daily life.

Nevertheless, our lust for recognition combined with our phenomenal inventive powers have pulled us into ever larger arenas, shared by increasingly large numbers of people. Since the invention of agriculture, we have radically changed our physical and social environments in almost every respect. But these recent 400 generations of change amount to a speck in evolutionary time. To most of the genes that mediate our behavior, we are still hunter-gatherers living in small, face-to-face clans, as we and our near relatives did over almost the entire past two million years. Evolutionary theorists call this earlier period—otherwise known as the Pleistocene epoch—our Environment of Evolutionary Adaptedness, or the EEA.[41] Notwithstanding the immense changes we have made to our living environments, our EEA genes remain surprisingly useful, testimony to the vast adaptive advantage of human intelligence.[42]

Yet some of our genetic inheritances have become dodo birds and pandas in the human-constructed physical and social environment. Rather than bedrock upon which we must unconsciously and unquestioningly build our lives, some of our traits and motivations have become like baldness or failing eyesight, natural human characteristics that most of us do not want and for which we find little use. The genes governing our small-group social capacity, once sufficient to bind together trusted communities, have become unsuited to our society of billions. Scientists flag it under "evolutionary mismatch theory" when our inherited genes are no longer suited to—or are downright harmful in—the contemporary environment.[43]

Some of our evolutionary mismatches are easy to recognize and tragic. Tay-Sachs disease is a fatal childhood neurological disorder resulting from the low-probability combination of recessive gene alleles from both mother and father. A single one of these recessive genes was once vital to survival; it probably protected many Eastern European Jews from tuberculosis. Similarly, cystic fibrosis, as a single recessive-gene mutation first appearing about 50,000 years ago, may have once safeguarded European children from fatal infection by bacteria causing diarrhea. Thirty thousand Americans who lost the genetic lottery have two CF alleles and now suffer from this horrible disease that usually ends life at about age thirty. Similarly, the recessive sickle cell anemia gene, occurring more frequently in the descendants of black Africans, is today a useless and costly adaptation to malaria, now conquered at very low cost in the advanced nations by off-patent medicines.[44]

We would prefer to think that our preferences, motivations, and behaviors, unlike our chances of inheriting a genetic disease, are always under our control. But our mismatched genes also give us involuntary, junk behavior. Our appetite for sweet, fatty foods is a perfect example. Before the time when a twenty-four-hour Dunkin Donuts could be found every few blocks, wild-berry feasts and mastodon kills were few and unpredictable, a situation that constrained our cravings. Only over the past few decades in the advanced nations have low-cost, good-tasting calories become inescapably abundant. Programmed by genes that were once essential to our survival, our taste buds tell us to pork out on junk foods that have little nutritional value. But our risk today is high blood pressure and diabetes, not famine. Walk into any American shopping mall and see the morphological effects. That two-thirds of Americans are now overweight or obese is solid evidence that our inherited dietary preferences are genetic relics that exact high social costs.[45]

Our ability to function best in small groups may be such a genetic relic. If it is, it has a great deal of company. Psychologist Julia Sherman provides evidence for more examples of what she terms "behavioral fossils." Seasonal affective disorder, which renders sufferers more depressed during months with less daylight, may once have helped hunter-gatherers cope with the winter by dampening motivation and conserving energy when little of value could be accomplished and food was scarce. Bipolar disorder (BD) may have been a similar adaptation and a useful social trait in a subset of the population living in climates featuring short summers and long, cold winters, typical during the 23 ice ages of our Pleistocene past. BD, according to this theory, forced a warm-season surge and cold-season suppression of activity, harmful behaviors in our world of electric light and central heating.[46] BD has a lifetime prevalence of five percent of the population, no small burden on sufferers.[47]

Junk-behavior theorists note that the minority of individuals burdened by a predisposition to a disorder are the cost of retaining a useful, average level of the associated more mild behavioral trait in a population. Today, those suffering at the harmful tails of the behavioral distribution curve would probably rather be happy during winter than play their part in ensuring that humans are prepared to quietly hole up in a cave during the next ice age.

The biologically ancient human herding instinct, suited to small, stable groups, is another case of what has become an evolutionary mismatch. Once upon a time, to be expelled from one's social unit was a major threat to survival, creating a strong behavioral tendency to herd, to conform. New members of a social unit tend to ingratiate themselves with popular members as a means to gain protection and preferred access to useful information. To be popular in a group was a shorthand indicator of one's reliability, reflecting the combined effort of prior evaluation by others.[48] Herding behind high-status people makes social organization and group decisions more efficient. While once it was useful for people to go along to get along, today that instinct has turned toxic. Teen girls who secretly starve themselves to emulate checkout-line magazine covers are driven by the human instinct to copy others who appear to be popular.

The persistence of herding genes probably explains how, among many other phenomena, we can get swept up periodically in irrational investment manias. Isaac Newton and I share the experience. During the 1998–2000 tech stock bubble, I was suckered by WorldCom for about a quarter-million dollars. Newton lost over one million in today's dollars investing in the South Sea trade bubble of 1720. "I can calculate the motions of the heavenly bodies," said one of history's greatest physicists, "but not the madness of people."[49]

Three Columbia University sociologists demonstrated the power of the herding instinct in an ingenious experiment involving the musical preferences of over 14,000 people as indicated by their downloads of 48 songs previously unknown to them. When the subjects weren't told how popular a song was said to be, the number of times they downloaded it was very closely related to its quality. When popularity rankings were made obvious, the number of downloads—the success of a song—was tightly related to its reported popularity and bore a three-times-more-random relationship to quality.[50]

As such data suggest, herding is central to the syndrome of OverSuccess and to the way we react to people we think outrank us. We are hardwired to pay greater attention to high-status, successful people and to be repulsed by low-ranking failures. Carefully designed research has shown that monkeys will forgo a fruit juice reward so they can watch their high-ranking peers; these monkeys must be bribed even to notice their social underlings. Monkeys actually prefer to look at a boring, neutral test pattern rather than at a social failure, requiring ten percent extra fruit juice to view the lowest-ranking member of their group. Similarly, recent fMRI studies show that humans involuntarily pay more attention to high status individuals.[51] Similarly, we humans pay to gawk at high-ranking famous people, whether we read the tabloids or listen to National Public Radio's high-minded *Fresh Air* celebrity interviews.

All kinds of signs show how we are in love with success and shun failure: a recent Google search for the terms "personal success" and "personal failure" returns a ratio of 9 to 1 for success. For we moderns, herding has become another costly junk behavior that overrides rational analysis in a world in which sham popularity can be manufactured by the entertainment industry or feigned by an Internet penny-stock tipper.

Our ancient, evolved psychological mechanisms are mismatched to a world without small, stable society. We are unconsciously biased to view the world as it was before the emergence of large, anonymous, fluid social groups and the written and electronic media that permit them to exist.[52] Evolutionary psychologist John Price suggests that in our small-group past, a person could usually retreat from social failure by finding a new role or new group in which he or she could make a contribution that would be appreciated by others. Today, the global economy and saturation of cultural space by big media force us to compete within what amounts to a social unit of two billion people. Without our ancestral environment of small, stable, face-to-face social groups, we have fewer places to retreat from failure.[53] American commercial culture bathes us involuntarily for hours each day in an unnatural concentration of the famous and successful. We are forced to endure unending status contests with hundreds of world-class personalities, from real to partially to fully fictional. Being recognized for something meaningful in a community of 150 is likely; being invisible among billions is a virtual certainty. Being an invisible loser is linked to clinical depression.

Depression itself may be another evolutionary mismatch. Although it is a harsh therapy, depression may once have been our best remedy for loss in a status contest, a cure for social defeat. So say psychologists Leon Sloman and Paul Gilbert in their textbook, *Subordination and Defeat*, in which they marshal extensive evidence that major depression helped govern and ameliorate social and status relationships over human evolutionary history. We are geneti-cally endowed with an automatic behavior, which Sloman and Gilbert call "involuntary defeat strategy," originating at least 250 million years ago with the reptiles. Involuntary defeat strategy forces us to adjust our responses and expectations when we fail in competition over food, territory, or mates—and over the most common human conflict, social rank. Depression suppresses the loser's motivation to continue to struggle against the odds for status domi-nance. Depression is our species' automatic means of increasing group cohe-sion, avoiding wasted energy in unwinnable status contests, and diminishing risk of serious injury in continued conflict. However, when a depression suf-ferer cannot dial down his expectations or remove himself from the competi-tive circumstance, the depression can persist and deepen rather than lift.[54]

German research scientist Edward Hagen provides evidence for a related model for depression that explains the malady's social utility. Hagen views major depression and its associated involuntary incapacitation as a means for the sufferer to "go on strike" and thus gain greater attention and social sup-port. The limited and dispersed populations in hunter-gatherer society made members highly dependent on each other's roles and talents. In such circum-stances depression's unfakeable signal of involuntary incapacity was a stronger bargaining tool to secure support than anger or logical persuasion would be. Hagen's bargaining model is testable and supported by research. For example, being depressed actually elicits greater help from others, but unfortunately only when the depressed person has a working social support network.[55]

British sociologist George Brown's lifetime of field research provides sub-stantial evidence that depression is an evolved and "normal" response to social defeat. Over the past thirty years, Brown and other researchers using his scru-pulous methods have conducted detailed personal interviews of people whose lives they follow over several years. In all human cultures the researchers stud-ied, the number of current symptoms of depression, and the prevalence of depression over a subject's previous year of life, are both tightly linked with the number of harsh life events the individual experienced. Severe losses—for example, such as that of a loved one, of money, of a valued role, of social defeat (humiliation, in Brown's words), and the inability to withdraw from a defeat (Brown calls this entrapment)—are the leading causes of depression. These causes are aggravated by low self-esteem. In one of Brown's study populations, almost fifty percent of women who were suffering both humiliation and entrapment later suffered depression. At least eighty percent of depression episodes follow severe loss or social defeat. Nearly all remissions from depression follow a positive event in the subject's life. Depression symptoms are relieved without medical intervention in two-thirds of those experiencing such life improvements.[56]

As I will show in Chapter 7, rates of depression surged with the advent of industrial society—and surged yet more in post-World War II America. Our "epidemic" of depression is the fingerprint of our genetic mismatch in a world of unceasingly fluid relationships, constant challenges to our status within new groups, the geographic dispersion of extended family and the supports family would otherwise provide, the message that only we are responsible for our life's outcome, the barrage of status comparisons we see in mass media, and the incessant modeling of unattainable, stratospherically high goals. The circumstances of modern American life that cause depression are far more frequent and continuous than in the EEA. Compared with animals, in whom depression first evolved, we are far more likely to become entrapped and unable to change our circumstances. Reptiles do not have stock options that become exercisable only after five years' subjugation by a bullying boss.

In our geographically rootless, atomistic society, with its wizened family and small-group networks, someone who becomes depressed about their failure in our two-billion-person global village is unlikely to be noticed and to gain social support from the same huge village. Our televisions, drive-through restaurants, and shape-shifting workplaces are dumb to our cries for help. Today's small-group remedy for personal failure is a gym membership, corporate retreat, or Facebook posting. These groups are qualitatively weaker, more focused on self-interest, and easier to exit than a truly functional social unit. Today, our social success and failure are disconnected from people we know, love, and trust.

BRAIN CIRCUITS AND REWARD-SEEKING ADDICTIONS

Our brain's motivational control system, too, is mismatched to twenty-first-century America. Emerging science is showing that activities we find psychologically rewarding—the things we want or act to get, ranging from food to sex to social attention—all stimulate parts of the same brain circuitry. We now know that addiction is a disease of the brain's reward system and that most rewards, including social attention, can become addictive.

Before about 1995, scientists were able to glean only spotty knowledge about the human motivational system by studying people suffering localized brain damage and making inferences from animal models. Since then, the National Institutes of Health and other funding sources have pumped hundreds of millions of dollars into brain research using new technologies such as functional magnetic resonance imaging (fMRI) and positron emission tomography (PET) scans that give us precise, real-time maps of human brain response to experimental and real-world stimuli. We can precisely correlate brain biochemicals and brain structures with our emotions, desires, and motivations—and recognize how our motivational programming is at odds with global success culture.

Assessing the flood of new data, Jonathan Cohen, Director of Princeton's Center for the Study of Brain, Mind, and Behavior, concludes that the economic model of humans as purely rational gain maximizers fails to fit the evidence. Our primitive emotional brains far more powerfully influence our lives and decision-making than we would care to admit. For example, empirical studies show that people make economic decisions that are clearly not in their objective self-interest.[57] We discount and downgrade the value of future money payments far more steeply than is rational. Quite rationally, we prefer to receive $110 in 51 days over $100 in 50 days, but we irrationally prefer the $100 today over $110 tomorrow.[58] Most people are less likely to accept a crisp, new $100 bill from a scary-looking person than from one who appears harmless. We are more likely to purchase a cereal labeled "99% whole grain" than an identical product marked "1% additives."[59] Brain imaging studies show that our immediate choices are driven by the emotional brain, whereas our choices among long-term options are made in the prefrontal cortex and make economic sense.[60] Baylor College neuroscientist Read Montague describes these behaviors as "pathologies in human decision-making."[61]

The problem is that our brains are a mish-mash of semi-compatible components added over millions of years of evolutionary trial and error. Portions of our motivational system are located in brain circuits that long predate the evolution of our conscious, rational minds—and are far more powerfully controlling. Our brains are not general-purpose computers, neutral blank slates ready to rationally tackle whatever task we assign; instead, they are more like bundles of behavioral and motivational autopilots. "The mind is organized into modules or mental organs," writes Stephen Pinker, "each with a specialized design that makes it an expert in one area of interaction with the world. The module's basic logic is specified by our genetic program. Their operation was shaped by natural selection to solve problems of the hunting and gathering life led by our ancestors in most of our evolutionary history."[62]

While we can voluntarily override our brain's motivational mechanisms to varying degrees, our conscious minds often trick us into thinking that our decisions are made under rational control.[63] These automatic brain mechanisms operate about one-half second before we are even aware of it.[64] From our EEA ancestors, we have inherited dozens, perhaps thousands of these hardwired brain modules, regulating breathing, heartbeat, gait, localization of high-calorie foods, sexual attraction, favoritism toward certain offspring and not others, three-dimensional visual representation, and the ability to detect and assess cheaters and threats, calculate odds, and gauge social ranking.[65] Our brains have been shown to include hardwired modules for language acquisition, representation of another person's beliefs, and even determination of the correctness of a logical proposition. Science has now localized brain modules down to the individual neuron. For example, 97 percent of the neurons in the Macaque monkey's middle face patch, likely homologous to the human fusiform face area, respond fifty times more strongly to faces than to hands or other non-face objects.[66]

Scientists have recently developed a detailed understanding of the evolutionarily ancient "attention-reward" brain module—technically, the mesocorticolimbic dopamine system. At least rudiments of this module are found in all mobile creatures, right down to hungry soil nematodes, who will slither right past their favorite bacteria without interest when their reward neurons are experimentally disabled. Remarkable new research provides good evidence that at least some part of the human reward system can automatically guide behavior independently of the cortex, the site of rational and conscious thinking. Swedish neuroscientist Bjorn Merker found that children missing up to eighty percent of their brains, often having little more than a brain stem, are capable of emotional response. One little girl's face lit up with joy when her baby brother was put into her arms.[67] Humans, until they are satiated, are automatically motivated by the reward system to seek food, water, sex, novelty, mastery, generosity—and social attention and status.

James Olds accidentally discovered the reward system in 1954 when he implanted electrodes directly into the mesolimbic dopamine pathways of rats. These "wirehead" rats self-administered brief and mild electric shock to satisfy their reward systems–without pause or boredom, without any interest in sleeping or eating, and in apparent rapture—until they had lost forty percent of their body weight and died of starvation. Olds' wirehead rats would not cross a walkway giving off a mild shock to get food, but they would shock themselves unconscious to earn their brain reward. Olds later replicated his findings with several other animals and with humans. Humans describe electrical stimulation to this area as orgasmic.[68]

Neuroscientists Read Montague and Gregory Berns suggest that our brains use dopamine, the key neurotransmitter of reward, as a "common currency" to instantaneously rank the value of an otherwise dizzying array of competing and incomparable, apples-to-oranges behavior choices—sleep versus sex, even save versus spend.[69] The attention-reward system is how our brains assign priority to an otherwise overwhelming panoply of things we would otherwise want.

Scientists have recently shown that the prospect of rewards as diverse as psychotropic drugs, money gain, gambling, shopping, chocolate, food, music, novelty, running, attractive faces, sex, pornography, romantic and maternal love, reputation gains, a reciprocated gaze, attention from others—even the punishment of cheaters, and acts of generosity and cooperation—all share a stimulatory overlap in precisely the same region of the brain.[70] Figure 2.1 shows the cocaine and sex overlap. Nicotine, cannabis, alcohol, cocaine, morphine, amphetamine, and love—all these stimuli initiate brain response with different neurochemicals and at varying points along the reward pathway, but all increase dopamine transmission to a single area, the nucleus accumbens.[71] This finding has large implications for how the rewards of status function in the brain as well. A recent, wonderfully elegant experiment has shown that rats perceive social status and social threat in the form of bullying through

Figure 2.1: MRI scans show the activation of nearly identical brain sites in cocaine addicts watching a film containing cocaine-craving cues (left) and non-drug users watching a pornographic film (right).[73]

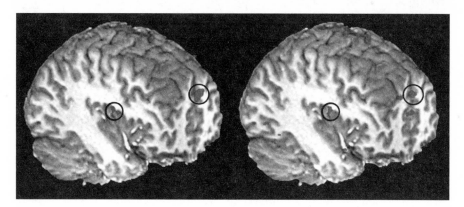

Patrick Zickler, *NIDA Notes,* "Cue for Cocaine and Normal Pleasures Activate Common Brain Sites," May 2001, 16(2), http://www.drugabuse.gov/NIDA_Notes/NNVol16N2/Cues.html

changes to dopamine signals to the nucleus accumbens. This experiment also showed exactly which biomolecules connect social defeat and depression.[72]

The prospect of an intangible social or emotional reward can be more intense than any object of physical desire. Once again, rats tell us a lot about the neurochemistry involved in social and emotional satisfaction. The brains of female rats register stronger reward signals for access to their 8-day-old pups than to cocaine.[74] In another experiment, rat moms about to nurse their pups experience a dopamine surge in the outer shell of the nucleus accumbens, with more loving rat moms experiencing more of a surge.[75] In the brains of human mothers, the reward system is activated by both maternal and romantic love. If love is blind, it is because it deactivates brain areas associated with negative emotions and social judgment.[76]

Nora Volkow, director of the National Institute on Drug Abuse, and her many co-workers have uncovered the reasons that physical and social pleasure sources and addictive materials and behaviors can substitute for one another. All rewards, however "natural," like eating and exercise, can become addictions, with the risk varying from person to person. Over the course of an addiction, the brain becomes less sensitive to dopamine release, depleting its ability to register the pleasure in the addictive substance or behavior. The structure and function of the brain regions controlling motivation and reward are altered. The longer the duration of cocaine abuse, for example, the greater the number of brain regions that are changed and the more a person's activity becomes limited to cocaine-seeking.[77]

The effect is similar for addictions to gambling or pornography. The prospect of a high may motivate people initially to engage in what becomes an addiction, but once the addiction is established, the brain's long-term memory continues to associate the target substance or behavior with its erroneous reward signals, putting addicted people at high risk of relapse, particularly when they are stressed, and even years after they have sworn off an addiction.[78] Harvard Medical School neuroscientist Steven Hyman sees addiction as the brain too powerfully remembering harmful substances or behaviors. "Addiction represents a pathological usurpation of the neural mechanisms of learning and memory that under normal circumstances serve to shape survival behaviors related to the pursuit of rewards and the cues that predict them."[79]

Volkow views addiction as involving four interrelated brain circuits: reward, centering in the nucleus accumbens; motivation in the orbitofrontal cortex; memory in the hippocampus and amygdala; and conscious control and inhibition in the prefrontal cortex. All four circuits are stimulated by dopamine. Drug abuse involves overactive response in the motivation, memory, and reward circuits, along with a reduction in conscious inhibition by the prefrontal cortex. Progression to addiction begins with the experience of an unnatural high, felt as dopamine is released into the synapses of nucleus accumbens. End-stage addiction, where drug-seeking becomes life's paramount goal, involves dopamine release in the prefrontal cortex and the amygdala and release of glutamate from the prefrontal cortex to the inner nucleus accumbens.[80] Glutamate (the same as in the monosodium glutamate used in Chinese food) is the brain's primary excitatory neurotransmitter.

The immediate effect of consuming alcohol or an addictive drug is an unnaturally intense surge in dopamine transmission. In the nucleus accumbens, this surge is three to five times the levels associated with natural rewards.[81] Addictive drugs thereby create a false positive reward prediction error signal, artificially pumping up dopamine release, and telling the brain that the drug will make us better off than we predict, even when the subjective experience is awful. Common to the promise of all natural and healthy rewards as well as addictive behaviors and substances is their ability to influence our wants and actions by increasing dopamine in the nerve synapses of the nucleus accumbens.[82]

Within one-twentieth of a second of its release into our synapses, dopamine registers at any of five types of dopamine receptors—D1 through D5—or else is scooped up by dopamine transporters for storage and later reuse. Cocaine is initially pleasurable because it blocks dopamine transporter action, keeping dopamine in the synapse and extending the reward experience. Amphetamine, an abuse drug even more toxic to the brain than cocaine, directly increases dopamine release into the synapse.[83]

Critical to reward and its disorders is the dopamine D2 receptor. Even months after drug abuse stops, dopamine release and D2 receptors remain depleted in the striatum. Reward sensitivity is reset and the impact of both natural and synthetic rewards is blunted. This is why addicts often spiral downward from feeling at one with the universe over the first few doses, to needing more just to evade bouts of depression, to wrecking their personal and financial lives to get one dose. Even long-abstinent addicts are bored more easily, are less motivated by normal pleasurable activity such as eating or conversation, and require more intense stimulation and larger rewards.[84]

"It is through activation of these circuits," Volkow writes about the dopamine reward system, "that we are motivated to do the things we perceive as pleasurable. If you have a decrease in dopamine receptors that transmit pleasurable feelings, you become less responsive to the stimuli, such as food or sex, that normally activate them. When these activities don't reward you enough, your brain signals you to do something that will stimulate the circuits sufficiently to create a sense of well-being. Thus, an individual who has low sensitivity to normal stimuli learns behaviors, such as abusing drugs or overeating, that will activate them."[85] I believe that some behavioral obsessions, compulsions, and addictions involved in OverSuccess—such as slot-machine gambling, pornography, pathological attention-seeking, hyper-materialism, and celebrity worship—mirror this pattern.

Individuals are born with significant variance in their numbers of reward system dopamine D2 receptors. For a given stimulus and associated dopamine release, those with fewer D2 receptors get less reward and have a biological need for more intense stimulus to obtain what they perceive as the same emotional satisfaction. Volkow views low-D2 brains as prone to addiction and obsession, providing a physical basis to explain the concept of "reward deficiency syndrome" first proposed by Kenneth Blum in 1995.[86] More recently, psychological tests have become well-accepted that measure "reward sensitivity," a personality trait that varies among individuals from high to low and is linked to variation in the dopamine reward system.[87]

Among people who have never taken either prescription stimulants or abused drugs, those with low D2 receptor density find Ritalin, a cocaine-like drug, most pleasant. Those with high D2 density find it unpleasant.[88] Nicotine addicts have fewer available D2 receptors in a portion of their dorsal striata.[89] Alcoholics have fewer D2 receptors than do healthy individuals.[90] Non-alcoholic people with higher levels of D2 receptor availability, but who have multiple alcoholic relatives, are nonetheless protected from familial risk of alcoholism.[91] People with high reward sensitivity crave food more frequently and intensely, are more likely to be overweight or suffer eating disorders, and show more activation in their brain reward systems when shown pictures of pizza and chocolate cake.[92] Obese people have 20 percent fewer D2 receptors in their reward pathways. The more obese someone is, the lower the density of his or her D2 receptors. Obese people whose D2 receptors were artificially signaled for eight days increased their resting metabolic rates and decreased production of body fat.[93] Volkow and her fellow researchers think that many obese people self-medicate, using food to compensate for decreased sensitivity of their brain reward systems.[94]

Experiments that manipulate D2 receptors have shown some striking results. Monkeys can be turned into workaholics when the action of their D2 receptors is blocked; they become unnaturally motivated and work their experimental levers like obsessives—harder, longer, and with fewer errors, regardless of the difficulty of obtaining their reward.[95] Using viral insertion, a current primitive form of gene therapy, scientists have successfully added D2 receptors into the brains of alcoholic rats, resulting in a dramatic reduction in alcohol preference and drinking. Unfortunately, the beneficial effect for the rats disappeared in eight days. Similarly, insertion of extra D2 receptors in the nucleus accumbens sharply curbs appetite for self-administered cocaine in rats. Another rodent experiment shows that mouse preference for and consumption of alcohol can be dialed up or down by increasing or decreasing the number of D2 receptors in their nucleus accumbens.[96]

To some extent, obsessive reward-seeking and D2 receptor deficits are inherited. People with a variety of addictive, obsessive, and compulsive disorders are at least twice as likely to have the dopamine D2 gene variant, the *Taq*A1 allele, in their bodies.[97] About one-third of us have either one or two copies of this A1 allele, which is associated with thirty percent fewer D2 receptor levels.[98] While there are contradictory studies, typical in the literature on low-effect genes, the weight of evidence links the A1 allele with increased impulsiveness, reward dependency, alcoholism, drug abuse, smoking, obesity, binge-eating disorder, post-traumatic stress disorder, gambling addiction, ADHD, novelty-seeking, detachment, social isolation—and verbal creativity.[99] The A1 allele also makes white male teens who do not associate with low-delinquency peers more likely to be violence victims.[100]

A good hint that a common cause unites many of these disorders and traits is that people with one disorder often have others. For example, violent criminals are overwhelmingly substance abusers. People with ADHD have atypically frequent family histories of depression. One-third to half of depressed people are abusers of nicotine, alcohol, and illegal drugs.[101] Dopamine signaling to D2 receptors in the nucleus accumbens is a necessary part of how we learn from both positive and negative experiences. A recent breakthrough study found that people with the D2 *Taq*A1 allele are less able to learn from their mistakes, although they learn equally as well from successes as people without the Al allele. Researchers at Baylor University recently showed that smoking addicts playing a simulated investment game were less able to learn from their investing mistakes than non-smokers, providing more evidence that addiction is, in part, a "reward prediction error" disease, with the brains of addicts ignoring signals that cause behavior change in non-addicts.[102] A reduction in dopamine signals triggered by harmful behaviors could be a biochemical basis for addiction, helping to explain why addicts and obsessives are less able to cease such behaviors.[103] It is likely that A1 carriers have lower self-control and reduced sensitivity to social cues.

Addiction, it appears, is a disease of the brain reward system, a fact that can help us understand why the behaviors associated with the OverSuccess syndrome work in us addictively.[104] But all people with low D2 receptor den-

sities are not addicts. And as with most human personality traits, the susceptibility to addiction involves dozens of genes and several neurotransmitters,
the effect of which can range from locking in one person's trajectory as an
addict to making addictive substances or behaviors repugnant to another. One
study showed that seven different genes governing dopamine, serotonin, and
norepinephrine expression were associated with pathologic gambling addiction.[105] Another study links at least 43 neurotransmitter genes with the propensity to addiction in general, each gene having a relatively small additive or
compounding influence.[106] Our life experience can literally place "epigenetic"
marker tags on our genes, switching on (or off) our genetic propensity to
addiction. Generally speaking, a propensity to addiction is about 50 percent
heritable.[107]

Addiction is no small matter in America. Yet while we appreciate how substance addictions have devastating personal, medical, and social effects, we
tend to downplay the behavioral addictions—wrongly so. Compulsive buying
may sound more like a joke than an addiction, but not to Elizabeth Roch, who
was fired from a top accounting firm for embezzling $241,061 to support her
habit. An anonymous male was compelled by his addiction to purchase two
thousand wrenches.[108] Now in jail, Uno Kim, a man addicted to gambling,
entered the home of two elderly New Hampshire gentlemen, drugged and
strangled them, robbed them of $36,000 in cash, then drove straight to the
Mohegan Sun casino.[109] The serial killer and rapist Ted Bundy, hours before
his execution, came clean about his own behavioral addiction to pornography,
saying, "I've met a lot of men who were motivated to commit violence just
like me. And without exception, every one of them was deeply involved in
pornography—without question, without exception—deeply influenced and
consumed by an addiction to pornography."[110]

A huge proportion of us are addicted to something. In Table 2.1, I've
assembled some reliable data showing the percentage of Americans who, at
some time during the prior year, were addicted to a substance or behavior
or who suffered obsessive-compulsive disorder or other repetitive behavioral
disorders I believe are biologically related to addiction. Not included in the
table are addictions for which there are no solid prevalence data, including
addictions to work, power-discordant relationships, cults, theft, love, pornography, perfectionism, and social attention.

Table 2.1: Prevalence of Selected Addictions and Related Disorders

Addiction	Percent Past Year Prevalence	Note
Nicotine[111]	15.0	29.8% of US adults use nicotine in some form
OCD[112]	7.9	Obsessive-Compulsive Disorder
Caffeine[113]	7	24% meet 3 of 4 caffeine-addiction criteria
Compulsive Buying[114]	5.8	
Compulsive Sexual Behavior[115]	5	Estimate only; ranges from 5–6%
Drugs, Alcohol, or Both[116]	4.6	Not including abuse prevalence
Rage[117]	3.9	Intermittent Explosive Disorder
Eating Disorders[118]	2.5	Anorexia, bulimia, binge-eating
Exercise[119]	2.5	
Gambling[120]	1.29	4% pathologic & problem gambling prevalence
Internet[121]	0.3–0.7	

Most addicts are dependent upon or abuse more than one substance or behavior, meaning that the percentages cannot be added up to establish an overall prevalence of addictions. However, it is reasonable to assume that at least one-quarter of Americans are currently addicted to something. Ernest Noble, former director of UCLA's Alcohol Research Center, estimates that alcoholism and addiction-related obesity, along with addictions to nicotine, and illegal drugs, afflict over one-third of Americans.[122]

Addiction to success—an obsession with high status or achieving it-should be on this list as well. I believe that at least one in four Americans are susceptible to a status-related pathology or obsession and that the behavior and thinking of tens of millions of us are significantly consumed by it.

While it would be an error to say that all human motivations, obsessions, compulsions, and addictions work in the same way, it is fair to say that a common brain circuit mediates how we respond to the prospect of reward—

SEROTONIN AND OVERSUCCESS8

Chapter 2: The Science of OverSuccess 51

whether that reward is natural or unnatural, healthy or unhealthy. OverSuccess offers us rewards—or so we think. We can become as consumed by the prospect of attention and social status as to nicotine, cocaine, or gambling. Our attention-reward system is equally subject to the effects of evolutionarily novel and more potent addictive substances and to the unnaturally intense behavioral and social stimuli found in our contemporary environment.

SEROTONIN AND OVERSUCCESS

Like our dopamine reward system, the neurochemical known as brain serotonin is linked to our status relationships and how we succeed or fail in life. Our serotonin system plays several key roles in our bodies and brains, including brightening mood, regulating status, inhibiting impulsive behavior, and down-regulating our appetites and aggressions. Lars Farde, a clinical neuroscientist and researcher at Sweden's Karolinksa Institute, has found that the density of serotonin brain receptors can vary by as much as several times from person to person, which can cause significant personality and behavioral differences among us. For example, men with fewer serotonin receptors are highly spiritual; those with a greater number are rationalists.[123]

Serotonin deficiency is linked with impulsivity, irritability, aggression, and criminality, with its effects on behavior twice as large for men as women. Low levels of serotonin are thought to increase sensitivity to negative stimuli and to reduce resistance to hostile impulses.[124] Serotonin's role in inhibiting aggression is persuasively demonstrated in breeding experiments involving wild rats and wild silver foxes: over the course of 25 generations of selection for docility and tameness, brain serotonin increased in both species.[125]

Serotonin is clearly linked to perceptions of our own social status. In a series of experiments with monkeys, UCLA neuroscientist Michael McGuire has provided a fascinating demonstration of serotonin's link to social status. The serotonin brain levels of socially dominant vervet monkeys are 50 percent higher than those in subordinates. When a dominant monkey is isolated from its group, its serotonin levels drop. Serotonin levels in a newly emergent leader increase to the levels of the former dominant. When the deposed alpha monkey is returned to the pack, its serotonin levels return to former high levels. In a follow-up experiment, after dominant male monkeys were removed from established groups, some randomly selected males were given serotonin-elevating drugs, such as Prozac, while others received serotonin-depleting drugs. In every case, the Prozac-enhanced monkey became dominant over the other. When the drugs were reversed among the animals, social dominance was upended as well.[126]

Failure to win status contests also depletes serotonin. Other monkey experiments show that chronic social stress probably causes long-term reduction in brain serotonin activity. Adult monkeys deprived of normal mothering during their first six months show reduced serotonin activity, along with an increased preference for alcohol, increased aggression, and reduced social bonding.

The relationship between serotonin and social dominance looks the same in humans as it does in monkeys. Based on measures of income and education, low social status contributes to chronic social stress and is linked to low serotonin activity.[127] As in monkeys, Prozac in humans increases sociability and dominance among normally functioning people.[128] People with higher serotonin blood levels are socially dominant, extroverted, and more successful.[129]

Natural born leaders, now hear this: a bedrock of your self-definition can be prestidigitated on or off by tweaking by a few milligrams the amount of a very inexpensive biomolecule in your bloodstream. But beware: the stresses associated with OverSuccess, I believe, blunt our serotonin systems. This partly explains the multi-decade rise in depression and antisocial behavior I explore in Chapters 6 and 7.

STRESS, SOCIAL DEFEAT, ADDICTION, AND DISEASE

Mice are teaching us a great deal about men. Over two-thirds of all animals used in lab experiments are mice. Mice are small and easy to handle and have short, two-to-three-year lifespans that allow researchers to "fast forward" the progression of human-like diseases. Ninety-nine percent of mouse and human genes are either identical or very similar. Search PubMed using the term "social defeat" and you will find over 180 journal articles, mostly involving mouse and rat experiments which, taken together, give us a robust mouse model for OverSuccess.

Typically among these social-defeat experiments, male mice are first allowed to live in cages alone or with a small group, comfortably and undisturbed, for several days. Then, once each day for ten days, these target mice are placed alone in a cage for five minutes with a larger male mouse of a type specially bred for aggressive behavior. An intense, bloody attack by the aggressor promptly ensues. The subordinate mouse faces a different aggressor each day to ensure that the experiment is not ruined by the establishment of a stable and more peaceful dominant-subordinate relationship between aggressor and target. To keep the violence bloody, but within ethical bounds, lab assistants referee the attacks, immediately replacing insufficiently or excessively brutal aggressors. After ten days of this little hell, the subordinate target mouse is usually "socially defeated."

Across these experiments, the physical symptoms of chronic and extreme social defeat are fairly consistent for mice and mammals. Even weeks after defeat, the effects upon mice, rats, hamsters, pigs, and monkeys include: reduced testosterone, obesity (in hamsters), reduced appetite and loss of body weight, cardiac arrhythmias, elevated blood lipids, immune system disturbances, disrupted stress hormone function, and increased inflammation. Evolution probably built this response into mammals with subordinate personalities to accelerate the healing of skin wounds after an attack by a dominant. But with chronic social defeat, the subordinate's immune system remains over-reactive, wasting metabolic energy and damaging tissue throughout the body.[130]

The brain effects of extreme, chronic social defeat for these animals include: suppressed hippocampal cell birth (slowing learning); increased circulating dopamine (which can damage and sensitize the reward system); reduced D2 dopamine receptor density at the nucleus accumbens; increased preference for drugs that stimulate the reward system, including alcohol, amphetamine, and cocaine; increased anxiety and fear of novelty; sensitization to minor stressors; increased social withdrawal; and other behaviors that closely mimic human depression.

In a critically illuminating experimental variation, these symptoms of social defeat are greatly reduced or even eliminated if defeated rats are returned to a familiar, stable group of cagemates.[131]

A fascinating, 20-year study of social defeat in monkeys shows that group cultural habits can mitigate most of the stress associated with being a subordinate. Starting in 1978, primate-stress expert Robert Sapolsky and his wife, Lisa Share, studied the social dynamics and stress levels in a typical troupe of olive baboons living in Kenya. Olive baboons are intensely hierarchical and aggressive, fighting over everything and routinely bloodying even non-threatening inferiors. Low-ranking troupe members live in a state of debilitating high blood-cortisol levels, rampant high stress, and demoralized submission. Then, in 1983, initiating what would become an inadvertent and remarkable natural experiment, the troupe found a pile of diseased meat in a garbage dump at a nearby human camp. The troupe's dominant males immediately gorged on the find, leaving none for their inferiors—and the dominants all died suddenly of tuberculosis.

Even though all the troupe's males were eventually replaced by new members, Sapolsky and Share were amazed to see that a new behavioral style not only emerged but persisted. Lower-ranking males were more tolerated and less harassed. Troupe members were comfortable being physically closer to one another, mutual grooming increased, and the troupe more rapidly welcomed newcomers. Unlike in the typical, non-pacific baboon troupes, the subordinate males did not exhibit elevated cortisol levels and did not display stress-related behaviors such as jaw grinding and defensive postures.

Sapolsky had often observed that, even within a particular monkey species, different groups had highly varied tendencies to inflict psychological stress on social subordinates.[132] But this natural experiment with baboons provided the first proof of cultural transmission of behavioral norms in non-human primates. Reduced imposition of stress on low-status individuals by those with high status is a learned behavior, passed on over the years by example and imitation.[133] "Being low ranking in a benevolent troupe is a hell of a lot better for your blood pressure than being low ranking in an aggressive troupe," says Sapolsky, drawing the parallel to humans.[134]

Civilized scientists do not run laboratory studies of social defeat by putting humans in cages with the likes of Sadaam or Stalin. But researchers do use epidemiological (real-world) data, tracking the life course of people subjected to prison, school, and workplace bullying. Also providing useful data are second-generation immigrants, who are cut off from the old-world community ties that remain intact in the first generation. In human social defeat, we see all the physical symptoms seen in mice, plus: sleep disorders, anorexia, bulimia, increased addiction and addiction propensity, increased sensitivity to status challenges, reduced self-worth, sense of failure, aggravated social withdrawal, and increased anxiety, schizophrenia, and depression. Here is the critical parallel with the rat experiment noted above: effects on people are aggravated by group instability; effects are buffered or eliminated if the socially defeated subordinate lives among familiar, non-aggressive peers.[135] Friends, social connections, predictability, advance warning, and a sense of control—even if it is ineffective—all mitigate the effects of stress and social defeat.

The link between social defeat and disease is stress. Bruce McEwen, who runs the neuroendocrinology lab at Rockefeller University, has played a leading role in explaining the relationship between stress and disease in humans. When we experience a threat, he has shown, adrenaline surges, followed by cortisol, our master stress hormone. Glucose is released to prepare the body for rapid physical response. Breathing and heart rate increase and blood pressure rises. Digestion and sex drive are suppressed. Extra oxygen is sent to the brain to keep us alert. Blood vessels near the skin tighten to reduce bleeding should we be wounded, causing our hair to stand on end. White blood cells marshal to fight potential infection. These responses are necessary and healthy; they prepare and protect us from a bison stampede, and they help us rescue our toddler from an aggressive elevator door. In such transient circumstances, our hormones mobilize to spur us to quickly resolve a problem. When the stress passes, our adrenaline and cortisol levels return to their baselines. Such moderate and intermittent incidents of stress make us stronger.

But in our world of traffic jams, impossible deadlines, unceasing uncertainty, and unremitting status challenges, our stress response can never switch off. Chronic stress—including stress from status conflict—is poisoning our bodies and brains with our own adrenaline and cortisol. Chronic stress reshapes and injures our brains' reward, motivation, memory, and conscious inhibition systems. The result is the modern panoply of degenerative diseases: insomnia, obesity, diabetes, atherosclerosis, decreased bone density, disregulated immune systems, depression, and brain-cell death. Chronic stress sometimes triggers "glucocorticoid resistance," leaving us with an over-reactive immune system and at greater risk of rheumatoid arthritis, allergies, and asthma. Sustained stress and social defeat and the elevated cortisol levels that sometimes result also suppress the birth of new cells in one of the brain's stress regulatory sites, the hippocampus, shrinking it, disabling it from performing its normal job of damping down the stress response, and sometimes contributing to depression symptoms.[136] Neuronal connections are decreased in the frontal cortex, impairing rational judgment. Some studies show increased growth and neuronal connections in the amygdala, which automatically processes fear and threat—these connections increasing propensity to anxiety. The result is a vicious cycle in which continuous stress reduces our ability to regulate our adverse reaction to it.[137]

Finally, chronic stress shrinks our telomeres, the mortality clocks located at the tip of most of our cell chromosomes. Telomeres become shorter each time our cells divide and reproduce, finally halting reproduction when they get too short. Shrunken telomeres sentence our cells to earlier death and make us die young.[138]

I want to avoid overstating my case. Most Americans do not suffer the extreme, chronic social defeat that the subordinate mice endured in the experiments. And for both mice and men, susceptibility to social defeat varies enormously among individuals.[139] People with high genetic susceptibility and harsh early life experiences can become socially defeated by patterns of aggression that others can laugh off. But in general, we see a dosage-related response in both animals and humans: the more intense social defeat results, the greater stress and greater pathology. The mouse model is useful to understanding OverSuccess because many of us live under the unrelieved stress that comes from a marathon of defeats in status contests, without the access we had two generations ago to the support of the extended family and the community. Like extreme and chronic social defeat, low social status and unstable dominance hierarchies—even without the violence of the mouse model—cause stress, and are both solidly linked to serious mental and physical disease and early death. A non-violent variation of the mouse-defeat experiment places a dominant aggressor and a subordinate rat in a single cage, but separated by a divider allowing the two to see, smell, and hear each other. Several days of even this non-physical contact produces chronic stress and social defeat in the subordinate. In this experiment, the stress results in disregulated cortisol levels and a shrunken anterior cingulate cortex (ACC), the brain region that in humans helps coordinate conflicting signals from the emotional and rational brains. The ACC is often shrunken in depressed people.

In perhaps the most definitive human study to date on status and brain injury, generally upper-class Pittsburgh-area residents were asked to rank their own social standings. Even after researchers statistically corrected for the respondents' actual social status, negative psychological states, the total volume of their brains' gray matter, and other potential explanations, those people who regarded themselves as having low status had significantly smaller-sized perigenual ACCs. This brain structure is 20 percent smaller in people who ranked themselves lowest in social status compared with those at the top.[140]

Severe psychosocial stress also damages our brain reward system and makes us more addiction prone—thus aggravating the OverSuccess syndrome. Indeed, both genetic and archaeological evidence shows that humans have used addictive plants and drugs such as nicotine, caffeine, opium, cocaine, and betel nut, likely to self-medicate against stresses such as food shortages and physical hardships.[141] Recent research has demonstrated that physical stress, like amphetamine, cocaine, morphine, alcohol, and nicotine use, causes the same long-term modification of the ventral tegmental area and other brain structures at the cellular level. Like drug abuse, sustained stress depletes dopamine receptors in the reward system and thereby increases the brain's susceptibility to substance addiction.[142] Nick Goeders, who directs Louisiana State University's postgraduate training program in stress and addiction neuroscience, thinks that the increased addiction among stressed people results from their attempt to self-medicate, using drugs to bolster their insufficiently rewarded brains.[143]

Dopamine levels are unquestionably affected by chronic stress, as a Wake Forest School of Medicine research team discovered in their study of monkeys that had lived in group housing for three months. Three months was long enough for stable social hierarchies to have become established. When tested to assess the density of their dopamine receptors and their vulnerability to cocaine addiction, compared with those living in isolation, the socially dominant monkeys living in stable groups had developed 22 percent more D2 receptors in their basal ganglia and had lower levels of dopamine in their neural cell synapses. This indicates greater efficiency in use of dopamine and better brain health.

Stable group living did not increase D2 receptor density in subordinate monkeys. Subordinates, but not dominants, became vulnerable to cocaine addiction. "Becoming a particular social rank may be as important as biological predispositions in determining vulnerability to drug abuse," write the study authors.[144] In female monkeys, chronic social stress and low rank depressed D2 receptor function.[145] Brief but repetitive episodes of social defeat yielded long-term neural changes and increased cocaine-binging in rats.[146] A similar experiment with rats shows that repeated psychological stress decreases D2 receptor density and is associated with depression-like behavior.[147] Another experiment found that bullied rats had altered dopamine reward systems and become socially withdrawn, exhibiting depressive behavior.[148]

A study of human alcoholics showed that severe stress activates or aggravates the genetic predisposition for a D2 receptor deficit.[149] Stress-induced cigarette craving is significantly stronger in people with genetic predisposition to D2 receptor deficit.[150] Acute stress sends substance abusers—even those clean for years—into relapse.[151] Compared with young adults who enjoyed early childhoods with low psychosocial stress, those with high-stress childhoods showed significantly greater dopamine release in the nucleus accumbens when subjected to a psychosocial stress test.[152]

For the past 25 years, Stanford biologist Robert Sapolsky has lived among Serengeti baboons, and what he learned from them has made him a leading expert in the brain biochemistry of status. When low-status baboons are denied sufficient social and kinship support, low-status baboons suffer higher brain-cortisol levels, indicating consistent and dangerous levels of stress. Significantly for our inquiry into OverSuccess, for both baboons and humans, maximum stress over status tends to occur among those frustrated in their attempts to move up the social hierarchy. Those either secure in power or accepting their subordinate role enjoy generally lower stress. For even those of high rank, an unstable dominance hierarchy is a source of chronic stress.

More important than rank, according to Sapolsky, is whether you live in a society where those of low rank are treated miserably and where rank is unstable. Both situations create more stress symptoms than low rank itself.[153] Sapolsky links the start of widespread and chronic social defeat in humans with the advent of agriculture. Agricultural surpluses enabled wider inequality, steeper hierarchies and, for the first time, extreme relative poverty. "I think that the punch line of the primate-human difference is that when humans invented poverty, they came up with a way of subjugating the low-ranking like nothing ever seen before in the primate world."[154]

In a simultaneously disturbing and fascinating study done at the California National Primate Research Center, rhesus monkeys were injected with the monkey analogue to the human immunodeficiency virus, then divided into four groups: subordinate and dominant personality; stable and unstable social groupings. The unstable groups were varied daily in size and membership. In the stable groups, the same three monkeys cohabited daily, allowing a dominance hierarchy to become established, then maintained with low effort on the part of the monkeys. There were more aggressive acts in the unstable groups. Subordinates in the unstable groups suffered weakened immune systems and more rapid progression of the viral infection. In the stable groups, both subordinates and dominants remained equally healthy for longer.[155]

Jay Kaplan and Stephen Manuck found that dominant male monkeys developed more extensive atherosclerosis than the subordinates did—but only when living in groups with unstable dominance hierarchies. Subordinate females always developed greater atherosclerosis than dominants, regardless of the group's social stability.[156] Unstable hierarchies undermined an animal-rights effort in the late 1980s, when well-intentioned activists persuaded the USDA to give its socially isolated research monkeys a respite from their individual cages by putting them together for an hour a week. That single hour, not long enough to establish a stable social hierarchy, was consumed by never-resolved brawling.

Unstable social hierarchies and unresolved conflict also degrade children's health. Anthropologist Marina Butovskaya and her co-workers spent weeks watching conflicts and reconciliations among boys seven to eleven years old in a Russian summer camp. Butovskaya found that ten minutes after an unresolved conflict occurred, the boys' saliva-cortisol levels were twice as high as they were for boys who had engaged in conflicts with a satisfactory resolution.[157]

Epidemiologists have irrefutably established the link between low social status and poor health in humans.[158] A study of over 36,000 Finnish workers shows the link between what the researchers call Effort-Reward Imbalance

(ERI) and health risk factors. For both men and women, a high ERI ratio puts a person at about 40 percent greater risk for heart and chronic diseases.[159] Another major study of this type followed over 8,000 white-collar British civil servants for eleven years. Those who most strongly felt that they were "being treated unfairly" at work suffered a 55-percent greater risk for heart disease, even after adjusting for age, demographics, ERI, employment grade, and the other risk factors for heart disease.[160] Lower social status, as measured by income, education, or occupation, correlates with higher mortality rates, low birth weight, obesity, heart disease, lung disease, incidence of smoking, asthma, cancer, diabetes, number of sick days taken on the job, accident rates, suicide, exposure to physical violence, and compromised mental health.[161] Ease of access to, and use of, medical care does not explain these data. The missing explanation involves the under-appreciated psychology of status.

Humans have depended upon stable social groups to reach our lofty achievements in complexity and excellence. We know that some individuals within every group are biologically driven to achieve dominance. But without efficient and sustainable emotional resolution of their contests for status, dominant individuals may win the fight, but risk surreptitious attack or group defection by losers. If conflicts are not resolved promptly, then stress levels will remain harmfully elevated among those in contention. To resolve this problem, animals, it appears, have the workings of a "natural conflict resolution" system, as seen among dozens of species from monkeys and dolphins to goats: they make physical contact. Within minutes of a fight, a losing chimp will approach the winner with an outstretched hand, ending in a mouth-to-mouth kiss; fighting dolphins will quickly begin rubbing gently against one another; winning bonobos initiate playful sex.[162] Humans, too, are built with a strong biological drive to face-to-face peacemaking within our social groups.

But hard evidence is emerging that the human body and brain are not evolved to indifferently accept prolonged social defeat and unresolved conflict over our place in the pack. We are poisoning our brains in an epidemic of intensified status competition and huge, weakly bonded, and unstable social groups. Chronic, mass social stress degrades our health, makes our brains' reward systems needy, and triggers dissatisfaction, depression, and behavioral and substance addictions among tens of millions of us who have genetic susceptibility. The size of the poppy crop in Afghanistan has little to do with it. Take away the heroin or cocaine, and those with injured reward systems will quickly find cigarettes or gambling to substitute. Success obsession, like many other mental disorders, cannot be pigeonholed as a failure of will. Success obsession is as biological as fever—and as preventable.

3

ENHANCEMENT TECHNOLOGY: THE NO-LIMITS NATION AND ITS FUTURE

I was [the] ideal result. It was a screwed-up idea, making genius people.
The fact that I have a huge IQ does not make me a person who is good or happy.[163]
—Doron Blake, 2001. Blake is the product of the now-defunct
"genius" sperm bank, Repository for Germinal Choice. Blake's 180 IQ
had him using a computer at age 2 and reading *Hamlet* in kindergarten.

PERSONAL SUCCESS IS A cultural notion that has changed over the past few centuries and, particularly, in America over the past few decades. But for the last 600 years, the Western world—and ultimately most of the rest of the planet—has been in thrall to an idea of success that took root early in the Renaissance: the idea of the individual as free agent, empowered to shape his or her own life and rise to the limits of his or her own talent and initiative. Through literature and philosophy and via accelerating scientific and techno-logical progress, we can trace success culture from its modern roots directly to our own turbocharged times. And now, in a way unique in human history, the science of genetic and physical enhancement is amplifying our hard-wired status-seeking drive.

Until now, human potential has been limited by natural constraints over our bodies and minds. But over the past decade, America has led the process by which these speed limits will be removed. Not later than about mid-century, we will have developed the technology we will need to take direct control over the genes that have limited success in ourselves and our children. Consistent with the pattern in every past debate over the adoption of a new technology, these genetic tools will move into broad use—and will profoundly alter the human species. Whether we're ready or not, we are about to embark on an unstoppable arms race in the enhancement of our bodies, social skills, and intelligence. If the United States resists embracing these controversial technologies, the leading edge will quickly pass to China or India, where public acceptance for human enhancement is already strong. The result? OverSuccess, integrated into our very DNA—at least for those of us who can afford it or are willing to risk it—will soon become a yet more intense syndrome.

A VISION OF LIMITLESS POSSIBILITIES, FOUNDED 1410

Today's prevailing American vision of personal autonomy, self-definition, worldly attainment, and limitless growth first emerged in complete form during roughly the first two decades of the fifteenth century. The epicenter was Florence in northern Italy. Converging there were all the ingredients for a new human-achievement agenda, some of the elements newly invented, with others freely borrowed from China, India, and Arabia: inexpensive communications media, the arts, humanism, rationalism, science, technology, accounting, trade, capitalism, university education, and scientific inventions. The concept of individual free agency was born. Your fate and status were no longer fixed immutably, your life no longer defined by outside forces. The focus of human ambition had shifted from the afterlife to the growing possibilities of this life, from the imagined to the real world. The growth of individualism and unchecked meritocracy was, for the first time, irreversibly underway.

Why do I plant the seed of success—and OverSuccess—in Florence circa 1410? In five years of research for his book, *Human Accomplishment,* Charles Murray catalogued the 1,560 most significant events in the sciences and technology and the 1,183 most significant people in the arts and sciences between 800 B.C. and 1950. The number of significant people shot almost straight up starting about 1450. From 1400 to 1600, these people were highly concentrated in the northern half of Italy. For every field of human endeavor, unbroken strings of progress began in the 1500s (for modern mathematics, it began in 1464 with the publication of Regiomontus' trigonometry text).[164] In about 1500, world economic product rose above subsistence levels for the first time in human history.

If there was a manifesto for the Italian Renaissance, it was philosopher Giovanni Pico della Mirandola's 1487 *Oration on the Dignity of Man.* A model of contemporary fame and glamour, Mirandola was renowned for his massive intellect, infallible memory, and physical beauty. He studied in five languages and endeavored to write theses on all of the 900 propositions he had culled from the world's body of knowledge. He offered to pay any scholar willing to travel to meet him and engage him in public debate on any subject. He was forced to flee to France when the Pope, worried that such disputations would challenge papal authority, put a stop to his proposed debates and threatened to burn him at the stake.[165] *Oration* was intended as Mirandola's introduction to the debates. In it he proclaims God's highest creation to be humans, who are, he avers, equipped by boundless powers of self-transformation, their constraints merely self-imposed. "Let a holy ambition enter into our souls," Mirandola declares; "let us not be content with mediocrity, but rather strive after the highest and expend all our strength in achieving it."[166] Mirandola sounds like the first American.

Now thumb forward a few thousand pages of history to America. Here the Christian faith—in its newly minted, individualist, anti-hierarchical, Protestant Reformation version—continued to provide the positive rationale for worldly success. In 1701, New England Puritan preacher Cotton Mather wrote, "Come, come, for shame, away to your business … Solomon, seeing that the young man was industrious, he made him a ruler … Let your business engross most of your time." Between 1836 and 1900, Presbyterian William

McGuffey, in more than 122 million copies of his *Readers*, instructed half of all American schoolchildren, unambiguously linking faith and good character to success: "God gives a great deal of money to some persons, in order that they may assist those who are poor."[167] In 1872, Methodism's founder, John Wesley, preached, "Gain all you can; save all you can; then, give all you can."[168]

Quintessential American Benjamin Franklin began the trend of secularizing the rationale for success, associating Puritan virtue directly with wealth and achievement. Industrious even about self-improvement, he ruthlessly scored himself each day on his progress toward achieving the virtue he had assigned himself that week, rotating through his list four times each year. Vigorous at self-promotion, he consciously developed the traits of frugality, practicality, affability, diligence, and positivism—retiring self-made from business at 42 to engage in civic and scientific pursuits, having risen over the course of his life from printer's apprentice to ambassador to European royalty. He invented bifocals, the Franklin stove, and the lightning rod. He was the role model for Andrew Carnegie's late-life altruism and for Horatio Alger's 130 novels. Franklin's writings led Thomas Mellon to leave his family farm for a life of entrepreneurship. Today, Franklin is the inspiration for Stephen Covey's seven best-selling habits. Franklin, anticipating science fiction writers and lab scientists two hundred years later, speculated about using science to extend the human lifespan.[169] Even more of his dreams promise to become true.

THE CERTAINTY OF BETTER HUMANS

The vanguard for tomorrow's idea of success is the contemporary movement known as transhumanism. The movement's goals are no less spectacular than Mirandola's: indefinite youth and vitality, the ability to choose not just your child's sex, but also that child's emotional makeup and body morphology, complete with new senses. An overarching goal of transhumanists is to see us acquire a level of intelligence that surpasses genius, opening up entirely new frontiers of endeavor and experience. Nick Bostrom, the Oxford University philosopher and co-founder of the World Transhumanist Association, describes what science and technological progress promises to establish as the next benchmark of human embodiment and personality: ". . . ageless, healthy, super-geniuses of flawless physical beauty, who are graced with a sparkling wit and a disarmingly self-deprecating sense of humor, radiating warmth, empathetic charm, and relaxed confidence."[170] As I will show, Bostrom is no wild dreamer.

The realistic possibility of such exactingly engineered superhumans will launch fierce and potentially violent moral and ethical contests over the commercialization of transhuman technologies. These coming conflicts are unavoidable, because the tools for making superhumans already exist. Nanotechnology, compact and embedded artificial intelligence, robotics, and genomics all loom as commercial certainties, with billions in annual dollars already flowing into their research and development. There is little doubt among lab scientists that, well within the lifetimes of many of us, these technologies will generate a social and economic Category 5 hurricane. My baby boomer cohort will likely be the last largely unaffected by brain and body modification that smashes the barriers that have heretofore limited the accelerated evolution of the human race.

Foremost among these tools is genomics, the science by which we will understand the function of all of our genes as an integrated whole. Assuming we don't destroy the planet or ourselves in the immediate future, within perhaps two to three decades we are certain to begin taking precise, rational control over human evolution.[171] René Descartes speculated in 1637 that science might make smarter, more competent and healthy and even immortal humans; his conjectures are no longer idle fantasy. Greg Stock, director of the program on medical technology and society at UCLA's School of Public Health and author of *Redesigning Humans: Our Inevitable Genetic Future*, pronounces with utter certainty, "the next frontier is not space, it is us."[172]

Even without the impending technological interventions that we will consider in the coming pages, the process of natural evolution itself has already powered the stunning acceleration of human enhancement over the past few hundred thousand years. As I noted at the start of Chapter 2, the history of rapid increases in our intelligence and our subtler sensitivity to complex status relationships begins about two million years ago. Since then, the average cranial size for humans and our nearest relatives has more than doubled, with the most rapid growth kicking in about 400,000 years ago.[173]

The oldest-yet-discovered symbol-using humans lived about 160,000 years ago, along the shore of a shallow Ethiopian lake that teemed with catfish, crocodile, and hippopotamus. An adult's skull found there indicates a man built like a soccer halfback. As evidence of the perennial human struggle to extract meaning from grief, the skull of a nearby child was ritually marked and polished from repeated and apparently loving handling after death.[174] When the discovery of these human remains was published in 2003, scientists finally had physical evidence to corroborate "molecular clock" estimates based upon mutation rates of our genes that were not under selection pressure—that is, not providing survival or reproductive advantage. These estimates backdate the first anatomically modern humans to one small population living in Africa about 200,000 years ago. New and more accurate dating methods now peg the first anatomically modern human skull, originally found in Ethiopia in 1967 by Richard Leakey, to 195,000 years ago.[175]

Recent molecular clock studies are confirming that we thoroughly modern humans are just evolutionary seedlings. A breakthrough in dating the origins of modern speech and language capability came in 2001 when a genetic defect was found to explain a rare, inherited speech and language disorder in some members of a British family. That finding led to the discovery in 2002 that the human version of the FOXP2 gene is necessary for speech by enabling fine motor control of the lower face.[176] Molecular clock calculations indicate that this gene emerged in humans roughly 120,000 years ago and must have conferred an overwhelming fitness and competitive benefit because it became so quickly universal.[177]

Archaeologists Christopher Henshilwood and Curtis Marean define modern humans by their use of symbolism to organize social behavior, a capacity made possible only by neural evolution. Our ability to deploy tools and our knack for fielding football teams don't distinguish us as human. Even birds make tools. Monkeys have invented social norms. The best bright line distinguishing the first known behaviorally and cognitively modern humans involves the creation of cave paintings, shared abstract and representational artistic styles, pigments, jewelry, personal ornamentation, and burial of the dead.[178] The earliest such evidence yet discovered—abstract symbolic engravings and perforated snail shells painted with iron oxide and likely worn as jewelry to signify social status—dates to 75,000 years ago in South Africa.[179] Use of iron oxide pigment, probably for symbolic ornamentation, dates to 164,000 years ago, also near the ocean in South Africa.[180] Use of rich artistic and cultural symbolic representation burst pervasively into the archaeological record just 40,000 years ago.

Human enhancement via evolution has continued to accelerate through even more recent history. The typical human body is markedly different than it was just 40,000 years ago: our teeth are at least ten percent smaller and our frames at least twenty percent less robust. In response to the spread of agriculture starting only 10,500 years ago, northern European genes have become better adapted than other peoples' to the diets and lifestyles that can predispose humans to heart disease and diabetes. Evidence includes the prevalence in northern Europeans of ABO blood groups, a resistance to infectious diseases associated with agriculture, the presence of enzymes that efficiently process alcohol, and other adaptations to diets rich in carbohydrates and saturated fats.[181] Adult ability to digest milk first evolved and became widespread starting in Europe no more than 7,000 years ago.[182] It was only about 6,000 years ago that the European white male first appeared on the planet, when the gene that causes white skin became predominant in response to reduced sunlight exposure.[183] Geneticists call this sort of process a selective sweep, when a new genetic attribute is so beneficial that it becomes common within only dozens of generations.

Without doubt, evolution of our brain structure, behavior, and intelligence is actively underway, probably more rapidly so in response to the radical changes we have made to our physical and social environments. In early 2006, UCLA geneticist Robert Moyzis led a team that mathematically screened two databases of the entire human genome. Moyzis and his co-workers found that 1,800 genes, about seven percent of the total, have been subject to rapid evolution over the past 10,000 to 50,000 years. A year later, a team led by paleoanthropologist John Hawks, using a newer and more extensive database, almost precisely confirmed this finding. The bigger news is the team's discovery that the rate of appearance of beneficial gene variations—the rate of human evolution—has accelerated by about one hundred times over the past 50,000 years, with one beneficial new gene variant appearing on average every two years. Human evolution is accelerating because more potentially beneficial mutations occur as human births increase, and because changes to the human physical and social environment have accelerated, increasing the probability that random mutations are helpful rather than harmful.[184]

While Hawks' analytic methods cannot identify many of the beneficial mutations of the past 5,000 years, there is every reason to believe that evolutionary acceleration continues. Human population and changes in our physical environment and the usefulness of intelligence and social skills have continued to increase, particularly over the past 600 years. One in six of these rapidly evolving genes are associated with brain function. But this figure misses even more recent lower-frequency and localized gene variants.[185] Another recent screening found that about 580 human genes in mid-selective sweep have emerged within the past 10,000 years.[186] The notion of humans as a fixed species is eroding into scientific unsupportability. Human evolution is recent, continuing, and possibly accelerating in response to conscious human intervention.

Many are alarmed by the prospect of humans shaping and radically accelerating our own evolution. But we are quite comfortable with the concept of domestication; we have been doing it to our plants, animals, and even ourselves for many centuries. We've known since the invention of agriculture how malleable genes can be and how easily a species can be transformed in service of human need. An unusual experiment run in the former Soviet Union demonstrated how quickly and powerfully domestication can change a species. Scientists bred wild silver foxes in captivity for 25 generations, the equivalent of about 600 human years, selecting for a single trait: friendliness to humans. Over this time, the foxes became as tame as spaniels. Along with tameness came an entirely unintended and consistent pattern of associated traits similar to those found in other domesticated animals—floppy ears; curly tails; colorless fur patches; earlier sexual maturity; smaller skulls, jaws, and teeth; and marked orthodontic problems. Behavioral changes included tail wagging, diminished fear response, significantly reduced levels of the corticosteroid stress hormones, and increased brain serotonin, the aggression inhibitor.[187]

Another study tracking genetic differences among dog breeds provides more evidence for the unexpected genetic impacts of domestication. A surprising 30 percent of dogs' genetic differences can be explained by systematic breeding programs that began only about 200 years ago, 50–75 dog generations. Over what is in evolutionary terms a short timespan, dog genes have diverged so extensively that the herding and hunting behaviors characteristic of some breeds can no longer be taught to others.[188] Seventy-five generations of domestication have been sufficient to partly separate some breeds into distinct species.[189]

We humans are already choosing our own genes. In only eight generations, humans have selectively bred themselves to double the incidence of the most common form of inherited deafness. Geneticist Walter Nance notes that, after the opening of the first schools to teach sign language in about 1800, deaf people began to marry one another. In the United States, 85 percent of profoundly deaf persons now marry another deaf person.[190] Nance thinks that the FOXP2 gene for speech spread rapidly starting 120,000 years ago, not because this gene conferred a pure survival advantage, but as a result of intentional selective mating. Says Nance, "If you were one of the first primates with an ability to communicate by speaking, wouldn't you want to select a partner who could whisper sweet nothings in your ear?"[191]

Over the past century, the industrial nations have made huge investments in efforts to increase intelligence. Psychologist and IQ researcher James Flynn has rigorously documented the gains that have resulted, which are so striking and difficult to explain that they have become known as the Flynn Effect. Flynn has shown that, in every nation where he could find reliable test data, median IQs have increased by a steady three points per decade. Increased test-taking familiarity has been ruled out as a cause. Raven's Progressive Matrices and Similarities—reliable intelligence subtests, given since 1877 in Britain and 1914 in the United States, that measure logical thinking and problem-solving ability without known rules—show gains so massive that the average person taking these tests in the gaslight era would score as retarded today.

Starting in the late 1800s, industrial societies made the purposeful and collective choice to shift teaching and living environments away from an emphasis on concrete experiences to focus on scientific thinking, use of symbols, and reasoning about the hypothetical. We have made what amounts to a cooperative cultural decision to augment a selected facet of intelligence: scientific thinking. Intelligence subtests for vocabulary and arithmetic, where we have *not* applied this increased emphasis, show only very small gains over the past fifty years. Indeed, average underlying general intelligence has not changed much over a century. What the Flynn Effect shows is how powerfully and rapidly group-determined cultural choices in environment and child-rearing can affect intelligence across our entire species.[192]

University of Birmingham orthodontist Peter Rock has recently extended the evidence for the rapid increase in human intelligence back to the Renaissance. Rock found that the volume contained by contemporary skulls is twenty percent larger than that of 84 intact skulls dated to 1348 and 1545. While improved nutrition has played a major role in increased body size over this time, foreheads have become strikingly more prominent and faces less so over the last 600 years.[193] The purpose of our larger foreheads is probably to house a larger frontal cortex, the primary locus of human intelligence.

A look back from the present to 1410—the advent of success culture—spans about 25 human generations. Could humans have bred and reared themselves for increased social sophistication and intelligence over just those 600 years? "Almost a certainty," Greg Stock told me. As I will show later in this chapter, the individual and societal returns from self-domestication for intelligence are huge and will only grow larger.

The Repository for Germinal Choice provides strong anecdotal evidence that self-domestication for intelligence works roughly as intended. Leave aside, for the moment, the troubling questions that surround this experiment in all-volunteer eugenics. Founded and funded by the late Robert Graham, inventor of the shatterproof eyeglass, the Repository aggressively solicited male donors endowed with advanced academic degrees, business success, and athletic prowess. The experiment resulted in the conception of 219 children between the late 1970s and 1999, when the repository closed. A non-scientific sample of 15 of these children reported that five ranked at the top of their classes, one had an IQ of 180, two were artistically gifted, and one was a skier of Olympic potential. Interestingly for those who believe that giftedness inspires misery, the crop is reported to be happier and better adjusted than average.[194]

Today, many couples and single mothers are using sperm banks, choosing donor characteristics that they feel will best augment their progeny's health, physical beauty, and intelligence. One facility, Fairfax Cryobank, permits prospective parents to select a sperm donor using pull-down menus covering race, hair and eye color, height, and doctoral degrees. At Cryos International in Denmark, which specializes in blond, blue-eyed post-grads and is currently the world's largest sperm bank, no more than 10 percent of potential donors make the cut. One young, highly sought-after Cryos sperm donor has already fathered over 110 children.

ENHANCEMENT TECHNOLOGY: THE VERY NEAR FUTURE

As we've seen, improving individual success odds by consciously manipulating our genetic makeup is not a new thing. What is new is the power and precise control we will soon gain over the genes that strongly influence how we look, think, and act. Regardless of our ethical trepidation, by about the middle of this century, parents—medically advised and aware of the trade-offs and risks involved—will select for athleticism, social dominance, perseverance, memory, creativity, and spatial and verbal intelligence in their children at the embryo stage. Some parents are already sorting among embryos to eliminate genetic defects and to choose their baby's sex. As of mid-2005, about 5,000 children worldwide had been born using the combination of in vitro fertilization (IVF) and pre-implantation genetic diagnosis (PGD).[195] IVF was first used to foster the birth of a human in 1977. PGD was first used in a human birth in 1990. IVF and PGD are now used to overcome parental infertility and to screen embryos at the eight-to-ten-cell stage for genetic defects, of which the average human is thought to have perhaps 300 that impair health to some degree.[196] As of late 2006, there were at least 200 American clinics offering IVF/PGD services to the public.[197] Over 100 clinics are using these techniques to help fertile couples select their baby's sex.

Clearly, in a society as individualistic as ours, there is no risk of designer babies all being square-jawed, blue-eyed extroverts. Cara and Gibson Reynolds, happily married dwarves living in Collingswood, New Jersey, decided against embryo screening to select for a healthy, dwarf baby only because of the cost and risks associated with Cara's age of 39 years. Cara bristles at criticism that she should want to purposefully dwarf her child. "You cannot tell me that I cannot have a child who's going to look like me. It's just unbelievably presumptuous and they're playing God."[198] Sharon Duchesneau and Candy McCullough, a deaf lesbian couple, successfully conceived two deaf children with the help of IVF and a sperm donor with a lengthy family history of deafness. A Johns Hopkins University survey found that three percent of PGD clinics admit to having used the technique to select for a disability.[199] IVF and PGD were recently used in combination to foster the birth of a baby with an immune system matching her sister's. This allowed blood taken from the baby's umbilical cord to be used to cure her sister's genetic disease, without risk of host-donor tissue incompatibility.[200]

For parents, IVF/PGD is now arduous and costly, at about $20,000 a pop. Unplanned triplets are another big-budget side effect. And, using present techniques, IVF babies are about 60 percent more likely to be born with birth defects than those naturally conceived. PGD also suffers high error rates and higher miscarriage rates.[201] I also do not want to tread blithely over the wrenching ethical and social perils of genetic entrepreneurialism that I will discuss later in this chapter. But new technology will reduce the medical risks in these procedures and price barriers will drop. Scientists are starting to make progress at overcoming today's poor understanding of complex traits such as intelligence and social facility, likely influenced by gene-environment interactions involving hundreds of genes.

Detailed information on most of the approximately 24,000 human genes—including gene sequence, proteins each gene encodes, and gene variance between individuals—can be found on the Annotated Human Gene Database, a public website.[202] The $135 million HapMap website, which went live in late 2005, provides a growing online library of most of the two million locations in the human genome where DNA varies among individuals and populations.[203] The U.K. and other economically advanced nations have announced planning for a multi-billion-dollar population database, including individual genotype, living environment, and decades of health history. This database will be a scientific bonanza for epidemiologists and a goldmine for trial attorneys and has therefore stirred up fierce political opposition. Another proposed gene database, the Human Variome Project, seeks to standardize and establish an open source for charting the collection and availability of data on the links between gene variants, mutations, diseases, and traits.[204]

Within a decade, searchable databases of the genotype, traits, and the medical, life, and environment history of hundreds of thousands of randomly selected and anonymous people will be posted for free public use. A global geekswarm will aggressively mine these databases for useful correlations. Early information from these databases is already driving the commercialization of both embryonic and adult gene enhancement and repair.

What will be the result of all this genetic information and dissemination? We will be engineering new babies—and, for those of us old enough to be born the old-fashioned way, we will be checking our own genes for potential upgrades. Once the cost comes down (and it will), and you have the data for your own genotype (and you will), you will Google your genes to predict your health, customize medical care, determine investment strategy, and select jobs, residence, and diet. It's already in the works, and Google will be part of it. In 2007, the information-search juggernaut co-funded 23andMe, a Bay Area startup that plans to build what its website describes as a fun, consumer-friendly, searchable genotype-phenotype database.[205]

Technology to enhance and repair our genes is already here. California-based Sangamo BioSciences is perfecting "zinc finger binding proteins" and "zinc finger nucleases" that latch onto and cut genes at precisely determined locations at the beginning and end of a mutated or undesirable section. Repair genetic material can then be introduced, with genes often self-healing the zinc-finger cut by incorporating the repair genetic material into the correct location. The company is using its technology in human clinical trials of a treatment for Lou Gehrig's Disease, the deadly muscle-wasting disease sometimes caused by an inherited genetic defect.[206] Challenges remain in the unfolding realm of gene repair, in areas such as the process of physically inserting large and delicate stretches of replacement DNA into cell nuclei, weeding out potentially cancerous cells containing erroneous repairs, and accounting for the status of the "epigenetic" control switches that turn gene activity on and off. But, year by year, research is making progress at generating the tools to repair and enhance genes in both embryos and adult cells.

A major impediment to screening embryos for multiple desired and unwanted traits is the small number (about a dozen) embryos produced for each IVF pregnancy. Controversy about it will rage, as it should, but prospects for the inexpensive and painless production of nearly unlimited numbers of embryos is only modestly speculative. Recent scientific history shows how rapidly this progress will continue to unfold.

As of late 2003, two teams of scientists converted mouse stem cells into egg cells and into primitive sperm cells that successfully fertilized a mouse egg, creating an embryo.[207] As of late 2004, scientists grew and multiplied mouse sperm stem cells in the laboratory, transplanting them into sterile males who were then able to reproduce and pass on the genetic traits contributed by the stem cells. This makes possible the genetic alteration and cultivation of mass quantities of identical sperm stem cells in a laboratory setting.[208] British biotech TriStem claims to have "retro-differentiated" blood immune cells back to stem cells, and from there into neuron, heart muscle, and new, genetically matched immune cells.[209] By 2006, a Canadian stem cell research team coaxed fetal pig skin cells to morph into cells that look and act like egg cells.[210] Also in 2006, a British team grew adult mice using mouse sperm cells derived from mouse stem cells.[211] In a late-2007 breakthrough described by stem-cell pioneer Robert Lanza as "the biological equivalent of the Wright Brothers first airplane," scientists retro-differentiated human skin cells into cells almost identical to stem cells, and then into heart, muscle, and brain tissue.[212]

Challenging cancer side effects and poor-yield problems remain, but the mass production of usable embryos from skin cells to stem cells to egg and sperm cells is coming. Within not more than two generations from today, commercial laboratories will convert various types of body cells from one or more adults or children into embryos in sufficient number to screen one pregnancy for thousands of genetic traits.[213] A human baby might then incorporate contributions from one or thousands of "parents." In at least the nations willing to tolerate the ethical quandaries and where residents are prosperous enough, parents and governments will buy and sell patented and unpatented genetic material from pull-down menus. Most of the genetic material that will form the basis of these choices will be manufactured, rather than biologically derived. Among elite social classes, biological parenthood may largely disappear.

We are backing step by step into this brave new world, starting with the perfectly defensible use of genetic testing to avoid deadly inherited diseases. Today, over a thousand genetic defects and other conditions such as deafness, dwarfism, and mental retardation can be detected from fetal cell tests. The acceptance by Ashkenazi Jews of fetal testing has resulted in the virtual elimination of Tay-Sachs disease, which afflicts people of only that specific ethnic makeup. Unfortunately, there is not yet sufficient regulation to assure the accuracy of such tests. The University of Washington maintains an online, searchable database of genetic diseases and clinics providing genetic tests.[214]

This discussion risks understating the extreme limitations in our understanding the workings of the three billion base pairs of information that make up the human genome. Scientists have recently warned against the over-simple notion that one gene produces one protein which produces one trait. Indeed, we are just beginning to gain understanding of how the activity of specific genes is suppressed or enhanced by "epigenetic" tags and folds in our chromosomes. Moreover, so-called "junk" genes, once thought to have little function, make up most of our genetic material and are likely to have complex functions we do not yet understand. Traits are also often influenced by gene variants typically inherited in groups known as haplotypes, yet another layer of complexity.

But complexity has not been an insurmountable barrier to particle physics and it will not prevent us from refining and advancing our success at genetic manipulation. In spite of the obstacles, before long we will literally draw life's blueprint and custom manufacture the repair or enhancement genes we want from bulk laboratory biochemicals. Today, you can phone 1-877-DNA-TOGO or visit their website to place your confidential order for customized genes for as low as $2.00 per base pair with a guaranteed 15-day delivery time for up to 1,500 base pairs. Integrated DNA Technologies advertises custom gene synthesis at a bargain 95 cents per base pair.[215] Another company with a snappy moniker, DNA 2.0, markets itself this way:

> Try our free Gene Designer software. Not only does it allow codon optimization using a choice of codon distribution tables, while minimizing DNA repeats and mRNA secondary structures etc. It is also a universal software tool for all your gene design needs. The software is available for download ... Gene synthesis allows you

to define exactly what specifications the gene should conform to, instead of consuming your time and effort in working around the limitations of the natural gene … We … will be very happy to walk you through the entire gene design process, making sure that your gene includes all of the features that you will need.[216]

The addition of an artificial 47th human chromosome is another potential means to repair genetic defects or to make possible population-wide genetic enhancement. An artificial add-on chromosome avoids the risk of inaccurate insertion of desired genetic material into a cell's genome. Artificial chromosomes in mice have been shown to replicate when cells divide and are passed to succeeding generations.[217] Lab experiments have shown the potential for use of artificial chromosomes to cure several genetic disorders.[218]

Up to here, I have discussed enhancement and repair of an individual's genotype by selecting from the menu of genes and haplotypes already found in humans. Once we get this taste for playing God, we may go even further and invent brand-new enhancement genes. This concept was demonstrated in mice, way back in 1999. Princeton neurobiologist Joe Tsien and his colleagues created a strain of smarter transgenic mice by increasing the number and activity of their NR2B genes. Tsien's mice could learn faster and remember longer, and do it farther into their old age than standard-issue mice; they could also pass these traits on to later generations.[219]

Pharmaceuticals are yet another route to cognitive enhancements in our motor systems, learning, memory, mood, and personality. Neuroscientist Tim Tully's company, Helicon Therapeutics, has a long-term memory-enhancing drug in clinical trials.[220] Ginkgo extract or a compound named PTZ improved memory in mice for up to three months per injection.[221] The prescription drug Provigil, already approved for treatment of narcolepsy, garners an estimated 90 percent of its sales from off-label use by test-taking students, long-distance truck drivers, and financial traders, all of whom report sharply increased focus, attention, and productivity—largely free of side effects.[222] The stimulant Ritalin improves concentration and spatial working memory, which is great for architects. The new, non-addictive amphetamine substitute atomoxetine accelerates motor learning, an effect helpful to musicians and athletes. Donepezil, designed to combat dementia, helped airplane pilots in a research study to perform far better than pilots on a placebo. If long-term experience with Donepezil proves it safe, would you want to fly with a pilot who had *not* taken it? If you're a college-bound student facing SAT test competitors who are fueled up on Provigil, will you handicap yourself by going drug-free?[223]

The prospects for human enhancement do not end with better bodies, personalities, and brains. Science is now at the edge of understanding means to dramatically lengthen healthy human lifespans. Aging, instead of being accepted as an inevitable aspect of life, will be viewed as a disease that inflicts physical and mental decline and causes unnecessary human suffering. Potential longevity strategies include: genetic and hormonal tinkering (in experiments, the worm *C. elegans* has had its lifetime extended by six times[224]); the restriction of caloric intake (tests of mice on a limited diet have led them to live 50 percent longer[225]); and the cellular-level repair of accumulated age-related injury.[226] Mice whose Klotho genes have been artificially extended produce more of a hormone that increases insulin resistance (a problem side effect) but live 19 to 31 percent longer.[227] Lower body temperatures also seem to increase longevity, according to a Scripps Institute study of mice whose body temperatures were artificially reduced by one-half to one degree Fahrenheit; they lived 12 to 20 percent longer, without apparent harm.[228] Researchers at Virginia-based Gencia Corporation are developing techniques to replace defective genes in mitochondria, the subcells inside most cells that burn sugars to produce energy. Unlike cellular genes, mitochondria have no means to repair the mutations that accumulate as we age. Mitochondrial gene repair offers another gateway to the lengthening of our lives.[229]

Longer, healthier lives will allow the more talented among us to accumulate greater knowledge and judgment, produce more, and remain longer in positions of leadership. With age-related impairment pushed back decades, the rhythm of natural succession will cease, and for the first time, four to five generations will be put into direct competition with one another. Within the lifetimes of our children, life extension and pharmacological and genetic enhancement will yield remarkable benefits. And, as we will see in the later pages of this book, they will intensify OverSuccess in ways we cannot yet imagine.

The increasingly robust scientific support for the prospect of better bodies, sharper minds, and longer lives has enhanced the credibility of the transhumanist movement. In 2003, I attended the first national conference of the World Transhumanist Association, held at Yale University. I expected a cult of Heinlein geeks, syncretic ontologists, and cyborg wannabees. All three and more were there. But two-thirds of the conference attendees were Ph.D.s who perfectly understood the science behind the progress they were making. They came to report on the pending union of humans and technology. In the first session, I sat next to a pony-tailed, sandal-clad, pencil-thin hippie-type fidgeting with the frazzled strands of his red, six-inch beard. Wonderfully exemplifying the latitudes that come with secure status, he turned out to be the University of Cambridge biogerontologist Aubrey de Grey, the world's leading scientist-advocate for what he calls "curing death." Speaking as rapidly as a radio announcer would machine-gun out the radioactive fine print for a car loan, he predicted that the first person who will live to the age of a thousand is alive today.

The world's largest single source of funding for human enhancement research comes from an organization dedicated to building a cadre of supermen (and superwomen): the U.S. Defense Department's Defense Advanced Research Projects Agency. DARPA funds a large portfolio of aggressive programs focused on augmented cognition, accelerated learning, stamina, extreme temperature and pain tolerance, and overcoming sleep deprivation.[230] Risking trademark infringement against Disneyland, DARPA's defense science office website proclaimed in 2002, "the magic begins with us."

With its ventures into mind over matter, DARPA is making carnival illusionists look like rookies. Research it has funded has already demonstrated telekinesis in monkeys. Externally detected brainwaves are translated into radio signals to control remote machines. Atlanta's Neural Signals, a private company, has achieved telekinesis in humans.[231] It is working, in a fashion, within humans too. An auto accident at age 19 left Eric Ramsey of Boston so paralyzed that he is able to communicate with the outside world using only eye movements. Now, with the aid of a wireless chip that uses Neural Signals' technology implanted just beneath the surface of his brain, Ramsey can "speak" a few basic syllables. The chip transmits the signals from a handful of neurons involved in moving the tongue and mouth to generate speech to an external receiver fitted with decoding software.[232]

Neuroscientist John Chapin, working under a DARPA contract, has created live, remote-control rats, with implants wired directly into the dopamine-reward pathways of their brains. Chapin can control their movements from his laptop, turning the rats into living bomb sniffers.[233] DARPA has sponsored development of a neural implant for sharks, designed to turn these animals into remote-control detectors of scent and electromagnetic fields in the open ocean.[234] DARPA has more recently discontinued its rat and shark experiments in favor of beetles whose wingbeats and direction can be governed by onboard software instructions and GPS signals. The insects will operate more surreptitiously in battlefield conditions than the larger animals. One team is working on a controller to be inserted into insects during their pupal stage, the hope being that the device will stably integrate into the insect's body as it develops into the adult flying stage.[235] From rats to insects to human beings, from DARPA to the science lab, "the scary part isn't that the technology is coming; it's that the major scientific breakthroughs have already been done. Now it's really just a question of engineering," says Chapin.[236]

THE MORAL CASE FOR CAUTION

Within a few years, benchmarks for human performance will begin to rise in concert with the accelerating commercialization of enhancement research. Many of us will be unwilling or unable to keep up with the genetically, pharmaceutically, and bionically enhanced Joneses. But once embryo screening and implantation become standardized pregnancy options—and that day is arriving very soon—parents will be confronted with an escalating norms race for their children-to-be. Many parents will want to help their children win. Others, however reluctant, will not want their children to be left behind; they will ditch the randomness of natural procreation and select for sex, health, height, eye color, and, later, complex polygenetic traits such as social facility, perseverance, and intelligence.[237]

During early years, enhancement technology will be available only at prohibitive cost or via black or gray markets, putting access off limits to the majority. Many parents will resist out of due caution or moral repugnance. But soon, within not more than two generations, the minority who refuse to adopt the radically more effective enhancement technology will be left so far behind as to foreclose their making a meaningful contribution to society. Tomorrow's losers will find themselves defeated by an OverSuccess more oppressive than anything we imagine today. In the end, few people will retreat from the near-certainty of the accelerated evolution of our species.

Formidable moral, social, and political questions will be raised about the new free-market eugenics. Will we come to view our children as designer objects, as we terminate pregnancies in the test tube or in the womb for those likely to be only average in height or intelligence? Will average become the new disability? Will parents' new power to engineer their children's success "undermine the ethical ideal of unconditional acceptance of children, no matter what their abilities and traits?" asks Oxford philosopher Nick Bostrom, summarizing the grave concerns of moral opponents. Will our longer lives further tax the planet's limited resources? Will the tenacious grasp on earned status by those with decades of additional vigor leave too little elbow room for the young?

Will we use drugs to banish struggles over our conflicting motivations—struggles that would otherwise make us wiser and stronger or lead us to unprogrammed creativity? Will we be coerced like major-league baseball players into keeping up with the genetically and pharmaceutically enhanced just to get hired? The scientists, entrepreneurs, and visionaries for whom human enhancement is gospel about to be fulfilled must lead us into a survey of their promised land with more caution and skepticism. We can probably all agree in theory that it is good that humans will be smarter and live longer. The trouble is, unless we heal the intensified OverSuccess that will accompany these benefits, we may not be happier.

Historian Francis Fukuyama, a member of the presidential bioethics council, warns, "the posthuman world could be one that is far more hierarchical and competitive than the one that currently exists, and full of social conflict as a result. It could be one in which any notion of 'shared humanity' is lost."[238] A conference organized specifically to oppose genetic enhancement warns of "new forms of discrimination, racism, and exclusion . . . that could radically alter the nature of humanity and undermine the foundations of civil society." These alarms are warranted.

The central moral concern about human enhancement is the potential social chasm—an organic Berlin Wall between those who can access and afford the new success technologies, and those who will be left behind in the escalating norms race. The potential for an unbridgeable divide between enhancement haves and have-nots is cause for such serious apprehension that many of the most ardent transhumanists—libertarian and liberal alike—support a state-funded enhancement welfare system to boost the bottom of the skills distribution curve. Once body and mind augmentation become standard practice, to what extent should social welfare systems include enhancement services to the disadvantaged? To what extent should public and private charity provide support for large populations of those who decline such enhancement or do not have access to it? Should parents be permitted to withhold from their children the enhancements that will, like it or not, be necessary for them to participate in the coming more complex social, political, and economic systems?

Our meritocracy will promptly sort out human capacities from the present lows to the coming new, much-higher highs, and we will confront the prospect of a caste system more pitiless than one the planet has ever known. Do a gut check on whether my warnings about the coming meritocratic caste system are overstated. Do you include in your regular business or private social affairs developmentally disabled people? What is your tolerance for the taxes necessary to fund humane social supports for the unenhanced if they made up, say, twenty or fifty percent of the American population?

Human history has been continuously darkened by the genocidal exterminations of millions of racial "others," most recently by Saddam, Hitler, and Stalin and as far back as the arrival of modern humans and the sudden disappearance of human Neanderthals from Europe. In 2001, philosopher George Annas was first to sound the alarm about the prospect of genetic genocide among new human-created human subspecies. For that reason, Annas called for the establishment of a global ban on species-altering modifications to the human germline.[239] The dangers of an incipient, science-backed, neo-eugenics are revealed in the hubris of this proposal published in and endorsed by the editor of *The American Journal of Psychiatry* just 65 years ago:

> I believe when the defective child shall have reached the age of five years—and on the application of his guardians—that the case should be considered under law by a competent medical board; then it should be reviewed twice more at four-month intervals; then, if the board, acting, I repeat, on the applications of the guardians of the child, and after three examinations of a defective who has reached the age of five or more, should decide that that defective has no future or hope of one; then I believe it is a merciful and kindly thing to relieve that defective—often tortured and convulsed, grotesque and absurd, useless and foolish, and entirely undesirable—of the agony of living.[240]

Such proposals, horrifying to us now, will become unnerving topics of policy debate in the near future. We are changing the very nature of what it means to be humans who live with immutable and naturally inherited limitations and die after six to ten decades—and there is no going back.

FROM CONTROVERSY TO NECESSITY

But the die was cast in 1410. We have, in fact, long since slipped our natural boundaries, radically altering our bodies, minds, and behaviors thanks to such technical and social advancements as vitamins, formal education, social stimulus in child-rearing, the unwritten norms that encourage us to thank our benefactors, and the written laws that require us to drive in the right-hand lane. Historically, new technologies of human enhancement usually track a course from secrecy to controversy, acceptance, and ultimately necessity. Consider vaccinations against smallpox as one instructive example. In the Britain of 1775, the disease afflicted 95 of every 100 people, killing one in seven. Yet smallpox vaccination was still being denounced as an unfair advantage until the end of the century.[241] General George Washington powerfully contributed to the American revolutionary war victory by secretly ordering the inoculation of his Valley Forge troops against smallpox in 1777, though he risked court martial for doing it. By the 1800s, the British government was organizing the mass inoculation of factory workers. These healthier and more productive workers made a signal contribution to that nation's hegemony. This adoption pattern will repeat itself frequently in our brave new century.

More recently, during the 1990s, consumer demand surged for classes of medicine that had been conceived to treat diseases and handicaps but now are employed primarily for human enhancement. One case is plastic surgery. Another is the use of the anti-depressant Paxil to increase social self-confidence. These two treatments, one surgical and one pharmacological, were once hidden embarrassments; now they are status symbols and prerequisites for success. Similarly, and more significantly for our purposes here, in vitro fertilization was controversial barely twenty years ago; today, there exists no movement to abandon any of these unnatural advantages now that they are safe, effective, and familiar. As for stem cell research or the use of drugs for off-label purposes, no restrictions will halt the market's acceptance of the results of enhancement technology. Our moral shepherds should stop kidding themselves that banning such scientific advances will work. Many people will not risk gutter-balling their careers or curtailing their children's potential by abstaining.

The mass shift to higher human intelligence is inevitable; overwhelming economic forces will trump moral resistance to it. Richard Lynn and Tatu Vanhanen's compelling book, *IQ and the Wealth of Nations*, documents that intelligence is prosperity's single most powerful determinant. More than culture, natural resources, climate, and economic system, intelligence explains 54 percent of the variance among the per capita gross domestic product of the 81 nations where the authors could find sufficient data.[242] University of Washington psychometrician Earl Hunt calculated desired IQ for 706 American job categories, finding that the proportion of today's jobs requiring above-average IQs of 105–125 are about twice the proportion of the population having those IQs.[243] Many countries will not wait long after the first mover (probably China, given its breakneck adoption of American success culture) to embrace safe and effective IQ enhancement as the most powerful available tool it has for economic advancement.

America and the other democratic nations will sidestep cautionary warnings about the horrors of state-sponsored eugenics—because individuals will make the choices, just as individuals, not the state, today opt in for plastic surgery and Paxil. The only open questions about genetic enhancement are exactly how soon, in which nations, and how openly it will occur. We Americans are inconsistent in our views on human enhancement; by an 87- to 13-percent margin, we oppose genetic engineering to select our baby's characteristics, but, by 81 to 19 percent, we favor drugs and surgery to extend our lives.[244] Our moral boundary seems to be use of biotech to preserve, but not enhance. But the minority will drag along the majority, just as trophy houses and SUVs supplanted split-level ranches and station wagons. After all, our drive to overcome our limitations has 600 years of unbroken momentum.

If the United States were to impose restrictions, East Asian nations such as China or India are virtually certain to rush ahead, given already strong government and popular support for genetic engineering there.[245] Some American critics call for such a halt. Bill McKibben from the political left and Leon Kass from the right argue forcefully that we should voluntarily stem the tidal wave of enhancement technologies that will lead us inevitably to the escalation of benchmarks in human achievement of all kinds—an escalation that is the subject of this book's next chapter.[246] However, if their entreaties succeed—which is unlikely—then America will only divert even more biotechnology investment to Asia. Just as we do our televisions and help desks, Americans will simply import the enhancement we need to succeed. If necessary, we will do so as surreptitiously as baseball players do their steroids. Whether or not America attempts to restrict it, political upheaval will accompany our inevitable enhanced future. The Republican and Democratic parties may fissure, with market and social libertarians and national security hawks driving moral conservatives and left-wing egalitarians into each other's arms.

By mid-century, aging will be a treatable disease. We will choose our children's IQ, talents, and metabolic efficiency. Dramatically more varied behavior and physical appearance will become choices based on fashion and lifestyle. New, more complex languages, cultures, and economies will diverge and disconnect from the old mainstream. We will complete our ongoing segregation into cognitive enclaves, and gone will be the fundamentally American premise that all of us are created equal. The enhanced elite will lead the world and set the dramatically higher benchmarks that those of us in the game will be compelled to emulate. OverSuccess will turn from an instrument of social defeat into an instrument of social torture.

But we have personal and political choices that can put enhancement in service of a future that will not only increase human accomplishment, but also augment happiness and satisfaction for most of us. For example, gene therapy can be put to use not only to make athletes more rich and famous, but also to cure bubble boy syndrome, chronic alcoholism, and chronic social defeat. I will turn to this and nineteen more cures for OverSuccess in this book's last chapter.

4

SUPERNATURAL BENCHMARKS

Simply moderate giftedness has been made worthless by the printing press and radio and television and satellites and all that. A moderately gifted person who would have been a community treasure a thousand years ago has to give up, has to go into some other line of work, since modern communications has put him or her into daily competition with nothing but the world's champions ... The entire planet can get along nicely now with maybe a dozen champion performers in each area of human giftedness.[247]
—Kurt Vonnegut, 1987

WE HAVE SEEN HOW the normal human desire for social visibility and America's individual achievement culture foster our drive for success. We have witnessed how technology is about to radically accelerate the pace of human improvement. Now we turn attention to the sharply rising benchmarks by which success is measured, and how they contribute to its pathologic form, OverSuccess.

The recent advent of the global economy has expanded the meritocratic talent pool by at least ten times. Gifted people from five continents now vie for the top spots in all of America's realms of competition, from business and science to sports and the arts. The winners, such as Kenyan marathoners and Indian software engineers, have now mapped the rarest and most sublime peaks of current human potential. The larger scale of the global economy and the emotionally immersive mass communications media (about which you will hear more in Chapter 5) have leveraged the value and public visibility of the winning talents. Yet in every field of endeavor, the number of top slots remains about the same. Monetary and power rewards for top performers are escalating so rapidly that ordinary people are unable to gain even fleeting recognition via their new status possessions. Google guy Larry Page, worth $20 billion, chartered private jets from all points of the globe to fly in his 170 guests (all of whom were asked to sign non-disclosure agreements) for his wedding celebration held at Richard Branson's $46,000-per-night private island, just off Virgin Gorda. The Google guys' own private 767 has been upstaged by the new high-water-mark in air travel, Prince Walid's personal Airbus A380, which will cost him $300 million before it is fitted with custom-ary palace amenities. The $50,000 SUV, only a few years ago a status symbol, is now reserved for the staff.

The gargantuan visibility and rewards given to winners have lured more qualified people into the chase for the hypertrophied spoils. The increased competition has made the pressure to acquire necessary skills invade all cor-ners of our lives. OverSuccessed parents are buying physical therapy for their perfectly normal two-year-olds, so that their children can pass admission tests to elite, gateway preschools. In every arena of endeavor, from pole vaulting to pediatric medicine to computational finance, preparation is more demanding, training regimens more sophisticated. Candidates with superior talents are identified earlier in life and provided more enriched learning environments; the new, higher performance benchmarks they master become the new norm. We live under a virtuous cycle where today's win is tomorrow morning's entry fee. Competition has intensified to the very edge of what we can tolerate. We learn early and thoroughly the hair's-breadth difference between winning and losing; everywhere, the gap between the celebrated victors and soon-forgot-ten runners-up has shrunk to hundredths of a second.

The big rewards and promiscuous visibility given to the most successful have lured even larger hordes of unqualified runners into the chase, resulting in a type of mass delusion among Americans: victory seems so everyday that we think we can win, too. Almost half of us think that we will become rich; almost a third think we will become famous. Many of us buy the constantly repeated lie that any American who really wants to can reach the top when, whether we admit it or not, at least half of the traits that determine whether we will ever join the winner's circle are inherited. Even the willpower of a blowtorch cannot deliver the traits that make Olympic athletes, theoretical physicists, and $2,000-an-hour management consultants if the potential for it isn't ordained by our DNA.

I learned this lesson firsthand when I decided I had what it takes to reach for Internet gold. What a fool I was to believe the new era hype, calculated to make the tech bubble look democratic and to suck in billions from dentists and plumbing contractors at PEs of infinity. Garage.com—so named because Hewlett-Packard had been launched in a residential garage—was running packed two-day conferences it called IPO (initial public offering) boot camps at $1000 a head. Here is the formula. First, build your advisory board by granting stock options to a Carnegie Mellon professor who is getting buzz about his recent paper on something massively parallel or nanotech. Then, for ten percent of the company, snag a CTO (chief technology officer) who is between jobs and willing to let you use his name on the business plan for a few months. Polish up your "elevator pitch," preferably not more than thirty seconds, on how you will disrupt the world and generate a market cap bigger than 3M's. One VC (venture capitalist) called the process "tornado diving": You jump off a tall building in hopes that a tornado will catch you and whisk you up to the promised land. "If it works, the results are impressive," he remarked.[248]

There I was, standing in the hotel lobby between bootcamp breakout sessions, cell phone to my ear, making a fake call so I would look important while waiting in line to pitch a C-list VC about my plan to disrupt democracy. I did manage to get a few meetings, one with a major Boston VC, but only because (as I later learned) the firm had funded a competitor to my project and wanted to milk me for intelligence. The founder of a Providence VC went ballistic and terminated the meeting when I turned what he thought unpatriotic by uttering the words "special interest." My only solace was that less than a year later the $30 million the Boston VC had pumped into the competitor was burned to flyash by a cocky, twenty-something CEO.

The garage startup model is dead. Intelligence and drive are no longer enough to succeed. Bring both brilliance and connections to the table, or bag it. Eric Schmidt, the CEO of Google, lays out the challenge honestly: "Colleges like Harvard and MIT and Stanford are part of a social network. You can be a brilliant entrepreneur, but if you go to a no-name school you don't have access to these networks. Take my word for it, the networks count for a lot in this industry. I keep reading in the business magazines that anybody can raise venture capital for an Internet company. Yeah, right. Anybody can raise capital for an Internet company if they know the same guys that I do."[249] If you are not a member of the right fraternity, don't bother waiting for your calls to be returned. You'll be staring up at a glass ceiling you don't even know is there.

THE GENETIC LOCKOUT

The downside of pure meritocracy is that you are unlikely to get into the right fraternity unless you inherited the right genes. Our genes control not only variation in physical appearance, but also in aptitude, behavior, and personality. We readily accept our inherited differences in hair or eye color, height, and facial appearance. We balk at digesting the hard fact that we also inherit about half of the social and intellectual talents that are the gateway to visible success. "Put concisely," comments psychologist and heritability researcher Thomas Bouchard, "all psychological traits are heritable."[250]

Studies of identical twins reared apart have provided our best insight so far into the extent that our resumes are pre-written by our genes. Even when they are separated at birth, have no contact with each other, and are raised in different environments, by adulthood identical twins are often stunningly similar in personality and intelligence, sometimes precisely sharing individual behavioral quirks. One pair of reunited twins who had never met before discovered that both dunked buttered toast in their coffee. Another pair habitually wore rubber bands around their wrists.[251] A third pair, adopted at infancy by different families, both named their favorite pet "Toy." One twin named his son James Alan; the other named his son James Allen. Identical twins have almost zero difference in the volume of brain gray matter in their frontal, sensorimotor, and language cortices. The structure of these brain regions is under very high genetic control and differences among individuals in these regions predict about 70 percent of differences in measured general intelligence.[252] From twin studies, we know that genes are a far more powerful predictor of happiness than income, health, social status, or other life outcome measures.

Table 4.1 summarizes data from several dozen studies that quantify the degree to which variation in selected human traits is heritable. Several qualifications apply to these data. First, while these figures are reasonably accurate

Table 4.1: Extent of Heritability of Selected Human Traits

Trait	Percent Heritable	Comment
Intelligence, Adult[253]	82–85	Environment is dominant influence until age 10. Heritability increases from 22% at age 5 to 82% at age 18. IQ heritability far lower in adolescents from poor families.[254]
Personality[255]	33–58	Traits studied: Extraversion, agreeableness, conscientiousness, neuroticism, openness.
Sexual Orientation, Homosexuality[256]	50–60	Literature survey, various studies cited.
Religiosity[257]	40	
Political Conservatism, Adult[258]	45–65	45 percent for females; 65 percent for males.
Vocational, Recreational Interests[259]	31–50	Bouchard reports numbers in the 31-38-percent range.
Happiness[260]	44–52	Subjective Well Being (SWB) measured.
Extraversion[261]	54	
Novelty Seeking[262]	55	Boredom susceptibility 40 percent.
Self-Esteem[263]	29–32	
Depression[264]	40–54	Heritability ranges up to 78 percent in adolescents.

Trait	Percent Heritable	Comment
Extreme Shyness[265]	70–80	
Extreme Narcissism[266]	65	
Extreme Self-Loathing[267]	60	
Antisocial Behavior[268]	41–46	Viding reports callous, unemotional traits at 70 percent.
Prosocial Behavior[269]	42	Altruism, empathy and nurturance.
Social Support, Female[270]	43–75	Relative problems, friend problems, relative support, confidants, friend support, and social integration measured.
Divorce Risk[271]	42, 30	Men, women, respectively.
Autism[272]	89	
ADHD[273]	76	Attention Deficit Hyperactivity Disorder.
Reading Disability[274]	48	
Schizophrenia[275]	80	
Bipolar Disorder[276]	72	
Female Obsessions, Compulsions[277]	33, 26	Percentages are obsessions, compulsions, respectively.
Addiction Propensity[278]	40–60	Literature survey of heritability of multiple addictions
Illegal Psychoactive Drug Use[279]	60–80	Heavy use, abuse or dependence, males only.
Gambling Addiction[280]	35–54	
Alcoholism[281]	48–58	
Regular Tobacco Use[282]	61–63	Respectively, males versus females born after 1940.
Heavy Caffeine Use & Addiction[283]	35+	Caffeine is the most widely used psychoactive substance.
Violent Criminal Behavior[284]	50	
Anorexia, Bulimia[285]	>50, 60	Female-only data; binge-eating is 50-percent heritable.
Binge-Eating[286]	51	Same for men and women.

Trait	Percent Heritable	Comment
Obesity[287]	86	Only women studied.
Weight[288]	25–40	
Height[289]	90	
Blood Pressure[290]	60	
Near- and Farsightedness[291]	89	
Cancer[292]	35	Varies greatly by type of cancer.

across large populations, genetic legacies may be higher or lower for each individual—with gestational and childhood environment and purely random effects playing the remaining roles. Second, these high heritability numbers are derived primarily from studies of twins. Where twins have identical genes, children inherit the randomized combination of their mother's and father's genes, which results in the averaging of more pronounced or extreme high or low traits and the blurring of trait inheritance. Third, twins separated at birth are nonetheless typically raised in similar environments. For example, American twins in a separated pair are likely to be given free public education, immunizations, vitamins, and eyeglasses to correct vision problems, all interventions that narrow the extent to which genes are expressed differently in different environments. Fourth, the same gene can also be tagged differently with "epigenetic" markers that boost or suppress their expression. These epigenetic regulatory settings can be inherited or can result from random effects or from the environment in the womb and beyond. Whereas genes are only slightly prone to mutation during our lifetimes, our epigenome remains only partially stable. Studies on identical twins reared in nearly identical environments have shown that, to some extent, differences in life outcomes and the incidence of disease—once thought to be the result of differences in environment—may instead be due to random changes to an individual's epigenome.[293]

These estimates of heritability may also be low. Studies for several personality traits using more rigorous techniques show heritabilities ranging from

40 up to 70 percent for anti-social behavior and 89 percent for the qualities of helping, sharing, and adherence to social and moral standards. Some aspects of our personality and attitudes may be almost entirely controlled by genes. While what we inherit from our parents may be exaggerated by twin studies, they accurately portray how greatly our genes govern our behavior and aptitudes.

Given these qualifications, I am comfortable reaching three conclusions. First, most of our automatic motivations and behaviors were evolved for a pre-agricultural world that largely no longer exists. Second, at least half of those motivations and behaviors are programmed by our genes rather than arising from the choices we consciously calculate. Third, for most of us, the escalating pressure to succeed collides with our not having inherited genes for a 180 IQ, marathon running, or perfect pitch. Environment, a realm over which we can exercise some control, may be less of an influence on our life history than is hoped by believers in human willpower. The bottom line is: few of us have the base pairs to achieve visible success. Our efforts to achieve America's high benchmarks—in almost every field—depend increasingly on physical and intellectual traits over which we currently have no control. Relief from these depressing conclusions can be found in adopting life goals rationally matched to our talents and in living and working in communities likely to respect and recognize our contributions.

THE ILLUSION OF ACCESSIBILITY

But humans and, particularly, Americans are an irrationally optimistic lot and our desire to reach, to paraphrase poet Robert Browning, can exceed our power to grasp. Economists, sociologists, and psychologists have repeatedly documented our normal propensity to overrate ourselves. Other than for depressed people, whose self-assessments are ironically accurate, when it comes to our own aptitudes and hopes, most of us are delusional optimists.[294]

Research by British evolutionary psychologist Daniel Nettle, who specializes in the psychobiology of status differences, confirms that we consistently overestimate our personal traits, our career prospects, our economic futures, and our influence over future events that involve us. We credit ourselves for our good fortune and blame outside circumstances for the bad. We remember our successes and forget our failures. We see ourselves as more likely than others to escape the consequences of risky actions. Our bullishness in the face of uncertainty tends to wilt only as we gain experience. Nettle believes that these tendencies are evolutionary advantages that allow us to act promptly when benefits outweigh costs and where there is insufficient time to gain accurate information to make a purely rational decision. "The presence of positive illusions, far from being a pathology, is related to good and robust mental health," he observes.[295]

But American culture puts our native optimism on steroids. In this regard we differ from people of other nationalities, as shown by sociologists Steven Heine and Takeshi Hamamura. Heine and Hamamura integrated 81 existing studies on their subject, finding that Americans tend to self-aggrandize, where East Asians do not. This cultural contrast was striking and highly consistent across almost all the studies. We Americans prime ourselves for success by thinking of ourselves as competent and uniquely talented, ready right now to prevail in our meritocracy. Asians think of themselves as succeeding best through self-improvement and by meeting consensual standards.[296]

Over recent decades, young Americans have become increasingly grandiose and delusional in their self-assessments. University of San Diego research psychologist Jean Twenge thinks the blame rests with the ill-considered self-esteem movement fostered in schools. Twenge has compared surveys of American college students over twenty-five years, finding that the student with average self-esteem in 1994 would be among the unusually self-aggrandizing of 1968.[297] Using more recent data, Twenge examined the responses of 16,000 college students to another survey, the Narcissistic Personality Inventory, with results gathered over the period 1982 to 2006. The NPI requires respondents to select as true or false statements such as "If I ruled the world, it would be a better place," "I think I am a special person," and "I can live my life any way I want to." Narcissists tend to lack empathy, are hostile toward criticism, have weak social relationships, enjoy inflated expectations and self-image, and are manipulative and self-promotional. Twenge found that two-thirds of students now score above the typical level of narcissism found in the early 1980s.[298] Students have become markedly more self-centered and egotistical over the past three decades.

Across the range of our endeavors, our expectations have grown increasingly out of whack with reality. For example, more than 70 percent of high school seniors rank themselves above average in leadership ability, only 2 percent of them below average. More than 90 percent of factory production workers think they are more productive than average.[299] Forty percent of professional sociologists expect eventually to be regarded as among the top ten in their specialization.[300] Two of every three black male high school athletes think they will make the pros, when the actual odds for a high school basketball player are 10,000 to one. Sixty percent of NCAA Division I college basketball starters believe they are destined to start for an NBA team, where the actual proportion is under five percent.[301] About three-quarters of all motorists think they drive more safely than the typical driver.[302] And perhaps most tellingly, when it comes to the delusions that pump up our success obsession, for every dollar that American gamblers think they are ahead in casinos, they are actually losing five.[303] We think of ourselves as financial winners even as our wallets are emptied.

Another unlikely gamble, one that warps lots of lives, is acting on the widely held magical belief, nurtured by OverSuccess, that entertainment-industry stardom is a single audition away. The blonds that land on the covers of the tabloids that glut every American grocery checkout line appear to do nothing but smile, shop, and vacation. Armies of young women are tricked into thinking that anyone with persistence, a winning attitude, and white teeth can become Jennifer Aniston. Parents are no less intoxicated by the Kool-Aid.

Each year, tens of thousands of mothers leave home and husband behind, dragging children as young as five to live for months or years at a time in soulless places like the Oakwood Toluca Hills apartments in Los Angeles, convenient to Studio City and the 24-hour drone of Route 101. These parents become unpaid, full-time personal aides, clothing, feeding, tutoring, and chauffeuring their aspiring child—with the overhead for their dreams sucking down tens of thousands of dollars of family savings annually. Their days are filled with voice classes, headshots, and endless waiting by the phone for audition calls. When the calls come, hundreds of these children fill up waiting rooms within minutes. California issued 120,000 entertainment work permits for minors in 2004, a year when only 1,800 members of the Screen Actors Guild of any age made more than $10,000. The hard reality is that no more than thirty to fifty actors can actually be classified by measure of income or fame as stars.[304]

Our ungrounded optimism is reflected in our political outlook. In my race for the state senate, I easily won election over an opponent whose platform focused on an income-leveling income tax; his spokesperson shared with me her incredulity that I had won so big in a poor town in the district. She failed to see that Americans do not harbor animosity toward wealth and success because so many of us believe that we will someday join the club. A *New York Times* poll asked Americans if it is possible to "start out poor, work hard, and become rich." Eighty percent said yes in 2005, up from 57 percent two decades earlier. This same poll also found that 45 percent of us think it at least somewhat likely we will personally become wealthy in the future.[305] Actual data tracking several thousand American families since 1968 found that only 5 percent rose into the top one percent of incomes at some point during their lives.[306] So, we over-estimate our odds of becoming wealthy by almost ten times. Only nine percent of Americans, including only nine percent of the lowest-income Americans, support a law limiting what people can earn. When we are asked to choose between two visions for our nation, one that guarantees the opportunity to succeed, the other guaranteeing security from failure, 76 percent of us prefer opportunity and only 20 percent choose security.[307] Though economic inequality in America has increased over past decades, our bullish illusions have grown. No wonder that John Edwards and his populist "two Americas" platform never polled over 15 percent even among Democratic voters in the 2008 presidential primaries.

Our political leaders have long conflated the shining American ideal of equal opportunity with the false notion that anyone can become rich and famous. Benjamin Franklin is renowned for being the first to popularize the American ideal of personal success, and for his admirable faith in the ability of the common person. Future president James Garfield spoke in 1869 to the graduating class of a business college, declaring that "The strata of our society resemble ... the ocean, where every drop, even the lowest, is free to mingle with all the others, and may shine at the last on the crest of the highest waves. This is the glory of our country."[308] During the 2004 Democratic primaries, before he retooled as a populist, John Edwards pitched himself uncontroversially to the very center of American values: "in our country, in our America, everything is possible."[309] Today, a candidate for president is considered unelectable without the rhetoric of relentless optimism, promising us loftier futures even as we sink in our ocean of debt.

American commercial culture saturates us with the illusion that success is at our fingertips. The glossy pages of *Architectural Digest* invite all of us to enjoy brunch on our marble verandahs overlooking the Caribbean, interrupted by cell phone calls from our agents. *People* and *Star* magazine show us how ordinary are the lives of the famous, caught shopping without makeup, pre- versus post-boob job, or in conjugal spat at the door of their SUV. We savor puncturing the famous to make their success accessible to us. The textures, tastes, and smells of peak status appear attainable because they are everywhere. The tabloids scream that fame is divorced from meaning or merit and that celebrity comes eventually to everyone, like a winning scratch ticket. The famous are just like the rest of us, separated only by a camera lens and a trip to the right real estate agent, car dealer, and plastic surgeon. Watching the cable news carnival one night, I caught these two ads almost back to back: the first for Cisco, saying "Welcome to the human network ... where anyone can be famous"; and the second for Macy's, declaring "Whatever makes you feel like a star." The result of years of such false promotions is the fact that an astounding thirty percent of us think we will someday become famous. Thirteen percent think it very likely.[310]

Commercial culture plants these illusions in infancy. The Disney Channel advertises its teen and pre-teen stars—smiling and surrounded by fans—as being "just like you." A *Nickelodeon* public service announcement intended to boost viewer self-esteem spotlights a real-life eleven-year-old, speaking with dead certainty to the camera, "I am going to be a big success. Miles Davis, watch out." The PSA fails to mention the genes and the decades of unglamorous practice and sacrifice that are required for the world's few Miles Davises to dazzle a serious music fan. We are transmitting to our children vivid, persuasive, and utterly false messages about the probability of visible success.

"I can do that," we say to ourselves, even when we can't, or when we'd be happier actually striving to do what we *could* do. Even as we are cautioned to refrain from addictive drugs, we are bombarded with images and messages that foster unlimited craving for wealth, adulation, and beauty. The sky is the limit. Be all you can be. Any American can become president. The real odds are more depressing. Is there an alterative to this cultural disinformation campaign? Yes, there is, as I'll explore in Chapter 10, where I show how nearly all of us can achieve success that is tuned to our actual talents and self-generated aspirations. But first we have to shed the gargantuan illusions infused into us by OverSuccess.

NO TIME FOR CHILDHOOD

In our world of hyper-competition, reaching high benchmarks demands that preparation begin earlier—much earlier. Anxious parents have become possessed in a relentless search for any available advantage for their progeny. Their quest starts with the first positive pregnancy test. Baby-naming consultants charging hundreds of dollars are retained to suggest monikers that account for phonetic rhythm, popularity, and originality. Parents are helpfully steered away from damagingly trendy names. Burt and Jennifer Alper selected the name Becket for their son. "That C-K sound is very well regarded in corporate circles. The hard stop forces you to accentuate the syllable in a way that draws attention to it," boasts Mr. Alper about the leg up he is confident he has given his child.[311]

Landing the right grad-school degree starts with the Baby Mozart CD, speaker pressed against Mom's stomach to infuse cognitive advantage directly into the womb. It may not be superstition. Recent evidence shows that six-year-olds can gain seven IQ points after eight months of music lessons—unfortunately from practicing, not listening.[312] As for the possibilities of visual stimulation, GeniusBabies says this about its Car Seat Gallery:

> This toy is easily installed (for BOTH front- and rear-facing infants) and features ten double-sided cards that are displayed and stored in four clear plastic pockets. The cards are comprised of

twenty research-correct graphics (ten in black & white, and ten in color) that can easily be changed and interchanged, providing a wealth of visual stimulation. Developmental Value: Encourages visual activity (scanning, focusing, tracking, orienting, and pattern recognition).

The epicenter of progeny status angst is probably Manhattan, where competition to get your three-year-old into the right preschool has driven parents neurotic. "Even the more reasonable folks are looking at their kindergartener's stick figures with a critical and competitive eye," says Steve Nelson, head of the Calhoun School, a top city private school.[313] The trend became noticeable in the late 1960s, cutthroat by the 1990s. Since 2002, the number of wealthy Manhattan children has been increasing and, like the Ivies, the number of private schools is static. Top Manhattan kindergartens are now accepting only one in seventeen applications, a more brutal ratio than Harvard's one in eleven. Some Manhattan parents admit anonymously to applying to ten or more recognized "feeder" nursery schools that are said to boost acceptance prospects at the right kindergartens. Amanda Uhry, president of Manhattan Private School Advisors, which provides counseling services for parents seeking preschool through high school admission for their kids, calls the 2009 admissions year "a minefield." Uhry's firm itself has a waiting list. Having friends on a school's board no longer guarantees admission. Moreover, most schools have terminated the practice of holding slots for siblings and children of alums. "Just because your sister is bright enough to get into a school doesn't really mean you are," says Uhry. "It kind of throws Clorox in the gene pool if you take kids who are substandard."[314]

As part of the admissions process at these schools, interviews—and interview prep—are the custom for even four-year-olds. Top preschools require testing for intellectual, social, and fine motor skills. The hard reality is that day-care kids with average IQs have no shot at acceptance at any of Manhattan's elite kindergartens. Said one disgusted mother whose son was wait-listed, "He's going to be pulling garment racks down Seventh Avenue."[315] A bustling new service has grown up around rehabilitating and tutoring four-year-olds who fall below the ninetieth percentile for auditory processing, tactile discrimination, or extroversion. Private occupational and physical therapists charging $200 per hour have waiting lists of perfectly normal boys.[316] Manhattan parents instruct their nannies to conceal these interventions and thus assure that their child appears effortlessly brilliant, properly reflecting their own intelligence.[317] In my preppy community well outside the New York commute radius, childhood is similarly penciled out of daily schedules choked by skill- and portfolio-building programs, and these waiting lists stretch beyond one year.

When it comes to college acceptance, benchmark escalation has reached the vicious-cycle stage. Adam Robinson, co-founder of Princeton Review, is a bird's-eye witness to the changes in SAT test prep since 1990. Back then, his company's Total Prep service cost $500.[318] Since then, Princeton Review and Kaplan Education Centers enrollments are up ten times and twenty times, respectively, making these services necessary, but no longer an advantage. Now, the bar is set at $5,000 for private SAT test tutoring. To gain a real edge, try IvyWise, which offers a $24,000, two-year program of application reviews, mock interviews, referrals to tutors and psychologists, and tailored guidance on athletic, extracurricular activities, internships, and the right hobbies.[319]

"These days, just having perfect grades and perfect SAT scores does not guarantee anything," said Victoria Hsiao, who works for a private admission counseling service. At Pomona College, nationally ranked number six in liberal arts, one-third of new admissions scored 800 on either their math or verbal SAT.[320] Hsiao warns against spending summers volunteering at the local hospital. "It's something every single high-school student does," she says, suggesting more adventurous pursuits more likely to break through to jaded college admissions officers. Putney Student Travel's $5,000 "global awareness" summer programs offer a far better subject for an application essay. In these programs, students study indigenous culture and help people with AIDS in Ecuador and Senegal.[321] What is the result of this admissions arms race? For all but an Olympics-bound polymath, getting into an elite college requires personal packaging, a managed portfolio of extracurricular activities, paid counseling to teach talking points and poise during interviews, and the abandonment of summer vacation.

Imagine the disappointment: being born on the wrong side of the tracks in elite Fairfield County, Connecticut. A parent lamented to me that one Ivy school has capped admissions from the county at sixteen. The surfeit of the super-achieving college-bound means that her Westport valedictorian tennis-star child did not even get wait-listed at the elite institutions they had hoped for. In 2007 the University of Pennsylvania rejected over one-third of valedictorians and seventy percent of near-perfect SAT scorers. Meanwhile, Ivy slots are barely increasing. To improve their odds, most students are applying to more colleges than ever before, and Ivy application numbers are breaking records. All the Ivies but one accepted their smallest-ever percentages of applicants in 2008.[322] Add to this cauldron of frustration the hyper-competitive screening process from which a new and larger wave of Ivy applicants flow from India and China, whose combined population of brilliant and motivated young people is ten times America's.

Fortunately for our economy, 38 of the world's top 50 research universities are in the United States.[323] America remains the global distillery and magnet for the educational elite. One-quarter of students leaving their home country for undergraduate and graduate education come to the U.S, which intensifies the competition among native-born Americans.[324] Over the past thirty years, foreign students as a percentage of all U.S. doctorate-degree recipients almost doubled, from 16 to 31 percent. Over these thirty years, foreign students accounted for nearly all the growth in new U.S. doctorates. In mathematics, computer sciences, engineering, and the physical and biological sciences, nearly half of new American doctorates are now earned by foreign students.

And the new Ph.D.s are increasingly staying here to compete after they graduate. Almost three-quarters of non-U.S. citizens with definite plans following doctoral graduation intend to remain here, up from fifty-seven percent in 1984. Among Chinese and Indians, almost nine in ten plan to work in the U.S. after graduation.[325] More Sierra Leonean doctors work in the Chicago metro area than in all of Sierra Leone. More African-born scientists and engineers work in America than in all of Africa.[326] Thirty percent of Mexicans with Ph.D.s live in the U.S. Three in four Jamaicans with post-grad degrees work in America. From both poor and rich nations, "it is the stars who are most likely to leave," (usually, for America), notes the *Economist* in a story tracking the trend.[327]

Pressures to compete globally have transformed American childhood. For children in America's middle and upper classes, structured activity has almost completely supplanted free exploration. During my youth, we neighborhood kids invented our own recreation and were not segregated by aptitude and age. My friends and I dammed up a swamp, explored and got lost in the woods, built tree forts and go-carts, bicycled to secret swimming holes, and played baseball in an ill-shaped gravel pit with no grass, drainage, or uniforms. Today, activities like this are considered dangerous wastes of time that do nothing to burnish one's grade-school curriculum vita. Today's elite class of children grow up on two-million-dollar playing fields that are safe enough to be immunized from trial lawyers, and supervised by paid, professionally trained adult coaches and referees. The average mom spends about an hour a day behind the wheel shuttling her kids to and from an ever-more-distant schedule of ballet lessons and soccer matches.[328] In the New York suburbs, an entrepreneur named Aresh Mohit does a booming business in the New York suburbs at $60 per hour teaching kids to ride a bike.[329]

Worried parents have invaded most childhood hobbies, morphing innocent and healthy pursuits into career-track battlefields. Each year now, nine million kids compete in the National Spelling Bee. The documentary *Spellbound* provides a very personal window into several of these contestants' lives. The winners and near-winners all enjoy extensive family support, high intelligence, and an intense commitment to perfection. The Hindu father of the ninth-place winner in *Spellbound* paid one thousand people to pray for his son—in addition to spending years before helping him memorize word roots from three languages.[330] Best-selling globalism booster Thomas Friedman, whose prescription for intensified competition among the world's smartest, best-educated people is more education and harder work, should check the daily schedules of a few upwardly mobile families to see where the increased hours would come from. Today, the seven-day, all-day scheduling regime begins when your child loses her first baby tooth.

A 2006 *New York Times* column, "How We Took the Child Out of Childhood," generated an avalanche of responses from parents frustrated by the very trend that so many of them have aggravated:

> "There is no 'child' in childhood anymore because kids have no down-time—especially the children perhaps most in need of down-

time: the achievers. If your child excels in school, he is placed in accelerated classes with crushing workloads. Weekends are gone. Homework takes up most of their waking hours. Gone are the days of family drives, lengthy Monopoly games, or all-day play dates," says Amy Kefauver.

"And the sports. Don't get me started. I haven't even broached the idea of trying to change the competitive mentality as it is so deeply entrenched. Junior high kids can choose a different sport three times during the school year, risk the humiliation of not being chosen for the team and, if chosen, must show up after school, 5 days a week, for two and a half hours!" write Rebecca and Rod Borrie.

"People have little time for their kids and compensate with their check books. It has come to be accepted that unless the kids are constantly being chauffeured to ballet or violin lessons that you are not a good parent. What rubbish. None of this is about the kids, alas. It's all about bragging rights for their parents. Ugh," writes Marjorie McCarthy.[331]

My post-Vietnam cohort ingested psychoactive substances and sought out forbidden experiences to break molds and upset the status quo. Today, there is no resistance to unrelenting career tracking. The young and the tracked now thoroughly embrace their parents' success coaching. Hyper-protective "helicopter parents" hover over their college-aged children's every move, cell-phoning daily, harassing administrators and professors about the school's plumbing and the faculty's teaching styles. Colgate University has been forced to implement a program to *reduce* parental involvement; the University of Vermont pays students to act as "parent bouncers."[332]

In one of his entertaining anthropological forays into upper-middle-class life, pundit David Brooks visited Princeton and Harvard and discovered what he dubbed "The Organization Kid." Ivy students, he wrote in an article in *The Atlantic*, are uniformly neatly dressed, clean-shaven, shampooed, and well mannered; their lives are aimed relentlessly at fast-tracking into challenging and rewarding careers. These academic draft horses seem untroubled at having to schedule appointments to chat with friends. "People don't have time or energy to put into real relationships," said one. A Princeton international relations professor, however, is troubled by the new conformity: "It's very rare to get a student to challenge anything or to take a position that's counter to what the professor says."[333]

Kid-market researcher Martin Lindstrom confirms the new conformity. Lindstrom helped Lego redesign its blocks to accommodate reduced interest in unguided creativity and greater interest in play by numbers. When young adolescents from eleven countries were asked if they agreed with the statement "I want to do things my own way," Americans ranked lowest in the world at 36 percent, Japanese highest at 82 percent.[334]

We fit our OverSuccessed young thoroughbred draft horses with blinders because the stakes have become so high and the focus on success must be so unrelenting. Boston Consulting Group, one of the world's elite global management consulting companies, recruits MBAs only from Harvard, MIT, Stanford, Dartmouth, and similar schools. BCG's regional office in Atlanta is allowed to stoop to eleventh-ranked Duke—if there are personal connections with the company. A close friend of mine who is a BCG partner describes the hiring process: a battery of interviews weeds out all but graduates demonstrating both analytical brilliance and charismatic personalities, characteristics frighteningly similar to David Bostrom's transhuman superman. The workloads for the new hires are typically 80 hours per week, which burns out most of them within a year. Survivors of these hurdles—from preschool to the newbies' eighty-hour workload—have a shot at partner and, at that point, a realistic chance at visible success in business.

BENCHMARK ESCALATION: BODIES

In athletics, as in the sciences, celebrity, business, and other fields of endeavor, more people are competing, competition has grown more intense, and performance gaps between top and near-top achievers can no longer be detected by the unassisted human senses. Visible winners are smarter, more talented, better mentored, better trained, and more willing to sacrifice from their very early years of life. For example, skateboard phenom Mitchie Brusco of Kirkland, Washington, branded "Little Tricky," began intense training at three. By age five, managed by his parents, he had his own fan website, earned manufacturer sponsorship endorsements, and performed in competitions across the country.[335] Targeted to athletes as young as four, a company called AdvoCare is marketing a performance-enhancing drink that contains the amount of caffeine in one and one-half cups of black coffee.[336] To pump up their kid's shot at professional sports stardom, parents are forking out $30,000 in annual tuition to the Bradenton, Florida-based IMG Academies, whose program includes years of one-on-one coaching, mental conditioning, and media training, with residential programs starting at age eight. Tiger Wood's father began his son's training at age 2, so that, at age 32, Tiger had already beat Arnold Palmer's age 62 career golfing championships.

Visible winners in sports must accept higher risks and Zen-level self-abnegation to achieve their goals. Ten years ago, "inversions," 360-degree mid-air flips, were banned from freestyle ski competitions because one bad landing can mean spending the rest of your life on a breathing machine. Today, all serious competitors have mastered the inversion. Almost half of Olympic contestants questioned in a survey said that they would be willing to take a drug that would give them a five-year wining streak, but then kill them.[337] Linebacker Greg Davis learned the risks of performance-enhancing drugs in high school. At five-foot-nine and 185 pounds, he was undersized for his position and took andro to increase his muscle mass and the stimulant ephedra to increase his endurance. First he suffered seizures; a year later, he lost consciousness behind the wheel, slamming into a tree, which saved him from a twenty-foot fall to certain death.[338] Davis took these extreme risks because in today's NFL, twenty percent of football players now weigh over 300 pounds, rare in the 1960s.

What is takes to become a visibly successful athlete has spiraled upward into the supernatural. Italian Reinhold Messner is, without dispute, history's greatest mountaineer, a rock star with about 2,000 solo ascents to his credit. At age five, his father coaxed him up his first peak. At age 42, Messner became the first person ever to have climbed all fourteen of the world's 8,000-meter peaks. He electrified the climbing world by pioneering the use of daring new techniques that depended on speed and lightness—no base camps, porters, expansion bolts, or oxygen tanks. He trained himself to climb for up to four days without food. In 1980, Messner became the first climber to scale Everest alone, carrying nothing but a small backpack. Asked at a celebration of the first of his two Everest ascents why he had not carried the Italian flag, Reinhold exploded in laughter, "I went up for myself. I took out my handkerchief: This is my flag. Nobody's going up for somebody [else] on Everest."

Messner's first 8,000-meter peak was Pakistan's Nanga Parbat, a searing experience that would have reduced most of us to psychological rubble. Messner was only slightly tempered. Heading down from the peak, he and his hypoxia-weakened brother survived the first overnight at 40 below zero, with nothing but a space blanket and without food or water. During the second day of descent, tragedy struck: Messner lost his brother to an avalanche. The event launched Messner into fame, wealth, forty books, corporate sponsors, and five boring years as a Green in the European parliament. Facing the physical limits of age—not to mention the amputations of the tips of his toes and fingers—Messner began a series of horizontal treks across some of the planet's most forbidding places. With a single partner, he became the first to cross the Antarctic continent on foot, a 1,550-mile distance. He then bagged 1,243 miles across Greenland. Now in his sixties, Messner has hit what he calls his sixth life stage, launching five museums devoted to mountaineering.[339] In later pages, I will sketch the lives of other personalities like Messner's, illustrating that achieving a modern success benchmark usually requires extraordinary feats in multiple domains, along with a charisma that allows the super-achiever to bond with audiences via mass media.

We can see in most sports this accelerating pattern of busting limits and setting new benchmarks. Over the past twenty years, cheerleading has evolved from bouncing sweater girls waving pom-poms into a highly competitive sport involving difficult and risky maneuvers, such as three-level pyramids and human basket tosses. More than 28,000 high school and college students landed in hospital emergency rooms as a result of cheerleading injuries in 2004, the injury rate per participant soaring by about 90 percent since 1990.[340] Southern Illinois University cheerleader Kristi Yamaoka nailed her fifteen minutes of fame when she fell fifteen feet from the top of a human pyramid. Landing headfirst on a wooden basketball court, she cracked her neck vertebra and skull. As she was being hauled off strapped prone to a stretcher and live on CNN and ESPN, Yamaoka moved her arms in cheer routine when the team fight song came on, earning herself 14,000 wildly cheering fans, a personal call from President Bush, and a spot on the *Today* show. She has fully recovered and returned to her studies in college.

The cost of two to four years' success in some sports is a lifetime of severe disability. Until 1912, Chinese girls whose parents wanted them to marry into wealth were subjected to foot binding, yielding tiny, wedge-shaped feet that were a fashion statement and indicator of dependency. The practice required a three-to-five-year-old to have all her toes but the largest broken and bent back under her soles, then wrapped tightly for years in cloth strips to prevent their growth. Some foot-bound girls were accompanied by the perpetual stench of their own rotting flesh because portions of their feet had died.[341] We now view the practice as barbaric. But we have demanded this same type of barbarism and self-abnegation from our women's gymnasts—at least until the sport's hidden brutality came to full public view in the early 1990s. Surging TV audiences for supernaturally lithe gymnastic performers led to training regimens in which "results are bought at any cost," says Joan Ryan, author of a book on the sport.

Romanian Bela Karolyi, who trained Mary Lou Retton and Kristie Phillips during the 1980s, represented the "new generation of American coaches who screamed, taunted, and demanded absolute subservience," said Ryan. To halt the onset of puberty and its career-killing spurt of body mass, gymnasts were forced to endure near-starvation diets. Because their estrogen was so depleted in adolescence, former gymnasts in their twenties now suffer from premature osteoporosis and the bone density of ninety-year-olds. Kathy Johnson, a 1984 medalist, did not begin menstruation until she retired at age 25. At 14, Kristie Phillips continued training in spite of a broken wrist by downing eighteen anti-pain pills daily. Kelly Garrison, worried that the pain from a fractured ankle would impede her performance at the 1988 Olympics, pounded the injury like hamburger meat to numb the pain. Another gymnast, Christie Henrich, died at age 22 from complications of anorexia and bulimia; she weighed only sixty pounds. Tiffany Chin, asked how it would feel if she did not win, replied, "I'd probably die." Her response to winning the U.S. figure-skating championship: "I didn't feel happiness. I felt relief."[342]

Over the past ten years, technology is increasingly being added to genes, training, and determination to engineer a win in athletic competition. To prepare for the 2000 Olympics, the U.S. speed-skating team lived half of each day at 7,300 feet, breathing pure oxygen during training, a regimen that forced skaters' bodies to produce more oxygen-carrying red blood cells. The team won eight medals, including two gold. For many sports, athletes now train on vibrating platforms, which increase muscle strength.[343] After the esteemed journal *Nature* reported that players wearing red in the 2004 Olympics consistently won more contests, many athletes have taken to wearing red uniforms. The red plumage is thought to elevate testosterone and augment the inner psychology of male dominance, while depressing performance in opponents.[344] The support teams for elite athletes now include sports psychologists utilizing therapies shown to improve self-confidence, task focus, anxiety control, and determination.

But while the inputs and effort needed to capture athletic gold are ever-escalating, incremental performance gains are shrinking to nearly zero. This pattern of intensifying competition and diminishing distinction between first and second place holds increasingly true across all endeavors. The narrowing year-over-year performance gaps in athletic world records (if we focus only on those not influenced by improvements in equipment) are an objective indicator of the trend. Figure 4.1 shows that, over the past century, an index of world

Figure 4.1

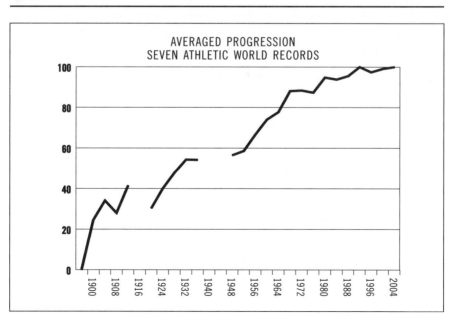

records for seven selected track-and-field events is flattening over time, as our most gifted and determined individuals approach the maximum potential of current human minds and bodies.[345] (There were no Olympics held during World Wars I and II.) Note the flattening of progress starting in 1968 and the topping in 1992. These transition dates are remarkably congruent with those of the many other OverSuccess indicators presented in Chapters 7 and 8, such as community and family breakdown, rising debt, and rising mental illness.

But this flattening is shortly to end, as "genetic doping" takes hold in athletics—and in every other competitive realm. Already, scientists have engineered a strain of "marathon mice" that produce more PPAR-delta, a naturally occurring protein that doubles growth of slow-twitch muscle fiber, making the mice able to run twice as far and twice as long; a drug that activates this protein is being tested in humans.[346] *New Scientist* reports on a young boy who won't even need genetic doping. He is already possessed of a rare mutation that dramatically enhances muscle growth, and is already deemed a likely winner in the 2016 Olympics. By age four, the boy could already support six-pound weights in both hands with his arms extended.[347] Only recently did scientists identify the traits that enabled Finnish cross-country skier Eero Mäntyranta to win two gold medals in the 1964 Olympics. His entire family, many of whom are also champion endurance athletes, shares a mutation that causes an excessive response to their bodies' naturally occurring hormone erythropoietin, producing a superabundance of oxygen-carrying red blood cells. Is it fair that athletes are disqualified for taking Epoetin, the synthetic form of this hormone, to achieve the same effect that comes naturally to Mäntyranta and his clan? H. Lee Sweeney, physiology chair at the University of Pennsylvania School of Medicine, thinks the 2004 Olympics was the last without genetically doped athletes.[348]

It's not just champion athletes that want the bodies of supermen and superwomen. For average Americans, too, body enhancement has been redefined over the past thirty years from competitive edge to necessity. Plastic surgery, initiated as a therapy for disfiguring injuries, is now used overwhelmingly to overcome aging and inherited characteristics. Once shunned as an act of vanity, the use of cosmetic surgery now receives approval from 55 percent of Americans, and our nation leads the world in annual cosmetic procedures.[349] In 2007, over 1.8 million total cosmetic surgical procedures were performed in the United States, 4.4 times the number in 1992. Between 1992 and 2007, breast lifts and augmentations increased eleven times, facelifts by three times. Over nine in ten procedures are performed on females.[350] MTV's hit reality show *I Want a Famous Face* follows hairdressers and go-go dancers through whole-body plastic surgery in their quest to rid themselves of their ordinary faces and bodies, which have been made intolerable by Hollywood's increasingly pervasive standards. Toward the end of episode 204, a woman named Kelly, her engineered boobs still far too painful to touch, holds up Jennifer Aniston's *People* magazine cover. "I hope I look more like this." Kelly frowns because she knows she doesn't and won't.

The proliferation of Internet sites like Models.com and the new global marketplace have made success far more elusive for gorgeous women seeking a career in modeling. So many contenders from so many places are competing for the same number of pedestals at such a higher level of required attractiveness. Thousands of flawless new competitors from Eastern Europe and Brazil are flooding the market, driving down fees even for such plum gigs as magazine covers. The biggest modeling fees still get paid out, but only to celebrities. Compared with ten years ago, ten times as many women now show up for auditions to model for a big designer like Calvin Klein. These jobs once paid $10,000 a day. Today non-celebrity models cover their own transportation and get to keep the gown. The lifespans of their careers have shrunk from eight years to one or two.[351]

The demand for flawless appearance at the top has spread to professions well beyond modeling. Television actors, celebrities, newspeople, and their producers are now being pushed to achieve far greater surface perfection than in the recent past. With its sharper, clearer, larger pictures, the high-definition television receiver requires that those who appear on it upgrade their makeup, hair, and props. Tiny cracks must now be completely removed from set walls. Makeup must extend beyond the face to the entire body, neck, chest, arms, and legs. To blur human flaws not concealed by better makeup, cameras are now equipped with "skin detail" that selectively soft-focuses skin tones.[352] Filmmakers using today's digital cameras must shell out up to $250,000 in post-production work to remove zits and wrinkles from stars' faces. During a Conan O'Brien interview, Anderson Cooper got days of big Internet buzz when he joked about first noticing a tiny fatty deposit under his lower left eyelid right after his CNN program switched to HD. His offhand remark indicates that it won't be long before we see a boomlet in this subspecialty of eyelid surgery. When a few people at the top move up the ladder in any new way, they haul everyone else up with them.

BENCHMARK ESCALATION: WEALTH DISPLAYS

Thirty years ago, Americans aspired to a comfortable, middle-class life. Just keeping up with the Joneses sufficed. One house, one car, and a weekend barbecue constituted full material contentment. Today, the old pyramid-shaped consumer products market has become an hourglass, with sales volumes increasingly concentrated at the extreme ends, the Wal-Mart and Tiffany price points. In their book-length study, *Trading Up: The New American Luxury*, Boston Consulting Group principals Neil Fiske and Michael Silverstein cheer the recent middle-income trend toward embracing BMW, Starbucks, and Williams-Sonoma.[353] Even prosaic consumer goods are going upscale. Whirlpool was taken completely by surprise in 2001 when it launched its Duet washer-dryer combination, at a retail price of $2,000; the product captured almost double its projected five-percent market share, even though its typical buyer earns only just above the national average. Explaining this phenomenon, J. Walker Smith, president of the market consulting firm Yankelovich Partners, says, "there's no aspiration to be middle class. Everyone wants to be at the top."[354]

Economist Robert Frank and sociologist Juliet Schor have amply demonstrated that consumer satisfaction depends not upon absolute performance or quality standards, but on standards set by our aspirational reference groups— that is, the class of people whose consumption patterns and lifestyles we seek to emulate. Over the past twenty years as economic inequality has increased, the wealth and incomes of these reference groups have been rising more rapidly than average incomes, meaning that, for the typical American, the gap between buying power and material goals is increasing. A 1986 Roper poll found that an inflation-adjusted income of $80,000 would make the typical American feel rich, but by 2003, that income benchmark had increased by 50 percent to $122,000.[355] Eighty-five percent of us want to be among the top fifth in income, with only fifteen percent satisfied by simply "living a comfort-able life."[356] Our OverSuccessed culture has taught us to covet the homes and lifestyles of the very rich and very famous, not those of our neighbors and peers.

Even with these rising aspirations, Americans grossly underestimate what it takes to be really rich. The public's median estimate of what it means to be wealthy is one million dollars.[357] That yardstick makes over eight percent of all Americans rich, a crowd the size of the combined populations of Mas-sachusetts and New York. The reality is that one million dollars' net worth is barely enough to support a couple in a middle-class retirement.[358]

Crossing the line into millionairehood sounds like a distinct achieve-ment—until you arrive there. When I hit my first million, no limos or TV crews arrived, and I was still schlepping my own garbage bags (and still do). To celebrate my new perch on this pile of psychic quicksand, my wife and I booked the most expensive room in the most expensive beachfront hotel on a Florida vacation island. We found ourselves sharing a poolside hot tub and a free Korbel with a delightful and perceptive couple, she a public school special-ed administrator, he an auto plant preventative maintenance technician, with grown children and plenty of discretionary income. If Richard Branson was on the premises, he did not join us for a toast. Fewer than one in four mil-lionaires think that one million dollars is enough to be considered rich.[359]

The Securities and Exchange Commission also apparently views mere millionaires as financial lightweights. In late 2006, the SEC proposed rais-ing from $1 to $2.5 million the "accredited investor" threshold of net worth, below which individuals are prohibited from investing in hedge funds and other pooled private investments. Stung by the insinuation that they are stu-pid, unsophisticated, and unrich, entry-level millionaires flooded the agency with objections to its proposal. In the words of one commenter, "Why should 99% of Americans, simply because they have less than $2.5 million of invest-ment net worth, be precluded from the same choices available to the 1% who are really rich?"[360]

Let's move up and see if the top one percent feels any better about them-selves. They enjoy an annual income starting at about $365,000 or have net assets of at least $5.8 million.[361] To an outsider looking up, these sums sound thoroughly comfortable, but the top one percent is still miles away from being able to display visible status. A mid-1990s Worth Roper Starch survey found that almost six in ten of those in the top one percent of earners did not even consider themselves rich. Only a quarter thought of themselves as upper class. Looking enviously above themselves, the bottom third of this top one per-cent—with annual earnings averaging about half a million dollars—describe American society as "unfair."[362]

In 2007, my wife and I celebrated a friend's wedding on Harbour Island, a charming little refuge in the Bahamas for celebs weary of over-exposure in Saint Bart's. We bedded down in a $1,000-a-night bungalow on a perfect, three-mile-long, pink-sand beach. But for the status-sensitive person, a dark cloud hangs over this paradise: just two hundred yards north on the beach lie five or so gated, twenty-room vacation compounds, each with a guest house and groundskeeper's cottage. I watched as two nannies on the seaside deck of one of these compounds fastidiously rolled out fresh white towels, beach toys, and wicker lunch baskets for the young children playing in the sand, whose parents' private jet and pilot were certainly on standby at the North Eleuthera airport. My wife and I had arrived by cattle car on a commercial flight. Lubricated by a couple of the hotel's trademark goombay smashes and feigning merely objective interest, I asked some of the guests what it takes to be rich. A pair of perfectly matched, blond and bronzed Palm Beach party girls concurred that a net worth under eight digits was "so 1980s." Ten mil-lion was thought to be the bare minimum to have any shot at being what they termed "fabulous."

Even at $10 million net worth, you remain anonymous in a crowd of at least 530,000 American households, one of every 230.[363] Ten million will buy you two CVS store buildings free and clear, maybe get you an all-black Amex card. You would still not have the economic clout to restructure the bottle-cap industry, get on the guest list for one of Henry Kravis' museum fund-raisers, or buy the governorship of a flyover state. To heap further insult on those in its psychologically oppressed bottom ranks, the number of inflation-adjusted decamillionaires has surged by four times since 1989.[364]

To be at least closer to genuinely rich is to have assets of at least $30 mil-lion.[365] Even at this level, there are still about 37,000 Americans, about one in 3,300 households. But here, in these lofty peaks above 99.9 percent of Americans, the intricacies of competitive wealth display require meeting formidable and ever-rising benchmarks. The costs of top-tier trophies—such as museum-quality paintings, watches of the type sold on Bond Street, multiple luxury homes, yachts long enough not to be embarrassing, and contributions required to chair Palm Beach charity events—as well as the number of Americans who can afford these more-rarified status symbols, have all generally increased by five to ten times since 1995.

Not only do the private jets of the bourgeoning ranks of genuinely rich clog Aspen Airport, but pulling off an impressive wealth display has become increasingly sophisticated and logistically complex. How do you manage the personal game park, the four homes in three nations, the Gulfstream and crew, vacation logistics for forty guests, the art collection on loan to various museums, the family foundation, publicity avoidance, staff management, and wealth counseling for two generations of potential heirs? A self-described "prominent Manhattan family" ran a recent ad in the journal *Science*, seeking a "Chief Medical Officer ... to research and coordinate family medical and healthcare issues ... [and to] act as liaison with leading medical researchers and consultants in academia and industry, with full responsibility for technical, financial and administrative functions."[366] This client, remember, is not a government but a family.

In 2006, *The Atlantic* ran a story, "Inside the Billionaire Service Industry," featuring Mary Louise Starkey and her Starkey International Institute, which offers an eight-week, $13,000 course in executive management. Without such people, many Americans with net worths north of $30 million are no longer able to orchestrate their personal lives. Graduates are snapped up as fast as they are minted by do-it-yourself spouses, desperate, bone weary, and overwhelmed by the complexities. A major challenge for those contemplating work in the billionaire-service industry is the need to maintain what the *Atlantic* article's author calls "relentless positivity in the face of constant, almost pornographic displays of wealth."[367]

Even for those not among the genuinely wealthy, your one house is likely to be bigger and more ostentatious than ever. Over the past fifty years, the average square footage per occupant in new homes has tripled from about 290 to 870.[368] Additionally, finish quality in new and remodeled homes has become more upscale, with such extras as tile, trim, higher ceilings, and architectural detail becoming commonplace. Homes costing over one million dollars, once rare, have become ordinary in hundreds of zip codes; by 2004, there were over one million million-dollar homes in the U.S.[369]

As prevailing tastes have improved, status homes have become larger, better located, and far more expensive. Homes with good ocean frontage in the best locations and without serious qualitative compromises now start at $15 million. The amenities arms race, which begins with the library and lap pool, now extends to the safe room, which exists not just to ensure the owner's safety, but primarily to mark him as liquid enough to warrant kidnapping. A physician couple turned their noses up at a recruiter for the regional hospital near where I live because even the area's most expensive existing homes lack the "volume rooms," dramatic entrances, and columned bathrooms that are standard in most metro areas. A genuinely wealthy friend of mine blasted a garage-sized wine cellar into the natural bedrock beneath his new home—one of his several residences. His subcontractor spent almost a year covering the cellar's walls and ceiling with a painstakingly established drapery of live moss imported from old wine caves in Hungary's Tokaji region.

On water as it is on land: "I used to think I had a good-sized boat," said Don Weston of his 100-foot motor yacht, a length that starts at $2 million—used. "Now it's like a dinghy compared to these others." Microsoft co-founder Paul Allen's 413-foot yacht, for a short period the world's largest, comes complete with a heliport and yellow submarine. Norberto Ferretti, one of the world's top yacht builders, explains the surging demand for private mega-boats. "Rich people can go to a beautiful hotel and pay $3,000 a night for a suite. The trouble is, when you go down the elevator, you're in the lobby with people who paid twenty times less. My clients don't like that."[370] Allen's yacht has already been upstaged by the crown price of Dubai's new private yacht, at 525 feet, longer than a World War II destroyer. As of 2007, more than 370 yachts 120 feet or longer were on order, twice the number in 2003.[371]

After his mega-cashout, AOL co-founder Steve Case launched Exclusive Resorts, an enterprise that put the trend toward increasing vacation cost and quality on the same parabolic curve as boats. For a $239,000 membership fee and annual dues of $14,000, members get fifteen vacation days in private residences at any of several dozen of the world's premium locations. Another company, Yellowstone Club World, takes the concept beyond the access affordable by mere millionaires, with offerings that include two yachts, a fleet of Gulfstreams and Citations, an English castle, a French chateau, a Scottish golf course, a Caribbean island, and a 1,600-acre Mexican beachfront. Buy-in starts at $3.5 million, with annual dues starting at $75,000, not including food and hourly operating costs for the boats and jets. The critical distinguishing feature is that membership is by invitation only.

Almost everything that was once free or ordinary has been made into an absurdly priced status consumable: the $700 sandal, the $800 haircut, the $4,000 pair of jeans. Stretch limos have reached the length of tractor-trailers. Tickets to a Rolling Stones concert can be $700 each. Lifestyle designers, charging fees of $400 an hour, select their clients' clothing, cars, and gifts, plan parties, and polish the images of those too busy to follow the dizzyingly obsolescent waves of fashion wrought by hypercompetitive marketers. With astonishing speed, new status objects are adopted, wholesaled, and discarded as uselessly common. BMWs have become Hampton Chevys. The higher you scale the mountain, the more demoralizing and distant your view of the peak. Millionaires, million-dollar homes, lattes, and luxury cars have all shrunk into marks of Babbittry.

BENCHMARK ESCALATION: COMPLEXITY AND SOPHISTICATION

The most valuable status markers require more than brute wealth. At the upper reaches of most hierarchies, the most impressive markers are detectable only to specialized audiences with the cultural background to read them.

Take the example of Art Basel, known as the "Olympics of the art world." Twice a year, rotating between Miami Beach and Switzerland, the world's leading galleries congregate for four days to sell original works by the twentieth century's masters. Anyone can buy a $20 ticket to gawk at the huge crowds, or spend a few hundred bucks on someone undiscovered. But to move up within this specialized hierarchy requires years of studious attention to markers in fashion and manner that change seasonally. It is good to be seen at the invitation-only parties held each evening around the pool at the Philippe Starck-designed Delano Hotel. Dominating its entrance lobby one year are ten two-story panels of silky white fabric, billowing seductively in the warm ocean breeze. Dressed in matching white and flanking these luscious panels are ten drop-dead-gorgeous young women who do nothing but stand silent and motionless through the hours of the party. Serious collectors are secluded in bungalows overlooking the pool, adding notches to their status belts by closing on pieces by Basquiat, Leger, Richter, Baselitz, and Walton Ford. Most buyers are entirely at sea in the impenetrably self-referential contemporary art world. In this million-plus range, most buyers keep their Yale-schooled art consultants closely in tow. Meanwhile, the handful of well-known living artists who top this evening's hierarchy sneer discreetly among themselves at the rich but hapless buyers.

Retaining visible success for longer than one fashion cycle often requires preeminence in multiple disciplines. A recent full-page ad in *The Economist* featuring Dr. John Halamka is selling us far more than the BlackBerry the doctor is sporting in the photograph:

> Being the CIO of Harvard Medical School is just one of my jobs and passions. I'm also an emergency room physician and a worldwide lecturer. No matter where I am, not matter what time zone, I need my virtual team at my fingertips … Without my BlackBerry smartphone, I couldn't … balance it all with being a rock climber, winemaker, husband and father.

Bill Gates' first act was to become the world's wealthiest person in fifteen years by achieving near monopolies in a string of software products. By the late 1990s, his company, Microsoft, was subject to antitrust litigation in North America and Europe, his products critiqued as inelegant and unoriginal, and his personal reputation in decline. He turned it all around by creating the Bill and Melinda Gates Foundation, at $35 billion by far the world's largest. The Gates Foundation has organized and funded fourteen medical "Grand Challenges" led by Nobel laureates that aim to do no less than invent and deliver new technology to eradicate the major diseases of the developing world. Gates' credibility is so great that the world's second-wealthiest person, Warren Buffett, pledged most of his net worth to the Foundation, an additional $30 billion, which was the largest charitable contribution ever. Gates has set an utterly unattainable benchmark of philanthropic power and entrepreneurial imagination in high-visibility competitive altruism.

Until recent years, wealthy philanthropists could make a big enough mark by building a hospital wing, bringing opera to one of America's top twenty cities, or endowing a graduate school. But for today's donor seeking high-visibility recognition, money only gets you in the door to the game. A philanthropist seeking to win wide acclaim must be no less than an intellectual leader pursuing a multi-disciplinary agenda for change. James Martin is another example. Born poor, he grew up to author or co-author 101 textbooks, found several global IT and management consultancies, and receive six honorary doctorate degrees. In retirement, Martin endowed his Institute for Science and Civilization with $100 million to "identify science and technology issues critical in shaping the future of world civilization." Showing off his multi-disciplinary facility, he tosses off aphorisms such as "we are forced to play God, and we are forced to be good at it."[372] Even with all this accomplishment, most of us have never heard of Martin.

Benchmark escalation in generosity has also affected those less conspicuous than the two paradigm-rocking entrepreneurs mentioned above. In 1996 Ted Turner lamented the existence of the Forbes 400—which encourages the retention of wealth—and the absence of a similar list of those giving the most money away in any one year. Taking Turner up on his challenge, the online magazine *Slate* created just such a list, the *Slate* 60, intended to encourage philanthropic competition among the very wealthy. It seems to have worked. Over the decade ending in 2006, in tandem with many OverSuccess indicators, the minimum and median contributions required to be included in *Slate's* list of 60 top donors have increased by three and four times, respectively.[373]

In an arena of accomplishment beyond the making and dispersal of money, trumpeter Wynton Marsalis is another example of the new, multi-disciplinary success. Marsalis, probably the world's greatest living jazz musician, extended himself into classical music, composing a string quartet and performing Bach at the Lincoln Center. He has recorded thirty albums and won a Pulitzer Prize and nine Grammys, one year winning Grammys in both the jazz and classical categories. *Time* magazine has named him among America's twenty-five most influential people. He got a standing ovation when he spoke at the National Press Club on race, class, and rebuilding New Orleans. I watched Marsalis charm an audience with his southern-fried colloquialisms and the aw-shucks deployment of his encyclopedic knowledge of jazz and his additional artfulness in demonstrating sprezzatura, the Italian term for making the difficult appear casual.

Advancement in science has also become vastly more complex over the past thirty years. Most research projects now involve more scientists, bigger budgets, dramatically more expensive equipment, more elaborate experimental design, and more rigorously documented procedures. Top journal articles have graphics with layer upon layer of information density, better statistical screening of data significance, conflict disclosures, and sentences composed almost entirely of technical terminology that did not exist thirty years ago. Whereas in the 1960s, a particle physics experiment might involve dozens of scientists, such an experiment can now include two thousand and require the clout to book time years in advance at the new $7 billion Large Hadron Collider in Geneva. More than ever, scientists must now also act as diplomats and politicians to coordinate the resources they need. The days of the lone wolf at the lab bench are largely over.

Even successful social fads have become subject to the trend toward increasing sophistication. Hipsters in media, the arts, and technology have mastered staying just ahead of the waves of fashion occurring in idioms of consumption, behavior, and language that erupt within hours into coolness and then die within weeks. Bill Wasik inadvertently documents this phenomenon in his *Harper's* story on the flash-mob fad he created in 2003. Flash mobs are short, precisely timed, and meaningless gatherings generated by a bulk e-mail message. For example, at 7:07 one evening, hundreds of people assembled around the balcony ringing the lobby of the Grand Hyatt on 42nd Street in Manhattan, applauded one another, then left just before the police arrived. Wasik's coup in benchmark sophistication was to have invented and perpetrated a fad, then announced his disdain for it, and finally, engineered a wave of fame-building publicity from it.[374]

Escalating benchmarks have both invaded and enriched nearly every part of American life—even bicycling. A generation ago, bicycling for fun meant putting on some casual clothing, grabbing the bike, and riding. Today, a recreational bicycler rarely appears without the full paraphernalia of a professional circuit competitor, complete with skin-tight jerseys and aerodynamic touring shorts ablaze with multiple corporate logos, camelback hydration systems, moisture-wicking socks, wind-tunnel helmet with variable position visor, and Bluetooth MP3 sunglasses with hydrophilic nosepad and reflective UVA/UVB photochromatic lenses. Even the most basic activities are no longer immune from rampant benchmark escalation. Walking now requires hours of shopping for stretch pants, iPod armband, and chest-mounted lighting system for walks after dark.

BENCHMARK ESCALATION: EDUCATION AND INTELLIGENCE

Education attainment and intelligence are increasingly linked to success in most fields. Since roughly the 1960s, we have used these attributes more than anything else to segregate ourselves. As we saw in Chapter 3, measured intelligence in Western societies has probably been increasing at an accelerating rate since the Renaissance, with more selectivity in mate choice and the resultant breeding for intelligence one likely explanation. Good data show that mate selection for intelligence has increased sharply over recent decades. Efforts to foster anti-discrimination, as well as affirmative action policies, falsely imply that society is treating and rewarding its members more equally.

While interracial marriages are on the increase, the trend to "assortative mating" (marriages within the same social class as measured by educational attainment) has increased markedly, by about 33 percent since 1960, according to UCLA demographer Robert Mare. Today, couples are four times as likely to share educational attainment as not to share it. The number of couples marrying across significant educational differences has dropped by almost half since 1960 and now accounts for only about ten percent of marriages. Among newlyweds, parity in educational attainment has increased rapidly since 1980, presaging further segregation by intelligence across the American population.[375] Intelligence as measured by IQ is similar between married couples to about the same extent as educational attainment.[376] These trends are supported by the tougher education gauntlets that more tightly segregate young people by intelligence, social class, and social skills, and by more efficient mating selection screens, such as singles ads and online dating. Given that education is the most stable indicator of social class, we can use these data to safely conclude that segregation by social class is also sharply increasing.

Educational stratification is intense. Of high school dropouts, 94 percent are married to someone with not more than a high school diploma. Sixty-nine percent of people with an advanced degree are married to someone with a bachelor's degree or higher. Of those with advanced degrees, 56 percent are married. By contrast, only 35 percent of adults without a high school education are married. In a survey of those with at least a college education, 90 percent say that intelligence is at least very important in a partner. A smaller number, just 66 percent, of people with a high school education or less consider intelligence a very important factor. When asked what they look for in a mate, people say that good looks, athletic prowess, and wealth do not approach intelligence as a value.[377]

Lower intellectual attainment has become downright repulsive for many people looking for a partner. Among the forty million Americans who visited online dating sites during a recent month, gone are surreptitious proxy questions like "What do you do?" that were used in the past to elicit education, class, and status credentials. The online dating site Emode.com posts your IQ next to your photo. TheSquare.com limits its personals to graduates of the 100 most selective colleges and universities; RightStuffDating.com applies a similar filter. Members almost universally describe themselves as witty, trim, healthy, accomplished in intriguing fields, travel lovers, and residents of the right zip codes. Given the standards these sites require, members depict themselves far more accurately than they would in a noisy bar. A typical posting reads: "Male, Redwood City, CA, Harvard AB and MBA, serial high tech entrepreneur, occasional author and strategy magazine editor, plays tennis, skis, works out, and does yoga ..."

MillionaireMatch.com segregates its members into those who make more than $100,000 a year and those who don't. Separating the wheat from the chaff in a different way, the number-three dating site (after Yahoo.Personals.com and Match.com), eHarmony.com, requires its posters to take a 40-minute personality test. As of mid-2005, it had rejected over one million people for depressive traits and exaggerated self-descriptions.[378] A dating site that propagandizes for the escalation of the physical beauty benchmark is

HotEnough.org, allowing you to join only if twenty-five current members rank your appearance at eight out of ten or higher. Clearly, relationship seekers are perfectly willing to subject themselves to potentially embarrassing status screens, including the disclosure of their measured intelligence.

Because educational attainment is more greatly valued, more people are getting degrees, and graduates are pedaling harder and going deeper into debt to get nowhere. In the 1960s, about ten percent of college graduates worked in jobs for which they were overqualified. By the 1980s, this number had doubled to twenty percent. The Bureau of Labor Statistics estimates that thirty percent of college grads are now working in jobs not requiring their degree.[379] Lifetime payoffs for higher education remain strongly positive, but these data look at past results. In coming years, the return on an investment in education will likely be choked off by a glut of college degrees.

In spite of the incessant refrain that the U.S. must graduate more scientists and engineers, America's 50,000 postdocs—recent Ph.D.s working in academic research laboratories before transitioning into their formal careers—are in a pitiable position, victims of escalating educational benchmarks. Typically in their early to mid-thirties, postdocs enjoy an average salary of just $38,000 for an average workweek of 51 hours—a rate that amounts to about half the hourly earnings of a licensed plumber in my area and about half the hourly fee my wife pays our diligent housecleaner.[380] Over the past twenty years, the number of postdocs has doubled, but the number of tenure and tenure-track positions they seek has barely budged.[381] Competition among postdocs has grown so fierce that only twenty percent now ever win such positions.[382] Those who do succeed must wait longer to do it: since 1970, the average age at which a researcher wins his or her first National Institutes of Health grant has increased from 34 to 42—and from 2000 to 2006, the success rate at getting a National Science Foundation grant dropped from 30 to 21 percent, because almost 50 percent more scientists are applying for them.[383] Over dinner, a Ph.D. engineer told me how demoralized he has become about his difficulties over several years in securing any permanent position, given the hundreds of applicants against whom he competes for every job at his education level. For postdocs, competition has made every state a rust belt.

America's science and engineering workforce is filled by less than one-third the number of degree holders at all levels in those fields. Over the past twenty years, we have continued to produce about three times the number of science and engineering graduates as the number of new jobs that open each year in these fields. The shortages reported by technology CEOs lobbying for expanded H1-B visas are not of higher-ed graduates, but of "brilliant," deeply experienced team players, says the Urban Institute's Hal Salzman. "Expanding our production of scientists and engineers just defies market reality."[384]

In endeavors requiring them, the extreme peaks of intelligence, nurturance, and educational attainment required to reach visible success are rising into ever-higher Everests. Consider Russian mathematician Grigori Perelman, who recently solved the Poincaré Conjecture, considered one of the world's seven toughest math problems, which had fiercely resisted proof since it was postulated in 1904. Perelman takes the prize for combining incandescent brilliance and outdoing J. D. Salinger for parlaying reclusiveness into global fame. For his achievement, Perelman had no interest in claiming publicity or the $1 million Clay Mathematics Institute prize. He does not respond to press inquiries, studiously avoids the public, and refused to attend the International Congress of Mathematicians to accept the Fields Medal he was awarded there. The Fields Medal is the Nobel Prize of mathematics. Perelman posted online a 61-page sketch of his proof, but apparently deeming it the province of mere mortals, he left it to other mathematicians to provide a full formal proof, which constituted nearly a thousand pages. The journal *Science* said his work "fundamentally altered two distinct branches of mathematics" and required the invention of a new mathematics of higher-dimensional topology, a branch of geometry.[385] Until recent generations, people like Perelman were invisible to most of us, or known by little more than name and career. Most of us now know them intimately.

Nobel Prize-winning physicist Richard Feynman provides a good illustration of the high benchmark demanded for lastingly visible success in the sciences. Feynman conceived quantum electrodynamics, ran the calculations shop for the Manhattan Project, and was thought by Robert Oppenheimer to be the most brilliant physicist of its brilliant phalanx of scientists. He is perhaps most visibly remembered for his tour de force at a congressional hearing on the 1986 *Challenger* shuttle disaster, when he asked for a glass of ice water and a pair of pliers and proceeded to vividly demonstrate the pliability problem with the shuttle's fatal O-ring. Biographer James Gleick describes Feynman's genius:

> Encounters with Feynman left marks on a series of young physicists and mathematicians, in the glare of a bright light, out-thought for the first time in their lives. They found different ways of adapting to this new circumstance. Some subordinated their own abilities to his and accepted his occasional bantering abuse in exchange for the surprising pleasure that came with his praise. Some found their self-image enough changed that they abandoned physics altogether ... To master—as modern particle physicists must—the machinery of group theory and current algebra, of perturbative expansions and non-Abelian gauge theories, of spin statistics and Yang-Mills, is to sustain in one's mind a fantastic house of cards, at once steely and delicate. To manipulate that framework, and to innovate within it, requires a mental power that nature did not demand of scientists in past centuries.[386]

What prodigies can do in math and physics, another can do at an even earlier age in music. Musician and teacher Samuel Zyman marveled about the talents of his young Juilliard student, composer Jay Greenberg, who was breaking a kind of sound barrier at age eleven. Zyman asked:

> How do you react when you encounter an early compositional gift so extraordinary that you can't even begin to comprehend it? How do you explain to others a compositional talent so exquisitely developed at such an early age that you can barely believe it yourself? What would you do if you personally met an 8-year-old boy who can compose and fully notate half a movement of a magnificent piano sonata in the style of Beethoven, before your very eyes and without a piano, in less than an hour? How do you let the world know that the same boy, at age 10, composed a probing, original viola concerto in three movements, fully orchestrated, in just a few weeks?[387]

By age fourteen, Greenberg's body of work already contained five symphonies and over a dozen piano sonatas. He composed his *Overture to 9/11* when he was eleven years old; it was performed that year by the Pittsburgh Symphony. He is already ranked by reviewers alongside Mozart and is the youngest-ever artist to be signed by the powerful IMG arts management group.

Asked to explain how he composes such prodigal work, Greenberg says, "It's as if the unconscious mind is giving orders at the speed of light. You know, I mean, so I just hear it as if it were a smooth performance of a work that is already written, when it isn't." Most of his written music is first completed in his head, then taken directly and unrevised to computer keyboard. More so than Mozart, Greenberg is being more methodically and intensively nurtured, and his living fame has already given him an audience in the millions.[388]

In a world of increasingly demanding endeavors, the global talent scouting, training, and sorting process recognizes and brings to public attention only increasingly celestial forms of brilliance. The slope upward to genius is now so nearly vertical that its attainment can be explained only as a form of magic.

HUMONGOUS WINNINGS, MINISCULE ODDS

While the global economy has greatly magnified the biggest prizes, many more people are competing for them, but the number of these prizes has remained about the same. So the odds of any one person's becoming visibly successful have dropped. In their persuasive book on the subject, *The Winner-Take-All Society*, Robert Frank and Philip Cook describe the increasingly extravagant rewards and visibility won by an increasingly small number of high performers. Though global markets are larger, the number of big winners remains about the same, because our brains are capable of remembering and venerating only a dozen or two top performers in any field, whether it be entertainment, science, politics, or business. While, over the ten years ending 2005, total inflation-adjusted gross revenues of the top 500 American companies grew by 57 percent and gross profits by 94 percent, streamlining has reduced the number of officer positions by 3.3 percent to just under 10,900.[389] The most valuable film stars, pitchers, and hedge fund managers are worth more because they can single-handedly determine success or failure in today's globally scaled projects. Intensely attractive and aggressively promoted rewards have created a surfeit of both talented and untalented people chasing roles as script writers, singers, and athletes, but a shortage of local plumbers and in similar fields without prospect of wealth, fame, or power.

For the few who reach America's status pinnacles, the trophies are golden. Just as significantly, the smaller prizes that were once distributed among many people are now concentrated among those global winners. As recently as the early 1980s, top-grossing film stars earned $2 million a movie. Today, that figure runs to about $20 million, now that films are seen by billions worldwide and cross marketing has become so finely honed.[390] Sirius Satellite Radio offers entire channels for the Rolling Stones, the Who, and Elvis, brands that can be leveraged across larger audiences and more platforms than in the recent past.

As for top business leaders, their rewards relative to the common person have grown by almost twenty times over the past forty years. In 1965, the pay ratio between CEOs and average workers was 24 to 1. By 2006, that ratio was 364 to 1, with the bulk of that escalation occurring in the last half of the 1990s—evidence that the winner-take-all trend is accelerating. Neatly capturing the cultural differences is the fact that, even though the European economy is larger than ours, America's top twenty executives earned three times as much as the top twenty in Europe.[391] Thirty years ago, the average, real pay for the top hundred American CEOs was $1.2 million; in 2006, it was $51 million.[392] In 2005, the 400 top-earning Americans averaged an income of $214 million each. Adjusted for inflation, the minimum earnings to make the top 400 has tripled since 1992.[393]

Over the past thirty years, economic mobility has declined noticeably, and the ordinary person has faced ever more daunting obstacles against breaking into the ranks of the successful. In 1978, 23 percent of men born into the bottom economic and social fifth made it into the top fifth at some point during their lives. Twenty years later, only ten percent of men born into the bottom quarter had made it into the top quarter. Three-quarters of students now attending the nation's top 146 colleges were born into the top socioeconomic quarter, with only three percent from the lowest quarter. Among Harvard students, median family income is now $150,000. Says *The Economist* in its 2004 feature issue on declining demographic mobility, "America is increasingly looking like imperial Britain, with dynastic ties proliferating, social circles interlocking, mechanisms of social exclusion strengthening and a gap widening between the people who make the decisions and shape the culture and the vast majority of working stiffs."[394] Counter to our idealistic expectations, the new meritocracy has aggravated rather than eased social sclerosis.

Intergenerational income elasticity (IGE), the extent to which a father's income advantage or disadvantage is passed on to his son, is a similar yardstick for the American promise of economic opportunity. Chicago Federal Reserve Bank economist Bhashkar Mazumder compared IGE among several industrial nations. In Canada and Finland, a son inherits only about twenty percent of a father's income ranking, indicative of societies with high economic mobility. Germany comes in at thirty percent. The U.S. figure is about sixty percent. In the U.S. the adult child of parents in the bottom ten percent has a scant 1.3-percent chance of being in the top ten percent and a 32-percent chance of remaining in the bottom ten percent. The adult child of parents in the top ten percent enjoys a 30-percent chance of remaining in the top ten percent and an only 1.5-percent chance of dropping into the bottom ten percent. These data "point to an especially high degree of rigidity at the bottom and top of the earnings distribution," writes Mazumder.[395] "[T]he U.S. may be exceptional for its relative *lack of mobility*."[396] While there are conflicting data about the extent to which this is the case, among the world's wealthy nations, America is clearly not among the socially and economically mobile. The true tale of poor Ben Franklin who grew up to dine with kings has become a fraudulent myth.

As it is in business and entertainment, so it is in sports. Seven-time Tour de France winner Lance Armstrong is world famous, taking down hundreds of millions in endorsement contracts. The 2003 race runner-up Jan Ullrich, who finished 61 seconds behind Armstrong's 83-hour, 42-minute time, is nearly anonymous. As Ned Edwards, once America's second-ranked squash player, said, "number two is the same as number sixty-two."[397]

Imagine yourself one of the hundred best golfers in the world. This achievement would make you an object of envy for millions of amateurs. But the workaday reality of such status is pretty humdrum. Laurel Kean, number 100 in winnings in the 2001 LPGA tour, drives her van 30,000 miles every year, shuttling between tournaments, sometimes sleeping in her car with her two dogs. She eats potpies from Kentucky Fried Chicken and is on the perpetual edge of an empty checkbook. Daniel DeBra, number 100 in the 2001 NGA tour, earned $10,761 in event, prize, and endorsement income, shares his hotel room with another golfer, buys his equipment at Sam's Club, carries his own clubs on course, and saves money by eating frequently at Subway and at free sponsor dinners. His wife subsidizes him with her salary. All of the top 100 winners refuse to quit the circuit, and few have anything less than love for their sport. But the glamour and paydays are limited to the top ten, the top three, and the top one.[398] Tiger Woods racked up $112 million in earnings in 2006.[399]

Across all sports, the gap between a lifetime of fame and wealth and a career coaching in high school often comes down to hundredths of a second. "The gap between best and second-best, or even best and tenth-best, is so slight that a gust of wind or a different running shoe might have accounted for the margin of victory," writes author James Gleick.[400] It does not make me more famous or powerful, but I find consolation in knowing that the naked eye sometimes cannot distinguish between a failing and a successful performance.

CRUSHED JUST BENEATH A BENCHMARK

There are no consolation prizes for the overwhelming majority of us who never reach the top—or even for those who come close. But success culture reserves its most merciless punishment on the big losers.

I've witnessed crushing failure in my role as one of the quarter-million American angel investors. Angels are often serial entrepreneurs themselves and typically provide the first outside funding for new, potentially high-growth companies that are too small for venture capitalists, too rapidly growing to live anymore off the founders' second mortgages and credit cards, and too risky for conventional lenders. In my area, angels and early stage companies from around New England come together in one of two different kinds of formats. In the first type, a group of us meet monthly in a boardroom setting and hear and discuss pitches that have been screened by our executive director.

The second format is even more fun. Called Peak Pitch, it's a ski day during which pairs of angels and startup CEOs share five-minute rides on a ski lift. The CEOs do the five-minute version of their pitch; the angels hand out tokens to their favorites. The top token getters win the potentially fate-changing opportunity to do their one-minute version to all hundred of us assembled over tuna sandwiches in the ski lodge. Our former governor, himself a one-time entrepreneur and reported to be worth about half a billion dollars, had co-founded the event two years before. But there he sat, a few months after being ignominiously defeated in his first reelection bid, like a wallflower at his empty table, the lodge buzzing all around him with dealmaking energy.

Hardball host Chris Matthews describes how viciously we ostracize political failure. "You have to win every time or you lose something. When you are a member [of Congress], they give you respect. The minute you lose, you owe it all back. It turns out they only lent it to you. My God, the way they look at you when you've lost. The way they *don't* look at you."[401]

"His whole life has been crushed," said a confidant of Ted Turner—swash-buckling entrepreneur, CNN founder, owner of 24 homes, creator of three personal foundations, the largest private landowner in America and, at $2.3 billion, the nation's 195th-wealthiest person—after he was pushed aside from a position of influence on Time Warner's board.[402] Being crushed by failure near the top is more than a metaphor. "If I lose a star, I will commit suicide," said chef Bernard Loiseau of the prospect of failing to maintain his restaurant's top GaultMillau rating. After his rating was dropped from 19 to 17 (out of 20), Loiseau did exactly that.[403]

American success culture's ranking system is binary: you are either number one or zero. Those few people with the genetic endowment, perseverance, social connections, educational attainment, timing, and luck can place themselves within striking distance of a status summit. Then there are the rest of us. Use this handy litmus test to clear up any confusion about your own ranking: royal purple if you are recurrently seen on TV or quoted in print, invisible if those on TV do not return your calls. Just up from plankton on the media food chain, I get interview calls from primarily state-based reporters once every few days. The resulting stories never break into the cable news crawl or above the fold in the national outlets. My relevance, limited as it was to local affairs, made it virtually impossible for me to get this book published. I was told by dozens of agents and publishers that if I were to become famous, they would become interested.

It's cruel, but your unrecognized potential and stale successes just do not count. There are simply too many qualified (and unqualified) contestants scrambling for every top spot. No talent spotters troll the hinterlands to rescue the invisible hordes of wannabes and nearly good-enoughs. In his book *Somebodies and Nobodies*, Robert Fuller captures this summary disposition of invisible persons. "At Washington cocktail parties people ask what you do for a living during the first 30 seconds of the conversation. When I was Executive Director of a national nonprofit working on transportation safety issues, I was of no interest to the would-be movers and shakers. They would simply walk away from me (sometimes without even a contrived exit line)."[404] Helpful hint: an ambiguous response, such as "I am in venture capital," ensures that you will not immediately be dispatched as irrelevant. But this deflects the brush-off for only a few more seconds, during which you'd better come up with a conversational hook about something involving yourself and the upper one-tenth of one percent.

Unfortunately, for the 60 million Americans who are convinced that they will someday become the next Michael Jordan, Catherine Zeta Jones, Yo-Yo Ma, or *American Idol* discovery, the global economy's billions of competitors, multiple winnowing gauntlets, transcendent performance benchmarks, and immense rewards all make the odds of achieving visible success more remote than at any other time in history.

For us 80 million baby boomers, the odds have grown even more dismal. For most of our lives, we were the center of attention, indulged with unlimited consumer and lifestyle options during America's peak as a superpower. Now, with our mammoth claim on the public retirement and medical systems, we are soon to become an intolerable deadweight on younger generations. In our forties and fifties, at the peak of our expertise, many of us can no longer find jobs in our fields. We are being replaced by younger people who are able to work long hours at starting salaries. We picketed for racial equality, but are now the largest class of discrimination targets in U.S. history. We are on our way down, not up. America will make failures of tens of millions of us if we do not create new roles for ourselves—outside the crushing rubric of OverSuccess.

5

FROM MICROEXPRESSION TO MEDIATED REALITY

In the very books in which philosophers
bid us scorn fame, they inscribe their names.
—Cicero, *Pro Archia Poeta*

WE SEEK STATUS THE way we seek food or sex, because our neurochemistry commands it. As I have shown, this motivation is made unnaturally more intense by the influence of American cultural values and the greater challenges of the American-made global economy. Now, in this chapter, we turn to the fourth key contributor to the emergence of OverSuccess: the increasingly potent forms of communication that successful people use to project their status. The media most effective at promoting OverSuccess are those that best carry the emotional messages of status comparison. Since the dawn of "modern" human intelligence, as evidenced by our first use of abstract symbols, the dominating forms of status communication have become progressively more powerful shapers of our lives, by three different measures: *emotion, speed,* and *ubiquity.* In our hyper-wired era, the media through which we communicate status affect us more deeply and reach more of us faster and more simultaneously. In short, contemporary media make winners and winning more compelling and visible than ever before. The escalating benchmarks of success, and the enticements to reach them, fill our psychologies and shape our goals in ways that were not possible under the less potent media mix existing even a few decades ago.

Human history includes thousands of significant media inventions and events, ranging from the engraved and painted snail shells used 75,000 years ago to signify status in South Africa, to homing pigeons and comic strips.[405] Twelve of these developments, I believe, have had the greatest impact on the pursuit of success:

1. spoken language and facial expression
2. written language
3. coinage
4. representational painting
5. print and literacy
6. music
7. photography
8. sound recording
9. radio
10. film
11. television
12. soon-to-be-perfected mediated reality

We could easily add to or subtract from this selection, but the increasing social impact of the dominating mix is clear. Each of these twelve has increased the successful individual's ability to rapidly convey emotionally immersive status messages to mass audiences and, as a side effect, define success and turn its pursuit into a mass obsession. Unlike the clay tablet or telegraph, all of these dozen remain in widespread use. They fill almost every crevice of our perceptual space, creating a contemporary media environment where success is more inescapable and necessary than air.

To roughly estimate a communication medium's social impact today, I rate each on three scales: emotional immersiveness ("emotion"), how quickly the medium's content permeates a given group ("speed"), and how omnipresent it is ("ubiquity"). I rate each category from one (weak) to three (strong).

For example, television is more emotionally immersive than representational painting, electronic communication is faster to permeate an idea or personality than word-of-mouth (given the same content), and printed word/literacy is more ubiquitous than handwritten manuscripts. In rating the increasing social impact of these dozen media, I intend to show that OverSuccess was not possible until about 1920, when film first made it possible to create fully emotional mass relationships with celebrities.

FACIAL EXPRESSION, BODY ADORNMENT, AND LANGUAGE
Emotion 3, Speed 1, Ubiquity 1

Charles Darwin was the first scientist to recognize the importance of facial expression as a sophisticated means to communicate status. In his 1872 bestseller, *The Expression of the Emotions in Man and Animals*, Darwin proposed that all mammals communicate emotion using a consistent repertoire of inherited facial expressions.[406] It was not until a century later that University of California Medical School psychologist Paul Eckman assembled the hard evidence to prove some of the elements of Darwin's second most fascinating theory. Humans and other primates share a facial musculature more complex than that of any other animals, which permits a greater number of more subtle facial expressions.[407]

Eckman began his lifetime of work on human facial expression in 1960, a research effort his peers at first considered greatly misguided. He demonstrated that specific facial expressions are recognizable across language and culture. Facial expression is the universal human language. Over his years of work, Eckman painstakingly catalogued 43 facial muscular movements and their 3,000 meaningful combinations. The face and head and its muscles have an extraordinary ability to instantly convey highly nuanced emotion. As brief as 1/20 of a second, these "microexpressions" are involuntary signals that convey genuine emotion; they cannot be faked or suppressed. Evolutionary psychologists call these expressions "credible" signals, conserved by our genes because they provide fitness benefits—for example, serving as indicators of who can be trusted or when threats are genuinely mortal.

Few people are able to read facial expression well enough to spot lying. However, a small number of individuals, perhaps one in one thousand, show an uncanny ability to do just that.[408] Responding only to the facial expressions he saw recorded on videotape, Eckman was able to describe the pre-presidential Bill Clinton, whom he admired, as "a guy who wants to be caught with his hand in the cookie jar, and have us love him for it anyway."[409] Within a few hours of study, most people can learn the basics of interpreting the repertoire of 3,000 facial expressions, spotting involuntary microexpressions like anger, disgust, fear, and a genuine smile. These expressions are readily identifiable when videotapes of faces are played at one-quarter speed. Sadness, to name one emotion, is revealed by the involuntary raising of the frontalis pars medalis, a muscle located in the inner eyebrow. A genuine smile involves involuntary muscle contraction at the corners of the eyes and lips. His work now well-accepted, Eckman was recently retained by the Transportation Security Administration to train airport security screeners to use microexpressions to spot troublemakers.

We make highly consistent, binding judgments about others after viewing a face for as little as 1/10 of a second, far too short a time for conscious deliberation. In an experiment that should frighten anyone who believes that election outcomes have a rational basis, people were asked to look at photos and pick the most "competent" among pairs of unfamiliar candidates contesting in hundreds of real elections. Those candidates deemed more competent won their real elections 70 percent of the time. People who took more than 1/10 of a second to make their choices—even as much time as they wished—were no more or less accurate in their predictions. The only group of people whose predictions were less accurate were those asked to carefully deliberate.[410]

Language is equally necessary for the management of complex group social relationships. Enabled by our larger brain, language made fame possible. As we saw in Chapter 2, Robin Dunbar found that among non-human social primates, a larger neocortex is associated with larger groups; Dunbar also thinks that human language evolved and spread quickly through our species to accommodate the social requirements of our larger groups. British primate researchers Karen McComb and Stuart Semple have provided solid evidence for Dunbar's conjecture, showing that the number of different vocalizations in a species' repertoire and time spent servicing social relationships both increase as the typical size of the group grows.[411]

Whenever their dates of origin, the use of body adornment and intricate language and facial expression are uniquely human traits that enable us to manage our exquisitely sophisticated social status relationships. Even with our many newer communication tools, the face-to-face media of facial expression, language, gait, posture, and personal ornamentation continue as our most precise means to make unconscious, split-second judgments about one another's relative status. These status-conveying media are as emotionally immersive as any ever invented; they are immediate, but reach no more than a small group of people within eye- and earshot.

WRITTEN LANGUAGE
Emotion 2, Speed 1, Ubiquity 1

The larger social organizations permitted by agricultural surpluses and the larger audiences permitted by written language mark a leap over face-to-face communication in the power to propagate one's personal success. Using common written language, individuals could for the first time directly communicate outside their immediate acquaintances, to advertise their literacy, publicize their accomplishments, memorialize their identities and their stories, and find visible roles as patrons of the written arts. Initially, it was the systematic domestication of plants and animals about 10,500 years ago, rather than the desire for wider fame, that created the need for written language. Once agriculture allowed the accumulation of economic surplus, humans could develop larger societies in fixed locations, establish highly specialized social roles, and rapidly accumulate knowledge—which required record-keeping and written language. Growing crops was at first a mixed blessing, increasing work hours and disease and reducing life expectancy, but its advantages were so great that it took agriculture only about a thousand years to become the dominant form of human organization.[412]

Clay tablets, used to document accounting records, appeared about 10,000 years ago. The first cities appeared in Mesopotamia about 8,000 years ago. The earliest known writing—the Balkan-Danube script—dates to about 7,000 years ago. Roughly 5,100 years ago, the Sumerians invented cuneiform, the world's first written language.

The big breakthrough, the first truly standardized, phonetic alphabet, appeared about 3,700 years ago in Syria. With the standardization of the Ionian phonetic alphabet in Greece in 403 BC came a historic leap beyond oral communication. Sufficient numbers of ancient Greeks could read and write so that, for the first time, a large number of humans shared a common and easy-to-learn means of durable and reliable communication. A small number of symbols could now convey an entire language, making written language accessible to most people, allowing for extended trade and common law, societal innovations that would encourage Greek citizens to advance their own place in society. Abstract ideas, metaphors, analogy, and precise representation of the spoken language became possible. A mass of ideas and facts far beyond what could be memorized could be recorded accurately and transmitted across geography and generations. Knowledge could rapidly accumulate and build upon itself.[413] More than two thousand years before Marshall McLuhan, Plato recognized that the medium is the message, crediting wider use of the written word with increasing logical thinking and reducing emotionalism.

Homer was among the first to use this new medium to spread his fame and status throughout the world and accurately into posterity. While the history is cloudy, Homer's personal scribe may have invented his own standardized Greek alphabet in roughly 800 BC, allowing him to record Homer's epic poems, the *Iliad* and *Odyssey*. Homer's fame is so massive that his work remains a foundation of Western literature, taught today in almost every high school.[414]

By 400 BC, written language became a powerful new means for individuals to augment their stature while alive and, for the first time, to immortalize their success. To become emotionally rich and to rapidly reach mass audiences, written language would await the later innovations of inexpensive printing, mass literacy, and more expressive formats such as the novel and incorporated pictures and color.

COINAGE
Emotion 1, Speed 1, Ubiquity 3

Legend has it that Alexander the Great slept as a boy with a copy of Homer under his pillow. Tutored by Aristotle, he is considered one of greatest conquering generals of all time. Over a ten-year succession of wars, before his death in 323 BC, he brought a region from Greece to Egypt to North India under his rule. The man's most enduring accomplishment was to disseminate Greek language and ideas through most of known civilization. But for a leader who strove to overcompensate for his perceived failings by viewing himself as a god, his second most noteworthy achievement was to establish the use of metal currency to magnify his own fame and status. The coins of his realm were among the first in history to portray a living human accurately, often depicting him in powerfully handsome profile.[415] From Alexander on, one of the best ways to signify your status and prominence, if not godliness, was to get your face on a coin.

Julius Caesar became the first Roman to appear on a coin during his own lifetime. After the puppet Senate gave him absolute power in 44 BC, he rushed to mint a coin depicting his head in profile, his face and neck etched by lines of wisdom and experience, his power conveyed by his crowning with an emperor's laurel wreath.[416] The coin's text, declaring him commander for life, was so politically inflammatory that the republicans in his Senate assassinated Caesar weeks after his coin was minted.

As a means of self-aggrandizement, coinage has the advantage of not requiring literacy or even a common spoken language. Ubiquitous distribution is guaranteed among all those who use money. While coinage now has the disadvantage of requiring that we die before we are celebrated, Caesar, George Washington, and Franklin D. Roosevelt show that getting our face into everyone's hands has remained a singular route to universal fame.

REPRESENTATIONAL PAINTING
Emotion 2, Speed 1, Ubiquity 1

A quick succession of technical inventions in the early 1400s—the perfection of lush and intensely brilliant oil paints, attributed to the Flemish master Jan van Eyck, and the use of lineal perspective to accurately portray dimensionality on a flat surface, rediscovered (from Greek mapmaker Ptolemy) by the Florentine Filippo Brunelleschi—enabled the creation of paintings possessed of an accuracy and emotional depth that had previously been limited to face-to-face encounters.[417] Highly representational painting attracted the attention of the period's nobility and the burgeoning merchant class, who would use this invention as a means to preserve their own images for posterity. They would often commission paintings of themselves in prayer to legitimize their status as patrons of the church, or would fill rooms likely to be seen by guests with family portraits to imply their noble lineage.

The most sought-after early Renaissance artists also actively cultivated their own fame. Previously thought of as craftsmen, the most gifted painters and sculptors made themselves into living legends. Lorenzo Ghiberti glorified himself by purposefully including his own likeness alongside biblical creation scenes in his masterpiece the second bronze Baptistry door in Florence, completed in about 1425. By the 1500s, Michelangelo promoted his own artistic and personal fame to frenzy levels, elevating himself to iconic status even among the Florentine working class. A savvy investor, he acquired and improved several properties in and around his city. He encouraged his extended family to dress, write, marry, and live like nobility. The first bad-boy artist, Michelangelo selected his own commissions, ignored the opinions of critics, refused honors, and rebuffed even the Pope's will. The artist forced his customers to pay outrageous fees to hire him, and then would not even depict his paying subjects' likeness in the art they sponsored. "No one will know how they looked in a thousand years," sniffed Michelangelo, less concerned about his patrons' posterity than his own.[418]

Demand for representational painting peaked in the 1630–1650 Netherlands, not incidentally the world's leading economy of that time, with a large and wealthy middle class intent on defining and advancing itself through art as a public relations tool. Two-thirds of the city of Delft's 4,000 households owned paintings—an average of ten per household. By the 1700s, European royalty flaunted their immense art collections to signify wealth and power.[419] The peak in the popularity of paintings was likely about 1780, when one of every twelve Londoners, still overwhelmingly poor and only partially literate, were drawn to visit a painting exhibition at the Royal Academy.[420] The comparatively broad social impact of representational painting may seem improbable today. Until the advent of color printing and museums that encouraged the masses to attend, paintings could broadcast the status of patrons and artists to only a limited audience. While representational paintings are slow to propagate success and are generally seen by few, we need only recall the *Mona Lisa* to understand their powerful emotional resonance.

PRINT AND LITERACY
Emotion 2, Speed 2, Ubiquity 3

Using his skills as a goldsmith, Johannes Gutenberg invented printing by moveable metal type in about 1437, though movable type employing woodblocks had been pioneered earlier in China in 1040 and in Korea in 1392. By 1450 in Europe, a handful of printed newsletters were already circulating; by 1500, middle-class literacy would emerge in England. By then, there were over 1,000 printers in 200 locations throughout Europe. On the printed page, the written word promised to become the most socially-potent media yet invented.

The first bestseller was, appropriately enough, a self-help book, *The Imitation of Christ*, written or transcribed in 1427 by a medieval monk, Thomas à Kempis. Kempis' counsel is that his readers live better by adhering to the examples set by Christ during his life. Printing made this book the number-one seller of the entire 1400s. Kempis' book continues to sell well today, consistently ranking in the top three thousand books in sales at Amazon.com, a remarkable 600-year record surpassed only by the Bible's.[421]

During the first half of the 1500s, copperplate etching and engraving (allowing lower-cost printmaking), colored woodcuts, and wax relief (allowing highly detailed medals) all began to flourish; for the first time, these technologies enabled the low-cost mass production and distribution of maps and images, including images of the successful.[422] To help solidify her power as monarch during the 1570s, Queen Elizabeth I promoted the fashion of wearing lockets containing medals bearing an idealized abstraction of her actual appearance. Later in life—her teeth blackened by decay from her love of sugar, her face pockmarked by smallpox, her head bald from use of lead-based makeup—she used mass distribution of images of herself to augment her living reputation. Like coins and painting, the printed reproduction of images allowed the successful to manage their own personae, freeing them from the sometimes reputation-damaging truth that comes with face-to-face communication.

In England by the second half of the 1500s, growing literacy and inexpensive access to the written word began to have marked social impact, standardizing roles and behaviors across large populations. Marriage and family manuals, mostly of the self-help genre, provided advice that was widely read and adopted. However, the greatest impact of print would wait another 200 years until the advent of widespread literacy, increased leisure time, the use of spectacles, and the gradual establishment and stabilization of language dialects. It fell upon the printers themselves to standardize the written language. The VHS-Betamax and Blue Ray-HD DVD format wars are just the modern examples showing that commercial interests, rather than neutral arbiters, have long played the major role in standardizing new communication media.

The first regularly published newspaper appeared in Antwerp in 1605, the first daily paper in Leipzig in 1650, followed by the first American newspaper, *Publick Occurrences, Both Foreign and Domestick*, published in 1690 in Boston, but shut down after its first issue hinted at corruption by the colonial government.[423] The first English paper, the *Daily Courant*, was published in 1702. By the mid-1700s, England had over 100 paper mills, with two in three males and one in three females being literate. By the late 1700s, England's one thousand for-profit libraries made the market for about half of all published books.[424] The first daily newspaper in America, the *Pennsylvania Evening Post*, appeared in 1783.

Low-cost, large-circulation newspapers became possible in 1814 with the invention of the steam-powered press. Mass literacy spread with the adoption of universal free public education, starting in Boston in 1821, thereby fostering the advantages and social urges of an emerging middle class. In 1833, Benjamin Day broke new ground with the first publication of the advertiser-supported *New York Sun*, selling it for one cent, almost free. During the decades after America's founding, newspapers focused almost exclusively on political debates, essays by leading intellectuals, and business transaction reports. The later mass-circulation papers dropped the literary writing style, popularizing and humanizing news to appeal to larger audiences. These papers featured crime and scandal, often fabricating events to stimulate reader interest. By 1880, newspapers had adopted widespread use of halftone printing, permitting the economical reproduction of photos. The number of American newspapers grew explosively during the thirty years ending in 1910, when the count of dailies peaked at 2,200. The first successful national magazine, *Godey's Ladies Book*, was launched in 1830, its color pages individually hand-tinted by 150 employees. By 1860, there were 260 U.S. magazines. This was the beginning of a boom that increased total magazine circulation by almost eight times—to three copies for every four Americans by 1905.[425] Their market penetration was now great enough to enable these media to replace local culture with mass commercial culture.

The fullest social impact of the printed word would await the invention of the novel. Critic Jacques Barzun credits the anonymous author of *La Vida de Lazarillo de Tormes* as inventor of this pathbreaking new form in 1554.[426] Book-length narrative breathed emotional depth into the printed word, while also exploring and defining middle-class life and propagating fame for authors.

Jean-Jacques Rousseau (1712–1778) is an exemplar of how writing could create living celebrity for an author. Already guaranteed a secure perch in history thanks to his writings on philosophy and politics, Rousseau is best known for setting forth the proposition that all men are born in nature free, equal, and virtuous, but corrupted by modern society and its institutions. He brazenly attacked the legitimacy of Europe's monarchies and religious monopolies just as some of them were poised to crumble. His memorable aphorisms inspired and suffused French revolutionary radicalism and rival anything from today's political shops. For example, princes encouraged involvement in the arts by their subjects, wrote Rousseau, "to wind garlands of flowers around the chains that bind them." Those same princes took an extreme dislike of *Émile*, his discourse on children's education; they ordered it burned. Authorities outraged by his words forced him on three occasions to flee for his life and safety to new European jurisdictions.[427]

 But Rousseau's unbounded vanity and hunger for notoriety impelled him to a new benchmark in literary success with publication in 1761 of his novel, *Julie: or the New Eloise*.[428] *Julie* was the eighteenth century's best-selling novel, with over seventy editions published before 1800. Demand was sometimes so insatiable that merchants were able to rent out the book by the day and even by the hour. With *Julie*, Rousseau pioneered a style of extreme, soul-baring emotionality, becoming history's first writer to create intense and personal relationships with his readers. The book is structured as a series of letters between two fictional lovers, which Rousseau claims in his preface to have edited rather than written. In spite of their checkered pasts and the stained world around them, the book's characters redeem themselves by exercising innate virtue. Readers identified so directly with Rousseau that they refused to believe that his characters were not real.

 Rousseau was deluged with unsolicited fan mail, then a novelty in history. According to French cultural historian Robert Darnton, "ordinary readers from all ranks of society were swept off their feet. They wept, they suffocated, they raved, they looked deep into their lives and resolved to live better, then they poured their hearts out in more tears—and in letters to Rousseau, who collected their testimonials in a huge bundle." Reader after reader recounted being disabled by emotion, unable to continue turning the pages. "At every page, my soul melted," said one. A baron suggested that reading was possible only in a locked room, permitting weeping unrestrained by the interruptions of concerned servants.

 Rousseau had mined the emotional power of print and literacy and made himself a personal object of desire as no author before. Wrote one male admirer, "Am I wrong to say that there is no equal to you on earth?" Readers begged Rousseau for advice, viewing him as a friend worthy of unguarded intimacy. Eighteenth-century groupies, language more polished than today's unsanitary illiterates, but infatuation no less intense, threw themselves at Rousseau's feet in letters and unannounced pilgrimages to his home.[429]

 In the centuries since Rousseau invented literary celebrity, print has become progressively less expensive and more popular—it is now essentially free of charge via the Internet, and literacy has become universal. Low-cost printing and universal literacy made the broadcast of individual success more rapid and ubiquitous. With the commercialization of emotionally unguarded writing styles, the incorporation of photography onto the page, and its power to be distributed simultaneously across the nation, print became immersive enough to alter our values, as I will show in the next chapter. Other than for face-to-face communication, the social impact of print was not to be exceeded until the advent of film and television.

MUSIC

Emotion 2, Speed 1, Ubiquity 1

The full social impact of music, as for representational painting, awaited the convergences by the second half of the 1400s, of several seminal inventions: advanced written notation, precise musical scales, polyphony and counter-point, tonal harmony, economical printing, and great improvements in the era's key musical instruments, the organ, harpsichord, and violin. Counter-point allows the emotional and intellectual intensity of two or more indepen-dent, simultaneous melodies. Printing enabled the distribution of music too complex to be carried by memory alone. Better instrumentation permitted musical richness and complexity and the display of a performer's virtuosity. Evolving through the 1600s and early 1700s, the establishment of a conven-tion of musical tonality (temperament) was as helpful to musicians and audi-ences as a standard alphabet was to Homer and his readers.

Renaissance musicians, like painters of the time, had thus acquired new and powerful tools that would enhance their patrons' status by association with these expressive magicians and would spread their own fame across the barriers of language. Composers themselves, once nearly anonymous, were now celebrated. Martin Luther described Josquin Desprez (1440–1521), an early master of polyphony, as a "wonder of nature." Bach, Mozart, and Beethoven were the pioneers in combining the new musical inventions and were revered during their lifetimes, as they are even today, as preeminent in Western music.

Nineteenth-century pianist and composer Franz Liszt showed that music, genius, and stage charisma could stir his audiences to outright hysteria—long before recordings and payola—and make him a preeminent cultural figure of his time. Just as Gutenberg's invention and the advent of widespread literacy fostered Rousseau's fame and impact, and lineal perspective and new paint compounds enabled Michelangelo's, so were musical temperament, notation, and polyphony predicates for Liszt's phenomenal success.

Originator of the solo piano concert *and* the benefit concert, Liszt was a "slim, strikingly handsome six-footer with a flowing mane of shoulder-length hair, a piano conjurer able to summon near orchestral effects and rouse audiences to … frenzied emotional states." The pounding to which he subjected his instrument would break strings and require him to switch pianos mid-concert. Women at his 1840s concerts would shriek in ecstasy, swoon, fling their jewels on stage, and fight over his green gloves he purposely left behind at concerts. Poet and Liszt contemporary Heinrich Heine described one concert he attended where a pair of countesses fought to exhaustion over Liszt's discarded snuffbox. He famously stopped playing during one concert when the Czar of Russia started speaking. Heine coined the term Lisztomania to describe the social effects of the first rock star, predating Elvis by 110 years.[430] Jimi Hendrix's smashed guitars and Elvis' stage sexuality had nothing but electricity over Liszt's performances.

The full social impact of music's powerful emotional content was limited by its slow permeation speed and moderate ubiquity. These deficits were fully overcome once music was married to recording, radio, film, and television.

PHOTOGRAPHY
Emotion 2, Speed 1, Ubiquity 1

Photography's worldwide popularity was triggered in 1841 by William Fox-Talbot's invention of the photographic negative, which allowed one photo to be reproduced in unlimited numbers. For the first time, mass propagation of reasonably detailed images became economical. Mathew Brady quickly became history's first famous photographer by building his career on the portraiture of notorious criminals, then celebrities. His 1850 book of celebrity portraits, *The Gallery of Illustrious Americans*, was among the first to make famous people emotionally accessible to mass audiences. By 1851, there were 100 photography studios in New York City. By the end of the 1800s, most American households had large collections of photographs of their families and of places around the world.

President Abraham Lincoln studied and used self-promotional photography for both campaigning and governing, a first among presidents. During the 1860 election, the Democrats made Lincoln's gangly physical appearance the centerpiece of their political attack against him. "We beg and pray you; Don't for God's sake, show his picture," went the theme song at opposition rallies. In a brilliant move of political ju-jitsu, Lincoln commissioned a Brady photograph of himself, standing solemnly with his left hand on a book, his face carefully lit to conceal his oddly chiseled features, his right fingers curled and shirtsleeve pulled slightly down to conceal his huge hands. Lincoln credited this single photo for his election victory.[431] Brady later lost his entire fortune bankrolling as many as twenty photographic teams to document the brutality of the Civil War. These photos stripped away the romanticism attached to war, profoundly affecting public opinion.

For the first time, microexpression had a rival: photography could precisely capture and transmit emotional and status signals. It radically eroded the concept of privacy, making the private public. As a stand-alone medium, photography ranks as moderate in emotional immersiveness; it spreads slowly and reaches only a tiny fraction of its potential audience. But married with faster and more ubiquitous distribution media, such as print, the Internet, and television, photography's social impact, as Brady showed in its early days, becomes high.

SOUND RECORDING
Emotion 2, Speed 2, Ubiquity 2

The first major recording star, Dan Quinn, emerged in 1892, his first twelve recordings all hitting number one. In 1902, opera singer Enrico Caruso became the first recording star to sell over one million records. Recordings became widely available after 1910, with their sales exploding to over 100 million units annually by 1918. By creating large and rich markets for exceptionally gifted singers and musicians, recordings transformed music, pushing the art of composition into the shadows. Performance and charisma became the central requirements for musical success. Today, music recordings that feature composition over performance and personality amount to just a tiny fraction of sales.

Consider Bing Crosby, whose astonishing popularity would not have been possible without sound recording. His flawless, mellow baritone made him the preeminent crooner of his era and history's most successful recording artist.[432] He recorded 1,600 songs and sold 400 million records, including "I'm Dreaming of a White Christmas," the very title of which causes his voice to play in most American heads. At Crosby's peak during the 1940s, he was probably the most famous man in the world. James Cagney describes Crosby's 1943 appearance before a crowd of 130,000 at Chicago's Soldier Field:

> Bing walked out to a reception for which the adjective "triumphant" is inadequate. He stood there in that very humble, charming way of his. ... After the audience explosion died down, Bing said, "Whadda yez wanna hear?" and they exploded again until the stadium walls nearly buckled. After they subsided, he said, "Ya wanna leave it to me?" and they blew up again. Finally, he said, "Hit me, Al," and our orchestra conductor, Al Newman, started his boys off on "Blues in the Night." They had played only the first two bars when the audience went into rapturous applause once more. Bing finished the song, and never in my life have I heard anything like it. I got the traditional goose pimples just standing there, listening. He did another, same thing.[433]

Like photography, sound recordings enable the mass distribution of authentic emotion, expanding the market for fame and establishing dramatically higher rewards and achievement benchmarks for artists. Consumers of recorded music, which is to say nearly all of us, define our social milieu and advance our own status by using our music choices to announce our distinctive tastes. As for me, I've already got the playlist for my own funeral party, a time when I figure that most people will be compelled to listen to my choices: a Bach oboe concerto, some Coltrane, Walter Piston, and Pat Metheny. My social-impact ratings for sound recording reflect its distribution as a stand-alone medium. Its emotional impact is moderate because it reaches only one sense, but it does so at high fidelity. Sound recording penetrates society with moderate speed and ubiquity, encumbered as it is with the necessity of physical or digital distribution. Of course, these ratings increase when recordings are integrated with broadcast and other media that reach more of our senses.

RADIO
Emotion 2, Speed 3, Ubiquity 2

In 1910, Lee DeForest's improvements to radio technology made possible his historic broadcast of Caruso's live performance at the Metropolitan Opera. By 1923, radio was reaching one percent of the U.S. population; by 1931, 20 percent; and by 1937, 75 percent. In an indication of radio's extraordinary social impact, the medium reached full market penetration more rapidly than any previous communication technology. By 1935, advertising sponsors were developing and controlling the content of many U.S. radio programs, a landmark in culture commercialization that would portend the market domination of most media over the coming decades. I rate radio as moderate in emotional impact because, like sound recording, only one of our senses is stimulated. Because radio allows simultaneous broadcast to many people, its penetration speed is obviously high. When measured by hours of use per day, its ubiquity is moderate compared with television or the Internet.

During the 1930s and 1940s, both Adolf Hitler and President Franklin Roosevelt were among the first to use radio to speak in their own voices directly and in real time to the entire populations of their nations. At 5' 8", Hitler was below average height; Roosevelt was confined to a wheelchair. Radio elevated these two men's stature and status, helping them to become among the most powerful people in human history, with Hitler's charisma dragging the world into the most deadly war ever, and FDR's sonorous exhortations uniting us through our fight against the Great Depression and then the war.

FILM

Emotion 3, Speed 2, Ubiquity 2

Only eight years after Louis Lumière opened the first motion-picture theater in France in 1895, New York City had more than 600 nickelodeons playing 5-cent silent films, and this transformational new medium was already taking hold. By the time D. W. Griffith released the first-ever feature film, *The Birth of a Nation*, in 1915, film was well on the way to removing the constraints of geography on culture and making us one. That same year, Hollywood's studio-controlled star system was born, with Charlie Chaplin earning $10,000 weekly, about $10 million annualized in today's dollars. By the 1920s, 40 million Americans made weekly visits to the packed movie houses, radically enlarging our experiences and changing our tastes, language, product preferences, even the shape of our bodies.

By 1926, Hollywood had discovered that it could completely bypass the vagaries of real cultural processes, as the studios mastered the use of promotion and publicity to manufacture stars. One of the first of these synthetic celebrities was the "Latin Lover," Rudolph Valentino, whose film image alone would cause women to scream and faint. Hysteria and suicides erupted worldwide in 1926 after Valentino died from a surgical infection. Rioting broke out among the 100,000 people attempting to view his body in New York City.[434] Valentino's elevation into celebrity Valhalla, a realm almost entirely disconnected from his actual earthly talents and accomplishments, is a preview of the absurd $7.6 million paid for U.S and U.K. market rights for the first photos of the Brangelina baby. Dan Wakeford, an executive at the tabloid *In Touch*, fed the frenzy for his readers when he declared, "This could possibly be the most beautiful baby in the history of the world."[435]

Combining highly realistic moving color images, sound, and music, film is the first medium since face-to-face communication that in my schema reaches a three rating for emotional immersion. Film's social impact is profound because it wholesales that immersion and captures both sight and sound with superb fidelity. Given film's immense worldwide popularity, an individual's status messages can now reach billions within weeks. If you doubt its effect, think about how film made icons out of these two otherwise ordinary male-dominance lines: "Go ahead, make my day" and "Hasta la vista, baby."

TELEVISION

Emotion 3, Speed 3, Ubiquity 3

Television technology was showcased at the New York World's Fair in 1939, the first year for regular broadcasts. NBC and CBS programming took off in the early 1940s, and by the middle of that decade, over twenty stations were operating profitably. In 1948, one percent of U.S. households were equipped with televisions; by 1955, 75 percent had TVs; by 1960, 90 percent had at least one set. The rate today is 98 percent. The astounding speed with which TV was adopted as a medium—seven years from its launch to universal market penetration and the fastest yet for any major communication technology, including the Internet—is the best indicator of television's extraordinary capacity to command attention. Forty-two million people witnessed the world's first murder televised live, when Jack Ruby shot Lee Harvey Oswald in 1963.[436]

Today, Americans expend just over 10 hours per day on all communications media, including television, radio, recorded music, newspapers, Internet, magazines, books, videotapes & DVDs, and videogames. Four of those hours are spent with the television switched on. The medium has become so effective at getting our attention that, by age 65, the average American will have spent nine full years of life watching. Television occupies more than half of the average American's waking, non-work life.[437] American kids, by the time they graduate from high school, will have spent twice as much time in front of a TV screen as in a classroom.[438] Television has turned us into spectators of a larger world beyond our reach. It has made living room couches into seedbeds for the transformation of American culture, filling cornfields with shopping malls, killing Rotary Clubs, and feeding the perception among the world's traditional societies that America is the source of all depravity. I recognize that these are strong statements; I will justify them in the next two chapters.

My own parents made a valiant but fruitless effort to turn my three siblings and me away from the evil box. For years, the only family TV was located in an unheated basement whose floor was often flooded by a few inches of water. Seating was limited to a flaming orange couch, with disintegrating foam erupting from its seams. My two sisters suppressed their fear of the mice who shared the Naugahyde island in our little subterranean Venice. We propped the TV legs above the waterline on blocks, then created an elevated wooden walkway so that we could traverse from door to couch to TV without getting electrocuted. The last to bark out "claim not!" the instant that *Lawrence Welk* or a *King Kong* rerun was announced would be forced to unhuddle from our blankets and venture across the walkway to change channels, risking the mild electric shock that often accompanied touching the dial. My brother so grokked the tube that he can still hum along with sitcom and ad music the first time he hears it.

Not only is television's social impact vastly greater than that of the most comparable form of entertainment of 300 years ago, live theater, but an evening of television costs 99 percent less than an outing in 1700 to enjoy, say, a Restoration comedy. The marginal cost of an extra hour of television viewing is approximately zero, as we see in Table 5.1.

Emotionally immersive like film, but also simultaneously and instantly broadcast nearly everywhere, television has the greatest social impact of any medium yet invented, earning a three on each rating scale.

Table 5.1: Entertainment costs over three centuries[439]

Entertainment	Cost as fraction of average day's wage
1700s theater	Greater than 1
1810 theater	1/3
1850 minstrel show	Slightly less than 1/3
1870 minstrel or variety show	1/6
1880 melodrama	1/13
1910 nickelodeon	1/40
1920 theater movie	Less than 1/40
1965 broadcast TV	1/360
2008 large-screen HDTV + cable or dish	1/35
2008 broadcast TV	1/800

MEDIATED REALITY
Emotion 3, Speed 3, Ubiquity 3

The Montreal-based cyborg Steve Mann coined the term "mediated reality" and lives out the new technology in his own life. Mann wears a computer, image projectors, and mini-cams covering one or both of his eyes; he can use real-time filtering software to screen out the billboards of brands he does not like seeing; he can see behind himself, perceive multiple views from the present or past at once, and read e-mail hands-free, to name a few of his features. Over twenty years of use, Mann had become so integrated with his technology that, when he was detached from it by over-scrupulous airport security in 2002, he became dizzy, disoriented, and unable to think clearly.[440] You can see pictures of Mann in his increasingly compact equipment at http://wearcam.org. Over the coming years, Mann's primitive cyborg getup and today's videogames and iPhones will morph into the entirely new medium of MR, which will wrap us in a blanket of sensation and perception more compelling and seductive than reality. Once that happens, success will become entirely intangible, and the successful will almost literally live in our heads.

Mediated reality has long been an object of sci-fi fantasy, with recent great examples being William Gibson's 1984 book *Neuromancer* and David Cronenberg's 1999 film *eXistenZ*, which forecast media so immersive that the boundary between medium and reality becomes impossible to identify. Progress toward that goal continues, and once MR overcomes its remaining technical challenges, it is certain to supplant TV as the dominant medium in terms of in social impact. Wearable hardware that displays fully accurate, three-dimensional representations of sight, sound, and other senses will become virtually unnoticeable. Today's "head mounted displays," bulky things that look like flattened binoculars, will etherealize into sunglasses with a built-in, see-through display.

Simulated touch and smell will be necessary parts of the MR revolution. Game controllers already on the market feature firearms with recoil and force-feedback steering wheels that mimic road vibration and torque. SensAble Technologies manufactures devices allowing artists and mold-makers to carve thin air, simulating the resistance of user-defined clay, while digitally capturing the work in CAD files. Nintendo's Wii, featuring a motion-sensitive game controller, sold 600,000 units in its first eight days on the market in 2006. California-based Immersion Corporation's "glove" allows users to feel the size, shape, and plasticity of computer-generated 3-D objects. To help foster the new technology, in 2006 Japan's Ministry of Internal Affairs and Communications invested $10 million in a plan to create virtual-reality TV technology, which will simulate 3D viewing, touch, and smell from a floor-mounted projector. The Tokyo Institute of Technology has developed a prototype machine that can both record and reproduce odors. Varying mixtures of 96 compounds are heated and vaporized to reproduce odors, sufficiently exact now to allow recognition of a green versus a red apple.[441]

The holy grail for MR will be fully noninvasive, direct-to-neuron displays of all five sensory simulations married to noninvasive neuron-to-computer controllers. Until about 2002, these notions were pure science fiction. Since then, Cyberkinetics, Inc., has received Food and Drug Administration approval to test implanted electrodes that are able to read signals from the brain's movement-planning area.[442] German neuroscientist Niels Birbaumer has developed a noninvasive device allowing paraplegics to use only thought to move a computer cursor to spell out sentences and surf the Internet. Using sensors pasted to the scalp, Birbaumer's Thought Translation Device reads a low-frequency brain wave, the slow cortical potential, but the tool requires that its user undergo painfully slow training.[443] A team at Berlin's Bernstein Center of Computational Neuroscience demonstrated a primitive "mental typewriter" in 2006, which features a wearable skullcap fitted with an array of EEG sensors; users can type with their thoughts at eight characters per minute. Emotiv Systems has prototyped an EEG helmet that would allow direct mind control of video games. Sony is apparently exploring noninvasive, direct-to-neuron display. In 2003, the company patented the concept of a device that fires precisely directed bursts of ultrasound at localized brain regions to elicit simulations of all the five senses, including taste and smell.[444]

The potential for mediated reality to graft itself permanently into our daily habits—and even to become the lives we prefer—is already being demonstrated by SecondLife.com, a massively multi-player online role-playing game (MMOG) launched in 2004 by Linden Lab. While it is primitive compared to where this medium will be at technical maturity, SecondLife is mediated reality's current state of the art. Total MMOG players for all games exceeded 30 million worldwide as of late 2007.[445] Freed of the immutable facts and constraints of their real lives, SecondLife players can construct their own appearance and personalities and can shape outcomes in their virtual worlds. Players build, buy, and sell real estate, clothing, skills, body shapes, and behaviors. SecondLife supports user-created political doctrines and social norms. Ads on Yahoo!, responding to the SecondLife market, hawk clothing to answer that last-minute what-to-wear question when your avatar meets that other avatar for your critical first date. Virtual characters, property, and powers are traded using real and virtual money on third-party websites.

Showing where the maturing medium of MR will lead, SecondLife makes irrelevant the boundary between real and virtual life. Real authors and virtual readers hold book-club discussions; real politicians troll for votes; players grapple with thefts, character assassinations, and hit men. Trial courts have sprung up to resolve conflict. Several real-world ad agencies have opened virtual offices on SecondLife, if only to evidence their digital grooviness.

And for many, life in game world is already better than reality. For the typical player, your game persona is often an idealized version of yourself: younger, hipper, and sexier. Sometimes the contrast is sad, as evidenced in a *Wall Street Journal* feature story on Ric Hoogestraat's SecondLife and his real existence. In virtual life, Ric has a muscular, 25-year-old body, a flourishing small-business empire, stimulating friendships, and an intimate marriage with another avatar. His real life consists of a $14-an-hour job at a call center, an aging body, deteriorating health, and a disintegrating marriage with his real wife, Sue. Over a ten-hour online session one Sunday—unaware of the food Sue had placed near his keyboard and stopping only for bathroom breaks—Ric evicted some deadbeat tenants in his shopping mall, negotiated some new leases, built a coffee shop, took a seaside Harley ride and a swim, counseled a lovelorn friend, and then shared his day's work with his virtual wife. His flesh-and-blood mate Sue sounds strangely understanding: "This other life is so wonderful; it's better than real life. Nobody gets fat, nobody gets gray. The person that's left can't compete with that." Indeed, a survey of 30,000 gamers found that 40 percent of men and 53 percent of women thought that their virtual friendships were as strong or better than those in real life.[446] Already, a third of SecondLife gamers clock more hours in their online roles than they do living their waking lives.

While SecondLife has plenty for those who want the seamier stuff, some MR sites offer exclusively red-light experiences. For about $150, at sinulator. com, you can buy an array of male and female sex toys that allow you and anonymous partners to hook up online, controlling one another's stimulatory apparatus in real time. Users can add visuals by selecting an online animated character and so "live out any fantasy" as "the characters react to your thrusting motion," according to the website. Get help if you are not at least mildly disgusted. To experience being a sociopath, visit sociolotron.com to rape or be raped and suffer the virtual consequences.

Mature mediated reality will bring all this and more to your bedroom, living room, or wherever you happen to be—without the distractions of clicking or external display screens. Instead of passively watching *West Wing* reruns, you will be the embedded reporter in North Korea or Mark Twain at a dinner party. You will alter history or the future in continuous, real-time, reality- or fantasy-based interactive relationships and plots. You will get trapped in licensed conspiracies with John Travolta. A pay-per-view Jack Welch will lead your company brainstorming session. Teens will party with a licensed Paris Hilton, sometimes in jail. MR subscribers will have X-ray vision, travel in atomic-scale space, or engage in sex so addictive, sanitary, and profitable that prostitution itself might join vinyl records in museums.

Mediated reality will make the very famous and the very successful more so. Our mediated personalities and social relationships might become more valuable and pleasurable than our real versions. The emotional intensity of MR will make it the first absolute rival to face-to-face communication. MR is certain to become the most socially potent communications medium yet to be invented. Its emotional immersiveness, speed, and ubiquity will surpass real human relationships within not much more than a decade or two.

COMMERCIAL CULTURE REPLACES REAL CULTURE

From the involuntary microexpressions of the human face to the rise of mediated reality, we could certainly debate the social-impact rankings that I've given my dozen top media that broadcast success and status. But the trend is abundantly clear. The impact of these media—especially the electronic-based ones—on our experiences is large and growing. Increasingly immersive and instantaneously ubiquitous media have progressively replaced some of the social and cultural functions of small, natural, face-to-face society. Our reference groups have become larger, of higher status, and our relationships with its members more tenuous. Through television, perhaps two billion people living under the influence of global culture share a set of one-way personal relationships. The purpose of these relationships is almost entirely commercial. Before the primacy of electronic media, cultures grew indigenously within groups of people who shared daily lives. Cultures that were successful at fostering group cohesion and survival prospered enough to hand down these qualities to generations following. The media that occupy so much of our lives today exist to sell us products, ideas, and personalities, replacing real culture with commercial culture. The result has aggravated our obsession with success.

Am I exaggerating the replacement of real culture by commercial culture, real life by mediated life? If you think so, tally up the time you spend interacting electronically with devices. The average player spends 22 hours weekly in online role-playing games, with some players clocking 80 hours weekly. One in five prefer their online existences to their real lives. Many players report that they have ended real relationships in favor of simulations. The American Medical Association recently weighed a recommendation that videogame addiction be given diagnostic status as a psychiatric disorder. Economist Edward Castronova, using Ebay auction prices for player-accumulated fantasy property such as real estate, characters, and powers, calculated that Sony's imaginary EverQuest economy—with almost half a million players— had a GDP per person almost equal to Russia's. Castronova estimates that the real-world market for virtual property is at least $100 million annually.[447] Some estimate the market at $1 billion, showing how deeply enveloped we have become in lives lived within commercial culture.

The Kaiser Family Foundation media-use survey found that American children's lives are now saturated by commercial culture to the dripping point. The typical American child age 8–18 lives in a home with eighteen media delivery devices, including "… three televisions, three VCRs, three radios, three CD/tape players, two video-game consoles, and a personal computer. The computer probably has an Internet connection and an instant-messaging program; the TV probably receives a cable or satellite signal." Half of American households with children have the TV on *all the time*, and that statistic shows little variance by income, race, or education. Six in seven children aged 8–18 have no parental rules limiting the time spent or content of television they watch.

If we add together all recreational screen, audio, interactive, and print media (and not double-counting overlapping media use), the Kaiser survey discloses that American children consume almost 6.5 hours of media content daily.[448] In the most comprehensive media use survey yet conducted, researchers at Ball State University's Center for Media Design shadowed 400 typical Americans for several months, finding that adults spend nine hours of their days using at least one form of media. We spend 21 percent of our waking hours working, 30 percent with media as our exclusive activity. Time allocation in the day of a typical seventh through twelfth grader is shown in Table 5.2.[449]

Commercial culture now occupies nearly half of our waking lives. It absorbs more of our waking hours, provides more compelling experiences, and imposes its own norms more effectively than ever in human history. As Ray Bradbury prophesied in *Fahrenheit 451*—never expecting his dystopia to become reality—commercial culture has overpowered genuine culture. Warned George Gerbner, then the dean emeritus of the Annenberg School of Communication, "For the first time in human history, children are hearing most of the stories, most of the time, not from their parents or school or churches or neighbors, but from a handful of global conglomerates that have something to sell."[450]

We can look back only a century to see how much commercial culture has changed our values and priorities. An 1898 survey found that children in their early teens most admired George Washington, Abraham Lincoln, Anne Sullivan (Helen Keller's teacher), Christopher Columbus, Julius Caesar, and other real figures from history and literature, but no entertainers or sports personalities.[451] By the 1990s, teens' most-admired lists consisted primarily of the com-

Table 5.2: Time Spent with Media and Selected Non-Media Activities

Media		Non-Media	
Watching TV	3:04	Hanging out with parents	2:17
Listening to music	1:44	Hanging out with friends*	2:16
Watching movies/videos	1:11	Exercising, sports, etc.	1:25
Using a computer	1:02	Pursuing hobbies, clubs, etc.	1:00
Playing video games	0:49	Talking on the telephone *	0:53
Reading	0:43	Doing homework *	0:50
		Working at a job *	0:35
		Doing chores *	0:32
TOTAL	**8:33**	**TOTAL**	**9:48**

* 7th to 12th graders only. Time uses overlap. Reprinted with permission. "Generation M: Media in the Lives of 8–18 Year-Olds – Report" (#7251), The Henry J. Kaiser Family Foundation, March 2005.

mercially managed personae of musicians and TV and movie stars—but not one political or historical figure.[452] Lycos' most continuously searched items over the period August 1999 through January 2005 confirms this trend. These searches consisted entirely of commercial pop-culture personalities, games, movies, and a few sports stars, with the only exceptions to the celebrity-search monopoly being marijuana, diets, illegal music-file swappers, Las Vegas, and the Bible.[453] Of Google searches in the U.S. in 2004, the top twenty men and women included not one political, scientific, or economic leader. Nineteen of the twenty were commercial pop-culture figures; one was an athlete. [454] Hold your lunch: once again in 2007, Britney Spears was the most popular Yahoo! search term, as it was for six of the prior seven years.

Prodded and corralled by commercial culture, we herd behind commercial role models. Our brain circuits confuse their synthetic popularity with trustworthiness. We try to conform to the vivid media fabrications of both real and imaginary people who are more perfect, gifted, powerful, wealthy, and successful than any we know in our real lives. The unreachable role models use ever more potent media to magnify their images ever more powerfully. We spend hours daily swamped in a world of unattainable status benchmarks. Said

The Wall Street Journal in a news story, "if happiness is relative, it's a wonder we Americans are not all miserable. No other people on the planet are bombarded with more images of the wealthier, the funnier, the more beautiful and the more successful."[455]

We have been transformed since 1410. Before the Renaissance, the religious and mythic exemplars for human ambition were objects of imagination, removed from everyday life and shaped over generations by enduring cultural values. Now, glossy magazines, movies, and television make living humans into gods on earth, constantly among us in high-definition detail, their personal habits and tastes better known to us than our own children's. As their proximity to us has increased, these profit-centers who are our heroes have become both role models and competitors. Our heroes are selling the desirability of their own fame. We have touched their Corinthian leather, and we want it for ourselves.

6

THE PRICE OF COMMERCIAL CULTURE

The guilt of murder may not stain their hands;
but the fouler guilt of making murderers surely does.[456]
—Horace Greeley, 1841, editor of the *New York Tribune*,
writing about his competitors

We have no obligation to make history. We have no obligation to make art.
We have no obligation to make a statement. To make money is our only objective.[457]
—Michael Eisner, former CEO and Chairman, Disney

SOME OF THE OLDER media that communicate status, such as face-to-face conversation, language, and literacy, are free public utilities; they serve public functions, and each of us has roughly equal access to them. We are therefore each personally responsible for their use or misuse. Not so the potent media mix that dominates contemporary American status relationships—namely newspapers, magazines, and the electronic media. These are operated largely to profit their owners. While I am a hardcore believer that these contemporary media should be governed by competitive free markets, I also believe that they continue to provide critical group cultural functions, such as providing information necessary for self-government, telling us what is important and what is not, and setting the very behavioral norms of our society.

Recall from Chapter 2 the idea that our species' phenomenal success at endeavors such as organized agriculture, warfare, and knowledge accumulation rests on genes giving us the unique ability to invent advantageous group cultural and behavioral norms that we can pass immediately to following generations. Human groups that adopt cultures supporting high aggregate health and productivity win over those that do not. Those who accept the validity of group selection theory must call upon the executives, producers, and shareholders who determine media content to balance profit with their personal responsibility for our species' prosperity and psychological wellness.

The overwhelming priority we place on individual success in America has corrupted the ethics of our merchants of culture. They have ditched their duty to balance profit and social obligation. They have distracted us from what is important with canned travel sections and an unending Roman circus of debauchery and celebrity malfeasance from O. J. Simpson to Laci Peterson to Drew Peterson and back to O. J. Simpson. In this chapter, I will lay out the solid evidence showing that the culture merchants must be fully aware of their breach of public duty and how their irresponsible decisions compound the harms of OverSuccess.

FAME FIXATION

My first awareness of the awesome power of culture merchants to make us worship their products goes back to my teen years and the time of Woodstock. In the summer of '69, my boyhood buddy Charlie Howes and I were manicuring lawns at the archetypal, old-money estates of Greenwich and Southport that look out over Long Island Sound. Occasionally, the reel of my three-gang Locke mower would lop off an azalea stem. I'd stick it back in the immaculate mulch, finish up, and be off to the next job before the gardeners noticed it wilting.

One August Friday, we cut out early, young men on a mission. Pumped for our long weekend, our musical orientation still more Beatles than Haight-

Ashbury, we packed up Charlie's red Chevy convertible with blankets and a beer cooler and headed for the Woodstock rock festival. By noon that Friday, the New York Thruway was already crawling several exits south of Max Yasgur's farm, the site of the concert. We were already beating Saturday night burger-eating contests in the Norwalk Mickey D parking lot by a mile. Unattached women wearing gossamer sun dresses spun like fairies in the median strip, their arms and faces raised to the sun. Strangers passed hash pipes through open car windows. Weekend-only freak flags were flying high in redneck dairy country.

When the state highway turned into a four-lane parking lot about eight miles from the farm, we abandoned the Chevy and grabbed our blankets and beers for the hike to the gate. As we fished for our tickets, a matched pair of Hell's Angels, as black and chrome as a Hudson Bay night, reared their bikes up on their back tires like stallions and plowed almost vertically into the chain-link fence. Down went the fence and at least $5 million in festival revenues, and we all streamed in. From then on, Woodstock would be a weekend of free love and free music, where, at least for three days, we could forget about our prison schools and errand-boy jobs for the military-industrial complex.

We set up our blanket and cooler on the freshly cut field. We had plenty of space, way down near center stage. On either side, towers of construction staging rising maybe 100 feet into the air supported dozens of industrial-strength loudspeakers, each the size of a VW bug. Through their records, I had already felt the Jefferson Airplane and Grateful Dead shake America's satisfied, 1950s complacency. Still idling at low volume with recorded folk singles, this battery of speakers would drive half a million people into mass euphoria with the music's power, and make Woodstock a moment historic enough to end up on *Alistair Cooke's America* series. Live music began late Friday afternoon. By Saturday midday, well over 200,000 people had crowded in. A couple traded space on our blanket for some pills of unknown provenance, probably stolen from a veterinarian's cabinet. Poor Charlie swallowed two, hoping they would provide him a portal to the free love proliferating around us. Instead, he was knocked prone until Sunday dawn.

A bit after midnight Saturday, Sly & the Family Stone took the stage and belted out their anthem, "I Want to Take You Higher." Body to body, in rapture and on cue, one-half million baby boomers simultaneously screamed "higher." Dancing feet ringed Charlie's tranquilized body. I shouted at him, "Get up, you'll never see anything like this again in your life." He flashed me the peace sign; he was grooving. In spite of the rain, mud, drugs, random sex, and the darkness and frenzy, the Woodstockers made sure that not a single person stepped on Charlie.

But the peace and harmony of Woodstock was not to be repeated; commercial culture had spotted a huge new market segment. My mom got me a lucky break writing a teen's-eye-view column for a local newspaper. My topic was the dozens of Woodstock-wannabe rock festivals that had sprouted throughout the Northeast in 1970 like backyard homegrown. With no backstage pass or connections, I spent many of that summer's weekends in the mud and dust with tens of thousands of young people seeking community and escape from their directionless, Wonder Bread lives in these last moments before the first oil embargo ended the Beach Boys' America.

For all the mud and organizational chaos, Woodstock was a success. It was the world's largest-ever music party and the national launch of the counterculture. It was not until the Powder Ridge Rock Festival, held at a Connecticut ski area in August 1970, that I became aware of how cynically music was being used to engineer our fixation on the famous.[458] A court injunction filed by locals fearful of another Woodstock blocked entry by the bands and shut off Powder Ridge's electrical power. Thirty thousand people showed up anyway, thinking the front-page and radio warnings of the festival's cancellation an anti-Aquarian conspiracy. A fifty-foot gauntlet of drug dealers set up for business in front of the stage. They came provisioned for a far larger crowd, openly hawking their products and prices to the arriving teenyboppers and very young adults. LSD was in such oversupply that the dealers were forced to give it away so that they did not have to risk taking it back on the highways buzzing with cops. "Free acid," they shouted to the earnest, trusting festivalgoers struggling to look hip, hair still just weeks beyond the influence of a barber, their drug experiences, for the most part, topping out at grass.

By Friday afternoon, the most ardent male groupies were squatted in the hot dust, staring through the chain-link fence protecting the empty stage, transfixed by the perceptual void. The record labels had inflated the rock-ers they came to see from bar acts and dance-hall rhythm-keepers into the north stars of the counterculture. Bathed in psychedelic stage light and amplified by diesel generators big enough to run a small hospital, the most famous lead guitarists had acquired the powers of Zeus, firing long soprano notes like lightning bolts into adolescent psyches yearning for meaning beyond the posters on their suburban bedroom walls. But nobody famous showed up—no Sly, Fleetwood Mac, Allman Brothers, or Janis Joplin, no Ten Years After.

When it became clear by late Friday night that there would be no music, drug use shifted from pleasure enhancement to pleasure substitute. Still in my role as local-news reporter, I made some notes by flashlight, then rolled out my sleeping bag and tried to sleep. But the mass hallucinogenic overdosing had stripped the teens down to their raw, unaddressed loneliness. Their tortured shrieks and moans jolted me upright and awake every few minutes until the groggy relief of dawn. Dr. William Abruzzi, who managed the medical tents at both Woodstock and Powder Ridge, shared his own shock at the experience:

> At one point we had 150 kids freaked out simultaneously. I'm not talking about the kid who is a little spaced out and saying, "Look, baby, I don't know where I am." I mean the horrendous kind, the paranoia, muscular activity, hostility, aggression, kind of frightened-out-of-their-minds scene that is unbelievable unless you've seen it happen ... The kids at Powder Ridge turned their hostility and frustration inward.[459]

We demand that the famous fill us. Powder Ridge was an accidental control experiment in fame deprivation.

Fast-forward two and a half decades and stop the tape at New Kids on the Block, an early '90s boy band manufactured by a producer specifically to appeal to the teen market. The yearning to be touched by synthetic gods that I saw at Powder Ridge had long since become the object of routine manipulation by the popular-music industry. The band's fans, early teenagers at the most socially insecure time of their lives, were calculatingly tortured into anguished frenzies of unrequited desire. Here is a portion of a fan letter, forgotten by a mail service and unread by its addressee, written to band member Jonathan:

Well anyway, about three or four years ago, I was a very happy person. Until I saw your cute little face on the cover of a tape that one of my friends had. Well ever since then, my life has been turned upside down. I mean, all I do anymore is think of you. I'm always miserable. I'm never happy. My grades have slipped rapidly, and every night I lie in my bed and cry. I asked my mom why the Lord made people so miserable ... I know you'd make me happy. Very happy. I mean, you wouldn't even have to try. It would make me happy to wait on you hand and foot. I don't care if I never get anything else in my life ... When do I get to meet you? Sometimes I think that if I don't get my turn soon, that I'm just gonna give up. I'm gonna kill myself. The only reason I haven't done it is because of my love for you.[460]

At least Rousseau read his fan mail. Another girl, a 16-year-old, on learning that her pop idol was to be married, ran herself a hot bath and slashed her neck, arms, and legs. She survived and explained her attempted suicide: "She's going to change him if he gets married ... I'm not going to live with that."

There is solid science behind our fixation with fame. Psychologists John Maltby and James Houran have painstakingly devised a "celebrity worship scale," which they used to show that eleven percent of people aged 10 to 68 suffer "celebrity worship syndrome," an obsessive-addictive disorder that affects men and women equally. CWS sufferers live in joyless worlds ruled by absurd pipedreams that they will be loved and made whole by stars they will never meet. Another ten percent of us have an intense, personal relationship with one or more star idols and agree with statements such as "I have frequent thoughts about my celebrity, even when I don't want to." Or, "I consider my favorite celebrity to be my soul mate." One percent of us fit in the borderline pathological group, agreeing with statements such as "If someone gave me several thousand dollars, I would consider spending it on a personal possession (like a napkin or paper plate) once used by my favorite celebrity" and "If my favorite celebrity asked me to do something illegal as a favor, I would probably do it."[461]

The celebrity mag *People*, launched in 1974 as fame fixation began to fill the void left by the erosion of stable community, is now number one in gross revenues of all U.S. magazines.[462] Its success is built entirely on our increasingly insatiable hunger for the illusion of connection with humans we will never meet. The magazine's tabloid spawn now blanket the magazine racks and twist our personal priorities. To fill demand, an industry of hundreds of paparazzi are on constant stakeout to grab unrehearsed pictures of celebrities doing everyday things like shopping, walking the dog, or exiting the courthouse.

Better than our delusional hobnobbing with celebrities, another means for us to self-validate against globalized benchmarks is to become famous ourselves. A 1998 poll found that 30 percent of American adults want to be famous.[463] Sixty-one percent of American tweens want to be famous, a number second only to India in a fifteen-nation survey.[464] For 51 percent of young American adults, the number-one or number-two goal in life is to be famous.[465] At any of 95 Club Libby Lu stores throughout the U.S., tween girls "can realize their dreams of being a rock star or a princess," boasts the chain's website. For $45.00, girls can hold little commemorative parties for themselves by purchasing the "On Tour" package, including the simulated wireless microphone/headset, backdrop poster of stage and stage lights, and personal makeover, including makeup, sparkles, sparkly pink tank-top and Hannah Montana-style blonde wig. Celebrity-Babies.com gets ten million monthly page views from infatuated visitors who brag about the hours they consume fawning over sunhats, strollers, and other minutiae of famous people's pregnancies. "Perfect couple, perfect family, perfect life! Perfect, perfect, PERFECT!" gushes a Brangelina fan. During 2005, over 100,000 people auditioned for *American Idol*, the Fox TV show, where 16- to 28-year-old amateurs can win up to one million dollars, their own CD, a *Rolling Stone* cover, and instant, if only transient, celebrity. To get a ten-second *Idol* audition and a microscopic shot at fame, people are willing to drive for hours, camp out for two nights on the sidewalks, and get banded like cattle for slaughter. "I just want to get noticed. I want to be seen. I wanna be on TV!" said *Idol* auditioner April Burnhart.[466]

Commercial culture has drained fame of meaning and value and made many of us desire it at almost any cost. Once reserved for the truly lasting monuments of human accomplishment, fame is now a commercial product with the shelf life and significance of a bag of potato chips. Fame is a means to visibility and recognition in a world where we have traded the intimacy of small, face-to-face community for global social hierarchies. With every small community lost, the ranks of the invisible and the unappreciated swell. Though the global market grows, our brains' social mechanisms are only slightly different than they were before the Renaissance. So we fill our heads with a few dozen stars instead of a few dozen neighbors and friends. The few of us who do become famous are showered with rewards—all paid for by a planet of anonymous losers.

For each celebrity that elbows into our mental bandwidth, we have one less space for a real person. While we yearn for it to be otherwise, celebrities cannot know or love us. We pay for fame fixation in personal emptiness and withered community. Yes, it's true that you merchants of culture are responding to a market need created by global society. But, untethered by self-restraint, you have converted the need into a dangerous obsession.

MEDIA VIOLENCE

An avalanche of evidence now shows that some portion of real violence in America is not just linked to but caused by the product and programming choices made by media decision makers. These conscious choices are emblematic of the collapsed ethical restraints central to the syndrome of OverSuccess. By consuming these products, we are all to blame for making success a license to foster the kind of violence that would put a no-name street criminal behind bars for life. The reviewers fawn over Eminem like a contemporary Shakespeare and load him with Grammys for his venomous doggerel. My repulsion for his music is, apparently, shared by terrorists. Human Rights Watch reports that the CIA blasted Eminem recordings at captive terrorists during their interrogations, hoping they would capitulate in the face of our cultural bilge, which probably served only to make them more certain of their hatred for us.[467]

In one of the Eminem songs that we made platinum, the rapper protagonist contemplates sodomizing his mother, slitting his father's throat, shooting toddlers, knifing prostitutes, and murdering his then-wife, Kim Mathers, before dumping her body off a pier. "Now bleed, bitch, bleed," go the lyrics. Live and onstage during his July 2000 hometown Detroit concert—with his wife in the audience—Eminem mockingly instructed her to commit suicide. The next night, she slit both her wrists.[468] Another top-grossing rapper who calls himself C-Murder, who is in fact serving a life sentence for murder, glorified his estimable status with a CD and video bootlegged directly from prison.[469]

Commercial culture's apologists have been successful in waving off concerns about media violence. Public opinion is tougher on the role modeling of drug abuse but, even here, commercial culture knows no restraint. Ralph DiClemente, a professor of public health at Emory University, checked a sample of youth music in five popular categories, finding that 77 percent of rap songs contained references to drug or alcohol abuse. And rap has a huge influence: of the fourteen styles of music prevalent in 2005, it was overwhelmingly the most listened to among 8- to 18-year-olds, more than double the next most popular genre.[470]

The critics gushed and ratings soared for *The Sopranos*, 2004 Emmy winner for best drama whose characters featured more endearing sociopaths than any previous shoot-'em-up on any screen. In one episode, a pregnant stripper is beaten to a bloody death in Tony Soprano's Bada Bing strip club parking lot. Reported a reviewer, "I counted a total of 13 blows, starting with one facial slap followed by one punch square in the face, then two vicious upper cuts to the stomach followed by five punches to the head while [she] lay unconscious on the pavement. [The assailant] then smashed her head three times into a reinforced steel guardrail and gave her one last punch to the head for good measure."[471] This is all perfectly OK in OverSuccessed America because the producers, the actors, and media conglomerate Time Warner all got rich and famous.

The film critic Michael Medved has noted that if the murder rate on the average TV night were real, everyone in America would be dead in fifty days. By age 18, the average young person has witnessed 220,000 televised acts of violence and 16,000 murders. UCLA's National Television Violence Survey coded three years of TV, finding that 61 percent of programs contain violence, with children's programming containing more violence than shows geared to adults. Perhaps more subversively, characters portrayed as "good" commit 44 percent of violence, humor is used in depictions of 43 percent of violent acts, and almost 75 percent of violent scenes show no immediate punishment for or condemnation of violence. Only 16 percent of violent TV acts show realistic consequences; 58 percent depict no pain, 47 percent no harm.[472] Remember that our teens spend an average of three hours each day watching people literally get away with murder.

MTV, which about three-quarters of American teens watch for over six hours each week, is also relentlessly violent. Fifteen percent of MTV's primary content, music videos, contains at least one overt act of interpersonal violence, with the violent videos showing six acts of violence per two- to three-minute segment. This means that MTV viewers see about 20 acts of personal violence per hour. In 80 percent of the videos, the main character is the aggressor and is nearly always someone teens perceive as an attractive role model.[473] No surprise that MTV also grabs teen attention with an average of 93 sexual scenes per hour.[474]

Over 300 laboratory, naturalistic, correlation, and longitudinal studies have characterized the impact of media violence on children; only a handful show no effect. I will single out one study led by Columbia University's Jeffrey Johnson that followed television watching and violence in 707 families for seventeen years. This was a longitudinal study, the most expensive type and the best at establishing scientific cause and effect. Johnson found that aggressive behavior, including assaults, fights, and robberies during early adulthood, increased with television viewing during adolescence. Among youths who watched television for more than three hours per day, the aggressive behavior rate was 29 percent, almost five times the rate for those who watched less than one hour per day. The effect was four times as pronounced for boys as for girls. Of the adult subjects who had watched less than one hour per day in their youth, 1.2 percent had committed an act of criminal violence, compared to 10.8 percent for those who had watched three or more hours per day. The study statistically controlled for factors such as psychiatric disorders, prior aggressive behavior, child neglect, neighborhood violence, family income, and education.[475] Highly similar results were found in a fifteen-year study that followed 329 Chicago-area children through adulthood.[476] A follow-up study by Johnson found that, by the age of 33, those who were the heaviest TV viewers at age 14 are more likely to have suffered obesity, sleep, aggression, attention and learning problems, and to have failed in school. Heavier TV viewing by adolescents with attention and learning difficulties does not explain their subsequent problems.[477]

Johnson explained to me why he thinks television causes increased violence among adults who watched more TV as children. "If middle and lower income individuals believe that the wealthy became wealthy by behaving in an unethical manner [as seen on TV], they may be more likely to see unethical behavior (even including aggression) as being an appropriate way to get ahead." Johnson thinks that commercial culture carries a toxic payload of adverse social teaching: atrophy of social skills, desensitization, disinhibition, imitation, and identification with the aggressor. TV shows aggressors using violence to win without paying any consequences. MTV has a particularly acute effect on violence because its viewers identify so fiercely with its stars.[478] Teens consider musicians even more than athletes as their heroes, and they rate the music's influence on their behavior and mores higher than they do religion or books.[479]

The link between videogames and violence is already firmly established, but because the videogame research field is younger, the evidence establishing cause and effect is still accumulating. In 1992, Doom became the first videogame to realistically simulate killing opponents. By 2001, videogames were out-grossing movie-theater ticket sales. Videogame hardware plus software chalked up $18.8 billion in U.S. sales in 2007.[480] One of the top-ten-selling videogames of all time is the Grand Theft Auto series. When it was released in 2002, GTA's Vice City scored over 1.4 million units sold in its first two days on the market, at the time, the fastest sales start for a video game in industry history. By 2003, 71 percent of boys and 34 percent of girls in the 13–17-year age group played the series.[481] GTA is rated for persons 17 and over. Not wanting to be like those moralizing prims against pool or pornography who never tried the stuff, I played some GTA-Vice City. Here's my blow by blow:

> Scene: Protagonist/player kicks bleeding, prostrate hooker in the groin, beats her with tire iron. Another hooker steps into car. Copulating sounds, car rocks and squeaks in rhythm. Hooker exits car. Player punches hooker in the face.

> Scene: Player beats and kills bleeding law enforcement officers, shoots policeman in pursuit. Realistic sound of spent shells dropping onto the street.

> Scene: Player perpetrates random violence against innocent bystander. White player administers kicks to the groin of a bleeding, overweight black man lying on the ground. Blood streams onto the pavement.

This product, which got its owners rich enough to buy islands in the right climates and famous enough to keynote industry conventions, glamorizes the brutal murder of women, while rewarding its boy players with "health points" for hijacking police cars, murdering policeman and prostitutes, gunning down innocent pedestrians, and delivering cocaine to crime bosses.

The 2004 version, GTA-San Andreas, provides a first-person experience of life as a retro 1990s street thug. Retail sales surpassed $100 million during this game's first five days on the market.[482] More complex, realistic, and engrossing than its predecessors, its players begin the game with low social status, and must earn "respect" by robbing the homes of innocents, slitting throats, performing drive-by shootings, gambling in sleazy casinos, dressing like pimps, scoring sex with hard-to-get prostitutes, learning masturbation tips, using vehicles to flatten pedestrians, recruiting gang members, and murdering cops. Each firearms kill helps move the player up the skill-level ladder from "gangster" to "hitman." Players learn proficiency in use of over thirty realistic and improvised weapons. The most successful game launch in history was GTA 4, chaulking up sales of $300 million and 3.6 million units in its first day.

The second most successful launch was Microsoft's Halo 3, a first-person shooter, with $170 million in sales on its first day. Game scenes are almost uniformly militarized landscapes, and players have a choice among a staggering variety of imaginative and beautifully detailed firearms. Said Bill Gates of his company's new game, "Halo is truly a cultural phenomenon ... an important milestone for ... video games as entertainment and as an art form ... our vision for the future of entertainment."[483]

The T-rated (i.e., intended for players aged 13-plus) Outlaw Golf features DD-cupped protagonists Trixie and Mistress Suki, a pair of foul-mouthed porn princesses who assault the player's golfer opponents over bad strokes, ripping the clothing off their sexual body parts. "Consider this a Christmas present," shouts one of them as she punches an opponent in the face. The core virtue of T-rated BMX XXX is that its adolescent male customers can look almost continuously through the almost undetectably thin thongs worn by a strip club hooker as she uses her bike to assault random pedestrians. By successfully attacking a sufficient number of victims, players are able to earn on-screen access to short films that were taped at real New York City strip clubs, depicting real strippers slithering and grimacing athwart BMX bikes.

A survey of the top-selling T-rated games found an average of 46 violent incidents during their opening ten-minute play-periods. In 98 percent of game segments, aggression goes unpunished; sixty percent of aggressors who injure others are rewarded. Most of the violence is lethal and shown in close, graphic detail.[484] In another random sample of 81 T-rated video games, two Harvard researchers found that 98 percent involved extensive intentional violence, 90 percent rewarded or required the player to injure game characters, and 69 percent rewarded or required the player to kill. Ninety-five percent of teenage boys play video games at least monthly. Boys average ten hours of play per week.[485]

The videogame industry defends itself by claiming that games are labeled for age-appropriateness and that consumers who are too young to play them cannot buy them. In reality, the industry's labeling system is notoriously lax. Forty-four percent of Everyone-rated games contain violence in over one-third of game scenes, yet do not contain the required labeling. A secret-shopper survey of retailers conducted by the Federal Trade Commission found that, when unaccompanied by an adult, 42 percent of children aged 13 to 16 were able to buy Mature-rated games. Via the Internet, four in five M-rated games are marketed to players 16 and under. The bottom line is that 70 percent of children 18 and under play Mature-rated games.[486] Activists had to spend years to achieve even the current fast-and-loose state of game ratings and enforcement, so fierce is culture merchants' resistance to social responsibility.

Do violent videogames cause real-world violence? Eighth and ninth graders with nonaggressive personalities who are heavy players of violent games are nearly ten times more likely to become involved in actual violence than teens who do not play the games. Teens who are heavy players of violent games show increased aggressive behavior and thoughts, decreased helping behavior, increased delinquency and fighting at school, poorer grades, and a greater likelihood of getting into arguments with teachers. In a study of more than 400 third through fifth graders, those who consumed more videogame violence early in the school year went on to become more verbally, relationally, and physically aggressive later in the school year.[487]

The link between violent media for teen and pre-teen aggression was made clear as far back as 1972.[488] Six major professional societies—the American Psychological Association, the American Academy of Pediatrics, the American Academy of Child and Adolescent Psychiatry, the American Medical Association, the American Academy of Family Physicians, and the American Psychiatric Association—have all concluded that the research data point "overwhelmingly to a causal connection between media violence and aggressive behavior in some children."[489] Over the past several years, hundreds of researchers and dozens of lay and scientific public health advocacy groups have repeatedly sounded the alarm about television violence to Congress and to the public.

The strength of the link between media violence and real-world aggression and violence is greater than the links between lead exposure and lower IQ in children, asbestos exposure and cancer, and secondhand tobacco smoke and lung cancer.[490] The same research methods were used in both the media violence and the health risk studies. Congress has responded to the evidence of such physical health risks by establishing tough liability laws and imposing tight exposure limits. Violent media is also a proven public health hazard, but the best we can muster to protect ourselves are product labels and V-chips.

Conscientious skeptics, as well as shills for commercial culture, argue that the mountain of evidence remains too weak to justify regulatory or legal action. They dismiss the hundreds of supportive studies that show a remarkable degree of consistency for the social sciences. Correlation between media violence and real violence is not causation, they correctly parry, but without acknowledging the even stronger evidence from experimental and longitudinal studies. Sounding perfectly reasonable to a poorly informed reporter on deadline, skeptics reply that violence-prone individuals choose violent media, or that poor parenting is the underlying explanation. Both of these assertions—the "reverse hypothesis" and the "shared causation model"—have been soundly disproved by the more rigorous evidence published over the past five years. Another favorite tactic among the skeptics is to evade reference to the immense body of supporting evidence while singling out a defect in one study or citing only the handful of contradictory studies.

Skeptics demand an artificially high burden of proof for media-violence risk. They rightfully say that only a few people who use violent media become violent and that real-world violence is caused by many factors. They fail to admit that, while the risk per person is small, almost all Americans are drenched daily in several hours of commercial media, making the aggregate exposure to violent media immensely high. Finally, and perhaps their most effective tactic, skeptics create doubt by demanding and getting "balance" in news reports on media violence. Such false balance creates controversy where little exists, treating a weak objection as equal in weight to solid proof. Paid shills for the Tobacco Institute and Exxon Mobil used exactly these techniques to delay action for years on smoking and global warming.

The toughest hurdle to action on media violence is our natural skepticism toward intangible processes. Without the need for persuasion, we instinctively guard against macroscopic physical threats, such as storms or large carnivores, and against noxious-smelling toxins. Yet it required centuries for us to accept the logic of precaution against germs and decades against radiation that we cannot see or smell. Though the risks caused by media-propagated violence are far greater than for many cancers and infectious diseases, we are doubtful about even solid evidence that a fixture in American living rooms for fifty years could inflict an unseen psychological disorder on enough viewers to cause a large public health and safety burden, or that the videogame versions of the cowboys and Indians kids once played in the woods could result in the death of real innocents.

Fortunately, very recent discoveries in neuroscience provide evidence for a direct, physical mechanism by which media violence causes real-world violence. This evidence may finally persuade commercial culture merchants to refresh their ethics and curb their toxic emissions. In 2006, Michigan State University media researcher René Weber and his team of neuroscientists published the first study showing how our brains automatically respond to violent videogame play. The team painstakingly coded level of violence for each frame of the first-person-shooter game Tactical Ops: Assault on Terror. Thirteen males, experienced in the game and screened for past violence, played the game in an fMRI machine. During frames showing violence, Weber's gamers show unusual activity in precisely the same brain regions that are more active in teens who have been diagnosed with aggressive and disruptive behavior disorders. Seconds before, during, and after violent play—and only during this tight time window—Weber found moderate activation in the brain's dorsal anterior cingulate cortex and great suppression in the rostral anterior cingulate cortex and the amygdala. These regions, along with the orbital frontal cortex, are involved in the regulation of emotion and, specifically, aggression.

In 1996, Giaocomo Rizzolatti and his team accidentally discovered mirror neurons located in our brain's premotor cortex, which fire both when we execute goal-directed movements, such as grasping a pen in order to write, and when we watch someone else do the same thing. Mirror neurons cause us to mentally rehearse each action we observe, which explains why yawns are contagious and why we feel empathy for others' pain. UCLA neuroscientist Marco Iacoboni has shown that mirror neurons are probably critical to imitation, teaching us to do what we see, but automatically and not under our conscious control. "This idea is especially dangerous now," says Iacoboni, "because we have discovered a plausible neural mechanism that can explain why observing violence induces imitative violence … [T]he strong imitative tendencies that humans have may lead them to imitative violence when exposed to media violence." Iacoboni warns that, through the action of mirror neurons, playing violent videogames may train our brains to feel pleasure and reward us with a sense of accomplishment for inflicting pain.[491]

Violent videogames do more than train teenage males to enjoy exploding skulls and spilling intestines. They teach the detailed mechanics of killing. Retired Lieutenant Colonel Dave Grossman, a West Point professor of military science and psychology, describes a 1997 incident in Paducah, Kentucky, in which fourteen-year-old Michael Carneal stole a pistol from a neighbor's locked garage, brought it to school, and opened fire on a morning prayer group.

> He fired eight shots. The FBI says that the average US law enforcement officer, at a distance of seven yards, hits with fewer than one bullet in five. Michael Carneal fired eight shots at a bunch of milling, scrambling, screaming children. He got eight hits. Five of them were head shots. Even more astounding was the kill ratio. Each kid was hit once. Three were killed; one was paralyzed for life. Never, to my knowledge, in the annals of law enforcement or military or

even criminal history can we find an equivalent achievement ... It turned out that while the kid had never fired a pistol before stealing that gun, he'd been a video-game fanatic. The family was well-to-do. He was the son of a well-respected local attorney, and they had arcade-quality games in the house. In addition to that, he spent a lot of time at the local arcade.[492]

Teen-rated videogames have taught our teens precision, rapid-fire killing technique, with intense gamers having become expert marksmen with real guns even on first use.[493] In a similar case, two boys aged 13 and 16, claiming to the police that they were bored and just imitating what they had learned by playing GTA, fired a .22 randomly at cars and trucks passing on Interstate 40 near their home in Newport, Tennessee, killing one person and wounding another.[494] When asked by a reporter to respond to concerns about videogame violence, a spokesman for Rockstar Games, GTA's maker, joked, "Seven million copies worldwide doesn't seem like much negative feedback."[495]

If you think that depravity's sub-basement has already been picked clean for raw material, then check out the indie documentary and hit DVD *Bumfights*. California filmmaker Ryan McPherson and his crew proffer vials of crack, cheap alcohol, a few bucks, and the promise of stardom to entice grungy homeless men into debasing and injuring themselves for fun on camera. Bloody fistfights, broken bones, tooth-pulling with pliers, a disastrous ride down concrete steps in a shopping cart, a used-condom-sucking contest, head-bashing into concrete walls, and self-immolation—all these are treated by the filmmakers as opportunities for humor. In one scene, a homeless addict, his ankle chained to a streetlamp, writhes on the pavement, struggling to reach a plate containing crack, a pipe, and a lighter placed a quarter-inch from his fingertips. Off camera, the filmmakers taunt the tortured addict. Interviewed on *60 Minutes*, chuckling and completely unburdened by remorse, McPherson watches a scene where his crew uses duct tape to bind and gag a sleeping homeless man.

The DVD inspired a national wave of bum hunting, with hundreds of copycat attacks against the homeless, many ending in death. Says hate crimes expert Brian Levin, a criminologist at California State University in San Bernardino: "This is the new sport. In many parts of the country, it's a rite of passage." Florida teens Jeffrey Spurgeon and three friends had watched *Bumfights* "hundreds of times." They are now spending decades in prison for kicking and clubbing to death a sleeping homeless man they came across in the woods while blowing weed. Spurgeon told CBS that he and his friends were imitating the show and killed the man "for fun." One *Bumfights* producer justifies himself by explaining, "this project is a means to an end. We want to be feature filmmakers. We're going to cash in and then cash out and go make some movies."[496]

What keeps us from driving these games, movies, music, and videos off America's store shelves and screens? The problem is not the First Amendment, which protects our right to unpopular speech, or the Second Amendment, which protects citizens' lawful right to own and use firearms. The problem is ethical neutering in an industry that insists on using its constitutional privileges to teach children racist and sexist violence, sadistic sex, murder, and cop-killing. For these culture merchants, to succeed is not to help build a better America, but to escalate realistic violence because it sells. To succeed in a broad swatch of American media is to knowingly harm our nation's next generation by teaching it that killing for fun is, as Bill Gates says, both entertainment and art.

For these and other reasons discussed in this chapter, the American Academy of Pediatrics recommends zero TV viewing for children under three. Do media big shots believe the American Academy of Pediatrics, or do they eat their own dog food? Eminem allows his young daughter to listen only to specially cleaned-up versions of his CDs.[497] Tom Cruise caps his two young kids' TV time at three and a half hours a week "if they're doing well in school." Steven Spielberg limits his children to an hour a day. Madonna caps TV time for her two young children.[498] The father of former Disney chairman Michael Eisner allowed his son only one hour of TV for each two hours of reading. Even *Hustler* magazine publisher Larry Flynt thinks children should be strictly denied access to his own pornographic materials.[499] These creatives who have collectively earned billions from media violence can read the scientific literature and want better for their own children. (Mr. Spielberg should be duly credited for his greater than ordinary redeeming content.)

Full disclosure: I am a big consumer of violent movies. I made opening night for all three *Aliens* movies. I found *Minority Report*'s pre-crime intercept scenes visually and intellectually dazzling, and David Cronenberg's *History of Violence* gets genuinely sensitive and intimate with its blood-soaked characters. Unfortunately, most of the "action" genre is aimed squarely at the adolescent market. I often leave the theater pinching the bridge of my nose and shaking my head in disgust for having being suckered by another plot concept whose tenuous promise was buried under ninety minutes of Armageddon so tiresome that I sometimes sleep through it.

OUR MEDIA-JAMMED BRAINS

Electronic media affect our brains psychologically, as well as physically. Advertising psychologists were first to learn how to command the attention of the TV viewer, not with content but with rapid zooms and pans, edits, dubs, music, bursts of color, sudden movement, and loud noises. Stanford University's Byron Reeves found that these "technical events," rather than TV's content, activate an involuntary orienting response, one that was probably designed to protect us from predators and can now be used to keep our attention hooked to the screen. MTV is the leader in use of technical events, at sixty per minute; public TV plods along at three to four.[500]

In film and television before 1970, cameras often fixed steadily on long threads of conversation, which look to today's viewers like still photographs. Cartoons on the commercial channels are a ceaseless frenzy, interrupted by even more rapidly paced ads for sugared cereals and candy. The movie *Matrix Reloaded*, featuring the protagonist, Neo, in high-speed hand-to-hand combat, simultaneously fending off one hundred moving opponents, was state of the art in 2003. The teen audience with whom I watched it was actually bored.

Are high-frequency technical events harmful? The evidence says yes. Most people are "attentionally blinded" for almost one second following one-tenth-second displays of violent and erotic images.[501] Steamy billboards are so distracting that they probably increase traffic accidents. Technical events can also jam our mental radar; TV-effects researcher Annie Lang finds that viewers cannot recall cuts to unrelated material of more than five per minute. Viewers, forced to continuously reorient themselves to new material without sufficient time to process it, are left mentally exhausted and unrewarded because they are unable to consciously recall much of what they had seen.[502] In 1997, 685 Japanese children were rushed to the hospital, many of them suffering from "optically stimulated epileptic seizures" after viewing the TV broadcast of a visually pyrotechnic sequence from a Pokémon videogame.[503] In early 2007, thirty TV viewers suffered seizures after viewing an advertisement for the 2012 Olympics. The cause was the bright images flashing at the 20–30-cycle-per-second rate that is known to be the most dangerous.[504]

Evidence is beginning to solidify that early-life TV viewing permanently rewires the brain. Preschoolers on a three-hour-plus daily TV diet had a thirty-percent increased risk of ADHD symptoms at age seven.[505] With one-sixth of American two- and three-year-old children and one-third of teens having a TV in their bedrooms, and with the average child watching three hours daily, we are running a risky nationwide social experiment.[506]

MERCHANDIZING BODY LOATHING

It's encouraging that teen pregnancy rates have dropped over the past decade. But the decline is the result of the menace of AIDS. It is not a sign of America's cultural health, and it is certainly not the result of any restraint by commercial culture in the use of sexualized children's bodies. Half of all girls aged 6–9 now use lip gloss or lipstick.[507] In your average shopping mall, you can probably find a store that sells first graders short-shorts with "Hot Stuff" written across the buttocks. A recent FAO Schwarz holiday catalogue featured Mattel's Lingerie Barbie, describing it like this: "Barbie exudes a flirtatious attitude in her heavenly merry widow bustier ensemble accented with intricate lace and matching peek-a-boo peignoir."[508]

Maybe Woodstock deserves some of the blame, but that was a long time ago. Maybe it's the media, or girls' clothing and toys, but the disturbing effect on real girls is apparent. As quoted in the 2002 book *Girl Culture*, Stephanie, a Long Island teen, explains why pregnancies are down among her set. "Most of the girls my age are virgins. They've all been brought up to not have sex till they're sixteen or seventeen … That's why they have oral sex. Oral sex to kids of my generation is not sex, technically … Sex to us is something that both people get pleasure from, and I don't think a girl gets pleasure from giving a guy head. . . It happens all the time, and we're fourteen."[509] Forty percent of boys aged 15–17 had received oral sex from a female; the rate is two-thirds among boys aged 18–19.[510]

Joan Jacobs Bromberg's penetrating book *The Body Project: An Intimate History of American Girls* uses adolescent girls' private diaries written between 1830 and the 1990s to chart the changing impact of commercial culture on teenage values and self-image. Teens of the 1800s wrote passionately about their belief in the primacy of character and spirituality—including service to others, self-control, belief in God, and learning—over physical appearance. By the 1920s, girls' chief concern was about increasing their sexual allure through clothing, cosmetics, and dieting. In the twentieth century, Hollywood and the fashion industry had bared women's arms and legs, requiring women to make demanding and costly dietary and beauty changes to keep up with rising personal appearance benchmarks. While these changes were heralded as marking greater freedoms for women, girls of the time privately described them as burdens.[511]

Today, OverSuccess is manifesting itself as OverSexualization. Advertising and commercial culture have almost entirely stripped the female torso and browbeaten girls and women into adoption of an unattainable, hyper-sexualized body image. If you doubt this, consider that an average woman's waist size is 30 inches, whereas a typical store mannequin measures 23 inches. Scaled up, Barbie comes in at a near-impossible 19 inches.[512] The average American woman is 5'4" tall and weighs 140 pounds; the average American model is 5'11" and at 117 pounds is thinner than 98 percent of American women.[513] The body mass index of *Playboy* centerfolds tracked between 1953 and 2001 shows that the gap between the real and idealized woman has become progressively wider.[514] *Seventeen* and *Teen People* relentlessly tell girls that they must be sexy, innocent, flawlessly beautiful, and impossibly thin—and, in the more recent deference to feminism, smart, successful, confident, independent, and popular. The culture merchants have raised the current benchmark to impossibly thin and impossibly successful.

These commercial messages impair female mental health. Research at Boston's Brigham and Women's Hospital shows that 50 percent of teen girls who read magazines targeted to their age level want to lose weight, whereas only 29 percent are actually overweight.[515] Teenaged girls who viewed commercials depicting women with the body type of today's models feel less confident, more angry, and more dissatisfied with their weight and appearance.[516] The greater the number of hours that teen girls watch movies, music videos, and daytime TV, the greater their degree of body dissatisfaction and desire to be thin.[517] Among college women, 70 percent feel worse about their body image after reading women's magazines.[518] Adult women are less satisfied with their own relative beauty after viewing ads containing female models, because the gap between their self-image and an advertiser-promoted ideal had been increased.[519]

Dr. Ira Sacker, director of the eating disorders clinic at Brookdale University Hospital in Brooklyn, New York, and co-author of the book *Dying To Be Thin*, reports a new body-image obsession among patients who still have most of their baby teeth. One of his patients was a six-year-old girl who was eating paper and running around her room to burn calories. "These aren't isolated cases anymore," says Sacker.[520] Studies compiled by the Harvard Eating Disorders Clinic show that 42 percent of first- through third-grade girls want to be thinner, while 40 percent of fourth graders are already dieting for thinness, and 81 percent of ten-year-olds are dieting, binge-eating, or fear getting fat.[521] Today, 78 percent of seventeen-year-old girls are unhappy with their bodies. Eight in ten adult women are unhappy with their appearance.[522]

Unattainable body-image benchmarks are damaging relationships between women and men. Evolutionary psychologist Douglas Kenrick ran a series of groundbreaking experiments establishing the link between media-created body image and male attitudes toward real women. Kenrick interrupted male students as they were watching either *Charlie's Angels* or the news, then asked them to rate the beauty of an average female student shown in a photo. The *Angels*-watchers scored the average female student lower than did news-watchers. Male students in another experiment were asked to view photos of *Playboy* models and of average women, then to rate their actual girlfriends. *Playboy*-viewers rated their girlfriends less attractive *and* reported loving them less.[523] Both men and women who viewed photos of models and average people found themselves depressed by looking at models of their own sex. Women in the company of attractive women, whether those attractive women are real or are photo or video images, rate themselves as less satisfied with their own appearance and attractiveness as a marriage partner.[524]

Recent research shows that the gap between body image among women and the unattainable ideal promoted by commercial culture at least partially explains the sharp increases in eating disorders and depression in the U.S. over the past century.[525] In America, women suffer depression at twice the rate that men do, where in cultures such as Egypt, Iran, India, and Uganda's, not subject to America's messages about female body obsession, rates of depression are about the same for the two sexes.[526] In the U.S., the lifetime risk of anorexia (associated with underweight women) is double for young men and women, compared with those one to two generations older—who grew up when body image was less aggressively shaped by commercial culture. The lifetime risk of bulimia (associated with obese women) is almost seventeen times higher for younger than for older generations. The lifetime prevalence of both eating disorders is three times higher among women than men, probably as a result of women's greater sensitivity to messages about physical appearance.[527]

For all of commercial culture's emphasis on thinness, watching television appears to cause both male and female teens to get heavier. When other potentially explanatory causes are removed from the analysis, people who watch a lot of TV are fifty percent more likely to become overweight.[528] A study of Massachusetts high school students considering or attempting suicide found that the largest group are girls who consider themselves overweight.[529] The advertising-effects researcher Jean Kilbourne laments that "girls are made to feel so terrible about themselves that they would rather be dead than fat."[530] Among females, one in five regular gym-goers are full-fledged or borderline anorexics or bulimics. "The situation is almost always the same," says Kristen Walsh, spokeswoman for the International Health, Racquet & Sportsclub Association, about the rise of compulsive exercise, or anorexia athletica. "A 20- or 30-something woman is using the club for several hours a day and has lost so much weight that other members are beginning to express concern." In extreme cases, the compulsive exerciser has little remaining body fat and disturbs other club members, not only because of her emaciation, but also because of the foul odor of her burning muscle.[531]

Wanting to be more beautiful is normal and healthy. But television, movies, magazines, billboards, and the Internet bombard women with digitally retouched, surgically enhanced, supernaturally proportioned, and unattainable bodies. Sara, a successful, 19-year-old, tall, blond, drop-dead-gorgeous Manhattan model, expresses guilt about her own physical beauty. "I don't think my modeling is good for society ... I'm making a bunch of little girls feel bad about their bodies and go anorexic ... But if a client is offering you ten thousand dollars to do a shoot for the day, are you going to say no?"[532] If a 19-year-old is fully aware of the ethical problems in commercial culture's messages, so are the industry heads who win success by inflicting body loathing and eating disorders on their own customers.

COMMERCIAL CULTURE AND PERVASIVE DISSATISFACTION

Over the past 40 years, we have radically restructured our daily lives around television. The average American adult spends about 4.5 hours each day watching.[533] TV viewing has consumed all of Americans' post-1965 gains in leisure time.[534] Four natural experiments provide great evidence as to the societal effects of this historically swift and massive time reallocation.

The first of these experiments occurred in an isolated Canadian town in central British Columbia that, before 1973, was the only settled area in North America without television. When Tannis MacBeth Williams, a psychologist at the University of British Columbia, learned that the town was about to get TV, she arranged a rigorous set of before and after studies, comparing the town (code-named NoTel in her study) and two matched Canadian towns that had TV all along. Williams found that the introduction of TV was associated with a reduction in child and adult problem-solving and creativity—by 40 percent in children in one experiment. Children became less perseverant and more easily bored during periods of unstructured time, overall aggression among second graders doubled, reading skills were delayed, and adult participation in public sports dropped in half.[535]

The second study explored the effects of the 1995 introduction of World Wrestling Federation broadcasts to Israeli television. Almost immediately, schools were reporting sharp increases in playground injuries. A survey of school principals found that students were imitating WWF moves, such as head banging, eye poking, hair pulling, crotch grabbing, and jumping onto opponents from desks. The result was a spike in broken bones, concussions, unconsciousness, and emergency-room visits. The child-on-child violence did not abate until an outcry from educational leaders forced a curtailment of WWF programming.[536]

In the third study, a Harvard research team, learning that TV was about to be introduced to the Pacific island of Fiji in 1995, jumped into action to determine the effect on native adolescent girls living there. The Harvard team compared rates of disordered eating in 1995, before TV could have had an impact, to rates in 1998, after Fijians' three years of exposure to programs such as *Baywatch*. Before television, Fijian culture fostered "robust appetites and body shapes," signifying health and prosperity. The island's body types did not change over the three years, but its girls' body image did. The rate of self-induced vomiting by girls trying to lose weight increased from zero to eleven percent. By 1998, 74 of the girls felt that they were "too big or fat." Interviews with the girls also disclosed increasing parent-daughter conflict, and not just over attitudes about body size. Before exposure to television, children spoke politely to adults; after TV arrived, impoliteness became more common. There is little doubt from this unique piece of naturalistic research that, with TV, comes another American export: body dissatisfaction, eating disorders, and bad behavior.[537]

In June 1999, Bhutan, the tiny Buddhist nation of two million tucked between China and India, became the last nation in the world to get television. By 2002, TV had become ubiquitous, consisting primarily of Rupert Murdoch's Star TV, featuring wrestling, MTV, Bollywood beauties, and the *X Files*. Half of Bhutanese children became heavy TV viewers, some up to 12 hours a day. Suddenly, after centuries of mutual respect and internal social peace, came an unprecedented wave of student disciplinary problems, drug use, embezzlement, materialism, theft, prostitution, and violence. One-third of Bhutanese girls now desire the white skin and blond hair they see on TV.

More than one-third of parents would rather watch TV than talk to their children. "TV is very bad for our country … it controls our minds … and makes [us] crazy," reads a typical letter to the editor in Bhutan's national newspaper. "The enemy is right here with us in our own living room. People behave like the actors, and are now anxious, greedy, and discontent."[538]

Research is starting to untangle why. We know that people feel relaxed and passive while watching TV. Even after they finish watching, TV viewers report feelings of passivity, low alertness, and depleted energy, and they find it more difficult to concentrate. Those describing themselves as addicted viewers are more easily bored and distracted and have greater difficulty paying attention than nonaddicts.[539] A journal article reviewing the evidence from five countries shows that, particularly in the United States, materialists—those whose primary life goals feature money, possessions, image, or status—watch lots of TV, compare themselves unfavorably to those they see on TV, and have lower life satisfaction. Although the studies in this review article do not untangle cause and effect, television's frequent images of wealth and beauty appear to make materialist viewers less satisfied with their own comparative economic status. The authors conclude, "television viewership, at least in the U.S., may play a significant role in making people unhappy with their lives."[540]

University of Texas marketing researcher L. J. Shrum and his co-workers have published some of the first experiments establishing cause and effect between TV viewing and formation of goals and values. Shrum's studies show that heavier viewers overestimate the extent to which Americans are millionaires and own tennis courts, private planes, maids, and plastic surgery.[541] Greater television viewing is strongly linked to a rise in materialistic values; and it is not simply that materialist people watch more television.[542] Shrum thinks that constant television exposure has altered the popular definition of success. Successful people seen on television excel in multiple attributes, and are often simultaneously beautiful, wealthy, and powerful. "Commercial culture sets and defines goals for people," Shrum told me. "These goals are often unconscious and we often pursue them unconsciously."[543]

Tightly controlled experiments show that when people are reminded of material or performance goals they cannot measure up to, their self-worth and altruistic behaviors are dampened. Subjects given lists of helping-related words were more likely to help someone pick up spilled pens. But people told that they were late for an appointment were less likely to stop to help someone slumped in a doorway. People prompted with an explicit role model, one against whom it is impossible to measure up, were less likely to volunteer. But when given a role model whose ambiguous but positive characteristics are more common and accessible, people were more likely to volunteer.

Another set of experiments draws out a fascinating contrast in people's behavior after they are unobtrusively prompted by accessible versus inaccessible role models. Leif Nelson and Michael Norton asked two groups of Princeton undergraduates to describe ten characteristics of the movie and cartoon character Superman (a positive but concretely defined role model) and a generic superhero (also a positive role model, but one whose powers were undefined). Students primed by the superhero agreed to volunteer for a real community service for twice as many hours as those who were primed by Superman. Ninety days later, when the students were asked to follow through on their offers to volunteer, the superhero-primed students were four times more likely to do so. Nelson thinks that altruism is squelched when unattainable role models make us subconsciously aware of our comparative shortcomings.[544]

Commercial culture saturates our mental environment with highly particularized, unattainable role models, most of them smarter, richer, more popular, and with better hair than we. We subconsciously compare ourselves to them, and wind up feeling subconsciously incapacitated and more worthless. As we consume commercial culture, its OverSuccessed benchmarks, and its global Supermen, we shrink into materialism, selfishness, and dissatisfaction.

THE CULTURAL CARTEL

Maybe the profusion of new media technologies will loosen the grip on American culture held by culture merchants who are obsessed by profit, career trajectories, and callous about their social responsibilities. In recent years, we have enjoyed a flood of new forms of media content and distribution. Instead of three national TV networks, we have DVD, video, the Internet, and hundreds of broadcast, cable, and satellite TV channels. On cable, I can watch the uninterrupted voice of the progressive left on Free Speech TV, its production values consisting largely of a brick wall and a potted ficus. I watched FSTV news anchor Amy Goodman impatiently wait out an extended, reverential standing-O at a DC Green Festival—for her content, certainly not for her glamour.

Matt Drudge has shown that someone with little more than an apartment and a server can tap national audiences in the tens of millions. Live365.com allows anyone to become an Internet radio broadcaster for only $9.95 per month. Blogs and YouTube allow anyone to become a reporter or entertainer, occasionally permitting the uncredentialed to have wide impact. Free of charge, Google can search 8 billion webpages for me in 0.29 second. On the printed page, writers have probed almost any imaginable subject, with over 2.8 million books now in print and over 150,000 new titles published each year—nearly all of them available on either Amazon or Ebay at eminently reasonable cost.[545] I can read refreshingly original investigative journalism from *Mother Jones*, *The New American*, and *The New Republic*, representing views from the anti-globalist left, the anti-globalist right, and the pro-globalist center.

And contrary to widely held belief, using standard antitrust yardsticks for ownership concentration, today's media remain highly competitive when compared with most other major U.S. industries. Media conglomerates have certainly grown, but at the same pace as the overall media industry.[546] Thus, the largest media companies do not have the power to fix prices and have not been able to freeze out new rivals.

But by more convincing measures, American media have become a de facto cultural cartel. Under the new theory that new types of media can substitute for one another (i.e., cable for newspaper for Internet), the Federal Communications Commission and antitrust regulators have become far more lax with respect to market share and vertical integration. We have more media outlets, but far fewer owners among those media from which most viewers and readers get their information and entertainment. While new types of media have proliferated, television and newspapers continue to dominate as our sources of news and political information, with television leading by far.[547] Internet news is almost exclusively content that is repurposed or purloined from print or TV news produced by the top eight conglomerates. New and old media have the same owners. As for blogs, with a few noteworthy exceptions, they contribute little original factual material. The Internet—and Web 2.0, with its pay-per-click, advertiser sponsorship, and free content—are certainly filling the space left open by shrinking traditional media, but these produce little original, high-quality, editor-curated content.[548] A tiny percentage of Americans regularly watch the likes of Free Speech TV or read *The New American* for serious nonfiction from independent sources.

At the national level, the commercial culture cartel is dominated by the eight largest global media companies: Time Warner, Walt Disney, News Corp, Bertelsmann, Sony, NBC Universal, CBS Corporation, and Vivendi. All eight (except for Vivendi, owner of Universal Music, number one in online, multiplayer video games, and minority owner of NBC Universal) are among the world's 500 largest firms and had combined 2006 media revenues of over $182 billion.[549] In 1983 fifty companies owned the majority of media outlets. Since the early 1990s, the top eight media companies have agglomerated almost every type of format and now typically own newspapers, magazines, book-publishing houses, movie and TV production divisions, broadcast networks, cable, satellite, videogames, and music and content licensing. The conglomerates are typically integrated horizontally and vertically, controlling content, distribution, and infrastructure. In the U.S., the big eight control access to two-thirds of all cable and network TV viewers. Three-quarters of all prime-time TV programming is broadcast under the aegis of the TV networks, almost double the concentration of 1989.[550]

Even media tycoons express concern about media concentration. Barry Diller, former chairman of Paramount, Fox TV, and Vivendi, lambastes media deregulation and concentration as a "disaster" for diversity, regionalism, and innovation. Diller has called for regulatory safeguards to ensure that 20 to 30 percent of media remain outside the control of media "oligarchs" whom he predicts will converge the industry unchecked into five or six firms that dominate both content and distribution.[551] Ted Turner, founder of CNN and former Time Warner board Vice-Chair, expresses the same concern. "There's really five companies that control 90 percent of what we read, see and hear. It's not healthy."[552] Turner has called for the federal government to bust up the media conglomerates, just as John D. Rockefeller's Standard Oil was in 1911 and AT&T was in 1982.[553]

The impact of this concentration of ownership is especially acute for local news and content. Between 1975 and 2002, the number of daily-newspaper owners dropped from 863 to 290. As of 2004, 22 companies owned 70 percent of all daily-newspaper circulation. Two-thirds of local newspaper markets are monopolies, and over 90 percent are either monopolies or duopolies. In radio, which is generally a local medium, ten companies control two-thirds of all US programming.[554] One company, Clear Channel, sits astride the industry, operating radio stations in 191 of the 289 Arbitron-rated markets. The 10 biggest companies own 30 percent of all television stations and reach 85 percent of households. Ninety-two percent of local TV markets are oligopolies with fewer than six competitors, and almost 40 percent are monopolies or duopolies. To an historic degree, the stories we tell, the images we remember, and the values we live by are selected by a small number of conglomerates that are driven hard by their stockholders to maximize quarterly profits.

CRIPPLING THE REPUBLIC FOR MARKET SHARE

I am watching Fox News, as I often do while exercising. Four talking heads grimace and bob in separate quadrants of the screen, two of them yelling over each other to be heard, a third begging the host to restore order. The host smiles at the melee, sure to pump up his ratings. At the bottom of the screen, the first layer of headline crawl keeps me up to the minute on Drew Peterson's missing wives; the second briefs me on Katie Couric's wardrobe controversy. Later that evening, number-one cable news host Bill O'Reilly is busy celebrating Bill O'Reilly, interviewing the producer of a TV special on Bill O'Reilly, then gloating about Bill O'Reilly's ratings and closing with a segment featuring man-on-the-street comments about Bill O'Reilly.[555] Guests on the cable news shows, particularly the women, are intensively coached about hair, makeup, and, if properly endowed, the all-important cleavage. It is critical to keep a phony smile pasted on your face and to look directly into the camera even when your credibility is going up in flames.

News coverage has become a Roman circus. As they have for many of us, the ethics of the culture merchants have been so rotted out by OverSuccess that they are willing to sacrifice one of humanity's most noble creations, the

American system of self-governance, for a shot at a ten share. Steve Coz, past editorial director for the tabloids *Star, National Enquirer,* and *Globe*, says that putting Laci Peterson on one of his covers bumped sales by 300,000 copies. So it made perfect sense that the *Enquirer* kept two full-time reporters on the Peterson story for over a year. Ron Frey, father of Scott Peterson's consort, Amber Frey, received over 5,000 phone calls from reporters. The immense publicity given the case flooded the Modesto, California, police department with more than ten thousand leads from TV viewers, including hundreds from psychics.[556] As of June 2004, before the verdict in the trial of Laci Peterson's husband Scott, two in three Americans were so well informed about the case that they had a definite opinion about the defendant's guilt or innocence.[557] When Scott Peterson's death sentence was handed down, the media pack moved immediately to Michael Jackson's pedophilia trial. To ensure absolute certainty that Americans would not miss any important detail about Jackson's penis, more than one thousand reporters were credentialed at the Santa Maria, California, courthouse.[558]

Market share trumps fact in the OverSuccessed news business. In a 2003 raid, the Iraqis captured American soldier Jessica Lynch, whose gun had jammed without her firing a single shot. An American military unit swept in and rescued her from an Iraqi hospital where she had been held and apparently treated well. But CBS News wanted a hero story to tourniquet their ratings slide, and it decided to pump up Lynch. In return for an exclusive, CBS's then-corporate parent Viacom was ready to offer the young Army supply clerk a book, movie, and MTV deal and a concert featuring her and some Viacom pop stars in her West Virginia hometown.[559] Lynch hit the magazine covers and split a million-dollar advance for a book with her ghostwriter, which hit number one during its first week of release and then became the subject of a TV movie. Even during the peak of the hype, Lynch publicly denied the story that made her famous. She told AP, "That wasn't me. I wasn't about to take credit for something I didn't do. I'm not that person." Media industry cynicism is so great that the story—as synthetic as PVC drainpipe—would still not stop until 2007, when Lynch spoke out again to deny the myth of her own heroism.

In its crass, lowest-common-denominator quest for eyeballs, American media are recruiting American enemies worldwide. As a rough yardstick for the growth of American commercial culture exports, delivery of U.S. film and video to foreign markets more than doubled between 1989 and 2005, from $8.5 to $19.5 billion in constant dollars.[560] In February 2004, when one billion people across the globe were watching the Super Bowl's half-time entertainment, how did our media portray our nation to the world? They featured MTV's top gangsta-rapper P. Diddy, dressed as a street pimp and drug peddler, grunting unintelligibly and grabbing his crotch for effect. Next, Justin Timberlake sang this at Janet Jackson: "Gonna have you naked by the end of this song." All this was apparently OK with MTV owner CBS until, in an unambiguously staged act of sexual assault, Timberlake ripped off Jackson's bra, exposing her breast on live television.[561] The FCC, needing to burnish President Bush's pre-election image among social conservatives, slapped CBS with a well-deserved fine, but only for the breast—not for promoting drug culture and sexual violence, and not for inflaming hatred of America among the planet's traditionalist societies.

Boston University Professors Margaret and Melvin DeFleur sought to learn what foreign teens thought about the United States just after 9/11. The DeFleurs are conservative and intensely patriotic military vets and were not out shopping at the time for an anti-imperialist narrative. In their surveys of middle- and lower-middle-class high school students in twelve nations, the DeFleurs found "consistently negative attitudes" toward the American people in all but Argentina, with harshly negative views in Bahrain and Saudi Arabia and, more surprisingly, in South Korea and Mexico. Tomorrow's adults view Americans, particularly American women, as violent, materialistic, dominating, intolerant, and immoral.[562] "These teenagers would write pages of information, spilling out the intensity of their negative feelings towards the United States." These impressions were formed largely from exposure to American movies, television, and popular music. "When they see a show like the *Sopranos* they think all American families are like that ... With married couples cheating on each other and doing drugs and giving sexual favors ... this is how they think American families really are!"[563]

As conservatives, the DeFleurs have the political cover to state the obvious: commercial culture has created a fertile recruiting ground for terrorists. While American media may be within their constitutional rights regarding nearly everything they produce, they are crossing a dangerous ethical boundary and failing in their patriotic duty. Ambassadors P. Diddy, Timberlake, and Jackson, along with the media that sponsor you: you are giving substance to our enemies' rhetoric and diminishing America's stature worldwide.

Over the past twenty years, major media have roughly doubled use of celebrity profiles, lifestyle vignettes, crime, disaster, and sensationalism. Hard news with public policy content has decreased from 65 to 50 percent of all coverage, even though by almost three to one, the public wants more. For every hour of cable news, we get 6 minutes of crime reports, 2 minutes on celebrities, and 25 seconds on science.[564] Election coverage has lobotomized candidates, filling the news with gaffe-baiting, tactical analysis, and daily polling. Only one of every six news stories covering the 2004 Democratic presidential primary tackled the candidates' voting records or positions. More than two in three featured poll numbers and tactics.[565] During the 2000 presidential election, reporters got 72 percent of airtime, with only 11 percent going to candidates speaking in their own words—a record low. Uninterrupted airtime for a candidate's own words has shriveled from an average of 42.3 seconds in 1968 to 9.8 in 1988 to 7.3 seconds in 2000.[566] It requires only about seven seconds to utter a sixteen-word statement, the length of this sentence.

The journalistic content vacuum as well as intensified competition for the power and status of office have compelled candidates to communicate with the public in the only way they can, via paid advertising. Most candidates must raise ever more money from favor-seeking interest groups to buy more 30-second TV ads. Most of these ads contain fewer words than this paragraph. Try explaining medical-cost drivers or national energy policy in thirty seconds. Now try it in seven seconds.

In the largest ever such study of the issue, University of Wisconsin professor Kenneth Goldstein and his co-workers coded the content of all political news coverage and advertising during the 2000 and 2002 elections. Goldstein's research covered TV stations that reached 75 percent of the U.S. population. Only four in ten newscasts carried any election coverage at all. On average, viewers saw four times the number of election ads as they did political news stories. Only 27 percent of the news stories contained information about issues or positions; the balance covered the horse race, tactics, and personal information. When stations did cover elections, the average story ran for 89 seconds. "Most local television stations ignored the 2002 campaign on most of their top-rated broadcasts," said Martin Kaplan, who worked with Goldstein on the project.[567]

Years of critical academic white papers have done little to alter the media's huge bias against the expressed wishes of the public for political coverage with more substance and less process. By the overwhelming margin of 77 to 17 percent, the public wants more information on candidates' positions on issues. According to the Project for Excellence in Journalism, in 2000 and 2004, about 55 percent of media coverage focused on campaign strategy, fundraising, and polls—a number that rose to 63 percent in the early part of the 2008 cycle. Just 17 percent of 2008 coverage involved the candidates' backgrounds or policy proposals. Online outlets, which are celebrated as the hope for the future, tilted coverage even more greatly away from issues.[568]

Biased more toward self-interest than to liberalism or conservatism, big media have turned increasingly to direct manipulation of news coverage and public policy. The media are highly dependent on governments for favors in reportorial access, below-market broadcast spectrum fees, regulatory exemptions, and antitrust leniency. Politicians in turn are dependent upon media, which have the power to grant coverage that is good, bad, or, still worse, nil. The unwritten quid pro quo is favorable coverage for officials who deliver favorable policy. The Center for Public Integrity, which uses Federal Election Commission data to track interest-group political spending, found that the broadcast industry and their trade associations spent almost $250 million on lobbying, campaign contributions, and junkets from 1998 through June 2004—all to influence federal policy and elections.[569] In a confidential Pew Center survey, four in ten journalists admitted that they have purposefully avoided or softened the tone of newsworthy stories that would harm the interests of their company. Half of investigative reporters and editors admitted that newsworthy stories are ignored for that same reason.[570]

While the specifics of every act of censorship or coverage in return for favors are usually well concealed, the public is fully aware of the pattern. Eight in ten viewers and readers are convinced that the media abuse their power to influence public opinion and public policy to advance their own political agenda.[571] The Gallup Organization has tracked continuous erosion in public trust in the media. Those who view the media as often inaccurate increased from 34 percent in 1985 to 62 percent in 2003, with little difference between conservatives and liberals.[572] A 2002 Pew Research Center poll found that 67 percent of Americans feel that journalists try to cover up their mistakes, up from 13 percent in 1985. The Project for Excellence in Journalism found that, compared with 1985, the public thinks the news media are "less professional, less accurate, less moral, less helpful to democracy, more sensational, more likely to cover up mistakes and more biased." Over half the American public thinks that the news media are either lying or deluding themselves as a result of financial self-interest or personal ambition.[573]

The public has grown deeply frustrated and alienated by television's content-free, celebrity-fixated, titillation-tinged, and self-interested slant on the world. *Orlando Sentinel* media critic Hal Boedeker was shocked by the 1,200 responses he got to an unscientific reader survey on local TV news. "People are really angry about local TV news. They're tired of being teased. They feel their time is being wasted. They're tired of anchors being cute. They're tired of repetition."[574] A scientific survey found the same reaction. Over half of viewers feel that TV news is endlessly repetitive, broadcasting the same stories "over and over again." Forty-five percent think that TV news is overly superficial, sensationalized, and tabloidized. Almost 40 percent feel that TV news is excessively and purposefully frightening and depressing. Thirty percent find news promotional teasers irritating and intentionally misleading. Almost 30 percent feel that local TV news wastes viewers' time, insults their intelligence, and is oversimplified.[575]

Increasing public frustration and anger mirror the private worries of national journalists. Two in three believe that financial pressures are "seriously hurting" news quality. Forty-five percent think that the news is now filled with factual errors.[576] "A journalism infatuated with celebrity is a limited journalism for informing the people," laments Bill Moyers. "I'm concerned that democracy is slowly dying of oxygen deprivation." Walter Cronkite grieves that "market forces on TV news has been so severe as to create a vacuum in news coverage which is exceedingly dangerous to democracy."[577] Former CBS News anchor Dan Rather despises the trend to shallowness, saying, "It's been one of the more important developments ... particularly of the last 10 to 15 [years] that we run stupid celebrity stories ... It has become pervasive, the belief that to be competitive, you must run a certain amount of celebrity news."[578]

On the critical, fact-based issues that have been so central to our nation's well-being over the past few years—such as federal debt, justifications for invading Iraq, immigration, or climate change—the media did not provide sufficient coverage for the public to form sound judgments. Andrew Revkin, who has covered climate change for *The New York Times* for over two decades, told me how stories on technical subjects manage to get any column inches at all. Even at his eminent journalistic outpost, science reporting must lead with a hot news hook, focus on emotion, oversimplify, and use false balance to create controversy. Until about 2007, stories on climate change ran only when a big name made an alarmist claim or charged corruption in high places. "The reader doesn't get served by that at all," declared Revkin.[579]

To pump up profits, television and newspapers, America's two leading news sources, have sharply reduced news staff. Nationwide, newspapers have about 2,200 fewer reporters than in 1990, and network TV reporters are down by one-third since the 1980s. Between 1994 and 2001, full-time radio newsroom employees were cut 44 percent, part-timers by 71 percent. Over the past 20 years, *Time* magazine has cut its news staff by 15 percent, while *Newsweek* has slashed its news team by 50 percent. More outlets are competing to provide fewer and more repetitive news stories.[580]

Declining local news coverage contributes to the ongoing loss of community and local social life that I discuss in other chapters. By withering the vitality of localism, commercial culture also robs us of the benefits of our uniquely decentralized form of government. The United States has 87,000 units of local government, laboratories of democracy that keep power dispersed and allow multiple approaches to problem solving. We are an economically stronger, more cohesive society because we can more readily tolerate differences by moving across municipal or state boundaries to live with others with whom we have closer political agreement. Local variety conflicts directly with the trend to centralization among media conglomerates, which prefer the operational efficiency of a homogenized national market.

Jack Fuller, former editor, publisher, and now president of Chicago's Tribune Publishing Company, delivered these wise and urgent words to his peers: "The central purpose of journalism is to tell the truth so the people will have the information that they need to be sovereign."[581] Warns Ilya Somin, author of a Cato Institute study subtitled *How Political Ignorance Threatens Democracy*, "On many issues, the majority is not only ignorant of the truth, but actively misinformed."[582] The evidence is in hand. Media programmers have swapped ethics for success, knowingly crippling the American republic in their amoral pursuit of market share.

THE STARVATION OF LOCAL POLITICAL LIFE

I first ran for elective office on an anti-tax, school-choice, accountable-government platform that fit the voters' appetite for change in 1994. Nine months of nonstop campaigning at dumps, strip mall parking lots, and Rotary barbecues—and the help of twenty phenomenal volunteers—scored me an upset victory over the incumbent senate president and a seat in the New Hampshire state senate, a full-time position paying $100 per year. I worked to keep myself accessible, installing an 800 number, so that all my constituents could easily reach me, personally returning every call within 48 hours. I wrote and organized legislative passage of our state's charter-school law, as well as a law ending the practice in which some towns auctioned off people's homes for unpaid taxes and pocketed the entire proceeds. For almost three years, I sometimes single-handedly fought off a "restructuring" law that compensated the state's largest electric utility for its assets of doubtful value with more than $1 billion in ratepayer money. I chaired the education committee and helped implement reforms making it easier for technical-school grads to transfer course credits to four-year institutions, which reduced costs for those taking that route to a college degree. I was named to chair my state party's platform committee.

As a way to stay connected, I genuinely enjoyed door-to-door campaigning. Usually, candidates on the hoof stick to where their likely voters live or work. I decided one day to do a Section 8 apartment complex, where I knew I would find few regular voters and still fewer Republicans. As I walked through the parking lot after I had finished knocking on all the doors, certain that I had not found a single vote, a man in his mid-40s named Stan Gilman approached me. Stan told me that he was a Vietnam vet and had various challenging medical problems but was particularly bothered by his teeth, some of which were obviously missing. Two years earlier, on his way home from work, he was assaulted by a punk who punched him in the face, knocking out several teeth and breaking his glasses. Stan cooperated with the local prosecutor, who succeeded in getting the court to order that the perpetrator reimburse Stan for his expenses, a few hundred dollars in dental work, and new glasses.

But Stan did not stop me to complain about his own circumstances. Stan wanted me to know that he had never seen a nickel from the court's order, which he thought was unfair. Stan told me that he was not worried about himself, but wanted to be sure that no one else was treated the way he was. Stan's troubles so touched me that I spent almost a year learning the intricacies of court administration and the probate system and wrote and passed our state's victim restitution law. I would never have known to do this if I had focused only on courting the constituents I knew would readily support me in my reelection campaign.

Responding to my door-to-door one Saturday morning in a neighborhood of young academics that vote in great numbers, one constituent grudgingly opened her screen door after recognizing me. She told me that she did not need to talk with me to learn about my positions and had no advice to offer me on any issue. She was a Democrat and did not need to hear any details about the Republican plan to install webcams in her bedroom to monitor her reproductive practices, shut down daycare centers, or allow strip mines in the national parks. She closed the door in my face, saying that she would find all she needed to know about me from the newspaper. Sadly, she could learn nothing at all about what her local representative was up to. The region's monopoly newspaper limited its coverage of state politics to occasional wire-service stories about the budget and a tired cartoon mocking the legislature's frugality. The local monopoly television station had been acquired by a chain that piped in local news from a city two states and two hours distant. I am years beyond any hard feelings about my forgotten press releases. My point is that because local political news coverage has been made so barren, local political life has withered to junk mail at election time.

Only three times since 1992 have I seen candidates genuinely break through public cynicism and attract big crowds and new activism: Ross Perot in 1992, John McCain in 2000, and Howard Dean in 2004. Before their iconoclasm imploded their candidacies, each made the uniquely persuasive case that he could win *and* was free of special-interest influence. (As of this writing, Barack Obama's story is promising, but incomplete.) I was naïve enough to think that I, too, could pull this off. For months, I led the polls in my primary campaign for governor. But I had become a definite distraction for my state's largest electric utility—with its billion-dollar ratepayer rip-off still in play in the legislature—and I would receive no help from the state's media in getting any coverage for my platform. In fact, they were party to a scheme to neatly derail my candidacy. The incumbent governor's political director, acting on a tip from a grassroots partisan, called the television station on which the well-funded incumbent was likely to spend several times more advertising money than I would. The station dispatched a reporter to interview a former business associate of mine who told the camera that I was psychologically unstable. My campaign knew nothing about the "story" built around this interview and was given no opportunity to respond until after it ran on the evening news. At that point, I could either (a) hold a press conference saying that I was not crazy, or (b) spend lots more money on TV ads on the station that ran the attack, charging my opponent with child abuse or whatever else some sleazy opp researcher could dredge up. Smart campaigns keep at least one slug of this trash in the can and ready for airing for just these type of circumstances.

The weekend before the primary, an unidentified backer of my primary opponent delivered the coup-de-grâce, pumping out 50,000 "push-poll" phone calls asking, "Would you vote for Senator Rubenstein if you knew that he was in favor of killing unborn babies?" Of course the media would not have the time or inclination to investigate this slur or uncover its perpetrators. By the time I left campaign politics in 2002, the situation had further deteriorated, with high office becoming a cool new trophy for those wealthy enough to buy all the media time they needed to define themselves and counter these types of attacks. Given a race with no incumbent, almost anyone willing and able to spend several times more than his rivals on polling, consultants, and TV ads can get elected.

I was spokesman and senior policy advisor for another candidate for governor who was narrowly defeated by such a trophy hunter. Our campaign tried for months to gain media coverage for a succession of policy proposals including broadband access, school choice, drinking water protection, healthcare quality, workforce housing, and state education funding. We got almost nowhere with earned media—that is, news coverage that candidates are able to get for free. But everything changed when we aired our first attack ad. The camera lights blazed and the microphones sprouted like sunflowers under a bird feeder. The press was intensely interested in every detail about our ads' air times, our budgets, and our polling data—but still they expressed no interest in my candidate's positions on the state's pressing issues.

What have big media allowed politics to become? They have systematically reduced hard news coverage, analytical depth, and investigative reporting. They splice together dueling sound bites snipped from press releases, making little effort to help readers separate fact from rhetoric. They have allowed politicians to become ever more comfortable making vacuous, transparently unsupportable statements—evading talk about the complications inherent in policy decisions, the inevitable hard choices, and the sensitive issues that could cost votes. Through their purposeful creation of the substance vacuum, they have fostered the regression of politics into vitriolic partisanship.

THE PRICE OF COMMERCIAL CULTURE

Entertainment and information are more abundant, higher in production value, and more affordable than ever before. For pocket change we can enjoy sublime music, inspired scholarship, and films that cost hundreds of millions of dollars to create. It took 48 man-years for Industrial Light and Magic to create the three-minute, digitally animated opening sequence for the 2006 disaster flick, *Poseidon*. What a privilege is life in America to be able to watch this for only $8.

But big media and commercial culture have come to dominate our cultural, political, and social lives. Few physical surfaces or social encounters remain free from a famous person or a brand. Armies of covert "buzz marketing" shills are paid to hang out in bars and movie-ticket waiting lines. Conversation with a stranger may well be a product pitch. Big media have starved local content and public awareness and interest in community life. Deprived of an important means to communicate within its own boundaries, local community is unable to sustain visible roles and pathways to respect for its people who are not celebrities. Commercial culture has populated our social reference groups with figures over whom we have zero influence and who are unapproachably more beautiful, wealthy, popular, smart, and successful than we are. We are made isolated and powerless. Commercial culture is depriving many Americans of the attainable, meaningful social roles that are vital to human mental and physical health.

Yes, we live in a 200-channel, 2.8-million-book media universe. But rather than quality and varied ideas, the big media that most of us consume give us celebrities, sex, violence, cheating, and status contests—commandeering the attention of our involuntary hunter-gatherer neural circuits. We experience more of this drama in a typical week than people of just five generations ago would in an entire lifetime.[583] American commercial culture has discovered that keeping our psyches on constant shock alert is the cheapest and most effective way to maximize market share. OverSuccess has removed compunctions against this societal abuse.

Can we calculate the cost of commercial culture on our lives and well-being? Attaching a dollar cost to media violence—one of the few areas of impact where there is at least some literature—is so dangerous a career exercise that no scientist has published a new estimate since 1993. Prolific media-violence researcher and pediatrics professor Victor Strasburger has surmised that media violence causes between five and fifteen percent of real-world violence, including domestic violence, rape, homicide, physical assault, and reckless behavior.[584] Based upon homicide levels before and after the introduction of television in the U.S. and Canada, researcher Brandon Centerwall has calculated that television causes half of all personal violence.[585] Today's more rigorous science would disallow both of these figures, which leaves the more recent and conservative work. Low-range data from multiple studies show that between 2 and 4 percent of interpersonal violence is explained by exposure to media violence.[586] Researchers at the Johns Hopkins Bloomberg School of Public Health estimate the annual economic cost of all interpersonal violence in the U.S. at 3.3 percent of gross domestic product—over 450 billion of today's dollars.[587] The arithmetic yields a range of $9 to $19 billion in yearly personal violence that is explained by exposure to media violence.

If a new type of criminal violence, food contamination, or a defective product caused impacts of this size, society would respond with wilting public outrage and crushing legal sanctions. Because statistics and epidemiology are required to measure the costs of commercial culture, the price tag is buried in our healthcare, justice, and debt service budgets. But rather than acting ethically in response to the overwhelming evidence that their products are sickening America (and the world), media CEOs have sought to actively misinform the public. Figure 6.1 shows that, as progressively more rigorous studies were indicating an increased linkage between media and real-world violence, media reports on the subject increasingly downplayed that link. It is not a coincidence that news reports about media violence became less truthful starting in about 1975, the 1965–1980 period being a turning point in ethical standards and for several other indicators of OverSuccess—as we will see in the next two chapters.

What about the other costs of commercial culture—brain development disorders, body-loathing, the sexualization of children, celebrity fixation, exaggerated fears, suffocating materialism, a crippled republic, inflamed foreign hostility to America, and desiccated local community? Certainly, every Saudi boy who watches *Desperate Housewives* does not become a jihadi, and every American girl who reads *Seventeen* does not become anorexic. But some are triggered to do so. Commercial culture that is stripped of ethical restraint contributes to all these problems and to some of the problems we will explore in the next chapter. There is no means even to provide estimates for most of the insidious costs of commercial culture, but in healthcare, justice, and lost productivity, they must run into the hundreds of billions of dollars.

You who shape commercial culture have harmed American well-being to boost your personal success. You have willfully ignored the abundant, objective evidence of those harms. You place your own careers and company profitability far above societal health. You are behaving exactly like the tobacco executives who once knowingly lied that cigarettes were healthy. Your ethical

Figure 6.1: Science Versus Media Spin on Media Violence

(the dashed line is the science, the solid line the misleading spin)
Brad J. Bushman and Craig A. Anderson, "Media Violence and the American Public: Scientific Fact Versus Media Misinformation," American Psychologist, June/July 2001; 56 (6/7): 477–489.[588]

neutering is both a symptom and a cause of American OverSuccess. Either you will adopt virtue and self-restraint as important behavioral norms, or Americans will be forced to turn to more coercive solutions.

[7

AMERICA'S OBSESSION: THE SOCIAL AND PSYCHOLOGICAL COSTS

Success is the one unpardonable sin against our fellows.
—Ambrose Bierce

NOW FOR THE BAD news: in this and the next chapter I will examine some of the personal and societal effects of OverSuccess. First, the caveats. Can I claim that all these consequences flow directly from the OverSuccess syndrome and that we would otherwise be cured of all of them? Can I supply rigorous proof that all the toxic effects I cite are caused by our success obsession? Of course not. For example, linking birth defects to our obsession with getting rich and famous, as I do, is admittedly a stretch. But many of us are working longer hours and delaying having children until later in our lives to advance our careers, to have more material goodies, and to give our kids a leg up with educational resources we could not afford as indebted young adults. And it's a fact that older parents pass along more chromosomal abnormalities to their offspring. Or consider traffic fatalities: even though they are thankfully down because of our safer highways and cars, I link some portion of these deaths to work stress and sleep deficits as we drive ourselves for success beyond our physical limits.

As I will show, about one-third of us exist every day with the psychological tax of OverSuccess. Many of us live in a state of perpetual status defeat in a world that increasingly fails to honor and justifiably recognize ordinary people. Some of us are overeating and becoming obese to self-medicate our dopamine deprivation, rewarding ourselves because no one else will. I will show that, while the links between our success addiction and the social and psychological effects may sometimes be modest, they are real and materially damage our lives and burden our economy. Viewed in combination, these effects make OverSuccess one of America's most costly problems.

AMERICA'S SOCIAL RECESSION

Perplexingly, the past decades of increasing material prosperity have not bought us greater well-being. Consider the December holiday season, glutted with more stuff, but emptied of social sustenance. It was back during the 1960s that Christmas divorced Christ, and American social health began its multi-decade decline. Today, holiday consumers line up in the pre-dawn sodium light outside the megastores, sometimes stampeding over each other when the doors open to seize deep-discount specials. In one incident, a bargain-hunter grabbed a competing shopper by the throat; in another, a shopper broke a rival's ankle. In an Orange City, Florida, Wal-Mart, shoppers in frenzied pursuit of a $29.87 DVD player knocked unconscious and stepped on a woman named Patricia VanLester, oblivious to cries for help from VanLester's sister. "They walked over her like a herd of elephants," said the sister. A mother and her two kids laughed as they tried to pry the DVD player from under the unconscious woman's body. Paramedics arriving on the scene to rescue the woman were compelled to shove through the mobbed shoppers, unable to convince them to move. "They were concerned about one thing, bargain shopping," said Mark O'Keefe, spokesman for the paramedic rescue team. Ironically, VanLester turned out to be a litigation scammer, a "frequent filer" who had racked up ten injury claims against Wal-Mart and other businesses. This time, her injury was inadvertent and real.[589]

Outbreaks of consumption fever are unfortunately not limited to the holiday season. In an August 2005 reprise of the Wal-Mart melee, the Henrico County, Virginia, school system put 1,000 surplus Apple laptops on sale at $50 each. Chaos ensued when 5,500 people waiting at the gates of a race track where the sale was held stampeded to get to the head of the line when the gates opened. The crowd trampled a woman named Starletta Wilson, crushing her child's stroller. An elderly man using a walker was shoved to the ground, the crowd literally walking on his body to secure the day's bargain. Police had to halt a driver using his car as a weapon to push through the crowd.[590]

New consumer technology can also incite these frenzies. Sony's Play Station 3 was in limited supply when it was released at the start of the 2006 holiday shopping season, generating the now-typical pre-dawn lines and violence. Police had to pepper spray a crowd of two hundred in near riot stage waiting at the Tyson's Corner Mall. Shoppers were trampled in Fresno. Five men beat and robbed a PS3 buyer as he exited a store in Manchester, Connecticut; one of the five thugs was seen being shoved out of the getaway car. Police had to ask Sacramento retailers to warn their customers to shop in groups and carry no cash. In Palmdale, California, police were forced to shut down a Wal-Mart to stop an unruly stampede of shoppers who had knocked down some toddlers.[591] What in America has changed to make well-fed crowds tip into madness over things that no one needs?

Growing unhappiness, depression, self-absorption, and civic decline are among dozens of objective measures of our psychological distress. Discount DVD players have obviously not mellowed us. David Meyers, the author of several of the most widely used student psychology texts, terms the contrast between our material abundance and our declining happiness "the American paradox."[592] Figures 7.1 through 7.5 picture the counterintuitive break between our rising incomes and our declining psychological and social well-being.

By any measure, our incomes have increased almost continuously since 1967.[593] In Chapter 1, I noted many other indicators of our greatly improved material well-being. But concealed just below the waterline of rising incomes and material comfort are stress-inducing changes in household economics.

Figure 7.1: America's Material Boom

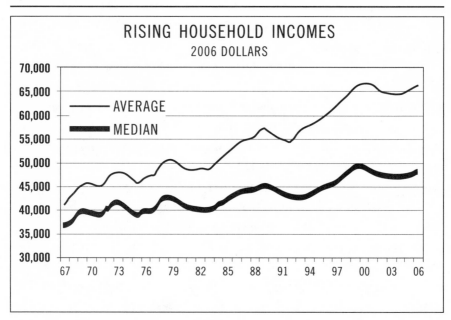

Over the last three decades, households have increased work hours, become dual-income dependent, diverged in income equality, reduced their savings, and increased their spending relative to income. Large income gains at the top have pushed up average income; the increasing divergence between average and median incomes is a good graphic indicator of this growing income inequality. See also Figure 8.1 showing the increasing share of income captured by those at the extreme top. For males, median full-time income has not risen since 1973. Typical household incomes have grown only because women are working more and earning more.

Meanwhile, we suffer under deepening personal and social recessions, which have gathered with unmistakable force during the last third of the twentieth century. Survey data from three sources document the steady erosion of personal life-satisfaction over this period. The DDB Needham Lifestyle Survey in Figure 7.2 shows that, from 1975 through 2005, the fraction of Americans aged 18–60 that were "generally" or "definitely" dissatisfied with their lives rose from 23 to 33 percent of us. *Eighteen percent of working-age Americans—30 million of us—now describe ourselves as definitely dissatisfied with*

Figures 7.2 and 7.3: Psychic Recession

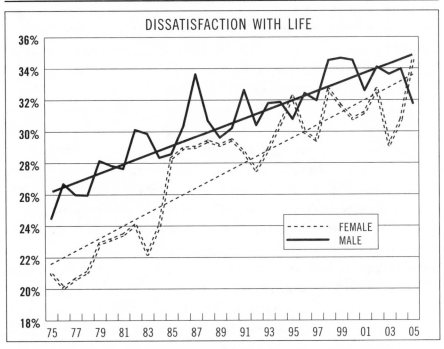

DDB Needham Lifestyle Survey, Age 18–60. Data used with permission.

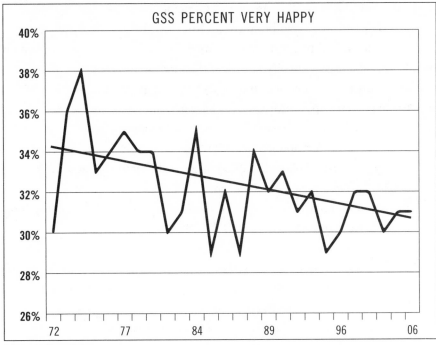

Data used with permission.

our lives. Another 30 million of us are generally dissatisfied. [594] The universally cited University of Chicago General Social Survey data (Figure 7.3) shows that, between 1972 and 2006, those "very happy" with their lives declined from 34.2 percent to 30.2 percent.[595] In two surveys taken a generation apart, Roper Starch Worldwide asked Americans if the present was better than the past. In 1974, 38 percent said that the "good old days" were better, a figure that jumped to 56 percent in 1994, with demographic groups of all races and income levels in agreement.[596]

Like canaries once used to provide early detection of toxic coal-mine gases, and like the frogs used today as indicators of environmental contamination, our young people are the most sensitive indicators of our social futures. MTV, whose business is youth, interviewed 5,200 16- to 34-year-olds living in fourteen developing and developed nations. MTV found that those in the developing nations are twice as likely to feel happy with their present lives as those in developed nations. More than 70 percent are happy in Argentina and Mexico, versus fewer than 30 percent in Britain and the United States, the lowest among the fourteen nations. Young people everywhere feel under intense pressure to succeed. In the developed nations—and acutely in the U.S.—this pressure is dashed against their increasingly diminished economic expectations.

A complex statistical teasing of the General Social Survey data used in Figure 7.3 shows that baby boomers are the least happy among the American generations. And this is despite boomers now having the highest median income and the least difficulty affording life's necessities than any other generation. "This is probably due to the fact that the generation as a group was so large and their expectations were so great," said study author Yang Yang, "that not everyone in the group could get what he or she wanted as they aged due to competition for opportunities." Duke University aging expert Linda George sees a similar explanation in boomers inability to abandon their quest for success. "They still seem to believe that they should have it all. They're still thinking about having a retirement that's going to let them do everything they haven't done yet." [597]

The American social recession can be seen in three datasets covering the years 1960–2005. The Index of National Civic Health and the Civic Health Index are combined onto the single Figure 7.4. The INCH index in Figure 7.4 portrays our thirty-five-year trend of declining political participation, trust, and group membership—as well as increasing divorce, and rises in

Figures 7.4 and 7.5: Social Recession

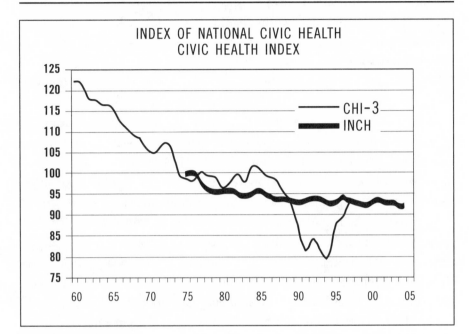

Data used with permission.

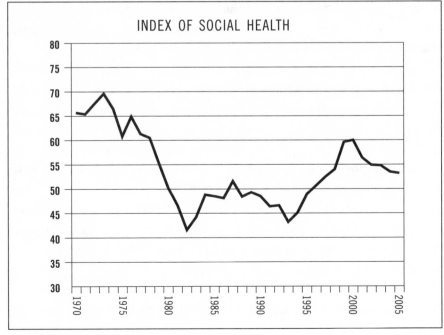

Data used with permission.

the number of unwed mothers, in crime, and in fearfulness. The CHI index includes 34 social health indicators selected by the leading scholars in the field. It shows a gradual and continuing thirty-year downhill slide in community participation, interest in joining organizations, levels of social trust, and willingness to socialize with others.[598]

The Institute for Innovation in Social Policy has maintained its Index of Social Health, composed of 16 indicators and shown in Figure 7.5. This index declined most steeply between its 1973 peak and its 1982 bottom, during the key transitional decade in the ascendancy of individualism—that is, self-definition and self-reliance. The index shows that America's social health has declined by 20 percent since 1970. Sandra Opdycke thinks that the troubling post-2000 declining trend has continued since 2005.[599] Among fifteen advanced nations, the U.S. now scores highest in a measure of societal individualism.[600]

As materialism and individualism have become culturally dominant, participation in public meetings, clubs, voluntary organizations, politics and voting, church attendance, socializing, and number of friendships have all declined. Robert Putnam, in his landmark book *Bowling Alone*, documents the decline in these indicators of what he calls "social capital." Social capital, interrupted by reversals during the Gilded Age of 1880–1910 and the 1930s, rose in America from the early 1800s until it peaked and then began another decline during the 1960s.[601] Putnam's data go back nearly two hundred years and provide further confirmation that OverSuccess began in the 1960s, roughly coincident with turning points in several OverSuccess indicators that I will cover in this and the next chapter. Putnam's critics charge that social capital is not in decline and that he ignores new types of social organizations that are replacing the old. But today's wine clubs, gym memberships, bird watchers' hikes, farmers' markets, blogs, and e-mail lists are qualitatively weaker as groups, more focused on self-interest, and easier to exit. Commitment to today's public causes often consists of pressing a button to authorize a credit-card contribution.

The hot social-networking website as of early 2008, Facebook, had 35 million visitors in a recent month. What Facebook calls friends are made with no more commitment than checking a box. Friends are often anonymous, with many users concealing or shaping their identities. Because communication among these friends lacks the richness of body language, facial expression, or vocal intonation, the medium does not facilitate the formation of trusting bonds. Particularly among its younger users, anonymity and the absence of an underlying face-to-face relationship tends to amplify behavior, diminish normal social restraint, and encourage use of sometimes reckless self-exposure to gain attention. Without these restraints, users sometimes attack others with hurtfully low social rankings and harsh comments, with limited consequences to the attacker. At a recent school forum I attended, a teen Facebook user commented, "you don't feel like you are alone, but you are."

Tom Sander, Executive Director of Harvard's Saguaro Seminar for Civic Engagement, continues to track *Bowling Alone*'s data on social capital. He finds no evidence of an upturn, other than a quickly evaporating boomlet in trust after the 9/11 attacks.[602] "Virtually every measure [of altruism] that shot up after 9/11 declined within three to six months," reports Tom Smith, director of the General Social Survey.[603] Notwithstanding 9/11 and a near-tripling in the amount of recruitment advertising per new soldier between 1998 and 2003, total new active-duty military enlistees dropped from 203,000 in 2000 to 163,000 in 2005.[604] In spite of record enlistment bonuses of $20,000 and a decline in educational and criminal record standards, in 2007 the number of new Army recruits dropped to the lowest level since it became an all-volunteer force.[605] Unlike during World War II, our collective willingness to sacrifice human life in defense of America does not match the lapel flag pins and the patriotic rhetoric. As of late 2007, trust in federal government institutions, other than the judiciary, fell to the lowest levels in modern American history.[606] Even the favorable, 15-year trend in crime reversed in 2005; in the two years following, violent crime was up by three percent, murder by 3.5 percent, and robbery by 10 percent.[607]

Social capital is dependent upon what sociologists call "generalized reciprocity," the expectation that if you do a favor for a stranger, some other stranger will repay the favor at some undetermined future time. From their opposite perches on the political spectrum, the liberal sociologist Putnam and the conservative philosopher Francis Fukuyama are both certain that trust and generalized reciprocity are fundamental to civilized society. Says Putnam: "Weakened social capital is manifest in the things that have vanished almost unnoticed—neighborhood parties and get-togethers with friends, the unreflective kindness of strangers, the shared pursuit of the public good rather than a solitary quest for private goods."[608]

And Fukuyama warns of the consequences: "A society dedicated to the constant upending of norms and rules in the name of increasing individual freedom of choice will find itself increasingly disorganized, atomized, isolated, and incapable of carrying out common goals and tasks."[609]

Generalized reciprocity and trust also make a society more efficient, allowing transactions to be consummated with a handshake while requiring less litigation and fewer pages of 200-word sentences that require $400-an-hour lawyers to write and understand.[610] Try slogging through the terms of a recent cardmember agreement to see whether directness and clarity or trickery and obscurity are the primary features of your relationship with your credit-card company. Attorney Philip Howard, in his important book *The Death of Common Sense*, observes how written bureaucratic rules are unworkable substitutes for the loss of shared norms of reasonableness, trust, ethics, promise keeping, and reciprocity.[611]

The trends in trust, like those for civic and social health, have all suffered roughly continuous declines over the past thirty-five years. The General Social Survey finds that trust in others has fallen steadily from 45 percent in 1972, when the question was first posed, to 32 percent in 2006, the lowest level yet. Trust in our major institutions (the press, medicine, Congress, and religion, although not the military) has been in free-fall since 1972.

Why has trust collapsed so precipitously? Using a rigorous statistical analysis, Putnam shows that the big two explanations for social capital decline since the early 1960s are television and the replacement of the pre–World

Table 7.1: Putnam's explanations for the decline in social capital, by percentage[612]

Generational change	35–40
Television	25
Time and money pressures on dual-income families	10
Suburbanization, commuting, sprawl	10
Unexplained	15–20

War II generation, now in their 70s and up, with baby boomers and younger generations. Compared with prior generations, we boomers are sharply more individualistic and are the least socially engaged of all the generations. We will continue to constitute more than one in four Americans until 2015, making our values dominant at least until then.

Other data confirm that declining trust in society's major institutions is most pronounced among boomers and later generations and among the more highly educated. Over the period 1958 to 2000, pre-boomer generations and Americans with less education and lower social and economic status enjoy flat to rising levels of trust.[613] So here is a critical question: why would baby boomers, who are younger, wealthier, and better educated, and who have most benefited from America's material gains, be the least satisfied with and most cynical about one another and about most of our major institutions?

Not included in the social health data above are many additional indicators that also point to ongoing social decline, starting in the 1960s. Weakened family and friendships, mental illness, child abuse, eating disorders, chronic sleep deprivation, public rudeness, materialism, debt burdens, stress and time pressure, declining ethical standards, cynicism, cultural pornography, violence, and more—all are evidence of continuing recession. Let's examine them in turn as we further assess the cost of OverSuccess.

WEAKENED FAMILY, LAPSING FRIENDSHIPS

Fearing for her personal safety after escaping her violent husband, our close friend Anne arrived at our door late one evening with her three children. No questions asked, we made beds for the kids in the spare room and got them to sleep. My wife, Susan, and Anne talked through tears until dawn. She and the family stayed with us for the several weeks it took for her fear and anger to subside. Yes, the police and the non-profits in our area could have taken fine care of Anne and of her kids' physical needs, and also provided professional counseling. But these helping institutions did not have the history and the trust that Anne had with us, and they would have added the shame of humiliation among strangers to Anne's burden of fear that night.

When we need help in a crisis or to discuss tough problems, the fortunate among us turn to close friends. But as a people, over the past twenty years our friendships have wilted away. Duke University sociologist Lynn Smith-Lovin co-led the first definitive study on changes in close friendship, using the most recent General Social Survey, widely agreed to be the best such dataset available. Her team found that, as recently as 1985, almost all of us had close friends. At that time, only ten percent of Americans said that they had absolutely no one with whom they could discuss important matters. By 2004, however, the number of these friendless Americans had jumped to 25 percent of us. Smith-Lovin found, in 1985, that the most frequently reported number of close friends was three; today, that number is zero. Including family members, the average number of close friendships dropped from about three to two. Those with at least one non-family friend dropped from 73 to 51 percent of us. Close non-family friendships dropped more rapidly for men than women. As neighborhoods and community bonds have withered, we lean far more heavily on family relationships for intimacy and support.[614] For half of us, when family bonds break, we wind up alone. And "being alone," says Lew Feldstein, co-chair with Robert Putnam of the Saguaro Seminar, "is about as likely as smoking or obesity to kill you."[615]

The shrinking space we are making for marriage and children may be the single most convincing correlate to the ascendancy of OverSuccess. Marriage and commitment to child rearing are fundamental reflections of the importance we place on life beyond self. But as we see from the data in Table 7.2, the bonds of marriage and family have weakened significantly since the 1960s. The percentage of households with children is now the lowest in American history. About 45 percent of first marriages are likely to fall to divorce or permanent separation. America has the fifth-highest divorce rate among 93 nations.[616] While American divorce rates have stabilized at our higher levels over the past two decades, married couples are significantly less likely than they were in 1980 to spend time interacting with one another over meals, with friends, shopping, or sharing projects or recreational activities. There is an immense literature proving that married couples are healthier and happier and pass on better health and social values to their children. Divorce and fatherlessness predict greater problems for children later in life.

Weakened family is driven by two key trends: increased competition and self-centeredness. Having fewer children permits more spending by adults on

Table 7.2: Indicators of Declining Commitment to Family

Indicator (percentage of total, other than bottom two rows)	1970	2005
Traditional families: married couples with children at home[617]	40	23
Never-married women, age 30–34[618]	6	24
Never-married men, age 30–34[619]	9	32
Births to unmarried mothers, 1960 & 2005[620]	5	37
Women never having given birth, age 40–44, 1976 & 2004[621]	10	19
Working moms, child 1 year or less, husband not present, 1975 & 2005[622]	31	56
Children living with single parent, 1960 & 2005[623]	9	28
Children living without biological father, 1960 & 2005[624]	17	34
Children living with married parents, reporting spouse rating marriage as "very happy," 1973–1976 & 1997–2002[625]	51	37
Divorces per 1,000 married women, age 15+, 1960 & 2004[626]	9	18
Marriages per 1,000 unmarried women, age 15+, 1970 & 2004[627]	77	40
Lifetime births per woman, 1960 & 2005[628]	3.65	2.05
Average number of children in families w. own children under 18[629]	2.28	1.82

their own current consumption, at the same time permitting more spending on braces, ballet, and boarding school to equip those fewer children to succeed in a more competitive world. According to the U.S. Department of Agriculture, raising one child to age 17 now costs over $260,000. For an upscale family, that cost through four years of college reaches over $500,000. While many couples still yearn to have children, for both men and women, education and early-career imperatives trump or defer the choice to have a family. Marriage and child rearing are crowded out by the 24/7 workplace, job transfers, and frequent corporate restructurings. The reluctance to have children can be selfless, even spiritual; many of us feel irresponsible about bringing a child into so demanding and uncertain a world.

Raising a family was once revered as a central purpose and source of satisfaction in adult life. While most parents continue to deeply value child rearing, having kids today seems to put a greater strain on marriage. Only 38 percent of new mothers with infants experience a high degree of enjoyment in their marriages, compared with 62 percent of childless wives. Children have become constraining frustrations, particularly for wealthier, higher-status parents accustomed to greater personal freedoms and more expansive goals than can be found in booster seats and coloring books. After having children, wealthier couples experience a drop in satisfaction with their marriages three times that of middle- and lower-income parents. Paralleling Putnam's generational change findings, the negative impact of children on couples' happiness was greater among boomers and younger parents. Couples who became parents during the 1990s experienced a decline in marital satisfaction twice that of new parents of the 1960s and 1970s.[630]

Simultaneously, we are more anxious about our competence in preparing our children for their futures. In Chapter 4, I discussed the stresses and pressures of rearing children in a world gone competitive from infancy. A survey of 13,000 parents by Florida State University professor Robin Simon found every category of parents more depressed than nonparents.[631] "Parents have more to worry about than other people do—that's the bottom line," laments Simon, herself a parent. "And that worry does not diminish over time. Parents worry about their kids' emotional, social, physical and economic well-being. We worry about how they're getting along in the world."[632] Simon suggests another contributor to the problem: the lack of outside help parents now find in our shriveled social networks.

Barbara Dafoe Whitehead of Rutgers University's National Marriage Project, in her essay on the decline of child-centeredness in America, writes:

> Increasingly, Americans see the years spent in active child rearing as a grueling experience, imposing financial burdens, onerous responsibilities, emotional stress, and strains on marital happiness. The *cri de coeur* is loudest among the most privileged. For upscale parents, it seems, every step of parenthood, from getting pregnant to choosing the right childbirth method to getting the kids into a nursery school to managing the Herculean task of college applications, is fraught with difficulty, anxiety and a growing sense of isolation from the adult mainstream.[633]

We could conclude from this that a renaissance in the nuclear family would portend a return in America to a golden age of social health. But through most of human history, this was never the structure for successful child rearing. A more likely healer is a return to the extended family that for eons sustained parents and children alike—a network consisting of parents, uncles, unrelated longtime neighbors, and particularly grandparents. Anthropologists Rachel Caspari and Sang-Hee Lee published striking data showing that the ratio of humans surviving into grandparenting age suddenly quintupled roughly 30,000 years ago. The authors' "grandma hypothesis" provides a simple and powerful explanation for (or at least a striking coincident indicator of) the rapid growth of human population, culture, and creativity in early Upper Paleolithic Europe.[634]

At the Wooden Shoe commune where I lived during the early 1970s, we revived the concept of the extended family, at least for a few years. A stressed-out parent could pass a misbehaving child into loving hands and receive instant respite. There was always someone close by to talk with if you had doubts about your competence or patience as a parent. No one was alone following the collapse of a romantic or a marital breakup. And today, no one should be alone when facing the challenges of sustaining a family. Far more than giving our kids cello lessons, a return to some form of extended-family parenting may be what our children most need. Extended families reduce risk of harm to children from bad parenting, economic shock, or a health crisis. In our quest for career opportunity, good schools, and safe neighborhoods, we have moved miles and hours away from our grandparents and from the possibility of extended family as supportive community. As we have substituted daycare and behavioral therapists for the family structures that were the norm for 30,000 years until the 1960s, we may have abandoned a major advantage that helped make us Earth's most successful species.

THE DEPRESSION EPIDEMIC

Martin Seligman, past president of the American Psychological Association, describes depression as "a disorder of individual helplessness and individual failure."[635] As we saw in Chapter 2, we are wired to seek attention and status and to redirect our behavior when confronted by failure. But American commercial culture and the high-flux, global economy have eroded stable, small-group society. We are enveloped in an electronic cloud of status superiors against whom we cannot escape comparing ourselves and from whom we get no response if we ask for help. We are saturated by vivid images of the rich and famous whose possessions, talents, and achievements make us feel puny and ineffectual. There are fewer places for ordinary people to be admired for their genuine talents and accomplishments. Our brains are simply not evolved to handle the overload of social isolation and status defeat.

E. Fuller Torrey and Judy Miller, authors of *The Invisible Plague: The Rise of Mental Illness from 1750 to the Present*, profusely document the coincidence of the rise of severe mental disease with industrialization and urbanization. They speculatively and wrongly rule out social causes for the rise.[636] The even sharper rates of increase in mental illness in America over the past three generations sound alarmist enough to be rejected out of hand—particularly given the lack of any scientifically accepted explanation. But a recent National Institutes of Health survey of almost 10,000 American adults provides very solid evidence that our nation is enduring an "epidemic" of mental disease. Those Americans born between about 1970 and 1985 are four times more likely than their grandparents to suffer any mental disorder during their lifetimes; they are seven times more likely to suffer major depression, six times more likely to become alcoholics, and 45 times more likely to become addicted to a drug.[637] The better reporting and relaxed diagnostic thresholds of more recent years do not come close to explaining these massive increases.[638]

In a composite analysis of hundreds of surveys involving tens of thousands of college students and children, research psychologist Jean Twenge found a huge and continuous increase in anxiety over the past fifty years. "By the 1980s, normal children were scoring higher than 1950s child psychiatric patients on self-reported anxiety," said Twenge. Increased anxiety was not related to economic conditions or poverty, but very strongly so with declines in the Fordham Index of Social Health (Figure 7.5), with declines in social capital five and ten years prior, and with threats such as the 1980s' rising crime rates.

Twenge links "skyrocketing" anxiety and depression among boomer and post-boomer generations to our entrapment between rising individualism and loss of our perception of control over our lives and environment. Her studies link weakening social capital to increases in measured individualism. Rising individualism is, in turn, linked to escalating depression and anxiety because we have no one to blame for our failure but ourselves.[639] Twenge also found a sharp increase over the past forty years among children and college students in the perception that their lives are controlled by outside forces. Loss of perceived control is closely associated with decreased self-control and increased aggression and depression.[640]

The most rigorous recent estimate for the prevalence of mental health disorders, including depression and substance addictions, is the National Comorbidity Survey Replication (NCSR) conducted in 2001–2003. The findings? A staggering 26 percent of Americans had suffered mental illness over the previous year, the rate rising to 51 percent of us when it is projected over a lifetime. Depression and related mood disorders constitute about half of all mental illness, with ten percent of us afflicted over the past year, 28 percent over the course of our lifetimes.[641] Depression has become by far America's leading cause of nonfatal medical disability. According to Thomas Insel, director of the National Institute of Mental Health, depression costs the U.S. $53 billion annually in treatment costs, lost life, and lost productivity.[642]

These alarming data have been attacked by critics as an artifact of overly loose diagnostic thresholds and survey methods, motivated by the self-interest of drug companies, researchers, and advocacy organizations. Allan Horwitz and Jerome Wakefield make the definitive case for this criticism in their recent book, *The Loss of Sadness: How Psychiatry Transformed Normal Sorrow Into Depressive Disorder*. They argue that a diagnosis of depression should not be given when the symptoms appear in proportionate reaction to a personal loss or social defeat, and when the symptoms clear up as a sufferer employs normal coping mechanisms or when his or her life simply improves. By their logic, people should not be diagnosed with depression if they show all its symptoms in reaction to, for example, a divorce, bankruptcy, or bullying, but recover two years later upon finding a new romance, job, or school. Horwitz and Wakefield charge that the methods used in the NCSR and similar surveys hype the numbers because interviewers who are without clinical training, and who are required to follow interview scripts blindly and precisely, capture people with depression symptoms, but not depression.[643] Ronald Kessler, who led the NCSR, told me that he vigorously disputes the notion that depression and other mental disorders are being over-reported. His clinicians went back and did blinded diagnostic interviews with a random sample of those surveyed, finding levels of prevalence unchanged.[644]

As I showed in Chapter 2, the emotional suffering occurring in depression is an evolved and therefore "normal" response to life's serious losses and defeats, designed to force us to abandon unattainable goals, accept defeat by a dominant, seek out a new role or social group, or alert others to our need for emotional support. Regardless of whether we classify the symptoms of this suffering as clinical depression or normal sadness, the rising incidence of these symptoms is evidence of increasing social stress, emotional loss, and status defeat. The appropriate response to America's depression epidemic is not to define it away. Instead, let's ask why the loss and defeat that provoke depression symptoms have spiked in recent decades.

America leads the world in mental illness. The World Health Organization surveyed over 60,000 adults in fourteen nations for prevalence of mental illness of all types, and—as shown in Figure 7.6—the United States tops even Ukraine, Colombia, and Lebanon, nations wracked by persistent political and economic turmoil. In the United States, the prevalence of mental illness is almost double that of the next-highest advanced nation, France. The United States also leads the world in every diagnostic category of mental disease, other than Ukraine, which is first in substance abuse disorders.[645] Another cross-national study shows that Americans suffer the highest rate of depression among the ten countries surveyed. Over the past century, depression has increased in all these ten countries, but mostly steeply in America.[646] In a striking comparison that hints strongly at the cause for increasing depression in America, past-year depression symptoms among women vary from a low of two percent in Basque Spain, where shared religion and traditional extended-family structures remain intact, to thirty percent in urban Zimbabwe, a nation torn by violence and instability.[647]

A major cause of our higher rates of depression is life within American culture. A recent National Institutes of Health survey found that almost all mental disorders occur at strikingly higher rates among white Americans and Mexican-Americans born in America, as compared with Mexican-Americans and other immigrants living here but born elsewhere. Over their lifetimes, white Americans are between three and four times as likely to suffer a mental disorder, depression, or alcohol addiction as are foreign-born Mexican-Americans.

Figure 7.6

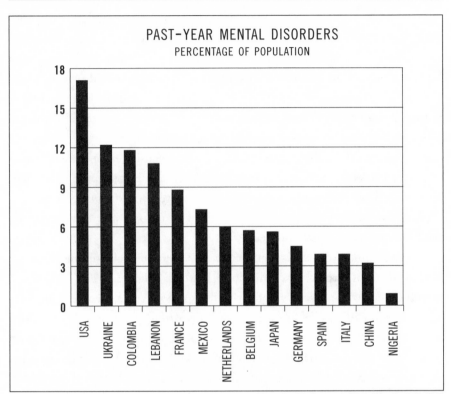

PAST-YEAR MENTAL DISORDERS
PERCENTAGE OF POPULATION

Data used with permission. Koen Demyttenaere, etal, "Prevalence, Severity, and Unmet Need for Treatment of Mental Disorders in the World Health Organization World Mental Health Surveys," *Journal of the American Medical Association*, June 2, 2004; 291(21):2581–90.

A white American is 23 times more likely to become a substance addict. Statistical tests show that higher stress, poor education, and poverty among first-generation Mexican-American immigrants do not explain the huge disparity. Emotional and financial support from other members of the traditional Mexican extended family seems to provide a protective effect that largely disappears once an immigrant becomes culturally Americanized.[648] An older, similar study found that the prevalence of major depression among the Amish of Lancaster County, Pennsylvania—who enjoy extremely tight community bonds but have no TVs or electricity—is about one-fifth to one-tenth that of their American neighbors.[649] America's fragmented social environment is making the world's wealthiest nation also a country of psychological failures.

SCHIZOPHRENIA AND SOCIAL DEFEAT

Accumulating evidence shows that chronic and severe social defeat may also help explain recent increases in rates of schizophrenia. In humans, monkeys, and rodents, it is well established that chronic social defeat is linked with higher sensitivity to and preference for rewards such as food or drugs, and with baseline hyperactivity of the dopamine reward system. In humans, higher reward sensitivity is, in turn, linked with increased schizophrenia in the ten to twenty percent of us who are predisposed to the disorder. On the level of brain biology, schizophrenics have more reward-sensitive dopamine systems and have a higher preference for amphetamines. Schizophrenic individuals who have never received medication show increased dopamine occupancy in their striatal D2 receptors. Use of marijuana, a dopamine-elevating drug, doubles the risk of schizophrenia.

There are numerous and specific reports of increased schizophrenia among people in social circumstances likely to increase social defeat. Those living in cities have a 72-percent greater risk for schizophrenia. People with average IQ bear a thirty-percent greater risk than those with high IQ. Second-generation immigrants have twice the risk of new arrivals to a country, with no evidence that predisposed individuals preferentially migrate. First-generation immigrants retain protective extended-family relationships and friendship networks that protect them not just from depression, as we saw in the last section, but from schizophrenia as well. Further evidence shows that a person's negative comparisons of his or her own status with that other people may contribute to the onset of schizophrenia. A final key piece of evidence: immigrants of low status in their birth country, those who are well-accepted by natives of their new country, and those living among larger groups of immigrants are all at lower or even no greater risk of schizophrenia.[650] People are better protected from psychological injury when they are not forced to adjust to lower status or when they live in a sustaining community. OverSuccess is removing these protections.

BODY MASS: RX FOR STATUS STRESS

Obesity has become impossible to ignore—on the sidewalk or in the nightly news. Government and health authorities have made a Herculean effort since the 1950s to warn Americans to control calories, to exercise, and to eat a balanced diet. Unlike admonitions against tobacco, these warnings have utterly failed. Americans are the most overweight and obese people in the world.[651]

Evidence of Americans' ballooning bulk is everywhere. Hospital body scanners are becoming obsolete because American body tissue has become too thick for ultrasound waves to penetrate. Restaurant seats are collapsing. Ambulance crews can no longer carry loaded stretchers. Hearses require beefed-up suspensions. In a 2005, a cruise boat sank in Lake George in New York State, causing twenty elderly passengers to perish—in part because their 174-pound average weight exceeded the 140-pound standard dating from when the boat was certified in 1979.[652] Since 1960, the average weight for American adults has increased by 25 pounds. The National Center for Health Statistics reports that between 1960 and 2006, obesity had almost tripled to 33 percent of the population. The number of us who are either overweight or obese increased from 45 to 66 percent—two of every three American adults. Eighty percent (!) of black females over forty are now obese or overweight.[653] Six percent of infants under six months are now overweight, a rate that has almost doubled since 1980.[654] Morbid obesity—where a person is more than 100 pounds overweight—is the fastest-growing category of weight status, tripling to nine million since 1986.[655] A jaw-dropping 80 percent of Americans are likely to become overweight or obese at some point during their lifetimes, and this estimate is conservative.[656]

Skeptics assert that the alarm about overweight is just another scare designed to attack the manufactured-food industry for its high-margin, high-calorie, low-nutrient products. The best study so far on the health effects of overweight—in which researchers followed more than one-half million participants aged fifty and over for ten years—lays this contention to rest. The study showed that overweight baby boomers and seniors who have never smoked face a 20- to 40-percent increase in the risk of early death. For the obese, the risk is two to three times higher. In 2003, overweight and obesity caused 14 percent of male cancer deaths and 20 percent of female. For the morbidly obese, cancer rates are elevated by at least fifty percent.[657] Excess weight will account for almost twenty percent of early death among boomers who have never smoked.[658] The healthcare costs of America's excess body mass runs to $93 billion per year, more than smoking.[659] Overweight people have 36-percent higher medical costs and 77-percent higher medication costs than other Americans.[660] Diabetes, a disease linked to obesity and lack of exercise, will afflict one in three children born in the U.S. in 2000. Half (!) of all black and Hispanic children will become diabetic.[661]

There are some obvious causes for this epidemic: more sedentary work and less active recreation, increased energy density in foods, reduced food costs, the supersizing of food portions, and more food advertising. The National Academy of Sciences has nailed down the link between obesity in kids and ads featuring characters like Tony the Tiger and SpongeBob SquarePants hawking high-calorie, low-nutrient foods.[662] Calorie-dense food is now everywhere: high school sports scrimmages end with a medieval banquet table groaning with branded junk food; pastry trays are a fixture at morning meetings. Coca-Cola's announced mission is to make its flagship product more available than water. We are consuming more calories than we need. The Centers for Disease Control and Prevention found that, between 1971 and 2000, women's calorie intake increased by 22 percent, men's by 7 percent—with all these added calories far beyond what we could burn off even with intensive exercise.[663] We do not know why women's food intake has increased so much more rapidly than men's, but a clue may be found in the increased stresses associated with women's having joined the full-time workforce.

Less obvious potential contributors to the body mass surge include reduced exposure to heat and cold in our increasingly airtight homes and workplaces: the closer indoor temperature is to 72 degrees, the less energy we need to burn to stay comfortable. Insufficient sleep is known to increase appetite and weight gain, and more of us are sleeping less; on average, we get about one hour less sleep than we did in 1970. Genetic predispositions to extra poundage, and the way they play out in the environment, are also a factor, with overweight and obese parents conferring these traits on their children via both genetic and epigenetic effects. While obesity is at least 65-percent heritable, it has been shown in studies of twin mothers that the one who is heavier during pregnancy will tend to have heavier children and grandchildren. Moreover, American mothers are becoming older, and older mothers tend to bear heavier children, with the child's odds of being obese increasing 14 percent for every five-year increase in the mother's age.[664] One in six Americans—up by about 50 percent over the past decade—already take at least one prescription psychoactive drug, many of which are known to cause weight gain.[665] Obesity has even been shown to be socially contagious, with one person in a friendship group making heaviness acceptable to another.[666]

But it is the increase in stress in our lives—a key driver of OverSuccess—that probably explains a good portion of why we are eating more. We learned in Chapter 2 that psychological stress, including status defeat, poisons the brain reward system and decreases its sensitivity to drugs, alcohol, and food. That means more of these substances are required for our stress-poisoned brains to experience the same level of pleasure—the "reward deficiency syndrome" that leads to overeating and to obesity.

Physiologist Mary Dallman and her colleagues found that rats subjected to chronic stress suffer continuously activated inflammation and immune system response. Normally, the immune response progressively stimulates production of glucocorticoids, hormones that circulate in the body and brain to dial down the inflammation and immune response. But under chronic stress, glucocorticoid signaling becomes impaired. Unable to tamp down their stress responses, these rats increase their consumption of sugar water and lard and develop pot bellies. Sound familiar? Increased corticoids are also known to cause weight gain in humans. Most intriguing of all, the rats' extra body weight then caused a reduction in their circulating stress hormones. The co-author of Dallman's study, Norman Pecoraro, draws the link to humans: "people are somehow stressed, and they are self-medicating because food is available."[667]

Both subordinate and dominant rats lose weight after enduring periods of socially stressful group confinement. However, when they are returned to their home cages, subordinate rats (but not dominants) regain more weight and put on more fatty tissue.[668] We may be eating more comfort food and adding bulk to salve our increased psychic discomfort. Debbie Wallis, a University of Liverpool research psychologist, confirmed this hypothesis in an experimental setting. After being subjected to an "ego-threat," people ate 23 percent more chocolate.[669] Another study shows that, after adjusting for other potentially explanatory variables—including family genetics, initial body mass index, height change, household income, and mental health—teen girls are almost 70 percent more likely to gain eleven or more pounds over two years if they initially rank themselves as low in social status, compared with their high-status peers.[670] The lawsuits fingering cheeseburgers for our obesity epidemic should name Over-Successed, status-stressed American culture as a co-defendant.

CHILD ABUSE IS INHERITED

The increasing emotional stress in American households over the past few decades and the startling pervasiveness of child abuse and neglect are clearly linked. Victims remain psychologically scarred for life; they even pass down their scars to their own children. We are beginning to understand how that legacy unfolds, right down to its specific biochemical mechanisms.

According to the most conservative numbers reported by the U.S. Department of Health and Human Services, in 2005 there were nearly 900,000 cases of "substantiated" child abuse and neglect, or 1.2 percent of all American kids. Rates of substantiated plus reported cases are higher, at almost five percent of children. The very good news is that, due to sharply reduced public tolerance for these crimes, the substantiated abuse and neglect rate has dropped by over twenty percent from its 1993 peak, driven largely by declines of more than 40 percent in the more readily detectable physical and sexual abuse categories.[671]

Critics charge that the higher five-percent rate of reported plus substantiated cases is merely an indication of the increased attention paid to the issue in recent years and the use of dirty tactics in custody disputes. But these data cover only circumstances brought to official attention and grossly underestimate the actual numbers. A sample of Tennessee adults, as well as adults in a random national survey, found that 40 percent of males and 30 percent of females reported they had endured physical and emotional abuse or neglect during their childhood.[672] Maxia Dong, a medical epidemiologist at the Centers for Disease Control and Prevention in Atlanta, has spent several years statistically teasing several seminal papers from the best database to date—the child-abuse histories of 8,100 mostly white, middle-class Kaiser Health Plan members, including detailed medical records for each. An astounding 25 percent of women and 16 percent of men had experienced contact sexual abuse during their childhoods. These numbers very closely corroborate data found in two previous studies.[673] Table 7.3 below breaks down Dr. Dong's child-abuse prevalence data.

Table 7.3: Percentage Prevalence of Childhood Abuse and Neglect by Type[674]

Physical Abuse	26.4
Sexual Abuse	21.0
Emotional Neglect	14.8
Emotional Abuse	10.2
Physical Neglect	9.9

Data used with permission.

Dr. David Finkelhor, Director of the Crimes against Children Research Center at the University of New Hampshire, thinks Dr. Dong's numbers are high and points instead to the National Comorbidity Survey estimate that 13 percent of women and 3 percent of men were sexually abused during childhood.[675] When we extrapolate from these lower sexual-abuse estimates, we still have a combined rate of abuse and neglect in the shocking 25-percent range, which indicates that victim demographics extend well beyond families in poverty. Overwhelmingly, the smallest set of 900,000 substantiated cases involves broken families and those in economic distress. Children living in families with incomes under $15,000 are twenty times more likely to be victims of abuse or neglect than those living in families with incomes of $30,000 or more.[676] But more detailed studies show that abuse and neglect are associated with multiple factors, not just poverty by itself. Families able to cope emotionally with the stresses of poverty are not at greater risk than nonpoor families. The risk factors for abuse and neglect include high life stress, economic and emotional insecurity, family unemployment, lack of trust, social isolation, high frequency of family moves, abuse perpetrated upon parents during their childhoods, fatherlessness, high-conflict divorce, parental depression, substance abuse, child disability, and unrealistic expectations about child development.[677]

Child abuse causes long-term damage, in both the physical and mental health of victims. A study that tracked over one thousand New Zealand children from birth through age 32 shows that adults who were subjected to serious abuse during their early childhoods suffer serious health consequences. As adults, children who are sexually or physically abused or rejected by their mothers during the first decade of life suffer a sixty-percent greater risk of harmful low-grade inflammation, a key predictor for later heart disease, diabetes, and chronic lung diseases. Psychosocial stress, father absence, and child abuse all hasten early development of sexual characteristics in girls, raising their risk of breast cancer. The average black American girl now begins breast development at age 9, years before she has the emotional maturity to handle sex. Child mistreatment need not rise to the level of physical or sexual abuse to result in the most serious harm. Recent research shows that child neglect— lack of minimal food, clothing or shelter, or lack of supervision or emotional support—between birth and age 2 is as strong a predictor of later aggression and violence as physical or sexual abuse at any age. [678]

The effects of child abuse on the brain are also becoming clearer. Martin Teicher, director of Harvard's Developmental Biopsychiatry Research Program, who has published dozens of papers related to child abuse and brain development, has found that early life stress such as child abuse suppresses development of the corpus callosum, the structure connecting the left and right brain hemispheres. For over ninety percent of us, the left brain is used for language and logical, analytical processing, the right brain for spatial and emotional processing, particularly of negative emotion. Abused right-handed children show significant suppression in development of their left brain cortex. Abused kids, whether right-handed or left-handed, show markedly greater asymmetry in the development and use of brain hemispheres compared with children not abused. Women who were sexually abused as girls have an 18-percent smaller left hippocampus, a brain region associated with memory and the ability to imagine one's future behaviors.[679] Asymmetric brain development and an underdeveloped corpus callosum probably contribute to a disconnection between conscious thought and emotional and social awareness, which is a core symptom of psychopathy. The adult prefrontal cortex, which inhibits behavioral signals and violent impulses from elsewhere in the brain, is also functionally and dimensionally stunted in child-abuse victims.

The amygdalae, a pair of almond-shaped structures in the more primitive "emotional" brain, help us focus our near-instantaneous attention on novel and ambiguous stimuli and on potential danger or threat. The amygdalae are activated as we experience fear, as we perceive fear and sadness in others, and as we learn to change our behavior in response to injury or punishment. While the results of studies on the subject vary greatly, major depression and severe child abuse may enlarge one or both of the amygdalae during the initial or acute stage of psychological response and cause it to shrink later, as part of a longer-term response.[680] Some studies show that depressed people's amygdalae are enlarged and show increased metabolism, perhaps related to their chronic hyper-vigilance to negative events. Teicher examined young adults with a history of serious sexual abuse and found that their left amygdalae were reduced in size by almost 10 percent.

Teicher thinks that these and other brain structural and functional changes in response to early child abuse are a programmed developmental response designed by evolution to "facilitate reproductive success and survival in a world of deprivation and strife." Conversely, Teicher thinks that loving parenting and freedom from intense early stress permits a child to develop less aggressive, more emotionally stable, and empathic brains.[681]

A set of rat experiments by Dr. Moshe Szyf and his McGill University coworkers provide firm support for Teicher's theory. Rat pups raised by mothers who frequently touch them grew a greater number of glucocorticoid stress receptors in their brains' hippocampii, which in turn dampened the release of stress hormones. But rat pups reared by moms who were too stressed out to lick and groom them developed fewer glucocorticoid receptors and released more stress hormones. These behavioral patterns persisted through the rats' lifetimes. In adult life, the maternally deprived rats were more fearful and defensive and were more stressed in adverse and novel circumstances. As adults, they showed more easily disrupted attention, as well as impaired memory, learning, and social-recognition skills. The effects are not always inherited, because pups born of low-nurturance mothers who were reared by high-nurturance mothers grew up to be unstressed and unfearful.[682] Other rat and monkey experiments show that lower levels of maternal care, even when within the normal behavior range, lead to mild impairment of social skills and outcomes.[683]

Differences in early care result in the lifetime fixation of one of two different behavioral repertoires—high- versus low-stress response to risk and novelty. At the biochemical level, this behavioral fixation happens via the semi-permanent attachment or removal of molecular tags at specific places on genes that are associated with regulation of these behaviors. Our genome includes the set of about 24,000 "coding" genes, the instructions by which our bodies manufacture proteins. The combination of our genes and these regulatory tags is called our epigenome. Epigenetic tags regulate which of these genes' activity is turned up or down in our various organs. In unloved rat pups, when a small molecular fragment called a methyl group attaches itself near the end of the gene that manufacturers glucocorticoid stress receptors, the gene becomes permanently suppressed. Methyl group tagging is an epigenetic effect we now know is controlled by the rat pups' early-life emotional environment. Cells pass on their epigenetic tag status as they reproduce, explaining how early life experiences can influence adult emotional makeup and behavior.

The authors of the rat experiments propose a theory very similar to Teicher's about children's long-term response to stressful upbringings. It is thoroughly demonstrated in humans that stressed-out parents are less nurturing parents. Weak and broken family ties during childhood result in higher stress response and increased mental and physical illness in adulthood. Less nurturing parents rear offspring that are better programmed to survive, reproduce, and succeed in a stressed, emotionally adverse world. The human epigenome is designed to function under nature's good assumption that our childhood and adult emotional environments will be similar. But the cost of success in an emotionally adverse world is increased mental and physical disease in later life. This pattern of lifelong imprinting of early developmental experience is shared across all forms of life, from plants that suffer early-life insect attack or drought, to reptiles, and to mammals.[684]

It would be a wild overreach to blame all child abuse on social stress and all stress on our obsession with success. Success often brings higher incomes and homes in safer neighborhoods. Children reared in better-off households in safe neighborhoods are exposed to less stress. And the developmental response of children to abuse varies greatly among individuals. Some brains are acutely sensitive, while some are inherently protected. But all else being equal, a stressed-out and unhappy, rather than an abusive, childhood causes subtle but fully real adult psychological problems, including major depression among susceptible people.

The connections between OverSuccess and child abuse are pristinely clear. Families under economic duress in America live under far greater emotional stress than those in other nations that offer far fewer public services. Our lack of noninstitutional community support is at the root of our socially isolated families who must confront challenges alone. The groundbreaking lab rat experiments are strong indications that the widespread social defeat that comes with American success culture causes increased child abuse and is tagging our children's stress receptor genes with methyl groups. The lasting epigenetic effects are passed to the next generation of adults, offering some explanation for our social withdrawal, and our high rates of mental disease, addiction, and chronic illness.

POSTPONED PARENTING AND ITS EFFECT ON BIRTH DEFECTS

Parenting later in life contributes to increased genetic abnormalities in children. The health consequences of our pressure-cooked lives, such as stress-related disease and sleep deprivation, are not news, and these pressures are also contributing to the phenomenon of Americans postponing parenthood. Other explanations for later-life parenting probably include the contribution of improved nutrition to reproductive longevity, fertility drugs, and healthier later life. For women, the average age at first childbirth is now the highest in U.S. history. Among white mothers in the age 35–44 category, birthrates jumped by almost 150 percent between 1980 and 2005, while rates have declined slightly for those in their twenties. The same change holds for white fathers: rates are up by about fifty percent for fathers 35 and over and down for those under 30.[685]

I can personally testify to the advantages of later-life parenthood; the benefits include greater life experience, more time, and more resources. But alarming new evidence shows that fathering by older males harms the brains of their children. Males add most of the new, nonfatal mutations to their children's genes because sperm cells are subject to more accumulated DNA errors than are egg cells. Sperm DNA in a twenty-year-old father has divided and been copied about 100 times—but more than 800 times in a fifty-year-old. More copies means more errors. In contrast, a mother's egg cells undergo only a few dozen divisions, regardless of her age.

Older fathers also accumulate a greater number of epigenetic markers that can contribute to brain development errors in their children. Autism and related disorders are now prevalent among children at an astounding rate of one in 150, and children conceived when the father is forty years or older are almost six times as likely to have an autism disorder compared with children of men fathering under age thirty. (Fortunately, there are no greater levels of autism correlated with conception by older mothers.) One in four cases of schizophrenia may be caused by the sperm of fathers over forty. Nonverbal IQ is significantly reduced for children of both mothers and fathers forty and over at age of birth, with later-life parenting explaining about two percent of variance in IQ.[686] Mothers giving birth at age 45 face a risk fifty times greater than those at age 20 of having a Down Syndrome baby. And if you're born to a mother under 25, you have twice the odds of living past 100.[687] Delaying parenting until you make partner or can afford a home in the Wellesley school district has its benefits. But success cannot (yet) buy back youthful reproductive cells.

RUDENESS AND WORSE

OverSuccess creates unnaturally intense pressure on us to think only about ourselves. How we treat ordinary strangers is a good index for the impact of our success obsession on American social health. Today's whipping boy is the retail sales clerk or flight attendant, strangers of unambiguously low status, never likely to wield power over our career or reputation and with whom we take the liberty to behave completely without respect or self-restraint. For example, while handing over a credit card in places like Bal Harbour or New-port Beach—and this requires study to pull off—it is bad form to indicate even awareness of the sales clerk.

Rudeness prevails even where there is no Cartier boutique. In the store she ran in our small New Hampshire town, my wife and her young clerk, Katie, stood behind the counter, carefully custom-packing a $3 gift box of candy for a thin-lipped, expensively dressed customer who was obviously an out-of-towner. Katie apologized for a slight bulge in the lid resulting from her effort to fill the box so that its contents looked more generous than its price would suggest, asking the customer if she'd like a gift bow to dress it up. Looking about the store to be sure no one else of import would witness her obnoxious behavior, the customer glared at the box, then lit into Katie with a venomous, out-of-the-blue attack because it bulged. My wife, consummate diplomat, defused the incident and let the customer know that Katie was recovering from surgery. The customer apologized, feebly, saying she had no way of knowing about the surgery—as if her behavior would have otherwise been acceptable.

While the residents of my little town value themselves for their sensitivity and tolerance, no one would ever dare do anything that could be remotely interpreted as disparaging to a black person, accidentally say "homosexual" rather than "gay," or boat past a loon at faster than wake speed. But seething just beneath this veneer of propriety is a new readiness to hair-trigger rage over inconsequential status slights. Over the past two years, in ways entirely new to my experience, I've witnessed people torch relationships over innocuous differences of opinion on a few words of text on a tourism website, or a disagreement over how to repair a bathroom door lock. I don't take much offense because I know that these people are passing on what they are getting from others. But, by failing to call people on their rudeness and allowing it to slip into our treatment of others, we allow our everyday behavior to make America a colder and crueler place.

Bad behavior has put New Hampshire's wonderful system of largely voluntary local government at risk. Many school boards and planning boards can no longer maintain required meeting quorums—thanks in part to long commutes that tax the evening hours of potential volunteers, and the regulatory complexity which now requires lay board members to be familiar with arcane subspecialties in engineering and law. But the rise of public vindictiveness is the most frequently noted change. People who do not get their way are far more likely to make it intensely personal. "The toxicity really discourages people from getting involved, whether it be battling another council member or School Board member or even a member of the public," says Rochester City Councilor Chuck Grassie, reflecting on changes he has witnessed in his thirty years of public service.

Longtime municipal attorney John Teague agrees that rudeness is now rampant in the public sphere and that public criticism used to be "coded with a basic respect. It was either done with a sense of humor or perspective. Now it carries with it this sense you're a bad person." Another municipal attorney, Walter Mitchell, laments the new take-no-prisoners attitude toward winning, recounting one community's inability to find enough local zoning board members after an aggrieved petitioner filed personal damages lawsuits against every member of the board. Nottingham Planning Board member Kay Kyle, suffering blood pressure spikes and headaches from meeting stress, finally resigned when a company representative publicly questioned her personal integrity.[688]

Psychologist Robin Kowalski, who has written three books about bad behavior, finds that swearing in public, aggressive driving, coughing or sneezing in a crowded space, public flatulence, vicious humor, and verbal harassment are all up over the past two to three decades. Kowalski blames the ascendance of "me first" in personal relationships and the examples set in entertainment media.[689] A survey by the civic organization Public Agenda found that 79 percent of Americans agree that rudeness has become a serious problem, with six in ten saying that the problem has worsened over the past few years. Forty-one percent of us admit to being rude ourselves. Those surveyed guess the causes to be crowding, the pressure to rush through daily life, the negative role models in the media, and the effect of our increasing anonymity in society.[690]

While there are no good data examining workplace rudeness, this also seems to be on the rise. "It's becoming much more socially acceptable to be mean and nasty to others," says Paul Spector, a professor of industrial and organizational psychology at the University of South Florida in Tampa and an expert on what's being called "desk rage." Spector thinks that bad behavior in the workplace has become more acceptable because cable TV news and enter-tainment shows like *The Weakest Link and American Idol* now portray nastiness as hip and because long work hours have ratcheted up our levels of stress.[691] "Air rage," too, seems on the rise. "The evidence is pretty clear," said Andrew Thomas, editor of *The Journal of Transportation Security.* "It fell off after 9/11, but has come back with a vengeance."[692] Lonny Glover of the Association of Professional Flight Attendants agrees that passenger behavior is getting worse, offering as illustration an incident where a drunken passenger got into a brawl with several others, then urinated in the aisle. Sara Nelson, a United Airlines flight attendant, witnessed a family whose flight had been canceled claw the arms of a customer service agent until they bled because the agent could not find them another flight.[693]

A *South Park* cartoon depicted two surly preteens on a shopping mall bal-cony passing time by entangling the strangers below in their unnaturally copi-ous and sticky phlegm. I admit the infantile humor made me laugh, a fact that gave my young nephew new respect for adults. But the *South Park* boys have inspired real-life copycats. Highway workers are being forced to clean up a new type of roadside waste virtually unknown in the 1980s: bottles and bags of human urine and feces chucked from moving cars.[694] In Las Vegas, city work-ers must now spray odor-eating enzymes along their thousand-megawatt strip to curb the stench from tourists who find it convenient to defecate directly on the sidewalks.[695]

At Little League games and the like, parents elbow into the sidelines to scream at coaches, referees, even their own children. Seeking vicarious suc-cess, some parents are pushing their children through athletic competitions like little greyhounds, and these adults not only bark but bite. A San Fernando father assaulted a coach for pulling his son from a game. Another parent in Las Vegas poisoned an opposing youth football team in Las Vegas. At a grade-school hockey game in Reading, Massachusetts, as four-year-olds watched, an enraged father beat a volunteer supervisor to death. An Albuquerque parent sharpened the faceguard of his son's football helmet, so that his son could slash five opposing players; the father got slapped on the wrist with two days in jail. Fred Engh, who heads the 2,200-chapter National Alliance for Youth Sports, says this sort of behavior has increased sharply since the mid-1990s.[696]

The nation's urban underclass provides an early-warning alert to yet more rudeness. Starting in 2005, American cities have been hammered by sharp increases in violence and murder. In Philadelphia, Houston, Boston, and San Francisco, drug and gang murders are down, but fights over petty disputes are now leading routinely to murder. In Milwaukee, a man shot and killed a neighbor because the neighbor's young son borrowed a soap dish without permission. Arrestees will often tell police they killed over a dirty look. "When we ask, 'Why did you shoot this guy?' it's, 'He bumped into me'; 'He looked at my girl the wrong way,'" says Philadelphia Police Commissioner Sylvester Johnson. "It's arguments—stupid stupid arguments over stupid things."[697]

SPREADING ETHICAL ROT

The number-one enabler of OverSuccessed behavior is our general abandonment of self-restraining personal ethics, among both ordinary people in their personal dealings and those who set our standards in public life. It starts at the top of the political system, where the game on all sides is to bludgeon the opposition for its moral failings. In this regard, the political right is as tarnished as the left. Rush Limbaugh, who lords over three hours of broadcast time each day and proclaims himself America's champion of personal responsibility and the accountability of all before the law, for years concealed his addiction to illegally obtained prescription painkillers. Laws barring left-wing debauchery such as drug abuse applied to Limbaugh only after he was outed by the *National Enquirer*. Bill Bennett, author of the bestselling *Book of Virtues*, admitted that he had been concealing $8 million in gambling losses, vowing to quit gambling only when faced with a washout in his credibility and a bear market in his $50,000-a-shot speaking fee.[698] Laura Schlessinger is radio counselor to seventeen million listeners and a strict moral conservative who quite properly lectures all callers that their first duty is to family. Her mother was found dead and badly decomposed in her home, weeks after she had died, possibly from starvation.[699]

Christian Coalition founder and TV preacher Pat Robertson entered into a gold- and diamond-mining venture with the genocidal Zairean dictator Mobutu Sese Seko. Robertson's onetime political deputy, Ralph Reed, blasted gambling as "a cancer on the American body politic ... It is stealing food from the mouths of children ... [and] turning wives into widows." Reed then took on a project to protect the monopolistic profits of a Louisiana casino, attempting to conceal his receipt of at least $350,000 in laundered consulting fees.[700] In 2002, Reed helped quash a Texas state board of education initiative to eject the in-school TV network, Channel One, and its ads for junk foods and sexualized movie trailers, from classrooms.[701] Christian values fell like confetti at a GOP convention to the lure of Channel One consulting fees. And the Catholic Church, as the entire world learned in 2004, admitted that for decades it had been harboring thousands of child-molesting pedophile priests. In an anonymous, multi-denominational survey of 300 pastors, 23 percent admitted engaging in extramarital sex.[702] A *Christianity Today* poll found that 37 percent of pastors routinely visit porn websites.[703]

Hypocrisy on the political left is in equally constant search for new low-lying territory. Under the guise of increasing minority economic opportunity, Jesse Jackson, one of our nation's leading black voices, repeatedly extorted large corporations for contributions to his presumably philanthropic Rainbow/PUSH organizations. A 2001 *Chicago Sun-Times* story documented multiple instances of Jackson's dropping a threat of a politically embarrassing boycott or his opposition to a big corporate merger requiring regulatory approval, but only after his cronies and family members were cut in on corporate deals worth tens or hundreds of millions of dollars.[704] Jackson has twisted the civil rights movement into his personal profit center. But the *Sun-Times'* revelations did nothing to dent Jackson's celebrity or political pull; three years later, he was sharing the podium with candidate John Kerry, trolling for black votes. Six years later and fully redeemed, Jackson had become a frequent Fox News Channel guest.

In 1993, Hillary Clinton was appointed by her husband, the president, to head what would become a star-crossed healthcare reform task force whose meetings included hundreds of healthcare industry representatives—but were illegally held in secrecy. After a federal judge ordered the meetings opened and its records made public, the task force fired up the document shredders to hide the composition of its membership. (Vice-President Dick Cheney must have plagiarized this blueprint for his energy task force.) While publicly railing against insurance-industry lobbyists to burnish her fraudulent populism, Mrs. Clinton had let them secretly write a healthcare plan that would benefit them.[705] While still first lady in 2000, she secured the lefty base she would need for her Senate run by prominently opposing an industry bill making it harder for consumers to use bankruptcy to shed debt burdens, but then took $140,000 in campaign contributions from the banking industry and, once elected Senator, switched positions and endorsed the bill.[706]

Former House Majority Leader Tom DeLay, the nation's third most powerful Republican until his resignation under a cloud of corruption litigation in 2006, was the primary architect of: (a) the earmarks explosion, where billions of dollars in federal spending benefiting the clients of favored lobbyists were inserted into budget bills in the dead of night without hearings or a vote; and (b) the "K-Street Project," where lobbyists were granted power to write legislation favoring their clients in return for not hiring Democrats and directing contributions primarily to Republicans. But having access to this powerful man trumped the integrity of my party and of the American political system: American Airlines, Bacardi, BellSouth, Coors Brewing, Philip Morris, R. J. Reynolds Tobacco, Reliant Energy, and many Republican House members contributed over a million dollars to his legal defense.[707] Unfortunately, in a nation where the news media prefer to chase market share with gavel-to-gavel coverage of ditzy celebrities, titillation, and violence, political duplicity is invisible to the public unless it rises to the level of firestorm. Even then, our appetite for accountability is limited to only one feeding frenzy at a time.

Infected through the route of politics, even health science has become corrupted at the highest levels. Two decades ago, the National Institutes of Health was an unsullied bastion of pure science. But in 1995, via an internal memo that was kept secret for eight years, NIH's then-director terminated the agency's longstanding prohibition on conflict-of-interest relationships. By late 2003, 94 percent of the NIH's high-ranking staff scientists were receiving undisclosed royalties, consulting fees, and stock option grants from drug companies with stakes in the outcome of NIH research. Dr. Stephen I. Katz, the head of a $500 million NIH institute that had conducted a human study of an experimental treatment for kidney inflammation, failed to halt the study promptly when a subject died from treatment complications—his reluctance perhaps influenced by the $170,000 in consulting fees paid to him by the drug's maker. Katz was paid at least $142,000 in consulting fees by another drug company to which his NIH institute awarded $1.5 million in grants. Katz claimed he was never informed of the grants.

In 1997 the Institutes' lead diabetes researcher, Dr. Richard C. Eastman, lobbied the Food and Drug Administration on behalf of a drug without disclosing that he was a paid consultant for its manufacturer. After reports linking the drug to liver injury, Eastman told the FDA, "[W]e continue to think that the drug is safe." Three years and $2.1 billion in sales later, the drug, Rezulin, was pulled from the U.S. market after being implicated in 556 deaths. Allergy and Infectious Diseases research head Thomas J. Kindt, who earned nearly $200,000 in annual salary from NIH in 2003, took $63,000 in consulting fees from Innovir Laboratories and was named co-inventor on one of its patents. Asked by the *Los Angeles Times* why the federal government received no consideration, Kindt said he had worked on the drug idea during his vacation time.[708]

For over twenty years until 2006, Dr. Trey Sunderland conducted Alzheimer's research for NIH. In 2000, Sunderland stated in a required disclosure form, "I do not have any outside positions to note." Meanwhile, between 1998 and 2004, Sunderland had collected $612,000 from Pfizer, without disclosing the fees to the public or obtaining the approval required. Sunderland used his stature and official position to pitch Pfizer's anti-Alzheimer's drug, Aricept, at over eighty medical conferences and in news releases and journal articles. Again, contrary to NIH rules, Sunderland shipped thousands of institute-owned spinal fluid samples to Pfizer and to a hospital where he was later to work. Yet in 2006 and without flinching, National Institute of Mental Health Director Thomas Insel recommended Sunderland be paid a $15,000 retention bonus. It was not until the *Los Angeles Times* published a series of stories and a House committee held bruising hearings that the NIH moved to fire Sunderland.[709]

Top-status scientists apparently set the example for the rest. In 2002 the NIH ran an anonymous survey of early and mid-career researchers, finding that one-third admitted to unethical behavior such as altering or concealing adverse data, purloining ideas, or breaking rules against subjecting volunteers to excessive risk. An alarming one in five mid-career scientists admitted to "changing the design, methodology or results of a study in response to pressure from a funding source," wrote the survey's authors. "Our findings reveal a range of questionable practices that are striking in their breadth and prevalence."[710]

Ethical rot also undermines American health by contributing directly to the obesity epidemic. The average American now consumes high-fructose corn syrup at the rate of 63 pounds per year. HFCS hit our food supply in the early 1980s, just as the obesity epidemic took off. It has become ubiquitous in such products as soda, fruit drinks, snacks, baked goods, breakfast cereals, candy, ketchup, granola bars, cough syrup, yogurt, pickles, applesauce, salad dressing, BBQ sauce, and ice cream, and now represents ten percent of our daily caloric intake, with sweetened soft drinks the largest single calorie source. One average-sized, 12-ounce soda can have 10 teaspoons of HFCS. Teenagers get one-third of their calories from the sweeteners in soda and fruit drinks, most of them HFCS. The fructose in HFCS is more readily converted to fat by the liver than glucose or other food sugars.[711] American teens are consuming HFCS at levels known to dangerously increase blood lipid levels, belly-fat accumulation, and insulin resistance, all of which elevate the risk of heart disease and Type-II diabetes.[712] There are many studies finding no metabolic distinction between fructose and other types of sugars, but most of these are funded by the food industry.

Ironically, high-fructose corn syrup would have a far smaller share of the sweetener market were it not for the Byzantine system of import quotas, tariffs, and subsidies imposed for decades by Congress on behalf of U.S. sugar growers. This distortion of the economic system by special interests doubles the price of sucrose sugar, costing Americans billions of dollars annually, benefiting a tiny number of individuals, and impoverishing developing-world sugar growers who could manufacture and sell sugar at lower prices. Without this dubious policy, HFCS would not be cost-competitive. I am comfortable saying that obesity is largely the result of political corruption that gives the food industry financial incentive to sell products that cause heart disease and diabetes, while shifting the massive healthcare burdens onto society.

Politics, science, and medicine hold no monopoly on ethical hypocrisy. In 1995, Dennis Kozlowski, then CEO of Tyco and paragon of corporate probity, flew to Texas to argue in front of a judge for tough penalties against an employee who had embezzled just under $1 million from the company. Kozlowski urged the court "to impress upon Mr. Shah and those others who commit similar crimes that wrongdoing of this nature against society is considered a grave matter by the Texas court and will not be condoned."[713] In 2002, three weeks after lecturing New Hampshire College graduating seniors that they "will be confronted with questions every day that will test your morals. Think carefully, and for your sake, do the right thing, not the easy thing," he was forced to resign from Tyco in disgrace after being accused of evading $1 million in New York City sales taxes and looting $600 million from his company.[714] Apparently, most of Kozlowski's charitable contributions for which he took personal credit were Tyco stockholders' money, not his. He loved being a celebrity philanthropist at dinners in his honor, but apparently could not spare any of the $466.7 million in total compensation he received during his three final years at Tyco.

Tyco stockholders were not by any means alone in suffering the erosion of trust in American capital markets. The bubble of the late 1990s was built on phony corporate-profit numbers that were sanctioned by the accounting industry, whose own profits depended increasingly on their management-consulting work for their audit clients. The dual roles played by big accounting firms created an impossible conflict of interest, giving them incentives to sign off on their clients' inflated numbers to win consulting business. Arthur Levitt, a former chairman of the American Stock Exchange and chair of the Securities and Exchange Commission between 1993 and 2001, made a prescient effort to prevent the accounting frauds that would bring down Tyco, Arthur Andersen, Enron, WorldCom, and Adelphia; he fought for years during the 1990s to impose rules limiting accounting firms' consulting work for audit clients. During the heat of his fight in 2000, Arthur Andersen's CEO, Bob Grafton, whose firm was busy pumping up Enron's numbers, threatened Levitt, saying, "If you go ahead with this, it will be war."

During the 2000 election cycle, the accounting industry showered Washington with $15.3 million in campaign contributions, with $386,377 in special attention to the 15 members of the Senate's securities subcommittee.[715] Sixty-nine members of Congress, including two-thirds of securities subcommittee members, received $1.14 million in accounting-industry contributions. All 69 signed stinging letters to Levitt demanding that he back off.[716] Of course, these 69 would say that the contributions they received in no way influenced their official actions. The contributors would say that in no way did they expect any such influence. It is easy to understand why a historically low one in four Americans approves of how Congress is doing its job.

What were the lessons learned from these accounting scandals? Ethical cripples in the spotlight moved like jackrabbits into newer gray areas. In 2004 *The Wall Street Journal* uncovered yet another ploy to pump up the quarterly numbers. Companies had taken up the tactic of filing lawsuits in distant venues against their retired employees, cutting off their promised medical benefits and justifying the move by arguing that the promise of "lifetime coverage" meant the life of their employees' union contract, not the life of the employee. As these members of America's greatest generation died off while waiting out years of tortured legal proceedings, the companies pocketed the savings they made by failing to pay promised benefits, assured that, even if they lose their cases, sanctions consist of no more than restoration of benefits.[717]

Unethical behavior was again central to the 2007–2008 collapse of the sub-prime home mortgage market. Subprime loans, which were typically sold to less creditworthy homebuyers, made inflated home prices affordable for novice and over-leveraged buyers, thanks to such tricks as 50-year terms, negative amortization (meaning that the loan balance goes up rather than down in early years), big future-year rate increases, and no documentation of borrowers' income claims. Ethical compromise remains thoroughly democratic. One study found that, in 60 percent of these no-doc or "liar loans," buyers had overstated their incomes by more than half. As a result, when buyers could not meet their obligations, dozens of lenders were shut down or bankrupted, the number of home foreclosures multiplied by several times in communities throughout the U.S., rocking the entire world's financial system. Once again, just as during the tech bubble, many Wall Street firms were riddled by conflicts of interest, profiting from both their analysis of the credit quality of these loans and their packaging of them for resale.

Politicians again had their hand in the till, as subprime mortgage companies spent millions lobbying state and federal legislators to block reforms that would ultimately have saved billions in losses. Regulators and Congress did nothing until they were caught in the camera lights. Says Josh Rosner, managing director at an independent investment research firm, "This is far more dramatic than what led to Sarbanes-Oxley"—legislation passed in response to the pop of the tech bubble—"both in conflicts and in terms of absolute economic impact."[718]

Capitalism on Wall Street has turned increasingly away from value-added services to financial engineering, untempered by any sense of obligation to America's long-term prosperity. Way back in the 1980s, leveraged-buyout (LBO) firms would pay a premium to gain control of moribund companies hampered by stodgy management and bloated overhead. The LBO firms would inject entrepreneurial energy, wring out cash, then sell the better-run company at its higher value. For the most part, this process was capitalism at its best. But getting in and out of these deals required years of hard work rebuilding and revamping these companies. Today, the ripest targets have been picked, competition is stiffer, and buyout premiums have cut prospective profits to passbook levels. As a result, leveraged buyout artists have invented a new model: pay a premium to buy the target and take it private; then, without stockholders to object to the dismemberment, recoup the cash outlay from the company within two or three years by bleeding it for exorbitant "management" fees and "dividend recaps," financed by loading the company with junk bond debt. By preserving just enough free cash flow to lure in new investors, the acquirer can cash out by taking the company public again.

Between 2003 and 2006, LBO firms used their target companies to borrow over $100 billion to pay themselves fees and dividends.[719] This shameless predation is just what America does not need: companies so loaded with debt that they cannot invest in next-generation products or survive the next serious downturn. But who cares about America when your $100 million share of the fees can buy you two nice houses and put your name on a business school?

From glass tower to kitchen table, situational ethics are the new rulebook for American behavior. Two weeks after Hurricane Katrina devastated the Gulf Coast, more than 4,000 websites had sprung up to scam generous Americans of their contributions.[720] The federal government, attempting to cover its butt for under-funding levee repair years earlier, handed out string-free $2,000 checks to each of the evacuees, most of whom had lost everything. Five weeks later, some New Orleans evacuees were spotted on Cape Cod, spending their taxpayer gift, not on rebuilding their lives, but swilling brown-bagged vodka and soaking up the local culture at a strip joint. "They were tipping me $5 a pop," said a lap-dancer named Angel. "I told them I felt bad taking their money. But I still took it."[721]

For a few months, the 9/11 attack had roused our better angels, but things quickly returned to business as usual. Nine in ten of the 219,000 claims to a federal program to compensate New York City residents for 9/11 dust-related damage turned out to be scams.[722] Following the attack, President Bush called upon Americans to fight the war on terrorism, not through personal sacrifice, but by continuing consumption as usual. Contrast this with America's response to President Roosevelt's call for sacrifice during World War II. In 1942, one month after being asked to do so, ordinary citizens had collected 800 million pounds of rubber, and within a year, Americans had planted 20 million victory gardens that would produce forty percent of the nation's vegetables. Twelve million of us had registered for the civilian defense corps.[723]

Take a good look in the mirror before wagging your finger at superlobbyist Jack Abramoff or the athletes on steroids. The distinction between them and us is only a matter of economic scale. At work, we have become a nation of sneaks, dissemblers, and pilferers. A 1999 Kessler International study of mid-level employees found that an astounding 79 percent steal from their companies, with nearly 87 percent admitting to falsifying their time sheets or getting paid for hours they did not work. A 2002 survey by a *New York Times* job market research team found that 89 percent of job seekers falsify their resumes. A 1997 survey by the Ethics Officers Association found that nearly half of U.S. workers anonymously admitted to unethical or illegal actions over the prior year, including expense account padding, discriminating against co-workers, paying or accepting kickbacks, secretly forging signatures, trading sex for sales, breaking environmental laws, not working while on company time, and lying to customers. Ernst & Young estimated the cost of employee theft and fraud at $600 billion in 2002.[724]

In our private lives too, we have also become rampant cheaters. Among married and engaged couples, one-third of women and one-quarter of men admit to financial infidelity, concealing substantial personal expenditures or investments from their partners.[725] Estimates of the annual cost of insurance fraud amount to $24 billion, with one in four Americans believing it is OK to defraud an insurance company.[726] A large survey found that 39 percent of doctors admitted to making false claims to insurance companies over the prior year, often in a noble effort to help their patients, but cheating insurance companies and the government nonetheless.[727]

Consumers will spend hours carrying out elaborate schemes to steal information, as my wife discovered in her design business. She would spend hours conferring with conspicuously jeweled women posing as customers, working to craft detailed architectural hardware specifications for their new trophy homes. As planned, these types did not end up buying anything from my wife, but had the temerity to call her a few days later, angrily demanding spec lists with manufacturers' product numbers after having been frustrated by the competition's incompetence. These "customers" were never in the slightest troubled in their refusal to purchase any products or pay anything for my wife's work.

It's not surprising that we learn the habits of ethical squalor long before adulthood. About sixty percent of high school and college students anonymously admit to cheating in academic work, according to a recent literature survey of a dozen studies.[728] Eighty percent of high school students earning A averages anonymously admit to academic cheating.[729] So where are young people learning the new rules for success? In 2004 seventeen fourth graders at a Boston public school wrote letters independently documenting their recollections that their principal had entered their classroom, asked the teacher to leave, and then told them to correct their previously completed state assessment tests. The teacher, Jennifer Day, blew the whistle to the state department of education. One month later, despite having received glowing performance reviews, she was terminated. Superintendent Thomas Payzant later cleared the principal of the charges, finding that all seventeen of the student letters describing the principal's instructions to cheat on their tests were in error.[730]

My Ivy League academic community was torn for months by bitter controversy over whether it was right that several high school students who broke into their teachers' offices and stole copies of final exams should have been reported to the police. Many in our town felt that the students should have been held above the law because their academic records would have been blemished. One sophomore captured the lessons we are teaching our children with devastating accuracy when he said, "[Cheating] is not such a big deal. It happens everywhere."[731]

Cheating on taxes costs the United States government at least $345 billion in 2001, up from $100 billion in 1990.[732] One-third to one-half of the taxpaying population participates in the game. High tax rates have nothing to do with it; after the tax cuts of 1981 and 1997, under-reporting of taxable income increased. Data on noncompliance are thin, but one of the easiest measures to track is the difference between the wage and salary expenses reported by businesses and the wage and salary income reported by individuals. This "tax gap" is a superb quantitative indicator of ethical decline among ordinary Americans, and it widened from 1 percent of all income in 1982 to 5.5 percent in 1998.[733] Another such indicator is our widespread failure to self-report personal income to the IRS. In 2001, 57 percent of all non-farm and 72 percent of all farm-related self-employment income went unreported.

Ethical standards have become pervasively weak in America because the small fish see the big ones get slapped on the wrists. If you get caught peddling an ounce of pot or hit a mandatory three-strikes sentence by ripping off a candy bar, you go to jail—just as it should be in a nation of laws. But our laws turn to ice cream in the summer sun if your crime is a stepping-stone to big-time power, wealth, or fame. Archer Daniels Midland executives who were convicted of a price-fixing scheme that cost consumers $500 million received two years in prison. Charles Keating, the notorious head of the Lincoln Savings and Loan, served four and one-half years in federal prison for looting $3.8 billion from U.S. taxpayers. Wall Street cheat Ivan Boesky got to keep $20 million of his ill-gotten gains and a $2.5 million California home. Tonya Harding was fined $160,000 and 500 hours' community service for her role in assaulting figure-skating rival Nancy Kerrigan—paying her fine from the proceeds of $600,000 she got for her TV confession.[734] Right after that, she joined O. J. Simpson and Mike Tyson on a list of America's twenty most-admired athletes.

As our relationships have become more opportunistic and transient, litigation has replaced ethics, self-restraint, and mutual trust. The United States has more lawyers per capita than any other country. The benign explanations for that questionable distinction include our greater civil rights and the complexity of our transactions. But between 1900 and 1970, certainly a period of growing rights and complexity, the number of lawyers and judges per capita in the U.S. actually decreased slightly. However, since 1970, that ratio almost doubled as a percentage of the civilian workforce. No other major profession has seen this level of growth.[735] Once again, note the key transition date, 1970. Note how frequently years during 1965 to 1980 recur as turning points in the ascendancy of American OverSuccess.

As a nation, we are thoroughly aware of our mass ethical gelding and it disturbs us—but we do not know how to turn it around. We think that *none* of our major institutions are doing a good job at maintaining moral and ethical standards. Eighty percent of us believe that government policy is for sale to the high bidder.[736] Religious institutions earn the top "good job" rating, but from only 29 percent of us; all other major institutions rank lower.[737] Just 11 percent of us think that our moral values as a nation are getting better; 82 percent view them as declining. Across political ideology, our moral pessimism is deep and longstanding, dating back to the mid-1960s and dropping to a historic new low in 2007.[738]

We now react not with outrage but with tired cynicism to our lavishly compensated virtue-mongers. We know that the ethical rot goes right to the grassroots. Americans have come to the corrosive realization that everybody does it. Deceit and crime are acceptable routes to success in sports, business, school, and our personal lives. Our nation's founding norms of self-restraint and integrity have given way to an amoral ethic of doing whatever it takes to rise. "Play by the rules" has become "do it if you can get away with it." Only when we curtail our own lying, cheating, stealing, and unwarranted harm to others will we reestablish humanity's most fundamental moral injunction: treat others as you would have them treat you. If we are going to address the social and psychological burdens of our success obsession, we each have to change our personal behavior.

8

AMERICA'S OBSESSION: THE ECONOMIC COSTS

If at first you don't succeed, try, try again.
Then quit. There's no point in being a damn fool about it.
—W. C. Fields

TO SELF-MEDICATE AGAINST status defeat, we are not just overeating, we are also over-spending and over-consuming. Suffocating materialism has ratcheted up our stress, maxed out our credit cards, and forced us to trade friends and sleep for almost nonstop work hours. The marketing industry, itself ethically blinkered by OverSuccess, has preyed upon the deficiencies we feel in comparison to hypertrophied success benchmarks, setting off an orgy of competitive consumption so unchecked that our garages no longer have space for our cars.

MATERIALISM FILLS THE SELF-WORTH GAP

As I have shown, many of us feel small and empty in the permanent flux of global social space. We receive precious few messages encouraging us to fill the gap by finding new friends or building stable community. Instead, we have become flaming materialists because marketers spend $250 billion each year persuading us to buy things. We are awash in advertising because it can change our behavior and overrule our preferences. In a blind test, the part of our brains that registers taste prefers Pepsi over Coke. Better marketing is so powerful that it makes our conscious minds pick Coke, the market leader. Among three- to five-year-olds, 76 percent preferred McDonald's fries in McDonald's packaging compared with 13 percent who preferred the identical fries without the packaging. In a test of identical carrots, kids preferred the branded version 54 to 23 percent. The more televisions in their homes, the more kids preferred the branded to the identical generic food item.[739]

Like kudzu on land or milfoil in lakes, invasive species without natural predators, advertising has choked our communication space. An American alive today will be exposed to between one and two million ads over his or her lifetime, and the number is rising. Over the past 15 years, the portion of the average TV broadcast hour devoted to advertising has increased by 36 percent, to almost one-third of airtime.[740] Almost every surface and every experience is branded. They advertise, and we consume—more than we ever did. The ocean of advertising in which we are compelled to swim has shifted our nation's priorities from the future to the present, in essence making us more like children and unable to delay gratification. We can translate our changed priorities into terms used by economists. The entire economy is the sum of personal consumption, government spending, private investment, and net exports (i.e., imports, which have been dangerously high since 2000). Consumer saving for the future has collapsed to below zero, and personal consumption as a fraction of the economy has grown to the highest levels since World War II, from an average of 62 percent during 1965 through 1980 to 70 percent during 2002 through 2007.[741]

Marketers obsessed with success at all costs have increasingly targeted children, too young to have developed defenses against ad-suasion. Television advertising directed at children has surged since the 1970s, now reaching $15 billion annually. The average American child now sees over 40,000 TV ads each year and nearly three-quarters of a million ads by age 18. In the past few years, even infants and toddlers have become marketing targets, so that by age three, kids already recognize over 100 brand names. "While older children and adults understand the inherent bias of advertising, younger children [under age 7–8] do not, and therefore tend to interpret commercial claims and appeals as accurate and truthful information," said psychologist Dale Kunkel, senior author of a recent American Psychological Association report on the effects of marketing on children. This is the basis for the APA's call for sharp restrictions on advertising to children under eight years old.[742]

For older children, marketing has grown more cunning. Masquerading as fellow teenagers, marketers put up fake personal pages and lurk around MySpace to learn current slang and make surreptitious product-placements. On a personal homepage purporting to be that of a teenager, a girl slouches on her bed with a branded item sitting innocently in the corner. Abercrombie & Fitch became a major force in teen apparel by insidiously integrating its brand into its customers' lives. The company published a catalogue that looked so much like a private scrapbook of partially clad teens that customers were willing to pay $10 to get a copy. A&F agents skulk around schools to recruit the most handsome and popular teens, hiring them as sales clerks and catalogue models.[743] The most successful brands geared to children retain teams of "cool-hunters" who prowl the malls and streets to spot trend leaders. Kids usually jump at an offer to proselytize brands among their peers without pay, taking this work more seriously than schoolwork in return simply for being listened to by an adult ad-agency employee.[744] Even stodgy Proctor & Gamble has plunged into stealth marketing, retaining 250,000 teen volunteers to report back to the company after talking up its new products to family and friends in return for free samples and discount coupons.[745]

Perseus Books made marketing history in 2006 with *Cathy's Book*, collecting product placement fees for conspicuously inserting Proctor & Gamble's makeup brands into its plot. David Steinberger, president of the book publisher's parent company, appears clueless when questioned about the propriety of this newest form of infection by commercial culture into every crevice of American life: "*Cathy's Book* surpassed our expectations and hit best-seller lists in every country." In 2008 HarperCollins Children's Books raised the bar with what it describes as a "ground-breaking deal" involving multiple corporate sponsors, a record company, and an ad agency for a series of tween books starring Mackenzie Blue, a girl character cloaked in the obligate cultural diversity and environmental do-gooderism, but invented for the primary purpose of moving products. Publisher Susan Katz is entirely untroubled that multiple references to branded products will appear on almost every page. "If you look at Web sites, general media or television, corporate sponsorship or some sort of advertising is totally embedded in the world that tweens live in," explains Katz. "It gives us another opportunity for authenticity." Authenticity has become a cluster of commercial brands around which preteen girls define their identities.[746]

As marketing has become more ubiquitous and cunning over the past three decades, we can track, generation by generation, the increasing embrace of materialism. An AARP poll found that 38 percent of those born before World War II covet wealth, compared to 70 percent of those born later. Of men born after 1970, the number rises to a nearly unanimous 82 percent.[747] A recent Pew Research Center poll found that getting rich is the number-one or number-two goal for a whopping 81 percent of 18- to 25-year-olds.[748] While only about two percent of baby boomers and five percent of Gen-Xers can be classified as clinically compulsive shoppers, this number rises to ten percent of Gen-Ys, those born between about 1980 and 2000.[749] Among college freshmen, since the late 60s, getting money has replaced finding personal values as students' top goal in life. Students saying it is either essential or very important to be "very well off financially" grew from 42 percent in 1967 to 74 percent in 2007. Forty years ago, 86 percent of students called "developing a meaningful philosophy of life" their primary objective; today, just 47 percent do.[750]

Among all Americans, Roper polling found that, between 1975 and 1996, those naming making a lot of money as essential to the good life increased from 38 to 63 percent. The importance placed on raising children, doing good for society, having an interesting job, and enjoying a happy marriage did not rise. We now see materialism as an essential component of the good life: another Pew poll charts the increasing number of consumer products over the past three decades that we once considered luxury items and now view as necessities.[751]

As a consultant to some of the globe's biggest consumer companies, Martin Lindstrom is unabashed about helping his clients drive their brands deeply into children's lives. Yet in *Brand Child*, his book about the lives and brand-affinities of the world's 8- to 14-year-olds, he expresses frank amazement and even regret over what marketers like him have wrought:

> Becoming rich, famous and popular is the goal for a substantial number of today's tweens who want to be discovered and thus saved from a world of boredom ... Somehow the brand has an ability to elevate them above the grayness of the everyday and add colour to their lives ... Unless you adopt the values embodied in the brand, you'll be a nobody ... Tweens choose their friends by the clothes they wear, the music they listen to and the electronic games they play ... It was initially the advertisers who envisioned turning brand into a form of religion, to increase their sales. And it has worked.

According to Lindstrom, 75 percent of American tweens want to be rich; along with people from India, they top the world charts for this indicator of materialism. And what do kids want to do with the money? They want to conform to commercially determined standards of appearance. American kids lead the world in thinking that they are defined not by who they are but by the brands of clothing they wear.[752]

Ad agency president Nancy Shalek describes how advertising is designed to prey on a child's natural status insecurity:

> Advertising at its best is making people feel that without their product, you're a loser. Kids are very sensitive to that. If you tell them to buy something, they are resistant. But if you tell them they'll be a dork if they don't, you've got their attention. You open up emotional vulnerabilities, and it's easy to do with kids because they're the most vulnerable.[753]

Designer brands such as Dolce & Gabbana, Armani, and Dior have launched lines for children as young as grade-school age. In her disturbing exposé *Branded: The Buying and Selling of Teenagers*, Alissa Quart follows Josie, a trend-leading cool-hunter for the tween fashion brand Delia*s. Josie offered this advice as she worked a Manhattan movie line: "If you are popular and outgoing, you can get away with wearing clothes without name brands. But [not] if you are second-tier socially." Echoes 13-year-old Becky Gilker, "If you don't wear those things you get criticized. The better brands you wear, the more popular you are."[754] A study of tweens in the Midwest shows that one-third are bullied because they wear clothing with the wrong labels. School guidance counselors report friendships being destroyed in fights over clothing brands.

To get the money to buy the right things, some middle-class teen girls go so far as to sell their bodies. "Compared to three years ago, we've seen a 70 percent increase in kids from middle- to upper-middle-class backgrounds," said Frank Barnaba, who works with the Justice Department and the FBI in getting help for sexually exploited kids. Bob Flores, who heads the Justice Department's Office of Juvenile Justice and Delinquency Prevention, confirms what Barnaba has found: "We've got kids in every major city and in suburbia all over the place being prostituted." One 17-year-old, who lives with her wealthy parents in an upscale zip code, was charging $400 to strip for men in hotel rooms and says, "Sex is a small price to pay for the freedom to spend money on what I want."[755]

Allen Kanner, a clinical psychologist who treats emotional disorders in children from both the inner city and affluent suburbs, has found in both groups an increasing, insatiable materialism. Until the early 1990s, kids spoke of their desires to become doctors, astronauts, athletes, and performing artists. Of today's kids, says Kanner, "[they] all say they want to make money. When they talk about their friends, they talk about the clothes they wear, the designer labels they wear, not the person's human qualities."[756] Today, the favorite pastime of 93 percent of teen girls is shopping. As adults, so dedicated have we become to our role as consumers that the average female worker's week includes six hours of shopping, but only forty minutes to play with her children.[757]

America's most prolific researcher on the psychology of materialism, Tim Kasser, has amassed data from dozens of studies on people in thirteen nations and found that, for all age groups and initial income levels, people whose primary life goals involve money, possessions, image, or status have lower self-esteem, higher insecurity, and shorter and more turbulent love and friend relationships. Materialists also have less empathy and are more likely to use their friends to get ahead. They are motivated by guilt and external pressure rather than internal commitment and the inherent pleasure of a pursuit. Materialists are more likely to engage in antisocial acts and to compete rather than cooperate. There is as yet no proof of causality, but there is little evidence that money buys happiness.[758] Indeed, sadness seems to increase spending. In a widely reported study, when two groups of research participants watched a neutral versus a sad video clip, those primed by the sadness-inducing clip were willing to spend four times more money for the same small consumer product. The study authors also found that sadness increases self-focus, the link found by Kasser to increased materialist desires.[759]

Kathleen Vohs, a marketing professor at the University of Minnesota, and her co-workers ran a series of nine simple and ingenious experiments, showing that subconscious reminders of the concept of money are linked to statistically large changes in behavior. In one experiment, she split people into two groups, one tasked with descrambling phrases including references to money, while the other group had neutral phrases. All were given two dollars apiece in quarters for their work. After a fake debriefing at what they thought was the end of the experiment, participants were asked to make a contribution to a student benefit fund. Those who had been reminded of money gave away half as many of their quarters.

In another experiment, Vohs gave a group of participants a dummy online survey, followed by a screensaver showing money floating underwater. Two control groups were given the same dummy surveys but neutral screensavers. After completing their surveys, participants were asked to set up two chairs for a chat with another participant. Those who had been reminded of money placed the chairs fifty percent farther apart than those who had not. People given subconscious reminders of money in other experiments were far more likely to choose to work alone, to work more persistently, and to offer less help to others.[760] In our consumer culture, we are bombarded with reminders of the value of money and of material goods. As a result, we have become more individualistic, self-reliant, and selfish than we would be if other messages dominated.

Boston Consulting Group principals Neil Fiske and Michael Silverstein are cheerleaders for the recent trend among middle-class consumers to trade up to luxury brands. They dispute that luxury-goods spending growth is driven by "mindless emulation," but rather by a desire to enhance pleasure, express individuality, explore new experiences, and engage in a form of consumer community. I agree that these are real and positive phenomena, but the authors do concede a substantial dark side to upscaling. Their survey of 2,300 consumers earning $50,000 and up found the group "highly aspirational *and* stressed, disconnected, and anxious." Fewer than four in ten respondents reported that they "feel like a part of my community," "have the right balance in my life," or "have a lot of close friends." Only three in ten were happy with their personal appearance and only 18 percent were happy in their romantic relationships.[761] One $50,000-a-year construction worker who scrimped for a year to own his set of $3,000 Callaway titanium-faced golf clubs admitted, "the real reason I bought them is that they make me feel rich." Our acquisition binge is a better reflection of our deficit in social capital than it is of our need for more material goods. Three in four Viking luxury cooktops installed are never used to cook.[762] The $50,000 tower room in my home is a nice showpiece and has a great view in all directions, but I never use it because I have no time. Commercial culture has preyed on our need for status and bulldozed America into a debt-propelled, competitive materialism.

COMPETITIVE CONSUMPTION

People first visiting my home always marvel at the 270-degree mountain views, gushing that my perch above such beauty must free my creativity and spiritual awareness. But other than those times when I can share the lovely landscape with friends, my view does none of those things for me, because I take it for granted and have adjusted my expectations to it. In the same way, most find that salary bonuses, leather seats, and even standing ovations devolve over time from being intoxicating rewards, to things we expect, and finally to ordinary necessities.

The scientific literature brims with evidence that satisfaction gained from new possessions or achievements largely evaporates over time.[763] A survey of lottery winners found that, after a year or two, they were not any more happy than nonwinners and were actually less fulfilled by seven different ordinary activities such as talking with friends, hearing a joke, eating breakfast, or getting a compliment. The winners' raised expectations made fulfillment harder to achieve as they had stepped up the ladder of difficulty.[764] As we rise, we replace our old goals with new and higher material or status goals, but we receive little long-term payoff in happiness if we attain them. Psychologists call this frustrating process the "hedonic treadmill."

When we move up the ladder of material success, we also raise the benchmark for all those who include us in their reference group. The psychological need for more visible success in the form of conspicuous consumption ripples out to neighbors who might otherwise have found contentment, as I once did, in my aluminum-sided duplex on Elm Street, across from a Vermont rail yard. Even the cognitive elite is not immune from this process. Harvard School of Public Health grad students and faculty were asked whether they would prefer to earn (a) $50,000 where others earn half that, or (b) $100,000 where others earn twice as much. Fifty-six percent preferred choice (a), earning relatively more but absolutely less. The study also asked the same type of question about educational attainment. Again, half of the respondents preferred a world where they had fewer degrees but more relative to others.[765] A recent survey of 16,000 employees found that satisfaction with any given level of income is lower when more people in your work group earn more than you do.[766]

A recent, beautifully designed brain-imaging experiment has, for the first time, found the biologic basis for our preference for higher relative rather than absolute incomes. Pairs of subjects, their heads in million-dollar fMRI machines, played and won an identical game, but were informed that they were being given different monetary prizes. Over the following ten seconds, the brain response in the ventral striatum, a key part of the reward center, was highest for the person getting the highest relative payment, independent of the amount of the actual payment.[767] We think we will be happier, not with more, but with more than others around us. We want to one-up the Joneses rather than satisfy any objective need.

Economists have conclusively demonstrated that this same process limits the aggregate happiness of entire nations. Once a nation reaches a threshold level of material comfort—about $15,000 in income per person—there is virtually no increase in average life-satisfaction that correlates with further increases in income. In the U.S., there is no increase in self-reported happiness once family income rises above $50,000. When measured by the amount of time each day that a person is happy, there is almost zero relationship between income and happiness.[768] Members of the *Forbes 400* list of wealthiest Americans, the Inuits of northern Greenland, and Kenyans living in dung huts without electricity or running water all report the same level of satisfaction with their lives. Though these groups have radically disparate material endowments, life-satisfaction for each is 5.7 or 5.8 on a scale of 1 to 7—all slightly greater than for the average American.[769]

Elizabeth Warren and Amelia Warren Tyagi challenge some of these findings, arguing in their thoroughly documented book, *The Two Income Trap*, that competitive consumption is a myth. Rising middle-class financial duress stems from parents' desire for the safe neighborhoods and good schools that can be found only where housing costs and property taxes are higher. The dual incomes required to pay for more costly housing drives the need for spending on daycare and a second car. The authors calculate that, after paying for these extras, the dual-income family has four percent less discretionary income than the single-income family did thirty years earlier.[770]

But families do not require wall-size televisions and in-dash navigation systems. Families do not require new homes with three times the floor area per occupant than they did fifty years ago. There is no doubt that land scarcity in desired neighborhoods and increases in the quality and size of homes have all contributed to the rising share of family income consumed by housing and property taxes. But size, quality, and the resulting higher taxes are all choices made by purchasers. Our family garages are stuffed with entirely new categories of possessions we barely use, forcing our cars out onto driveways and streets and making expensive three-car garages and walk-in attics new necessities. In the area where I live, the material glut overflows into a chain of secondhand stores that cannot operate without 20-yard compactors to dispose of the huge excess contributions of unwanted clothing, toys, and furniture—beyond what the store could ever sell. Craigslist has postings for free items by the tens of thousands. The material deluge pours out over our nation's boundaries onto container ships loaded with mountains of perfectly functional computers and cell phones bound to India for scrap.

This hyper-abundance did not exist 30 years ago. Today, we are rushing upscale to Starbucks and BMW to get better-quality items and a temporary status booster shot. The coffee and the car are genuinely better. But as we buy and display them, we also downgrade the status of those among us who buy Dunkin' Donuts and Dodge. When they see what we buy, we force them to climb onto the treadmill and the vicious cycle escalates, ending for almost everyone in status defeat.

THE COST OF PERCEIVED INEQUALITY

The United States has the greatest domestic income inequality among the 22 most advanced nations.[771] But apart from this fact, why does the recent literature show that the medical and psychological burdens of inequality at any level are so much higher in America? Great inequality has prevailed elsewhere in the world and at other times in history, but is not associated with the high levels of personal status and social health disorders we endure in America. Are these problems explained by inequality in actual status—or by inequality in perceived status?

To help explore that question, consider, first, some tasty data points on increasing income inequality in America. Between 1982 and 2001, the top 20 percent of households snared 89 percent of all gains in net-worth and 67 percent of all gains in income. The top one percent enjoyed a net-worth increase of 63 percent. The bottom 40 percent suffered a decline in net worth of 44 percent.[772] Over the twelve years ending in 2002, for every one additional income dollar scored by the bottom 90 percent of Americans, the top 14,000 households took in an extra $18,000.[773]

As of 2006, economic inequality between the classes had exceeded the peak that our nation last reached in 1928. Figure 8.1 shows the increasing share of total personal income captured by top income groups. Since 1975, when equality was greatest over the past century, the top 1 percent has increased its share of all income by 2.5 times. The share earned by the top tenth of one percent is up by 4.5 times; the share of the top hundredth of one percent is up by 6.5 times.[774] Edward Wolff, who makes inequality research his specialty, predicts that these wealth and income gaps will widen further in coming years.[775] The steep rate of income gain at the top (but nowhere else) permits the widely advertised but soaringly inaccessible material benchmarks we sampled in Chapter 4.

Figure 8.1

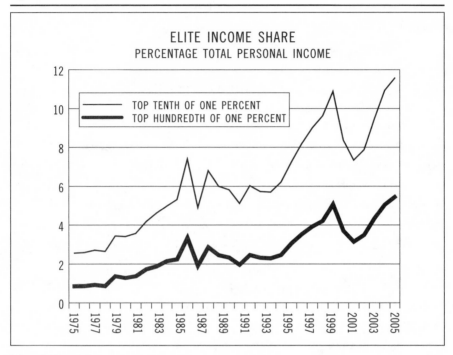

Data used with permission.

To add insult to inequality, American families have also become subject to greater income volatility, a measure of the risk of sharp and unexpected income changes in any one year. Income volatility more than tripled between the early 1970s and the late 1990s.[776] Like income inequality and income volatility, health inequality has also increased over past decades. While premature mortality has declined for all races and income groups over the past four decades, the mortality (and therefore, health) disparities between the highest and lowest income groups have increased sharply—for whites, from equity in 1960 to 60-percent greater premature-death rates in 2000.[777]

It is no wonder that perceived inequality is also on the rise. Since 1988, Americans perceiving themselves to be members of the economically disadvantaged "have-nots" increased from 17 to 31 percent of us. Over this period, those viewing America as divided into haves and have-nots increased from 26 to 37 percent.[778] Even the bottom third of the top-one-percent Americans—those with annual earnings averaging about half a million dollars—describe

American society as unfair. About one-third of us, including some who are wealthy, are psychologically wounded by perceived inequality.

There is little doubt in the literature that, at the individual level, low status in income, social class, and education are causes of poorer physical health and shorter lifespan, even for those who have lifelong access to quality medical care. But the relationships among income inequality, perceived inequality, and general-population happiness and health have required more work to understand.

Economists have recently joined psychologists and doctors to firmly establish the link among income inequality, happiness, and health. Andrew Oswald, a University of Warwick economist, and David Blanchflower, a Dartmouth College economist and member of the Bank of England's interest-rate-setting monetary policy committee, have plowed this new ground in several studies. They found a moderately strong link between income inequality and happiness. The greater the inequality within an American state, the greater the unhappiness among its inhabitants. In another study among European nations, Blanchflower and Oswald found an unambiguous link between self-reported happiness, high blood pressure, and blood cortisol levels. The citizens of happier nations have markedly lower blood pressure. Given that high blood pressure is a strong predictor of heart disease, we can safely say that efforts in the tiny Asian nation of Bhutan to measure and improve what it calls its "Gross Domestic Happiness" will generate a payoff in reduced healthcare costs.[779]

Crime is probably a cost not of actual poverty but of perceived inequality. John Lynch, a McGill University social epidemiologist, and his co-authors analyzed 98 peer-reviewed studies on income inequality, general-population health, and crime, finding a solid relationship between income inequality and the incidence of crime, particularly murder.[780] Economists at the World Bank performed a rigorous statistical analysis of crime rates in 39 nations over three decades, carefully controlling for potential explanatory variables such as absolute income level, ethnic diversity, police per capita, and young male population share. These economists found that income inequality is a strong predictor of and a cause of higher homicide and robbery rates, both among and within countries.[781] Among our fifty states, however, poverty has only a weak statistical connection with violent and property crime.[782]

To complicate matters, when Lynch examined data for nations and communities around the world, he found only mixed evidence for a link between income inequality and population health—except in the United States. The link between inequality and health is virtually nonexistent in wealthy social democracies such as northern Europe and Canada. The current inequality-health relationship is not stronger anywhere in the world than among states and cities within the United States. In a study of 282 American cities, Lynch and University of Michigan health statistician George Kaplan found that residents of places with wider economic disparities are less healthy. Regardless of their actual income, greater inequality is associated with poorer health for all income groups—including the wealthy. Most surprisingly, for every income group, including the wealthy, it is healthier to live in a low-income, low-inequality city than in a high-income, high-inequality one. To explain this, Lynch and his co-authors speculate that "the quality of the psychosocial environment" can buffer the harmful perceived effects of actual inequality.[783] I believe that the stronger social capital in places like Canada or Norway may be that buffer. We do not know whether this stronger social capital creates the political support for, or is a consequence of, those nations' expansive social welfare systems. I believe the former.

To check the Lynch-Kaplan findings, Marilyn Winkleby and her Stanford School of Medicine colleagues tracked mortality among 8,000 men and women in eighty California neighborhoods over seventeen years. Each individual and neighborhood was classified into high, middle, and low socio-economic status (SES), as measured by levels of personal income and education. Indeed, the risk of death among low-SES people living in high-SES neighborhoods was about 70-percent higher than when they lived in low-SES neighborhoods. Among all nine combinations of individual and neighborhood class, low-SES individuals living in high-SES neighborhoods fared worst. Confoundingly, low-SES people had generally greater access to healthcare and information resources by living in the high-SES neighborhoods. These findings did not change appreciably after the data were statistically adjusted for risk factors such as age, smoking, alcohol use, heart disease, and obesity. The authors conclude that the only plausible explanations are psychosocial, such as higher perceived inequality and the sense of deprivation that comes from having low relative status.[784] Another study looking at California women found that those who perceived themselves as having lower status in their community—regardless of their actual status—suffered increased anxiety, stress, pessimism, and blood pressure.[785]

Lynch dug even deeper and checked for *changes in the strength* over time of the link between inequality and general-population health. Lynch compared economic inequality and age-at-death among the fifty U.S. states over the past six decades. Age-at-death is a good proxy for population health status.[786] Figure 8.2 presents the Lynch data. In the U.S., income inequality has become an increasingly strong predictor of general-population health since the 1960s. The data in Figure 8.2 show that, over the last four decades, some unidentified feature of American inequality—but not rising inequality itself—has grown more toxic, with that toxicity increasing from none to strong. (An r-value of zero indicates no relationship; 0.4 or higher is considered strong in the social sciences.) Let's keep looking for what the cause might be.

Figure 8.2

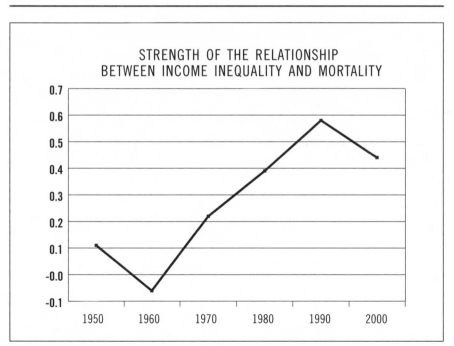

r-value of the Gini inequality index compared with all causes, age-adjusted mortality among the 50 states.

Lynch JW, Smith GD, Harper S and Hillemeier M, "Is Income Inequality a Determinant of Population Health? Part 2. U.S. National and Regional Trends in Income Inequality and Age- and Cause-Specific Mortality," *Milbank Quarterly*, June, 2004; 82(2):355–400, Table 3.

Over the past twenty-five years, Michael Marmot, chair of the World Health Organization's Commission on Social Determinants of Health, has made rigorous study of the effect of social status on human health, specifically among British civil servants. Marmot found that white-collar bureaucrats who are perfectly well-fed and well-housed and who have full access to medical care—but who have lower job rankings—live shorter, less healthy lives. Marmot's work leads us to the conclusion that highly ranked people live longer and healthier lives because they enjoy personal power and autonomy.

In 2006, Marmot co-authored one of the year's most acutely perplexing studies. Adjusted for purchasing power, Americans spend nearly 2.5 times more on healthcare per capita than the British. Yet as shown in Table 8.1, an upper-income, white American aged 55–64 is 75-percent more likely to suffer heart disease or cancer and 53-percent more likely to suffer diabetes than a similar English person. Both groups have near-universal access to healthcare and, via statistical adjustment, both are equally likely to be smokers, heavy drinkers, or obese. This gap in health status is similar for all income groups. Poorer access to healthcare and higher incidence of disease earlier in life among high earners in the U.S., along with other potential explanations, have too small an effect to explain America's stunningly worse health status.[787]

Table 8.1: Risk-Adjusted Health Status for High-Income Persons, Ages 55–64

Percent Lifetime Prevalence

	U.S.	England	U.S. Greater By %
All heart disease	12.1	6.9	75
Cancer	9.5	5.5	73
Diabetes	9.2	6.0	53
Heart attack	3.3	2.5	32
Hypertension	38.2	31.6	21
Stroke	1.8	1.6	13
Lung disease	5.1	4.8	6

James Banks, Michael Marmot, Zoe Oldfield, and James P. Smith, "Disease and Disadvantage in the United States and in England," *Journal of the American Medical Association*, May 3, 2006; 295(17):2037–45

Harvard social epidemiologists Ichiro Kawachi and Bruce Kennedy suggest that highly unequal social and economic settings engender resentful status comparisons and the psychological stresses underlying these health disparities.[788] Richard Wilkinson, a professor of epidemiology and public health at Britain's University of Nottingham Medical School, who published the seminal paper on social epidemiology in 1992, thinks it "likely that reducing the burden of low social status would do more than any other policy for improving national standards of health."[789] Kawachi, Kennedy, and Wilkinson's speculations probably overreach. But they would be on the mark if they were to finger the OverSuccessed America that emerged between 1965 and 1980, the America that has taxed our physical and psychological health in decades since.

Though egalitarians such as Wilkinson wish it otherwise, research has shown that government-provided income support and free healthcare do not overcome the adverse health effects of low status rank. Something more immutable is at work. Nancy Adler, a professor of medical psychology who chairs the MacArthur Foundation Network on SES and Health, examined a random sample of 500 Americans and another of over 10,000 London white-collar workers. She found that self-perceived social-status differences were more important determinants of health than actual status differences.[790] Stanford's Robert Sapolsky, who has spent a career researching primate social stress, often recounts a study of a group of nuns born into differing social and economic rank. The nuns all took their vows as young adults, subsequently living through their adult lives with identical food, housing, healthcare, and work hours. Amazingly, even in old age, their disease, dementia, and longevity were all tightly correlated with their social status as children 50 years earlier. Something as intangible as perceived status has a critical impact on human well-being.

In the rich nations, and particularly in America, the psychological burden of perceived status deprivation is greater than that of actual poverty and actual inequality. The effects of perceived status differences cannot be erased by income-equalizing tax policies, free healthcare for all, or even perfect material equality. Of course, perfect equality in material and social rank are not possible and not desirable. As I discussed in Chapter 1, status hierarchies are a healthy and necessary feature of properly functioning groups. Without rank, we would waste too much time making decisions and be embroiled constantly in physically dangerous power contests. But our brains are not evolved to indifferently accept prolonged, in-your-face status deprivation. As we'll see in this book's last chapter, both the cause and cure for OverSuccess can be found in the voluntary social and cultural norms that guide how we treat our neighbors of differing rank. It's the culture, stupid.

SWAMPED BY DEBT

Over the past few decades, Americans have become willing to absorb strikingly higher financial risk in their pursuit of OverSuccess. The invention of ingenious and useful new financial instruments is a partial and favorable explanation. Some of these instruments, as we discovered in the wake of the 2006–2008 housing bubble collapse, are far from benign and are evidence of the lengths to which OverSuccessed players in the financial industry will go to advance their careers and quarterly profits at the expense of customers, stockholders, and the entire U.S. economy. But it is enveloping materialism and the death of delayed gratification that are at the root of the rise of debt. Starting in the early 1980s, household, corporate, and government debt growth abruptly accelerated, saddling today's America with the most highly leveraged major economy in world history. Our total debt far exceeds our national assets, and we continue to consume far more than we earn. There will be hell to pay for this unsustainable borrowing binge.

In the early 2000s—when the handwriting was already boldfaced on the wall—we staved off a deflationary pop in the debt bubble only with another massive new surge in borrowing. Between then and mid-2007, zero-percent auto financing, 100-percent loan-to-value mortgages, and high-risk lending to people of blatantly marginal creditworthiness were the tottering props under our debt-fueled consumer economy. Since the 1965 to 1980 turning point, the indicators of OverSuccessed borrowing and lending have progressively worsened for households:

Personal savings

- Between 1950 and 1984, our personal savings rate, as a percentage of disposable personal income, averaged just under nine percent. Savings rates then plunged in an approximately straight line to the present zero percent. Recent savings rates are the lowest since the Great Depression.[791]
- As of 2004, median family financial assets of any kind totaled just $23,000.
- Half of all American households have *zero* retirement savings.[792]

Household debt-to-asset ratio

- The total household debt-to-asset ratio for the average family rose in a nearly straight line, tripling from 6 percent in 1950 to 19 percent in 2006.[793]

Household debt-to-income ratios

- Total household debt including mortgages, as a percentage of disposable personal income, rose from 33 percent in 1950 to a record 128 percent today, with a surge in the ratio starting in 1984.[794]
- Total household debt service including mortgages, as a percentage of disposable personal income, rose from 9 percent in 1950 to over 14 percent today, the highest percentage in U.S. history.[795]
- Unlike during the recessions of 1975, 1980, and 1991, Americans continued to spend, rather than rebuild, their balance sheets during and after the recession of 2001.[796]

Personal bankruptcy (as of just before the 2005 change in the bankruptcy law)

- Rates increased by almost 400 percent since 1981, reaching the highest levels since the Great Depression, with almost 1.6 million filings in 2004.[797]
- For the decade ending 2001, most of the growth in the number of personal bankruptcies was among baby boomers aged 35 to 54.[798]

Home mortgage foreclosures (as of just before the housing bubble popped)

- These rates have increased by 15 times since the 1950s.[799]

- In 1975, the median first-time homebuyer provided 18 percent of a house's purchase price in cash. That figure recently bottomed at two percent, when forty-five percent of borrowers put no money down.[800]
- Just before the housing bubble popped in 2006, over sixty percent of newly originated California home loans were interest only.[801]

The explosion of credit cards

- In aggregate, we carry almost eight credit cards per household for a total of 900 million nationwide. The average household received over 70 junk-mail credit-card solicitations in 2006.[802]
- Nearly half of households carry credit-card debt. Sixty percent of households with credit-card debt (which averages $5,100 per household and has the highest interest rate of any type of consumer debt) do not pay it off at the end of the month.[803]
- Half of all people taking on more credit-card debt do so because their spending exceeds their income. Customers who pay off their balance in full each month, thereby incurring no fees or interest, are called "deadbeats" by industry insiders.
- Two-in-three bankruptcy filers acknowledge poor money management or excessive spending (and only one-in-three, loss of income or high medical bills) as the causes. Credit card lenders were largely responsible for creating the bankruptcy explosion by pushing out pre-approved cards to consumers with increasingly marginal credit. Because it became more difficult for consumers to evade past debts, the 2005 bankruptcy law should have reduced borrowing but did not because consumers remained shortsighted and took advantage of easier credit. [804]

The weight of debt on the young

- Today's 20-somethings are the most indebted younger generation in U.S. history. The average 25–34-year-old household is now spending 24 percent of its income on debt payments. For the average 18–24-year-old, that figure is nearly thirty percent, double the levels of 1992.[805]

Figure 8.3

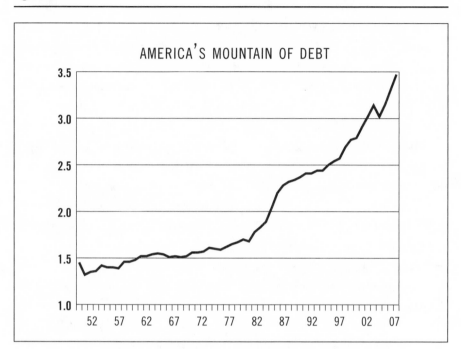

Total household, corporate, and government debt outstanding divided by Gross Domestic Product, 1950–2007

- The average undergraduate is saddled with almost $20,000 in debt; the graduate with a professional degree has $91,000.[806]
- For young adults, increased debt is caused by the trend of living large now rather than saving, and by the high costs of getting to the first rung of the career ladder. Low salaries and the temporary nature of entry-level jobs often do not support high education-debt payments and high living costs in the urban areas offering better jobs.[807]

For the entire American economy, total household, business, and government debt stood at $49 trillion at the end of 2007. As shown in Figure 8.3, this is a record 347 percent of gross domestic product and double the level of debt in 1981. Most ominously, debt as a percentage of GDP now exceeds the previous record 264 percent set early in the Great Depression.[808] The American government has set the example for its citizens in its profligate accumulation of debt. Since 1969, when it was in approximate balance, federal spending has topped federal revenue every year but two.[809] The federal government's debt load is increasing by over one billion dollars a day. By late 2007, America's combined trade and federal budget deficits reached a staggering eight percent of GDP. Over just the past two decades, we have metamorphosed from the world's largest creditor to the world's largest debtor; we now consume 75 percent of the entire world's savings surplus. The International Monetary Fund warns that U.S. consumption is soaking up an unsustainable portion of the world's investable capital and that U.S. indebtedness threatens the stability of the entire world economy.[810] This type of IMF warning was previously meted out to third-world kleptocracies, not the world's largest economy.

Worse, our $49 trillion in total household, business, and government debt as reported by the Federal Reserve Board deeply understates America's borrow-and-spend addiction. The data do not include the present value of unfunded future federal liabilities, of which Medicare, Medicaid, and Social Security comprise the lion's share, at $66 trillion. Seventeen trillion of this is the prescription drug benefit, rammed through Congress in the middle of the night in 2003 by politicians from both parties.[811] America's actual liabilities therefore total at least $115 trillion—a total burden of about $370,000 for every American man, women, and child and far in excess of national assets. On the day that foreign lenders grow leery of providing our daily $2 billion net borrowing fix, America will be bankrupt.

In 2002, the Treasury Department commissioned the original version of the study that quantified the federal "fiscal gap," the unfunded future Medicare, Medicaid, and Social Security liability. The study was censored by the Bush Administration before its publication, its unpalatable conclusions emerging almost a year later only when the Federal Reserve Bank of Cleveland published the authors' analysis. The Clinton Administration censored a similar study in 1994.[812] My party, the GOP, once the party of fiscal responsibility, in 2005 proposed borrowing yet another trillion dollars to reform Social Security, calling it privatization. But like the prescription drug benefit, it was just another expansion of the program and its unfunded costs.[813] The Democrats' contribution to reform is to make certain that no one interested in public office dares mention the obvious need for benefit cuts.

Washington is doing just as the public wishes. By 62 to 36 percent, voters prefer more spending on education and healthcare over balancing the budget.[814] Any pol with the spinal calcium to tell the whole truth about America's actuarial holocaust would be repaid with millions of dollars of attack ads from labor unions and the AARP. As shown by the slope in Figure 8.3, America's goals changed in the early 1980s. We decided to live dangerously beyond our means without regard to the future. With the support of both political parties and a solid majority of the public, we are spending our toddlers into a mountain of debt so that we can have now what we cannot possibly afford.

GAMBLING FOR SUCCESS

The extraordinary growth of the gambling industry is more compelling evidence of the penetration of OverSuccessed values in America. Gamblers are lured in by the false hope of escape from financial Dullsville, and casino owners purposefully addict their own customers to bankrupt them. Since 1991, when legalized casinos spread outward from Las Vegas and Atlantic City, the amount Americans lose on all betting, including lotteries, casinos, and racetracks, has increased from $27 billion to an estimated $91 billion in 2007.[815] Americans now spend more money on gambling than on movies, videos, DVDs, music, and books combined.

Many people gamble for recreation and are not harmed financially or psychologically by their losses. I love the Las Vegas strip, as dazzling as Times Square, but clean and warm year-round, the interior design and restaurants in its billion-dollar casinos sometimes superb. But there are now over 1,000 casinos and 800,000 video slot machines in the U.S., more than anywhere else in the world. Entirely unlike those on the strip, most casinos are factory-like, windowless places, filled by rows of people sitting for hours on padded barstools monotonously pushing the button on a random-number generator. Many gamble in a delusional and cheerless effort to escape financial hardship. Of people earning less than $20,000 per year, 45 percent purchased an average of $552 in lottery tickets over the past year.[816] To gamble away $552 of an income of under $20,000 is an act of desperation, not casual entertainment, as the gambling industry would have us believe. Pay a Friday evening visit to a convenience store in a working-class neighborhood and watch the faces of people whose hard-earned food money and dreams of escape from paycheck-to-paycheck living evaporate with a forearm's length of losing scratch tickets.

At least three million American adults gambled last year because they are addicted to it.[817] As we saw in Chapter 2, many addictions involve the same brain regions and neurochemicals. Pathologic gamblers and drug addicts share a deficient response in their brains' dopamine reward systems.[818] Addictions to alcohol, cocaine, and gambling are equally powerful and destructive in their effects on addicts' lives and those of their families, and on our workplaces and communities. Some addicts now play in $35 reusable diapers specifically designed to absorb nine cups of urine, worn so that these gamblers don't need to leave their machines to go to the bathroom for an entire night.[819] Over roughly three years, a gambling addict will spiral downward in a pattern of increased debt, reduced workplace productivity, job loss, theft and embezzlement, bankruptcy, depression, medical problems, family violence, divorce, violent crime, and suicide. The total social and economic cost of gambling addiction is estimated to be $32 to $54 billion, half the societal cost of drug abuse.[820]

The social impact of these personal tragedies can be seen in the communities surrounding casinos. Walk a block beyond the casinos in Atlantic City to see the pawn shops and shuttered businesses. The ads illustrating family fun leave out the family misery. Nevada's suicide, bankruptcy, and child-abuse rates are all among the worst in the nation.[821] Rates of aggravated assault, rape, robbery, larceny, burglary, and auto theft increase by an average of eight percent in counties with a casino.[822] Anecdotes put a face on the misery: an Illinois woman suffocated her seven-week-old child to collect insurance money to feed the slot machines. A Mississippi woman killed her husband and mother in a suicide pact made in despair over her gambling debts. A Massachusetts school principal stole $20,000 in student funds to support his habit. Gambling addict Uno Kim bound, drugged, and murdered two elderly brothers, Theodore and Gury Joseph, ransacked their home for $30,000 in cash, and drove straight to the Mohegan Sun Casino in Connecticut to pay off his gambling debts.[823] News stories on tragedies like these number in the thousands.[824]

I often debate spokespeople from the "gaming" industry, so renamed by its public relations people. No argument, no data, no hardship story will deflect these flaks from their chant that gambling is voluntary and that government should not restrict personal freedoms. Their rhetoric about freedom is nakedly cynical. They fill statehouses across the nation with their lobbyists, who beg for monopoly franchises and restrictions on competition. They plead innocence regarding the hidden trick behind many of their video slot machines, whose simulated reels stop mid-play on a win for 1/20th of a second, too short for conscious perception, long enough to subliminally trick the customers they will bankrupt into thinking they are winners.[825] Gambling is not voluntary for addicts. About half of casino profits are extracted from problem and pathologically addicted gamblers, who are not free to stop themselves.[826] The Joseph brothers and the Illinois infant did not die voluntarily.

The wildfire legalization of gambling, in the face of the incontestable science establishing its social harm, calls into question the ethics of gambling-industry management and the politicians who vote to legalize it. Their ethical blinkering parallels the media industry's nonresponsiveness to research proving the link between media violence and real violence. Politicians wave pitchforks at drug dealers who prey on the weak dopamine systems of meth addicts, even as they pander to gambling-industry campaign contributors whose video slot machines prey on those same dopamine systems. Few of our leaders are even embarrassed by the double standard.

OVERWORKED?

Controversy swirls around the claim that Americans are overworked. There is no dispute that working hours became dramatically more humane between 1900 and the mid-1960s. Since then, depending on the data source and how it is analyzed, some studies show that the average individual workweek has increased, while some show a slight decrease. But there is no dispute that *household* total hours worked have increased sharply. Is it because life's necessities have become more costly, that these necessities (such as a college education for the kids, two cars, and a computer) have increased in number and sophistication, or that our aspirational benchmarks have gone global? The answer is probably all three.

Today, nearly eight in ten working-age households have two breadwinners, double the percentage in 1970. Since 1989, driven by this massive trend toward dual incomes, the typical family has increased its paid work hours by thirteen percent.[827] Even among those with dual incomes, families are clocking more total paid work hours: 91 hours per week now, versus 81 hours in 1977. Combined daily personal time has shriveled since 1992 from 3.7 to 2.2 hours.[828] Total job-commuting time per household jumped by almost fifty percent since 1983.[829] Extreme commutes of three-hours-plus per day have almost doubled since 1990 to 3.4 million workers.[830]

But this huge increase in work hours is primarily a phenomenon of America's upper classes. Over the past few decades, the American workforce has become more bifurcated, with those nearer the bottom increasingly underemployed and those nearer the top increasingly overworked and overstressed. In the early 1980s, the bottom fifth of earners were most likely to clock 50 or more hours a week. Today, the situation has reversed entirely, with the top fifth by income, education, and job responsibility over twice as likely to work long hours as the bottom. Among full-time, college-educated males, long hours have increased from 22 to 31 percent.

The new badge of workplace OverSuccess for those at or near the top is the "extreme job," thoroughly characterized by an extensive Harvard Business School study. You've got an extreme job if you are always on, have 24/7 duties, work at a radically accelerated pace, must perform what were once multiple jobs, experience unpredictable workflow, work across multiple time zones, constantly travel, and have a workweek of at least 60 hours. Of the top six percent of Americans by pay, six in ten work at least 50 hours per week. One in three of the high earners, the extreme workers, work at least 60 hours. Twenty percent of high earners now work over 70-hours-plus per week, a percentage that is up sharply over just five years ago.

People love these love-hate jobs not just because of the high pay, but because of the opportunity to excel in a high-impact arena and the intellectual excitement of working with other highly talented people. Overwhelmingly, the most important benefit extreme workers report is the "adrenaline rush." As in extreme sports culture, extreme workers rhapsodize about testing their limits and operating at the edge of their abilities. Many extreme jobholders report that their home lives have become a source of guilt because they find their best friends and their most stimulating relationships at work.

On the dark side, seven in ten extreme workers think that their work regimen hurts their health; two in three do not have time to get enough sleep or maintain their homes. Half do not have time for a satisfying sex life. The nearly half of extreme jobholders who work in globalized companies admit that they are too drained at the end of their day even to hold a conversation with their spouses. "My dad's always exhausted," says one teen, orphaned by an extreme job. "He's gone when I get up, and not back when I go to sleep." A young financial analyst describes his work as consuming his entire life. When he finishes his workday, he doesn't even bother leaving the office, except to sleep, eat, and bathe. One managing director at an investment bank routinely takes work calls in the middle of the night and spends so much time on the road that he sees his family only on weekends. Another extreme worker, an entertainment company creative director, "cannot remember" his last vacation; he describes his work as defining his entire identity and delegates his entire social life to staff. The load is so unsustainable that about half of extreme workers do not want to continue at their pace beyond another year.[831] Yet most of them do because quitting would leave them without a life.

The "winner-take-all" phenomenon, and the new primacy of meritocracy that I explored in Chapter 4, also drive the compulsion to overwork. Peter Kuhn of the University of California at Santa Barbara and Fernando A. Lozano of Pomona College found that changes in financial incentives have contributed to the growth of extreme work over the past twenty-five years. The big prizes for the long hours are available only at the top, and those prizes have become much larger. Individual and team performance incentives roughly doubled in pervasiveness among large companies since 1979. Job security protections have dropped by over half.[832]

Work life has become shoehorned into all hours of personal life by ubiquitous wireless connectivity, 24/7 e-mail, cell phones, and multi-disciplinary, project-based teams spanning the world's time zones that can summon an extreme jobholder to work at any hour. A McKinsey survey of top American executives found that 20 percent describe themselves as being borderline overwhelmed by the larger volumes of e-mail, phone messages, and meetings to which they are required to respond.[833] But while many extreme workers bemoan the extreme costs, many companies not only expect employees to overwork but boast of it, claiming it gives them their edge in the marketplace.

An ad for the accounting firm Grant Thornton shows a time-lapse scene of its office tower, with most of its lights staying on through the night—while windows in surrounding buildings go dark. The message is that Grant Thornton's employees know that analyzing a merger or responding to a regulatory emergency does not stop at five o'clock. Moans an IT slave whose job is to support the infrastructure necessary for these analysts, "Because of technology we can never leave work. We have lost our evenings, weekends, and vacations ... Pagers in the restaurant, cell phones on the beach, laptops in hotels? While HR professionals advise corporations on the need to balance work and life outside of the office, their admonitions are ignored."[834]

Americans are working harder than people in other countries and taking fewer vacations too. Whereas we worked about equal hours as those in the other advanced nations in the early 1970s, the average American adult now works fifty-percent more hours than does his or her French, German, or Italian counterpart.[835] According to the World Tourism Organization, Americans take only thirteen days of vacation each year, the fewest among the industrialized countries and half that of the next lowest nation. About half of American workers do not take all their allotted vacation time. One in three managers report that their bosses expect them to be accessible for work during vacation times. One in four managers return from vacations more stressed than before he or she left.[836]

The overtime for overwork has to come from someplace, and one of those places is family. Spouses in dual-income families with children spend twelve minutes a day talking with each other.[837] The average child spends *zero* minutes per week talking with the whole family and only 45 minutes with anyone in the family.[838] Sixty-seven percent of American workers say that they do not have enough time for their children; 63 percent say they do not have enough time for their spouses. In a three-year study following parents' self-rated stress and their children's illness symptoms and blood levels of immune function indicators, for each notch up on a scale of psychosocial stress in parents, children suffer a 40- to 70-percent increase in illness.[839] Asked about their number-one wish to improve their lives, children 8 to 18 want their parents to be less tired and stressed.[840]

The stress of overwork is getting to us. One in three Americans and one in four of those aged 35–54 describe themselves as suffering extreme stress over the prior month, naming work and money pressures as the top causes. Three in four of us say our pressure-cooker lives are causing physical and psychological symptoms such as fatigue, sleeplessness, headache, and anger. Thirty-six percent of us say that our stress makes us feel like crying.[841] "We've got a cultural problem with leisure time. We are an overworked, overtired, underpleasured culture," said Herbert Rappaport, a Temple University psychology professor.[842] "People are very emotional about work, and they're very negative about it," says David Rhodes, a principal at human-resource consultant Towers Perrin. "The biggest issue is clearly workload. People are feeling crushed."[843] Says former ad-agency CEO and now work/life consultant Mary Lou Quinlan, "I listen to women every day. Boomer women tell me that they're nearing the breaking point. The life that they bought into as college graduates in the late 1960s and early 1970s has brought them success but often not a lot of satisfaction."[844]

To compensate for the losses entailed by overwork, our workplaces have become substitute extended families. In her book *Married to the Job*, Silicon Valley psychologist Ilene Philipson reports the grim awakening among her patients forced by layoffs or demotions to confront the barrenness of their lives outside work. Work is so demanding that many professionals have abandoned all but a dry husk of personal life—no friends, no family relationships, no sex. Philipson nicely identifies companies that have caught on to their employees' unmet emotional needs. Common among *Fortune* magazine's 100 best employers are "not only corporate child care, free food, and weekly parties, but take-home meals, school tuition, full-service gyms, concierge services, support groups, company rock bands, paid time off for volunteer work, massage, sabbaticals, in-house stores, and all-company trips to tropical islands." The former office manager at a high-tech firm describes the traumatic loss of being fired from her employee-friendly workplace: "My husband was just a man and I know there'll be other ones out there. But I know there'll never be another PeoplePoint."[845]

But our workplace extended families can be outsourced, offshored, downsized, and bought or sold on an hour's notice. We put on brave faces at work, and our economy is stronger for it, but for many of us, our emotional foundations are rubble in a world of continuous high pressure and unpredictable organizational change. We Americans are unquestionably delivering the results demanded by the global economy. Corporate profits as a percentage of national income are highest in at least 80 years.[846] But, oddly, for those of us enabling these record profits, our success is not making us feel successful. A large survey taken in 1994 and again in 2005 found that the percentage of American workers describing themselves as very or extremely successful dropped from 40 to 28 percent. Those describing themselves as very productive dropped from 63 to 41 percent.[847] We are meeting higher performance benchmarks, but we feel increasingly like failures. For many of us, those benchmarks have become too demanding, are rising faster than we can rise to meet them, and allow no airspace for the sweet and slow times of life.

HURRY SICKNESS

The 24-hour business cycle has migrated from the coasts and into the heartland. Infants and the aged are the few among us not ruled by the imperative to work harder, do more, and go faster. To avoid being thought irrelevant, we must answer "very busy" to the casual question "how are you doing." From three-minute speed dates to three-second download times to 19-millisecond stock trading windows, our choice is to accelerate or to fail.

To win in the global economy, projects never stop and work teams live on three continents. Software engineers, investment bankers, and managing editors pass work like batons from Santa Clara to Düsseldorf to Hyderabad. Team coordination requires 6:00 a.m. and 10:00 p.m. conference calls. And time compression is not limited to multi-national companies. Most families I know with school-aged kids complain of the unceasing, seven-day pressure to cram in school, extracurricular activity, transportation coordination, homework, and meals. I find it insane that it often requires several weeks' notice for my son to schedule three hours of play with a friend who lives in the same town and goes to the same school.

To do more, given the immutability of the 24-hour day, requires abandoning adequate sleep. AOL executive Tina Sharkey drags herself from bed at 5:30 in the morning to prepare for reading with her son. "The only place I can give is sleep," she says.[848] According to the National Institutes of Health, the average American gets 6.8 hours of sleep a night, compared with 7.7 hours in

1970 and 8.8 hours in 1920. The trend has grown worse over just the past few years. According to the National Sleep Foundation, 40 percent of adults operate with less than seven hours of sleep on weekdays, up from 31 percent in 2001. Half of us report losing an average of three-quarters of an hour of sleep a night due to stress, caused primarily by work and money worries.[849] About half of us are not getting the seven- to eight-hour nightly rendezvous with the sandman considered optimal for most adults. America's overscheduled three-to ten-year-olds are operating on a nightly sleep deficit of about one hour.[850] More evidence of our sleep deficit can be seen in our electric meters: twenty years ago, U.S. electricity demand would spike after 7 a.m. when people rose for the day to shower and cook breakfast. Today, demand surges starting at 5 a.m. Here in New England, since 1985, the demand for electricity at 5 a.m. is up by 65 percent relative to midnight.

Insufficient sleep is linked to increased heart disease, obesity, diabetes, accidental injury, mood disorders, weakened sex drive, and immune system dysfunction. Mathematical, verbal, and general intelligence, attention span, reaction time, memory, and problem solving all suffer. Sleep deprivation is known to temporarily disrupt connections between the amygdala, which provides automatic processing of fear and other negative emotions, and the rational and tempering prefrontal cortex. Otherwise healthy sleep-deprived people react more like those with depression or post-traumatic stress disorder.[851] The greater our accumulated sleep debt, the greater our self-confidence that we are functioning unimpaired, making us more dangerous on the roads or in the operating room.[852] Sixty percent of adults acknowledge driving while drowsy during the past year, with 37 percent admitting to falling asleep behind the wheel.[853] The National Highway Traffic Safety Administration conservatively estimates that 100,000 crashes annually—ten to thirty percent of all accidents—are directly caused by driver fatigue. The result is an estimated 1,550 deaths (about 12 percent of the annual deaths caused by drunk driving), 71,000 injuries, and $12.5 billion in monetary losses from sleep-deprived driving alone.[854]

Hurry sickness has removed patience from our behavioral repertoire. CNN, in an attempt to keep viewers from reaching for their remotes during ads, tested viewer reaction to a digital timer at the bottom of the screen, counting down to the end of the ad in a blazing blur of hundredths of a second. Otis Elevator notes that the paint wears off their "DOOR CLOSE" buttons before any others because urban elevator riders can no longer tolerate the three-second mechanical delay.[855] The daily activity of information workers is so badly fragmented that they spend an average of only three sustained minutes on any task before being interrupted or switching tasks.[856] In the words of a junior investment banker, "Waiting an hour to respond to an e-mail is just not acceptable."[857]

Intensified competition among the 7,000 hedge funds has left derivatives traders less than one second to execute their trades before a rival snaps up a transient arbitrage opportunity. Dave Cummings would be out of business had he not moved Tradebot's computers from Kansas City to New York to shave 19/1000 of a second in execution time from his trades. Forty of his competitors followed him within a year.[858] Our BlackBerries, now worn like six-guns in hip holsters, provide cell phone, fax, e-mail, wireless broadband, TV, camera, and laptop computer functionality everywhere significant. A study of motorist behavior at suburban New York stop signs shows that the number of drivers not stopping at all rose from 29 percent in 1979 to 97 percent in 1996.[859] A quarter of motorists do not stop at stop signs, even when pedestrians are in the process of crossing the street.[860] My little maelstroms at five-minute PDF downloads (pre-broadband) would raise the sheetrock screws in my office, though obtaining such documents ten years ago would have consumed hours of library time. Food manufacturers now compete to shave precious seconds from American mealtimes with frozen, crustless peanut-butter-and-jelly sandwiches, yogurt in squeeze tubes, soup eaten from soda cans, dashboard and desktop meals—all costing several times more, consuming more resources, creating more trash, and compounding family budget stress.

We even talk faster to cram our thoughts down our shorter attention spans. Because Americans speak more rapidly than we did three decades ago, court stenographers have learned to work faster.[861] To sound cutting-edge, the TV series *The West Wing* purposefully sped up dialogue just beyond comprehensibility.[862] Symphony orchestras are playing louder and faster music, given that audiences have lost tolerance for anything languid or subtle. Fifty-four percent of us read our e-mail while talking on the phone.[863] Our handwriting has become illegible; I can barely read my own. We even have fun faster. The average Grand Canyon visitor now spends only 22 minutes at this world wonder before moving to the next spot in their tight vacation schedule. And while we tell pollsters that our most favorite activity is sex, we average only three minutes a day doing it.[864]

The pursuit of love unfolds on these same compressed time lines. Seattle-based HurryDate offers speed-dating parties where, for $35, you play musical tables at a restaurant as you squeeze in 25 back-to-back three-minute cold calls on Cupid. Given that our mate-qualification brain module sizes up a person of interest within as little as one-tenth of a second, speed dating is probably an improvement over meat shopping at bar scenes. *The Wall Street Journal* reports on the newest trend in dating for the acutely time constrained: the working date. Busy couples bring laptops and cell phones to each other's apartment, order in for dinner, and agree on a protocol to allow interruption, maybe breaking at 10:00 p.m. for actual conversion or sex.

Downtime is history. So are the rewards of sustained attention. Cooking, talking, eating, sex, viewing the miracles of nature—we do it all so fast that we miss the experience. Our desires grow faster than our gains. Tens of millions of us have narrowed our priorities and suffer growing relative deprivation, as OverSuccess robs us of the pleasures and purposes of ordinary life. If we are to tame OverSuccess, then living large will require us to live, for at least parts of most days, smaller and slower.

9

THE MALE BURDEN
OF OVERSUCCESS

I am seen, therefore I am.[865]
—Jean-Paul Sartre, 1972

MALES ARE AFFECTED BY status contests, failure, and OverSuccess differently than females, because males are conspicuously unlike females. During most of human history, whether as hunters or industrial laborers, males were able to benefit from their greater physical size, strength, and endurance because men could produce more. But over the past few decades in the United States, technology and offshoring have eliminated most work requiring the male advantages. The new knowledge, collaboration, and multi-tasking economy gives females the edge. Male psychology takes a bigger beating from the increased status challenges that are endemic to hyper-competition, escalating global success benchmarks, and our emotion-laden immersion in the cast of winners broadcast by commercial culture. For males at the top, life remains good—less so for the rest. One lapel-grabbing indicator of the problem is the increasing incidence of headline-grabbing acts of extreme violence by males subjected to severe status defeat.

MALE BRAINS, FEMALE BRAINS: NEUROCHEMISTRY RULES

No teacher, coach, or parent can miss the differing play styles of first-grade boys and girls. On average, boys play with objects, prefer win-lose games, are more physical, prefer larger groups, are more argumentative, and tend to form dominance hierarchies. Girls play in smaller, more cooperative, and more egalitarian groups, and excel in the emotional and interpersonal. As evolutionary theorists explain, males are superior at spatial and abstract tasks because ancient males were better able to hunt protein by predicting the trajectories of a hurled rock and a zigzagging rabbit. Females are better at recalling concrete knowledge because Paleolithic women were superior at identifying edible plants or the meaning of a baby's cry. Throughout their lives, females have consistently better social skills and are more sensitive to facial expressions. Men are detail-oriented systems thinkers who tinker until they find rules. Women quickly grasp situations using intuition and empathy.[866] Compared with men and boys, women and girls are better able to conceal their emotions, delay gratification, and resist temptations and distractions. Across all age groups, females are more prone to feelings of shame and guilt than males.[867]

As I shall show, these differences are immutably biological. The male Y-chromosome has a tiny gene dubbed SRY which very early in fetal life launches a cascade of irreversibly defining events, starting with the development of the testes which, at about eight weeks after conception, are busy pumping out the master male hormone, testosterone in concentrations as high as during puberty. Circulating throughout the developing fetus, testosterone makes the male body and the male brain. Simon Baron-Cohen, a cognitive neuroscientist at Cambridge University, measured levels of testosterone in the fetuses of boys and then followed their development for eight years. Higher fetal testosterone in boys is linked to less eye contact with their mothers at age one, a smaller vocabulary at age two, delayed social development at age four, and poorer social skills and reduced ability to understand others' viewpoints at age eight. Fetal testosterone slows the growth of the brain's left hemisphere and accelerates growth of the right.[868] Male brains are consistently asymmetrical, in a way visible even to the naked eye in brain scans; in females, the two hemi-spheres look alike.[869] Even on day one of life, before cultural biases could pos-sibly have any impact, Baron-Cohen found that boys look more at mechanical objects, girls at faces.

Virginia Tech's Harriet Hanlon and her co-workers studied brain activity in hundreds of normal children aged two months to 16 years. For girls, the brain areas involved in language and fine motor skills mature about six years earlier than they do in boys. For boys, the brain areas involved in spatial activ-ity mature about four years earlier.[870] Even hearing ability differs dramatically: "Every systematic evaluation of children's hearing has confirmed that girls hear significantly better than boys," says Leonard Sax, founder and director of the National Association for Single Sex Public Education.

The difference between male and female brains strongly influences pat-terns of drug use and behavioral and substance addictions. Men are more likely to use drugs to find pleasure, whereas women use them to alleviate physical or emotional pain.[871] Compared with women, adult men are about one-third more likely to use alcohol, fifty percent more likely to use illegal drugs and tobacco, two to three times more likely to have a drug addiction, and four times more likely to have an alcohol addiction.[872]

One explanation for these variations is that the male brain grows more dopamine receptor neurons—the critical mediators of reward and motivation. Amphetamines cause males to release about three times more dopamine in the nucleus accumbens than do women. The higher male responsiveness to this pleasure-pathway drug may explain why amphetamine abuse among men is sixty-percent higher than among women, and why males experience greater pleasure from the drug.[873] Stanford University researchers have found the likely explanation for why males are more prone to addiction to videogames. Even among males and females with similar motor skills and previous expo-sure to videogames, males mastered the games faster and racked up higher scores. The male brains found the games more rewarding and potentially more addictive because key portions of their brain reward system, including the right nucleus accumbens, the right amygdala, and the orbitofrontal cor-tex, all showed greater activation during videogame play than did women's.[874] Taken together, this research is showing that portions of the brain reward system differ markedly between the sexes and that, because of this biological difference, men are more reward-sensitive than women.

While average general intelligence is the same between the sexes, men and women achieve it via radically different brain structures. Generally, the brain's information-processing regions are comprised of gray-matter cells and the connections among these regions are white matter. Men have about 6.5 times the volume of intelligence-related gray matter that women do. Women have almost 10 times the intelligence-related white matter. The distribution of intelligence-related gray and white matter also differs fundamentally between the sexes. About 85 percent of gray- and white-matter areas associated with intelligence are found in women's frontal lobes, whereas the frontal lobes of men contain only 45 percent of such gray matter and none of the white matter involved with intellectual performance.[875] These hormonal and anatomical differences may explain why, on average, males are better at mental rotation, map reading, and maze navigation.

Anatomical differences have been documented in every region of the male and female brain.[876] Women show more convoluted folding of brain structures in the frontal, parietal, temporal, and occipital regions.[877] On average, compared with women, men have less brain tissue located in the orbitofrontal cortex region, an area associated with behavioral inhibition. Male brains have a larger parietal cortex, which is involved in spatial processing, and larger amygdalae, involved in automatic emotional processing. Females have a larger hippocampus, which helps to store navigational landmarks. White matter in female brains is more concentrated in the corpus callosum, the link between the right and left brain, perhaps explaining why females are more verbal than males. Figure 9.1 shows that women use both brain hemispheres in processing language, where men use only their left hemisphere.

Baron-Cohen thinks that the female brain is designed to be better at identifying and responding to other people's mental states; he calls this the empathic brain. The male brain is designed to decipher rules that can be used to predict the behavior of systems, which he calls the systematizing brain. Baron-Cohen classified 1,761 healthy men and women regarding these mental habits, finding that roughly thirty percent of men and women were equally empathizing and systematizing. Of the rest, the empathizers were three-to-one female, and the systematizers were more than three-to-one male.[878]

Figure 9.1: How Male and Female Brains Process Language
Male versus female brain activity hot spots (shown in white) while listening to a passage from a John Grisham novel[878]

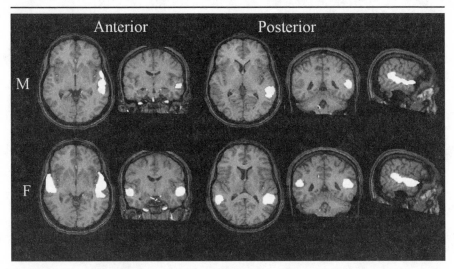

Adapted from Michael Phillips, Mark Lowe, Joseph T. Lurito, Mario Dzemidzic, and Vincent Matthews, "Temporal lobe activation demonstrates sex-based differences during passive listening," *Radiology,* 2001, 16(2)

Even in adulthood, tweaks to our hormone balance can have profound effects on our behavior, even turning us into different people. The National Public Radio program *This American Life* broadcast a fascinating interview with an anonymous man whose body, during a four-month medical treatment, ceased to produce any testosterone. He found his personality entirely altered—and the experience unexpectedly pleasant. His testosterone at zero, he discovered remarkable contentment in a life utterly without desire or motivation.

> Everything that I identify as being me, my ambition, my interest in things, my sense of humor, the inflection in my voice. … The quality of my speech even changed during the time I was without testosterone … [I lost] envy, the desire to judge the self. I approached people with a humility that I have never displayed before … When you have no testosterone you have no desire. When you have no desire you have no content in your mind. You don't think about anything … [I would sit] in bed staring at the wall for three or four hours at a time … I had no interest … I did not want my food to taste good or interesting … [I was] unable to distinguish between

what is and is not interesting ... Every mundane thing seemed to
have purpose and therefore beauty ... Everything [was] beautiful
from the bugs to the cracks in the sidewalks ... [but] in the most
flat-line, boring way possible ... It doesn't matter if you have nothing if you want nothing.

On the flip side is Griffin Hansbury, a woman who used testosterone injec-
tions to raise her blood levels to twice that of the highest levels found in adult
males. Adult males usually have blood levels of testosterone averaging around
600 nanograms per deciliter, about 20 times that of females. The high dose
was successful in rendering Hansbury physically and socially a man.

The world just changes ... Everything I looked at, everything I
touched turned to sex ... [even] the Xerox machine ... I felt like
a monster ... I was just a jerk ... a misogynist ... I became interested in science. I was never interested in science before ... I found
myself understanding physics in a way I never had before ... I have
a hard time crying ... [and miss] the close relationships I had with
women.[880]

Research has confirmed the conclusions drawn from these individual stories with hard science. James M. Dabbs, chair of the Georgia State University
social/cognitive program, who has published about 50 studies on testosterone and behavior, has found that men and women with relatively high testosterone levels are more engaged, direct, outgoing, focused, and independent;
they have higher energy and tend toward dominance, persistence, and com-
bativeness. "High-T" individuals, whether male or female, spend more time
thinking, with particular focus on concrete and immediate problems; they feel
more frustrated when they cannot get things done. They are more confident
in business settings and make more positive first impressions within the first
20 seconds of meetings. In one experiment, a single administration of one-
half milligram of testosterone under the tongues of young women significantly improved their ability to perform a mental 3-D rotation test.[881] Men
whose testosterone levels are suppressed during treatment for prostate cancer
show increased verbal memory as well as reduced performance on a spatial-
rotation test.[882]

High levels of testosterone are also unambiguously predictive of high status. Success in life's pursuits increases testosterone, while failure reduces it.[883] Testosterone rises when you watch your team win at a sporting event and drops when they lose. Futures traders with higher T-levels at the opening bell make more winning trades which, in turn, further boost T levels. High-T men and women, when placed in low-status positions—likely hurt and distracted by their demotions—perform more poorly on spatial and verbal tasks.[884]

Marked sex differences are found in the mood-regulating brain chemical serotonin, whose functions are complex and poorly understood. Men's brains produce fifty percent more serotonin than women's. Compared with men, women have more of the most common type of serotonin receptor and lower levels of the brain chemical that returns circulating serotonin to the nerve cells that store it.[885] These differences may someday help explain why women suffer twice the rate of major depression as men.[886]

The sex differences in our brain morphology and neurochemistry show that our gender identity, social status, and personalities are not built on foundations of granite. Nor are they molded like clay to our conscious will. Instead, they are controlled by a few milligrams of biochemicals whose up or down regulation can strip us of our gender-typical behaviors, make us unrecognizably different people, and either drive or shut down our life's work and obsessions.

GENDER GAP: HEALTH

The same hormones that make males into better systems thinkers also exact a heavy toll in greater illness, stress, debility, and mortality. In a barbaric procedure used during the 1930s, male residents of homes for the developmentally disabled were castrated as punishment for masturbation; a follow-up study forty years later found that those men who were castrated and deprived of most of their testosterone lived 10.2 years longer than those who were not. Testes cost males the same number of years as a two-pack-a-day cigarette habit.[887]

Men have weaker immune systems and die earlier. A baby girl born in America in 2004 can expect to outlive a baby boy by 5.2 years.[888] In every age group, men have poorer health as well as a higher death rate than women for all fifteen leading causes of death except Alzheimer's disease. Men smoke more, drink harder, abuse more drugs, drive less safely, and use less preventative medical care. Men seek out and receive less social support than women. Even working-age men with more than a college education—those with the means and knowledge to better care for themselves—suffer a 56-percent-greater age-adjusted death rate.[889] Age-related shrinkage in areas of the brain involved in thinking, planning, and memory is more pronounced in elderly men.[890] Because they are greater risk-takers, men are almost twice as likely to die by accident and more than twice as likely to be struck by lightning.[891] Even at ages one to four, well before they can take up hang gliding, the risk of accidental death is 45-percent higher for boys.[892] Evolutionary theorists explain that because women's time investment in offspring is far greater than that of men, women are more choosy in their mating strategy, more concerned about personal heath, and more averse to physical risk.

The gender gap in mental and physical health status is growing worse for males, and probably contributes to the more adverse rates and trends in male suicide. Women are three times as likely to attempt suicide, but when men try to kill themselves they choose more lethal means and are over four times as likely to succeed.[893] After age 75, their power and status wizened, males commit suicide at ten times the rate of females. Thankfully, suicide rates have declined for both sexes over the past fifty years, except among the young. Table 9.1 shows the alarming trend in suicide rates for teen and young adult males and the more benign trend for females, other than for girls and young women, who are most sensitive to the body image pressures of our sexualized commercial culture.

Again, evolutionary theorists have an explanation for why men are dying more often at their own hand. In the hunter-gatherer environment of our ancestors, bottom-ranked males (but not females) were likely denied any chance to reproduce, in a pattern seen among some nonhuman social primates. Perhaps because low rank in ancient times was so devastating to male reproductive success, fifty percent of low-status adolescent boys today suffer from serious thoughts of suicide, compared with only ten percent of those

Table 9.1: Changes in U.S. Suicide Rates by Age Group and Sex[894]
1950 and 2004 data are the rate per 100,000 U.S. residents

Age Group	1950 Male	1950 Female	2004 Male	2004 Female	% Increase (Decrease) Male	% Increase (Decrease) Female
5–14	0.3	0.1	0.9	0.5	200	400
15–19	3.5	1.8	12.6	3.5	260	94
20–24	9.3	3.3	20.8	3.6	124	9
25–34	13.4	4.9	20.4	4.7	52	(4)
All Ages	21.2	5.6	18.0	4.5	(15)	(20)

with high status. Among girls, status rank has no such sharp effect on suicidal ideation.[895] The higher expectations our society places on males for success and the harsher psychological penalties to which young men are subjected for failure may explain the sharply diverging gender gap over the past fifty years in suicide rates among young adults.

GENDER GAP: BRILLIANCE

Evolution has made males the extreme sex, the human testbed for both home runs and wipeouts. It is well known that males, far more often than females, exhibit extreme traits, both extraordinarily high and low, and particularly those involving social behavior and intelligence. How have males come to bear this blessing and burden?

Over millions of years and in almost every known human society, males have done the fighting. Males are physically larger and stronger … and more expendable. Females, more so than males, must survive long enough to reproduce and rear children through extended years of dependency to ensure our species' survival. As the more expendable sex, evolution has assigned males the greater proportion of nature's higher-risk mutational experiments. Nature has pulled this off by locating many of the genes governing intelligence and social behavior on the female X-chromosome. Normal XX females have two versions of these genes, one contributed by the male and the other by the female parent; normal XY males have just one. The two versions, called alleles, perform the same function, but are often not identical. With two alleles of a gene, X-linked traits in females are more subject to averaging of the differing effects of the two alleles or to quieting the allele with the more extreme effects. With a single allele governing these X-linked traits, male social behavior and intelligence are less subject to this averaging or quieting, making males the extreme sex.[896]

While, on average, women and men are about equally intelligent as measured by overall IQ scores, male intelligence is more broadly distributed at both ends of the spectrum. In 35 of 37 different intelligence tests given to broadly representative national populations, males show a greater spread in scores. There has been little change in these results over the thirty-two years during which these tests were administered. In some tests of mathematics and sciences aptitudes, males outnumber females in the top one percent by ratios of several times and more. In some tests, no females scored in the top one percent.[897] At the level of a 145 IQ—which is a one-in-one-thousand score—males outnumber females by eight to one.[898] The same over-representation of males exists among scorers at the very bottom. Mental and learning disabilities are more frequent among males by up to several times.

So there are more male polymaths and more male dolts, albeit in small numbers, but enough so that history's most significant persons are overwhelmingly male. Think of Galileo, Darwin, Aristotle, Plato, Newton, Einstein, Edison, Confucius, Basho, Shakespeare, Beethoven, Mozart, Michelangelo, and Leonardo—all of whose work required their extraordinary intelligence. Men are almost 98 percent of those that appear most frequently in 175 authoritative histories of leading figures in the arts, sciences, and invention over the past 3,000 years. Even on closer examination within non-Western cultures and artistic fields of endeavor, male dominance remains at between 92 and 100 percent.

As cultural barriers to female accomplishment have been removed in recent years, male hegemony at the highest levels of excellence has dropped, but only slightly to 95 percent during the 1900–1950 period. Four percent of Nobel Prize winners were female during the first half of the 1900s, three percent during the second half.[899] Among academic scientists who had earned their doctorates over the thirty-year period ending in 1995, women were awarded one patent for each fourteen held by men. In a statistic that shows both the improvement in the status and opportunities afforded to women, as well as the continuing gender gap, for the decade ending in 1995, women were awarded patents at about half the rate as men.[900] When in 2007, literary agent John Brockman, who has very good taste in big thinkers, invited the Western world's leading scientists and intellectuals to submit brief essays on the question "what are you optimistic about?" of his 160 big thinkers, 21 were female.[901]

I do not tread with ousted Harvard President Larry Summers and *Bell Curve* co-author Charles Murray into this politically incorrect territory to make a claim about male superiority. And I will certainly not resolve ongoing disputes about the adverse effect of past and present bias on female accomplishment at the rarified levels. Regardless of cause, males continue to outnumber females here, imposing higher expectations and competition on males. I am not gloating about male dominance in extreme intelligence. For both males and females, America's take-no-prisoners meritocracy makes the absence of inherited intelligence an increasingly impermeable barrier to success in many fields. To a greater extent in global than local society, only those endowed with the most extraordinary talents and motivation can rise to visible success. Aspirants to alpha status in art, science, and invention face a small number of extraordinarily determined and untouchably gifted competitors who set the benchmarks. But for males, as I will show later in this chapter, biology makes failure here more painful. More brilliant males make more male losers.

GENDER GAP: EDUCATION

Their widening lag in educational attainment is making males the new second sex. "Girls outperform boys in elementary school, middle school, high school, and college, and graduate school," says Michael Thompson, a school psychologist and author of *Raising Cain*, a book on the educational problems of boys.[902] Terrill Stammler, principal of Maryland's Rising Sun High School, says, "Every time I turn around, if something good is happening, there's a female in charge. Boys are missing from nearly every leadership position, academic honors slot, and student-activity post at the school."[903] Christina Hoff Sommers, in her book *The War Against Boys*, cites an assessment of 99,000 sixth through twelfth graders on the extent to which they had forty "building blocks for healthy development," such as supportive families, adult role models, connections to schools, assertiveness, motivation to achieve, and social confidence: on thirty-seven of the forty criteria, girls outshone boys.[904] A recent survey of 48,000 sixth through twelfth graders in Maine shows that, compared with girls, boys are more bored and less interested in their schoolwork, are more pessimistic about their futures, and have lower career aspirations.[905]

In virtually all problem areas other than eating disorders and attempted suicide, school-aged boys are worse off than girls. Boys at all levels are far more likely than girls to be disciplined, suspended, held back, or expelled. Two-thirds of special-education placements are boys.[906] The reading disorder dyslexia is two to three times more common among boys.[907] And while the most common "psychiatric disorder" among children, ADHD, is thought to affect boys and girls about equally, boys' symptoms are more obvious and more socially disruptive, leading to a doubled rate of diagnosis among boys.[908]

American schools have come to favor innate female characteristics. "The traditional high school is set up to some degree in a way that plays to girls' strengths. They tend to be neater, pay attention longer. Boys are more likely to actively challenge a teacher," says Gerald Freitag, superintendent of schools in Franklin, Wisconsin.[909] Almost eight in ten K–12 teachers are female, which affords boys fewer male role models who are succeeding in educational set-tings.[910] The typical academic pacing and teaching styles of American educa-tion are better suited to girls. Overwhelmingly, schools take no account of the slower maturation rate of the male brain.

Unintentionally, most American schools are shaping a darker future for males. A socially dangerous disparity in academic achievement confirms these observations. Since about 2001, girls began to outscore boys in state testing programs, for the first time even in mathematics, where boys had previously done better.[911] The twelfth-grade National Assessment of Educational Prog-ress (NAEP), as close as it gets to the nation's report card, shows that 40 per-cent more girls than boys score "proficient" or above in reading. Girls surpass boys in reading and writing at all three NAEP test grades. Girls now tie boys in NAEP math scores, other than in high school, where girls and boys are now almost equal.[912] Boys are 33-percent more likely to drop out and 60-percent more likely to stay back a grade than girls. Boys resist the career-track social opportunities in schools as well, with girls about fifty-percent more likely to participate in extracurricular activities, except in athletics.[913]

As shown in Table 9.2, women now dominate higher-education enrollments. Whereas in 1960 about four in ten of those graduating from college were women, today those four in ten are men.[914] Starting in the year 2002 and even among U.S. citizens, the majority of doctorates are awarded to women.[915] The thoroughly warranted effort since about 1980 to advance gender parity at all levels of education is working—to the distinct disadvantage of males.

A NEW MALE UNDERCLASS?

Relative to women, men's economic value has been in eclipse in the United States for over thirty years. Inflation-adjusted median earnings for full-time male workers have been flat since 1972. The increased earnings for the top twenty percent of men mask a decline for the bottom eighty percent.[916] Over this period, male income instability, a measure of the risk of unexpected income declines, has also increased markedly.[917] In contrast, earnings by women working full time are up by 33 percent.[918] For the first time, as of 2005, median annual earnings for never-married, childless women and men aged 25–44 were statistically identical.[919] I use this comparison because both sexes are equally unburdened by traditional female home and childcare duties and in a

Table 9.2: Percentage of Higher-Education Degrees Earned by Females

Year	College	Masters	MD, DDS, Law	Doctorate
1960/61	39	32	3	11
2007/08	58	61	51	51
2016/17	60	63	53	56

career stage most reflective of current social conditions. The growing education gap makes it virtually certain that women who commit to their careers as intensely as men do will very soon outearn men. Even among married couples, one-third of wives now earn more than their husbands, compared with 10 percent in 1970.[920] Women now slightly outnumber men in management, professional, and related occupations.[921]

Helen Fisher, a Rutgers anthropologist and evolutionary biologist, also thinks that the past thirty years' economic and social changes will soon make women the first sex, as their genetic predispositions become competitive advantages. Fisher's premise is that women integrate information more rapidly than men, are more comfortable with ambiguity and nuance, and have better interpersonal skills. Men prefer to segment and sequence their work, but America's increasingly collaborative, fluid, multi-tasking workplaces are better suited to women's stereotypical skills. Our new gender-neutral society and service economy threaten men's traditional roles as soldiers, protectors, goods producers, and breadwinners.[922]

Psychologically, men are less well-equipped to cope with financial failure. During steady economic times for a family, husbands are three times more likely than women to manage the family finances. But when a married couple is subjected to the status humiliation of bankruptcy, the wife is twice as likely to run the checkbook and three times as likely to assemble the paperwork necessary for credit counseling.[923] Men, moreover, are less able to cope with their wives' financial independence: marriages in which both spouses earn at least 40 percent of family income are 57-percent more likely to end in divorce.[924] The explanation? Perhaps males become more uncertain of their role and doubtful of their competency when their wives are economically independent.[925]

With career opportunities far greater than those afforded to their mothers and grandmothers, women are more confident of their capacity to provide for themselves and are more willing to end an unsatisfying marriage. Wives now initiate 61 percent of divorces, husbands 33 percent. In even the mid-1990s, 56 percent of divorced wives and only 23 percent of husbands said that they wanted the split more than their former spouse.[926] Men apparently no longer feel the imperative they once did to support their ex-wives and families, with fifty-six percent of divorced mothers with custody receiving *zero* child-support money from the father.[927] Among the explanations for the failure of divorced fathers to support their children are the widespread erosion of ethics and personal responsibility, the severe financial duress experienced by the divorced, and child-custody practices that shut divorced men out of their children's lives. Whatever the cause, the traditional male provider and protector is becoming an endangered species.

Andrew Hacker, a sociologist and professor of political science at Queens College in New York, wrote a book called *Mismatch: The Growing Gulf Between Women and Men* that offers a detailed and well-documented look at the new economic and emotional relationships between husbands and wives. "Marriages are weaker and briefer than at any time since this nation began," writes Hacker, who thinks that traditional marital roles—the man providing sustenance and the woman providing emotional support—are no longer functioning. "The burden usually fell on the woman to make the pairing work. Thus when it came to consoling and commiserating, the man expected the bulk of the attention would be bestowed on him. … Until about the middle of the last century, men of all classes accepted fatherhood as a duty. This meant not only being a reliable provider but remaining with your family even when other options beckoned."[928]

Hacker thinks that white women are following an earlier pattern set by black women in cutting their lives loose from undependable men.[929] Increasing numbers of young white men are joining the ranks of the distressingly large number of black men who have failed school, thereby becoming less reliable providers and husbands and forcing women to support themselves outside of marriage. The lower men are on the income scale, the more pronounced the male dropout phenomenon. Among college-bound high school seniors with family incomes under $20,000, 62 percent are women and 38 percent are men.[930]

Men are also suffering because manufacturing has shriveled as a portion of the American economy, from one in three jobs in 1950 to one in ten today, making males increasingly unable to secure a solid middle-class life without higher education. For the fewer low-skill, entry-level jobs remaining, wages are being further depressed by the surge in illegal immigration and by the increasing price pressures created by the genuinely globalized economy. For example, auto-parts maker Delphi declared bankruptcy in 2005 in an express effort to reduce labor costs nearer to world levels, its $27 hourly wage unsustainable against China's $3. Boxed out, greater numbers of men are simply giving up on themselves. America faces the real prospect of a large, permanent underclass of men trapped in subsistence or shacked up in their boyhood bedrooms with their aging parents.

Preliminary evidence portends a growing army of demoralized male slackers. Figure 9.2 shows changes over the past twenty years in the percentages of young black and white men and women who are neither in school nor looking for work. The graph indicates how both young black and white women have dramatically increased their engagement in responsible life, starting in the early 1990s. Whereas young black men's disengagement trend leveled off and began to decline in the mid-1990s, young white men have increasingly drifted

Figure 9.2

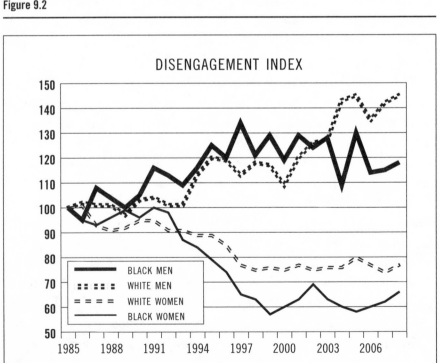

DISENGAGEMENT INDEX

BLACK MEN
WHITE MEN
WHITE WOMEN
BLACK WOMEN

Age 16–24, Percent Not Working and Not in School; Index: 1985=100

into disconnection with productive society, with the trend spiking after the year 2000.[931]

Andrew Sum directs the Center for Labor Market Studies at Northeastern University and has examined differences in labor force participation between males and females for over a decade. He laments the malign neglect paid to the economic crisis facing working-class men. "If this was happening to women, you would have fourteen task forces, five presidential commissions and Ted Kennedy jumping up and down. It's been largely ignored because it's not politically correct to raise it."[932]

What should we do to stop our young men from dropping out of school, work, fatherhood, and civic life? Tom Mortenson, senior scholar at the Pell Institute for the Study of Opportunity in Higher Education, winces at the question: "We are doing nothing to turn this situation around … It's going to get worse [for] as long as I'm alive."[933] As I will show in the next chapter, we can reverse this dark prognosis by giving boys access to schools better tailored to their brains, and by fostering economic and social alternatives to the global hierarchies that bury ordinary people—while at the same time further improving the lives of women.

LEADERS OF THE PACK: SEX, VIOLENCE, AND DOMINANCE

The American male can take heart that his pecking-order battles are far less bloody than among at least some other mammals—and that humans are far less physically violent than in centuries and eras past. Nonetheless, compared with women, men remain the more aggressive status-seekers and are more acutely sensitive to the crushing failure of status defeat.

For both men and our mammalian brothers, competition for sex is at the heart of our status sensitivity. Male marsupial mice are highly territorial and fight viciously against rivals for territory and mates, with the resulting stress killing every male, both winner and loser, before their mates even give birth. When marsupial mice are emasculated, they are freed from testosterone stress and live twice as long. The male elephant seal clocks in at 5,000 pounds, seven times the female's weight. Despite her small size, she controls the males and simultaneously tests for their genetic fitness—by withholding sex. This triggers a brutal and usually mortal male fight for her attentions, the female accepting copulation only with the often badly wounded winner. Four of five male elephant seals die in these fights before maturity and nine of ten fail to have any progeny.[934] During their mating season, sexually mature male fallow deer endure hours-long bellowing contests to establish dominance. Failing a win by that means, they resort to bloody fights, averaging one each two hours. These mating seasons cost the males an acute deterioration in their body condition. At great nutritional expense, they spend most of the rest of each year growing a new set of antlers, designed exclusively for fighting and dominance displays. The winning 5 percent of deer commandeer 80 percent of all mating opportunities.[935] Human dominance wars differ only in lethality and sophistication, not in kind or ultimate motivation.

Temüjin is history's most powerful single human. After quelling Mongolia's warring tribes and consolidating his rule, he coined a new name for himself, Genghis Khan, or Universal Ruler. In 1218, Khan next set his sights on expanding peaceful trade with the neighboring Muslim empire of Khwarezmia. When his diplomatic caravan arrived in the city of Otrar, its governor, Inalchuq, made a poor choice in his response, murdering most of the delegation. Khan dispatched a second peaceable delegation; this time, Khwarezmia's Shah beheaded all but one. Patience exhausted, Khan then launched a ruthless two-year war against Khwarezmia, pillaging Otrar and personally executing many of its inhabitants, in Governor Inalchuq's case by pouring molten silver into his eyes and ears. The Universal Ruler's army went on to capture the empire's capital city, traversing its protective trenches by filling them with the bodies of its soldiers and inhabitants, then raping and murdering the rest. The Shah fled in secrecy, rather than face certain dismemberment as his city fell. Unappeased, Khan sent 20,000 men on a two-year mission to find and kill him.[936] Historian George Vernadsky paraphrases Khan instructing his lieutenants in the art of dominance: "The greatest pleasure is to vanquish your enemies and chase them before you, to rob them of their wealth and see those dear to them bathed in tears, to ride their horses and clasp to your bosom their wives and daughters."[937]

But Khan's brutal power displays were a means to a higher end. After he died in 1227, his sons' armies spent the next fifty years conquering two-thirds of the known world and establishing history's largest empire. Khan's armies prevailed in nearly every one of dozens of recorded battles, exterminating the populations of those who resisted, and building such a fearsome reputation that most surrendered without a fight. But once a population was subjugated, both Khan and his sons became benevolent, instituting religious freedom, the rule of law, paper money, a postal system, public schools, meritocracy, and free trade. Geneticists estimate that eight percent of all men now living in the region of his empire and one in 200 of all males now living on earth have inherited some of Khan's genes.[938] At bottom, male dominance in elephant seals and humans—whether by violence or benevolence—is all about immortality.

Among *homo sapiens*, as with most primates and many mammals, the males of the species share an intense, hardwired motivation to attain status dominance. For humans, this fact is evident across culture and history. In his two books, *The Inevitability of Patriarchy and Why Men Rule*, sociologist Steven Goldberg has rigorously demonstrated that males have nearly always dominated competitive hierarchies. While there are exemplary exceptions by such leaders as Golda Meir, Margaret Thatcher, and Carly Fiorina, male dominance has prevailed without exception in all societies for which there is direct evidence.[939] Having worked personally with gifted female leaders, I'd prefer this not to be the condition going forward, but the outcome will be a tug-of-war between genes and culture. Showing how uncomfortable we are with the fact of male dominance, *The Guinness Book of World Records* lists Goldberg's first book as having been rejected by the highest-ever number of publishers (55) before one accepted.

Across cultures, more highly ranked men are taller, stronger, more mature, more self-confident, and have greater earning power. Alpha males engage in culture-specific dominance displays and have facial features such as wide foreheads and strong jaws.[940] Donald Trump, with his concrete and steel towers, faux pompadour, and power to fire quivering apprentices on a whim and in view of millions, makes an archetypal American dominance display. At the moment Ronald Reagan took control and said, "I paid for that microphone," he had secured the presidency against a weaker man.

As explanation for the hunger males have to dominate, Darwinians cite the differing returns between the sexes for reproductive success. No matter how intense their effort, females can bear no more than about a dozen children during a lifetime—yielding only modest differential reproductive return for high status. In contrast, high-status males like Temüjin and the Ph.D. sperm-bank donor we met in Chapter 3 can successfully ensure their genes' survival by spreading them among hundreds, perhaps thousands, of children.

In a study of 37 contemporary cultures, evolutionary psychologist David Buss found that men, regardless of their age, prefer as sexual partners younger women who are at the peak of their reproductive years. Women in every culture Buss studied prefer somewhat older men who have more physical resources and the ambition, industriousness, and social status required to accumulate more resources in the future.[941] A survey of 729,000 members of the online dating service Match.com found a pronounced difference in preferences between men and women. Men of high income and educational attainment are more than twice as willing as women to date down the income and education strata. Consistent with Buss' findings, women are far more rigid in demanding mates who match their own income and education attainments.[942] Women even use comedy to identify potential mates likely to reach high status later in life. Women, but not men, are strongly attracted to members of the opposite sex who are good at making jokes, which is an unfakeable indicator of both social facility and intelligence.[943] But these preferences for high-resource men are likely to blur as women increasingly match men in economic independence.[944]

Laura Stroud and her co-workers at Brown University's Centers for Behavioral and Preventative Medicine ran two novel and highly revealing experiments showing how differently the two sexes react to challenges to their status. Men's cortisol levels spiked in reaction to achievement-related stressors, whereas women's rose when they faced social rejection.[945] When both sexes were asked to count backwards by seven, men's blood pressure and heart rate increased by more than women's; women's increased by more when they were asked to describe what they dislike about their own bodies.[946]

As a result of the differing mating and reproductive strategies between the sexes, evolution has made the male more sensitive to the rewards of high social status and the failure to achieve it. Status and dominance display—outward evidence of success—are vitally more important for men. But just as there are more hyper-intelligent males, that males rule is not evidence of superiority over women. Nor do these gene-deep realities mean that men are getting the better deal. Except at the very top, American men are slipping badly relative to women in health, education, marriage, work, and status.

EXTREME MALE VIOLENCE: A PATHOLOGICAL RESPONSE TO STATUS DEFEAT

The fingerprints of the Mars-Venus difference can also be found in the FBI's comprehensive criminal-arrest database. Men are massively more prone to crimes involving physical violence; they are charged with 82 percent of all violent crimes and 89 percent of murders. But, when it comes to surreptitious, nonviolent property crimes, where the smaller female body size and lesser strength is not a disadvantage, women are nearly men's equals. Women are charged with 53 percent of embezzlements, 45 percent of frauds, and 39 percent of forgery/counterfeiting crimes.[947] Evolutionary psychologist Anne Campbell explains that females are driven to crime more to overcome economic hardship, where males more often commit crimes to seek thrills, impose dominance, or use stolen property to project status.[948]

For men, status defeat is far more socially toxic than economic hardship and is a certain contributor to America's high levels of male violence. When exposed to severe status insult, psychologically sensitive males are increasingly resorting to extreme acts of violence intentionally made visible to the public. Despite our having by far the highest incarceration rate of any country in the world, among the advanced industrial nations the United States ranks number one in murder and assault, number two in rape, and number three in robbery per capita.[949] Violent crime rates have declined (until 2005) to the present still-high levels only because the number of violence-prone young males has grown smaller, and more of them have been locked up. Another credible theory explaining the decline in violent crime is that violence is linked to exposure to lead during childhood. American children have ingested radically less of the metal since it was fully banned from gasoline in 1986.[950]

However, the most horrible forms of personal violence, while mercifully rare, have been on the rise since the 1970s. We are shocked by their increasing lethality, monstrousness, and frequency. Particularly horrific is planned murder in our schools.[951] Figure 9.3 shows the trend.[952]

Many theories have been offered to explain the Columbine High School massacre of April 20, 1999. Some say that the killings could have been prevented if the parents of one of the perpetrators, Dylan Klebold, had been alert to the firearms poorly concealed in their son's room and clothing. Or if police had investigated reports that the second killer, Eric Harris, had made death threats and openly fantasized about building bombs. Or if Harris had not been taking Luvox, an anti-depression drug reported by its manufacturer to induce mania in four percent of children and young people who take it.[953] Or

Figure 9.3

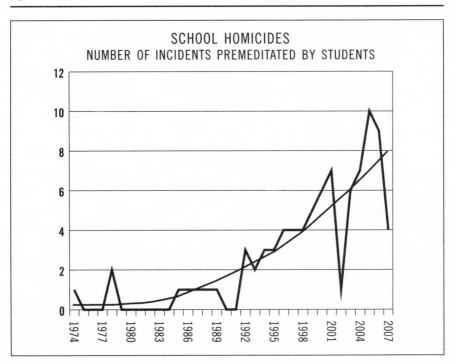

SCHOOL HOMICIDES
NUMBER OF INCIDENTS PREMEDITATED BY STUDENTS

Data: 1974–1999 Vossekuil et al., 2000–2007 Trump

if the pair had not been superbly trained to hit moving targets with firearms by the then-popular videogame Doom. Or if they had not been subject to their peers' incessant and vicious taunting.[954]

In a set of five home videos, carefully left behind for discovery in Harris' bedroom, the two teens offer their own explanations for why they murdered thirteen people and then killed themselves. Klebold vents his rage against "stuck up" kids who put him down ever since his years in daycare. Harris, the mastermind, expressed bitterness toward his military family and their constant moves, each new school forcing him to start out "at the bottom of the ladder ... [where peers constantly mocked] my face, my hair, my shirts." In page after page of his handwritten journal, released to the public in 2006, he vents his disdain for most of the human race, which he deems beneath him. He reports his hair-trigger sensitivity to inconsequential status slights, such as when people butt in movie lines or fail to step aside as he walks a school hallway. Six months before Columbine, Harris wrote this:

> I think I will choose to kill and damage as much as nature allows me to ... I want to burn the world, I want to kill everyone except about 5 people who I will name later, so if you are reading this you are lucky you escaped my rampage because I wanted to kill you ... Everyone is always making fun of me because of how I look, how f***ing weak I am ... well I will get you all back: ultimate f***ing revenge here. You people could have shown me more respect, treated me better, asked for my knowledge and guidance more, treated me more like a senior, and maybe I wouldn't have been so ready to tear your f***ing heads off. Then again, I have always hated how I looked ... That's where a lot of my hate grows from, the fact that I have practically no self-esteem, especially concerning girls and looks and such ... HATE! I'm full of hate and I love it ... It'll be f***ing hard to hold out until April. If people would give me more compliments all of this still might be avoidable ... but probably not. Whatever I do people make fun of me, and sometimes directly to my face.[955]

But all these potential explanations miss another that compels us to review our cultural priorities. Klebold and Harris's T-shirts bore the acronym NBK, referring to the film *Natural Born Killers*. Lead Columbine investigator Kate Battan spent months reviewing the evidence, including Harris' journal and the never-made-public bedroom videos. Battan concludes that Klebold and Harris were motivated primarily by a desire to achieve fame in avenging their loser status. "All the rest of the justifications are just smoke," she concluded. Deputy District Attorney Steve Jensen seconded, "It is obvious that these guys wanted to become cult heroes of some kind."

"We're going to kickstart a revolution," said Harris, seeking to upend a school status hierarchy with them at the bottom. Klebold bragged to his video camera that Hollywood would engage in a bidding war to tell his tale: "Directors will be fighting over this story." Harris expressed concern that they would be seen as also-rans after the school shootings in Oregon and Kentucky. "Do not think we're trying to copy anyone. [Our plan is] not like those f***s in Kentucky with camouflage and .22's. Those kids were only trying to be accepted by others."[956] Hundreds would have died had the timers not failed on the killers' propane bombs planted in the cafeteria and in their cars outside the school doors. Columbine begs us to reflect on a culture that spends billions advertising escape from inferiority through fame and the achievement of fame through violence.

In a videotape he carefully scripted for posthumous public consumption, Cho Seung-Hui, the perpetrator of the April 16, 2007, Virginia Tech massacre-suicide, credits the Columbine attackers as heroes and "martyrs." Cho was intelligent, sullen, hermetically introverted, zit-faced, agonizingly self-conscious, and, like Harris, suffered blanket rejection by the opposite sex. Before moving to America from his native Korea in 1992, Cho and his family lived in near-squalid conditions in the lowest-priced apartment in the basement of his building. His two infantile plays, dramatized on YouTube postings days after the massacre, reveal his violent psychology and hint that he may have been sexually abused when he was younger. Even at age 23, he described himself a boy, which is often an indicator of prior sexual abuse.

Cho rarely spoke or replied to anyone he encountered. He was taunted by unkind high school and college schoolmates for his Asian face and his speech problems. A college classmate described a revealing scene in an English class, when Cho's teacher asked him to read his work aloud. As typically occurred when he was spoken to, Cho looked down in silence. Finally, after the teacher threatened him with an F for nonparticipation, Cho began to read in a strange, deep voice that sounded "like he had something in his mouth," the classmate recalled. "As soon as he started reading, the whole class started laughing, pointing at him and saying, 'Go back to China.'"[957]

Why did Cho massacre 32 people and then kill himself? He had ample opportunity to turn to the abundant mental-health and counseling resources on campus. He suffered from untreated schizophrenia. His alarming and violence-prone mental state had been repeatedly reported to campus authorities. He had been tagged for stalking two women. It might have helped if campus staff (properly screened for competence) had been allowed to keep self-defense firearms. In the days following the massacre, the media got Cho's motives all wrong, describing his videotapes as incoherent, anti-Christian rants against no one in particular. Yet Cho's words are absolutely clear. He took 32 innocent lives, most apparently randomly, to avenge his crushed status.

> Do you know what it feels like to be spit on your face and to have trash shoved down your throat? Do you know what it feels like to dig your own grave? Do you know what it feels like to have your throat slit from ear to ear? Do you know what it feels like to be torched alive? Do you know what it feels like to be humiliated and impaled upon a cross and left to bleed to death for your amusement? You have never felt a single ounce of pain your whole life. Did you want to inject as much misery as you can into our lives as you can just because you can? You had everything you wanted. Your Mercedes wasn't enough, you brats? Your golden necklaces weren't enough, you snobs? Your trust fund wasn't enough? Your vodka and cognac weren't enough? All your debaucheries weren't enough? Those weren't enough to fulfill your hedonistic needs? You had everything.
>
> You sadistic snobs. I may be nothing but a piece of s**t. You have vandalized my soul, raped my heart, and torched my conscience. You thought it was one pathetic boy's life you were extinguishing. I did it for them. I did it to make you stop what you did to me ... Did you think I wanted to do this? Do you think I ever dreamed of dying like this? In a million years, I didn't want to do this. I didn't have to do this. I could have left. I could have fled. I didn't. But no, I will no longer run. It's not for me. It's for my children, for my brothers and sisters ... Thanks to you, I die like Jesus Christ, to inspire generations of the weak and the defenseless people.[958]

Trying to answer the questions "why did this happen?" and "how can we stop future Columbines?", the U.S. Secret Service and the Department of Education published a definitive study of the thirty-seven planned school shootings and killings during 1974–2000. In every case, the perps are male, but there is otherwise no consistent profile. However, 71 percent of the attackers were "bullied, persecuted or injured," many tormented at levels that would reach actionable harassment if the incidents occurred in an adult workplace. Before their attack, almost all had suffered a major loss, two-thirds of them experiencing some type of failure or status injury. Most attackers planned ahead, three out of four of them identifying their individual targets beforehand. The problems that beset them rarely involved academics, with four in ten earning A's and B's, and only five percent failing school.

Fortunately, there are practical things we can do to prevent most acts of school violence. First, we can act on the warnings. Before almost every school shooting, more than one person has become concerned about the attacker's potential for violence. In eight in ten cases, a peer knows about plans for the attack before it happens. Almost half of attackers are coaxed or helped by peers. Adults are rarely informed beforehand. In one case, a shooter told his friends that he would simply brandish a gun in school to ward off his bullies; his friends persuaded him that he would have to actually shoot to get the relief he sought.[959]

Second, we can end our tolerance for bullying. School bullying is far more serious than an unpleasant rite of passage like braces or acne that adults can chuckle about from a comfortable distance. Victims of bullying suffer serious social withdrawal and major depression.[960] As I will show in the next chapter, we will not stop school violence until all of us, particularly students, stop colluding through our silence. We need to start exerting and expecting strong peer pressure against both the bullies and the attackers before they hurt others. The solution will come from cultural rather than institutional change.

What drives extreme violence in schools also drives it among adults. Contemporary America holds a near-monopoly on the most attention-getting form of individual violence: serial killing. Over the last century, between 75 and 85 percent of the world's serial killers were Americans and 90 percent were men.[961] Pointing again to the key decades of transition in our social norms, victimization rates by serial murderers exploded by about 35 times between the 1950s and 1980s.[962]

Charles Starkweather was socially encumbered by his bowlegs, his short and weak stature, a speech defect, and his poor, uneducated parents. He grew into young adulthood as a garbage collector, feeling trapped at the bottom of society. During his trial for viciously killing eleven people from 1957 to 1958, he fought to block an attempt to have the court declare him insane. Insanity would allow the public to dismiss him and his newfound James Dean rebel persona that gave him self-worth and public visibility. Starkweather's monstrosity was the inspiration for *Natural Born Killers*, a media product itself linked to at least a dozen copycat murders. From death row, Starkweather wrote this about himself: "They hated me because of the way I looked, and because I was poor and had to live in a goddamned shack; it didn't matter that we all loved each other; that my mother worked hard away from home to help support us children and washed our clothes and cooked and got us off to school. All these goddamn kids cared about was: 'what kind of job does your old man have? What kind of house do you live in? What do your legs look like? Are you taller than any girl in school?'"[963]

Bobby Joe Long was raised by his attractive and unloving single mother, sleeping with her in the same bed until age thirteen, other than during the many nights when he was displaced by her sexual interludes with strange men. His alcoholic father was absent from his life. Long and his mother moved constantly, usually living in single rooms in other people's homes. He survived numerous accidental blows to the frontal regions of his skull. His congenital gynecomastia branded him with an effeminate appearance, causing him to grow female-like breasts during adolescence. This, along with severe facial scarring from an auto accident early in life, left him subjected to constant torment in school. Long became the frequent instigator of brutal fights in school. Starting in his teens, Long raped at least fifty women, killing nine.[964]

John Wayne Gacy, a.k.a. the Killer Clown, grew up subjected to constant degradation by his violent, alcoholic father, who himself was obsessed by a well-founded personal fear of not measuring up in life. He routinely beat the boy's mother, despised homosexuals and, over almost nightly dinner-table arguments, never failed to remind his son that he saw him as a sickly, stupid failure and a homosexual. In one of his periodic fits of rage, he shot his son's beloved dog. Gacy, as a result of being slammed in the head by a playground swing, suffered blackouts starting at age 11. The father accused the son of faking these blackouts to gain attention.

In his double life, Gacy was a successful businessman, popular community volunteer, homosexual rapist, and serial killer at age 26. He was caught and sentenced to ten years for sexually assaulting a teenage male employee. In the classic psychopathic pattern, he became a model prisoner and persuaded the parole board that he was fully reformed, securing release after only 18 months. Then, in his constant search for recognition, Gacy constructed a new mask of normalcy, married his second wife, started a successful contracting company, became a Democratic party precinct captain, and gained considerable esteem for his charity work, dressing as Pogo the clown to entertain hospitalized children. His costume served a second purpose: tricking unsuspecting victims into entering his house and donning handcuffs. Once they were helpless, Gacy subjected his victims to torture, mutilation, and rape. In 1978 he was arrested for the murder of 33 teenage boys, young men, and male prostitutes. Once in prison, Gacy treasured the media scrapbook he kept documenting the attention he so craved.[965]

These snapshots of the depraved provide clues to help explain the sharp increases in extreme violence over recent decades. Status defeat plays an unambiguous contributory role. A study profiling the psychologies of 64 predominantly American mass murderers found a consistent pattern of major personal rejection or loss in the hours or days before their violence exploded.[966] Forensic psychotherapist James Gilligan, director of Harvard's Center for the Study of Violence, and for 25 years a prison psychiatrist, writes, "I have yet to see a serious act of violence that was not provoked by the experience of feeling shamed and humiliated, disrespected and ridiculed, and that did not represent the attempt to prevent or undo this loss of face."[967]

Forensic psychiatrist Helen Morrison has professionally profiled more than eighty serial killers, usually in long one-on-one interviews, sometimes over a period of many years. In her book, *My Life Among the Serial Killers*, Morrison speculates that many serial killers are addicted to killing, that they cycle through stages of fantasy, execution, and depression or let-down when the killing fails to resolve their psychological problems. Morrison does not reach the conclusions I do regarding the relation among murderousness, child abuse, head injury, and status defeat, but most (not all) of the serial killers profiled in her book suffered hideous abuse as children.[968]

But additional explanations must be involved because most child abuse does not lead to serial killing. Evidence points to a direct, genetic explanation for a connection between child abuse, greater male sensitivity to status defeat, and male's consequential proneness to violence. Jonathan Pincus, chief of neurology at the Washington, D.C., Veteran's Administration Hospital and professor of neurology at the Georgetown University School of Medicine, has examined 150 murderers and serial killers. He found that two in three had suffered some combination of mental illness, neurological damage, and child abuse. Ninety-four percent had experienced severe physical and sexual abuse. As we saw in Chapter 7, roughly one in ten American males has been subjected to childhood physical or sexual abuse.

For many of its victims, child abuse grows into a deep well of intense anger. Brain damage, particularly to specific areas of the frontal cortex, the higher brain's center for emotional impulse inhibition, reduces the capacity to restrain this anger before it turns to violence. Pincus makes an analogy to an infant born with a cataract in one eye. Unless the cataract is removed early, the infant will never develop the brain circuits necessary to support vision for that eye. Like Teicher, Pincus theorizes that an abusive, emotionally deprived upbringing irreversibly skews juvenile brain development toward the behaviors needed to survive in a harsh world.[969] Experiments with primates provide solid evidence that childhood emotional deprivation triggers a genetic predisposition toward lower brain serotonin and increased aggressiveness, anxiety, depression-like behavior, and reactivity to stress.[970]

The strongest link between genes and violence yet shown in humans involves monoamine oxidase A (MAO-A), an enzyme that regulates the concentration of brain neurotransmitters including serotonin, norepinephrine, and dopamine. As I explained earlier in this chapter, males are more likely to have an "extreme" version of the gene encoding for production of MAO-A because it is located on the X-chromosome. Like many, the MAO-A gene comes in a variety of forms, some high and some low producing. About one-third of white males have MAO-A-low. If seriously abused as children, males with the MAO-A-low gene are almost ten times more likely to be convicted of a violent crime as adults. MAO-A-low also makes abused males, but not females, more impulsive as adults. Healthy, normal males, but not females, with the MAO-A-low gene typically have significant impairment of the brain's key impulse-control circuit. People with MAO-A-low genes have significantly smaller amygdalae, increased reactivity to negative stimuli in the left amygdala, and diminished conscious inhibition reactions in several parts of the cortex. The diminished inhibitory effect of MAO-A-low genes is far more pronounced in men than women. People with low MAO-A levels in their cortical and subcortical brain regions report greater aggression, with low MAO-A levels accounting for over one-third of the variability in aggressive, antisocial behaviors.[971]

Psychopathy, itself linked to child abuse and thereby to status defeat, is yet another explanation for some serial killing. Robert Hare, creator of the widely used Psychopathy Checklist, estimates that there are nearly two million psychopaths living in America and that they are responsible for at least half of all serious crime. The characteristics Hare uses to diagnose a psychopath are these: profoundly lacking empathy or remorse, emotionally cold, self-centered, grandiose, deceitful and manipulative, superficially charming, impulsive, irresponsible, excitement-seeking, and highly reactive to insults.[972] Behavioral therapy for psychopaths released from prison has proven spectacularly unsuccessful.[973] Psychopaths often enthusiastically accept the behavioral therapy they receive in prison, using it as psychopath "finishing school" to become yet more effective manipulators. Many scientists in the field believe that many or most psychopaths are born with this disease for which there is, as yet, no known cure. "Lock them up till they die," says Jonathan Kellerman, the psychologist and author of the Alex Delaware series of psychological-thriller novels.[974]

Hare describes a category of "sub-criminal" psychopath who operates largely undetected and without resorting to violence, thereby avoiding prosecution. Nonviolent psychopaths nonetheless exact a high cost on society through their unscrupulous business dealings and emotional damage to their victims. We even admire and reward the more intelligent psychopaths—the greedy, self-absorbed, risk-taking types—with election to high office, fat IPOs, and sell-out performances. We pay in the billions annually for psychopaths who operate detected and undetected among us. While Hare estimates that about half of psychopaths had warm, nurturing parents, systematic research shows that psychopaths are disproportionately exposed to traumatic events such as child abuse.[975] Childhood emotional trauma or compounding brain injuries seem to mutate the psychopath's baseline manipulative behavior into violence.

Psychopathy has recently been linked to reduced functionality or size in the brain's amygdala, our first-line fear-detection and empathy center. James Blair, a pioneer in this field who heads the affective cognitive neuroscience program for the National Institute of Mental Health, has studied the relationship between violence and localized brain-activity deficits in the frontal cortex and the amygdala. Blair sees a fairly consistent pattern of reduced amygdalic activity in people who commit planned acts of violence. They fail to detect their victims' fear, do not learn from being punished, and lack empathy. The brain amygdalae of psychopathic individuals show less activation in response to the fearful expressions of others.[976] While Blair cannot show a cause-and-effect relationship, he has firmly established the clear link between reduced amygdalic activity and psychopathy. Martin Teicher's work, showing reduced size in the left amygdala of young adults who were seriously sexually abused as children, provides more evidence for a link between child abuse and psychopathy.

Blair distinguishes psychopathic from unplanned, reactive, or impulsive violence, linking the latter to generalized frontal cortex activity deficits.[977] Jordan Grafman, chief of cognitive neurosciences at the National Institutes of Health, has shown that physical damage to the prefrontal cortex (PFC) is associated with impulsive violence. People who are abnormally aggressive or violent show an eleven-percent reduction in PFC gray matter.[978] The frontal functioning in psychopaths is typically intact, however, other than reduced function in a more localized area called the orbitofrontal cortex, which does not mature until late adolescence.[979]

Serial killing and extreme violence probably result from an acutely toxic combination of multiple causes: inherited and acquired psychopathy, frontal lobe injury, developmental brain defects, child abuse, severe social-status insult, and the pathological search for recognition to compensate for the social deficit these men feel. Psychologically harsh, early childhood experiences may be epigenetic triggering events or may aggravate an otherwise-dormant neural predisposition. It is vital to remember that most abused and bullied children and most people with un-average brain function are not psychopaths and do not become violent. But we can no longer ignore the link among child abuse, violence, and America's overstressed, OverSuccessed, socially isolated parents. By my rough calculations, we are preparing perhaps one million of our boys to live out the plot in Grand Theft Auto.[980]

We cannot exclusively blame extreme violence in America on the failure of its perpetrators to exert their wills and exercise self-control. And, as even anti-gun lefty Michael Moore admits in *Bowling for Columbine*, ready access to guns is not the cause of our violence epidemic. Nor is poverty by itself an explanation for violence, other than in extreme and rare circumstances.

So how can we protect ourselves? We are certainly not lacking in police or prisons. Unquestionably, and for even those opposing the death penalty, locking up violent offenders until they are no longer violent—for life, if necessary—is the right way to protect the public from known criminals. But prison cannot protect us from the violence of newly spawned offenders. No, the way to prevent violence in men—at least in those not wired for criminal psychopathy—is to change the culture. We should carefully consider several recent experiments showing that even brief, friendly human contact can reduce aggression by a person who has been socially rejected.[981] The sum of our billions of small, daily choices in how we treat one another shapes America's most important social safety net. Any of these choices can become the tipping point that prevents or incites an act of extreme violence.

SAVE THE MALES

While both sexes bear the costs of OverSuccess, biology puts the heavier burden on males. As we've seen in this chapter, males are genetically more sensitive to status contests and status defeat. Today's American male is overwhelmed by both. Status defeat is more psychologically devastating for men than poverty is, and it almost certainly contributes to our high levels of male violence. For most men—who are not violent—the intelligence and social-skills economy is making traditional male roles obsolete. Rising success benchmarks are boxing out all but gifted males. When not in violence, we pay the cost for the displacement of ordinary men in their deteriorated mental and physical health, further weakening our social capital.

In his epic study of fame, *The Frenzy of Renown*, Leo Braudy nails at least a part of the explanation for what ails men today: "In a world preoccupied with names, faces, and voices," Braudy writes, "fame promises acceptability, even if one commits the most heinous crime, because thereby people will finally know who you are, and you will be saved from the living death of being unknown."[982] Most of us, men and women alike, are irrelevant failures in a culture drowning in the images and stories of famous, important people, whose gleaming influence, wealth, talent, and beauty are avoidable only where there is no paper, electricity, or conversation. The horror is that in an America where only preeminent status makes us fully alive, the most twisted among us will kill to be seen.

10

HEALING THE OBSESSION

Most people would succeed in small things,
if they were not troubled with great ambitions.[983]
—Henry Wadsworth Longfellow, 1857

SO HOW CAN AMERICANS seek achievement and visibility in healthier ways? How can we recognize virtue and value among the millions of generous and competent people who will never appear on a magazine cover? How can we adjust our social norms to better fit human psychological tolerances—so that one person's success does not make many others miserable? How can America continue to lead the world in progress and excellence—while reducing social and personal failure?

We cannot downshift our way back to some rose-colored past of small towns, horseshoe tournaments, and aproned moms stirring at the hearth. For most of us, the pastoral, socially circumscribed life was mean and short, best left idealized in the *Farmer's Almanac.* Nor can we engineer social change by even well-meaning central command. The twentieth century's experiments with socialism and gunpoint egalitarianism left over thirty million dead. Stifling progress and capping rewards would stunt America's continuing adventure. I, for one, would not trade high-speed ski lifts, artisan chocolate, and

RSS feeds for Wonder Bread, Bakelite, and a bowling renaissance. Whatever we do to temper meritocracy and globalism, we must remain committed to the biological and social truth that our urge for personal success is what drives the human enterprise forward.

The prospect of being admired among our peers is so strong that to achieve it, artists will work in damp garrets for a lifetime without pay. Michael Bloomberg and Jon Corzine will spend major fortunes on the slightly favorable odds of being elected to a job paying little more than the cost of a nice one-week vacation. Our urge to be recognized does us great collective good, bestowing humanity with gifts of art, invention, altruism, and material progress that are cherished long after the individual contributor is forgotten. More of us are free to attempt such great accomplishments than at any other place and time. America has created history's preeminent engine for the accelerating accumulation of these goods. On balance, our country is a gift to all humanity.

At America's founding, we became the pilots of a new culture of freedom and individual success that was irreversibly launched in fifteenth-century Europe. But with the early 1920s came movies, manufactured celebrity, and the advent of consumerism. When the first television generation came of age in the 1960s, community began its collapse, and our nation's social and psychological health slid into continuing decline. By the early 1980s, success obsession became malignant, as materialism, debt, ethical rot, and pure meritocracy swamped our older, better-balanced values. With the 1990s came the global economy and the escalating benchmarks set by its stratospherically gifted performers. With these changes came OverSuccess, which has turned too many of us into hopeless failures.

History seems to be a seesawing balancing act between the sometimes opposing goods of individual and social success. Today in America, we have reached a poisonous extreme where personal success matters more than the society that makes it possible. Every one of us who cares about something more than ourselves must make changes in our own lives and work to recruit others into the cause of restoring America's best values. Just as we have used our intellectual gifts to increase our command over food supplies and pathogens to defeat hunger and disease, so should we thoughtfully intervene to improve our social, cultural, and psychological environments. Within our power are some easy personal steps that we can take immediately. As we learn to live these, we can press for the difficult and time-consuming political and institutional changes that are necessary to reduce the costly burdens of Over-Success.

Fortunately, there are dozens of things we can do to cure what ails success in America—even as we preserve freedom and opportunity—and without New Age expectations about human nature. What follow in this chapter are my suggested cures for OverSuccess. Some of them are obvious but unavoidably necessary; others are controversial. Some require an act of Congress, others no more than a smile at a stranger.

SORRY, PLEASE, AND THANK YOU

The healing can begin right now with three small courtesies: saying sorry, please, and thank you. They take so little of our time, sweeten every interaction, and make us feel more connected and responsible for one another. Small acts of kindness and deference require only that we put aside our self-importance for a moment.

Breast cancer took my wife's closest friend, who left behind her two children and a husband. Her death was the result of her doctor's failure to diagnose her condition and the resulting one-year delay in treatment. Before her death, but long after it could do her any good, and in service to humanity, she decided to confront the doctor who cost her her life. In a display of brutal arrogance, the doctor told her he would treat her identically if given another opportunity. His inability to say he was sorry left behind an anger that will never heal and that money cannot compensate.

Doug Wojcieszak's brother also died of a gross medical error. The doctor responsible concealed the error to protect himself from liability. Wojcieszak is not a doctor, attorney, or insurance company executive, but he wanted to turn his grief and anger into something that would increase our social health. He founded the SorryWorks! Movement, whose goal is to substitute an apology for a lawsuit. The University of Michigan Hospital joined SorryWorks! in 2002, and since that time, UM doctors who have made medical errors approach the patient and family with genuine humility, admit their mistake, and apologize. The hospital conducts an investigation into the root cause of the error, improves its internal processes, and offers reasonable compensation to the patient. As a result of the SorryWorks! program, patients are so often willing to forego their right to litigate that UM has halved pending lawsuits and cut its annual litigation expense from $3 million to $1 million.[984]

At this very instant, we can each take action to close the open sewer of bad manners, vulgarity, and disrespect created by our get-to-the-top-by-walking-on-someone's-face society, and which has spread from commercial culture and into our workplaces and our children's mouths. Reestablishing politeness does not require curtseying and cloying formality. It means apologizing when called for. It means saying "thank you" to a token-taker at the toll booth, even though you will never see her again. We can all fit six seconds (I timed it) into our schedules to hold the door for a stranger. We can show respect for other people's time by returning their phone calls. Big shots too busy to return calls can show respect by not publishing their phone numbers. We can stop yelling into our cell phones in public places to show how important we are. We'll be remembered for something other than being obnoxious, while avoiding aggravating someone else's status insecurities. A henchmen for rap star Lil' Kim took exactly this offense, opening fire on a Brooklyn man and wounding him in the leg when he refused to lower his voice while talking on his cell phone.[985]

To you socially comatose coughers: is there anyone home? The aerosol of phlegm in your projectile cough makes people around you cringe in repulsion. I am constantly astounded that you are oblivious to the reactions. Your bacteria is not a gift to your neighbors. Please cover your mouth—and with something other than your hands. This small consideration could save someone from a week sick in bed.

I have a special deficit in my ability to comprehend seat kickers. Short of being an undiagnosed epileptic, you have no excuse for using your knees to bruise the kidneys of the person riding in front of you. And think of the lapful of acrid airline coffee on the person behind before reclining your seatback with such vengeance. On the street, those among us who are smokers are already lepers, but we can be aware that we force someone to stoop down and pick up our discarded butts off the sidewalk. We can all remember the simple rule taught in preschool and in all religions: treat others as you wish to be treated.

I make no claim to sainthood based on politeness (or anything else). I have fantasized about having a megaphone loud enough to boom the very voice of God through the car roof of the brain-dead dawdler, too oblivious to the perfectly clear breakdown lane to free his ten-car retinue from life-threatening passing maneuvers. (My father would pull briefly alongside when he finally got the chance, looking through the dawdler's window—not to glare, but struggling to understand the mind that would perpetrate this commuters' version of Chinese water torture on random strangers.)

America needs a high-profile campaign to foster politeness—using humor, true anecdotes, and (yuk) celebrity conversions, but not preachiness. Maybe some of the original cast of *Animal House* would sign on. The Mormon Church has an admirable, long-running TV ad series promoting tenderness and civility, showing ordinary people doing kind things for strangers. The campaign's politeness mascot could be the "Gentleman Bandit," a Manchester, New Hampshire, bank robber who, in mid-crime, actually paused to hold the door for a woman while bolting with the cash.[986] Courteous crime may be catching on. Three years later in the same city, a jewel thief made off with a $4500 diamond ring, but not before saying "thank you" to the store clerk who handed it to him.[987] I can see the campaign slogan: there's always time for politeness.

SAVORING NOW

My wife and I were hosting a nearly flawless election party in the hilltop field in front of our home. Creampuff clouds drifted across the bright blue summer sky. My volunteers were happily cranking out the barbecue, bean salad, and cold beer just fast enough to keep up with the overflow crowd of six hundred. Everyone felt the sizzle of live politics, the state's top names circulating among the guests, sizing each other up for future alliances. The reporters and camera crews, like well-fed sharks, were temporarily at ease in their gaffe hunt. A photographer for my local paper, which supports exclusively liberals, snapped my face from acute angles, hoping as usual for a ghoulish shot they could publish to poison my PR. (They did not get the shot that day.) I was completely freed of the usual distractions that come with hosting a big event, because the volunteers were totally on top of everything and the buzz was that this was the place to be.

While I was physically present, I missed most of my own perfect party. Instead of enjoying the perfect now with each friend and friendly adversary, I was in air-traffic-control mode, scanning for more important people the instant my conversational partner's eyes were not fixed on mine. (Voters rightfully hate this because it means the politician is pretending to listen to them. To avoid this offense, professionally handled candidates have a staffer "on body." The staffer does the scanning and knows exactly when to gently break into the conversation, getting a phone number and promising that Senator X or Governor Y will be back in touch when there is more time to thoroughly discuss the matter.) Genuinely important people need never be interrupted like this because they know not to talk so long as to make it necessary.

None of us should live like that, stripping our lives of moment-to-moment consciousness. The good life entails not having bagged some desired steady state, but a readiness for possibility. Even if we rise, living with nothing but a goal always in mind will deny us the infinitely greater pleasures of the process. Our shortcut social tactics should never screen out the fascinating, off-brand people who could become our close friends or help us conceptualize a breakthrough. Instead, we can open the doors to our gated lives. We can strike up conversation with the introverted teen silent on his skateboard, or the person with an ideology opposite our own. That way, we will learn and enrich the world.

HEROES WITHOUT PUBLICISTS

Today you are a nobody unless your face is painted in LCD on a building in Times Square. Our constant diet of supersized junk celebrities and million-watt success icons deprives us of our real heroes. We need to stop drooling over the artificially famous and pay more attention to the millions of generous, highly competent, but anonymous people who make the world work.

Even if by no more than a few moments of private refection, we can honor those people doing good and quiet jobs. We can send a friendly note to the guys at the district highway garage who worked until dawn pushing back the snowbanks so that they do not thaw into the road and form a dangerous ice patch. We can take notice of how, even going 30 miles per hour, these drivers can pull up their blades and miss each reflector post. Or the daycare worker driving to work in her nine-year-old car and whose patience and love teaches a child how to share a toy. We can thank the factory preventative-maintenance technician who increases product quality by an amount that only a statistician can detect, but enough to help keep 100 jobs here. We can put some sunshine inside the cubicle walls of the Dakota tech support who, without stock options, cheerfully and competently gets your 100-percent consumer-proof software working.

Any of us could become a hero—and with zero advance planning. Just after midnight one night in 2003, thirteen-year-old Ethan Billings and his father woke to discover that their Center Ossipee, New Hampshire, home was burning down. They pushed out a bedroom window screen and jumped to safety. Young Billings immediately climbed back into the house to rescue his eight-year-old sister, Clarissa. Meanwhile, the boy's four-year-old sister, Savannah Rose, had run from her bedroom into the burning kitchen, immobilized and screaming in panic. Once again, Ethan crawled back through the smoke and into the burning kitchen, carrying his little sister outdoors to safety.

Two towns from where I live, a couple of teenage boys driving over a bridge watched as a stranger's car swerved through a guardrail and plunged into the icy river. Without hesitation or any equipment, the teens stopped their car and jumped into the river, rescuing a mom and her two kids who would otherwise have drowned. In a similar brave incident, though one with a sad ending, dentist Gerard Soucy stopped his car on an icy New England highway, the first person on the scene to help the victims of a rollover accident. Approaching the vehicle to help, Soucy was hit and killed by a truck that had swerved onto the shoulder.[988] Most of us have very deep respect for people like Soucy and his family, and, by reflecting a bit, we can find considerate ways to show it.

Eighty-four-year-old Donald Tullis never earned more than $6 per hour, but he committed his entire life to caring for his youngest son, Tim, 50, who is autistic. Tullis slept in a bed a few feet from Tim, tied Tim's shoes, shaved him, made the afternoon popcorn, and let Tim sort through the junk mail—the kind of daily routines that anchor those with autism. Tim adored his father who, in turn, beamed with pride at his son's progress. Rather than showing concern for himself and focusing on the pain of his arthritis, the ageing Tullis worried about what would happen to his son when he could no longer care for him.

One afternoon, Tim came home from the sheltered workshop he attended to find Donald gone, and searched from room to room, calling "Daddy, Daddy." Donald Tullis had been taken to the hospital and later died. Tim found a temporary home with Marianne and Larry Badaczewski and their young family, who take in people like Tim until permanent placements can be found. About twenty percent of the nation's 4.3 million people with developmental disabilities are cared for at home by a family member over sixty years old. "I wish I had a thousand more like Marianne," said Rose Warman, who runs a program that helps care for people like Tim.[989] Maybe some of us can be among those thousand more.

RATIONAL GOAL-SETTING

We'd feel more successful if we would select aspirations tuned to our qualifications. Misleading biochemical and cultural lures have sucked in too many underqualified contestants whose efforts would be better expended on attainable goals. As we saw in Chapter 4, almost half of us believe we are either now or will someday be wealthy, when the actual number is five percent. Two in three black male high school athletes think themselves destined for the pros, where the actual odds are 10,000 to one. An astounding 30 percent of us operate under the illusion that we will someday become famous.

The reality is that equal opportunity is a lie. About half of our personality and aptitudes are inherited, and even those born with the aptitudes for a demanding endeavor may lack degrees from the right schools or the right social networks to overcome the class barriers in our increasingly stratified America. This does not mean that every introvert should abandon public speaking or that entire industries will no longer be built upon discoveries

made by the unpedigreed. But reality counsels that we should not beat ourselves up over failure to be what we are not meant to be. Precious few of us
have bodies that use oxygen as efficiently as Lance Armstrong's, and even
fewer of us have minds like Jay Greenburg's that play unwritten symphonies in real time.[990] Wasted effort would be saved and national productivity
increased if America's armies of aspiring actors and NBA starters did a reality
check on their skills.

Gregory Miller and Carsten Wrosch have run several studies showing that
simply giving up in the face of unattainable goals is far healthier than per-
sisting and failing. Miller followed teen girls for one year, finding that those
unable to retreat from failure to reach a cherished life goal had elevated blood
levels of cortisol and C-reactive protein, a biomarker for heart disease, diabetes, and shortened lifespan. Miller and Wrosch found large differences in
self-reported life-satisfaction between people with a high versus low ability
to abandon unattainable goals. Low ability to abandon such goals has the
same impact on personal life-satisfaction as moving from the United States to
Uzbekistan, or from Switzerland to the United States.[991] Yang Yang's analysis
of the General Social Survey happiness data I cited in Chapter 7 shows that
happiness among Americans peaks between age sixty and seventy. The best
explanation is that the young-elderly are happier because their expectations
have diminished to more closely match their actual circumstances. Members
of the baby boom generation—their expectations and goals least congruent
with their reality—are least happy of all.

We can be healthier and happier by abandoning OverSuccess and selecting and pursuing goals better matched to our talents, stage in life, and current
resources. Rationally selected goals challenge our personal skills, training, and
aptitudes. They are neither too easy nor impossibly difficult. A good rule of
thumb recommended by psychologists is that we select challenges at which we
are about fifty-percent likely to succeed. Of course, we do not know our capacities until we test drive them, and when we're confronted with failure to achieve
a goal, we should try harder and then smarter. But if failure persists, certainly
before we reach the point of psychological depression, we are wise to redirect
our energy and select more achievable goals. Rather than wallowing in failure,
we should take on transitional activities if we haven't ascertained what our new
goals might be. Those of us who have what it takes to reach excellence and pre-

eminence in highly challenging fields should persist in their quest. Those of us less endowed should concentrate on finding success within reach.

Even if we choose goals considered to carry low status, we need not compromise our ultimate personal fulfillment. Some low-status goals provide immense but unrecognized value to society. New York University's Amy Wrzesniewski studied hospital janitors, finding that some described their jobs in glowing terms, seeing themselves as improving people's lives and performing tasks critical to the functioning of their units.[992] The former CEO of a billion-dollar company told me he was never happier than when he and his wife opened a small pet store in their hometown. America's onetime number-six bicyclist told me that he grew to enjoy his sport only after finally coming to terms with the reality that he would never be number one.

In my years as a tree surgeon, I finished work each day soiled and sweaty. Upper-middle-class women, hands held equestrian as if their nail polish were still drying, would sneer at me in the teller line as I deposited the day's checks for looking as I did. But I was lucky enough to get jobs where I could select and shape the mature trees around a home or on a topographically interesting public place. The work required intense physical exertion and the constant judgment of a sculptor. My crew loved their work so much that they would sometimes cut short lunch to get back at creating the beauty we could envision. Years later, customers would often approach me to thank me for my work. I sold the business in my twenties out of concern for the physical risks, but mostly because of my sensitivity to my craft's low status. In the years since, I have come to revalue it. We can find profound satisfaction in goals that suit us, rather than the OverSuccessed goals we sometimes irrationally impose on ourselves.

THE SCIENCE-BASED RECIPE FOR HAPPINESS

Being happy—that is, enjoying a meaningful and satisfying life, as opposed to one that is merely filled with pleasure—is the best alternative to wallowing in the fruitless wants and fantasies of OverSuccess. Happy people live longer (nineteen-percent longer, according to one forty-year study), have healthier immune systems, are more creative and helpful, earn more money, have stronger marriages, are better leaders, have more friends, are more socially adept, cope better with difficulties, are better able to multi-task, and are more altruistic. Age, health, income (beyond $50,000 in the U.S.), intelligence, beauty, race, education, and gender have little impact on happiness. However, long-lasting and disabling illness, the death of a spouse, or job loss can have multi-year deleterious effects on happiness. Kenyans living in dung huts without TVs are among the happiest people in the world. If, as we've seen, material and status success brings little lasting happiness, what does? Fortunately, a well-developed body of research provides us with sound guidance.[993] You are more likely to be happy if you:

- Accept yourself for who you are.
- Have control over the major elements of your life.
- Find and engage in purposeful, meaningful work and activity in which you are competent and where you can grow. (More about this critical worklife alternative to OverSuccess is just below.)
- Help others. Be of service to something larger than self. Develop a second or third career in voluntary or philanthropic activity built around personal strengths. This is especially relevant to skilled baby boomers being pushed aside in paying careers by age discrimination.
- Focus on the process of reaching personal goals, not just achievement.
- Find faith, spirituality, or religion. Whether it is a delusion or not, the belief in God and an active faith strengthens nations and makes us happier.
- Be married. Forty percent of married people say they are very happy compared with 24 percent of those unmarried.
- Live a rich social life with multiple strong friendships. Build an extended family to strengthen family life, including nonrelatives if we feel close to them.
- Get sufficient sleep and aerobic exercise.
- Act happy to be happy. There is some evidence to support "behavior induction," the purposeful replacement of negative emotions, bodily motions, facial expressions, and vocalizations with positive ones. Reflect daily on positive experiences and people. To trigger positive

emotions, say "ah" instead of "uw," smile rather than frown, and walk with a confident gait instead of a desolate shuffle.

- Do not expect accumulating pleasures to provide happiness. (More about the happiness-inducing alternative to pleasure seeking is below.)

Contrary to folk wisdom, the desire for status success, and even wealth and fame, does not preclude happiness, as long as we balance the pursuit of status with other meaning-related goals. Research has shown that people whose goals combine high material and nonmaterial aspirations are as happy as those with low material and high nonmaterial goals.[994]

In our work lives, *the* central alternative to OverSuccess is finding a career that is a calling. To accomplish this, leading happiness researcher and former American Psychological Association president Martin Seligman first suggests identifying your "signature strengths." A free, online version of Seligman's 245-question VIA Signature Strengths Survey is accessible at www.AuthenticHappiness.com.[995]

Once you know your signature strengths, find a way to apply them in specific jobs and activities that put you in a psychological zone called "flow." Mihaly Csikszentmihalyi developed the concept and has contributed over two decades of research and written several books on flow experience. Csikszentmihalyi first noticed flow in painters who, after hours of absorption with one canvas, would jump right to a fresh one, spending no time in contemplation of their completed work. Flow is about the process, not the finished product. You can find it in work that applies your well-developed skills and that challenges you but is not overwhelming. This work is so engrossing that your self-awareness disappears for hours.[996] By designing our educational systems and work environments around the concepts of signature strength and flow, America could accelerate innovation and achievement while increasing our aggregate happiness.

Several experimental approaches have shown that accumulating pleasurable experiences does not produce happiness, whereas doing things to develop your potential or to help others does. Michael Steger, director of the laboratory for the study of meaning and quality of life at the University of Louisville, and his co-workers compared the effect of "eudaimonic" versus "hedonic" activities on the self-reported happiness of college students. Eudaimonic activities included volunteering, making a contribution of money, listening carefully to or confiding in another person, thinking about long-term life goals, persevering in attaining a difficult goal, and expressing gratitude. Hedonic activities included having sex for pleasure, buying something for yourself, getting drunk or high, eating for taste rather than hunger, or being entertained at a party, sporting event, movie, or by listening to music. The eudaimonic or meaning- and purpose-enhancing activities had large effects on short-term happiness. Purely pleasurable activities had no significant effects on either short- or longer-term happiness.[997] Another recent set of experiments provides strong hint of a causal relationship between contributing even modest sums of money to others and increases in happiness, whereas spending more on oneself results in no lasting increases. This is so even though nearly two-thirds of people in one experiment thought that spending more money on themselves would make them happier.[998] Most people do not know what they can do to make themselves happier—which means that we can put to good use right now the existing body of happiness science.

Happiness science has engendered a movement whose champions are working to establish an American "national well-being index" to parallel the gross domestic product index. If, as I showed in Chapter 7, American GDP is rising while mental health, social capital, and satisfaction with life are declining, we need a more inclusive indicator to help shape our national goals. For example, rebuilding New Orleans adds to GDP but does not account for the physical and psychological losses of its devastation by Katrina. Likewise, prison construction grows the economy but is not offset by the cost of the status defeat and crime that have made new prison buildings necessary. In 2004, Seligman and University of Illinois happiness researcher Ed Diener began to construct a national well-being index, to be composed of indicators for social capital, health, purposeful lives, work satisfaction, volunteering, altruism, crime, corruption, marriage stability, religiosity, optimism, engagement, freedom, and human rights.[999] In early 2008 Gallup-Healthways used some of these concepts, launching the world's first ongoing well-being index.

If the idea of a happiness index sounds embarrassingly kumbaya to you, just recall that our Declaration of Independence summoned us to found an America that would protect our rights to life, liberty, and the pursuit of happiness. We are doing well at the first two; we can do better at the third.

IMPROVED MENTAL HEALTHCARE

In these pages we have seen compelling evidence that OverSuccess contributes substantially to the high prevalence of mental illness in America, with rates here at least twice those in the rest of the industrialized world. The social burden is often under-recognized. As measured by lost years of healthy life, mental illness and addiction are the leading sources of disease burden globally, topping cardiovascular disease and cancer.[1000] Each year, one in ten American adults will be afflicted by depression or a related disorder. Almost one-third of us are likely to suffer a serious or moderate mental disorder sometime during our lifetimes. Those born between 1970 and 1985 are four times more likely than their grandparents to suffer any type of mental disorder, up to ten times more likely to suffer depression, six times more likely to become addicted to alcohol, and 45 times more likely to be addicted to drugs.[1001]

Improving the nation's mental-health status will not be easy. While most of us who suffer mental illness do seek out and find some type of care, we often delay getting help for years. Just over half of alcohol addicts will eventually seek out mental healthcare, but typically six years after the onset of their disease. About ninety percent of those suffering major depression eventually seek out care, but eight tortured years after symptoms begin. And when care is obtained, it is usually ineffective. Of those who do seek timely treatment within one year of the onset of their symptoms, only about one-third receive even minimally adequate care. Mental illness is unlike the degenerative and age-related diseases that consume most of America's healthcare dollars because it can debilitate people in the prime of productive life and linger with the sufferer for decades.[1002]

Mental illness and addiction are not failures of willpower or indications of character weakness. Mental illness can be just as serious and just as organic as cancer or Parkinson's. As evidence of this seriousness, depressed people commit suicide at 25 times the rate of others.[1003] As I have shown, depression and addiction are substantially caused by physical differences among our brains and cause long-lasting physical damage to both our brains and bodies.

America would not tolerate two-thirds of broken bones or cases of tuberculosis going untreated. We should demand that Congress and insurance companies equalize the availability and utilization of medical care for the organ above our shoulders that consumes 20 percent of our resting metabolic energy and contains 40 percent of our cells. Mental disorders such as schizophrenia, major depression, and obsessive-compulsive disorder are now as diagnosable and treatable as general medical conditions. Fortunately, more people are getting treated for depression, because it has been destigmatized, because effective drugs are now available to treat it, and because drug companies have advertised those treatments to consumers. On the dark side, addiction treatment—a largely public function—has dropped since 1990. As a nation, we must realize that it is no longer morally or financially defensible to arbitrarily ration mental healthcare (but not general healthcare) as a cost-containment strategy.

The National Alliance for the Mentally Ill is the nation's leading advocate for equitable mental-health treatment and for ending social stigma against those suffering from mental disorders.[1004] NAMI can provide more information for those wishing to become active in the fight to reduce mental illness in America.

PLACEBOS AND BRAIN TRAINING TO TREAT OBSESSIONS?

U.S. sales of the selective serotonin reuptake inhibitors, such as Prozac, Paxil, Zoloft, and Effexor, were about $12 billion in 2007, with 233 million prescriptions written—more prescriptions than any other class of medication—with the U.S. by far the world's leading market.[1005] With lower side effects than the older antidepressants that they have largely displaced, the SSRIs marked a milestone in rational drug design, and are a blessing for many depression sufferers. However, like all compounds, SSRIs have unwanted side effects, including serious ones such as a doubled risk of suicidal thinking and a doubled risk of bone fractures in the elderly.[1006]

Recent research, buried by the very drug companies that market the SSRIs, provides compelling evidence for the effectiveness of another powerful means to reduce depression—one with zero side effects. Dr Irving Kirsch, a University of Connecticut psychologist, used the Freedom of Information Act to pry loose the less favorable drug-company clinical studies submitted to the FDA in support of approval of six of the top-selling SSRIs. Kirsch found that, among moderately depressed patients, sugar pills produced a nearly identical rate of symptom improvement. SSRIs delivered clinically significant benefit over sugar pills only for the most severely depressed patients. In the aggregate, zero-cost, zero-side-effect sugar pills delivered 80 percent of the response of the drugs.[1007] Patients receiving no medicine at all (but thinking that they might be) get very nearly the benefit of those spending the $12 billion annually. Similarly, Parkinson's Disease patients who took a placebo increased their brain dopamine production by as much as those taking their regularly prescribed levodopa.[1008]

The placebo effect is now viewed as holding so much medical promise that the National Institutes of Health set aside $5 million to study it. Doctors often report anecdotally that their patients do better when they are given a positive prognosis and when they talk up the positive benefits of an administered drug.[1009] A recent survey of Israeli medical practitioners found that a surprising sixty percent routinely use placebos for patients suffering from pain, anxiety, vertigo, sleep problems, asthma, and drug withdrawal. The Israeli study found placebos either generally or occasionally effective.[1010] In another placebo experiment, subjects who were told that ordinary skin lotion applied to the arm would reduce the pain of a mild electric shock felt less pain, even though pain signals to their brains were unchanged. The brain regions that respond to real pain medication responded in identical fashion to the belief that pain would be reduced.[1011] Men who had been injected with a compound that creates moderate jaw pain experienced relief from an injected placebo of saline water that was described to them as a pain reliever. PET brain scans found that this placebo activated the brain's natural pain-suppressive opiod system, causing the brain to release its own pain-relieving endorphins.[1012] Patients who were given a placebo they were told cost $2.50 per pill felt it relieved pain better than an identical pill they were told cost 10 cents, which again shows the power of suggestive power.[1013] Safe and effective illusion will someday be used under carefully controlled protocols and administered by responsible practitioners to synchronize our obsessions with reality.

Recent evidence also shows that we can use willed mental activity to diminish perceived pain. Using mental exercises, experimental subjects were successfully trained to control blood flow to their rostral anterior cingulate cortex, an area of the brain that registers pain. Sufferers of chronic pain for whom other approaches did not work reported being able to reduce perceived pain by about half. The training took only 39 minutes to learn, but required lying down in a two-million-dollar real-time fMRI machine and worked only if the subjects were able to see a real-time display of their own localized brain response. Old-fashioned and technically simpler biofeedback monitoring and attempting to control breathing and heart rate proved ineffective.[1014]

My hunch is that placebos and meditation are effective, albeit crude forms of brain training that, in the future, will be combined with new technology to take us beyond managing physical pain and allow us to control addictions and other learned psychological disorders. Before long, accessible and affordable real-time brain-scanning technology will become available, giving us another tool to help us quickly damp down Brangelina, Branson, or Bentley envy, or whatever other cues trigger our personal success obsession.

PSYCHOPHARMACOLOGY

I believe that we can and must provide safe and effective medication to people suffering from recognized behavioral addictions and obsessions, including those associated with OverSuccess. First, however, we must overcome the laugh factor already associated with Paxil being prescribed for social introversion. Second, we must address the side effects against which the therapeutic benefits of almost every drug must be balanced. For example, seven percent of Parkinson's disease patients taking Mirapex, which is used to increase dopamine function, wind up addicted to gambling, sex, or shopping while taking the drug.[1015]

Relying on pharmacology to relieve normal social distress is a remedy inferior to treating its underlying causes. But those causes are sometimes immutable. And there are many precedents for using medical intervention to improve the normal human condition. For example, we administer painkillers during childbirth without controversy, though childbirth is not a disease. It is also natural, as we have seen, for humans to be overoptimistic. We overestimate our own skills and the odds of our success and, to our economic detriment, we sharply underestimate the value of long-term compared to short-term financial gains. Moreover, as we've seen, the psychological gains from an increase in income, new possessions, or achievements evaporate within just a few months. We compete irrationally for relative status, even if we get no absolute gain. In the absence of more valuable markers, we compete even for worthless symbolic crumbs.

Before the historically recent human achievement of hyper-abundance, survival was our species' primary goal. We needed brain chemistry to motivate these irrational behaviors, spurring us to want more food, sex, and visual stimulation because future shortages were certain. Now, we have enough calories, soft porn, and television so that getting more makes us fatter and hyper-stimulated, but not happier. As we've seen, our natural ambition is to seek recognized status within the small, face-to-face groups for which our brains have evolved. Now, the global economy taunts us with its Olympian goals and massive rewards for its top slots. Our innate psychology drives us to imitate famous and successful people whose characteristics are misleadingly souped up by plastic surgeons and publicists. Now, American culture is a marketing machine that tells our status-conscious brains to want ever more numerous, sophisticated, and hard-to-get trophies. We are under intense biological and cultural pressure to succeed, but contemporary America's extraordinary standards make visible success virtually impossible for most of us to achieve.

I've described the widely accepted evidence that our innate drives are mediated, in large part, by brain biochemicals, such as dopamine, serotonin, testosterone, and cortisol. All of them play roles in shaping our health, motivations, and behavior. But our chronically stressed, status-obsessed world sometimes causes our native neurochemistry to harm us. Our brains were not built to damp down our desire for higher status in the face of hyper-abundance, supernatural benchmarks, and 24/7 pressure from commercial culture. For perhaps sixty million Americans, including a big slice of the boomer generation, our ferocious pursuit of more success may be natural, but it is not buying us more health or happiness.

Just as we were morally justified in using technology when we were faced with smallpox—a physical disease that emerged as a result of larger, denser human populations—so are we morally justified in using technology to inter-vene against psychological disorders that have emerged as a result of global society. For some of us, nonmedical interventions to success obsession are ineffective. Some of us wrestling with OverSuccess will want to use soon-to-be perfected pharmaceuticals to modulate this evolutionary mismatch between culture and motivation. Should we deny sixty million OverSuccess sufferers the right to take a pill allowing them to walk past the fashion maga-zines without triggering a six-year bout with anorexia, or to feel content living in a house with aluminum siding?

Even given our justifiable concerns about medicating social disabilities, America has come to broadly accept the use of legal drugs such as Prozac and Strattera to make us happier and more personable. No less a figure than the director of the National Institute of Drug Abuse concedes that the physi-cal structure and biochemical functioning of parts of a drug addict's brain have become permanently altered, and if an addict is to successfully resist relapse, his or her treatment may require the use of a substitute drug that does not provide a high. Our rapidly increasing knowledge of the biochemical and genetic bases for disease will soon deliver safer and more precisely act-ing drugs that will adjust our neurochemistries to mitigate the obsessions we endure over status.[1016] We should welcome such progress.

I have shown that some of the same brain pathways are involved in drug addiction and status obsession. The pharmaceuticals to treat both have com-mon neurochemistries. Buprenorphine attaches itself to brain opiod receptors, making addicts feel better and at the same time blocking the action of opiate abuse drugs. Naltrexone also blocks the opiod receptors and is used to treat alcohol addiction. An Israeli research team has shown that the transplantation of human cells that increase local production of glial cell line-derived neuro-trophic factor (GDNF) into the nucleus accumbens of cocaine-addicted rats suppresses the rats' appetite for cocaine.[1017] Rimonabant, a still-experimental drug, dampens the cravings of food and nicotine addicts. Inhaling oxytocin, the brain neurotransmitter associated with love and mother-infant bonding, makes people more trusting. Oxytocin may one day help America's millions of child-abuse and neglect victims learn to connect again with trustworthy people.[1018]

Such drugs will be double-edged swords; they may aggravate the very social tensions we hope to heal. Some of us will use these drugs to control irrational and self-destructive urges for unattainable status. But cure will become enhancement will become necessity. In the end, we will use drugs, not just to cure mental disease, but also to deliver context-sensitive personality adjustments. We will fine-tune our demeanor, language, and body scent to social circumstances. Group leaders will neurochemically bulk up when entering a meeting room, just as those gifted with charisma now do naturally. Like good hair color, no one but our pharmacist will know for sure.

Even in their more advanced forms, the use of motivation-adjusting drugs will entail risks and trade-offs. Roy Wise, who studies the neurobiology of drug addiction for the National Institute of Drug Addiction, warns that "if you block all dopamine, it blunts all the pleasures of life ... We need to make small adjustments to [drug addicts'] lives, like technicians fine-tune the ratio of fuel and oxygen in a racecar."[1019] But in consultation with our doctors, each of us should have the right to choose whether or not to use these drugs that are soon to enter our formularies—whether to shape our own status or to ameliorate the impact of other people's status on us. We will soon regulate our status psychology—up and down, as needed—just as we do blood pressure.

GENE THERAPY

Justifiably intense debate surrounds the prospect of improving human well-being by intentionally modifying our genetic characteristics. Before exploring this approach as it relates to OverSuccess, I want to dispel any inference that gene therapy should be used to remove the effects of ordinary daily stressors. Until a large body of clinical experience has accumulated, gene therapy should be restricted to those diagnosed by a professional as unusually susceptible to, or with a history of, mental disorders resistant to conventional treatments. But the conceptual objections to gene therapy for mental disorders are already moot because, as we'll see in the following paragraphs, two types are already in use: somatic-cell gene therapy, and most controversially, germline modification.

Germline modification has been used since 1990 in the form of in vitro fertilization and pre-implantation genetic diagnosis and other techniques to sort out genetic defects at the egg, sperm, or embryo stage in thousands of American births. Use of these techniques constitutes germline modification because the resulting genetic choices are incorporated into every cell of the new baby's body and are passed on to all subsequent generations. Somatic-cell therapy is less radical, in that it is used to treat genetic defects in living individuals: corrective genetic material is inserted into specific human body tissue and cells, but not reproductive cells, meaning that somatic-cell genetic changes are not passed on to subsequent generations—and are therefore not species-altering.

Somatic-cell gene therapy has progressed slowly since it was launched on an experimental basis, also in 1990. It remains a major challenge to deliver the corrective genetic material and get it to incorporate permanently into the right places on the chromosomes within the nucleus of target cells. Research has focused on the use of modified viral material to carry the therapeutic genetic payload to its intended destination. Viruses are nature's wizards at navigating through the body and getting through cell walls, but viral genetic payloads do not always successfully "transfect" the target cells. So far, the genetic transmission rates have been low, the beneficial effects quickly reverse themselves, and the host immune responses make repeated treatments impossible.

But there is progress. A gene therapy cure may be at hand for children born with severe combined immunodeficiency (SCID), or "bubble boy" disease. SCID is caused by various mutations that deprive sufferers of a functioning immune system. When immune-matched donors are not available for bone marrow transplants, these children typically die during early childhood. Ten of eleven SCID-afflicted children given gene therapy in 1999 are alive today, eight with operating immune systems.[1020] However, enthusiasm for the technique has been severely dampened because four of the eleven children to date have been stricken by leukemia. Unwanted genetic material from the virus apparently randomly integrated into non-target body cells, or else the inserted genes became overactive.[1021] Three of the four sick children were successfully treated with chemotherapy, but all gene-therapy research using humans was halted in the U.S., though it continues in England, using a non-carcinogenic viral vector.[1022]

In an early, phase-one trial, twelve humans with Parkinson's disease had corrective genetic material injected into their brains' subthalamic nucleus. The intent was to down-regulate an overactive brain function characteristic of the disease. After one year, the typical patient enjoyed a 25-percent reduction in PD symptoms with no reported harm.[1023]

Success with these somatic-cell gene-therapy experiments will almost certainly lead to treatments which will permanently correct genetically controlled psychological and motivational disorders. Gene therapy will eventually be used to adjust excessive brain reward system and dopamine response to status pressure. As we discussed in Chapter 2, research on rats and humans has shown that individuals with lower than average brain populations of D2 dopamine receptors are more prone to substance and behavioral addictions. Alcohol and addictive drugs increase brain dopamine production, and extended alcohol or drug abuse decreases D2 receptors in some parts of the brain. Using the viral insertion technique, researchers have used somatic-cell gene therapy to successfully add D2 receptors to the brains of alcoholic rats, resulting in a dramatic reduction in their desire for and consumption of alcohol. The effect disappeared in eight days, but the concept of gene therapy to correct substance addiction was proved.[1024] Another gene-therapy experiment identified a means to block the ability of rats' livers to metabolize alcohol, which offers one more potential route to treating alcoholism. However, as I have already noted, because boosting traits into the normal range increases psychological health does not mean that traits above normal are even better. Adding extra D2 receptors to the striata of normal mice dulled their working memories and made them slower learners. [1025]

As we learned in Chapter 2, chronically bullied and socially defeated mice show long-term increases in social withdrawal and depression-like behavior. This behavior is dependent upon increased levels of brain-derived neurotrophic factor (BDNF) in the nucleus accumbens, a key area of the brain reward system. Gene therapy that deleted BDNF production in a brain area supplying the nucleus accumbens eliminated the socially withdrawn and depression-like behavior in the bullied mice. BDNF may facilitate changes in neural architecture of the reward system in response to status stress. We don't yet know the effects of BDNF adjustment in humans, although depressed people have sharply higher levels of BDNF in their nucleus accumbens.[1026] Do not try this at home.

The most profound ethical challenge of germline modification is that it would pass unpredictable and potentially irreversible genetic changes on to future generations who would have no say in the choice. A passage in the American Medical Association's ethical code nicely summarizes the fundamental tensions inherent in using gene therapy for social ends:

> Efforts to enhance "desirable" characteristics through the insertion of a modified or additional gene, or efforts to "improve" complex human traits … are contrary not only to the ethical tradition of medicine, but also to the egalitarian values of our society. Because of the potential for abuse, genetic manipulation to affect non-disease traits may never be acceptable and perhaps should never be pursued. If it is ever allowed, at least three conditions would have to be met before it could be deemed ethically acceptable: (1) there would have to be a clear and meaningful benefit to the person, (2) there would have to be no trade-off with other characteristics or traits, and (3) all citizens would have to have equal access to the genetic technology, irrespective of income or other socioeconomic characteristics.[1027]

The first use condition set forth by the AMA is sound and would be fulfilled via the FDA's drug and therapy regulatory process. The second and third provisions are excessively restrictive, in my view. Individuals already make wrenchingly tough trade-off decisions with many medical interventions, with examples including diabetes-related amputations and toxic cancer treatments. Moreover, restricting access to gene therapy until it is made universally available would prevent early adopters from helping to more rapidly debug and drive down the high costs of new technology.

As I discussed in Chapter 3, because customers in nations such as China will lead the market forward regardless of American institutional or political caution, the barriers to use of gene therapy will be technical, not ethical. Unlike muscular dystrophy or cystic fibrosis, which are single gene defects, intelligence and mental disorders are complex traits, not susceptible to simple on-off genetic manipulation. A recent experiment successfully creating a strain of smarter fruit fly illustrates these difficulties. While it took only twenty generations of selectively breed a super fly better able to remember flavors, the flies were less able to compete for limited food.[1028] Similar trade-offs will complicate cures for mental disorders. For example, people with mild schizophrenia, who suffer from paranoia and jumpy speech but not hallucinations or delusions, more evenly use both their left and right brains and perform better on standardized tests for creativity. Long-term administration of Ritalin to juvenile rats causes adult depression and reduces motivation and persistence.[1029] A genetically manipulated strain of mathematicians might also turn out to be functional incompetents. A side effect of eliminating all schizophrenia and ADHD may be the suppression of imagination and rapid perception, because mild ADHD makes people more alert to random environmental stimuli. Curing a mental disorder may also cure a person's talent or distinctiveness.

The silver fox experiment cited in Chapter 3, in which a wild animal was selectively bred for only tameness without selection pressure on other traits, also changed the animal in several other unpredicted ways. Genetic tinkering to enhance a complex trait may come with unwanted baggage. For example, it sounds appealing to genetically banish physical pain, but about a dozen people worldwide suffering from Hereditary Sensory and Autonomic Neuropathy Type-5 would differ. A woman named Gabby Gingras, who cannot sense pain, had to have one eye and all her teeth removed as a result of unintentional self-mutilation.[1030] Similarly, relief from all psychological pain would also have intolerable consequences. Imagine banishing all guilt.

Our defense against such excessive and irresponsible use of gene therapy is the simple fact that most of us are innately reasonable. Most people using gene therapy will choose body and personality enhancements that are intermediate to high, but not extreme in degree, and will alter only those disorders that are seriously disabling. Few of us will want no pain, no guilt, nine feet of height, or a ceaselessly sunny disposition.

Gene therapy, beginning with embryo and somatic-cell gene modification, will hit the market within ten years. Within twenty years, it will be commonplace. Two hundred years ago, killing bacteria and immunizations against viruses were taboos, thought to be hubris and dangerous violations of the natural order. But just as antibiotics became a life-transforming reality, so will scientists improve genetic technologies to make them practical, and so will government regulate them for safety and effectiveness. A combination of regulation, subsidies, and private philanthropy will address the social challenges of national genetic inequity. Genetic technologies will ultimately become as familiar as telephones and as well-accepted as eyeglasses.

Gene therapy and enhancement promise to put us at the cusp of a second major burst of species-changing evolution, as powerful as the natural advances that made us human. Yes, these new genetic tools will unleash an inevitable arms race in intelligence, but they will also provide the means to survive it psychologically. We can and should perfect genetic technology. Those of us who choose to use it will be able to temper the automatic motivations and obsessions that are unsuited to our hyper-competitive society and that drag down our emotional well-being.

THE PROMISE OF EPIGENE THERAPY

Our genes can also become differently tagged with epigenetic markers that boost or suppress their expression within our organs, offering a lower-risk means for us to dial up or down psychological traits affected by OverSuccess. Happily, new research is showing that epigenetic markers are not permanently fixed like genes and can be altered throughout a person's lifetime. In one example of how epigene therapy may one day be used to treat emotional problems, Dr. Moshe Szyf and his McGill University co-workers injected the anti-fungus drug Trichostatin A into the brains of older rats, knocking controlling methyl groups off their glucocorticoid receptor genes, and completely reversing the behavioral effects of lack of affection and care during childhood. Their epigenetic controls biochemically reversed, the formerly fearful, stress-sensitive rats behaved like high-nurturance, low-stress rats. Showing this mechanism to be well-characterized, the opposite effect was achieved when the essential amino acid L-methionine was injected into older rats which had been well-nurtured as pups. The amino acid caused methyl group tags to be attached to the rats' glucocorticoid receptor genes, switching the rats into a high-stress behavior pattern.[1031]

Dr. Arturas Petronis, who leads the University of Toronto's Epigenetics Laboratory, is searching for the links between the epigenome and major depression in humans.[1032] His team had already provided early evidence for epigenetic links to schizophrenia and bipolar disorder, which explains the difficulty scientists have experienced over the past decade nailing down genetic explanations for diseases like these. The same gene variant may poorly predict the odds of an associated disorder as a result of differences in epigenetic tagging. "[Epigenetics] has profound implications in aging, neurological disorders, and child development," says Peter Jones, director of the Norris Comprehensive Cancer Center at the University of Southern California. Jones is also a founding member of the U.S. Human Epigenome Project, launched in 2005 to work alongside a similar European project. Like the various gene-mapping projects already underway, these epigenome projects will likely find links between epigene status and disease, including mental illness and the behavioral obsessions incident to OverSuccess.[1033] Congress should support funding to accelerate epigenome mapping.

MEDIA REFORM

We can go a long way toward healing OverSuccess by refashioning a part of the American media landscape in service of healthier society. We can take advantage of the flood tide of new communication technologies to restore space for genuinely local media outlets, thereby providing visibility and recognition for millions more deserving Americans. The public can demand that for-profit media pay market prices for their use of the public airwaves. We can use these proceeds to fund greatly expanded offerings of diverse, high-quality educational, cultural, and public affairs programming. We can enforce existing law to hold media conglomerates to a higher standard of public service.

As we've seen, the average American spends 4.5 hours daily watching TV and almost ten hours with all forms of media. Commercial culture has replaced the time we once spent in two-way relationships with real people. It has suffocated real culture in a richly engrossing, synthetic social world of richer, more famous, thinner, more physically perfect, more powerful, more materialist, more violent, and more corrupt role models. To grow market share, commercial culture has back-burnered quality, shouldered aside diversity of viewpoint, cut budgets for local content, providing instead a wasteland of visual cacophony, sex, violence, and vapid celebrity. The loss of localism has seriously damaged our communities and starved people of the recognition they deserve for their modest but vital and socially sustaining deeds. Impoverished political coverage threatens our ability to weigh complex issues and to govern ourselves effectively. Commercial culture has incited one billion people living in traditionalist societies around the world to hate America, partly because of how our success-obsessed media managers falsely portray us at Super Bowl halftime. The culture merchants have exchanged American icons, trading the Statue of Liberty for Paris Hilton.

We can have a media that enriches and strengthens, rather than debases and stupefies us. Five practical and possible media reforms can improve our political, social, and psychological health.

End the Spectrum Giveaway. The nation's airwaves are owned by the public, but the most desirable spectrum real estate is largely given away to the media conglomerates with few restrictions. We should capture the full market value for commercial use of this public asset and use the proceeds for public benefit. And the public should be granted free use of a far greater portion of the airwaves than the slivers now available for uses such as Wi-Fi, cordless phones, and garage door openers. Many people do not know that the airwaves are already public property, which the Communications Act of 1934 made explicit. Title III, Section 301, reads, in part, as follows:

> It is the purpose of this Act, among other things, to maintain the control of the United States over all the channels of interstate and foreign radio transmission; and to provide for the use of such channels, but not the ownership therefore, by persons for limited periods of time, under licenses granted by Federal authority, and no such license shall be construed to create any right, beyond the terms, conditions, and periods of the license.

The federally licensed electromagnetic broadcast and communications spectrum may be worth as much as $770 billion. Measured by value, only 12 percent of this public property has ever been auctioned. Most of the remaining 88 percent has been simply granted without charge in the form of quasi-perpetual licenses, in "perhaps the largest corporate welfare giveaway in U.S. history," according to Michael Calabrese, a spectrum policy wonk at the New

America Foundation.[1034] There is little public outcry about the giveaway because 56 percent of us believe erroneously that broadcasters already pay license fees for use of the public spectrum.[1035] Just as we do for offshore oil properties, we should auction limited-duration spectrum licenses for all frequencies—other than those held for public use—with proceeds flowing to the public treasury and to fund independent media, as described below.

After full conversion to digital TV in 2009, a significant part of the "beach-front property" portion of the broadcast spectrum, formerly reserved almost exclusively for UHF TV channels 14 to 51, will no longer be used. This premium-quality spectrum—called "white space"—is highly valuable because it offers the optimum combination of ability to carry high data payloads, travel long distances and over hills, and penetrate concrete walls and thick vegetation at very low power levels. The availability of white space provides an extraordinary opportunity to extend free, unlicensed public use to a part of the spectrum that will allow creation of Internet broadband with sufficient speed and capacity to carry television, radio, voice, and data.

Companies such as Microsoft, Google, and Intel, along with several public-interest groups, have predicted that, after a go-ahead by the Federal Communications Commission, personal white-space devices would hit the consumer market within a year. WSDs would look like an iPhone or a laptop computer and would be enabled with broadband-everywhere Internet connectivity. WSDs already being engineered would communicate with each other like walkie-talkies over a range of several hundred feet, a distance that would be extendable to several dozens of miles with the installation of a nearby $100 radio transmitter. The result would be what enthusiasts call "Wi-Fi on steroids." WSDs would use off-the-shelf military technology to hunt for frequencies not occupied by licensed broadcasts, wireless microphones, and other uses that share this part of the spectrum. Sascha Meinrath, a telecom visionary at the New America Foundation, sees WSDs self-linking into a "mesh" communications network, where each user granting permission would allow any other user to route messages, like a baton in a relay race, through their device's idle capacity. Bandwidth will likely be in the gigabits-per-second range, a thousand times the capacity of current consumer broadband, and ample enough to support a free wireless Internet broadcasting network.[1036]

Needless to say, the broadcasting industry finds this world-changing vision rather threatening. Led by the National Association of Broadcasters, the industry is fighting social and technological progress with regulatory delay, fear-mongering, lobbying, and abundant campaign contributions. As they have for years, the incumbent media and telecom oligopolies would prefer to continue pumping up their quarterly profits by under-investing in consumer bandwidth, jacking up prices, maximizing control over both distribution pipes and content, and retarding development of new technologies. As a result, the U.S. has slipped to fifteenth in the world in broadband penetration rates.[1037] The public and Congress should demand an end to the stranglehold these retrograde companies have been able to maintain over our spectrum.

The combination of ending spectrum giveaways and the free, unlicensed public use of white space would create more competition and more choices, reduce barriers to entry for small and more specialized media, permit low and no-cost communication space for ordinary people and local affairs, and reduce domination of our psychological space by commercial culture.

Fund Independent Media. Even with free public use of white space, spectrum auction proceeds would yield billions of additional dollars per year for the public treasury. (Even as is, proceeds have averaged over $5 billion per year since 1994 when spectrum auctions began; for comparison, funding for the Corporation for Public Broadcasting has averaged about $400 million per year.) A portion of this public revenue should be reserved to fund independent, noncommercial content, programming, and distribution. The market alone has proven unable to provide all the media we need to have a healthy society and a strong republic. Like orphan drugs that are of great value to a small number of people, all worthwhile media products are not commercially viable or supportable by private grants.

How could Congress address the thorny problem of allocating independent media funds without being confined by mass taste and without being consumed by debates over partisan bias, *Piss Christ*, and other controversial cultural products? To get a variety of independent media that reflects and explores the best of America, we should avoid the French Ministry of Culture's approach and its 12,000 culturecrats. Nor do we need another Public Broadcasting Service, which is certainly a valued public asset, but too large and institutionally straitjacketed to provide the greater viewpoint diversity we need. Instead, to keep government out of actual decisions about production, programming, and distribution technology, multiple and diverse audience and peer panels could determine how best the money should be spent. Or, funds could be allocated on a matching basis to projects that demonstrate their merit by their ability to secure partial private funding. In Belgium and the Netherlands, civic groups and listener associations are guaranteed media access time in proportion to the size of their memberships. An American version of that idea could use public independent-media funds to pay for production and distribution access via cable TV or broadcast radio and TV at market rates. These approaches would help counter the starvation we currently experience in local political and social coverage.

How do we know that the public will not demand more *Desperate Housewives*? Perhaps we underestimate the American people. A RoperASW poll in 2004 found that the public believes PBS to be the most valuable service taxpayers receive, second only to national defense. Seventy-nine percent feel that existing government funding for PBS is "money well spent."[1038] And the public does not feel that PBS by itself is enough public programming. A 1999 Lake Snell Perry & Associates poll found that nearly eight in ten Americans support the use of spectrum license fees to fund more educational, public affairs, and local programming.

Enforce the Public Interest Doctrine. Massive and continuous public pressure would be required, but Congress and the FCC should reinvigorate enforcement of the public interest doctrine that applies to broadcasters and communications services providers. Sections 307 and 309 of the 1934 Communications Act empower the FCC to license spectrum use for a limited period to an applicant if the service would serve "the public interest, convenience, and necessity." Congress purposely never defined the meaning of the term "public interest." Even though the Supreme Court declared, "It is the right of the viewers, not the right of the broadcasters, which is paramount," seventy-five years of relentless pressure by holders of spectrum licenses has forced Congress and federal regulators to void almost all specific or enforceable public service requirements.[1039]

Either the Communications Act should be repealed in its entirety to end the charade, or license holders should be required to provide more educational, public affairs, and local program content, greater depth of information, and more viewpoint independence and diversity. The notion of providing "equal time" for two opposing views should not be reinstated because almost every issue requires illumination by, for example, more voices than those of just a Democratic and Republican spokesperson or a land developer arguing against a neighborhood antidevelopment organizer. These requirements are particularly essential if we never do manage to auction off the spectrum as we should or win greatly more funding for independent media. Libertarians and conservatives should be frank with themselves: the public interest doctrine goes unenforced not because of Congress' devotion to free markets, but because big media and big telecom spent $485 million to influence federal politicians between 1997 and 2006. Presidents and presidential contenders George W. Bush, John McCain, Joe Lieberman, Barack Obama, Hillary Clinton, John Edwards, John Kerry, Al Gore, Howard Dean, and Chris Dodd all received at least three-quarter-million dollars from companies seeking to evade their duty to serve the public interest.[1040]

Frankly, until candidates have another option than relying on deep-pocketed special interests to fund their elections, the enforcement of the public interest doctrine and the free, unlicensed public use of white space are both political pipe dreams. Perhaps a grand trade, one for the other, might be feasible.

Enforce Antitrust Law. Mass media provides a constitutional function in shaping the culture, social values, public opinion, and public knowledge that are necessary for self-government. We must therefore enforce antitrust law to ensure that prices remain competitive and that new competitors with diverse viewpoints can enter the market. In its 1945 *Associated Press* decision, the Supreme Court declared that "the widest possible dissemination of information from diverse and antagonistic sources is essential to the welfare of the public, [and] that a free press is a condition of a free society."[1041] Even with the explosion of new forms of Internet news and information, Americans continue to obtain most of their information directly or indirectly from the media conglomerates and the local television and newspaper outlets they own. As we saw in Chapter 6, these sources are either monopolies or tight oligopolies which have reached dangerously cozy relationships with those in power: they trade coverage (but lazy coverage) for light regulation.

Existing antitrust doctrine and enforcement intensity are sufficient for the software or automobile industries because competition has remained sufficient to allow new competitors into these markets and to drive price competition and product innovation. This is not the case for media. As Ben Bagdikian, the Pulitzer Prize winner and former dean of UC Berkeley's School of Journalism, says, "[a]t issue is the possession of power to surround almost every man, woman, and child in the country with controlled images and words, to socialize each new generation of Americans, to alter the political agenda of the country."[1042] Viewpoint, information, and idea diversity are admittedly difficult to measure objectively, but these criteria must be added to conventional antitrust market and pricing power analyses. I can tolerate Microsoft's near-monopoly in desktop operating systems and applications, knowing that the ever-present threat of new technology holds the company reasonably accountable to consumers. But none of us should tolerate having only one or two viewpoints available in each media market. This parched media landscape is not sufficient to protect us from tyranny and ignorance.

If antitrust law is to be expanded to cover media content and diversity of media sources, the public must rise up in sufficient numbers to overcome the four million dollars that big media and big telecom now spend *each month* to retain control over federal policy. Fortunately, concern about media consolidation has recently spread from academic theorists to the rest of us. In 2003, the FCC was deluged by 2.3 million letters and e-mails in opposition to then-chairman Michael Powell's proposed rules to allow further media consolidation. As it turns out, Powell probably knew at the time that media consolidation kills local news coverage: Adam Candeub, then an FCC attorney, told the Associated Press that FCC management ordered the destruction of "every last piece" of the 2004 report that revealed the problem. The exhumed report, leaked in 2006 by an unidentified FCC staffer, found that local ownership increased news content by over five minutes and local news by over three minutes.[1043]

Ask Media to Take Voluntary Action. To restore health to the American republic, a more pluralistic free press must replace the "he said versus she said" pulled from dueling press releases with more independent analysis and much more fearless investigative reporting. Daily newspapers should do what only they can do, instead of mimicking television in a failing effort to stanch their declining readership. Staff and budget cutting is failing to restore financial health to the industry. Newspapers must reverse course and bring back the skilled journalists necessary to restore local coverage, filling their pages with protein and cutting the empty calories of travel and lifestyle filler, which we can already find in far more depth from specialized sources. Publishers and editors should give their best reporters more time to probe, more space to analyze, and more latitude to draw meaty conclusions. To restore health to American culture, local media should reverse the downward spiral of celebrity, debasement, sensationalism, and violence and begin once again to illuminate local and community life.

TOXIC CULTURE TORTS

If media violence is not to be tempered by voluntary self-restraint, and not by politicians muzzled by campaign contributions, society may be left with no option but to litigate. We have established torts for illness caused by chemical contamination and for failure to warn about the hazards of cigarette smoking. As you weigh the concept of liability for harm caused by toxic cultural products, consider this hypothetical scenario.

Imagine that a virulent new strain of flu virus is making the rounds, costing America billions in lost workdays and healthcare. A terrorist cell manages to culture a bulk quantity of the live virus while it is still circulating naturally, releasing it on a busy Friday evening in a terminal at LAX. The perpetrators are recorded in the act via concealed airport surveillance monitors. Thousands more people who would otherwise be unaffected get and spread the flu. There is no means to trace any one person's flu to the perpetrators. When the terrorists go on trial, forensic epidemiologists use dispersion models to generate a conservative estimate of workdays lost, medical costs incurred, and early deaths among young, elderly, and sick populations with compromised immune systems.

Should the perpetrators be given a pass from financial liability because there is no means to prove that any one person got the flu as a result of what they did, and because the cause-and-effect pathway is complicated and requires statistics to elucidate and quantify? Many of us on that jury would probably vote to hold the terrorists liable for the full calculated costs resulting from their act. So should we seriously consider the ramifications of holding the entertainment industry liable for knowingly releasing toxic cultural products into the American psychological landscape.

For those of us doubtful about this form of liability, consider these deaths and attempted murders, plotted by media and executed in real life:

In Las Vegas, four youths ambushed and shot two police officers, explicitly stating that they were inspired to do so by the lyrics to *Cop Killer*, a 1992 recording by rapper Ice-T. The perpetrators were chanting exactly those lyrics during their arrest.[1044] The protagonist in the recording is sitting in his car by the side of the road at night, headlights off, sawed-off shotgun loaded, savoring his plan to kill a random police officer who would stop to check.

In Jackson County, Texas, nineteen-year-old Ron Howard shot and killed Texas state trooper Bill Davidson as he approached Howard's vehicle after pulling him over for a defective headlight. Howard told authorities that he was hypnotized by gangsta-rapper Tupac Amaru Shakur's *2 Pacalypse Now*, playing in his car tape deck as he fired his Glock pistol at the trooper. Lyrics from three songs on the tape feature the rapper-protagonist delighting in the act of using his Glock and Tech 9 to kill cops. Even after he was sentenced and put in prison, Howard told the trooper's wife that he wanted to realize the rapper's lyrics by killing her and her family.[1045] Citing First Amendment speech protection, the courts ruled against a liability claim filed by Davidson's widow.

In Mississippi and Louisiana, following six sequential viewings of the Oliver Stone film *Natural Born Killers*, teenagers Sarah Edmondson and her boyfriend Benjamin Darras randomly shot two people, killing one and paralyzing the other from the neck down. At least a dozen other random killings have been linked to Stone's movie, with several of the killers quoting lines from the film, dressing like its characters, and using their names while committing the murders. None of several liability claims involving murders inspired by the film have prevailed in the courts.

In 1984 in Indio, California, 19-year-old John McCollum was found dead from a self-inflicted gunshot wound to the head, his earphones still on. McCollum had been listening to Ozzy Osbourne's 1981 song "Suicide Solution," also linked to two other cases of teen suicide. Parents of the three victims all filed suit, all of which were dismissed by the courts on the basis of First Amendment protection.

In 1981 in Texas, 14-year-old Troy Dunaway followed the explicit instructions for autoerotic asphyxiation given in a *Hustler* magazine article, "Orgasm of Death." He was found dead in his closet, hanging by his neck with a belt looped around the doorknob and the magazine at his feet. The courts found that *Hustler's* First Amendment rights trumped any responsibility for consequences.[1046]

There is no positive means to determine whether these specific murders, maimings, and suicides were caused by bad parenting, bad choices, genetic susceptibility, or the instigation or role models provided by the media. In Chapter 6, I have shown the slam-dunk proof that media violence causes increased real-world violence. But it would of course be impossible to pin down an absolute cause and effect for specific incidents. Liability claims and regulatory restrictions resulting from cases like the five I describe here always get tossed by the courts because *almost* all forms of expression are properly protected by the First Amendment. But free speech rights are not absolute. They do not protect perjury, inciting imminent unlawful conduct, aiding and abetting a crime, speech or writing that is an integral part of the commission of a crime, solicitation of a crime, libel or slander, harassment, extortion, blackmail, threats, fraudulent or negligent misrepresentations, disclosure of national defense secrets, or false or misleading advertising.[1047]

There are two seemingly insurmountable problems with media violence litigation. First, if we assume that free speech protections do not apply to media violence, how would it be possible for us to objectively distinguish between, say, use of the same photo of an act of violence for scientific, expressive, or purely gratuitous purposes? Would a Renaissance masterpiece portraying Christ bleeding on the cross fall inside the protection line? Would Mel Gibson's version, in *The Passion of the Christ*? Would the horrific maiming presented in Ken Burns' television series chronicling the Civil War? All of these works depicting violence might incite copycat acts, and all must be protected speech—just as, sadly, the hateful and lethal lyrics of Tupac Amaru Shakur must be protected. Consumer boycotts and voluntary self-restraint by the media, while weak, remain the best solutions involving least potential harm to our constitutional speech liberties.

Second, media violence litigation has failed in every case. As of early 2008, judges have categorically struck down every ban or restriction on violent videogame sales, giving the industry an 11–0 win record.[1048] In 2001, an Indianapolis city ordinance restricting youth access to violent videogames was ruled unconstitutional in federal circuit court. Writing for the court, Judge Richard Posner ruled that " ... studies do not find that video games have ever caused anyone to commit a violent act, as opposed to feeling aggressive, or have caused the average level of violence to increase anywhere."[1049] In late 2007, U.S. District Court Judge Robin Cauthron struck down an Oklahoma law banning the sale to minors of materials containing inappropriate violence, writing, "[there] is a complete dearth of legislative findings, scientific studies, or other rationale to support passage of the Act." A PubMed search on the words "videogame violence" shows that these judges' findings are blatantly false. The courts have struck down a Washington State law banning the sale of videogames portraying realistic cop killing, citing the First Amendment and lack of evidence of harm. Similarly, U.S. District Court Judge Ronald Whyte found that, unlike cigarettes, alcohol, and pornography, the sale to minors of the videogame Postal II is protected by the First Amendment. In this game, players win by shooting schoolgirls in the knee, setting them on fire, and urinating on them.[1050] It is banned in New Zealand.

Given that consumer boycotts and calls for media self-restraint have been wholly ineffectual, where do we turn for relief? A handful of shoestring anti-media-violence groups offer healthy advice, but have little impact. Voluntary labeling, V-chips, and videogame sales restrictions to minors have all been failures. The Federal Communications Commission's more recent moves to enforce its own anti-obscenity regulations are long overdue, but only broadcasters using spectrum licensed by the FCC, such as free radio and TV, can be regulated in this manner. As a result, cultural debasement is migrating even faster to satellite and Internet broadcasters, exemplified by Howard Stern's move to regulation-free satellite radio.

Are innocent American victims required to suck it up and absorb their share of the annual 9- to 19-billion dollar cost of media violence? Kevin Saunders, a Michigan State University law professor, has thus far unsuccessfully defended local regulations restricting exposure of violent media to children, but he thinks that one or more of three legal approaches will ultimately prevail. First is the imposition of restrictions narrowly tailored to prevent harm to minors. Second are restrictions against violent videogames that convey no information or ideas, but are simply forms of entertainment like baseball or card games, and therefore do not enjoy First Amendment speech protection. The third legal approach would be restrictions against violence that fails to meet community moral standards that (like some portrayals of sex) are forms of obscenity not enjoying speech protection.[1051] If sex can be subject to community standard restrictions, so should violence.

In an extensive review of media violence case law, Roger Williams University School of Law Professor John Charles Kunich has found no media violence liability theory yet to survive appeal.[1052] But Rod Smolla, a University of Richmond law professor who litigated the seminal *Hit Man* case in 1999, is slightly more sanguine.[1053] The court found that the publisher of *Hit Man: A Technical Manual for Independent Contractors*, which glorifies and graphically describes how to operate a murder-for-hire business, knowingly "assisted" and "encouraged" reader, James Perry, in the commission of an actual triple murder. The publisher reportedly settled the liability claim on appeal, paying $5 million to the victims' family, while avoiding the establishment of any media-violence case law.[1054]

Smolla cautions that *Hit Man* involves extremely unusual circumstances not likely to apply to major media companies. He does advance other theories of liability for violence induced by toxic culture where children are involved. First, media companies may not knowingly or recklessly market material harmful to minors. Second, a social utility test applies to obscenity, where protection of children from harmful or dangerous material outweighs speech rights. Third, some types of violent material may create liability if it is deliberately, knowingly, and with reckless indifference marketed to children too young to make moral distinctions or distinguish fantasy from reality. Fourth, courts have refused to give speech protection to some types of grotesque sex and excretory depictions. Smolla does not envision a successful liability claim where a violent media product directed at adults is designed to inform or entertain, even if it triggered highly susceptible individuals to commit violence in imitation of it.

Smolla told me that he sees no hope for my theory, that is, using statistical approaches to allocate liability among vendors of media violence.[1055] However, statistical association is well accepted by the courts in establishing liability in cases involving pollution by toxic substances. Liability in these cases is calculated using factors such as the size of the population exposed to the toxic substance, the quantities of the exposure, the degree of increased risk from the exposure, and the costs of the illness associated with it. The Federal Judicial Center, established by Congress to help judges improve court administration, has published a sound guide to the use and admissibility of population-harm-incidence data, including data from the social sciences.[1056] Anthony Roisman, whose long career has been devoted to establishing liability in complex environmental litigation, thinks the causal links shown in recent scientific literature between real-world and media violence overcome the multi-step evidentiary hurdles proposed by the FJC.[1057] My hope is that—where there is no First Amendment protection, for example where media violence is directed at young children—financial liability be statistically imposed against media perpetrators as much as against the flu-spreading terrorists.

Defenders and perpetrators of toxic commercial culture argue that the antidote to objectionable speech is more speech, thereby acknowledging that toxic culture is indeed harmful and that they intend to continue spewing it across the world. They spend millions each day to influence Congress to protect their right to coach our kids to kill cops. They say that viewers should exercise personal responsibility, stop crying victimhood, and stop blaming the media's First Amendment litigation victories for our character weaknesses. But why does personal responsibility apply to parents, but not to them? Toxic culture merchants are making their customers and society ill. They can ratchet back the cultural pollution they started mass producing in the 1970s. They have the power to remove anorexia from the magazine racks and cop killing from the

Xbox. But until they finally embrace ethical norms and restrain themselves, they must be held accountable at law for the costs of the externalities they impose on society.

Libertarians say boycott them by hitting the "off" button. But TV Turnoff Week is a toothless sideshow, and *Saw* has generated five sequels, a videogame, and over half a billion dollars in gross revenue. I lament elsewhere in this book that America has become history's most litigious society, but in the absence of a self-restraint norm, we subsidize pollution if we do not compel the polluter to compensate the injured. In OverSuccessed America, unbounded by self-restraint, there is no accountability without litigation. As was the case with tobacco, the legal route to establishing financial liability for media violence will be long and frustrating, but ultimately successful. A couple of billion-dollar judgments will persuade toxic culture merchants to once again find value in virtue.

THE DANGEROUS IDEA OF SCHOOLS FOR BOYS

America can improve our children's educational destiny for both genders and mitigate the greater male burden of OverSuccess by abandoning scientifically disproved dogma about equality between the sexes. As we saw in Chapter 9, males and females are born with significantly different brains, behaviors, and learning styles. Males are more greatly injured by the increased status defeat associated with OverSuccess. In the new collaborative, fluid, multi-tasking economy, males are falling badly behind, particularly in educational attainment. The sit-still-and-listen format in most grade-school classrooms is tolerated well by girls but is entirely ill-suited for many boys.

Dr. Leonard Sax, founder and director of the National Association for Single Sex Public Education, is the leader of a nascent national movement to end school sex discrimination against boys. His ideas are taking root. As of the 2008–2009 school year, 360 single-sex public schools or schools offering gender-segregated classrooms were in operation, most having opened or converted since 2001. Washington State's 2003 Principal of the Year Benjamin Wright converted his Thurgood Marshall elementary school to sex-segregated classes in 2000. Within one year, reading scores increased for girls and jumped dramatically for boys. Wright is enthusiastic about this form of segregation:

> We outscored the entire state in writing. Once we changed it from just those two single-sex classes to the whole school, the environment in the school changed overnight. Here's what we found: Kids really became kids. The girls participated in physical education like they had never participated before. ... The name-calling, the social behavior completely changed. The focus on academics went way, way up. So what I'm telling you about single-sex education today—I am not the researcher, I am not the legal beaver—but I'm telling you, I'm the practitioner, and I'll tell you it works. It not only works. In my opinion, it is the only way to fly in America right now when we have so many kids that are not making it.

For single-sex schools and classrooms to succeed, Sax cautions, major curriculum revision and staff training are necessary. Teachers must be carefully selected for suitability to the new classroom environments.[1058]

Another solution to the challenges faced by boys in school is to bring gender balance to classroom teaching. Eight in ten K–12 teachers are female— five of six are female at the elementary level.[1059] In the words of one male elementary school teacher in Maine, "As ... the only male classroom teacher in the entire school, I see the value of male teachers in the lower primary grades everyday ... In my opinion, the value really lies in having boys see adult men in their lives valuing literacy. Quite simply, boys need to see men reading and writing on a daily basis." But the trend among teachers is for more to be female. Chris Galgay, president of the Maine teacher's union and the only male teacher and in fact the only male adult in his Sumner, Maine, elementary school, says, "[Teacher gender imbalance is] not getting better, it's getting worse."[1060]

Parents should be empowered to choose classrooms better suited to boys' brains. Their options should include public funding for vouchers redeemable at private schools, charter schools, or public schools within schools. When all parents have the right to seek the kind of education they want for their sons— and daughters—public schools will more rapidly adjust to new knowledge about learning and to the needs of kids. The OverSuccessed teacher unions that have blocked this reform for decades are motivated by self-interest, not the national interest.

THE FAIR TAX

Americans aggressively deploy material possessions to signal status success. Leather seats, lavish houses, and longer yachts induce retaliation by competitors in the form of yet more expensive display consumption. This serves only to increase the cost of status for everyone and the likelihood of defeat in status contests. In 1985 economist Robert Frank proposed a policy to curb the vicious cycle of competitive consumption, the progressive consumption tax.[1061] Such a tax would direct consumer spending preferences away from visible status markers. By making hundred-thousand-dollar vacations and Prada bags more expensive, we would redirect our money to less visible, socially healthy uses, such as savings and investment.

Despite a mass campaign to discredit it, the concept of a national consumption tax has gained considerable support over the past few years. It would increase America's abysmally low household savings rate and level the playing field for our exports. One version, the Fair Tax, would replace federal taxes on income, payroll, corporate profits, capital gains, and gifts with an approximate 30-percent tax on consumer purchases of new goods and services. The Fair Tax would be made somewhat progressive via a monthly "prebate" check sent to all low-income households.[1062] The savings in record keeping, tax compliance, and reduced tax evasion alone could exceed $500 billion annually.

Many social commentators prefer the more aggressively redistributive tax systems of the European social democracies. The higher and more progressive taxes there act to levelize material inequality, suppress competitive consumption, and fund more public benefits. But simply imitating the social democracies puts the American engine of invention at risk of stalling out. From this engine will come clean energy sources big enough to displace fossil fuels, ways to combat cancer and depression with far lower side effects, and the next new waves of cultural innovation.

RESPONSIBLE WEALTH DISPLAY

Writing this book definitely complicated my most recent new car purchase. I spent a day test-driving two Lexus sedans. Both models were understated and gorgeous. But I could not write the check. I wound up instead with a loaded Camry. I got all the features I wanted, Bluetooth, NAV, leather, hybrid engine, decent body styling, but a bit less muscular than I would prefer.

My problem is that cars are used in public psychological space. I felt I had to make a choice not to wield my wealth as a social weapon. Many people in my community measure their place, in part, by the newness and price of their own car compared to that of other vehicles in the area. I nixed a luxury car because I did not want to inspire envy in a neighbor. I did not want to force others to turn their heads, as many do when they see a luxury brand cruise by, to feel subconsciously less comfortable for a moment, or to make an unnecessary purchase beyond their means.

My new car was socially responsible in another way, too. Almost every luxury auto gets poor gas mileage, and burning more gasoline will bring increasing drought, catastrophic weather events, and coastal flooding, likely displacing or causing suffering among tens of millions of people who live near the equator. Knowing the harm to others, luxury manufacturers continue to sell and consumers to buy cars with uselessly huge engines. Billions of people around the world look to wealthy Americans as examples of how to live. In the face of accumulating dire information about global resource exhaustion, the wealthy bear a heightened responsibility to be aware that their multiple 10,000-square-foot houses and sending staff off on a cross-continental flight to fetch a bottle of wine for dinner are bad for our species. If every human lived like the average American, it would require the resources of five Earths. The lifestyle of an American in the top one-tenth percent of our society would require dozens of Earths.[1063]

My favorite new peeve in consumption display is garishly huge jewelry stones. Women now wear rings with cut stones (some real) three-quarters of an inch across. Making certain to be noticed, the hand bearing the ring is waved in your face during conversation like a conductor's baton. Tastelessness seems to aggravate conspicuous excess. Someone ought to tell the ladies carrying those purses with the huge gold-plated G how much they look like hookers.

I have no personal problem with wealth. If it has been accumulated without resort to corruption, it usually indicates that value has been delivered to society. Wealth can be put to fine private uses and enable great personal pleasure. But for the sake of the national savings rate and our collective mental health, we should back off aggressive, in-your-face public displays of possessions such as cars, watches, jewelry, and personal accessories which cause those of us who are status-sensitive to engage in consumption-display wars we cannot afford to win. We should avoid triggering useless benchmark escalation that leaves most of us losers. Manufacturers and marketers, too, can play a role, building a profitable new market segment around responsible wealth display. Product design would ditch today's emphasis on overscaling and ostentation, instead emphasizing functional quality and pure aesthetics. In former times in my native New England, brahmins would often wear flannel shirts and work pants in public, not just to conceal their wealth, but because they considered it a personal duty to foster community cohesion. Metaphorically at least, isn't it time we all put on a flannel shirt?

GUILT IS GOOD

When I was growing up, my mother turned our four Connecticut acres into a Noah's Ark for animal castoffs. Over the years, she cycled through sheep, goats, geese, chickens, horses, rabbits, dogs, and cats. We four kids learned to love and care for this menagerie, taking pride in our ability to coax lovable but quirky personalities out of each to its capacity. My brother taught his pet rooster to perch on his shoulder. The two would sit in shared bliss watching *Green Acres* reruns when no one else cared to. My younger sister, wanting to maintain her storybook peaceable kingdom fantasy long into her teens, taught her cat and bunny rabbit to sleep together like lion and lamb. I taught an unruly draft horse fated for the dog-food factory to become a hunt club steeplechaser. We didn't know it, but through these experiences my mom taught her kids several moral lessons, including responsibility and compassion for the weak.

Today, commercial culture has invaded most of our children's time, and it has stepped in with its own lessons. Today's kids watch Michael Jackson on television smiling and waving to the crowd on the way into his pedophilia trial. They listen to Eminem, showered with attention and money for glorifying misogyny. In America, our children learn that those who should be shamed are shameless, that villains are role models, and that antisocial behavior is rewarded by fame and undeterred by guilt.

The individualistic values of the 1960s gave it a bad name, but guilt needs a comeback. Not the neurotic kind of guilt that used to make Woody Allen hilarious before he tried to be Bergman, but the healthy guilt that makes us cringe when we contemplate injuring or stealing from another person. According to George Washington University psychologist June Tangney, author of the book *Shame and Guilt*, healthy guilt depends on our ability to anticipate and understand other people's feelings. Healthy guilt restrains us from insulting people. Healthy guilt makes us declare our income because we know that every dollar we do not pay in income taxes is another dollar our government will borrow from the Chinese and on which our kids will pay interest. In a study tracking children as they grew into adulthood, guilt-prone fifth graders lived more successful lives and had lower rates of criminality and higher rates of college attendance and community service. For all its lifetime benefits, guilt is the only success technique I've not seen in a book about success.

Because our proneness to guilt is more a learned than an inherited emotional trait, parents play a big role in their children's moral development. Beyond age seven or eight, there is little difference among children or adults in knowledge of moral rules. Sinners and saints are both equally aware of the rules against lying, cheating, and stealing, for example. However, there are large differences in the extent to which we apply these moral rules. A critical role for parents, then, is to internalize healthy guilt in their children when they are young, a process that is largely complete by age eight to ten. After those years, our proneness to guilt remains nearly unchanged through old age.

Tangney usefully distinguishes guilt from shame. Shame associates hurtful behavior with its effects on the self, rather than on others. The primary effect of shame is to hold oneself in lower regard. Shame does not inhibit bad behavior or motivate the sufferer to repair the damages, but instead causes denial, withdrawal, self-harm, anger, and aggression. Whereas guilt can induce and preserve positive behavior, shame can be toxic—as we saw in the last chapter, with severe public shaming sometimes leading children to later acts of extreme violence.

Tangney suggests that parents' lessons to their children should focus on how bad behavior affects others, rather than how it affects the self. Teaching that focuses children on their failings builds shame, whereas teaching that focuses on others' feelings develops healthy guilt. More powerfully than with words, parents should teach by example, admitting their own mistakes, apologizing and making reparation in real-life situations as they occur, such as leaving a note on the windshield of the car you accidentally dent, rather than driving away and saying that the insurance company will pay for it anyway. Parents should help children learn how to correct injury they may have caused others. Good parents deliver even disciplinary messages in the context of a loving, supportive relationship. "You don't have to feel really bad to be a good person," says Tangney. "Moderately painful feelings of guilt about specific behaviors motivate people to behave in a moral, caring, socially responsible manner."[1064]

American parents make extraordinary effort to get their children into good schools and help them become status winners as adults. Parents would do well reserving a bit more of that time for the subtle moral lessons that will determine the health of the next generation's social commons.

WE ARE THE COOPERATION POLICE

We saw in Chapter 2 how humans are unique among the planet's species in our willingness to sacrifice to help our group mates, even those with whom we have no genetic relationship. Our global dominion can be credited largely to our establishment of cultural customs that foster this pro-group cooperation. I have called these cultural customs extended cooperation, a key feature of which is our automatic propensity to help enforce our shared customs by punishing those who violate them, even if we get no benefit whatsoever. In OverSuccessed America, too few of us are stepping up in moments of need to protect extended cooperation, which threatens its collapse. As science has come to show, extended cooperation is a delicate and sensitive enterprise that can break down even with small losses to its voluntary police force. Consider these pages a recruitment call to fill out the dangerously thinning ranks of America's extended cooperation police.

Well-replicated experiments show that we humans are typically generous to strangers, even when we know that our good deeds will remain anonymous and we have no prospect of future benefit. We selflessly and anonymously reward strangers for their cooperative behavior. We are also wired to play a second-party role, sanctioning those who do not fairly share resources—even when we will be hurt by doing this. Scientists term this sanctioning behavior "costly punishment," costly because we pay a price in lost resources or in the scorn of the sanctioned, and do not expect anything in return. Finally—and most critically to the survival of healthy cultural customs—we play a third-party role in enforcing extended cooperation, by punishing those who fail in their second-party duty to inflict costly punishment on cheaters.[1065] So we are both enforcers of cooperation and enforcers of the enforcers.

Some human societies do not enforce very well. Emory University anthropologist Joseph Henrich and his co-workers ran a series of elaborate cross-cultural experiments on costly punishment, testing individuals living in fifteen highly diverse societies from around the world as to their willingness to inflict costly punishment on those who behave unfairly. In one of these experiments, an anonymous player divides a day's local wages with a second player. If a third player, acting as an anonymous arbiter, feels that player one has offered too little money to player two, the arbiter can dock player one, but forfeits a known portion of his own pay by doing so. While this willingness to costly punish for unfairness exists at some level in all societies, it varies greatly. The Lamalera people from Indonesia strongly sanction violations of fairness, whereas the Machiguenga from Peru show almost no concern about fairness in their own or other people's behavior.[1066] Moreover, those societies whose members are more willing to inflict costly punishment are also more generous.[1067] "You evolve into a more cooperative being if you grow up in a world where there are punishers," says Henrich.[1068]

Urs Fischbacher and Ernst Fehr, experimental economists and game theorists at the University of Zurich, were the first to develop a more complex behavioral model that convincingly explains how extended cooperation can survive in groups larger than a few dozen people. Fischbacher and Fehr have shown that cooperation collapses beyond a handful of people when there is no punishment of cheaters. It collapses entirely in groups larger than a few dozen people—*if we fail to punish those who fail to punish cheaters.*[1069] Extended human cooperation depends not only on generosity and sanctions against those who are not generous, but also on third-party moral policing, where a sufficient number of us prod each other to share the policing burden so that it does not fall too heavily on the too few who do it without prodding.

In the most elaborate cross-cultural experiments to date on the enforcement of cooperative norms, University of Nottingham economist Benedikt Herrmann and his co-workers were surprised to find great differences among even economically advanced societies. In these experiments, upper-middle-class university undergrads from 15 different countries played anonymous cooperation games using real money. In societies found by the World Values Survey to have weaker civic cooperation norms—including Greece, Saudi Arabia, Oman, Russia, and Belarus—players inflicted mild punishment on freeloaders, but more heavily punished those more generous than themselves. Players from Greece and Oman punished generosity so strongly as to wipe out the higher collective payoffs that result from effective punishment of cheaters. The freeloading players in the low-cooperation countries probably punished the generous to block the establishment of a high contribution requirement. In the nations with stronger norms of cooperation—including the U.S., Britain, Germany, Denmark, Switzerland, Australia, and China—players more harshly punished freeloaders, but rarely punished players for being generous. Herrmann found that these patterns of punishment and reward were highly consistent among players within a particular society, showing that prevailing societal values have a strong and continuing influence on our everyday cooperative behavior.[1070]

Exciting physical evidence is emerging from labs that shows the biochemical basis for extended cooperation. PET brain scans record a significant spike in activity in the nucleus accumbens, the Grand Central Terminal of our dopamine reward system, when we contemplate punishing violators of social norms.[1071] Men (but not women) experience activity spikes in their brain reward centers as they watch people being physically punished for unfairly distributing winnings.[1072] Our dopamine system also responds, in graduated fashion, to the size of both the rewards we receive for cooperation and the sanctions we dish out to norm violators. We are hardwired to feel good when we enforce social standards, even when we get hurt doing it.[1073]

Clearly, our species is predisposed to extended cooperation thanks to an evolved brain mechanism—but one that is heavily influenced by culture. The Henrich cross-cultural studies show that extended cooperation is strengthened or weakened by varying cultural norms, which are the sum of individual behaviors, the imitation of those behaviors, and the social institutions that develop around normative behavior. The Herrmann experiments show that strong extended cooperation is not guaranteed, even in economically advanced societies. Extended cooperation depends upon the expectation by most group members that most individuals will cooperate. If norm enforcement becomes too costly, too great a burden on those doing it, too frequently necessary, or ineffective, then extended cooperation will break down.[1074]

The experimental evidence tells us what we need to do to sustain the norms and customs that will help to heal us from the estranging and antisocial aspects of OverSuccess. First, cooperative norms become established as a result of the voluntary personal sacrifices made by a small number of our generous peers. Second, cooperative norms become widespread only if our interactions within our groups are continuous and recurrent. Third, we must prosecute the small infractions of our cooperative norms, or people will give up on them, losing their faith that the norms will be applied regularly and fairly. If we lose that confidence, then big violations will become too frequent and impossible to control. Think of this as the broken windows theory of social health. While doing small things such as repairing broken windows, removing graffiti, and arresting squeegee men may or may not explain the dramatic drop over the 1990s in major crimes in New York City, evidence and experience shows that enforcing social norms makes a profound difference in social order and civility if we do it consistently.

Because our ethical standard bearers have become scarce, apart from the force of law, America is drifting dangerously close to becoming a punishment-free world. We take the money and run, tolerate rudeness, and allow bullies to roam free in our schools and workplaces. Our rootless mobility and our tenuous, commercially dominated and overscaled communities mean that we can expect no more than weak and temporary relationships with each other. So we keep to ourselves and stay out of everyone else's business. Beneficial norms are in collapse. OverSuccess puts at risk literally what makes us human: the most rigorously structured experiment to date shows that chimps, our closest living genetic relative, do not share our aversion to unfairness and our inbuilt preference toward extended cooperation.[1075]

Today in America, we have grown over-reliant on our formal institutions as a substitute for extended cooperation. When Hurricane Katrina temporarily shut down those institutions in New Orleans, our failing behavioral norms became glaringly obvious. The breakdown was not just looted TV sets, stinking feces everywhere, and the dead left untended. And well before the subprime mortgage collapse, almost everyone knew that a fraud was being perpetrated, by everyone from homebuyers falsifying their incomes, to brokers waving off concerns about the rate reset clauses, to Wall Street analysts assuring investors that subprimes were little more risky than T-bonds.

Here is the change we can make. Whether after a hurricane, before a financial collapse, or in countless routine social transactions, we will make a healthier America by stepping in ourselves when someone is needed to enforce social order and by prodding passive bystanders to do the same. We can politely ask the parents at the table next to us to impose discipline on their unruly children. We can speak to the husband who is doing nothing to stop his wife from harassing the innocent sales clerk. We can ask the flight attendant to provide a handkerchief for the projectile cougher sitting four rows behind us. By living up to our social-policing obligations, we will help bring lasting success to American life by making the social order our everyday business.

Humans are unique because we are not Hobbesian beasts, caged only by despotic and coercive government. Instead, we are and should be constant busybodies in defense of healthy common behavior via our corrective nudges to those around us. We can encourage the busybodies by more readily accepting those nudges when they are directed at us. Restoration of American social health demands that each of us make it our daily business to apply peer pressure to spread the costs of maintaining a reasonable degree of shared trust. We are the extended cooperation police, without whom all else fails.

BELIEF IN HIGHER PURPOSES

Atheist Richard Dawkins has famously and neatly capsulized the problem of a worldview without faith: "The universe we observe has precisely the properties we should expect if there is, at bottom, no design, no purpose, no evil and no good, nothing but blind pitiless indifference."[1076] Whatever its scientific defensibility or its past and present misuse by evil people, from a purely practical standpoint, faith and religion have worked very well for Americans as a means of cultivating social cohesion and as a calling to purposes higher than material self-interest. From conservative to liberal, 85 percent of Americans say that spiritual faith gives meaning and purpose to their lives. More than nine in ten of us believe in God or a universal spirit.[1077] An almost unassailable body of scientific research has established that religious people are happier, suffer less depression, and cope better with adversity. These beneficial effects are strongest for the more fundamentalist religions that more strongly emphasize hope.[1078] At least in the United States, faith and the belief in higher purposes seem to support both progress and social health. No matter how we might define our faith or how we might experience a summons to our spirit, for the sake of our individual well-being and the common good, each of us should open our hearts to our higher purpose.

The quest for higher purposes has benefited societies through history. From past centuries of trial and error, we can see that the core values of societies matter in a big way. In his definitive tome on the lofty subject of human accomplishment and excellence, Charles Murray shows that the most successful societies—as measured by their production of the seminal achievements in the arts, sciences, and technology—foster these characteristics: freedom of expression, market economies, dense networks of voluntary association, extended cooperation, and belief in a transcendental purpose to life. Murray's chief conclusion is that if a society is to make a lasting contribution, then personal and cultural embrace of truth, beauty, and virtue must prevail. In societies where faith or religion are unimportant, people are not motivated toward pursuits beyond their lifetimes. Such societies are consistently very low producers of what Murray calls the "transcendental goods" embodied in lasting accomplishment and excellence.[1079]

Compared with those of most contemporary nations, America's core values empower us to flourish both economically and spiritually. Ronald Inglehart, a social scientist at the University of Michigan, is the leader in examining value differences among modern societies. Inglehart and his dozens of collaborating investigators have run four different iterations of the ongoing World Values Survey, using roughly same sets of 250 questions and now covering 99 nations. Among the world's nations, the United States is exceptional in simultaneously embracing progress, individuality, and faith. Inglehart's fascinating "cultural map of the world," a graphical summary of the 2005 World Values Survey, can be viewed at www.worldvaluessurvey.org.[1080] America shows that, contrary to Marx's predictions, religious belief and the search for transcendental meaning can indeed flourish in a post-industrial society.

But our country's OverSuccessed, winning-at-all-costs politics have turned America's unusual dual strengths into enemies. Faith has been placed in opposition to science and turned into a partisan wedge issue, risking both our economic and spiritual futures. Among residents of 34 mostly Western nations, Americans are second only to Turkey in believing that evolution is a false concept. Three of ten candidates for president raised their hands at a 2007 GOP debate when asked if they rejected evolutionary theory. As the evidence supporting evolution has mounted into an overwhelming body over the past twenty years, belief in evolution has declined to only forty percent of us, whereas in Iceland, eighty percent accept evolution as true.[1081] This disparity is genuinely dangerous, and if we are to thrive as a nation, we must do a better job of reconciling exponentially growing knowledge with our continuing spirituality.

American churches and transcendental practices could do more collective good by de-escalating the fight over disagreements, such as biblical literalism or homosexuality. Whether Mormon, Unitarian, Buddhist, or anything in between, our faith leaders should unite across religions and denominations to show their agreements as to how each of us can use living faith as a daily guide to personal behavior and fulfillment. Our political and spiritual leaders should also acknowledge the great common ground between believers and those whose quest for a meaningful life and a higher purpose does not demand belief in God. Whether our spiritual work involves helping others in simple ways, discovering, developing one's own capacity to create or discover, finding deep meaning, or leaving a positive legacy, each of us can integrate into our daily lives a chosen purpose greater than ourselves.

BUILDING NEW VILLAGES

How we shape the groups and organizations in which we work, play, and volunteer will profoundly influence the course of American OverSuccess. The social design of these groups must take conscious account of how each of its members can be recognized and valued for his or her strengths and contributions. Writ large, when socially healthy organizations come to number in the millions, we will have cured OverSuccess. Only then will we move past our obsession with the grand and unattainable goals on which commercial culture lavishes its attentions and the private economy bestows its rewards, and whose crumbs leave satisfying roles for too few of us.

The village is my working model for a socially healthy organization. For some of us, the village may be a genuine small town or neighborhood where stable and nourishing relationships are built on physical proximity. For most, it will be businesses and voluntary associations that are structurally and culturally shaped primarily to provide human psychological sustenance. In these new villages, our largest compensation for our work in fulfilling the group's mission will be the achievement of our personal goals and the recognition we receive for making a difference. This vision is in no way meant to diminish the importance of the few extraordinary individuals who will change the world by conquering brain cancer, replacing fossil fuels, or defining the next great musical genre. The motivation and rewards for such lasting accomplishments must assuredly continue. But the village is the nursery for the everyday experiences and roles that make life good: our median strip gardens, bike paths, community suppers, finance committees, humane societies, janitors, auto mechanics, laboratory technicians, nurses, and accountants—without which and whom the world cannot work. To heal OverSuccess, America needs millions more such places, where millions more ordinary people can be recognized for doing good things.

Before we turn to real-world examples of new villages and how they are indeed healing us, consider their four key attributes:

- They have about 20 to 200 members.
- They must be created or redesigned in very high numbers.
- Their members are bound together by a common higher purpose.
- Their leaders treat subordinates as valued and respected companions.

Our new villages should be neither too large nor too small. Recall from Chapter 2 the Dunbar number, 150—the number of people beyond which we each can no longer recall who is trustworthy and who is competent in a specific role. Because the human social brain has a fixed memory for people, groups begin to fragment when they have more than about 150 to 200 members. New villages should also not be too small and include at least 20 members, thereby providing space for its members to specialize and to buffer other members when conflict arises. New villages do not require abandoning cities or dismantling General Electric. Inside such large organizations, we can proliferate new villages, each with its own mission, culture, and leadership aligned with that of its parent organization.

New villages must also be myriad, spread across every field of commercial, recreational, and voluntary endeavor. Being highly numerous, they can then become places for people of every type of talent and for most Americans to be recognized and valued once again. New villages must also align themselves around inspiring goals. Both individuals and groups can thrive only when they are focused on a higher purpose. Who will create all these groups? Any of us with the influence to reshape an existing organization or to form a new one.

Finally, new villages must have healthy hierarchies, allowing members psychological sustenance no matter what their rank. In Chapter 2, we explored the work of primate-stress expert Robert Sapolsky, whose research on status relationships within groups is extraordinarily applicable to humans. Sapolsky found great variation between different baboon troupes in the tendency of dominant members to inflict psychological stress on subordinates. This tendency, Sapolsky found, is a learned behavior, is stably controlled by group cultural norms, and is passed on to following generations. In Chapter 8, I noted the lifelong work of British social epidemiologist Michael Marmot, who has shown that perfectly well-paid, well-fed, white-collar civil servants with full access to healthcare—but who have lower job-status rankings—live shorter, less healthy lives than those with higher job status. These burdens are unnecessary. There will always be status hierarchies in groups, but as Sapolsky has shown, status relationships can be more or less hurtful, depending upon the group cultural norms guiding how we typically treat others of differing rank. The adoption of these norms appears random in baboons. It is conscious in humans. To reduce psychological stress among subordinates, Marmot advises that organizations build in meaningful responsibility and self-direction for all members, particularly those down the hierarchy.[1082]

W. L. Gore, the global manufacturer of Gore-Tex fabric and thousands of other high-tech, materials-based products, maintains a culture that emphasizes a light corporate touch and close bonds in its hierarchical relationships. It is a large, rapid-growth company with 7,800 employees and over $2 billion in annual sales and is consistently ranked one of the world's top employee-friendly workplaces, rating "astonishingly highly" and always in the top ten in *The London Times'* annual survey of best global companies to work for. Almost ninety percent of its employees feel that they make a valuable contribution to the business's success and would miss the company if they left.[1083] Gore employees also own most of the company. This kind of employee ownership is not unusual: over 11,000 U.S. companies are wholly or substantially owned by their employees. Employee ownership can strengthen new village attributes by flattening unnecessary hierarchies and strengthening commitments to team and mission.

Gore is a "flat lattice" organization. Employees have no formal rank or title. "There are no chains of command nor pre-determined channels of communication. Instead, we communicate directly with each other and are accountable to fellow members of our multi-disciplined teams," says the company in describing its corporate culture. Gore associates, as they are called, use their own judgment in selecting new projects or products, becoming leaders and launching products only if they are able to recruit team members from within the company to join them.

In his description of how he structured the company he co-founded, Bill Gore laid out the imperative that has kept the entire company at the scale of the village:

> You can't do this in very large groups. The size of the group where I think it becomes difficult, and to some degree impossible, is the point where it isn't any longer possible for everyone in the organization to know everyone else. This begins to happen somewhere in the range of 150 to 200 people. At about this number you begin to hear conversations change from *we* decided, *we* did, or *we* planned, to *they* decided, *they* told us. That is the signal that the organization is not together ... Sticking to this limitation of 150 to 200 in a team requires some special skill and determination ... [I]t is a waste of the human resource to fail to do this.[1084]

The company builds plants large enough for no more than 150 to 200 employees, forcing new groups to break off into new buildings when they rise above that number. This big company gains major economic advantage by maintaining groups small enough to preserve the benefits of face-to-face relationships, personal knowledge, and earned trust. Bill Gore could build what became a $2 billion company around small groups because humans thrive in organizations scaled to suit our need for durable, face-to-face relationships.

Surveys routinely report that employees' number one source of workplace stress is their immediate supervisor. University of Kent evolutionary psychologist Mark Van Vugt thinks that human psychology is simply mismatched to prevailing corporate organizational structure, where leadership is rigid, static, and imposed from above. In small-group organization, which prevailed during most of human evolution, leaders were selected by consensus because their skills were appropriate to the task at hand and could be sanctioned and removed by followers. Status differences between leaders and followers were minimal. Van Vugt cites Sir Richard Branson's Virgin Group—comprising over 200 operating companies, 50,000 employees, and $20 billion in sales—as another corporate exemplar in its use of small groups and flattened hierarchies.[1085] On its website, Virgin describes itself as having "minimal management layers, no bureaucracy, a tiny board . . . [o]ur companies are part of a family rather than a hierarchy." Once again, weaving new villages into global enterprises works: British consumers rank Virgin as their favorite brand.

Former New Hampshire Senator Gordon Humphrey is hard at work in a two-front war against OverSuccess—fighting against commercial culture and advocating for new villages. A rarity among those who have tasted power in Washington, Humphrey kept his promise, limiting himself to two terms.

Back home, his political ambition still raging, he ran and lost two intensely fought campaigns for governor. I helped him on one of these runs. After a year of licking his wounds, he redirected his life to a new set of goals that did not include fame: he purchased WKXL-1450, one of the remaining New Hampshire radio stations not already owned by a media conglomerate.

After three years' work, WKXL remains an economic experiment, but it stands as a model for how media can once again help build local community. WKXL takes no national feeds. Its on-air personalities—almost all live—are polite, civilized, and calm. In a setup that is highly unusual for a small station, it has two local news reporters and offers hours each day of in-depth coverage of everything local: politics, business, culture, religion, high school sports, social affairs, and voluntary organizations. The county's sheriff hosts a program on law enforcement and social problems. An academic type reports on local lectures. The director of a local arts high school interviews students. What makes the financial numbers almost work is that volunteers host and produce about 40 percent of programs. Humphrey finds that these volunteers are passionate about their subjects and need little guidance as to quality. He wants to make his station a model for a new media format that others can use and has plans to branch into community TV. He explained to me why he is so deeply committed to local broadcasting:

> Individual citizens and small organizations doing good things go unrecognized. Virtue and merit go largely unrewarded. Exemplars simply aren't exemplars if they are invisible. My focus on community is to give worthy local residents and organizations visibility and provide public validation for their good deeds. Surely, this is as vital to a healthy society as is the making of public policy.

The four attributes of new villages apply equally well to those in the voluntary and nonprofit sectors, where opportunities to improve American social health are often more abundant than in the business world. Long Island steamfitter Don Perks, like many of his brother union members, helped build the World Trade Center. Also like too many in his trade, he was a heavy on-the-job drinker and addicted to alcohol. His own wife and children lived in fear of his alcoholic rages. A string of car wrecks finally persuaded Perks to get help and stop drinking—and to change his entire life. He wrestled down his once belligerent personality and completed the intense training required to become a substance abuse and addiction counselor. In 1990 he took over as director of his Steamfitters Local Union 638 Member Assistance Program.

Before the MAP, when it came to on-the-job personal problems, "don't ask, don't tell" was the prevailing workplace culture. Brothers would openly spike their coffee with vodka, crack a six-pack for lunch, and cover for one another after accidents. When their problems began to overwhelm them, they had nowhere to turn but an ineffective, managed-care substance abuse program. The main agenda for the union's managed-care provider, remote from the scene and with little understanding of a steamfitter's life, was to hold down costs by turning away people asking for help. For those who did get assistance, the mandate was to cut treatment short, before it could work. When the MAP took over, it substituted a self-insurance program, doubling the effectiveness of the former managed-care program, with about seventy percent of brothers asking for help succeeding at staying clean. The program combines a 30-day in-patient detox and rehab program and a 24/7 member-to-member hotline. It costs less because multiple detox and rehabs are less frequently required, and because workplace productivity, job safety, and skilled-worker retention are all way up.

The MAP works because it comes with a culture transplant that can thrive only in village society. Steamfitters can feel comfortable admitting their problems to one another, can ask a peer for help, and are able to watch over each other on and off the job. Instead of calling managed care, each worker can talk to someone he knows and trusts. "They can say anything they want. They can cry," Perks told me. After 9/11, demand among members for help with alcohol and drug problems tripled, and it has not yet abated. "This was our building," Perks says about the World Trade Center complex. "We had 1,000 guys working there, 1,000 of our guys collecting body parts." He can channel his anger at the attack—something he cannot do much about—into being useful and responsible. "I help who I can when I can."[1086] Perks' efforts show how a small, close-knit organization committed to an urgent mission has strengthened America both socially and economically.

Most of our new villages don't involve life or death matters, but they do cultivate missions held just as intensely by members, as I see firsthand in one of my favorite hobbies. I spend as many free sunny days as possible hiking New Hampshire's thousands of one-of-a-kind mountain trails. Rarely do I encounter fallen logs, eye-level branches, washouts, or unreasonably loose rocks. The people who maintain these trails lug tools miles from the nearest road, dig drainage trenches, and move rocks and logs without power equipment. They return home after this grubby, backbreaking work covered in brown sweat and the bites from clouds of merciless black flies. Over eighty percent of this trail maintenance is provided by small groups of loosely coordinated volunteers.

For the past twenty years, Craig Sanborn has led one of these crews, nicknamed the Cardigan Highlanders. The Highlanders are about a dozen volunteers who are responsible for thirteen miles of the state's trails. I asked Sanborn how he keeps his crew and himself motivated. "Pride of workmanship, camaraderie, and fun," he told me. "A wise leader listens and justifies decisions to followers. There is give and take." After the volunteers put in their first three days of work, Sanborn awards them their Highlanders tartan neckerchief. No other people in the world get one. His report in the state parks division exercises a very light managerial touch because the Highlanders have long demonstrated their commitment to quality. Sanborn and his volunteers get no money, advancement opportunity, or recognition outside their little community. Their rewards are the type that can flow only from autonomy, responsibility, and a recognized place in a small group that is doing something very well and that very few people do. The hunger for these intangibles is so powerful that New Hampshire can offer a valuable public service that brings delight to others at no charge to taxpayers.

Humans are built to seek status success within groups, and we are exquisitely sensitive to our place within them. But in America, and more recently in the world's emerging meritocracies such as China, our reference groups have gone global. OverSuccess does not work because too few of us can ever succeed. Socialism is not an answer because we will never be equal. The solution is to multiply the number of America's status ladders by ten thousand times. We can shed the mental-health burden that comes with supernatural success benchmarks by creating a profusion of new and revitalized social and organizational niches. Each will define its own relevant skills, talents, goals, role models, and reference benchmarks. With a profusion of new social niches, we will have a wider variety of success yardsticks that are not comparable to one another, a "multiple intelligences" approach to success. We will crack open the narrow wealth-beauty-fame-power rubric I see every time I log on to AOL. There will be places for more people to meaningfully contribute and be recognized, more ways to succeed. Competition will remain intense, but channeled throughout myriad niches where each of us will have the opportunity to shine.

Creating new villages and healthy hierarchies will be a bottom-up, grassroots endeavor. It will be fiercely resisted by global society's success oligopolists. The Communist Party did not tear down the Berlin Wall. AT&T did not voluntarily permit alternatives to its black rotary phone. *People* magazine will never remove celebrities from its cover. The franchise is too profitable to cede sales or cultural space to small society. The success oligopoly's job is to prevent us from turning our attention to the millions of talented people who will give far more as soon as we give them some social oxygen.

As W. L. Gore and the Cardigan Highlanders show, small, empowered, myriad groups with vital missions will make us happier and healthier. They will help the large organizations into which they can be coordinated deliver high profits and valuable services. We need these new villages by the millions. But make-work stage sets will not do. They must be real and varied enough so that we actually live and produce in them. They must be stable and local enough so that they are trellises for our sustained relationships. The new villages we need are benevolently led, human-scaled, and provide meaningful roles and attainable success opportunities for most of us. Each of us should take a role in building them.

SOCIAL VIRTUE: RESTORING THE FORGOTTEN HALF OF THE AMERICAN REVOLUTION

American progress has depended upon constitutionally protected rights and freedoms and upon a revolutionary model of voluntary behavior. America's visionary founders risked one of history's boldest leaps of faith in humankind, knowing that our republic's success was to be contingent on how Americans integrated the virtues of self-restraint, civic involvement, and generosity into their daily lives. The words of our system's architects make their hopes and trepidations clear:

Only a virtuous people are capable of freedom. As nations become corrupt and vicious they have more need for masters.

—*Benjamin Franklin*

A nation as a society forms a moral person, and every member of it is personally responsible for his society ... It is in the manners and spirit of a people which preserve a republic in vigour ... degeneracy in these is a canker which soon eats into the heart of its laws and constitution.

—*Thomas Jefferson*[1087]

The preservation of the sacred fire of liberty and the destiny of the republican model of government are justly considered, perhaps, as *deeply*, as *finally*, staked on the experiment entrusted to the hands of the American people.

—*George Washington, from his first inaugural address,*
likely drafted by James Madison[1088]

We have no government armed with power capable of contending with human passions unbridled by morality and religion. Avarice, ambition, revenge, or gallantry would break the strongest cords of our Constitution as a whale goes through a net. Our Constitution was made for a moral and religious people. It is wholly inadequate to the government of any other.

—*John Adams, 1798 address to the military*[1089]

George Washington taught by example when he relinquished his status as the nation's president, declining the public's intense wish that he become America's new king. John Adams toiled for years in frustration and lonely separation from his beloved wife to assure the structural and financial soundness of the new nation. Tocqueville, visiting America in the early 1800s, was amazed at the willingness of Americans to help one another, as well as their disinclination to take advantage of one another. This embedded sense of social virtue, these norms of honesty and trust—and the freedom they permit—must be credited for America having become the wealthiest and most powerful nation on earth only 150 years after its founding.

Today, we are failing to meet the founders' expectations. We have allowed our obsessive pursuit of individual success to starve personal and social virtue.

OverSuccess has become a cankerous barrier to our individual and national well-being and imposes costs far greater than we recognize. When we tailgate into submission the geezer in the passing lane, we lose far more than the few seconds we gain. When we let our cell phone ring in the theater, dozens of people's transport to a beautifully imagined reality is broken. Being brusque with an anonymous call-center clerk spreads surliness through another lunchroom. These small, selfish annoyances model, legitimize, and mirror the larger ethical breaches that have swamped confidence in our institutions. We cluck-cluck at Dennis Kozlowski, the Tyco pirate, but there is no qualitative difference between his imperial theft and the shabby little larcenies that most of us admit to in anonymous surveys. Over the days and decades, these behaviors add up to our selfish, uncivil, and unhealthy society.

On the most fundamental level, healing OverSuccess will require a renewal of America's founding values as embodied in our everyday, personal behavior. That doesn't mean just faithfully attending church on Sunday, but living Christ's example when we are confronted by an ethical challenge on Monday. It doesn't just mean giving generously to United Way, but in our treatment of those who can't afford it or don't want to. Healing OverSuccess is less about complying with the letter of the law, more about exceeding society's minimum standards for behavior. Some of the remedies I have proposed require tough institutional change, but each begins with adjustments to our everyday behaviors and attitudes. Healing OverSuccess calls for a revolution in the smallest things, a revolution repeated millions of times hourly across the nation in our personal, work, and public lives.

My father suffered from Parkinson's disease in the last decade of his life. He made a living arrangement with his former second wife's relatives so that, in return for caring for him in his home, they would be given his house when he died. On paper, this blended, three-generation family looked like a recipe for dysfunction—an introverted, Ph.D. abstract expressionist and four working-class, country-music lovers who had never heard of the Met. But they came in loving aid to my father. This extended family put down roots in my dad's community, and their kids did well in school. My dad would charge up his chair battery and travel three blocks without sidewalks, across a field and through a secret break in a chain-link fence, so he could cheer on the family's boy at bat, just as if he were his own son.

When my dad died, I flew down to Virginia to grieve and to put things in order. But the agreement he had made with his new family was never put on paper. The only legally binding will left the house to my siblings and me, and its sale would have netted us about $50,000. When I sat down with my dad's adopted family in the living room filled with cardboard boxes containing what was left of a life, they all crumpled into tears when I explained what the will directed. Hard workers, they nonetheless had no savings, and the cost of housing in the town was far beyond their means. When it came to my father's agreement with them, all I had to go on was their word. The choice was difficult for me because I had to persuade my brothers and sisters to give up money they really needed and give it to strangers whose word they had absolutely no reason to trust. I made the pitch to them, and we agreed to give away the house. A family we barely knew got a vital boost, and the world is a little fairer. This was a lesson and a test for me. I know I passed, because of how much better I felt than if I'd taken the $50,000.

The essential ingredient in every cure for OverSuccess is the forgotten half of the American Revolution—our commitment not just to individual freedom but to each other's well-being. As the founders so frequently reminded their new nation, the premise of our freedom and prosperity lies, not only in our exquisite constitution, but also in our widespread personal commitment to the voluntary norms of self-restraint and civic generosity. The founders were our first role models, living examples of the social virtues without which our nation's strength and greatness could not have been built. As Franklin, Jefferson, Madison, and Adams so presciently warned us, free society cannot persist without pervasive social virtue.

As we've seen in these pages, our brains are wired to seek recognition through generosity and good works—and to patrol against antisocial behavior. As we've also seen, the idea of success in America no longer supports what made our species and our nation successful. For the cure, we must look to our personal behavior, not to our OverSuccessed leaders. The leaders who will inspire us to virtue will emerge from the grassroots, among those outside the camera lights, those whose good works and small sanctions are witnessed and appreciated by only a few people, or one person, or even no one at all. Healing OverSuccess must begin with the things we do in small social and economic spaces. In reward for their efforts, the pioneers of modern American virtue will get a natural dopamine rush, a few extra minutes of sleep, and maybe a grateful nod.

But over time, our small actions will win big results. Expectations will shift and more people will follow our examples. Perhaps once or twice in our lives, each of us will face a major test, one that will force us to choose between the values of OverSuccess and the values of the village. It might be an unsafe drug that would go to market were we not to act, our rejection of a suspiciously low container price from a Chinese manufacturer, or an opportunity to make a sacrifice that is right and good and that will change a stranger's life. If virtue is to prevail once again, millions of us must make a personal commitment to intervene today. Once it infuses our everyday attitudes and behavior, renewed virtue will rise again to the top. Within only two or three generations, we will be back on our way toward making America that shining city upon a hill.

ENDNOTES

1. Bertrand Russell, *The Conquest of Happiness*, 1996, Liveright Publishing Corporation, page 70. Originally published by Routledge Press, 1930.

2. Sarah M. Lewis, Christopher K. Cratsley and Kristian Demary, "Mate recognition and choice in *Photinus* fireflies," *Ann Zool Fennici*, December, 2004; 41:809-21. Christopher K. Cratsley, "Flash Signals, Nuptial Gifts and Female Preference in *Photinus* Fireflies," *Integrative and Comparative Biology*, June, 2004; 44(3):238–41. Fredric V. Vencl, "Allometry and Proximate Mechanisms of Sexual Selection in *Photinus* Fireflies, and Some Other Beetles," *Integrative and Comparative Biology*, June, 2004; 44(3):242-49. "News of the Wild: Looking for Miss Light," *National Wildlife Magazine*, Feb/Mar, 1996; 34(2).

3. Glenn E. Weisfeld & Craig A. Wendorf, "The Involuntary Defeat Strategy and Discrete Emotions Theory," in Leon Sloman & Paul Gilbert (eds), *Subordination and Defeat: An Evolutionary Approach to Mood Disorders and Their Therapy*, 2000, Mahway, New Jersey: Lawrence Erlbaum Associates, pages 121-145.

4. Stephanie Coontz, *The Way We Never Were: American Families and the Nostalgia Trap*, New York: Basic Books, 1992. Lifespan is measured as life expectancy at birth.

5. Alfred Crosby, Jr., *Epidemic and Peace, 1918*, Westport, CT: Greenwood Press, 1976.

6. Jemal A, Ward E, Hao Y, Thun M., "Trends in the leading causes of death in the United States, 1970-2002," *Journal of the American Medical Association*, September 14, 2005; 294(10):1255-9.

7. Greg Easterbrook, "Bush Faces Hostile Environment," *Los Angeles Times*, October 14, 2003.

8. Steven Pinker, "A History of Violence: We're getting nicer every day," *The New Republic*, March 19, 2007, pages 18-21.

9. R. D. Plotnick, E. Smolensky, E. Evenhouse and S. Reilly, "The Twentieth Century Record of Inequality and Poverty in the United States," http://www.ssc.wisc.edu/irp/pubs/dp116698.pdf. U.S. Census Bureau, "Historical Poverty Tables, Table 5. Percent of People By Ratio of Income to Poverty Level: 1970 to 2005," September 6, 2006, http://www.census.gov/hhes/www/poverty/histpov/hstpov5.html. Recent range is that percent of Americans living at or below 100 percent of federal poverty level.

10. U.S. Census Bureau, "Poverty in the United States: 2002," Figures 1 and 6, September, 2003, http://www.census.gov/prod/2003pubs/p60-222.pdf.

11. Economic Research Service, U.S. Department of Agriculture, "Household Food Security in the United States, 2005 / ERR-29," November, 2006, page 9, http://www.ers.usda.gov/publications/err29/.

12. Since 1950, median personal income has increased by 79 percent. U.S. Census Bureau, "Historical Income Tables – People," Table P-4, All Races, April 22, 2004, http://www.census.gov/hhes/income/histinc/p04.html. The 79 percent cost-of-living adjusted median income gain since 1950 (50 percent of the population with higher and 50 percent with lower income gains) is more conservative than the 117 percent average personal income gain over that period.

13. See note on average new home sizes in Chapter 4 for sources and calculations.

14. Chicago-based Spectrem Group estimates that there were 9.2 million millionaire households in the U.S. as of mid-2007. Wealth here includes net financial and other assets, such as investment real estate and privately held businesses, but not including primary residence. Kevin Phillips, *Wealth and Democracy: A Political History of the American Rich*, New York: Random House, 2002, page 121. Calculation accounts for adjusting 1900 dollars for inflation. The growth in wealthy households was particularly pronounced over the past two decades. Between the years 1983 and 2001, the proportion of households with net worth of $1, $5 and $10 million, respectively, increased by 92, 240 and 300 percent. Source: author's calculations from Edward N. Wolff, "Changes in

Household Wealth in the 1980s and 1990s in the U.S.," May, 2004, Table 2, page 30, http://www.levy.org/2/bin/datastore/pubs/files/wp/407.pdf.

15. U.S. Census Bureau, "Table HINC-05. Percent Distribution of Households, by Selected Characteristics Within Income Quintile and Top 5 Percent in 2006," August 28, 2007, http://pubdb3.census.gov/macro/032007/hhinc/new05_000.htm.

16. Stephen Moore and Julian Simon, *The Greatest Century That Ever Was*, Cato Institute, 1999, http://www.cato.org/pubs/pas/pa364.pdf, the source for data in this section on American comparative material well-being not otherwise footnoted.

17. Reality News Online, May 25, 2005, number of 2005 auditions.

18. Tiggemann, M., and Pickering, A. S., "Role of television in adolescent women's body dissatisfaction and drive for thinness," *International Journal of Eating Disorders*, 1996; 20:199-203. Screening for Mental Health, Inc, April, 2003, http://www.mentalhealthscreening.org/eat/eat-fact.htm.

19. Prescription stimulants: Terrance Woodworth, Deputy Director Office of Diversion Control, Drug Enforcement Administration, Congressional Testimony, May 16, 2000, http://www.dea.gov/pubs/cngrtest/ct051600.htm. Report: International Narcotics Control Boardfor1995,page34,http://www.incb.org/pdf/e/tr/psy/2005/psychotropics_comments_en.pdf. Serial killers: Michael Newton, author of the *Encyclopedia of Serial Killers*, personal communication, August 29, 2003.

20. Mark Jacobs, et al, "The Other Side of the Mountain," *The New York Times Magazine*, December 18, 2005, pages 65-73. *The New York Times Magazine*, "Regular Reader Study, 2002," http://nytmarketing.com/mediakit/docs/readership/magazine/magazine_readership_study.pdf. Almost half of Sunday *Times* readers have a post-graduate degree; the average reader falls comfortably into the top five percent in household income at $162,600 in 2002. The US Census pegs the lower limit of top five percent household earnings at $150,012 in 2002.

21. Raksha Arora, "A Nation More Divided: Ranks of "Have-Nots" Swell," *Gallup News Service*, July 20, 2004. Additional data for Princeton Job # 04-060-20 provided by the company.

22. Tiggemann, M., and Pickering, A. S, "Role of television in adolescent women's body dissatisfaction and drive for thinness," *International Journal of Eating Disorders*, 1996; 20:199-203. Screening for Mental Health, Inc, April, 2003, http://www.mentalhealthscreening.org/eat/eat-fact.htm.

23. Photo by Nick Ut, *AP*, http://en.wikipedia.org/wiki/Image:TrangBang.jpg.

24. http://cdd.stanford.edu/. Jim Fishkin first proposed deliberative polling in 1991 and has used it successfully throughout the world. Poll results often change sharply after participants engage in structured discussion of various points of view presented by credible advocates.

25. American Psychiatric Association, *Diagnostic and Statistical Manual of Mental Disorders*, 4th edition, 2000, Washington DC. Consult the manual for the complete symptom criteria.

26. S. Dakin, P. Carlin, D. Hemsley, "Weak suppression of visual context in chronic schizophrenia," *Current Biology*, October, 2005; 15(20):R822-R824. Anna Gosline, "Creative spark can come from schizophrenia," *NewScientist*, July 24, 2004, page 14.

27. William Hazlitt, "Disappointment," in *Lectures on the Literature of the Age of Elizabeth*, 1820, cited in Geoffrey Keynes, editor, *Selected Essays*, London: Nonesuch Press, 1930.

28. Henry M. McHenry and Katherine Coffing, "Australopithecus To Homo: Transformations in Body and Mind," *Annual Review of Anthropology*, 2000; 29:125-146. Table 1, comparison of brain mass/body mass ratio between *Homo ergaster* and *Homo sapiens*.

29. David Sloan Wilson and Edward O. Wilson, "Rethinking the Theoretical Foundation of Sociobiology," *The Quarterly Review of Biology*, December, 2007; 82(4):327-348. David Sloan Wilson, Mark Van Vugt, and Rick O'Gorman, "Multilevel Selection Theory and Major Evolutionary Transitions: Implications for Psychological Science," *Current Directions in Psychological Science*, in press.

30. Flinn, M. V., Geary, D. C., & Ward, C. V., "Ecological dominance, social competition, and coalitionary arms races: Why humans evolved extraordinary intelligence," *Evolution and Human Behavior*, January, 2005; 26(1):10-46.

31. Jung-Kyoo Choi and Samuel Bowles, "The Coevolution of Parochial Altruism and War," *Science*, October 26, 2007; 318(5850):636-640.

32. R. B. Alley, "Ice-core evidence of abrupt climate changes," *Proceedings of the National Academy of Sciences of the United States of America*, February 15, 2000; 97(4):1331-1334.

33. Samuel Bowles, "Group Competition, Reproductive Leveling, and the Evolution of Human Altruism," *Science*, December 8, 2006; 314(5805):1569-72. See Tables S3 and S4 in the supplemental materials for hunter-gatherer death data.

34. Brian Hayden, "Fabulous feasts: a prolegomenon to the importance of feasting," In, *Feasts: Archaeological and Ethnographic Perspectives on Food, Politics, and Power*, Eds. Michael Dietler and Brian Hayden, Washington: Smithsonian Institution Press, 2001, pages 23-64.

35. Bob Holmes, "Manna or millstone," *NewScientist*, September 18, 2004, pages 29-31.

36. James Perodie, "Feasting for Prosperity: A Study of Southern Northwest Coast Feasting," In *Feasts: Archaeological and Ethnographic Perspectives on Food, Politics, and Power*, Eds. Michael Dietler and Brian Hayden, Washington: Smithsonian Institution Press, 2001, pages 185-214. Roheim, G., *The Origin and Function of Culture*, Nervous and Mental Disease Monograph no. 69, 1943, New York: Nervous and Mental Disease Monographs, page 12.

37. Charlie L. Hardy and Mark VanVugt, "Nice Guys Finish First: The Competitive Altruism Hypothesis," *Personality and Social Psychology Bulletin*, September, 2006; 32(10):1402-1413.

38. Dunbar, R. I. M., "Coevolution of neocortical size, group size and language in humans," *Behavioral and Brain Sciences*, 1993; 16(4):681-735. Dunbar, R. I. M., "Determinants of group size in primates: A general model," in Runciman, W. G., Maynard Smith, J. & Dunbar, R. I. M. (eds.), *Evolution of social behaviour in primates and man*, 1996, Oxford: Oxford University Press. Christopher Allen, "The Dunbar Number as a Limit to Group Sizes," March, 2004, http://www.lifewithalacrity.com/2004/03/the_dunbar_numb.html.

39. Lewis R. Binford, *Constructing Frames of Reference: An Analytical Method for Archaeological Theory Building Using Hunter-Gatherer and Environmental Data Sets*, 2001, Berkeley: University of California Press, Table 8.01, pages 245-251. Group type cited is Regional Periodic Aggregations, for example a male initiation ceremony. Binford's Regional Aggregations are composed of two smaller sizes, the "most aggregated" and "most dispersed" groups. The "most dispersed" group is the subsistence living unit in intimate daily contact and numbering in the range of 10-20 persons.

40. M. Gullestad and M. Segalne, *Family and Kinship in Europe*, London: Pinter, 1997.

41. The Pleistocene epoch began about 1.8 million years ago and ended about 11,000 years ago at the end of the last ice age.

42. I should note that the EEA-mismatch concept has been shaken by very recent evidence that humans have continued to evolve over the past thousands and even hundreds of years.

43. Peter Gluckman and Mark Hanson, *Mismatch: Why our world no longer fits our bodies*, London: Oxford University Press, 2006. Gluckman and Hanson discuss several modern mismatches: the falling age of puberty versus the increasing age of social maturity, and medicine giving us lives longer than those of our cellular repair systems.

44. Jared Diamond, "The Cruel Logic of our Genes," *Discover: Exploring the Mind*, Discover Publications, 1990, pages 24-31.

45. Centers for Disease Control, "Prevalence of Overweight and Obesity Among Adults: United States, 2003-2004," January 30, 2007. Kelly D. Brownell and Katherine Battle Horgren, *Food Fight: The Inside Story of the Food Industry, America's Obesity Crisis, and What We Can Do About It*, New York: McGraw-Hill, 2004, pages 24-27.

46. Julia A. Sherman, "Evolutionary Origin of Bipolar Disorder (EOBD)," *Psycoloquy*, June 25, 2001. Julia A. Sherman, "Is Bipolar Disorder a Behavioral Fossil?" *Psycoloquy*, 2002; 13:24.

47. Ronald C. Kessler, Patricia Berglund, Olga Demler, Robert Jin, Kathleen R. Merikangas, Ellen E. Walters, "Lifetime Prevalence and Age-of-Onset Distributions of *DSM-IV* Disorders in the National Comorbidity Survey Replication," *Archives of General Psychiatry*, 2005; 62:593-602, Table 3. Lifetime risk of BD I and II disorders is projected at 5.1 percent of the U.S. population.

48. Joseph Henrich and Francisco J. Gil-White, "The evolution of prestige: freely conferred deference as a mechanism for enhancing the benefits of cultural transmission," *Evolution and Human Behavior*, May, 2001; 22(3):165-96.

49. Christopher Reed, "The Damn'd South Sea," *Harvard Magazine*, May-June, 1999.

50. Salganik MJ, Dodds PS, Watts DJ., "Experimental study of inequality and unpredictability in an artificial cultural market," *Science*, February, 10, 2006; 311(5762):854-6.

51. Robert O. Deaner, Amit V. Khera and Michael L. Platt, "Monkeys Pay Per View: Adaptive Valuation of Social Images by Rhesus Macaques, *Current Biology*, published online, January 27, 2005. CF Zink, Y Tong, Q Chen, DS Bassett, JL Stein, and A Meyer-Lindenberg, "Know your place: neural processing of social hierarchy in humans," *Neuron*, April 24, 2008; 58(2):273-83.

52. Satoshi Kanazawa, "The Savanna Principle," *Managerial and Decision Economics*, 2004; 25:41-54.

53. John Price, Leon Sloman, et al., "The social competition hypothesis of depression," *British Journal of Psychiatry*, 1994; 164:309-315.

54. Leon Sloman & Paul Gilbert (eds), *Subordination and Defeat: An Evolutionary Approach to Mood Disorders and Their Therapy*, Mahway, New Jersey: Lawrence Erlbaum Associates, 2000. The authors clearly note that their "involuntary defeat strategy" model does not explain all depressions.

55. Edward H. Hagen, "The bargaining model of depression," in Hammerstein, Peter, Eds. *The genetic and cultural evolution of cooperation*, 2002, Cambridge: MIT Press.

56. George Brown, "Social Roles, Context and Evolution in the Origins of Depression," *Journal of Health and Social Behavior*, September, 2002; 43(3):255-276.

57. Cohen JD and Blum KI, "Overview: Reward and decision. Introduction to special issue," *Neuron*, 2002; 36(2):193-198.

58. George-Marios Angeletos, David Laibson, Andrea Repetto, Jeremy Tobacman and Stephen Weinberg, "The Hyperbolic Consumption Model: Calibration, Simulation, and Empirical Evaluation," *Journal of Economic Perspectives*, Summer, 2001; 15(3):47–68.

59. De Martino B, Kumaran D, Seymour B, Dolan RJ., "Frames, biases, and rational decision-making in the human brain," *Science*, August 4, 2006; 313(5787):684-7. These decision-making errors result from what scientists call the "decision framing effect."

60. McClure, Samuel M., Laibson, David I., Loewenstein, George, Cohen, Jonathan D., "Separate Neural Systems Value Immediate and Delayed Monetary Rewards," *Science*, October 15, 2004; 306(5695):503-507.

61. P. Read Montague, Brooks King-Casas, and Jonathan D. Cohen. "Imaging Valuation Models in Human Choice," *Annual Review of Neuroscience*, July 21, 2006; 29:417-448.

62. Stephen Pinker, *How the Mind Works*, New York: Norton, 1997, page 21.

63. Michael Gazzaniga, *The Mind's Past*, 1998 [2000], Berkeley: University of California Press, page xiii.

64. Benajmin Libet, *Mind time: The temporal factor in consciousness*, 2004, Cambridge: Harvard University Press.

65. Joshua New, Max Krasnow, Danielle Truxaw, and Steven J.C. Gaulin, "Spatial adaptations for plant foraging: women excel and calories count," *Proceedings of the Royal Society: Biological Sciences*, August 21, 2007; 274:2679–2684.

66. Nancy Kanwisher, "What's in a Face," *Science*, February 3, 2006; 311(5761):617-8. Michael Gazzaniga, *The Mind's Past*, 1998 [2000], Berkeley: University of California Press, page xiii.

67. Bjorn Merker, "Consciousness without a cerebral cortex: a challenge for neuroscience and medicine," *Behavioral and Brain Sciences*, May 1, 2007; 30(1):63-81. Bruce Bower, "Consciousness in the Raw: The brain stem may orchestrate the basics of awareness," *Science News*, September 15, 2007; 172(11):170.

68. James Olds, "Pleasure centers in the brain," *Scientific American*, October 2-7, 1956; 195(4):107-108. Olds, J. & Milner, P., "Positive reinforcement produced by electrical

stimulation of septal area and other regions of rat brain," *J. Comp. Physiol. Psychol.*, 1954; 47:419-427.

69.   Montague PR and Berns GS, "Neural economics and the biological substrates of valuation," *Neuron*, 2002; 36:265-284. Daniel H. Lende & E.O. Smith, "Evolution meets biopsychosociality: an analysis of addictive behavior," *Addiction*, April, 2002; 97:447-458. McClure, SM, Daw, N, Montague, PR, "A computational substrate for incentive salience," *Trends in Neuroscience*, 2003; 26(8):423-428.

70.   Dr. Anna Rose Childress, "Opiates, Brownies, Sex and Cocaine: Seeking the Brain Signature for Desire," *Irvine Health Foundation Lecture Series*, Jan. 29, 2003, http://www.ihf.org/lecture/childress_trans.html. Fisher HE, Aron A, Mashek D, Li H, Brown LL, "Defining the brain systems of lust, romantic attraction, and attachment," *Arch Sex Behav.*, October, 2002; 31(5):413-9. Rilling JK, Gutman DA, Zeh TR, Pagnoni G, Berns GS, Kilts CD, "A neural basis for social cooperation," *Neuron*, July 18, 2002; 35:395-405. Jorge Moll, Frank Krueger, Roland Zahn, Matteo Pardini, Ricardo de Oliveira-Souza, and Jordan Grafman, "Human fronto-mesolimbic networks guide decisions about charitable donation," *Proceedings of the National Academy of Sciences U S A*, October 17, 2006; 103(42):15623-8. This PNAS study is the first to decisively prove that monetary generosity stimulates the shared brain reward system. Martin Werme, Chad Messer, Lars Olson, Lauren Gilden, Peter Thorén, Eric J. Nestler, and Stefan Brené, "Delta*FosB* Regulates Wheel Running," *The Journal of Neuroscience*, September 15, 2002; 22(18):8133-8138. This last study involves rats, but there is now little reason to suspect it would not be the same in humans. K Izuma, DN Saito and N Sadato, "Processing of social and monetary rewards in the human striatum," *Neuron*, April 24, 2008; 58(2):284-94. Jasmin Cloutier, Todd F. Heatherton, Paul J. Whalen and William M. Kelley, "Are Attractive People Rewarding? Sex Differences in the Neural Substrates of Facial Attractiveness," *Journal of Cognitive Neuroscience*, June, 2008; 20:941-51.

71.   Marina E. Wolf, "LTP May Trigger Addiction," *Molecular Interventions*, August, 2003; 3(5):248-52.

72.   O. Berton, C. A. McClung, R. J. DiLeone, V. Krishnan, W. Renthal, S. J. Russo, D. Graham, N. M. Tsankova, C. A. Bolanos, M. Rios, L. M. Monteggia, D. W. Self, E. J. Nestler, "Essential role of BDNF in the mesolimbic dopamine pathway in social defeat stress," *Science*, February 10, 2006; 311, 864-868.

73.   Source: research published in: Garavan, H.; Pankiewicz, J.; Bloom, A.; Cho, J-K.; Sperry, L.; Ross, T.J.; Salmeron, B-J.; Risinger, R.; Kelley, D.; Stein, E.A., "Cue-induced cocaine craving: neuroanatomical specificity for drug users and drug stimuli," *American Journal of Psychiatry*, 2000; 157(11):1789-1798. Figure published in: Patrick Zickler, NIDA Notes, "Cues for Cocaine and Normal Pleasures Activate Common Brain Sites," May, 2001; 16(2), http://www.drugabuse.gov/NIDA_Notes/NNVol16N2/Cues.html.

74.   Mattson BJ, Williams S, Rosenblatt JS, Morrell JI, "Comparison of two positive reinforcing stimuli: pups and cocaine throughout the postpartum period," *Behavioral Neuroscience*, 2001; 115:683-94.

75.   Frances A. Champagne, Pablo Chretien, Carl W. Stevenson, Tie Yuan Zhang, Alain Gratton, and Michael J. Meaney, "Variations in Nucleus Accumbens Dopamine Associated with Individual Differences in Maternal Behavior in the Rat," *Journal of Neuroscience*, April 28, 2004; 24(17):4113-4123.

76.   Bartels A, Zeki S., "The neural correlates of maternal and romantic love," *Neuroimage*, March, 2004; 21(3):1155-66.

77.   Porrino, Linda J.; Daunais, James B.; Smith, Hilary R.; Nader, Michael A., "The expanding effects of cocaine: studies in a nonhuman primate model of cocaine self-administration," *Neuroscience & Biobehavioral Reviews*, January, 2004; 27(8):813-20.

78.   Nora D. Volkow, Joanna S. Fowler, "Addiction, a Disease of Compulsion and Drive: Involvement of the Orbitofrontal Cortex," *Symposium of the UCLA Neuropsychiatric Institute and Brain Research Institute*, February 8, 2002, http://www.mentalhealth.ucla.edu/esyllabus/volkow1.pdf.

79.   Hyman, Steven E., "Addiction: A Disease of Learning and Memory," *American Journal of Psychiatry*, 2005; 162:1414-22.
80.   Kalivas, Peter W., Volkow, Nora D., "The Neural Basis of Addiction: A Pathology of Motivation and Choice," *American Journal of Psychiatry*, 2005; 162:1403-13.
81.   Volkow, Nora D.; Fowler, Joanna S.; Wang, Gene-Jack, "The addicted human brain: insights from imaging studies," *Journal of Clinical Investigation*, May 15, 2003; 111(10):1444-1451.
82.   Hyman SE, Malenka RC, Nestler EJ., "Neural Mechanisms of Addiction: The Role of Reward-Related Learning and Memory," *Annual Review of Neuroscience*, July 21, 2006; 29:565-598.
83.   Gene-Jack Wang, personal communication, February 25, 2005.
84.   Volkow, N.D.; Fowler, J.S.; Wang, G.-J.; Swanson, J.M., and Telang, F., "Dopamine in drug abuse and addiction: results from imaging studies and treatment implications, *Arch Neurol*, November 1, 2007; 64(11):1575-9. Diana Martinez, Rajesh Narendran, Richard W. Foltin, Mark Slifstein, Dah-Ren Hwang, Allegra Broft, Yiyun Huang, Thomas B. Cooper, Marian W. Fischman, Herbert D. Kleber, and Marc Laruelle, "Amphetamine-induced dopamine release: markedly blunted in cocaine dependence and predictive of the choice to self-administer cocaine," *American Journal of Psychiatry*, April, 2007; 164(4):622-629. The cocaine study shows that amphetamine produces a blunted dopamine release in the striata of cocaine-dependent people. The alcohol study shows similarly that amphetamine produces a blunted dopamine release in portions of the striata of alcohol-dependent people and that alcohol dependence is associated with a reduced count of D2 receptors in those portions of striatum.
85.   Nora D. Volkow, Gene-Jack Wang, Frank Telang, Joanna S. Fowler, Jean Logan, Millard Jayne, Yeming Ma, Kith Pradhan, and Christopher Wong, "Profound Decreases in Dopamine Release in Striatum in Detoxified Alcoholics: Possible Orbitofrontal Involvement," *Journal of Neuroscience*, November 14, 2007; 27(46):12700-12706. This study provides recent evidence of decreased reward sensitivity in addicts. Detoxified alcoholics, but not control subjects, show at least 50 percent reduced reward response to the active ingredient in Ritalin in their ventral striatum, a central structure in the brain reward system. Robert Mathias, "Pathological Obesity and Drug Addiction Share Common Brain Characteristics," *NIDA Notes*, October, 2001; 16(4).
86.   Blum K, Sheridan PJ, Wood RC, Braverman ER, Chen TJ, Comings DE., "Dopamine D2 receptor gene variants: association and linkage studies in impulsive-addictive-compulsive behaviour," *Pharmacogenetics*, June, 1995; 5(3):121-41.
87.   Pickering AD, Gray JA., "The neuroscience of personality," In: *Handbook of Personality: Theory and Research*, 2nd Edition, Pervin LA, John OP, eds, 1999, New York: Guilford, pages 277–299.
88.   Volkow ND, Wang G-J, Fowler JS, et al. Prediction of reinforcing responses to psychostimulants in humans by brain dopamine D2 receptor levels," *American Journal of Psychiatry*, 1999; 156:1440-1443. Dalley JW, Fryer TD, Brichard L, Robinson ES, Theobald DE, Laane K, Pena Y, Murphy ER, Shah Y, Probst K, Abakumova I, Aigbirhio FI, Richards HK, Hong Y, Baron JC, Everitt BJ, Robbins TW., "Nucleus accumbens D2/3 receptors predict trait impulsivity and cocaine reinforcement," *Science*, March 2, 2007; 315(5816):1267-70. This rat experiment shows conclusively that those with fewer D2 receptors in the nucleus accumbens were more impulsive and self administered more cocaine.
89.   Fehr, Christoph, Yakushev, Igor, Hohmann, Nina, Buchholz, Hans-Georg, Landvogt, Christian, Deckers, Hanna, Eberhardt, Alexandra, Klager, Marie, Smolka, Michael N., Scheurich, Armin, Dielentheis, Thomas, Schmidt, Lutz G., Rosch, Frank, Bartenstein, Peter, Grunder, Gerhard, Schreckenberger, Mathias, "Association of Low Striatal Dopamine D2 Receptor Availability With Nicotine Dependence Similar to That Seen With Other Drugs of Abuse," *American Journal of Psychiatry*, March 3, 2008; 165:507-514.
90.   Volkow, Nora D.; Wang, Gene-Jack; Maynard, Larry; Fowler, Joanna S.; Jayne, Budd; Telang, Frank; Logan, Jean; Ding, Yu-Shin; Gatley, Samuel J.; Hitzemann, Robert; Wong,

Christopher; Pappas, Naome, "Effects of alcohol detoxification on dopamine D2 receptors in alcoholics: a preliminary study," *Psychiatry Research: Neuroimaging Section*, December, 2002; 116(3):163-72. Martinez D, Gil R, Slifstein M, Hwang DR, Huang Y, Perez A, Kegeles L, Talbot P, Evans S, Krystal J, Laruelle M, Abi-Dargham A., "Alcohol dependence is associated with blunted dopamine transmission in the ventral striatum," *Biological Psychiatry*, November 15, 2005; 58(10):779-86. The alcohol study shows similarly that amphetamine produces a blunted dopamine release in portions of the striata of alcohol-dependent people and that alcohol dependence is associated with a reduced count of D2 receptors in those portions of striatum.

91.   Nora D. Volkow, Gene-Jack Wang, Henri Begleiter, Bernice Porjesz, Joanna S. Fowler, Frank Telang, Christopher Wong, Yeming Ma, Jean Logan, Rita Goldstein, David Alexoff, and Peter K. Thanos, "High Levels of Dopamine D_2 Receptors in Unaffected Members of Alcoholic Families: Possible Protective Factors," *Archives of General Psychiatry*, September, 2006; 63:999-1008.

92.   Beaver JD, Lawrence AD, van Ditzhuijzen J, Davis MH, Woods A, Calder AJ., "Individual differences in reward drive predict neural responses to images of food," *Journal of Neuroscience*, May, 10, 2006; 26(19):5160-6. Franken IH, Muris P., "Individual differences in reward sensitivity are related to food craving and relative body weight in healthy women," *Appetite*, October, 2005; 45(2):198-201.

93.   Petra Kok, Ferdinand Roelfsema, Marijke Frölich, Johannes van Pelt, Marcel P. M. Stokkel, A. Edo Meinders, and Hanno Pijl, "Activation of dopamine D2 receptors simultaneously ameliorates various metabolic features of obese women," *American Journal Physiology Endocrinology and Metabolism*, June 27, 2006; 291: E1038-E1043. Bromocriptine was the compound used in this experiment to stoke D2 receptors. Do not do this at home.

94.   Wang, G.-J.; Volkow, N.D.; Logan, Pappas, N.R.; Wong, C.T.; Zhu, W.; Nerusil, N.; Fowler, J.S., "Brain dopamine and obesity," *Lancet*, February 3, 2001; 357:354-357. Wang GJ, Volkow ND, Thanos PK, Fowler JS., "Similarity between obesity and drug addiction as assessed by neurofunctional imaging: a concept review," *Journal of Addiction Disorders*, 2004; 23(3):39-53.

95.   Zheng Liu, Barry J. Richmond, Elisabeth A. Murray, Richard C. Saunders, Sara Steenrod, Barbara K. Stubblefield, Deidra M. Montague, and Edward I. Ginns, "DNA targeting of rhinal cortex D2 receptor protein reversibly blocks learning of cues that predict reward," *Proceedings of the National Academy of Sciences*, August 17, 2004; 101(33):12336-12341.

96.   Thanos, Panayotis K.; Volkow, Nora D.; Freimuth, Paul; Umegaki, Hiroyuki; Ikari, Hiroyuki; Roth, George; Ingram, Donald K.; Hitzemann, Robert., "Overexpression of dopamine D2 receptors reduces alcohol self-administration.," *Journal of Neurochemistry*, September 9, 2001; 78(5):1094-1103. Thanos PK, Michaelides M, Umegaki H, Volkow ND, "D2R DNA transfer into the nucleus accumbens attenuates cocaine self-administration in rats," *Synapse*, April 16, 2008; 62(7):481-486. Panayotis K., Thanos, T, Seth N. Rivera, Katrina Weaver, David K. Grandy, Marcelo Rubinstein, Hiroyuki Umegaki, Gene Jack Wang, Robert Hitzemann, Nora D. Volkow, "Dopamine D2R DNA transfer in dopamine D2 receptor-deficient mice: Effects on ethanol drinking," *Life Sciences*, May 27, 2005; 77:130-139.

97.   Gene-Jack Wang, Nora D. Volkow, Panayotis K. Thanos, Joanna S. Fowler, "Similarity between obesity and drug addiction as assessed by neurofunctional imaging: a concept review," *Journal of Addiction Disorders*, 2004; 23(3):39-53. Cocaine, amphetamines, alcohol and heroin addicts all show significant reductions in D2 receptors in the striatum. Noble Ernest P., "D2 dopamine receptor gene in psychiatric and neurologic disorders and its phenotypes," *American Journal of Medical Genetics Part B*, January, 2003; 116B(1):103-25. Persons with D2A1 allele have almost 40 percent fewer D2 receptors in their striatum. Roughly 40 percent of alcoholics, nicotine and illegal drug addicts and obese people have the D2A1 allele, where roughly 15 percent of non-alcoholic, non-drug abusers have the allele.

98.   Berggren U, Fahlke C, Aronsson E, Karanti A, Eriksson M, Blennow K, Thelle D, Zetterberg
       H, Balldin J., "The taqI DRD2 A1 allele is associated with alcohol-dependence although
       its effect size is small," *Alcohol and Alcoholism*, June, 2006; 41(5):479-485. Scandanavian
       population, unscreened for alcoholism, large sample size of 264 people. A1A1 (two-copy)
       incidence is 3 percent, A1A2 (one-copy) incidence is 31 percent of the population.
99.   D2Al allele associations. **Impulsiveness:** Limosin F, Loze JY, Dubertret C, Gouya L, Ades
       J, Rouillon F, Gorwood P., "Impulsiveness as the intermediate link between the dopamine
       receptor D2 gene and alcohol dependence," *Psychiatr Genet.*, June, 2003; 13(2):127-9.
       Reward dependency: Lee HJ, Lee HS, Kim YK, Kim L, Lee MS, Jung IK, Suh KY, Kim
       S., "D2 and D4 dopamine receptor gene polymorphisms and personality traits in a young
       Korean population," *Am J Med Genet.*, August 15, 2003; 121B(1):44-9. **Alcoholism:** MR
       Munafo, IJ Matheson1 and J Flint, "Association of the DRD2 gene Taq1A polymorphism
       and alcoholism: a meta-analysis of case–control studies and evidence of publication bias,"
       Molecular Psychiatry, January 9, 2007; 12:454–461. Smith L, Watson M, Gates S, Ball D,
       Foxcroft D., "Meta-Analysis of the Association of the Taq1A Polymorphism with the Risk
       of Alcohol Dependency: A HuGE Gene-Disease Association Review," *American Journal
       of Epidemiology*, January 15, 2008; 167(2):125-38. This meta-analysis found a 22 percent
       greater alcoholism likelihood among those with two D2A1 alleles. **Alcohol, cocaine,
       heroin and methamphetamine:** Nora D. Volkow, Joanna S. Fowler, "Addiction, a
       Disease of Compulsion and Drive: Involvement of the Orbitofrontal Cortex," *Symposium
       of the UCLA Neuropsychiatric Institute and Brain Research*, Institute February 8, 2002,
       http://www.mentalhealth.ucla.edu/esyllabus/volkow1.pdf. **Drug abuse, smoking, obesity
       and post traumatic stress disorder:** Noble, 2003, above. Jason P Connor, Ross McD
       Young, Bruce R Lawford, John B Saunders, Terry L Ritchie, and Ernest P Noble, "Heavy
       nicotine and alcohol use in alcohol dependence is associated with D2 dopamine receptor
       (DRD2) polymorphism," *Addictive Behaviors*, June 9, 2006. **Food reward intensity:** Epstein
       LH, Temple JL, Neaderhiser BJ, Salis RJ, Erbe RW, Leddy JJ., "Food reinforcement, the
       dopamine D2 receptor genotype, and energy intake in obese and nonobese humans,"
       Behavioral Neuroscience, October, 2007; 121(5):877-86. Food reinforcement was found to
       be greatest in obese persons with the genotype. **Binge eating disorder:** C Davis, RD
       Levitan, AS Kaplan, J Carter, C Reid, C Curtis, K Patte, R Hwang, and JL Kennedy,
       "Reward sensitivity and the D2 dopamine receptor gene: A case-control study of binge
       eating disorder, "*Prog Neuropsychopharmacol Biol Psychiatry*, April 1, 2008; 32(3):620-8. This
       study found that obese individuals and those with binge eating disorder were more likely
       to be TaqA1 carriers and more likely to be more reward sensitive. **Pathologic gambling
       addiction:** Comings DE, Rosenthal RJ, Lesieur HR, Rugle LJ, Muhleman D, Chiu C,
       Dietz G, Gade R., "A study of the dopamine D2 receptor gene in pathological gambling,"
       Pharmacogenetics, June, 1996; 6(3):223-34. Sixty-four percent of more severe pathological
       gamblers had the D2A1 allele, versus 18 percent of those scoring zero on the South Oaks
       gambling scale. Cohen MX, Young J, Baek JM, Kessler C, Ranganath C., "Individual
       differences in extraversion and dopamine genetics predict neural reward responses,"
       Cognitive Brain Research, December, 2005; 25(3):851-61. People with the D2A1 allele had
       brains whose dopamine systems were significantly more responsive to gambling reward.
       ADHD: Serý O, Drtílková I, Theiner P, Pitelová R, Staif R, Znojil V, Lochman J, Didden
       W., "Polymorphism of DRD2 gene and ADHD," *Neuro Endocrinology Letters*, Feb-April,
       2006; 27(1-2):236-40. David E. Comings, "Clinical and Molecular Genetics of ADHD and
       Tourette Syndrome: Two Related Polygenic Disorders," *Annals of the New York Academy
       of Sciences*, 2001; 931:50-83. This study found that 46 percent had D2A1 allele. Smith
       KM, Daly M, Fischer M, Yiannoutsos CT, Bauer L, Barkley R, Navia BA., "Association of
       the dopamine beta hydroxylase gene with attention deficit hyperactivity disorder: genetic
       analysis of the Milwaukee longitudinal study," *Am J Med Genet.*, May 2003; 119B(1):77-85.
       Novelty seeking: Berman, Steve; Ozkaragoz, Tulin; Young, Ross McD.; Noble, Ernest P.,
       "D2 dopamine receptor gene polymorphism discriminates two kinds of novelty seeking,"
       Personality & Individual Differences, October, 2002; 33(6):867-882. **Detachment and social
       isolation:** Farde, L., J.P. Gustavsson & E. Jönsson, "D2 dopamine receptors and personality

traits," *Nature*, 1997; 385:590. **Verbal creativity:** Reuter M, Roth S, Holve K, Hennig J., "Identification of first candidate genes for creativity: a pilot study," *Brain Research*, January 19, 2006; 1069:190-197.

100. Kevin M. Beaver, John Paul Wright, Matt DeLisi, Leah E. Daigle, Marc L. Swatt and Chris L. Gibson, "Evidence of a Gene X Environment Interaction in the Creation of Victimization: Results From a Longitudinal Sample of Adolescents," *International Journal of Offender Therapy and Comparative Criminology*, July 17, 2007; 51:620-645. The effect was not shown for black or female teens.

101. Brady, Kathleen T., Sinha, Rajita, "Co-Occurring Mental and Substance Use Disorders: The Neurobiological Effects of Chronic Stress," *American Journal of Psychiatry*, 2005; 162:1483-93.

102. Chiu PH, Lohrenz TM, Montague PR., "Smokers' brains compute, but ignore, a fictive error signal in a sequential investment task," *Nature Neuroscience*, March 2, 2008, Epub ahead of print.

103. Tilmann A. Klein, Jane Neumann, Martin Reuter, Jürgen Hennig, D. Yves von Cramon, Markus Ullsperger, "Genetically Determined Differences in Learning from Errors," *Science*, December 7, 2007; 318(5856):1642-1645. Individuals had either one or two copies of the A1 allele.

104. Kalivas, Peter W., Volkow, Nora D., "The Neural Basis of Addiction: A Pathology of Motivation and Choice," *American Journal of Psychiatry*, 2005; 162:1403-13.

105. Comings DE, Gade-Andavolu R, Gonzalez N, Wu S, Muhleman D, Chen C, Koh P, Farwell K, Blake H, Dietz G, MacMurray JP, Lesieur HR, Rugle LJ, Rosenthal RJ., "The additive effect of neurotransmitter genes in pathological gambling," *Clin Genet.*, August, 2001; 60(2):107-16.

106. David E. Comings, "Clinical and Molecular Genetics of ADHD and Tourette Syndrome: Two Related Polygenic Disorders," *Annals of the New York Academy of Sciences*, 2001; 931:50-83.

107. Eric J. Nestler, "Psychogenomics: Opportunities for Understanding Addiction," *The Journal of Neuroscience*, November 1, 2001; 21(21):8324-8327.

108. Lucinda Hahn, "Buyer's remorse," *Chicago Magazine*, April, 2002; 51(4):44-53.

109. Mark Hayward, "All-out effort lead to killer," *New Hampshire Union Leader*, November 8, 2004.

110. James Dobson, *Life on the Edge*, Dallas: Word Publishing, 1995, pages 196-197.

111. Substance Abuse and Mental Health Services Administration, "Results from the 2003 National Survey on Drug Use and Health: National Findings," 2004, Rockville, MD: Office of Applied Studies, NSDUH Series H–25, DHHS Publication No. SMA 04–3964, Figures 4.1 and 4.7 notes, year 2003, ages 12 and over. Bridget F. Grant; Deborah S. Hasin; S. Patricia Chou; Frederick S. Stinson; Deborah A. Dawson, "Nicotine Dependence and Psychiatric Disorders in the United States: Results From the National Epidemiologic Survey on Alcohol and Related Conditions," *Arch Gen Psychiatry*, Nov 2004; 61:1107-1115. Grant et al report nicotine dependence at 12.8 percent of adults. According to National Institute of Drug Abuse, "Nicotine Addiction: NIH Publication No. 01-4342," August, 2001, thirty-five million Americans attempt to quit tobacco use each year.

112. Bridget F. Grant; Frederick S. Stinson; Deborah A. Dawson; S. Patricia Chou; W. June Ruan; Roger P. Pickering, "Co-occurrence of 12-Month Alcohol and Drug Use Disorders and Personality Disorders in the United States: Results From the National Epidemiologic Survey on Alcohol and Related Conditions," *Arch Gen Psychiatry*, April, 2004; 61:361-368.

113. Griffiths, R.R., Juliano, L.M., & Chausmer, A.L.. "Caffeine pharmacology and clinical effects," in: Graham A.W., Schultz T.K., Mayo-Smith M.F., Ries R.K. & Wilford, B.B. (eds.) *Principles of Addiction Medicine, Third Edition*, Chevy Chase, MD: American Society of Addiction, 2003.

114. Koran LM, Faber RJ, Aboujaoude E, Large MD, Serpe RT, "Estimated prevalence of compulsive buying behavior in the United States," *American Journal of Psychiatry, October,* 2006; 163(10):1806-12. The 5.8% prevalence number represents less than or equal to two standard deviations below mean behavior. Contrary to previous estimates, prevalence is

very similar for men and women. Compulsive buying is not recognized in the DSM-IV; however, diagnostic criteria have been proposed. Point prevalence of 5.8% is reported. Phone survey of 2,513 adults. The most restrictive diagnostic criteria yields 1.4% prevalence for compulsive buying. Kyrios, M.; Frost, R. O.; Steketee, G., "Cognitions in Compulsive Buying and Acquisition," *Cognitive Therapy & Research*, April, 2004; 28(2):241-258. Siskos, Catherine and Burt, Erin, "Slaves To the Sale," *Kiplinger's Personal Finance*, November, 2002; 56(11):108-113. Donald Black, a psychiatrist and a professor of psychiatry at the University of Iowa, finds from his clinical work that female shopping addicts focus on clothing and personal accessories; males on technology and investments.

115.   Thomas M. Mick and Eric Hollander, "Impulsive-Compulsive Sexual Behavior," *CNS Spectrums*, 2006; 11(12):944-955, http://www.cnsspectrums.com/aspx/article_pf.aspx?articleid=914. These numbers are estimates rather than the result of a systematic population study. CSB is thought to be three times more common in men than women.

116.   Substance Abuse and Mental Health Services Administration, "Results from the 2003 National Survey on Drug Use and Health: National Findings," 2004, Rockville, MD: Office of Applied Studies, NSDUH Series H–25, DHHS Publication No. SMA 04–3964, Figure 7.1, year 2003. Bridget F. Grant; Frederick S. Stinson; Deborah A. Dawson; S. Patricia Chou; Mary C. Dufour; Wilson Compton; Roger P. Pickering; Kenneth Kaplan, "Prevalence and Co-occurrence of Substance Use Disorders and Independent Mood and Anxiety Disorders: Results From the National Epidemiologic Survey on Alcohol and Related Conditions," *Arch Gen Psychiatry*, August, 2004; 61:807-816. Grant et al report combined drug and alcohol dependence at 4.07 percent of adults.

117.   Ronald C. Kessler, Emil F. Coccaro, Maurizio Fava, Savina Jaeger, Robert Jin, Ellen Walters, "The Prevalence and Correlates of *DSM-IV* Intermittent Explosive Disorder in the National Comorbidity Survey Replication," *Archives of General Psychiatry*, June, 2006; 63(6):669-678. IED is significantly comorbid with mood, anxiety and substance addictions.

118.   Hudson JI, Hiripi E, Pope HG, Kessler RC., "The Prevalence and Correlates of Eating Disorders in the National Comorbidity Survey Replication," *Biological Psychiatry*, 2007; 61:348-358. Lifetime prevalence for anorexia nervosa, bulimia nervosa, and binge eating disorder are .9%, 1.5%, and 3.5% among women, and .3% .5%, and 2.0% among men. I have estimated about 50 percent non-comorbitity between BN and BED.

119.   Hausenblas, H and Symons Downs, D, "How much is too much? The development and validation of the Exercise Dependence Scale," *Psychology and Health*, 2001; 17:387-404.

120.   Shaffer HJ, Hall MN, Vander Bilt J., "Estimating the prevalence of disordered gambling behavior in the United States and Canada: a research synthesis," *American Journal of Public Health*, September, 1999; 89(9):1369-76, Table 3. Past-year prevalence of level 3 gambling disorder among adults is 1.29 percent. This number is almost certainly low given that it is derived from studies taken in the 1994-1997 period before slot-machine casinos had spread throughout the U.S. Shaffer HJ, Hall MN., "Updating and refining prevalence estimates of disordered gambling behaviour in the United States and Canada," *Canadian Journal of Public Health*, 2001; 92(3):168-172.

121.   Aboujaoude E, Koran LM, Gamel N, Large MD, Serpe RT, "Potential markers for problematic internet use: a telephone survey of 2,513 adults," *CNS Spectrums*, October, 2006; 11(10):750-5. Accepted diagnostic criteria for "Internet addiction" do not exist. Random survey of 2,513 U.S. adults. The range is from tightest to most relaxed potential diagnostic criteria.

122.   Noble Ernest P., "D2 dopamine receptor gene in psychiatric and neurologic disorders and its phenotypes," *American Journal of Medical Genetics Part B*, January 1, 2003; 116B(1):103-25.

123.   Borg J, Andree B, Soderstrom H, Farde L., "The serotonin system and spiritual experiences," *American Journal of Psychiatry*, November, 2003; 160(11):1965-9.

124.   Todd M. Moore, Angela Scarpa and Adrian Raine, "A Meta-Analysis of Serotonin Metabolite 5-HIAA and Antisocial Behavior," *Aggressive Behavior*, 2002; 28:299-316. The

link between low brain serotonin and antisocial behavior is moderate, about one-half of a standard deviation.

125. Westergaard, G. C.; Mehlman, P. T.; Suomi, S. J.; Higley, J. D., "CSF, 5-HIAA and aggression in female macaque monkeys: species and interindividual differences," *Psychopharmacology*, 1999; 146(4):440-446.

126. Michael McGuire, Lynn Fairbanks, Michael Raleigh, "Life-history strategies, adaptive variation, and behavior-physiology interactions: the sociophysiology of vervet monkeys," *Sociophysiology*, P. Barchas, (Ed.), 1996, New York: Oxford Press.

127. Karen A. Matthews, Janine D. Flory, Matthew F. Muldoon and Stephen B. Manuck, "Does Socioeconomic Status Relate to Central Serotonergic Responsivity in Healthy Adults?" *Psychosomatic Medicine*, 2000; 62:231-237.

128. Wai S. Tse and Alyson J. Bond, "Serotonergic intervention affects both social dominance and affiliative behaviour," *Psychopharmacology*, April 4, 2002; 161:324-330.

129. Michael T. McGuire and Michael J. Raleigh, "Behavioral and Psychological Correlates of Ostracism," *Ethology and Sociobiology*, 1986; 7:187-200.

130. Michael T. Bailey, Harald Engler, Nicole D. Powell, David A. Padgett, and John F. Sheridan, "Repeated social defeat increases the bactericidal activity of splenic macrophages through a Toll-like receptor-dependent pathway," *American Journal of Physiology - Regulatory, Integrative and Comparative Physiology*, June 27, 2007; 293:R1180-R1190. Ronit Avitsura, Steven G. Kinsey, Kineret Bidora, Michael T. Bailey, David A. Padgett, John F. Sheridan, "Subordinate social status modulates the vulnerability to the immunological effects of social stress," *Psychoneuroendocrinology*, September-November, 2007; 32(8-10):1097-105. Personal communication with Dr. Steven G. Kinsey, Ph.D., Virginia Commonwealth University, October 28, 2007. Over-reactive immune system response does not occur in other types of rodent social defeat experiments.

131. de Jong JG, van der Vegt BJ, Buwalda B, Koolhaas JM., "Social environment determines the long-term effects of social defeat," *Physiology & Behavior*, January 31, 2005; 84(1):87-95.

132. Robert M. Sapolsky, "The Influence of Social Hierarchy on Primate Health," *Science*, April 29, 2005; 308(5722):648-52.

133. Robert M. Sapolsky and Lisa J. Share, "A Pacific Culture among Wild Baboons: Its Emergence and Transmission," *PLoS Biology*, April 13, 2004; 2(4):534-41.

134. Shostak, Elisabeth, "PW Talks with Robert Sapolsky," *Publishers Weekly*, February 19, 2001; 248(8):82-3.

135. Bjorkqvist K., "Social defeat as stressor in humans," *Physiology & Behavior*, June, 2001; 73:435-442, http://www.vasa.abo.fi/svf/up/articles/social_defeat.pdf. Selten JP, Cantor-Graae E., "Social defeat: risk factor for schizophrenia?" *The British Journal of Psychiatry*, August, 2005; 187:101-102, http://bjp.rcpsych.org/cgi/content/full/187/2/101.

136. Eberhard Fuchs and Gabriele Flügge, "Chronic social stress: effects on limbic brain structures," *Physiology & Behavior*, August, 2003; 79(3):417-427. Colla M, Kronenberg G, Deuschle M, Meichel K, Hagen T, Bohrer M, Heuser I., "Hippocampal volume reduction and HPA-system activity in major depression," *Journal of Psychiatric Research*, October, 2007; 41(7):553-60. MacQueen GM, Campbell S, McEwen BS, et al., "Course of illness, hippocampal function, and hippocampal volume in major depression," *Proceedings of the National Academy of Sciences U S A*, 2003; 100:1387-92. Bell-McGinty S, Butters MA, Meltzer CC, et al., "Brain morphometry in geriatric depression: long-term neurobiological effects of illness duration," *American Journal of Psychiatry*, 2002; 159:1424-7. Sheline YI, Gado MH, Kraemer HC., "Untreated depression and hippocampal volume loss," *American Journal of Psychiatry*, 2003; 160:1516-8. The majority of studies in this area report that longer depression duration is associated with reduced hippocampal volume. Contradictory findings are reported on hippocampal volume and depression severity.

137. Bruce McEwen & Elizabeth Norton Lasley, *The End of Stress as We Know It*, Washington, DC: Joseph Henry Press, 2002. Bruce McEwen & Elizabeth Norton Lasley, "Allostatic

Load: When Protection Gives Way to Damage," *Advances in Mind - Body Medicine*, Spring, 2003; 19(1):28-33.

138. Elissa S. Epel, Elizabeth H. Blackburn, Jue Lin, Firdaus S. Dhabhar, Nancy E. Adler, Jason D. Morrow, and Richard M. Cawthon, "Accelerated telomere shortening in response to life stress," *Proceedings of the National Academy of Sciences*, December 7, 2004; 101(49):17312–17315.

139. Vaishnav Krishnan, Ming-Hu Han, Danielle L. Graham, Olivier Berton, William Renthal, Scott J. Russo, Quincey LaPlant, Ami Graham, Michael Lutter, Diane C. Lagace, Subroto Ghose, Robin Reister, Paul Tannous, Thomas A. Green, Rachael L. Neve, Sumana Chakravarty, Arvind Kumar, Amelia J. Eisch, David W. Self, Francis S. Lee, Carol A. Tamminga, Donald C. Cooper, Howard K. Gershenfeld, and Eric J. Nestler, "Molecular Adaptations Underlying Susceptibility and Resistance to Social Defeat in Brain Reward Regions," *Cell*, October 19, 2007; 131:391–404.

140. Peter J. Gianaros, Jeffrey A. Horenstein, Sheldon Cohen, Karen A. Matthews, Sarah M. Brown, Janine D. Flory, Hugo D. Critchley, Stephen B. Manuck, and Ahmad R. Hariri, "Perigenual anterior cingulate morphology covaries with perceived social standing," *Social Cognitive and Affective Neuroscience*, May 4, 2007; 2(3):161-173. Of the 100 people checked, none ranked themselves at the very top or bottom in social standing. No size relationship was found in this experiment between any part of the amygdala or hippocampus. Self-rankings used the MacArthur Subjective Social Status Scale, http://www.macses.ucsf.edu/Research/Social%20Environment/notebook/measure.html.

141. Sullivan RJ, Hagen EH, Hammerstein P., "Revealing the paradox of drug reward in human evolution," *Proceedings of the Royal Society B*, March 19, 2008, published online. Sullivan RJ and Hagen EH, "Psychotropic substance-seeking: evolutionary pathology or adaptation?" *Addiction*, 2002; 97:389-400.

142. Saal, Daniel; Dong, Yan; Bonci, Antonello; Malenka, Robert C., "Drugs of Abuse and Stress Trigger a Common Synaptic Adaptation in Dopamine Neurons," *Neuron*, February, 2003; 37(4):577-582. Marina E. Wolf, "LTP May Trigger Addiction," *Mol Interv.*, August, 2003; 3(5):248-52. Inge E M de Jong and E Ronald de Kloet, "Glucocorticoids and vulnerability to psychostimulant drugs: toward substrate and mechanism," *Annals of the New York Academy of Sciences*, June, 2004; 1018:192-8.

143. Nick E. Goeders, "The impact of stress on addiction," *European Neuropsychopharmacology*, December 2003; 13(6):435-441.

144. Morgan D, Grant KA, Gage HD, Mach RH, Kaplan JR, Prioleau O, Nader SH, Buchheimer N, Ehrenkaufer RL, Nader MA., "Social dominance in monkeys: dopamine D2 receptors and cocaine self-administration," *Nature Neuroscience*, February, 2002; 5(2):169-174.

145. Shively CA, Grant KA, Ehrenkaufer RL, Mach RH, Nader MA., "Social stress, depression, and brain dopamine in female cynomolgus monkeys," *Ann NY Acad Sci*, 1997; 15:574–577.

146. Covington HE, Kikusui T, Goodhue J, Nikulina EM, Hammer RP, Miczek KA., "Brief Social Defeat Stress: Long Lasting Effects on Cocaine Taking During a Binge and Zif268 mRNA Expression in the Amygdala and Prefrontal Cortex," *Neuropsychopharmacology*, February, 2005; 30(2):310-21.

147. Kram, Martin L.; Kramer, Gerald L.; Ronan, Patrick J.; Steciuk, Mark; Petty, Frederick, "Dopamine receptors and learned helplessness in the rat: An autoradiographic study," *Progress in Neuro-Psychopharmacology & Biological Psychiatry*, May, 2002; 26(4):639-645.

148. O. Berton, C. A. McClung, R. J. DiLeone, V. Krishnan, W. Renthal, S. J. Russo, D. Graham, N. M. Tsankova, C. A. Bolanos, M. Rios, L. M. Monteggia, D. W. Self, E. J. Nestler, "Essential role of BDNF in the mesolimbic dopamine pathway in social defeat stress," *Science*, February 10, 2006; 311:864-68.

149. Madrid GA, MacMurray J, Lee JW, Anderson BA, Comings DE., "Stress as a mediating factor in the association between the DRD2 TaqI polymorphism and alcoholism," *Alcohol*, February, 2001; 23(2):117-22.

150. Erblich J, Lerman C, Self DW, Diaz GA, Bovbjerg DH., "Stress-induced cigarette craving: effects of the DRD2 TaqI RFLP and SLC6A3 VNTR polymorphisms," *Pharmacogenomics Journal*, 2004; 4(2):102-9.

151. Saal, Daniel; Dong, Yan; Bonci, Antonello; Malenka, Robert C., "Drugs of Abuse and Stress Trigger a Common Synaptic Adaptation in Dopamine Neurons," *Neuron*, February, 2003; 37(4):577-582.

152. Pruessner JC, Champagne F, Meaney MJ, Dagher A., "Dopamine release in response to a psychological stress in humans and its relationship to early life maternal care: a positron emission tomography study using [11C]raclopride," *Journal of Neuroscience*, March 17, 2004; 24(11):2825-31.

153. Abbott, D.H.; Keverne, E.B.; Bercovitch, F.B.; Shively, C.A.; Mendoza, S.P.; Saltzman, W.; Snowdon, C.T.; Ziegler, T.E.; Banjevic, M.; Garland Jr., T.; Sapolsky, R.M., "Are subordinates always stressed? a comparative analysis of rank differences in cortisol levels among primates," *Hormones & Behavior*, January, 2003; 43(1):67-82. Robert M. Sapolsky, "The Influence of Social Hierarchy on Primate Health," *Science*, April 29, 2005; 308(5722):648-652. In this review article, Sapolsky shows how rank produces varied stress effects in different species and populations and that there are no simple, one-size-fits-all models. For example, low status often does not induce high social stress.

154. Robert M. Sapolsky, *Why Zebras Don't Get Ulcers: A Guide To Stress, Stress-related Disease and Coping*, Second Edition, New York: WH Freeman, 1998.

155. John P. Capitanio, Kristina Abel, Sally P. Mendoza, Shelley A. Blozis, Michael B. McChesney, Steve W. Cole, and William A. Mason, "Personality and serotonin transporter genotype interact with social context to affect immunity and viral set-point in simian immunodeficiency virus disease," *Brain Behavior and Immunity*, August 22, 2007, in press.

156. Kaplan JR, Manuck SB, "Status, stress, and atherosclerosis: the role of environment and individual behavior," *Ann N Y Acad Sci.*, 1999; 896:145-61.

157. Marina L. Butovskaya, Elizaveta Y. Boyko, Nelly B. Selverova and Irina V. Ermakova "The Hormonal Basis of Reconciliation in Humans," *Journal of Physiological Anthropology and Applied Human Science*, July, 2005; 24:333-337.

158. Michael Marmot, *The Status Syndrome: How Social Standing Affects Health and Longevity*, New York: Henry Holt, 2004. For thirty years, Marmot has directed the Whitehall study of British social servants, finding that those with high-status job rankings were healthier and lived longer. Hewstone, Miles, Rubin, Mark and Willis, Hazel, "Intergroup Bias," *Annual Review of Psychology*, 2002; 53(1):575-604. Robert M. Sapolsky, Why Zebras Don't Get Ulcers: A Guide To Stress, Stress-related Disease and Coping, WH Freeman, New York, NY., Second edition, 1998.

159. Kouvonen A, Kivimaki M, Virtanen M, Heponiemi T, Elovainio M, Pentti J, Linna A, Vahtera J., "Effort-reward imbalance at work and the co-occurrence of lifestyle risk factors: cross-sectional survey in a sample of 36,127 public sector employees," *BMC Public Health*, February 7, 2006; 6:24.

160. Roberto De Vogli, Jane E Ferrie, Tarani Chandola, Mika Kivimäki and Michael G Marmot, "Unfairness and health: evidence from the Whitehall II Study," *Journal of Epidemiology and Community Health*, May 13, 2007; 61:513-18.

161. Paul Henry, "An Examination of the Pathways Through Which Social Class Impacts Health Outcomes." *Academy of Marketing Science Review* [Online] 2001; (3), http://www.amsreview.org/articles/henry03-2001.pdf.

162. Aureli F., de Waal F.B.M (eds.), *Natural Conflict Resolution*, Berkeley: University of California Press, 2000. Lee Duatkin, "Kiss and make up," *NewScientist*, May 7, 2005, pages 35-37.

163. David Plotz, "The Nobel Sperm Bank Celebrity," *Slate*, March 16, 2001, http://slate.msn.com/id/102689.

164. Charles Murray, *Human Accomplishment: The Pursuit of Excellence in the Arts and Sciences, 800 B.C. to 1950*, New York: HarperCollins, 2003, pages 163-204, 263, 301. Murray selected these most significant accomplishments on the basis of their frequency of appearance in 175 authoritative histories of the various fields. I define "unbroken strings of progress" in

a field to be a continuous string of significant accomplishments separated by no more than 50 years.

165. Robert Appleton Company, *The Catholic Encyclopedia*, Volume X, 1911, Online Edition by Kevin Knight, 2003, http://www.newadvent.org/cathen/10352a.htm.

166. Giovanni Pico della Mirandola, *Oration on the Dignity of Man*, 1487, Paragraph 6, translated from the Latin by Richard Hooker, 1994, http://www.fordham.edu/halsall/med/oration.html.

167. Richard M. Huber, *The American Idea of Success*, Wainscott, New York: The Pushcart Press, 1987, pages 12, 25. Mather and McGuffey quotations.

168. John Wesley, "The Use of Money," Sermon 50, 1872, http://gbgm-umc.org/umw/wesley/serm-050.stm#III, verbs made present tense.

169. Walter Isaacson, *Benjamin Franklin: An American Life*, Simon & Schuster, 2003. Richard M. Huber, *The American Idea of Success*, Wainscott, New York: The Pushcart Press, 1987, page 15.

170. Nick Bostrom, "Human Genetic Enhancements: A Transhumanist Perspective," http://www.nickbostrom.com/ethics/genetic.pdf.

171. Gregory Stock, *Redesigning Humans: Our Inevitable Genetic Future*, Boston: Houghton Mifflin, 2002.

172. World Transhumanist Association, annual convention debate, June 2003.

173. Flinn, M. V., Geary, D. C., & Ward, C. V., "Ecological dominance, social competition, and coalitionary arms races: Why humans evolved extraordinary intelligence," *Evolution and Human Behavior*, January, 2005; 26(1):10-46.

174. White, T.D., B. Asfaw, D. DeGusta, H. Tilbert, G.D. Richards, G. Suwa, and F.C. Howell, "Pleistocene Homo sapiens from Middle Awash, Ethiopia," *Nature*, 2003; 423:742-747. Robert Sanders, "160,000-year-old fossilized skulls uncovered in Ethiopia are oldest anatomically modern humans," *UC Berkeley News*, June 11, 2003, http://www.berkeley.edu/news/media/releases/2003/06/11_idaltu.shtml.

175. McDougall I., Brown F. H. & Fleagle J. G., "Stratigraphic placement and age of modern humans from Kibish, Ethiopia," *Nature*, February 17, 2005; 433(7027):733-736. Of the two skulls found here, only Omo I is anatomically modern. No evidence is reported for cultural or behavioral practices as advanced as that from the 160,000-year-old find, although such evidence would not be surprising to me.

176. Wellcome Trust, "The FOXP2 Story," April 28, 2003, http://www.wellcome.ac.uk/en/genome/genesandbody/hg05f004.html.

177. Enard W, Przeworski M, Fisher SE, Lai CS, Wiebe V, et al., "Molecular evolution of FOXP2, a gene involved in speech and language," *Nature*, August 14, 2002, 418:869–872. The human FOXP2 gene is almost certainly not alone in being necessary for speech, but may have improved human ability to vocalize existing language.

178. Henshilwood, Christopher S.; Marean, Curtis W, "The Origin of Modern Human Behavior," *Current Anthropology*, December, 2003; 44(5):627-651.

179. Henshilwood, Christopher; D'Errico, Francesco; Vanhaeren, Marian; Van Niekerk, Karen; Jacobs, Zenobia, "Middle Stone Age Shell Beads from South Africa," *Science*, April 16, 2004; 304(5669):404. Henshitwood, Christopher S.; d'Errico, Francesco; Yates, Royden; Jacobs, Zenobia; Tribolo, Chantal; Duller, Geoff A. T.; Mercier, Norbert; Sealy, Judith C.; Valladas, Helene; Watts, Ian; Wintle, Ann G., "Emergence of Modern Human Behavior: Middle Stone Age Engravings from South Africa," *Science*, February 15, 2002; 295(5558):1278-80.

180. Marean, C., Bar-Matthews, M., Bernatchex, J., Fisher, E., Goldberg, P., Herries, A., Jacobs, Z., Jerardino, A., Karkanas, P., Nilssen, P., Thompson, E., Watts, I., Williams, H., "Early human use of marine resources and pigment in South Africa during the Middle Pleistocene," *Nature*, October 18, 2007; 449(7164):905-8.

181. Jared Diamond, "Evolution, consequences and future of plant and animal domestication," *Nature*, 2002; 418:700-706.

182. Burger J, Kirchner M, Bramanti B, Haak W, Thomas MG., "Absence of the lactase-persistence-associated allele in early Neolithic Europeans," *Proceedings of the National Academy of Sciences USA*, March 6, 2007; 104(10):3736-41.

183. "European Skin Turned Pale Only Recently, Gene Suggests," *Science*, April 20, 2007; 316:364.

184. Hawks, J., Wang, J.T., Cochran, G., Harpending, H.C. and Moyzis, R.K. "Recent acceleration of human adaptive evolution," *Proceedings of the National Academy of Sciences, USA*, December 26, 2007; 104(52):20753-8. To ensure that the variations are both beneficial and recent, only those present in 22 to 78 percent of the population were included in the analysis. Most of these new variations are not shared between the world's major races, strong evidence for the recency of their emergence.

185. Wang ET, Kodama G, Baldi P, Moyzis RK., "Global landscape of recent inferred Darwinian selection for *Homo sapiens*," *Proc Nat Acad Sci USA*, January, 2006; 103:135-140.

186. Voight BF, Kudaravalli S, Wen X, Pritchard JK, "A Map of Recent Positive Selection in the Human Genome," *PLoS Biology*, March, 2006, 4(3): e72, http://biology.plosjournals. org/archive/1545-7885/4/3/pdf/10.1371_journal.pbio.0040072-S.pdf.

187. Lyudmila N. Trut, "Early Canid Domestication: The Farm-Fox Experiment," *American Scientist*, March-April, 1999; 87:160-169. More exactingly stated, existing genes for a fox tameness phenotype became prevalent as successive generations were selected for success in the domesticated environment.

188. Elaine Ostrander, Leonid Kruglyak, et al, "Genome Resources to Boost Canines' Role in Gene Hunts," *Science*, May 21, 2004; 304:1093-1095.

189. Not quite distinct species, yet, because most breeds can be forced to mate and interbreed.

190. Walter E. Nance, Michael J. Kearsey, "Relevance of Connexin Deafness (DFNB1) to Human Evolution," *American Journal of Human Genetics*, June, 2004; 74(6):1081-1087.

191. "Did sign language increase deaf population?" *Reuters*, Wednesday, April 28, 2004.

192. James R. Flynn, *What Is Intelligence? Beyond the Flynn Effect*, 2007, New York: Cambridge University Press. Raven's shows three or more geometric patterns, asking you to pick among three or more for the pattern that comes logically next. Similarities includes questions like asking for the common feature of a slice of bread and a plate (both can be used as a means to eat cheese). Flynn thinks that developing nations' IQ scores will catch up with the west as their teaching and living environments become similar to those of industrial nations.

193. Rock, W. P.; Sabieha, A. M.; Evans, R. I. W., "A cephalometric comparison of skulls from the fourteenth, sixteenth and twentieth centuries," *British Dental Journal*, January 14, 2006; 200(1)33-37.

194. David Plotz, "The "Genius Babies" Grow Up: What happened to 15 children from the Nobel Prize sperm bank?" *Slate*, May 30, 2001, http://slate.msn.com/id/106575/.

195. Michael Le Page, "Barriers to embryo testing go down," *NewScientist*, June 4, 2005, page 17. Note the distinction between birth counts using IVF+PGD versus much larger numbers for IVF only. In the U.S. alone, 120,000 IVF procedures were provided in 2003.

196. USDHHS, "Newborn Screening: Toward a Uniform Screening Panel and System," http://mchb.hrsa.gov/screening/summary.htm. At this link, you can see a proposed uniform screening panel, ranking of the approximately top 100 genetic defects by severity, detectability, treatability, etc. Armand Marie Leroi, *Mutants: On Genetic Variety and the Human Body*, New York: Viking Books, 2003.

197. Baruch S, Kaufman D, Hudson KL, "Genetic testing of embryos: practices and perspectives of U.S. IVF clinics," *Fertility and Sterility*, September 20, 2006.

198. Lindsey Tanner, "Some ponder 'designer' babies with Mom or Dad's defective genes," *Associated Press*, December 21, 2006.

199. Liza Mundy, "A World of Their Own: In the eyes of his parents, if Gauvin Hughes McCullough turns out to be deaf, that will be just perfect," *Washington Post*, March 31, 2002, page W22. Darshak Sanghavi, "Wanting Babies Like Themselves," *The New York Times*, December 5, 2006. Baruch S, Kaufman D, Hudson KL, "Genetic testing of embryos: practices and perspectives of U.S. IVF clinics," *Fertility and Sterility*, September 20, 2006.

200. Ben Harder, "Born to Heal: Screening embryos to treat siblings raises hopes, dilemmas," *Science News*, March 13, 2004, page 168.
201. Michael Reilly, "IVF increases the risk of birth defects," *NewScientist*, February 14, 2007. A study of 1,394 IVF babies delivered in Ontario, Canada, found 2.62 percent born with genetic abnormalities versus 1.87 percent of naturally conceived babies. Mastenbroek S, Twisk M, van Echten-Arends J, Sikkema-Raddatz B, Korevaar JC, Verhoeve HR, Vogel NE, Arts EG, de Vries JW, Bossuyt PM, Buys CH, Heineman MJ, Repping S, van der Veen F., "In vitro fertilization with preimplantation genetic screening," *New England Journal of Medicine*, July 5, 2007; 357(1):9-17. In a randomized, double-blind study, one-third fewer women using PGD/IVF had live births compared with IVF-only women.
202. H-Invitational Database, Annotated Human Gene Database, September 27, 2007, http://www.jbirc.aist.go.jp/hinv/ahg-db/index.jsp.
203. The International HapMap Project, October 17, 2007, http://www.hapmap.org/.
204. The Human Variome Project, http://www.variome.org/?p=Home.
205. www.23andMe.com.
206. Sangamo BioSciences, Inc., http://www.sangamo.com/index.php. As I wrote this, I held securities in this company.
207. Rick Callahan, "Scientists Create Sperm From Stem Cells," AP, December 10, 2003. Hübner, K., et al., "Derivation of oocytes from mouse embryonic stem cells," *Science*, 2003; 300(5620):1251-1256. Lab-grown embryonic stem cells have been shown to spontaneously differentiate into many types of cells, including germ cells from which eggs and sperm ultimately develop.
208. "Researchers Grow Sperm Stem Cells In Laboratory Cultures Advance Could Lead To New Infertility Treatments, Source of Adult Stem Cells," *NIH News*, November 30, 2004.
209. Ilham Saleh Abuljadayel, "Induction of stem cell-like plasticity in mononuclear cells derived from unmobilised adult human peripheral blood," *Current Medical Research & Opinion*, August 1, 2003; 19(5):355-375.
210. Dyce PW and Julang Li, "From skin cells to ovarian follicles?" *Cell Cycle*, July, 2006; 5(13):1371-5.
211. Nayernia K, Nolte J, Michelmann HW, Lee JH, Rathsack K, Drusenheimer N, Dev A, Wulf G, Ehrmann IE, Elliott DJ, Okpanyi V, Zechner U, Haaf T, Meinhardt A, Engel W., "In vitro-differentiated embryonic stem cells give rise to male gametes that can generate offspring mice," *Developmental Cell*, July, 2006; 11(1):125-32.
212. Kazutoshi Takahashi, Koji Tanabe, Mari Ohnuki, Megumi Narita, Tomoko Ichisaka, Kiichiro Tomoda, and Shinya Yamanaka, "Induction of Pluripotent Stem Cells from Adult Human Fibroblasts by Defined Factors," *Cell*, November 16, 2007; 131(4):1-12. Okita K, Ichisaka T, Yamanaka S., "Generation of germline-competent induced pluripotent stem cells," *Nature*, July 19, 2007; 448(7151):313-7. Steve Johnson, "Bay Area professor aids in stem cell breakthrough," *San Jose Mercury News*, November 20, 2007.
213. However, animal clones grown from embryos derived from adult or somatic cells are often diseased or abnormal. The accumulated epigenetic profiles of the genetic material in the adult cells may be an explanation for these problems and will be barrier to making babies from snips of mom and dad's skin tissue.
214. The site is funded by the National Institutes of Health, http://www.geneclinics.org.
215. Integrated DNA Technologies, www.idtdna.com.
216. DNA 2.0, Inc, http://www.dnatwopointo.com/commerce/misc/syn.jsp.
217. Sylvia Pagán Westphal, "Just add a chromosome . . . ," *NewScientist*, June 19, 2004, page 10.
218. Bunnell BA, Izadpanah R, Ledebur Jr HC, Perez CF., "Development of mammalian artificial chromosomes for the treatment of genetic diseases: Sandhoff and Krabbe diseases," *Expert Opinion on Biological Therapy*, February, 2005; 5(2):195-206.
219. Ya-Ping Tang, Eiji Shimizu, Gilles R. Dube, Claire Rampon, Geoffrey A. Kerchner, Min Zhuo, Guosong Liu and Joe Z. Tsien, "Genetic enhancement of learning and memory in mice," *Nature*, September 2, 1999; 401(2):63-69.

220. Tim Tully, Rusiko Bourtchouladze, Rod Scott and John Tallma, "Targeting the CREB Pathway for Memory Enhancers," *Nature Reviews, Drug Discovery*, April, 2003; 2(4):. In clinical trials as of mid 2004.
221. Fernandez F, Morishita W, Zuniga E, Nguyen J, Blank M, Malenka RC, Garner CC., "Pharmacotherapy for cognitive impairment in a mouse model of Down syndrome," *Nature Neuroscience*, April, 2007; 10(4):411-3.
222. *The Economist*, "Supercharging the brain," September 16, 2004.
223. Anjan Chatterjee, "Cosmetic neurology: The controversy over enhancing movement, mentation, and mood," *Neurology*, September, 2004; 63:968-974.
224. Marilyn Chase, "Scientists Extend Worms' Life Span by Altering Genes," *The Wall Street Journal*, October 24, 2003, page B2, reporting on research published in Cynthia Kenyon, et al, *Science*, October 24, 2003.
225. M. Beckman, "Dieting Dwarves Live It Up," *Science, SAGE KE*, 2001.
226. Aubrey D.N.J. de Grey, "The foreseeability of real anti-aging medicine: focusing the debate," *Experimental Gerontology*, September, 2003; 38(9):927-34.
227. Kurosu H, Yamamoto M, Clark JD, Pastor JV, Nandi A, Gurnani P, McGuinness OP, Chikuda H, Yamaguchi M, Kawaguchi H, Shimomura I, Takayama Y, Herz J, Kahn CR, Rosenblatt KP, Kuro-o M., "Suppression of aging in mice by the hormone Klotho," *Science*, September 16, 2005; 309(5742):1829-33.
228. B. Conti et al., "Transgenic Mice with a Reduced Core Body Temperature Have an Increased Life Span," *Science*, November 3, 2006; 314: 825-8.
229. Khan SM, Smigrodzki RM, Swerdlow RH., "Cell and animal models of mtDNA biology: progress and prospects," *Am J Physiol Cell Physiol*, February, 2007; 292(2):C658-69.
230. Defense Advanced Research Projects Agency, Defense Sciences Office, http://webext2.darpa.mil/dso/index.htm.
231. John P Donahue, "Connecting cortex to machine: recent advances in brain interfaces," *Nature Neuroscience*, November, 2002; 5:1085-1088. Eric Eisenstadt, DARPATech 2002 Symposium, http://www.darpa.mil/DARPATech2002/presentations/dso_pdf/speeches/EISENSTADT.pdf; and Neural Signals, http://www.neuralsignals.com, accessed July 15, 2003.
232. Jim Giles, "From thoughts into words . . . ," *NewScientist*, November 17, 2007, page 10.
233. Will Knight, "Remote-controlled rats to sniff out explosives," *NewScientist*, April 25, 2005.
234. Susan Brown, "Stealth sharks to patrol the high seas," *NewScientist*, March 4, 2006, page 31.
235. Jessica Marshall, "The fly who bugged me," *NewScientist*, March 8, 2008, pages 41-3.
236. Jocelyn Selim and Pete Drinkell, "The Bionic Connection," *Discover*, November, 2002; 23(11):49-52.
237. Richard Lynn, *Eugenics: A Reassessment*, Westport: Praeger Publishers, 2001. As I do, Lynn argues that economic pressures are certain to make embryo selection pervasive, with only 10-20 percent of parents ultimately using sexual intercourse to procreate. This book is a ruthless, frightening, but logically sound defense of the inevitability of the new, high-tech eugenics.
238. Francis Fukuyama, *Our Posthuman Future: Consequences of the Biotechnology Revolution*, Farrar, Straus and Giroux, 2002, page 218.
239. George Annas, "Genism, Racism, and the Prospect of Genetic Genocide," presented at the World Conference Against Racism, September 3, 2001.
240. Foster Kennedy, "The Problem of Social Control of the Congenital Defective: Education, Sterilization, Euthanasia," *American Journal of Psychiatry*, July, 1942; 99:13-16.
241. Braudel, F., *The Structures of Everyday Life: The Limits of the Possible*, New York: Harper & Row, 1979, page 79, as cited in Murray, 2003.
242. Richard Lynn and Tatu Vanhanen, IQ and the Wealth of Nations, 2002, Westport: Praeger.
243. "IQ Mismatch," *Science*, January 5, 2007, 315(5808):21.

244. Fast Company-Roper Starch, survey of college-educated Americans, 1999, www.fastcompany.com/online/27/survey.html.

245. Darryl R. J. Macer, Azariah, J. & Srinives, P., "Attitudes to Biotechnology in Asia," *International Journal of Biotechnology*, 2000; 2:313-332. Lynn, 2001, page 294 cites a 1994-1996 survey of physicians and geneticists in 36 nations, finding that fewer than one-third in the United States and other Western democracies supported genetic counseling to reduce harmful gene prevalence in the population. Such a strategy was supported by 100% in China and 87% in India.

246. Bill McKibben, *Enough: Staying Human in an Engineered Age*, Times Books, 2003; and, Leon Kass, *Life, Liberty and the Defense of Dignity: The Challenge for Bioethics*, San Francisco: Encounter Books, 2002.

247. Quoting fictional character Rabo Karabekian in Kurt Vonnegut, *Bluebeard*, 1987, Delacorte, as quoted in Robert H Frank and Philip J Cook, *The Winner-Take-All Society*, 1995, 1996, Penguin Books, p1.

248. Geoffrey Moore, Mohr Davidow Ventures partner, sharing tips at a Garage.com bootcamp.

249. Dinesh D'Souza, *The Virtue of Prosperity: Finding Values in an Age of Techno-Affluence*, New York: Simon & Schuster, 2000, pages 86-87.

250. Thomas Bouchard, Jr., "Genetic Influence on Human Psychological Traits," *Current Directions in Psychological Science*, August, 2004; 13(4):148-151.

251. Steven Pinker, "Human Nature and Its Future," Testimony Before The President's Council on Bioethics, March 6, 2003.

252. Thompson, Paul M.; Cannon, Tyrone D.; Narr, Katherine L.; van Erp, Theo; Poutanen, Veli-Pekka; Huttunen, Matti; Lönnqvist, Jouko; Standertskjöld-Nordenstam, Carl-Gustaf; Kaprio, Jaakko; Khaledy, Mohammad; Dail, Rajneesh; Zoumalan, Chris I.; Toga, Arthur W., Genetic influences on brain structure, *Nature Neuroscience*, December, 2001; 4(12):1253-1258. Genetically identical twins have almost 100 percent identical gray matter distribution in frontal, sensorimotor and perisylvian language cortices. The study authors note their small sample size of 40 individuals.

253. Thomas Bouchard, Jr., "Genetic Influence on Human Psychological Traits," Current Directions in *Psychological Science*, August, 2004; 13(4):148-151. Turkheimer, Eric; Haley, Andreana; Waldron, Mary; D'Onofrio, Brian; Gottesman, Irving I., "Socioeconomic status modifies heritability of iq in young children," *Psychological Science*, November, 2003; 14(6):623-628. Bouchard's cited low 80 percent IQ heritability contrasts the more widely published 50 percent plus range because study data is often skewed by use of school-aged study populations where shared environmental effects are greater. See: Thomas J. Bouchard, Jr., Matt McGue, "Genetic and Environmental Influences on Human Psychological Differences," *J Neurobology*, 2003; 54:4-45. Flynn, 2007, thinks that part of the high adult IQ heritability is due to those whose genes give them IQs having greater access to enriched environments which amplify measured IQ differences, meaning that the environmental effect on intelligence is larger than reported in twin studies.

254. Harden KP, Turkheimer E, Loehlin JC., "Genotype by environment interaction in adolescents' cognitive aptitude," *Behavior Genetics*, March, 2007; 37(2):273-83. Twin studies typically under sample low-income children. Correcting for this, the authors of this study found that IQ is very strongly genetic for children raised by better off parents, and up to 80-90 percent environmental for children raised by poor families. Intelligence heritability is therefore very high when environmental contribution is optimal, the circumstances in OverSuccessed families most relevant to my argument.

255. Thomas J. Bouchard Jr. and John C. Loehlin, "Genes, Evolution, and Personality," *Journal of Behavior Genetics*, May, 2001; 31(3):243-273, Table III. Data cited is for U.S. populations.

256. Rahman, Q. and Wilson, G.D., "Born gay? The psychobiology of human sexual orientation," *Personality and Individual Differences*, June, 2003; 34(8):1337-1382. Kirk, K.M.; Bailey, J.M.; Martin, N.G., "Etiology of male sexual orientation in an Australian twin sample," *Psychology, Evolution & Gender*, December, 2000; 2(3):301-311.

257. Bouchard TJ Jr, McGue M, Lykken D, Tellegen A., "Intrinsic and extrinsic religiousness: genetic and environmental influences and personality correlates," *Twin Research*, 1999; 2(2):88-98.

258. 258 Thomas Bouchard, Jr., "Genetic Influence on Human Psychological Traits," *Current Directions in Psychological Science*, August, 2004; 13(4):148-151.

259. Lykken DT, Couchard TJ Jr., McGue M, Tellegen A., "Heritability of interests: a twin study," *Journal of Applied Psychology*, 1993; 78(4):649-61. Thomas Bouchard, Jr., "Genetic Influence on Human Psychological Traits," *Current Directions in Psychological Science*, August, 2004; 13(4)148-151.

260. Lykken, David and Tellegen, Auke, "Happiness Is a Stochastic Phenomenon," *Psychological Science*, May, 1996; 7(3):186-189.

261. Thomas Bouchard, Jr., "Genetic Influence on Human Psychological Traits," *Current Directions in Psychological Science*, August, 2004; 13(4):148-151.

262. Yoon Mi-Hur and Thomas Bouchard, Jr., "The Genetic Correlation Between Impulsivity and Sensation Seeking Traits," *Behavior Genetics*, September, 1997; 27(5):455-463.

263. Kendler KS, Gardner CO, Prescott CA., "A population-based twin study of self-esteem and gender," *Psychol Med*, November, 1998; 28(6):1403-9.

264. Nestler, E.J. et al., "Neurobiology of depression," *Neuron*, 2002; 34:13-25. Agrawal A, Jacobson KC, Gardner CO, Prescott CA, Kendler KS., "A population based twin study of sex differences in depressive symptoms," *Twin Research*, April, 2004; 7(2):176-81. Epidemiology Data Center, "Genetics of Recurrent Early Onset Depression," March 6, 2003.

265. Gregory Stock, *Redesigning Humans: Our Inevitable Genetic Future*, 2002, Boston: Houghton Mifflin Company, page 230, Note 103.

266. Stock, page 230, Note 103.

267. Stock, page 230, Note 103.

268. Thomas Bouchard, Jr., "Genetic Influence on Human Psychological Traits," *Current Directions in Psychological Science*, August, 2004; 13(4):148-151. Essi Viding, "Genetics, Early Life Experiences, and Violence: Preventive Strategies," New York Academy of Sciences Symposium, April 24-26, 2004, http://www.nyas.org/ebriefreps/main.asp?intSubsectionID=699#07.

269. Rushton, J. P., "Genetic and environmental contributions to prosocial attitudes: A twin study of social responsibility," *Proceedings of the Royal Society of London. Series B. Biological Sciences*, November 30, 2004; 271:2583-2585.

270. Kendler KS., "Social support: a genetic-epidemiologic analysis," *Am Journal of Psychiatry*, October, 1997; 154(10):1398-404.

271. Jockin V, McGue M, Lykken DT., "Personality and divorce: a genetic analysis," *Journal of Personal and Social Psychology*, 1996; 71(2):288-99.

272. Rapin I, Katzman R., "Neurobiology of autism," *Ann Neurol*, 1998; 43:7-14.

273. Castellanos, F.X. and R. Tannock, "Neuroscience of Attention Deficit/Hyperactivity Disorder: The Search for Endophenotypes," *Nature Reviews Neuroscience*, 2002; 3:617-628. Sherman, D.K., W.G. Iacono & M.K. McGue, "Attention-deficit hyperactivity disorder dimensions: a twin study of inattention and impulsivity-hyperactivity," *J. Am. Acad. Child. Adolesc. Psychiatry*, 1997; 36:745-753.

274. Plomin R & Craig I., "Human behavioural genetics of cognitive abilities and disabilities," *BioEssays*, 1997; 19:1117-24.

275. Thomas Bouchard, Jr., "Genetic Influence on Human Psychological Traits," *Current Directions in Psychological Science*, August, 2004; 13(4):148-151.

276. Martin E.P. Seligman, Elaine F. Walker and David L. Rosenhan, *Abnormal Psychology*, Fourth Edition, New York: W.W. Norton, 2001, page 265.

277. Jonnal AH, Gardner CO, Prescott CA, Kendler KS., "Obsessive and compulsive symptoms in a general population sample of female twins," *Am J Med Genet.*, December 4, 2000; 96(6):791-6.

278. Eric J. Nestler, "Psychogenomics: Opportunities for Understanding Addiction," *The Journal of Neuroscience*, November 1, 2001; 21(21):8324-7.

279. Kendler KS, Karkowski LM, Neale MC, Prescott CA., "Illicit psychoactive substance use, heavy use, abuse, and dependence in a US population-based sample of male twins," *Arch Gen Psychiatry*, March, 2000; 57(3):261-9.

280. Eisen SA, Lin N, Lyons MJ, Scherrer JF, Griffith K, True WR, Goldberg J, Tsuang MT., "Familial influences on gambling behavior: an analysis of 3359 twin pairs," *Addiction*, September, 1998; 93(9):1375-84. Raylu N, et al. "Pathological Gambling: A Comprehensive Review," *Clinical Psychology Review*, September, 2002; 22(7):1009–61.

281. Prescott CA, Kindler KS., "Genetic and environmental contributions to alcohol abuse and dependence in a population-based sample of male twins," *Am J Psychiatry*, January, 1999; 156(1):34-40.

282. Kendler KS, Thornton LM, Pedersen NL., "Tobacco consumption in Swedish twins reared apart and reared together," *Arch Gen Psychiatry*, September, 2000; 57(9):886-92.

283. Kendler KS, Prescott CA., "Caffeine intake, tolerance, and withdrawal in women: a population-based twin study," *Am J Psychiatry*, February, 1999; 156(2):223-8.

284. 284 Christopher M. Filley, James P. Kelly, and Bruce H. Price, "Toward an understanding of violence: neurobehavioral aspects of unwarranted interpersonal aggression," *Neuropsychiatry, Neuropsychology, and Behavioral Neurology*, February 2001; 14:1-14.

285. The Editors, "Genetic Study of Anorexia Nervosa Fueled by NIMH Grant," *Eating Disorders Review*, November-December, 2002; 13(6):1-3. Bulik CM, Sullivan PF, Kendler KS., "Heritability of binge-eating and broadly defined bulimia nervosa," *Biological Psychiatry*, December, 1998; 44(12):1210-8.

286. Reichborn-Kjennerud T, Bulik CM, Kendler KS, Roysamb E, Maes H, Tambs K, Harris JR., "Gender differences in binge-eating: a population-based twin study," *Acta Psychiatr Scand.*, September, 2003; 108(3):196-202.

287. Bulik CM, Sullivan PF, Kendler KS., "Genetic and environmental contributions to obesity and binge eating," *International Journal of Eating Disorders*, April, 2003; 33(3):293-8.

288. Kelly D. Brownell and Katherine Battle Norgen, *Food Fight: The Inside Story of the Food Industry, America's Obesity Crisis, and What We Can Do About It*, 2004, Chicago: Contemporary Books, page 23.

289. Robert Plomin, John DeFries, Gerald McClearn, and Michael McGuffin, *Behavioral Genetics*, New York: W.H. Freeman, 2000.

290. Stock, page 103.

291. Christopher J. Hammond, Toby Andrew, Ying Tat Mak, and Tim D. Spector, "A Susceptibility Locus for Myopia in the Normal Population Is Linked to the PAX6 Gene Region on Chromosome 11: A Genomewide Scan of Dizygotic Twins," *The American Journal of Human Genetics*, August, 2004; 75(2):294-304.

292. Stock, page 224, Note 57.

293. Albert H.C. Wong, Irving I. Gottesman and Arturas Petronis, "Phenotypic differences in genetically identical organisms: the epigenetic perspective," *Human Molecular Genetics*, 2005; 14(1):R11-R18.

294. Roth, D.L., & Ingram, R.E., "Factors in the Self-Deception Questionnaire: Associations with depression," *Journal of Personality and Social Psychology*, 1985; 48:243-251.

295. Nettle, D., "Adaptive illusions: Optimism, control and human rationality," In D. Evans & P. Cruse (Eds.), *Emotion, evolution and rationality*, Oxford: Oxford University Press, 2004, pages 193-208.

296. Steven J. Heine, "In Search of East Asian Self-Enhancement," *Personality and Social Psychology Review*, February, 2007; 11(1):4-27. Heine, S. J., & Hamamura, T., "In search of East Asian self-enhancement," 2004, unpublished manuscript, University of British Columbia, provided by author. Heine's published paper reports his larger meta-analysis of 131 studies showing that Westerners self-aggrandize more than Asians to a statistical medium to large degree (Cohen's d), solidly confirming the results in the unpublished paper.

297. Jean Twenge, "Birth Cohort, Social Change and Personality: The Interplay of Dysphoria and Individualism in the 20th Century," in Daniel Cervone and Walter Mischel, eds.,

Advances in Personality Science, New York: Guilford Press, 2002, pages 206 and 212. Twenge found a two-thirds standard deviation increase in self-esteem among college students over the period 1968 to 1994.

298. Personal correspondence with Twenge. Twenge, J. M., Konrath, S., Foster, J. D., Campbell, W. K., & Bushman, B. J., "Egos inflating over time: A cross-temporal meta-analysis of the Narcissistic Personality Inventory," *Journal of Personality*, 2007, in press.

299. Robert H Frank and Philip J Cook, *The Winner-Take-All Society*, New York: Penguin Books, 1995, 1996, page 104.

300. Frank R Westie, "Academic Expectations for Professional Immortality: A Study in Legitimation," *Sociological Forum*, Summer 1972, pages 1-25.

301. John Simons, "African-Americans are a dominant presence in professional sports: Do blacks suffer as a result?" *US News and World Report*, March 20, 1997.

302. Leonard Evans, *Traffic Safety and the Driver*, 1991, Chapter 12, http://www.scienceservingsociety.com.

303. NORC, "Report to the National Gambling Impact Study Commission," 1999, Appendix D, Table 20, http://www.norc.uchicago.edu/new/pdf/d.pdf. NORC's survey discloses that gamblers thought themselves to be just over $5 billion ahead in past year casino gambling. Christianson Capital Advisors estimates gross annual casino wager at just under $25 billion for 1999.

304. http://www.bizparentz.com/index.html. Adrian Nicole LeBlanc, "Hollywood Elementary," *The New York Times*, June 4, 2006.

305. Marjorie Connelly, "How Class Works," *The New York Times*, May 15, 2005. Another one percent in this poll classified themselves as already wealthy.

306. Thomas A. DiPrete, "Is this a Great Country? Upward mobility and the chance for riches in contemporary America," *Research in Social Stratification and Mobility*, 2007; 25(1):89-95.

307. Ichiro Kawachi and Bruce Kennedy, *The Health of Nations: Why Inequality is Harmful to Your Health*, 2002, New York: The Free Press, pages 165-166.

308. Richard M. Huber, *The American Idea of Success*, Wainscott, New York: The Pushcart Press, 1987, pages 18, 40.

309. CNN, February 4, 2004. This was before Senator Edwards shifted to his populist platform in mid-2007.

310. The Harris Poll, #43, August 9, 2000, http://www.harrisinteractive.com/harris_poll/index.asp?PID=103.

311. Alexendra Alter, "The Baby-Name Business," *The Wall Street Journal*, June 22, 2007, page W1.

312. E. Glenn Schellenberg, "Music lessons enhance IQ," *Psychological Science*, August 15, 2004; 15(8):511-514.

313. Steve Nelson, "Parents, Don't Let Your Kids Become Boring High Achievers," *Valley News*, April 20, 2003, page A8.

314. Elizabeth Green, "Legacy Is Losing Out in Kindergartens," *New York Sun*, December 11, 2007. Manhattan Private School Advisors, http://www.privateschooladvisors.com.

315. Kay S. Hymowitz, "Survivor: The Manhattan Kindergarten," *City Journal*, Spring, 2001.

316. Marcia Vickers, "Commentary: Why Can't We Let Boys Be Boys?" *Business Week*, May 26, 2003.

317. Hymowitz, 2001.

318. Princeton's "Total Prep" SAT and PSAT service costs $1,049 as of early 2005.

319. Alissa Quart, *Branded: The Buying and Selling of Teenagers*, Cambridge: Perseus Publishing, 2003, pages 149-159.

320. "America's Best Colleges, 2006, *U.S. News & World Report*.

321. June Kronholz, "Cram Sessions: For High Schoolers, Summer Is Time to Polish Resumes," *The Wall Street Journal*, April 21, 2005, page A1. Hsiao quote from this article.

322. Source: Accepted.com, April, 2008.

323. Jiao Tong University Institute of Higher Education, "Academic Ranking of World Universities," 2004, http://ed.sjtu.edu.cn/rank/2004/2004Main.htm.

324. National Academy of Sciences, *Policy Implications of International Graduate Students and Postdoctoral Scholars in the United States*, 2005, Washington: The National Academies Press, page 102.

325. Hoffer, T.B., V. Welch, Jr., K. Williams, M. Hess, K. Webber, B. Lisek, D. Loew, and I. Guzman-Barron, "*Doctorate Recipients from United States Universities: Summary Report 2004*," 2005, Chicago: National Opinion Research Center, Tables 11, 31 and 32. http://www.norc.uchicago.edu/issues/sed-2004.pdf. A slight drop post-doc stay rate is reported post 9/11.

326. David H. Shinn, "Reversing the Brain Drain in Ethiopia," *Addis Tribune*, December 6, 2002.

327. "Outward Bound," *The Economist*, September 26, 2002, http://www.economist.com/world/na/displayStory.cfm?story_id=1352810.

328. "High Mileage Moms," Surface Transportation Policy Project, May, 1999, http://www.transact.org/report.asp?id=183.

329. Hilary Stout, "Family Matters: Hiring Someone Else To Potty-Train Your Kids, Teach Them to Ride a Bike," *The Wall Street Journal*, March 31, 2005, page D4.

330. Jeffrey Blitz, *Spellbound*, 2003, Sony Pictures.

331. Peter Applebome, "How We Took the Child Out of Childhood," *The New York Times*, January 8, 2006.

332. Justin Pope, "Schools weaning students away from their 'helicopter parents,'" *AP*, August 29, 2005.

333. David Brooks, "The Organization Kid," *The Atlantic Monthly*, April, 2001, pages 40-54.

334. Martin Lindstrom and Patrician Seybold, *Brand Child*, 2003, London: Kogan Page, page 197.

335. SkateboardDirectory.com News, "'Little Tricky', Skateboarding's New Generation Rising," http://skateboarddirectory.com/articles/480292_little_tricky_skateboardings.html. Little Tricky was five in 2003.

336. Advocare.com website, October 3, 2005. Use of drop down menu selected for kids 11 and under and sports performance yielded the company's KickStart product marketing to kids as young as age 4.

337. Mark Compton, "Enhancement Genetics: Let the Games Begin," *DNA Dispatch*, July 2001, cited in Bill McKibben, *Enough: Staying Human in an Engineered Age*, 2003, Times Books, page 4.

338. Chris Mooney, "Teen Herbicide," *Mother Jones*, May/June, 2003, pages 18-19.

339. Caroline Alexander, "Murdering the Impossible," *National Geographic*, November, 2006, pages 42-67.

340. Brenda Shields and Gary Smith, "Cheerleading-related injuries to children 5 to 18 years of age: United States, 1990-2002," *Pediatrics*, January, 2006; 117(1):122-9, http://pediatrics.aappublications.org/cgi/content/abstract/117/1/122. Mueller FO, Cantu RC, "Special section on cheerleading," in: National Center for Catastrophic Sports Injury Research: twenty-fourth annual report: fall 1982-spring 2006, July 9, 2007, http://www.unc.edu/depts/nccsi/AllSport.htm.

341. Cummings SR, Ling X, Stone K., "Consequences of foot binding among older women in Beijing, China," *American Journal of Public Health*, October, 1997; 87(10):1677-9. Pictures of bound feet can be found here: Candace Hutchins, "Chinese Foot Binding," http://www.ccds.charlotte.nc.us/History/China/04/hutchins/hutchins.htm.

342. All references to women's gymnastics from: Joan Ryan, *Little Girls in Pretty Boxes: The Making and Breaking of Elite Gymnasts and Figure Skaters*, Warner Books, 2000.

343. Skip Rozin, "Sports, Science and the Spirits of Competition," *The Wall Street Journal*, August 12, 2004, page D8.

344. Hill RA, Barton RA, "Psychology: red enhances human performance in contests," *Nature*, May 19, 2005; 435(7040):293. The authors' theory about red is disputed.

345. Data is the progression of Olympic world records from 1896 to 2004 for 100 meter, 1500 meter, marathon, 400 meter hurdles, long jump, high jump and discus. Data are other than Olympic for 100 meter after 1996, for marathon after 1984, for long jump for 1992

only. I selected these sports because improvements are objectively measurable over time and not significantly related to changes in equipment, i.e., improved skates or pole jump pole materials. Data gaps are World Wars I and II, where Olympic contests were not held. Data are normalized so that 1896 records are set at zero and 2004 or most recent records at 100, then averaged. Sources: International Olympic Committee records, www.olympic.org; International Association of Athletics Federations, www.iaaf.org; and www.MarathonGuide.com.

346. Wang Y, Zhang C, Yu RT, Cho HK, Nelson MC, et al., "Regulation of Muscle Fiber Type and Running Endurance by PPAR," *PLoS Biology*, October, 2004; 2(10):e294.

347. "In sport, are good genes just another cheat?" *NewScientist*, August 28, 2004, page 3.

348. H. Lee Sweeney, "Gene Doping," *Scientific American*, July, 2004.

349. The American Society for Aesthetic Plastic Surgery, 2002 survey, http://www.face-lift-surgery-resource.com/html/news.html.

350. American Society of Plastic Surgeons, http://www.plasticsurgery.org/media/statistics/2007-Statistics.cfm. http://www.plasticsurgery.org/media/statistics/1997_cosmetic_procedure_trends.cfm.

351. Rachel Dodes, "Strike a Pose, Count Your Pennies," *The Wall Street Journal*, February 3-4, 2007, page 1.

352. Emily Nelson, "High-Definition TV Causes Worry Lines For Stars, Producers," *The Wall Street Journal*, January 8, 2004, page A1.

353. Neil Fiske and Michael J. Silverstein, *Trading Up: The New American Luxury*, London: Penguin, 2003.

354. Gregory L. White and Shirley Leung, *The Wall Street Journal*, March 29, 2002.

355. David W. Moore, "Half of Young People Expect To Strike It Rich," *Gallup News Service*, March 11, 2003. Roper 1986 number is $50,000 adjusted to $80,000 using BEA consumer expenditures price deflators for 1986 and 2003.

356. Juliet B Schor, *The Overspent American*, Harper Perennial, 1999 (1998), page 13.

357. David W. Moore, "Half of Young People Expect to Strike It Rich: But expectations fall rapidly with age," Gallup News Service, March 11, 2003.

358. Fidelity.com, Retirement Income Planner. Assumes retirement at age 65, $1,000,000 in liquid assets, $54,000 in after-tax income requirement, partially provided by Social Security income.

359. Spectrum Group millionaire survey, January 7, 2008. (Those with net financial assets of at least $500,000.)

360. Securities and Exchange Commission, March 9, 2007, http://edgar.sec.gov/comments/s7-25-06/s72506.shtml.

361. Tom Herman, "There's Rich, and There's the Fortunate 400," *The Wall Street Journal*, March 5, 2008, page D3. Wealth: Edward N. Wolff, "Changes in Household Wealth in the 1980s and 1990s in the U.S.," May, 2004, Table 5, page 33, http://www.levy.org/2/bin/datastore/pubs/files/wp/407.pdf. 2001 data. The average wealth of the top one percent of households is $12.6 million, author's calculations from, Gerhard Fries, "Disclosure Review and the 2001 Survey of Consumer Finances," Federal Reserve Board, 2003, http://www.federalreserve.gov/pubs/oss/oss2/papers/asa2003f6.pdf.

362. Richard Todd, "What It Takes (and what it means) to be Wealthy Today," *Worth*, November, 1996.

363. Robert Frank, *Richistan: A Journey Through the American Wealth Boom and the Lives of the New Rich*, 2007, New York: Crown.

364. Source: New York University wealth expert Edward Wolff estimate for the year 2004. Decamillionaire household wealth in 1989 adjusted for inflation.

365. Merrill Lynch & Co. and Capgemini Group, "World Wealth Report 2007."

366. Positions Open, *Science*, June 2, 2006, page 1408.

367. Sheelah Kolhatkar, "Inside the Billionaire Service Industry," *The Atlantic*, September, 2006; 298(2)97-101.

368. The average new home's square footage measured 983 in 1950, 1,645 in 1975 and 2,241 in 2007. Meanwhile the number of persons in the average household decreased from 3.37 to 2.94

to 2.57 over that period. Sources, National Association of Home Builders for square footage. Grebler, Leo, Blank, David M., and Winnick, Louis, *Capital Formation in Residential Real Estate*, 1956, Princeton: Princeton University Press for NBER, page 119 for 1950 square footage data. US Census Bureau, "Average Number of People per Household, by Race and Hispanic Origin, Marital Status, Age, and Education of Householder: 2006," Table AVG-1, March 27, 2007, http://www.census.gov/population/socdemo/hh-fam/cps2006/tabAVG1.xls; http://www.census.gov/hhes/www/housing/ahs/01dtchrt/tab2-3.html. Given that only 27 percent of present dwelling units were built before 1950, average space per person including both new and existing homes has probably at least doubled over the past fifty years.

369. "Selected Housing Characteristics: 2004," U.S. Census Bureau. Owner-occupied housing only.

370. Yacht asking prices at www.YachtWorld.com, January, 2008. Yacht quotes in, Robert Frank, "Making Waves: New Luxury Goods Set Super-Wealthy Apart from the Pack," *The Wall Street Journal*, December 17, 2004, page A1.

371. Robert Frank, "Stalkers of the High Seas," *The Wall Street Journal*, October 19, 2007, page W2.

372. Brad Lemley, "Computers Will Save Us: The Future According to James Martin," *Discover*, June 2001, 22(06).

373. "The 2006 Slate 60: The 60 largest American charitable contributions of the year," *Slate*, February 16, 2007, http://specials.slate.com/slate60/2006/. Author's analysis. Over the period 1996-2006, the minimum and median contributions necessary to be included increased from $10 to $30 and from $15 to $60 million, respectively. Data is not inflation adjusted.

374. Bill Wasik, "My Crowd, Part 1," *Harper's*, February 22, 2006, http://www.harpers.org/MyCrowd_01.html

375. Christine R. Schwartz and Robert D. Mare, "Trends in Educational Assortative Marriage From 1940 to 2003," *Demography*, November, 2005, 42(4):621-46, http://repositories.cdlib.org/ccpr/olwp/ccpr-003-05. See figures 2, 3 and 4.

376. Watson, David; Klohnen, Eva C.; Casillas, Alex; Nus Simms, Ericka; Haig, Jeffrey; Berry, Diane S.. "Match Makers and Deal Breakers: Analyses of Assortative Mating in Newlywed Couples," *Journal of Personality*, October, 2004; 72(5):1029-1068. IQ was found to be similar between marriage partners to about the same extent as educational attainment (42% versus 45% similarity) taken in this 2000 survey of recently married couples, with markedly higher similarity in verbal than in other types of intelligence.

377. Gardyn, Rebecca, "The Mating Game," *American Demographics*, July/August, 2002; 24(7):32-37.

378. Jane Spencer, "Sorry, You're Nobody's Type: Dating Sites Are Rejecting Some Applicants Upfront; Flunking the Personality Test," *The Wall Street Journal*, July 30, 2003, page D1. Dating site traffic ranking by Alexa.com, November, 2007.

379. Ichiro Kawachi and Bruce Kennedy, *The Health of Nations: Why Inequality is Harmful to Your Health*, 2002, New York: The Free Press, page 97.

380. Geoff David, "Doctors without orders," *American Scientist*, 2005; 93(3), http://postdoc.sigmaxi.org/results/.

381. National Science Foundation, "Selected Data on Graduate Students and Post doctorates in Science and Engineering," Fall, 1994, Supplementary Data Release Number 13: Postdoctoral Appointees and Other Nonfaculty Research Staff, Table C-21. In 1987, there were 24,819 postdocs engaged in science, engineering and health research.

382. Sigma Xi, "Sigma Xi Postdoc Survey Offers Surprising Insights," April 6, 2005, http://www.sigmaxi.org/about/news/postdoc.shtml

383. Julie Rehmeyer, "Chasing Money for Science," *Science News*, March 31, 2007, page 206. Yudhijit Bhattacharjee, "Data Point: Higher Stakes," *Science*, December 15, 2006; 314:1665.

384. B. Lindsay Lowell and Hal Salzman, "Into the Eye of the Storm: Assessing the Evidence on Science and Engineering Education, Quality, and Workforce Demand," The Urban Institute, October, 2007, http://www.urban.org/uploadedPDF/411562_salzman_science.pdf. Yudhijit Bhattacharjee, "New Analysis Questions Push for More Degrees," *Science*, November 16, 2007, 318:1052.
385. Dana Mackenzie, "Breakthrough of the Year: Poincaré Conjecture Proved," *Science*, December 22, 2006; 314:1848-9. Josh Brodie, "Perelman explains proof to famous math mystery," *DailyPrincetonian.com*, April 17, 2003. Sharon Begley, "Major Math Problem Is Believed Solved By Reclusive Russian," *The Wall Street Journal*, July 21, 2006, page A9.
386. James Gleick, *Genius: The Life and Science of Richard Feynman*, New York: Pantheon Books, 1992 [1993], pages 145 and 316.
387. Samuel Zyman, "New Music From a Very New Composer, *The Julliard Journal*, May, 2003.
388. http://www.fromthetop.org/Programs/Performers.cfm?pid=1586.   Without   doubt, impressive for an 11 year old, but not at the time a Mozart.
389. Catalyst,"2005 Catalyst Census of Women Corporate Officers and Top Earners of the Fortune 500," 2006, http://www.catalyst.org/files/full/2005%20COTE.pdf. U.S. Department of Commerce: Bureau of Economic Analysis, "Gross Domestic Product: Implicit Price Deflator," December 20, 2007. *Fortune*, "A database of every year of Fortune's list of America's largest corporations," http://money.cnn.com/magazines/fortune/fortune500_archive/full/1955/index.html. Officer positions at the top 500 companies decreased from 11,241 to 10,873 over the ten years ending 2005. Midyear 2005 and 1995 deflators were applied to total gross revenues and total reported profits of all Fortune 500 companies for the years 2005 and 1995.
390. "The Celebrity 100," *Forbes*, June 23, 2006.
391. Institute for Policy Studies, "14th Annual CEO Compensation Survey," August 29, 2007, http://www.ips-dc.org/reports/070829-executiveexcess.pdf. United for a Fair Economy, "Ratio of CEO Pay to Average Worker Pay Reaches 301 in 2003," April 14, 2004. The 301 multiple is down from the bubble peak of 475, "Executive Pay," *The Economist*, Sept. 30, 2000, page 110. Data from *Business Week* survey executive pay at the top 360 U.S. corporations.,
392. *Forbes*, "Special Report, CEO Pay," May 3, 2007. "Ever higher society, ever harder to ascend," *The Economist*, January 1, 2005.
393. Tom Herman, "There's Rich, and There's the Fortunate 400," *The Wall Street Journal*, March 5, 2008, page D3.
394. "Faltering meritocracy in America," *The Economist*, December 29, 2004.
395. Bhashkar Mazumder, "The Apple Falls Even Closer To The Tree Than We Thought," in Samuel Bowles, Herbert Gintis, and Melissa Osborne Groves, ed., *Unequal Chances: Family Background and Economic Success*, Princeton: Princeton University Press, 2005, page 80. Tom Hertz, "Rags, Riches, and Race," in Samuel Bowles, Herbert Gintis, and Melissa Osborne Groves, ed., *Unequal Chances: Family Background and Economic Success*, Princeton: Princeton University Press, 2005, Table 5.10, page 186.
396. Bhashkar Mazumder, " Revised Estimates of Intergenerational Income Mobility in the United States," Federal Reserve Bank of Chicago, November, 2003, http://www.chicagofed.org/publications/workingpapers/papers/wp2003-16.pdf. Author's emphasis. Mazumder's estimate is 60 percent. Lee and Solon's U.S. IGE estimate is 44 percent: Chul-In Lee and Gary Solon, "Trends in Intergenerational Income Mobility," August, 2005, unpublished working paper, http://www-personal.umich.edu/~gsolon/workingpapers/trends.pdf. Lee and Solon find no decrease in economic mobility since 1977. On balance, however, the evidence points to a decrease.
397. Carole Hyatt & Linda Gottlieb, *When Smart People Fail: Rebuilding Yourself for Success*, New York: Penguin Books, 1993, page 29.
398. John Strenge, "Who Wants to be 100th on the Money List?" *Golf Digest*, April 2002.
399. Jonah Freedman, "The 2007 Fortunate 50," *Sports Illustrated*, May 31, 2007.
400. James Gleick, *Genius: The Life and Science of Richard Feynman*, New York: Pantheon Books, 1992 [1993], page 128.

401. Chris Matthews, quoted in *Esquire* magazine, date unknown, author's emphasis.
402. Joe Flint and John Lippman, "Stripped of Power at Empire He Built, Ted Turner Quit," *The Wall Street Journal*, January 31, 2003, page B1. "The 400 Richest Americans," *Forbes*, September 20, 2007.
403. UPI, February 26, 2003.
404. Robert W. Fuller, *Somebodies and Nobodies: Overcoming the Abuse of Rank*, Gabriola Island, Canada: New Society Publishers, 2003, page 54, parentheses authors'.
405. Irving Fang, "The Media History Project," http://www.mediahistory.umn.edu/timeline. Fang's timeline lists over 4,000 media inventions and events dating from prehistoric times to the present. Some information in this chapter not otherwise cited is drawn from this source.
406. Paul Ekman (Ed), *Charles Darwin's The Expression of the Emotions in Man and Animals*, New York: Oxford University Press, 1998.
407. A bibliography on shared human-primate facial expression is here: http://www.learnlink. emory.edu/~npatel2/bibliography.htm
408. Ekman, P., & Rosenberg, E.L. (Eds), *What the Face Reveals: Basic and Applied Studies of Spontaneous Expression Using the Facial Action Coding Systems (FACS)*, New York: Oxford University Press, 1997; and, J.N. Browndyke, 2002, http://www.neuropsychologycentral. com/interface/content/resources/page_material/resources_general_materials_pages/ resources_document_pages/neuropsychosocial_factors_in_emotion_recognition.pdf.
409. Malcolm Gladwell, "The Naked Face: Can you read people's thoughts just by looking at them?" *The New Yorker*, August 5, 2002.
410. Charles C. Ballew, II and Alexander Todorov, "Predicting political elections from rapid and unreflective face judgments," *Proceedings of the National Academy of Sciences*, USA, November 13, 2007; 104(46):17948-53. Todorov A, Mandisodza AN, Goren A, Hall CC, "Inferences of competence from faces predict election outcomes," *Science*, June 10, 2005; 308(5728):1623-6. The experimenters also asked viewers to pick the most competent, likeable, and trustworthy candidate, but only perceptions of competence accurately predicted election outcomes.
411. Karen McComb and Stuart Semple, "Coevolution of vocal communication and sociality in primates," *Proceedings of the Royal Society B*, July, 2005; 1:381-85.
412. Jared Diamond, *Guns, Germs and Steel: The Fates of Human Societies*, New York: WW Norton, 1999 [1997]. Agriculture was adopted independently and closer to simultaneously than earlier believed, specifically, agriculture appears to have been independently invented in New Guinea 10,000 years ago. B. Bower, "New Guinea Went Bananas: Agriculture's roots get a South Pacific Twist," *Science News*, June 21, 2003, page 389.
413. Anthony Snodgrass, *Archaic Greece: The Age of Experiment*, Berkeley: University of California Press, 1980, pages 78-83.
414. Barry Powel, *Homer and the Origin of the Greek Alphabet*, Cambridge: Cambridge University Press, 1991.
415. Tim Spalding, *Alexander in Images*, 1999, http://www.isidore-of-seville.com/ ImagesofAlexander/Antiquity_Coins_Alex.html.
416. Lawrence University, 1996, http://www.lawrence.edu/dept/art/buerger/catalogue/060.html.
417. Anita Albus, *The Art of Arts: Rediscovering Painting*, New York: Knopf, 2000. Joseph W. Dauben, "The Art of Renaissance Science: Galileo and Perspective," VHS video, 1991. Kemp, M., *The Science of Art: Optical Themes in Western Art from Brunelleschi to Seurat*, New Haven: Yale University Press, 1990, as cited in Murray, 2003, page 214.
418. Ross King, *Michelango and the Pope's Ceiling*, Penguin Books, 2003. William E. Wallace, *Michelangelo: The Complete Sculpture, Painting, Architecture*, Beaux Arts Editions, 1998. Tyler Cowen, *In Praise of Commercial Culture*, 1998 [2000], Cambridge: Harvard University Press, pages 93-94.
419. Cowen, 1998, pages 109 and 112.
420. Charles Murray, *Human Accomplishment: The Pursuit of Excellence in the Arts and Sciences, 800 B.C. to 1950*, New York: HarperCollins, 2003, page 47.

421. Amazon.com, February 10, 2008.
422. Roger Baynton-Williams, "A Short History of Print Art 1500-1860," http://www.mapforum.com/05/print.htm.
423. A facsimile of all three pages of this newspaper is provided by the Massachusetts Historical Society, http://www.masshist.org/database/query3.cfm?queryID=219.
424. Cowen, 1998, pages 60-63, and M. Emery, E. Emery, with N. L. Roberts, *The Press and America: An Interpretive History of the Mass Media*, 8th ed., Boston: Allyn and Bacon, 1996.
425. Ben H. Bagdikian, *The Media Monopoly*, Boston: Beacon Press, 2000, page 161 and Richard Ohmann, *Selling Culture: Magazines, Markets, and Class at the Turn of the Century*, Verso Books, 1996, page 29.
426. Jacques Barzun, *From Dawn to Decadence: 500 Years of Western Cultural Life 1500 to the Present*, New York: HarperCollins, 2001, page 111.
427. Mary Ann Glendon, "Rousseau & the Revolt Against Reason," *First Things*, October, 1999; 96:42-47.
428. Rousseau's last major work was an autobiography intended, in part, to burnish his reputation sullied by critics such as Voltaire. Displaying his grandiose self-image, here are the opening lines of *The Confessions of Jean-Jacques Rousseau*, Book 1, 1781, translated by W. Conyngham Mallory, http://www.swan.ac.uk/poli/texts/rousseau/confcon.htm:

    I have begun on a work which is without precedent, whose accomplishment will have no imitator. I propose to set before my fellow-mortals a man in all the truth of nature; and this man shall be myself. I have studied mankind and know my heart; I am not made like any one I have been acquainted with, perhaps like no one in existence; if not better, I at least claim originality.

429. Robert Darnton, *The Great Cat Massacre: And Other Episodes in French Cultural History*, New York: Basic Books, 1984, pages 242-249. Rousseau probably does not exaggerate in this passage from *Confessions*, Book 11: "Women especially had become so intoxicated with the book and its author that there were few of them, even at the highest rank, whom I could not have had, had I attempted their conquest."
430. Elliot Ravetz, "The Book of Liszts: Finally, A Biography That Does Justice To All Facets of Franz Liszt's Messy Life and Protean Work," *Time Magazine*, Sept. 2, 1996., reviewing Alan Walker's biographic trilogy; and, H.C. Schonberg, *The Great Pianists from Mozart to the Present*, New York: Simon & Schuster, 1987.
431. Mary Warner Marien, *Photography: A Cultural History*, London: Lawrence King Publishing, 2006, pages 106-107. Leo Braudy, *The Frenzy of Renown: Fame and Its History*, New York: Random House, 1986, [1997], pages 493-496.
432. Crosby can be considered the best selling recording artist in history by measuring his unit sales against the U.S. population during his career. Measured by unit sales, only the Beatles top Crosby.
433. James Cagney, *Cagney by Cagney*, New York: Doubleday, 1976.
434. Donna Hill, "Rudolph Valentino Chronology," 2000, http://www.geocities.com/~rudyfan/rv-chron4.htm.
435. Jason Zengerle, "Not Since Jesus," *New York Magazine*, April 10, 2006.
436. Ronald L. Goldfarb, *TV or Not TV: Television, Justice, and the Courts*, New York: New York University Press, 1999.
437. Two confirming sources for this television viewing time data: Veronis Suhler Stevenson Communications Industry Forecast, cited in Martin Peers, "Buddy, Can You Spare Some Time?" *The Wall Street Journal*, January 26, 2004, page B1; and, Gallup News Service, Jan 7, 2000.
438. Gallup Youth Survey, November 19, 2002. Sege, R., and Dietz, W., "Television Viewing and Violence in Children: The Pediatrician as Agent for Change," *Pediatrics*, 1994; 94(4).
439. Adapted from Todd Gitlin, *Media Unlimited: How the Torrent of Images and Sounds Overwhelms Our Lives*, 2001, New York: Henry Holt and Company, page 20, citing Richard Butsch, *The Making of American Audiences: From Stage to Television, 1750-1990*, Cambridge University Press, 2000, pages 295-297. 2006 data author's calculations.

440. Lisa Guernsey, "At Airport Gate, a Cyborg Unplugged," *The New York Times*, March 14, 2002.

441. Tokyo Institute of Technology, July 15, 2006, http://silvia.mn.ee.titech.ac.jp/MNL_index. htm.

442. Cyberkinetics, Inc., "BrainGate Clinical Trial," April 20, 2004, http://www.cyberkineticsinc. com/newbraingate.htm

443. See: http://www.locked-in.com/installation/video_eng.html. Jeffrey Winters, "Communicating by Brain Waves," *Psychology Today*, May/June, 2003. http://www.psychologytoday.com/htdocs/prod/PTOArticle/PTO-20030724-000002.asp.

444. U.S. Patent Number 6,536,440, Method and system for generating sensory data onto the human neural cortex; U.S. Patent Number 6,584,357, Method and system for forming an acoustic signal from neural timing difference data; U.S. Patent Number 6,729,337, Method and system for generating sensory data onto the human neural cortex.

445. http://www.mmogchart.com.

446. Alexandra Alter, "Is This Man Cheating on His Wife?" *The Wall Street Journal*, August 20, 2007, page W1.

447. TerraNova, December 9, 2004, http://mypage.iu.edu/~castro. Julian Dibbell, "The Unreal Estate Boom," *Wired*, January, 2003, http://www.wired.com/wired/archive/11.01/gaming.html.

448. Donald F. Roberts, Ulla G. Foehr, Victoria Rideout, "Generation M: Media in the Lives of 8-18 Year Olds," Kaiser Family Foundation, March, 2005, page 38, http://www.kff.org/ entmedia/loader.cfm?url=/commonspot/security/getfile.cfm&PageID=51809.   Twenty-three minutes of media time use is books. Most kids are media-multi-takers, consuming more than one at the same time, explaining the 8.5 total hours spent with all media. Over half of 8-10 year olds have one or more of a VCR, DVD, radio, CD player or video game in their own bedrooms. More than two-thirds have a television.

449. Adapted from: Roberts, *et al*, 2005, Box 5.1, page 38.

450. George Gerbner, "Reclaiming Our Cultural Mythology: Television's global marketing strategy creates a damaging and alienated window on the world," *In Context*, Spring, 1994, page 40.

451. Tyler Cowen, *What Price Fame?*, Harvard University Press, Cambridge, 2000, page 47.

452. Linda Lyons, "No Heroes in the Beltway," Gallup Organization, July 30, 2002.

453. Aaron Schatz, "The Lycos 50 Elite," http://50.lycos.com/elite.asp.

454. Google.com, "2004 Year-End Google Zeitgeist: Search patterns, trends, and surprises," http://www.google.com/press/zeitgeist2004.html.

455. *The Wall Street Journal*, October 23, 2002.

456. Horace Greeley, *The Tribune*, 1841.

457. Kim Masters, *The Keys to the Kingdom: How Michael Eisner Lost His Grip*, 2000, New York: Morrow. The quote dates to former Disney CEO Eisner's days at Paramount.

458. Some great Powder Ridge photos are here: http://www.chronos-historical.org/rockfest/ PowderRidge/index.html.

459. William Abruzzi, "The rock doctor tells about 985 freakouts," *Life Magazine*, August 14, 1970.

460. Cintra Wilson, *A Massive Swelling: Celebrity Re-examined as a Grotesque, Crippling Disease and Other Cultural Revelations*, 2000, New York: Penguin Books, page 13.

461. McCutcheon, Lynn E.; Ashe, Diane D.; Houran, James; Maltby, John, "A Cognitive Profile of Individuals Who Tend to Worship Celebrities," *British Journal of Psychology*, July, 2003; 137(4):309-312. McCutcheon, Lynn E.; Lange, Rense; Houran, James, "Conceptualization and measurement of celebrity worship," *British Journal of Psychology*, February, 2002; 93(1):67-87. Maltby, J., Houran, M.A., & McCutcheon, L.E, "A Clinical Interpretation of Attitudes and Behaviors Associated with Celebrity Worship," *Journal of Nervous and Mental Disease*, 2003; 191:25-29.

462. *People* Magazine gross revenues: "Top 300 Magazines, 2006" AdAge.com, October 28, 2007.

463. Harris Poll #46, September 9, 1998, http://www.harrisinteractive.com/harris_poll/index. asp?PID=162.

464. Martin Lindstrom and Patrician Seybold, *Brand Child*, 2003, London: Kogan Page, page 25.

465. The Pew Research Center, "How Young People View Their Lives, Futures and Politics: A Portrait of 'Generation Next,'" January 9, 2007, http://people-press.org/reports/display. php3?ReportID=300.

466. www.Celebrity-babies.com, May 15, 2008. Susan Saulny, "What Price Fame? 2 Nights on a Street," *The New York Times*, August 24, 2003; and, Meriah Doty, "At the 'American Idol 3' auditions: Disappointment, thrills and a lot of waiting, *CNN*, August 22, 2003, http://www.cnn.com/2003/SHOWBIZ/TV/08/22/idol.tryouts/

467. Gil Kaufman, "Eminem, Dr. Dre Music Allegedly Used To Rattle Detainees In Secret Prison," *MTV.com*, December 20, 2005.

468. William Shaw, "The Super Anti-Hero," *Blender*, August, 2002, www.blender.com/articles/article_380.html. "Eminem Files for Divorce," *NYRock*, August 17, 2000. Ben Schmitt, "Eminem's Wife Attempts Suicide," *Rolling Stone*, July 10, 2000.

469. Josh Grossberg, "C-Murder's Jailhouse Raps Slammed," EOnline, February 25, 2005.

470. Donald F. Roberts, Ulla G. Foehr, Victoria Rideout, "Generation M: Media in the Lives of 8-18 Year Olds," Kaiser Family Foundation, March, 2005, Table 4-1, http://www.kff. org/entmedia/loader.cfm?url=/commonspot/security/getfile.cfm&PageID=51809.

471. Adam Buckman, "Did 'Sopranos' go too far?" *New York Post*, April 5, 2001.

472. Smith, S. L., & Donnerstein, E., "Harmful effects of exposure to media violence: Learning of aggression, emotional desensitization, and fear," in R. G. Geen & E. Donnerstein (Eds.), *Human aggression: Theories, research, and implications for social policy*, 1998, New York: Academic Press, pages 167-202, cited in: U.S. Department of Health and Human Services, Youth Violence: A Report of the Surgeon General, 2001, page 88.

473. Michael Rich, Elizabeth R. Woods, Elizabeth Goodman, S. Jean Emans, and Robert H. DuRant, "Aggressors or Victims: Gender and Race in Music Video Violence," *Pediatrics*, April, 1998; 101(4):669-674.

474. S. Robert Lichter, Linda S. Lichter, Daniel R. Amundson and Trevor Butterworth, "Hollywood Cleans Up Its Act: Changing Rates of Sex and Violence in Entertainment Media," Center for Media and Public Affairs, March, 2002.

475. Jeffrey G. Johnson et al, "Television Viewing and Aggressive Behavior During Adolescence and Adulthood," *Science*, March 29, 2002; 295:2468-2471.

476. L. Rowell Huesmann, Jessica Moise-Titus, Cheryl-Lynn Podolski, and Leonard D. Eron, "Longitudinal Relations Between Children's Exposure to TV Violence and Their Aggressive and Violent Behavior in Young Adulthood: 1977 - 1992," *Developmental Psychology*, March, 2004; 39(2).

477. Jeffrey G. Johnson, Patricia Cohen, Stephanie Kasen, Judith S. Brook, "Extensive Television Viewing and the Development of Attention and Learning Difficulties During Adolescence," *Archives of Pediatrics and Adolescent Medicine*, May, 2007; 161(5):480-6.

478. Personal correspondence from Jeffrey G. Johnson to author, January, 15, 2003.

479. Roberts, D. F. & Christenson, P. G., "Popular music in childhood and adolescence," in Singer, D. G., Singer, J. L. (Eds.), *Handbook of Children and the Media*, Thousand Oaks, CA: Sage Publications, 2001, pages 395-414.

480. "Annual U.S. Video Game Sales," NPD Group, January 31, 2008.

481. Steve Crabtree, "Grand Theft of Innocence? Teens and Video Games," The Gallup Organization, September 16, 2003.

482. "October U.S. Games Sales Up 35 Percent," *Reuters*, November 12, 2004.

483. Blake Snow, "Halo 3 becomes fastest selling video game ever," *GamePro.com*, October 4, 2007.

484. Smith, S.L., Lachlan, K.A., & Tamborini, R, "Popular Video Games: Quantifying the Presentation of Violence and its Context," *Journal of Broadcasting and Electronic Media*, 2003; 47(1).

485. Kevin Haninger and Kimberly M. Thompson, "Content and Ratings of Teen-Rated Video Games," *Journal of the American Medical Association*, February 18, 2004; 291:856-865.

486. Federal Trade Commission, "Marketing Violent Entertainment to Children," April, 2007, http://www.ftc.gov/reports/violence/070412MarketingViolentEChildren.pdf.

487. Douglas A. Gentile, David A. Walsh, Paul R. Ellison, Michelle Fox, Jennifer Cameron, "Media violence as a risk factor for children: A longitudinal study," Paper presented at the American Psychological Society 16th Annual Convention, Chicago, Illinois, May, 2004, http://www.psychology.iastate.edu/faculty/dgentile/pdfs/Gentile_et_al_APS_2004.pdf. Even college students become more violent after playing "E" for everyone games–even though they know the game violence is not real. Heavy game users also increased their presumption that other's intent was aggressive.

488. Lefkowitz, M. M., Eron, L. D., Walder, L. O., & Huesmann, L. R., "Television violence and child aggression: A follow-up study," in G. A. Comstock & E. A. Rubenstein (Eds.), *Television and social behavior, Volume III*, 1972,: Washington, D.C.: U.S. Government Printing Office. A group of third graders were followed for 11 years, with heavier exposure to TV violence predicting higher levels of aggression at age 19.

489. "Joint Statement on the Impact of Entertainment Violence on Children: Congressional Public Health Summit," July 26, 2000, www.aap.org/advocacy/release/jstmteuc.htm.

490. Stephen J. Kirsh, *Children, Adolescents, and Media Violence: A Critical Look at the Research*, 2006, Thousand Oaks, CA: Sage Publications, pages 273-287. Anderson, C. A., & Bushman, B. J., "Media violence and societal violence," *Science*, March 29, 2002; 295:2377-2378. B. J. Bushman, C. A. Anderson, *Am. Psychol.*, 2001; 56:477, www.psychology.iastate.edu/faculty/caa/abstracts/2000-2004/01BA.ap.html. Gentile, Douglas A.; Lynch, Paul J.; Linder, Jennifer Ruh; Walsh, David A., "The effects of violent video game habits on adolescent hostility, aggressive behaviors, and school performance," *Journal of Adolescence*, February 2004; 27(1):5-22. Craig A. Anderson, "An update on the effects of playing violent video games," *Journal of Adolescence*, February, 2004; 27(1):113-122. Anderson, C.A., "Violent video games: Myths, facts, and unanswered questions," *Psychological Science Agenda: Science Briefs*, October, 2003; 16(5):1-3. The best-yet meta-studies peg the effect-size relationship between media violence and real-world aggression and aggressive behavior, respectively, at .31 for TV and movies, .26 for video games, with more recent and more rigorous studies yielding higher numbers. A "large" TV-violence effect size of .46 is reported by Kirsh, page 282, for violent TV viewing by children under age 5. Scientists would classify these effect sizes as "moderate" and effect sizes as roughly "small" for the following: lead exposure and lower IQ, asbestos exposure and cancer, second-hand smoke and cancer, calcium intake and bone mass, breast self-examination and early cancer detection, and failure to use condoms and HIV. All of the small effect-size risks have generated public policy response.

491. Marco Iacoboni , "Media Violence Induces Imitative Violence: The Problem With Super Mirrors," Edge: What Is Your Dangerous Idea?, January, 2006, http://www.edge.org/q2006/q06_11.html#iacaboni.

492. Dave Grossman, *On Killing: The Psychological Cost of Learning to Kill on War and Society*, Back Bay Books, 1996.

493. Dave Grossman and Gloria DeGaetano, *Stop Teaching Our Kids to Kill*, Three Rivers Press, 1999.

494. Jim Balloch, "Teens plead guilty in I-40 shootings," *Knoxville News*, August 29, 2003.

495. Stephen A. Crockett Jr., "For Young Fans, the Name Of the Video Game Is Gore," *Washington Post*, August 24, 2002, page A01.

496. *60 Minutes*, CBS, October 1, 2006. Michael Squires and Juliet V. Casey, "Film cashes in on street scenes: Video selling fast, but advocates for homeless critical," *Las Vegas Review-Journal*, May 05, 2002. Jay Stapleton, "Teens get from 22 to 35 years in prison for homeless beating," *Daytona Beach News Journal*, April 25, 2006. To see dozens of *Bumfights* clips without financially rewarding the producers, visit YouTube.com and search "bumfights." Producers Ryan McPherson, Zachary Bubeck, Michael Slyman and Daniel Tanner plea

bargained to an admission of guilt for having arranged a 2003 bumfight without a permit. They were fined $500 each and ordered to perform community service at a homeless shelter – which they failed to perform.

497. According to the blogger who writes KimMathers.com.
498. *Adbusters*, http://adbusters.org/campaigns/tvturnoff/updates/a_wasted_life.html.
499. Eric Schlosser, *Reefer Madness: Sex, Drugs, and Cheap Labor in the American Black Market*, 2003, New York: Houghton Mifflin, page 202.
500. Jerry Mander, *Four Arguments for the Elimination of Television*, Quill, 1978, cited in, Kalle Lasn, *Culture Jam: How to Reverse America's Suicidal Consumer Binge – and Why We Must*, Harper Collins, 1999 [2000], page15. Mander originally coined the term "technical events" with reference to television production.
501. Most, S.B., Chun, M.M., Widders, D.M., Zald, D.H., "Attentional rubbernecking: Involuntary attention to emotionally negative pictures induces blindness for targets," *Psychonomic Bulletin and Review*, August, 2005; 12(4):654-61.
502. Lang, Annie; Zhou, Shuhua; Schwartz, Nancy; Bolls, Paul D.; Potter, Robert F., "The Effects of Edits on Arousal, Attention, and Memory for Television Messages: When an Edit Is an Edit Can An Edit Be Too Much?" *Journal of Broadcasting & Electronic Media*, Winter, 2000; 44(1):94-109. Lang, A., Dhillon, K., & Dong, Q., "The effects of emotional arousal and valence on television viewers' cognitive capacity and memory," *Journal of Broadcasting and Electronic Media*, 1995; 39(3), 313-327. Lang, A., Geiger, S., Strickwerda, M., & Sumner, J., "The effects of related and unrelated cuts on viewers' memory for television: A limited capacity theory of television viewing," *Communication Research*, 1993; 20:4-29.
503. Kubey, Robert & Csikszentmihalyi, Mihaly "Television Addiction is no mere metaphor," *Scientific American*, February 2002; 286(2):74-80.
504. "Flicker illness." *NewScientist*, November 10, 2007, page 77.
505. Christakis, Dimitri A.; Zimmerman, Frederick J.; DiGiuseppe, David L.; McCarty, Carolyn A., "Early Television Exposure and Subsequent Attentional Problems in Children," *Pediatrics*, April, 2004; 113(4):708-713. Obel, Carsten; Henriksen, Tine Brink; Dalsgaard, Søren; Linnet, Karen Markussen; Skajaa, Elisabeth; Thomsen, Per Hove; Olsen, Jørn, "Does Children's Watching of Television Cause Attention Problems? Retesting the Hypothesis in a Danish Cohort," *Pediatrics*, November, 2004; 114(5):1372-1374. The Obel study shows no statistically significant evidence for a TV-ADHD relationship. But few in this Danish population viewed more than 2 hours per day.
506. Jordon A, Woodard E, "Electronic childhood: the availability and use of household media by 2- to 3-year-olds," *Zero to Three*, 2001; 22(2):4-9; and, Victor C Strasburger and Edward Donnerstein, "Children, Adolescents, and the Media: Issues and Solutions," *Pediatrics*, January, 1999; 103(1):129-139. 35% of age 12-17 year olds have a TV in their bedroom.
507. Camille Sweeney, "Never Too Young for That First Pedicure," *The New York Times*, February 28, 2008.
508. Deborah Roffman, "Barbie's lost innocence reflects America's lost innocence," *The Union Leader*, December 26, 2002, page A23.
509. Lauren Greenfield, *Girl Culture*, San Francisco: Chronicle Books, 2002.
510. William D. Mosher, Anjani Chandra, and Jo Jones, "Sexual Behavior and Selected Health Measures: Men and Women 15-44 Years of Age, United States, 2002," Centers for Disease Control, September 15, 2005, Table 3. Data is "had ever" received oral sex.
511. Joan Jacobs Brumberg, *The Body Project: An Intimate History of American Girls*, New York: Random House, 1997, pages xxv and 98.
512. Anorexia Nervosa and Related Eating Disorders, Inc., July 21, 2003, http://www.anred.com/males.html.
513. Screening for Mental Health, Inc, April, 2003, http://www.mentalhealthscreening.org/eat/eat-fact.htm.

514. Voracek M, Fisher ML., "Shapely centrefolds? Temporal change in body measures: trend analysis," *British Medical Journal*, December 21, 2002; 325(7378):1447-8.
515. Field, A.E., Cheung, L., Wolf, A.M., Herzog, D.B., Gortmaker, S.L., & Colditz, G.A., "Exposure to the mass media and weight concerns among girls," *Pediatrics*, 1999; 103:36-41.
516. Hargreaves, D., "Idealized Women in TV Ads Make Girls Feel Bad," *Journal of Social and Clinical Psychology*, 2002; 21:287-308.
517. Tiggemann, M., and Pickering, A. S., "Role of television in adolescent women's body dissatisfaction and drive for thinness," *International Journal of Eating Disorders*, 1996; 20:199-203. Marika Tiggemann and Julia K. Kuring, "The role of body objectification in disordered eating and depressed mood," *British Journal of Clinical Psychology*, September 2004; 43:299-311.
518. Richins, M. L., "Social comparison and idealized images of advertising," *Journal of Consumer Research*, 1991, 18, 71-83; and, Then, D, "Women's magazines: Messages they convey about looks, men and careers," Paper presented at the annual convention of the American Psychological Association, Washington, D.C., August, 1992.
519. Marsha Richins, "Social comparison and the idealized images of advertising," *Journal of Consumer Research*, 1991; 18:71-83.
520. AP, "Experts: More kids worried about weight, looks," July 7, 2001.
521. Linda Searing, "Even Young Kids Now Fixate on Weight," *HealthScoutNews*, undated, http://preventdisease.com/news/articles/young_kids_fixate_on_weight.shtml.
522. Tiggemann, M., and Pickering, A. S., "Role of television in adolescent women's body dissatisfaction and drive for thinness," *International Journal of Eating Disorders*, 1996; 20:199-203. Screening for Mental Health, Inc, April, 2003, http://www.mentalhealthscreening.org/eat/eat-fact.htm.
523. Kenrick, D. T., Gutierres, S. E., & Goldberg, L. L, "Influence of popular erotica on judgments of strangers and mates," *Journal of Experimental Social Psychology*, 1989; 25:159-167.
524. Kenrick, D. T., Montello, D. R., Gutierres, S. E., & Trost, M. R., "Effects of physical attractiveness on affect and perceptual judgments: When social comparison overrides social reinforcement," *Personality and Social Psychology Bulletin*, 1993: 19:195-199.
525. Marika Tiggemann and Julia K. Kuring, "The role of body objectification in disordered eating and depressed mood," *British Journal of Clinical Psychology*, September 2004; 43:299-311. Considerable evidence supports the theory of "body objectification," unattainable external norms (such as impossibly thin) contributing to the higher incidence of eating disorders and depression in women.
526. Stice, E., Review of the evidence for a sociocultural model of bulimia nervosa and an exploration of the mechanisms of action," *Clinical Psychology Review*, 1994; 14(7):633-661.
527. Hudson JI, Hiripi E, Pope HG Jr, Kessler RC., "The prevalence and correlates of eating disorders in the National Comorbidity Survey Replication," *Biological Psychiatry*, February 1, 2007; 61(3):348-58, Table 3. Odds of suffering anorexia during one's life was double for those aged 18-29 compared with 60 plus years, but did not reach statistical significance. The bulimia data is statistically significant.
528. Fleming-Morn M, Thiagarajah K, "Behavioral interventions and the role of television in the growing epidemic of adolescent obesity—data from the 2001 youth risk behavioral survey," *Methods of Information in Medicine*, 2005; 44:303–309.
529. Overlan, L., "Overweight girls at risk," *Newton Tab*, July 2, 1996, page 15.
530. Jean Kilbourne, "The More You Subtract, the More You Add: Cutting Girls Down to Size," Chapter 14, in Tim Kasser and Allen Kanner, Eds, *Psychology & Consumer Culture: The Struggle for a Good Life in a Materialistic World*, APA Press in October, 2003, in publication.
531. Brenda Goodman, "Stop That Treadmill," *Psychology Today*, May-June, 2004; 37(3):15.
532. Greenfield, 2002. Source for Mary Cady and Sara quotes.

533. U.S. Census Bureau, *Statistical Abstract of the United States: 2000*, Tables 17, 722, 909, 910, 911, 931, 932, 937, *Statistical Abstract 2001*, Tables 1125, 1126, in . . . Comments of the Consumer Federation of America and Consumers Union before the Federal Communication Commission, January, 2, 2003, http://www.consumersunion.org/pdf/CFA-CU-jan202.pdf. Adult hours per year spent watching network plus cable TV is 1,495, newspapers, 152.

534. Putnam, 2000, pages 222-223.

535. Joy, L. A., Kimball, M. M., & Zabrack, M. L., "Television and children's aggressive behavior," in Tannis MacBeth Williams (Ed.), *The Impact of Television: A Natural Experiment in Three Communities*, New York: Academic Press, 1986, pages 303-360.

536. Dafna Lemish, "The school as a wrestling arena: The modeling of a television series," *Communication: European Journal of Communication Research*, 1997; 22(4):395-418.

537. Becker AE, Burwell RA, Gilman SE, Herzog DB, and Hamburg P, "Eating behaviours and attitudes following prolonged exposure to television among ethnic Fijian adolescent girls," *British Journal of Psychiatry*, 2002; 180:509–514.

538. Cathy Scott-Clark and Adrian Levy, "Fast forward into trouble," *The Guardian*, June 14, 2003. "Bhutan, The Last Place," *Frontline World*, May, 2002, http://www.pbs.org/frontlineworld/stories/bhutan/index.html.

539. Kubey, Robert & Csikszentmihalyi, Mihaly, "Television Addiction Is No Mere Metaphor," *Scientific American*, February, 2002; 286(2):74-80.

540. Sirgy, M.J., Lee, D., Kosenko, R., Meadow, H.L., Rahtz, D., Cicic, M., Jin, G.X., Yarsuvat, D., Blenkhorn, D.L., and Wright, N., "Does television viewership play a role in perception of quality of life?" *Journal of Advertising*, 1998; 27:125-142.

541. O'Guinn, Thomas C. and L J. Shrum, "The Role of Television in the Construction of Consumer Social Reality." *Journal of Consumer Research*, March, 1997; 23(4):278-294.

542. Shrum, L. J., James E. Burroughs and Aric Rindfleisch, "Television's Cultivation of Material Values," *Journal of Consumer Research*, 2005; 32(3):473-9. Heavy viewers enjoyed a low materialist program (*Gorillas in the Mist*) as much as they did a high materialist program (*Wall Street*), showing that content quality did not explain the link between heavy TV viewing and materialism.

543. Personal communication, March 18, 2005.

544. Leif D. Nelson and Michael I. Norton, "From student to superhero: Situational primes shape future helping," *Journal of Experimental Social Psychology*, July 2005; 41(4):423-430.

545. Personal communication with Andrew Grabois, Senior Director, Publisher Relations & Content Development, R.R. Bowker Co.

546. David Waterman, "CBS-Viacom and the Effects of Media Mergers: An Economic Perspective," *Federal Communications Law Journal*, 2000; 53:531.

547. Comments of the Consumer Federation of America and Consumers Union before the Federal Communication Commission, January 2, 2003, http://www.consumersunion.org/pdf/CFA-CU-jan202.pdf.Lydia Saad, "Local TV Is No. 1 Source of News for Americans," *Gallup News Service*, January 5, 2007. Our daily news sources are: local TV for 55 percent of us, local newspaper for 44 percent, network TV news for 35 percent, cable TV news 34 percent, public TV news 28, Internet 22 percent, talk radio 20 percent.

548. Andrew Keen, *The Cult of the Amateur: how today's internet is killing our culture and assaulting our economy*, 2007, London: Nicholas Brealey Publishing.

549. *Fortune.com*, "The 2006 Global 500," http://www.finfacts.ie/Private/curency/fortune500.htm and from company 2006 filings. Rankings and media gross revenues in billions: Time Warner #122, $43.7b; Walt Disney #180, $31.9b; News Corp #256, $23.9b; Bertelsmann #287, $22.2b; Sony #362, $17.9b; NBC Universal #414, $16.2b; CBS Corporation #468, $14.3b; Vivendi >#500, $12.0b. Sony and Vivendi gross revenues are entertainment/media only. Rankings for Sony, NBC and Vivendi are if the entertainment/media operations were stand alone firms. Another dozen American firms, such as Hearst, New York Times Company, the Washington Post Company, Cox, Advance, Tribune Company, Clear Channel

and Gannett, with gross revenues of $2 to $8 billion are involved in two to three media sectors. Thus, under two dozen firms control most media content and distribution..

550. Project for Excellence in Journalism, "The State of the News Media 2004," March 14, 2004, http://www.stateofthenewsmedia.org/index.asp.

551. Richard Tait, "Diller a Critic of Relaxing Rules," *Financial Times*, May 5, 2003; and, *Reuters*, October 22, 2003.

552. John Nichols and Robert W. McChesney, "FCC: Public Be Damned," *The Nation*, May 15, 2003.

553. Ted Turner, "My Beef With Big Media: How government protects big media–and shuts out upstarts like me," *Washington Monthly*, July/August, 2004.

554. FCC Commissioner Michael J Copps, Jan 22, 2003, Remarks to NATPE Family Programming Forum

555. "O'Reilly Factor," Friday January 17, 2003.

556. Maureen Orth, *The Importance of Being Famous*, New York: Henry Holt, 2004, page 2, 7-9.

557. Dana Rohinsky, "Will Peterson Get Off Scott-Free?" *Fox News*, June 10, 2004.

558. As of March 1, 2005.

559. Orth, page 21.

560. Bureau of Economic Analysis, "U.S. International Services: Cross-Border Trade 1986-2006, and Sales Through Affiliates, 1986-2005," Table 1, Trade in Services, 1992-2006, http://www.bea.gov/international/xls/tab1b.xls (for 2005 film and television tape rental exports);Table5.1,OtherPrivateServices,1989,http://www.bea.gov/international/xls/tab5a.xls (for 1989 film and television tape rental receipts); Table 10.17, Sales of Services to Foreign Persons by U.S. MNCs Through Their Nonbank MOFAs, Industry of Affiliate by Country of Affiliate, 2005, http://www.bea.gov/international/xls/tab10b.xls (for 2005 delivery by U.S. foreign affiliates for foreign markets of motion picture and video industries). Table 10.1, Sales of Services to Foreign Persons by U.S. MNC's Through Their Nonbank MOFA's, SIC-Based Industry of Affiliate by Country of Affiliate, 1989, http://www.bea.gov/international/xls/tab10a.xls (for 1989 delivery by U.S. foreign affiliates for foreign markets of motion pictures, including television tape and film); We can get a rough idea as to growth in U.S. "exports" of commercial culture to foreign markets by combining direct exports and delivery by foreign affiliates to foreign markets of film and video. The sales by affiliates data and the export data are not entirely comparable because sales by affiliates may include activity such as financing, consulting, etc, reported by entities whose business is categorized as film and video. 1989 data adjusted to 2005 dollars using BEA's GDP price deflator. Other commercial culture "exports" for which comparable data is not reported include sound recording, newspapers, periodicals, books, broadcasting, cable and program distribution, arts, and entertainment.

561. Federal Communications Commission, "Notice of Apparent Liability for Forfeiture," September 22, 2004. Toby Forage, "Janet & Justin get hot," news.com.au, February 2, 2004.

562. Margaret H DeFleur and Melvin L. DeFleur, "The Next Generation's Image of Americans: Attitudes and Beliefs Held by Teen-Agers in Twelve Countries," College of Communications, Boston University, unpublished report, September, 2002, http://www.bu.edu/news/releases/2002/defleur/report.pdf. The 12 nations surveyed: Saudi Arabia, Bahrain, South Korea, Mexico, China, Spain, Taiwan, the Dominican Republic, Pakistan, Nigeria, Italy, and Argentina.

563. Sheera Frenkel, "Negative Perceptions Prevail - Study Finds Foreign Teenagers Harbor Anti-American Sentiment," *The Student Underground* (Boston University), November 1, 2002, quoting Margaret and Melvin DeFleur.

564. Thomas E Patterson, "Doing Well and Doing Good: How Soft News and Critical Journalism Are Shrinking the News Audience and Weakening Democracy and What News Outlets Can Do About It," John F Kennedy School of Government, 2000, http://www.ksg.harvard.edu/presspol/publications/pdfs/softnews.pdf. Constance Holden, "Science Off the Air," *Science*, March 28, 2008; 319:1741.

565. The Center for Media and Public Affairs, "Network News Focus: Flubs, Fluff—Not Functional," February 9, 2004, http://www.cmpa.com/pressrel/EW200403.htm.

566. Center for Media and Public Affairs, "The Incredible Shrinking Sound Bite: Network Election News Study Finds Decline in Candidate Airtime," September 20, 2000, http://www.cmpa.com/pressrel/electpr5.htm, citing Kiku Adatto, "Soundbite Democracy: Network Evening News Presidential Campaign Coverage, 1968 and 1988," Research Paper R-2, Joan Shorenstein Barone Center for Press, Politics, and Public Policy, June 1990.

567. Norman Lear Center, "Political Ads Dominate Local TV News Coverage," Lear Center Local News Archive, November 1, 2002; and, Norman Lear Center, "Over Half of Local News Broadcasts Ignored 2002 Midterm Election Campaigns," July 23, 2003.

568. Project for Excellence in Journalism, "The Invisible Primary-Invisible No Longer: A First Look at Coverage of the 2008 Presidential Campaign," October 29, 2007, http://www.journalism.org/node/8187.

569. Robert Morlino, "Broadcast Lobbying Tops $222 Million," The Center for Public Integrity, October 28, 2004. The exact total is $248.9 million.

570. "Self Censorship: How Often and Why; Journalists Avoiding The News," The Pew Research Center for the People and the Press, April 30, 2000, http://people-press.org/reports/display.php3?ReportID=39.

571. Sacred Heart University Polling Institute, "New Poll Probes Questions on Trusting the Media," March 11, 2003.

572. Mark Gillespie, "Public Remains Skeptical of News Media: Majority of Americans believe news organizations often get facts wrong," *Gallup News Service*, May 30, 2003. Sixty-eight percent of self-described conservatives and 61 percent of liberals believe the media is often inaccurate. Trust in media rises sharply as education levels increase.

573. Project for Excellence in Journalism, "The State of the News Media 2004," March 14, 2004, http://www.stateofthenewsmedia.org/index.asp.

574. Karl Idsvoog, "Let's Blow Up Our Brand: The Dangerous Court of Today's Broadcast Newsrooms," in Kristina Borjesson, Ed, *Into the Buzzsaw*, Amherst, New York: Promethius Books, 2002, pages 248-249.

575. Insite Media Research, 2000, http://www.tvsurveys.com/billofrites/summary.htm.

576. "The State of the News Media 2004," The Pew Research Center for the People and the Press, May 23, 2004, http://www.stateofthenewsmedia.org/prc.pdf

577. Mary Lenz, "Cronkite, Moyers share views on journalism, democracy," On Campus at UT Austin, October 12, 1999; 27(3).

578. David Croteau and William Hoynes, *The Business of Media: Corporate Media and the Public Interest*, Thousand Oaks, CA, Pine Forge Press 2001.

579. Personal communication, November 1, 2006.

580. Project for Excellence in Journalism, "The State of the News Media 2004," March 14, 2004, http://www.stateofthenewsmedia.org/index.asp.

581. Jack Fuller, "Journalism at the Millennium," speech delivered to the Committee of Concerned Journalists, November 6, 1997, Northwestern University, Chicago, IL.

582. Ilya Somin, "When Ignorance Isn't Bliss: How Political Ignorance Threatens Democracy," *Cato Institute*, September 22, 2004, http://www.cato.org/pubs/pas/pa525.pdf.

583. Todd Gitlin, *Media Unlimited: How the Torrent of Images and Sounds Overwhelms Our Lives*, 2001, New York: Henry Holt and Company, page 15.

584. Comstock GC, Strasburger VC., "Media violence: Q & A," *Adolescent Medicine*, 1993; 4:495-509.

585. Brandon Centerwall, "Television and violence: the scale of the problem and where to go from here," *Journal of the American Medical Association*, June 10, 1992; 267(22):3059-3063.

586. Stephen J. Kirsh, *Children, Adolescents, and Media Violence: A Critical Look at the Research*, 2006, Thousand Oaks, CA: Sage Publications, pages 273-287. Craig A. Anderson, *et al*, "The Influence of Media Violence on Youth," *Psychological Science in the Public Interest*, December, 2003; 4(3):81-110, http://www.psychologicalscience.org/pdf/pspi/pspi43.pdf.

George Comstock and Erica Scharrer, "Meta-Analyzing the Controversy over Television Violence and Aggression," in Douglas A. Gentile, ed, *Media Violence and Children*, 2003, Westport: Praeger, pages 205-226. The best-yet meta-studies peg the effect-size relationship between media violence and real-world aggression and aggressive behavior, respectively, at .31 for TV and movies, .26 for video games, medium strength effects. For TV violence and actual interpersonal violence, the low range of effect sizes across several studies run from .15 to .20, small, but statistically significant, and larger than the effects of broken homes or abusive parents on violence. Squaring the effect sizes yields a variance range of about 2 to 4 percent, the portion of actual interpersonal violence explained by exposure to violent media.

587.   Hugh Richard Waters, Adnan Ali Hyder, Yogesh Rajkotia, Suprotik Basu, Alexander Butchart, "The costs of interpersonal violence—an international review," *Health Policy*, 2005; 73:303–315. A more detailed document from World Health Organization: http://whqlibdoc.who.int/publications/2004/9241591609.pdf. Data is given in 2007 dollars relative to the 2007 GDP.

588.   Brad J. Bushman and Craig A. Anderson, "Media Violence and the American Public: Scientific Facts Versus Media Misinformation," *American Psychologist*, June/July, 2001; 56(6/7):477-489.

589.   Rick Brooks and Chard Terhune, "Holiday Horror: The Mall Can Be A Dangerous Place," *The Wall Street Journal*, December 19, 2003, page A1; Alicia Caldwell, "Blitz sale floors woman," *The Orlando Sentinel*, November 28, 2003; and, "Trampled Shopper Has History of Injury Claims Against Stores," *Associated Press*, December 7, 2003.

590.   Laurie   A   Duncan,   "$50   iBooks   Cause   Stampede!"   tuaw.com, http://www.tuaw.com/2005/08/16/50-ibooks-cause-stampede. "Mob Scene, Several Hurt in Rush for Cheap Laptops," *NBC12News.com*, August 16, 2005.

591.   Peter Svensson, "Violence Mars PlayStation 3 Launch," *Associated Press*, November 18, 2006.

592.   David Myers, *The American Paradox, Spiritual Hunger in the Age of Plenty*, New Haven: Yale University Press, 2000. The concept for the juxtaposed income and social health data is Meyers'.

593.   U.S. Census Bureau, "Historical Income Tables," Table H-5, Race and Hispanic Origin of Householder - Households by Median and Mean Income: 1967 to 2006, All Races, 2006 Dollars, http://www.census.gov/hhes/www/income/histinc/h05.html. Other than for recessionary hiccups, personal incomes have increased continuously over this time period, but at a slower rate.

594.   Author's analysis and fitted trend lines of DDB Needham Lifestyle Survey data responses. Chart shows the average percent responding "generally agree" plus "definitely agree" to two questions, "If I had my life to live over, I would sure do things differently," and "I wish I could leave my present life and do something entirely different." Male trend line R^2 = .78; Female trend line R^2 = .82. Average survey sample size 2,664 responses per year. Database courtesy of Robert D. Putnam and Chris Calhoun of DDB Needham.

595.   University of Chicago, General Social Surveys, 1972-2006, Cumulative File, July 23, 2007, http://sda.berkeley.edu/D3/GSS06/Docyr/gs06.htm. Author's analysis and fitted trend line. Trend line R^2 = .28. Average survey sample size 1,860 responses per year surveyed. General Happiness, Question 157: "Taken all together, how would you say things are these days–would you say that you are very happy, pretty happy, or not too happy?"

596.   Well-known happiness researcher Ed Diener, who has published over fifty papers, books and book chapters on the subject, reports that "subjective well being," is relatively high in the United States and in other individualistic nations, although depression and suicide rates are higher. Diener thinks that the spectrum of happiness versus unhappiness is greater in individualistic versus collectivist nations. See Ed Diener's web site, http://www.psych.uiuc.edu/~ediener/faq.html.

597.   MTV Networks International, "Wellbeing Study Reveals Fascinating Insights into Global Culture: Telling a Tale of Two Worlds for Kids and Youth," November 20, 2006. Yang

Yang, "Social Inequalities in Happiness in the United States, 1972 to 2004: An Age-Period-Cohort Analysis," *American Sociological Review*, April, 2008; 73(2):204-226. These results differ from mine, particularly the author's reported uptrend in happiness since 1995, as a result of the complex statistical procedures used in this study, particularly the author's adjustments for compositional or cohort demographic changes in younger generations. Quote sources: "With Age Comes Happiness, Sociological Study Shows," American Sociological Association, April 16, 2008. Lindsey Tanner, "Survey of 28,000 Americans of All Ages Finds Elderly the Happiest," *Associated Press*, April 19, 2008.

598. Chart data: The National Commission on Civic Renewal, "Hopeful Signs in America's Civic Health," September 27, 1999, page 6. The Index of National Civic Health (INCH) was created by The National Commission on Civic Renewal, co-chaired by William Bennett and former Senator Sam Nunn and was discontinued in 1997. The National Conference on Citizenship, "America's Civic Health Index: Broken Engagement," September 18, 2006, http://www.ncoc.net/conferences/2006civichealth.pdf. The newer Index of Civic Health is an ongoing project of the National Conference on Citizenship. I have used the 37 measure Civic Health Index dataset, without three "controversial measures" (online chat activity and two indicators of political knowledge) considered by project authors and statisticians as not reflective of any trend to improving civic health. In personal communications in 2003 and 2007, Peter Levine, Director, of the Center for Information & Research on Civic Learning & Engagement at the University of Maryland and statistician for both indices, explained to me that the INCH uptrend during 1994-1997 is the illusory result of a change in the way the political participation survey questions were asked. He provided me data showing a continuation of the political participation downtrend through 2000. He told me that, while the methodologies of the two indices are different, my chart presents a valid comparison.

599. Marque-Luisa Miringoff and Sandra Opdycke, "The Index of Social Health of the United States, 1970-2005," Institute for Innovation in Social Policy, undated, http://iisp.vassar.edu/ish.html. Indicators worsening since the 1970s are: child poverty, child abuse, teen suicide, unemployment, average weekly wages, health insurance coverage, elderly out-of-pocket health costs, food stamp coverage, affordable housing, and income inequality. Six indicators have improved since 1970: infant mortality, teen drug abuse, elderly poverty, homicides, alcohol-related traffic fatalities.

600. Gregg Scott, Joseph Ciarrochi & Frank Deane, "The Increasing Incidence of Suicide: Economic Development, Individualism and Social Integration," in The Erosion of the Social Link in the Economically Advanced Countries, Patrick Hunout et al, *The International Scope Review*, 2003; 5:9.

601. Robert D Putnam, *Bowling Alone: The Collapse and Revival of American Community*, New York: Simon & Schuster (Touchstone), 2000 (2001).

602. Personal communication, Tom Sander, September 17, 2003. Saguaro data also shows a more enduring upturn in one item, volunteering by 18-25 year olds, but without increases in other types civic engagement among this cohort. http://www.ksg.harvard.edu/saguaro

603. Lawrence Kaplan, "American Idle," *The New Republic*, September 12, 2005, page 22.

604. Department of Defense, "Numeric Goals and Achievement," December 31, 2006, http://www.defenselink.mil/prhome/docs/numgoals06.pdf. "DOD Needs to Establish Objectives and Measures to Better Evaluate Advertising's Effectiveness," Government Accounting Office, September, 2003, http://www.gao.gov/new.items/d031005.pdf.

605. Robert Burns, "Army Has Record Low Level of Recruits," *Associated Press*, October 31, 2007.

606. Jeffrey M Jones, "Low Trust in Federal Government Rivals Watergate Era Levels," *Gallup News Service*, September 26, 2007.

607. FBI, "Preliminary Annual Uniform Crime Report, 2006," December 18, 2006, http://www.fbi.gov/ucr/prelim06/.

608. Putnam, page 403.

609. Francis Fukuyama, *The Great Disruption: Human Nature and the Reconstitution of Social Order*, New York: Simon & Schuster, 1999, page 15.
610. Francis Fukuyama, *Trust*, New York: Free Press, 1995.
611. Philip K. Howard, *The Death of Common Sense: How Law Is Suffocating America*, New York: Random House, 1994.
612. Putnam, 2001, page 283.
613. Russell J. Dalton, "The Social Transformation of Trust in Government," *International Review of Sociology*, March, 2005; 15(1):133-154, Figures 2 and 3. Data from 1958-2000 American National Election Studies.
614. Miller McPherson Lynn Smith-Lovin and Matthew E. Brashears, "Social Isolation in America: Changes in Core Discussion Networks over Two Decades," *American Sociological Review*, June, 2006; 71(3):353-75, http://www.asanet.org/galleries/default-file/June06ASRFeature.pdf.
615. Lew Feldstein, remarks to the New Hampshire legislature, November 8, 2007.
616. Gulnar Nugman, Heritage Foundation, http://www.divorcereform.org/gul.html. The U.S. divorce rate is exceeded only by that Russia, Belarus, Guam and the Maldives. Paul Amato, Alan Booth, David Johnson, and Stacy Rogers, *Alone Together: How Marriage in America Is Changing*, Cambridge: Harvard University Press, 2007. The decline in social interaction between spouses between 1980 and 2000 is about one-third of a standard deviation, considered a "moderately strong" effect. The authors (Table 3) also found this effect not related to generational change and within every age group.
617. Bureau of the Census, "Current Population Survey, 2005: Annual Social and Economic Supplement," http://www.census.gov/population/socdemo/hh-fam/cps2005.
618. CPS, 2005.
619. CPS, 2005.
620. Hamilton BE, Martin JA, Ventura SJ., "Births: Preliminary data for 2005, National vital statistics reports," National Center for Health Statistics, December 28, 2006, 55(11). Barbara Dafoe Whitehead and David Popenoe, "The State of Our Unions: The Social Health of Marriage in America," July, 2006, Figure 12, http://marriage.rutgers.edu/Publications/Print/PrintSOOU2006.htm.
621. U.S. Census Bureau, "Current Population Survey Reports, Table H1. Percent Childless and Births per 1,000 Women in the Last Year: Selected Years, 1976 to Present," October 23, 2003. U.S. Census Bureau, "Fertility of American Women: June 2004," December, 2005.
622. U.S. Census Bureau, The 2007 Statistical Abstract, "Table 585. Labor Force Participation Rates for Wives, Husband Present by Age of Own Youngest Child: 1975 to 2005."
623. Whitehead and Popenoe, 2006, Figure 10.
624. Whitehead and Popenoe, 2006, page 25.
625. David Popenoe and Barbara Dafoe Whitehead, "The State of Our Unions 2005," The National Marriage Project, July, 2005, http://marriage.rutgers.edu/publicat.htm, page 22.
626. Whitehead and Popenoe, 2006, Figure 5. This measure of the divorce rate peaked in 1980 at 22.6/1,000 married women.
627. Whitehead and Popenoe, 2006, Figure 1.
628. Whitehead and Popenoe, 2006, Figure 8. Hamilton BE, Martin JA, Ventura SJ., "Births: Preliminary data for 2005, National vital statistics reports," National Center for Health Statistics, December 28, 2006, 55(11).
629. U.S. Census Bureau, "Families and Living Arrangements, Table FM-3. Average Number of Own Children Under 18 Per Family, By Type of Family," March 27, 2007.
630. Jean M Twenge, W. Keith Campbell, Craig A Foster, "Parenthood and Marital Satisfaction: A Meta-Analytic Review," *Journal of Marriage and Family*, August, 2003; 65(3):574–83. This definitive study brings together data from 148 previous studies on marital satisfaction ranging back into the 1950s.
631. Ranae J. Evenson and Robin W. Simon, "Clarifying the Relationship Between Parenthood and Depression," *Journal of Health and Social Behavior*, December, 2005; 46:341–58.
632. Robert Roy Britt, "Kids are Depressing, Study of Parents Finds," *LiveScience.com*, February 7, 2006.

633. Barbara Dafoe Whitehead and David Popenoe, "The State of Our Unions: The Social Health of Marriage in America," July, 2006, http://marriage.rutgers.edu/Publications/Print/PrintSOOU2006.htm.

634. Rachel Caspari and Sang-Hee Lee, "Older age becomes common late in human evolution," *Proceedings of the National Academy of Sciences of the USA*, July 27, 2004; 101(30): 10895–10900.

635. Martin E.P. Seligman, Elaine F. Walker and David L. Rosenhan, *Abnormal Psychology*, Fourth Edition, New York: W.W. Norton, 2001, page 258.

636. E. Fuller Torrey and Judy Miller, *The Invisible Plague: The Rise of Mental Illness from 1750 to the Present*, Rutgers University Press, 2002.

637. Ronald C. Kessler, Patricia Berglund, Olga Demler, Robert Jin, Kathleen R. Merikangas, Ellen E. Walters, "Lifetime Prevalence and Age-of-Onset Distributions of *DSM-IV* Disorders in the National Comorbidity Survey Replication," *Archives of General Psychiatry*, June, 2005; 62:593-602, Tables 3 and 4. The authors acknowledge risk of methodological error in their age cohort versus lifetime risk estimates, but are certain that prevalence of mental illness has increased for more recent generations.

638. Jerome C. Wakefield, Mark F. Schmitz, Michael B. First, Allan V. Horwitz, "Extending the Bereavement Exclusion for Major Depression to Other Losses: Evidence From the National Comorbidity Survey," *Archives of General Psychiatry*, April, 2007; 64(4):433-40. The authors reviewed the NIH survey data generating the seven times increase in major depression. They found that reaction to normal grief resulting from events such as job loss or divorce may account for 25 percent or more of major depression diagnoses. If this is so, depression prevalence would still have increased five times among those born after 1969.

639. Jean Twenge, "Birth Cohort, Social Change and Personality: The Interplay of Dysphoria and Individualism in the 20th Century," in Daniel Cervone and Walter Mischel, eds., *Advances in Personality Science*, New York: Guilford Press, 2002, pages 196-218. Twenge, J. M., "The age of anxiety? Birth cohort change in anxiety and neuroticism, 1952-1993," *Journal of Personality and Social Psychology*, December, 2000; 79: 1007-1021. Twenge found an anxiety increase of over one standard deviation over the study period.

640. Twenge, J. M., Zhang, L., & Im, C., "It's beyond my control: A cross-temporal meta-analysis of increasing externality in locus of control, 1960-2002," *Personality and Social Psychology Review*, 2004; 8:308-319.

641. Ronald C. Kessler, Patricia Berglund, Olga Demler, Robert Jin, Kathleen R. Merikangas, Ellen E. Walters, "Lifetime Prevalence and Age-of-Onset Distributions of *DSM-IV* Disorders in the National Comorbidity Survey Replication," *Archives of General Psychiatry*, June, 2005; 62:593-602, Table 3. Ronald C. Kessler, Wai Tat Chiu, Olga Demler, Ellen E. Walters, "Prevalence, Severity, and Comorbidity of 12-Month *DSM-IV* Disorders in the National Comorbidity Survey Replication," *Archives of General Psychiatry*, June, 2005; 62:617-627, Table 1. Mood disorders include: depression (major depressive disorder), dysthymia, and bipolar disorder.

642. Susan Landers, "Depression cited as the top cause of medical disability," *AMNews*, April 2, 2007.

643. Allan V. Horwitz and Jerome C. Wakefield, *The Loss of Sadness: How Psychiatry Transformed Normal Sorrow Into Depressive Disorder*, 2007, New York: Oxford University Press.

644. Personal communication with Dr. Ronald Kessler, November 28, 2007.

645. Koen Demyttenaere, etal, "Prevalence, Severity, and Unmet Need for Treatment of Mental Disorders in the World Health Organization World Mental Health Surveys," *Journal of the American Medical Association*, June 2, 2004; 291(21):2581-90, http://jama.ama-assn.org/cgi/content/full/291/21/2581. Data shown in the figure is prevalence of 12-Month World Mental Health-Composite International Diagnostic Interview/Diagnostic and Statistical Manual of Mental Disorders, Fourth Edition Disorders by Severity Across Countries. Total shown is taken from Table 3, the sum of serious and moderate 12-month prevalence. Schizophrenia not included. Sufferers of serious disorders were "out of role" for a at least 30 days; moderate sufferers, typically 9-19 days. China average of Beijing and Shanghai data.

646. Myran M. Weissman and Marc J. Gameroff, "Cross-National Epidemiology of Mood Disorders: An Update," 2002, unpublished study, www.pasteur.fr/applications/euroconf/ depression/weissman.pdf; and Kessler RC et al., "The epidemiology of major depressive disorder: Results from the National Comorbidity Survey Replication (NCS-R)," *Journal of the American Medical Association*, June 18, 2003; 289:3095-105.

647. George Brown, "Social Roles, Context and Evolution in the Origins of Depression," *Journal of Health and Social Behavior*, September, 2002; 43(3):255-276. See Figure 3 for cross-cultural data.

648. Bridget F. Grant; Frederick S. Stinson; Deborah S. Hasin; Deborah A. Dawson; S. Patricia Chou; Karyn Anderson, "Immigration and Lifetime Prevalence of *DSM-IV* Psychiatric Disorders Among Mexican Americans and Non-Hispanic Whites in the United States: Results From the National Epidemiologic Survey on Alcohol and Related Conditions," *Arch Gen Psychiatry*, Dec 2004; 61:1226-1233, Table 3.

649. Seligman, et al., 2001, page 257.

650. Jean-Paul Selten and Elizabeth Cantor-Graae, "Hypothesis: social defeat is a risk factor for schizophrenia?" *British Journal of Psychiatry*, December, 2007; 191(51):s9-s12.

651. Other than for women in some Arab countries where force-fed girls are considered more desirable wives.

652. Ben Schmitt, "The Sinking of the Ethan Allen: Tourists too much for boat to handle," *Detroit Free Press*, October 6, 2005.

653. National Center for Health Statistics, "Health, United States, 2006," Table 73, release date, April 5, 2006. Youfa Wang and May A. Beydoun, "The Obesity Epidemic in the United States—Gender, Age, Socioeconomic, Racial/Ethnic and Geographic Characteristics: A Systematic Review and Meta-Regression Analysis," *Epidemiologic Reviews*, May 17, 2007.

654. Juhee K, et al., "Trends in Overweight from 1980 through 2001 among Preschool-Aged Children Enrolled in a Health Maintenance Organization," *Obesity*, July, 2006; 14:1107-1112. The cause is probably overweight mothers and formula feeding rather than breast feeding.

655. Roland Sturm, "Increases in clinically severe obesity in the United States, 1986-2000," *Archives of Internal Medicine*, October, 2003; 163(18):2146-8.

656. Ramachandran S. Vasan; Michael J. Pencina; Mark Cobain; Matthew S. Freiberg; and Ralph B. D'Agostino, "Estimated Risks for Developing Obesity in the Framingham Heart Study," *Annals of Internal Medicine*, October 4, 2005; 143(7):473-480. The 80 percent estimate may be low because only whites are included in the study and other ethnic groups presently have higher rates of overweight or obesity.

657. Calle EE, Rodriguez C, Walker-Thurmond K, Thun MJ., "Overweight, obesity, and mortality from cancer in a prospectively studied cohort of U.S. adults," *New England Journal of Medicine*, April 24, 2003; 348(17):1625-38. Morbid obesity is characterized by a BMI or 40 or greater.

658. Adams, Kenneth F., Schatzkin, Arthur, Harris, Tamara B., Kipnis, Victor, Mouw, Traci, Ballard-Barbash, Rachel, Hollenbeck, Albert, Leitzmann, Michael F., "Overweight, Obesity, and Mortality in a Large Prospective Cohort of Persons 50 to 71 Years Old," *New England Journal of Medicine*, August 22, 2006; 355(8):763-78, http://content.nejm.org/cgi/reprint/NEJMoa055643v1.pdf.

659. Finkelstein EA, Fiebelkorn IC, Wang G., "National medical spending attributable to overweight and obesity: how much, and who's paying?" *Health Affairs*, May 14, 2003; W3:219-26.

660. Sturm R, Wells KB, "Does obesity contribute as much to morbidity and poverty or smoking?" *Public Health*, 2001; 115:229-295; and Sturm R, "The effects of obesity, smoking, and problem drinking on chronic medical problems and health care costs," *Health Affairs*, 2002; 21:245-253, both cited in, Kelly D. Brownell and Katherine Battle Norgen, *Food Fight: The Inside Story of the Food Industry, America's Obesity Crisis, and What We Can Do About It*, 2004, Chicago: Contemporary Books, pages 45-46.

661. Yale University Schools of Public Health and Medicine, "The Diabetes Epidemic: The Case for Changing Diabetes," November, 2005, page 17. Narayan, K.M., Gregg, E.W., Engelgau, M.M., et al. "Translation research for chronic disease: the case of diabetes," *Diabetes Care*, 2000; 23:1794-8.

662. Committee on Food Marketing and the Diets of Children and Youth, J. Michael McGinnis, Jennifer Appleton Gootman, Vivica I. Kraak, Editors, "Food Marketing to Children and Youth: Threat or Opportunity?" The National Academies Press, 2006. This 516 page review examined 123 studies, concluding that there is a strong link (not causality) between advertising and food preferences, short-term consumption and overweight/obesity for children aged 2-11. Licensed characters are used in half of food marketing to kids.

663. JD Wright, J Kennedy-Stephenson, CY Wang, MA McDowell, CL Johnson, " Trends in Intake of Energy and Macronutrients – United States, 1971-2000," National Center for Health Statistics, Centers for Disease Control and Prevention, February 6, 2004, http://www.cdc.gov/mmwr/preview/mmwrhtml/mm5304a3.htm. Men's caloric intake increased to 2,618 per day, women to 1,877 per day, most from increased carbohydrate and sugar consumption.

664. Alison Motluk, "Supersize surprise," *NewScientist*, November 4, 2006, pages 34-38.

665. Paula Caplan, "The pills that make us fat," *NewScientist*, March 8, 2008, page 18.

666. Christakis NA, Fowler JH., "The spread of obesity in a large social network over 32 years," *New England Journal of Medicine*, July 26, 2007; 357(4):370-9.

667. Dallman MF, Pecoraro N, Akana SF, La Fleur SE, Gomez F, Houshyar H, Bell ME, Bhatnagar S, Laugero KD, Manalo S., "Chronic stress and obesity: a new view of 'comfort food,'" *Proceedings of the National Academy of Sciences*, 2003; 100(20):11696-701. K. Ramsayer, "Sweet Relief: Comfort food calms, with weighty effect," *Science News*, September 13, 2003, pages 165-166.

668. Kellie L. K. Tamashiro, Mary M. N. Nguyen, Michelle M. Ostrander, Stacy R. Gardner, Li Yun Ma, Stephen C. Woods, and Randall R. Sakai, "Social stress and recovery: implications for body weight and body composition," *American Journal of Physiology - Regulatory, Integrative and Comparative Physiology*, November, 2007; 293(5):R1864-R1874.

669. Wallis, D.J.; Hetherington, M.M., "Stress and eating: the effects of ego-threat and cognitive demand on food intake in restrained and emotional eaters," *Appetite*, August, 2004; 43(1):39-46.

670. Adina R. Lemeshow, Laurie Fisher, Elizabeth Goodman, Ichiro Kawachi, Catherine S. Berkey, and Graham A. Colditz, "Subjective Social Status in the School and Change in Adiposity in Female Adolescents: Findings From a Prospective Cohort Study," *Archives of Pediatric & Adolescent Medicine*, January 1, 2008; 162(1):23-28.

671. U.S. Department of Health and Human Services, Children's Bureau, "Child Maltreatment (1993, 1997, and 2002): Reports from the States to the National Child Abuse and Neglect Data System, 1993, 1999 and 2002," 2004, Washington, DC: U.S. Government Printing Office. U.S. Department of Health and Human Services, Administration on Children, Youth and Families, "Child Maltreatment 2005," 2007, Washington, DC: U.S. Government Printing Office, http://www.acf.hhs.gov/programs/cb/pubs/cm05/index.htm. Conversion with Dr. David Finkelhor, Director of the Crimes against Children Research Center at the University of New Hampshire.

672. Scher, Christine D.; Forde, David R.; McQuaid, John R.; Stein, Murray B., "Prevalence and demographic correlates of childhood maltreatment in an adult community sample," *Child Abuse & Neglect*, February, 2004; 28(2):167-180. Briere, John; Elliott, Diana M., "Prevalence and psychological sequelae of self-reported childhood physical and sexual abuse in a general population sample of men and women," *Child Abuse & Neglect*, October, 2003; 27(10):1205-1222.

673. Additional recent studies support very high abuse prevalence. A national survey found that of children aged 2-17, 53 percent had suffered a physical assault and 8 percent a sexual victimization during the prior year. Source: David Finkelhor, Sherry L. Hamby, Richard Ormrod and Heather Turner, "The Juvenile Victimization Questionnaire: Reliability,

validity, and national norms," *Child Abuse & Neglect*, April, 2005; 29(4):383-412. In another random survey of children 2-17, 71 percent suffered abuse or victimization in the past year. Source: Finkelhor D, Ormrod R, Turner H, Hamby SL., "The victimization of children and youth: a comprehensive, national survey," *Child Maltreatment*, February, 10, 2005; 10(1):5-25. These studies are both self-report.

674. Maxia Dong, et al., "The interrelatedness of multiple forms of childhood abuse, neglect, and household dysfunction," *Child Abuse & Neglect*, 2004; 28(7):771-84, Table 1.

675. Molnar BE, Buka SL and Kessler RC, "Child sexual abuse and subsequent psychopathology: results from the National Comorbidity Survey," *American Journal of Public Health*, May, 2001; 91(5):753-60.

676. U.S. Department of Health and Human Services, Administration for Children, National Center on Child Abuse and Neglect, "Third National Incidence Study of Child Abuse and Neglect," September, 1996.

677. Black, D. A., Heyman, R. E., & Smith Slep, A. M., "Risk factors for child physical abuse," *Aggression and Violent Behavior*, 2001; 6:121-188. Heyman, R.E. & Smith Slep, A.M., "Risk factors for family violence: Introduction to the special series," *Aggression and Violent Behavior*, 2001; 6:115-119. Schumaker, J.A.; Smith Slep, A.M., & Heyman, R.E., "Risk factors for child neglect," *Aggression and Violent Behavior*, 2001; 6:231-254. Michelle D. DiLauro, "Psychosocial Factors Associated with Types of Child Maltreatment," *Child Welfare*, January-February, 2004; 83(1):69-99. High frequency of residential moves association with child abuse found in abstract of Maxia Dong, et al paper in Am J Epidemiology, June 2004. McLloyd, V.C., "Socioeconomic disadvantage and child development," *American Psychologist*, February, 1998; 53:185-204. Conger RD, Ge X, Elder GH Jr, Lorenz FO, Simons RL, "Economic stress, coercive family process, and developmental problems of adolescents," *Child Development*, April, 1994; 65(2):541-61. Poverty has no statistical effect on child emotional development when a low stress environment and high-quality parenting is available. Poverty, however, is often tightly linked with stressors.

678. Andrea Danese, Carmine M. Pariante, Avshalom Caspi, Alan Taylor, and Richie Poulton, "Childhood maltreatment predicts adult inflammation in a life-course study," *Proceedings of the National Academy of Sciences*, January 23, 2007; 104(4):1319-24. The sixty percent greater risk is after statistically removing other potentially explanatory factors, such as low IQ, low childhood social status, adult level of stress, etc. Maltreated children are the 9 percent of the 1,037 children studied suffering the greatest number of abuse and maltreatment experiences during their first decade of life. Sandra Steingraber, "The Falling Age of Puberty in U.S. Girls: What We Know, What We Need to Know," Breast Cancer Fund, August, 2007. Kotch JB, Lewis T, Hussey JM, English D, Thompson R, Litrownik AJ, Runyan DK, Bangdiwala SI, Margolis B, Dubowitz, H, "Importance of early neglect for childhood aggression," *Pediatrics*, April, 2008; 121(4):725-31. Aggressive behaviors included arguing, fighting, bullying, threatening others, destroying property, and cruelty.

679. Vythilingam M, Heim C, Newport J, Miller AH, Anderson E, Bronen R, Brummer M, Staib L, Vermetten E, Charney DS, Nemeroff CB, Bremner JD., "Childhood trauma associated with smaller hippocampal volume in women with major depression," *American Journal of Psychiatry*, December, 2002; 159(12):2072-80.

680. Bruce McEwen, "Glucocorticoids, depression, and mood disorders: structural remodeling in the brain," *Metabolism*, May, 2003; 54(5 Supplement 1):20-3.

681. Martin Teicher, et al., "The neurobiological consequences of early stress and childhood maltreatment," *Neuroscience & Biobehavioral Reviews*, January, 2003; 27(1-2):33-44. Martin Teicher, et al., "Childhood neglect is associated with reduced corpus callosum area," *Biological Psychiatry*, July, 2004; 56(2):80-85. Martin Teicher, "Scars That Won't Heal: The Neurobiology of Child Abuse," *Scientific American*, March, 2002; 286(3):68-65. Where not otherwise noted in this section on the relationship between brain structure and function and child abuse, Dr. Teicher's work is the source.

682. Weaver IC, Cervoni N, Champagne FA, D'Alessio AC, Sharma S, Seckl JR, Dymov S, Szyf M, Meaney MJ., "Epigenetic programming by maternal behavior," *Nature Neuroscience*, August, 2004; 7(8):847-54.

683. Frances A Champagne and James P Curley, "How social experiences influence the brain," *Current Opinion in Neurobiology*, December, 2005; 15:704-709. Champagne F, Francis D, Mar A, Meaney M., " Variations in maternal care in the rat as a mediating influence for the effects of environment on development," *Physiology & Behavior*, August, 2003; 79:359-371. Weaver A, Richardson R, Worlein J, De Waal F, Laudenslager M., "Response to social challenge in young bonnet (Macaca radiata) and pigtail (Macaca nemestrina) macaques is related to early maternal experiences," *American Journal of Primatology*, 2004; 62:243-259.

684. Zhang TY, Bagot R, Parent C, Nesbitt C, Bredy TW, Caldji C, Fish E, Anisman H, Szyf M, Meaney MJ, "Maternal programming of defensive responses through sustained effects on gene expression," *Biological Psychology*, July, 2006; 73(1):72-89.

685. Joyce A. Martin, Brady E. Hamilton, Paul D. Sutton, Stephanie J. Ventura, Fay Menacker, and Martha L. Munson, "Births: Final Data for 2003," National Vital Statistics Reports, September 8, 2005, 54(2), Tables 4, 20. Hamilton BE, Martin JA, Ventura SJ., "Births: Preliminary data for 2005," National Vital Statistics Reports, National Center for Health Statistics, December 28, 2006, 55(11).

686. Abraham Reichenberg, Raz Gross, Mark Weiser, Michealine Bresnahan, Jeremy Silverman, Susan Harlap, Jonathan Rabinowitz, Cory Shulman, Dolores Malaspina, Gad Lubin, Haim Y. Knobler, Michael Davidson, Ezra Susser, "Advancing Paternal Age and Autism," *Archives of General Psychiatry*, September, 2006; 63:1026-1032. Malaspina, Dolores; Reichenberg, Avi; Weiser, Mark; Fennig, Shmuel; Davidson, Michael; Harlap, Susan; Wolitzky, Rachel; Rabinowitz, Jonathan; Susser, Ezra; Knobler, Haim Y., "Paternal age and intelligence: implications for age-related genomic changes in male germ cells," *Psychiatric Genetics*, June, 2005; 15(2):117-125.

687. Leonid Gavrilov and Georgeanne Patmios, March 30-April 1, 2006 presentation at the Population Association of America annual meeting, Los Angeles.

688. Adam D. Krauss, "Fewer running for local boards; more running away," *Foster's Daily Democrat*, July 29, 2006.

689. Robin Kowalski, "The Escalation of Incivility in Western Culture," in *The Erosion of the Social Link in the Economically Advanced Countries*, Patrick Hunout et al, *The International Scope Review*, 2003; 5:9.

690. Public Agenda, "Land of the Rude: Americans in New Survey Say Lack of Respect is Getting Worse," April 3, 2002, http://www.publicagenda.org/aboutpa/aboutpa3vv.htm.

691. Paul Spector, personal communication, November 16, 2007. Jacqueline Stenson, "Desk rage: Workers gone wild; Job stress fuels backstabbing, tirades, even assault," MSNBC, December 20, 2006.

692. Chuck Bennett, "Air Passengers' Fury Is All the Rage," *New York Post*, June 12, 2007.

693. Susan Carey, "Cranky Skies: Fliers Behave Badly Again As 9/11 Era Fades," *The Wall Street Journal*, September 12, 2007, page A1.

694. "Highway workers lament increase of human waste," *Associated Press*, December 16, 2003.

695. "Las Vegas Officials Worried About City's Foul Stench," *Associated Press*, May 24, 2004.

696. Tim Dahlberg, "Violence Plagues Youth Sports: Overbearing Parents Creating Dangerous Situations on the Field," *Associated Press*, June 4, 2001.

697. Kate Zernike, "Violent Crime Rising Sharply in Some Cities," *The New York Times*, February 12, 2006. www.sheriffs.org/docs/Violent_Crimes_Rising_Sharply.pdf.

698. Joshua Green, "The Bookie of Virtue," *Washington Monthly*, June, 2003.

699. John Sutherland, "Virtue is its own drawback: One pops pills. Another gambles. Another lets her mother die alone," *The Guardian*, October 20, 2003.

700. Jack Newfield, "Ralph Reed's Gamble," *The Nation*, June 24, 2004.

701. Peter Stone, "Ralph Reed's Other Cheek," *Mother Jones*, November/December, 2004, p18.

702. Frank York and Jan LaRue, *Protecting Your Child in an X-Rated World: What You Need to Know To Make a Difference*, Tyndale House Publishers, Wheaton, Illinois, 2002, page 179.

703. *Christianity Today*, "Leadership Survey," December 2001.

704. Chuck Neubauer and Abdon M. Pallasch, "Jackson's Protests Benefit His Family, Friends," *Chicago Sun-Times*, February 4, 2001, page 2.

705. Peter and Timothy Flaherty, *The First Lady: A Comprehensive View of Hillary Rodham Clinton*, Washington, DC: Vital Issues Press, 1996, Chapter 9.

706. Elizabeth Warren and Amelia Warren Tyagi, *The Two-Income Trap: Why Middle Class Mothers and Fathers Are Going Broke*, 2003, New York: Basic Books, pages 123-126. She was the only Senator not voting on the bill, being with her husband during his heart surgery.

707. Philip Shenon and Robert Pear, "As DeLay's Woes Mount, So Does Money," *The New York Times*, March 13, 2005.

708. David Willman, et al., "Stealth Merger: Drug Companies and Government Medical Research," *Los Angeles Times*, December 7, 2003.

709. David Willman, "Panel Challenges NIH Handling of Rules Violations: House members call disciplinary action tepid in the 'largest scandal' in agency history," *Los Angeles Times*, September 14, 2006. Jocelyn Kaiser, "House Panel Finds Fault With How NIH Handles Tissue Samples," *Science*, June 3, 2006; 312(5781), 1733. David Willman, "$508,050 From Pfizer, but No 'Outside Positions to Note'" *Los Angeles Times*, December 22, 2004.

710. Brian Martinson, Melissa Anderson and Raymond de Vries, "Scientists behaving badly," *Nature*, June 9, 2005; 435(7043):737-738.

711. Naila Moreira, "Soft Drinks as Top Calorie Culprit," *Science News*, June 18, 2005; 167(25).

712. Stanhope KL, Havel PJ., "Fructose consumption: potential mechanisms for its effects to increase visceral adiposity and induce dyslipidemia and insulin resistance," *Current Opinion in Lipidology*, February, 2008; 19(1):16-24. Heather Basciano , Lisa Federico and Khosrow Adeli, "Fructose, insulin resistance, and metabolic dyslipidemia," *Nutrition & Metabolism*, February 21, 2005; 2:5, http://www.nutritionandmetabolism.com/content/2/1/5. Lee S Gross, Li Li, Earl S Ford and Simin Liu, "Increased consumption of refined carbohydrates and the epidemic of type 2 diabetes in the United States: an ecologic assessment," *American Journal of Clinical Nutrition*, May, 2004; 79(5):774-779. Reported health risks are associated with fructose consumption at 17 percent of total calories. Soft drinks are now sweetened primarily with HFSC, which is about half fructose, placing American teen consumption at the established harm level.

713. "Tyco chief urged prison time for embezzler," *Associated Press*, January 1, 2003.

714. Kevin McCoy, "Kozlowski's fall from grace," *USA Today*, June 7, 2002.

715. Center for Responsive Politics, 2000 Election Cycle, accountant's contributions, www.opensecrets.org.

716. Arthur Levitt, *Take On the Street*, New York: Pantheon Books, 2002, pages 287-305; quote, page 128.

717. Ellen E. Schultz, "End Run: Companies Sue Union Retirees to Cut Promised Health Benefits," *The Wall Street Journal*, November 10, 2004, pages A1, A10 and A12.

718. Gretchen Morgenson, "Crisis Looms in Mortgages," *The New York Times*, March 11, 2007. Glenn R. Simpson, "Lender Lobbying Blitz Abetted Mortgage Mess," *The Wall Street Journal*, December 31, 2007, page A1.

719. Barton Biggs, "The New Kings Have No Clothes," *Newsweek International*, September 18, 2006.

720. "Officials Warn of Katrina Relief Web Scams", AP, September 13, 2005. Extrapolated through yearend 2007 as 2006 rate of $25 billion

721. Maggie Mulvihill and Dave Wedge, "Evacuees binge on Cape: Spend fed cash on booze, strippers," *Boston Herald*, October 18, 2005.

722. Maggie Haberman,"Feds: Phonies cleaned upon WTC aid,"*New York Daily News*,February 20, 2003, http://www.nydailynews.com/news/local/v-pfriendly/story/61086p-57094c.html.

723. Putnam, 2001, page 269.

724. David Callahan, *The Cheating Culture: Why More Americans Are Doing Wrong to Get Ahead*, New York: Harcourt, Inc., 2004, page 180.

725. "Nearly One in Three U.S. Adults in a Committed Relationship Has Lied to His or Her Partner About Spending Habits, New Survey Finds," Martindale-Hubell, October 11, 2005, http://www.martindale.com/xp/Martindale/About_Us/Media/archive/051011.xml.

726. Christopher Oster, "Insurance-Fraud Survey Confirms Industry Worries," *The Wall Street Journal*, February 12, 2003, page D2.

727. Wynia MK, Cummins DS, VanGeest JB, Wilson IB., "Physician manipulation of reimbursement rules for patients: between a rock and a hard place," *Journal of the American Medical Association*, April, 2000; 283(14):1858-65.

728. Athanasou, James A. and Olabisi, Olasehinde, "Male and female differences in self-report cheating," *Practical Assessment, Research & Evaluation*, 2002; 8(5), http://ericae.net/pare/getvn.asp?v=8&n=5.

729. Data: 2000 *Who's Whom Among American High School Students* cited in David Callahan, *The Cheating Culture: Why More Americans Are Doing Wrong to Get Ahead*, New York: Harcourt, Inc., 2004, page 204.

730. Anand Vaishnav and Peter Schworm, "MCAS cheating allegations seen as unsupported," *Boston Globe*, July 15, 2004.

731. Tovia Smith, "New Hampshire Split Over High School Cheating," *National Public Radio*, September 29, 2007.

732. Internal Revenue Service, "National Taxpayer Advocate, 2006 Report to Congress," December 31, 2006, http://www.irs.gov/advocate/article/0,,id=165806,00.html. Internal Revenue Service, "IRS Updates Tax Gap Estimates," February 14, 2006, http://www.irs.gov/newsroom/article/0,,id=154496,00.html.

733. Bruce Bartlett, "Unpaid Taxes," *National Center of Policy Analysis*, April 16, 2001.

734. David Callahan, *The Cheating Culture: Why More Americans Are Doing Wrong to Get Ahead*, New York: Harcourt, Inc., 2004, pages 238, 245-247, 248, 255, 257, 261.

735. U.S. Census Bureau, "The 2008 Statistical Abstract," Table 598, Employed Civilians by Occupation, Sex, Race, and Hispanic Origin: 2006, http://www.census.gov/compendia/statab/tables/08s0598.pdf. Putnam, 2000, page 145.

736. *ABC News* poll, March 2001.

737. George H. Gallup Jr., "Which National Principles Keep America Strong?" *The Gallup Organization*, November 4, 2003.

738. Gallup, Moral Issues poll, September, 2007, http://www.gallup.com/poll/1681/Moral-Issues.aspx. Lydia Saad, "Morality Ratings the Worst in Five Years," Gallup News Service, May 25, 2006. Joseph Carroll, "Society's Moral Boundaries Expand Somewhat This Year," Gallup News Service, May 16, 2005. George H. Gallup, Jr., "Public's View of Morals: Bad and Getting Worse," The Gallup Organization, June 10, 2003. Lydia Saad, "Democrats and Republicans Agree That U.S. Morals Are Subpar: Outlook for morals worsened over past year," Gallup News Service, May 21, 2004.

739. Thomas N. Robinson, Dina L. G. Borzekowski, Donna M. Matheson, Helena C. Kraemer, "Effects of Fast Food Branding on Young Children's Taste Preferences," *Archives of Pediatric & Adolescent Medicine*, August, 2007; 161(8):792-7.

740. Reuters, "Report finds record amount of 'clutter' on TV," December 23, 2003.

741. Bureau of Economic Analysis, "Gross Domestic Product," Table 1.1.5, 1929-2007, February 28, 2008.

742. Brian Wilcox, et al, "Report of the Task Force on Advertising and Children," American Psychological Association, February 20, 2004.

743. Martin Lindstrom and Patrician Seybold, *Brand Child*, 2003, London: Kogan Page, pages 17 and 81.

744. Alissa Quart, *Branded: The Buying and Selling of Teenagers*, 2003, Cambridge: Perseus Publishing, page 23.

745. Gary Ruskin, "Request for Investigation of Companies That Engage in 'Buzz Marketing,'" letter to Federal Trade Commission, October 18, 2005, http://www.commercialalert.org/buzzmarketing.pdf.

746. Motoko Rich, "In Books for Young, Two Views on Product Placement," *The New York Times*, February 19, 2008. PR Newswire, "HarperCollins Children's Books Signs Tina Wells to Publishing Deal," February 19, 2008.

747. Susan Jacoby, "The Allure of Money, America's Love-Hate Relationship With the Almighty Dollar," *Modern Maturity*, July-August, 2000.

748. The Pew Research Center, "How Young People View Their Lives, Futures and Politics: A Portrait of 'Generation Next,'" January 9, 2007, http://people-press.org/reports/display.php3?ReportID=300.

749. Jim Roberts, "Huge Increase of Compulsive Buying in Generation Y," *Baylor Business Review*, March, 2004, http://www.baylor.edu/bbr/index.php?id=16311.

750. Higher Education Research Institute, University of California at Los Angeles, "CIRP Freshmen Survey Trends," April 2, 2007, http://www.gseis.ucla.edu/heri/PP/PR_TRENDS_40YR_NASPA-ACPA_04-07.ppt.

751. Pew Research Center, "Luxury or Necessity? Things We Can't Live Without: The List Has Grown in the Past Decade," December 14, 2006, http://pewresearch.org/pubs/323/luxury-or-necessity. This upward trend tracks 14 consumer products and has continued roughly consistently over the past three decades, accelerating a bit in the past decade, other than for car, clothes dryer and TV, which have been considered necessities by most of us at stable levels.

752. Martin Lindstrom and Patrician Seybold, *Brand Child*, 2003, London: Kogan Page, pages 25, 33, 77, 81, 82 and 85.

753. Quoted in, Gary Ruskin, "Why they whine: How corporations prey on our children," *Mothering*, 1999; 97:42.

754. Quart, 2003, pages 23, 94.

755. "Law-Enforcement Officials Note Marked Nationwide Increase in Teen Prostitution; Trends Show Kids Getting Younger, More from Middle-Class Homes," *Newsweek*, August 10, 2003.

756. Miriam H. Zoll, "Psychologists Challenge Ethics Of Marketing To Children," *American News Service*, 2000, http://www.mediachannel.org/originals/kidsell.shtml. Bruce Bower, "Buyer Beware: Some psychologists see danger in excessive materialism," *Science News*, September 6, 2003, pages 152-154.

757. Victor C Strasburger and Edward Donnerstein, "Children, Adolescents, and the Media: Issues and Solutions," *Pediatrics*, January, 1999; 103(1):129-139.

758. Tim Kasser, Richard M. Ryan, Charles E. Couchman, Kennon M. Sheldon, "Materialistic Values: Their Causes and Consequences," in Tim Kasser and Allen Kanner (eds), *Psychology & Consumer Culture: The Struggle for a Good Life in a Materialistic World*, 2003, Washington, DC: APA Press, Chapter 2.

759. Association for Psychological Science, "Misery Is Not Miserly: Why Even Momentary Sadness Increases Spending," *ScienceDaily*, February 8, 2008.

760. Kathleen D. Vohs, Nicole L. Mead, Miranda R. Goode, "The Psychological Consequences of Money," *Science*, November 17, 2006; 314(5802):1154-56.

761. Fiske and Silverstein, pages 72-73.

762. Fiske and Silverstein, pages 5, 96.

763. Loewenstein, G. and Schkade, D., "'Wouldn't it be nice? Predicting future feelings'" in Kahneman, D., Diener, E. and Schwartz, N., *Well-being: the foundations of hedonic psychology*, 1999, New York: Russell Sage Foundation.

764. Brickman, P., Coates, D., and Janoff-Bulman, R., "Lottery winner and accident victims: Is happiness relative?" *Journal of Personality and Social Psychology*, 1978; 36: 917-927.

765. Solnick, Sara and David Hemenway, "Is More Always Better?: A Survey About Positional Concerns," *Journal of Economic Behavior and Organization*, 1998; 37(3), 373-383, cited in Ichiro Kawachi and Bruce Kennedy, *The Health of Nations: Why Inequality is Harmful to Your Health*, 2002, New York: The Free Press, pages 52-53.

766. Brown, Gordon D. A., Gardner, Jonathan, Oswald, Andrew J. and Qian, Jing, "Does Wage Rank Affect Employees' Wellbeing?", IZA Discussion Paper No. 1505, March 2005, http://ssrn.com/abstract=678868.

767. K. Fliessbach, B. Weber, P. Trautner, T. Dohmen, U. Sunde, C. E. Elger, and A. Falk, "Social Comparison Affects Reward-Related Brain Activity in the Human Ventral Striatum," *Science*, November 23, 2007; 318:1305-8.

768. Daniel Kahneman, Alan B. Krueger, David Schkade, Norbert Schwarz, Arthur A. Stone, "Would You Be Happier If You Were Richer? A Focusing Illusion," *Science*, June 30, 2006, 312(5782):1908-10.

769. Ed Diener and Martin E.P. Seligman, "Beyond Money," *Psychological Science in the Public Interest*, May, 2004; 5(1):1-31. Inglehart, R. and Klingemann, H-D., "Genes, culture, democracy and happiness," in Diener, E. and Suh, E. (eds.) *Subjective Well-being Across Cultures*, 2000, Cambridge MA: MIT Press. Ed Diener, Jeff Horwitz and Robert A. Emmons, "Happiness of the Very Wealthy," *Social Indicators*, 1985, 16:263-274.

770. Warren and Tyagi, 2003, page 208, note 121.

771. David Jesuit and Timothy Smeeding, "Luxemburg Income Study Working Paper No. 293: Poverty and Income Distribution," Encyclopedia of Population, Michigan: Macmillan Library Reference, March 2003, Figure 1, http://www.lisproject.org/publications/liswps/293.pdf; and OECD Employment Outlook 1994 and 1997 as cited in Robert Topel, "Unions and Collective Bargaining," Autumn 2002, http://gsbwww.uchicago.edu/fac/robert.topel/teaching/33032topic2-a02.pdf. David Jesuit told me that if public benefits and transfers were taken into account, relative U.S. income inequality would likely be greater.

772. Edward N. Wolff, Ajit Zacharias and Asena Caner "Levy Institute Measure of Economic Well-Being: United States, 1989, 1995, 2000, and 2001," May, 2004, http://www.levy.org/2/bin/datastore/pubs/files/limew/limew0504.pdf. Edward N. Wolff, "Changes in Household Wealth in the 1980s and 1990s in the U.S.," May, 2004, Table 2 and 3, pages 30-31, http://www.levy.org/2/bin/datastore/pubs/files/wp/407.pdf. However, inequality in wealth as measured by net worth did not change over the period 1989-2001.

773. David Cay Johnston, "Class in America: The very rich leave the plain rich behind," *The New York Times*, June 6, 2005. These 14,000 households earned at least $5.5 million in 2004.

774. Emmanuel Saez and Thomas Piketty, "Income Inequality in the United States, 1913-1998," *Quarterly Journal of Economics*, 2003; 118(1):1-39. Data provided by the authors in April, 2008 is updated through 2006. I use data from table A-3; incomes include capital gains. I estimate that income inequality exceeded the 1928 peak based upon 2006-2007 income trends at the top.

775. Robert Frank, "U.S. Led a Resurgence Last Year Among Millionaires World-Wide," *Wall Street Journal*, June 15, 2004, page 1.

776. Jacob Hacker, Suzanne Mettler, Dianne Pinderhughes, Theda Skocpol, "Inequality and Public Policy," Task Force on Inequality and American Democracy, American Political Science Association, 2004, unpublished paper, https://www.apsanet.org/imgtest/feedbackmemo.pdf. See Figure 2 for U.S. income volatility measure developed by Jacob Hacker and Nigar Nargis.

777. Krieger N, Rehkopf DH, Chen JT, Waterman PD, Marcelli E, et al., "The Fall and Rise of US Inequities in Premature Mortality: 1960–2002," *PLoS Medicine*, February, 2008; 5(2):e46, http://medicine.plosjournals.org/perlserv/?request=cite-builder&doi=10.1371/journal.pmed.0050046. Table 2: in 1960 whites in the lowest 20 percent of counties by income were no more likely to die prematurely (before age 65) than those in the highest 20 percent of counties. By 2000, the rate of premature deaths among whites in the lowest income counties was 60 percent higher. Table 5: similarly, in 1960 white infants (under age one) in bottom 20 percent of counties were 20 percent more likely to die than those in the highest 20 percent of counties. By 2000, infants in the lowest income counties were 50 percent more likely to die.

778. Raksha Arora, "A Nation More Divided: Ranks of "Have-Nots" Swell," *Gallup News Service*, July 20, 2004. Additional data for Princeton Job # 04-060-20 provided by the company. "Have-nots" reported as 17, 24, 31, 27 and 31 percent for the years 1988, 1998, 2000, 2002 and 2004, respectively. "Haves" declined from 59 to 57 percent over this period.

779. David G. Blanchflower and Andrew J. Oswald, "Does Inequality Reduce Happiness? Evidence from the States of the USA from the 1970s to the 1990s," March, 2003, unpublished study, http://www2.warwick.ac.uk/fac/soc/economics/staff/faculty/oswald/. David G. Blanchflower and Andrew J. Oswald, "Hypertension and Happiness Across Nations," National Bureau of Economic Research, Working Paper No. 12934, February, 2007.

780. Lynch JW, Harper S, Smith GD, et al, "Is Income Inequality a Determinant of Population Health. Part 1. A Systematic Review," *Milbank Quarterly*, November 1, 2004; 82:5-99.

781. Pablo Fajnzylber, Daniel Lederman, and Norman Loayza, "Inequality and Violent Crime," *Journal of Law and Economics* April, 2002; 45(1):1-40, http://econ.worldbank.org/files/15757_FajnzylberEtAlInequalityCrime.pdf.

782. Steve Kangas, "Myth: Getting tough on crime reduces crime," http://www.huppi.com/kangaroo/L-toughcrime.htm.

783. Lynch J, Kaplan GA, Pamuk ER, Cohen RD, Heck KE, Balfour JL, Yen IH, "Income inequality and mortality in metropolitan areas of the United States," *American Journal of Public Health*, 1998; 88(7): 1074-80. The observations in the paragraph reflect 1990s data, the most recently generally available.

784. Winkleby et al., "Low Individual Socioeconomic Status, Neighborhood Socioeconomic Status, and Adult Mortality," *American Journal of Public Health*, December, 2006; 95(12).

785. Ghaed SG, Gallo LC., "Subjective social status, objective socioeconomic status, and cardiovascular risk in women," *Health Psychology*, November, 2007; 26(6):668-674.

786. Lynch JW, Smith GD, Harper S and Hillemeier M, "Is Income Inequality a Determinant of Population Health? Part 2. U.S. National and Regional Trends in Income Inequality and Age- and Cause-Specific Mortality," *Milbank Quarterly*, June, 2004; 82(2):355-400, Table 3. 1950 and 1960 data have very high (.5 and .7) p-values; subsequent year data have a very low probability of being by chance.

787. James Banks, Michael Marmot, Zoe Oldfield, and James P. Smith, "Disease and Disadvantage in the United States and in England," *Journal of the American Medical Association*, May 3, 2006; 295(17):2037-45. The table is taken from data in Banks, Marmot et al, 2006, Table 3 and shows percent lifetime prevalence of selected diseases for the top one-third of earners in both countries. Health status is adjusted for obesity, smoking and heavy drinking risk factors.

788. Ichiro Kawachi and Bruce Kennedy, "Income inequality and health: pathways and mechanisms," *Health Services Research*, April, 1999; 34(1 Part 2):215-27.

789. Personal communication, November 17, 2003.

790. Operario, Don; Adler, Nancy E.; Williams, David R., "Subjective social status: reliability and predictive utility for global health," *Psychology & Health*, April, 2004; 19(2):237-246. Adler NE, Epel E, Castellazzo G, Ickovics J, "Relationship of subjective and objective social status with psychological and physiological functioning: Preliminary data in healthy white women," *Health Psychology*, November, 2000; 19(6):586-592. Singh-Manoux, A., Adler, N.E., & Marmot, M.G., "Subjective social status: Its determinants and its association with measures of ill-health in the Whitehall II study," *Social Science and Medicine*, 2003; 56:1321-33.

791. Bureau of Economic Analysis, "National Income and Product Accounts, Table 2.1, Personal Income and Its Disposition," February 28, 2008.

792. Brian K. Bucks, Arthur B. Kennickell, and Kevin B. Moore, "Recent Changes in U.S. Family Finances: Evidence from the 2001 and 2004 Survey of Consumer Finances," *Federal Reserve Bulletin*, February, 2006; 92:A1-A38, Table 5, http://www.federalreserve.gov/pubs/oss/oss2/2004/bull0206.pdf. 51.3 percent of households have zero retirement savings, not including Social Security.

793. Brian K. Bucks, Arthur B. Kennickell, and Kevin B. Moore, "Recent Changes in U.S. Family Finances: Evidence from the 2001 and 2004 Survey of Consumer Finances," *Federal Reserve Bulletin*, February, 2006; 92:A1-A38, Table 10, http://www.federalreserve.gov/pubs/oss/oss2/2004/bull0206.pdf. Paul Kasriel's blog, February 11, 2008, http://www.financialsense.com/economy/northern/kasriel/2008/ec021108.pdf.
794. Federal Reserve Board, "Flow of Funds Accounts of the United States," March 6, 2008, Tables F.100 and L.1.
795. Federal Reserve Board, "Household Debt Service and Financial Obligation Ratios," December 12, 2007, http://www.federalreserve.gov/releases/housedebt/default.htm.
796. US Bureau of Economic Analysis, "Table 2.1. Personal Income and Its Disposition," March 27, 2007. Sam Gerdano, executive director of the American Bankruptcy Institute, quoted by AP, June 24, 2003.
797. Data: Administrative Office of the U.S. Courts and US Census Bureau. For the year ending September 30, 2004, there were 1.584 million non-business filings, a rate of 539 per 100,000 people. In 1981, there were 312,000 personal filings, a rate of 135 per 100,000 people. I have not provided bankruptcy data for 2005 and following years because the October 2005 effective date of more stringent bankruptcy law caused a stampede in 2005 filings and made filings in subsequent years more difficult.
798. Suein Hwang, "New Group Swells Bankruptcy Court: The Middle-Aged," *The Wall Street Journal*, August 6, 2004, page 1.
799. Peter J. Elmer and Steven A. Seelig, "The Rising Long-Term Trend of Single-Family Mortgage Foreclosure Rates," Federal Deposit Insurance Corporation, 1998, http://www.fdic.gov/bank/analytical/working/98-2.pdf. Current foreclosure rate: Mortgage Bankers Association, "Delinquencies and Foreclosures Increase in Latest MBA National Delinquency Survey," March 13, 2007. Foreclosure rates rose in a roughly straight line from an average of eight-hundredths of one percent during the 1950s to 1.19 percent as of Q4 2006. The roughly straight line increase is interrupted by a spike during the speculative "go-go" investment climate of the 1960s. The cited Federal Reserve Board study found that mortgage foreclosure rates are only weakly related to unemployment, interest rates, or home value appreciation, but strongly correlated with greater borrower tolerance for high loan-to-value ratios and with higher borrower incidence of life shocks such as divorce or uninsured health crises. The slope of the increase in foreclosure rates closely mirrors that of personal bankruptcy rates and the percentage of consumer disposable income spent on gambling, more evidence of the growing acceptance of risk as a price of growing consumption.
800. National Association of Realtors, "Survey Shows Buyers And Sellers Use Technology And Want Personal Services," November 11, 2006.
801. Ruth Simon, "Concerns Mount About Mortgage Risks," *The Wall Street Journal*, May 17, 2005, page D1.
802. The Nilson Report, December, 2007.
803. Brian K. Bucks, Arthur B. Kennickell, and Kevin B. Moore, "Recent Changes in U.S. Family Finances: Evidence from the 2001 and 2004 Survey of Consumer Finances," *Federal Reserve Bulletin*, February, 2006; 92:A1-A38, Table 11, http://www.federalreserve.gov/pubs/oss/oss2/2004/bull0206.pdf.
804. Reuters, "Americans Struggle with Credit Card Bills," March 5, 2004. Michelle J White, "Bankruptcy Reform and Credit Cards," *Journal of Economic Perspectives*, Fall, 2007; 21(4):175-199, http://www.econ.ucsd.edu/~miwhite/JEPIII.pdf.
805. Tamara Draut and Javier Silva, "Generation Broke: The Growth of Debt Among Young Americans," Demos, October, 2004, http://www.demos-usa.org/pubs/Generation_Broke.pdf. A banker told me that his peers in the credit card industry know that college students cannot payoff their accumulated credit card debt, expecting parents to bail them out at the end of college to avoid embarrassment. College lender Nellie Mae found that the average undergraduate carried four credit cards in 2004.

806. Robert Shireman, Lauren J. Asher, Ajita Talwalker, Shu-Ahn Li, Edie Irons, and Rowan Cota, "Addressing Student Loan Repayment Burdens," Project on Student Debt, February, 2006, http://projectonstudentdebt.org/files/pub/WHITE_PAPER_FINAL_PDF.pdf.

807. Allan C. Carlson, "'Anti-Dowry'?: The Effects of Student Loan Debt on Marriage and Childbearing," The Howard Center for Family, Religion and Society, December, 2005, http://www.profam.org/pub/xfia_cur.htm. Seventy-six percent of self-described happy couples in their mid-30s are free of heavy debt burdens, where only thirty-five percent of unhappy couples are free of heavy debt. High debt loads probably explain some of the delay in marriage and child-rearing and increased marital stress and divorce among young adults over the past fifteen years.

808. Federal Reserve Board, "Flow of Funds Accounts of the United States," March 6, 2008, http://www.federalreserve.gov/releases/z1/Current/z1.pdf.

809. Office of Management and Budget, "Budget of the United States Government, 2006," Table 1.1, http://www.whitehouse.gov/omb/budget/fy2006/pdf/hist.pdf.

810. Elizabeth Becker and Edmund L Andrews, "I.M.F. Says Rise in U.S. Debts Is Threat to World's Economy," *New York Times*, January 8, 2004.

811. Gokhale, Jagadeesh and Kent Smetters, "Measuring Social Security's Financial Problems," NBER working paper 11060, January 2005. Gokhale, Jagadeesh and Kent Smetters, "Fiscal and Generational Imbalances: New Budget Measures for New Budget Priorities," Washington, DC: The American Enterprise Press, 2003. Niall Ferguson and Laurence Kotlikoff, "The New New Deal," *The New Republic*, August 15, 2005, page 19.

812. Laurence J. Kotlikoff, "Is the United States Bankrupt?" *Federal Reserve Bank of St. Louis Review*, July/August, 2006; 88(4):235-49. See pages 239-240 for a discussion of avoidance of the national bankruptcy issue by both political parties.

813. Congressional Budget Office estimate, February, 2005, added borrowing over 2009-2015 to fund private accounts.

814. Ipsos Public Affairs poll, reported by *Associated Press*, March 31, 2004.

815. International Gaming & Wagering Business, November, 2007. Christiansen Capital Advisors, "Gross Annual Wager of the United States: 2003," http://www.cca-i.com/Primary%20Navigation/Online%20Data%20Store/Free%20Research/2003%20Revenue%20by%20Industry.pdf.

816. David W. Moore, "State Lottery Tickets Most Popular Form of Gambling," *Gallup News Service*, February 2, 2004. The $552 is twice the amount wagered by those earning $30,000 to $50,000.

817. Shaffer HJ, Hall MN, Vander Bilt J., "Estimating the prevalence of disordered gambling behavior in the United States and Canada: a research synthesis," *American Journal of Public Health*, September, 1999; 89(9):1369-76, Table 3. Past-year prevalence of level 3 gambling disorder among adults is 1.29 percent. This number is almost certainly low given that it is derived from studies taken in the 1994-1997 period before slot-machine casinos had spread throughout the U.S.

818. Reuter J, Raedler T, Rose M, Hand I, Glascher J, Buchel C., "Pathological gambling is linked to reduced activation of the mesolimbic reward system," *Nature Neuroscience*, February, 2005; 8(2):147-8.

819. Dirk Meissner, "Diapers in casinos a troubling symbol of problem gambling, says researcher," *Canadian Press*, May 10, 2007.

820. Earl L. Grinols, *Gambling in America: Costs and Benefits*, 2004, New York: Cambridge University Press, page 175.

821. Fordham Institute, The Social Health of the States, 2003. Bankruptcy: FDIC State Profiles - Fall 2003, Nevada, November 21, 2003.

822. Earl Grinols and David Mustard, "Casinos, Crime, & Community Costs," *Review of Economics and Statistics*, February 2006; 88(1):28-45. This study examined crime rate data in every US county between 1977 and 1996, statistically controlling for population density, race, age, sex, income, and other potentially explanatory variables. This study post-dates

the 1999 National Gambling Impact Study Commission finding that it could reach no conclusion on the subject because of lack of quality research.

823. The Supreme Court of New Hampshire, The State of New Hampshire v. Uno Kim, opinion issued March 28, 2006.

824. Hundreds of news clips on the effect of gambling crime and addiction are here: http://www.noslots.com/Gambling_Releated_Crimes.htm.

825. Tim Falkiner and Roger Horbay, "Unbalanced Reel Gambling Machines," unpublished paper presented at the International Pokies Impact Conference, Melbourne, Australia, September 9, 2006, http://www.gameplanit.com/UnbalancedReels.pdf. In early 2008, the province of Ontario, Canada removed slot machines that do this.

826. Robert Williams, et al., "Final Report: The Demographic Sources of Ontario Gaming Revenue," Prepared for the Ontario Problem Gambling Research Centre, June 23, 2004, page 42. Henry Lesieur, "Pathological and Problem Gambling: Costs and Social Policy," Testimony before the Rhode Island House Gambling Commission Hearings, Slide 22, October 15, 2002.

827. Edward N. Wolff, Ajit Zacharias and Asena Caner "Levy Institute Measure of Economic Well-Being: United States, 1989, 1995, 2000, and 2001," May, 2004, page 6, http://www.levy.org/2/bin/datastore/pubs/files/limew/limew0504.pdf. 1989 and 2001 household paid work hours, respectively, 2080 and 2340.

828. James T. Bond, Cindy Thompson, Ellen Galinsky and David Prottas, "National Study of the Changing Workforce," Families and Work Institute, 2002.

829. Pat S. Hu and Timothy R. Reuscher, "Summary of Travel Trends: 2001 National Household Travel Survey," US Department of Transportation, December, 2004, http://nhts.ornl.gov/2001/pub/STT.pdf. Number trips to/from work per household (Table 6) multiplied by average commute travel time (Table 26), shows a net increase from 126 to 186 hours per year from 1983 to 2001.

830. Clara Reschovsky, "Journey to Work: 2000," U.S. Census Department, March, 2004, Table 2.

831. Sylvia Ann Hewlett and Carolyn Buck Luce, "Extreme Jobs: The Dangerous Allure of the 70-Hour Workweek," Harvard Business Review, December 1, 2006.

832. Kuhn, Peter J. and Lozano, Fernando, "The Expanding Workweek? Understanding Trends in Long Work Hours Among U.S. Men, 1979-2004," December, 2005, NBER Working Paper No. W11895, http://www.econ.ucsb.edu/~pjkuhn/Research%20Papers/LongHours.pdf. Data is for other than self-employed men, aged 25-54.

833. "Global Survey of Business Executives," The McKinsey Quarterly, July, 2005, http://download.mckinseyquarterly.com/exglosurv_0705.pdf.

834. Michael Mandel, Steve Hamm, Carol Matlack, Christopher Farrell and Ann Therese Palmer, "The Real Reasons You're Working So Hard... and what you can do about it," BusinessWeek, October 3, 2005. Quote is a reader response dated December 28, 2005.

835. Edward C. Prescott, "Why Do Americans Work So Much More Than Europeans?" Federal Reserve Bank of Minneapolis Quarterly Review, July, 2004; 28(1):2–13. Data is from OECD for adults working in the "above-ground" market sectors for the period 1993-1996 and 1970-1974. The author ascribes the increase in American work hours to lower marginal tax rates.

836. "Employers Recognize Work-Life Balance, But Do Employees? Hudson Survey Finds More Than Half of Workers Don't Use All Vacation Time," Hudson, April 18, 2007. American Psychological Association, "Stress in America," October 24, 2007, http://apahelpcenter.mediaroom.com/file.php/138/Stress+in+America+REPORT+FINAL.doc. Joe Robinson, "Ah, Free At Last: Whoops! Time's Up," Washington Post, July 27, 2003, page B1. Data cited is a 2007 Hudson survey and a 2003 survey of 700 companies. Explanations include job insecurity, guilt pangs and unspoken hints from bosses.

837. Mary Pickett, "Health News," Harvard Medical School/Aetna InteliHealth, September 8, 2003, http://www.intelihealth.com/IH/ihtIH/WSIHW000/333/7228/369040.html.

838. William J. Doherty, "Overscheduled Kids, Underconnected Families: The Research Evidence," paper provided by author, October, 2003.

839. Casertaa, Mary T., Thomas G. O'Connor, Peter A. Wyman, Hongyue Wang, Jan Moynihan, Wendi Cross, Xin Tu, and Xia Jin, "The associations between psychosocial stress and the frequency of illness, and innate and adaptive immune function in children," *Brain, Behavior, and Immunity*, February 26, 2008 (epub ahead of print).

840. Ellen Galinsky, President, Families and Work Institute, testimony before the U.S. Senate Health, Education, Labor & Pensions Committee, Subcommittee on Children & Families, April 22, 2004, http://familiesandwork.org/3w/testimony.doc.

841. American Psychological Association, "Stress in America," October 24, 2007, http://apahelpcenter.mediaroom.com/file.php/138/Stress+in+America+REPORT+FINAL.doc

842. Jared Sandberg, "Sun, Beach, Sand – I Think I'd Rather Be Back in the Office," *Wall Street Journal*, July 30, 2003, page B1.

843. Quoted in: Andrew Curry, "Why We Work," *U.S.News & World Report*, February 24, 2003, pages 49-52, 54-56.

844. Mary Lou Quinlan, "Idea Fest: The New Business Conversation Starts Here. 23 Bright Ideas for a Stellar 2003," *Fast Company*, January, 2003, page 95.

845. Ilene Philipson, *Married to the Job: Why We Live to Work and What We can Do About It*, 2002, New York: The Free Press, pages 26, 112-115. PeoplePoint is a fictitious name for a real company.

846. Bureau of Economic Analysis, "National Income by Type of Income, Table 1.12," April 27, 2007. This BEA data series extends from 1929-2006. Corporate profits are pre-tax.

847. Jeffrey L Johnson, "Time in America Study," December, 2005, http://www.daytimer.com/About-Day-Timers/Press-Releases/where-did-the-time-go/16140126096B45DB96A9B9645F6955BD/False.

848. John Jurgensen, "When Life Begins at 5: A New Wake-Up Call," *The Wall Street Journal*, March 25-26, 2006, page P9.

849. American Psychological Association, "Stress in America," October 24, 2007, http://apahelpcenter.mediaroom.com/file.php/138/Stress+in+America+REPORT+FINAL.doc

850. National Sleep Foundation, "Summary Findings of the 2005 Sleep in America poll," March, 2005. Jane Spencer, "The Quest to Banish Fatigue," *Wall Street Journal*, July 1, 2003, page D1.

851. "Lack of sleep's a lot like mental illness," *NewScientist*, October 27, 2007, page 22.

852. Varsha Taskar, "Health Effects of Sleep Deprivation," *Clinical Pulmonary Medicine*; January, 2003; 10(1):47-52. *The Economist*, December 21, 2002, pages 111-113. Bruce Bower, "Sleeper Effects: Slumber may fortify memory, stir insight," *Science News*, January 24, 2004; 165:53. Liesl Owens, "Siestas in space?" *National Space Biomedical Research Institute*, January 3, 2002.

853. National Sleep Foundation, "State of the States Report on Drowsy Driving," November, 2007.

854. National Sleep Foundation, "Less Fun, Less Sleep, More Work, An American Portrait," March 27, 2001, http://www.sleepfoundation.org/PressArchives/lessfun_lesssleep.html. National Highway Traffic Safety Administration, "Alcohol-Impaired Driving ," March, 2008, 2006 data. Drunk drivers caused 13,470 highway deaths in 2006.

855. James Gleick, *Faster: The Acceleration of Just About Everything*, New York: Random House, 1999, 2000, page 27.

856. Gonzalez, V. and Mark, G., "Constant, Constant, Multi-tasking Craziness: Managing Multiple Working Spheres," *Proceedings of ACM CHI'04*, April, 2004, pages 113-120, http://www.ics.uci.edu/~gmark/CHI2004.pdf.

857. Sylvia Ann Hewlett and Carolyn Buck Luce, "Extreme Jobs: The Dangerous Allure of the 70-Hour Workweek," *Harvard Business Review*, December 1, 2006.

858. Aaron Lucchetti, "Firms Seek Edge Through Speed As Computer Trading Expands," *Wall Street Journal*, December 15, 2006, page A1.

859. Robert D Putnam, *Bowling Alone: The Collapse and Revival of American Community*, New York: Simon & Schuster (Touchstone), 2000 [2001], page 143.

860. Cody BE, Hanley MP., "Stop sign violations put child pedestrians at risk: a national survey of motorist behavior at stop signs in school zones and residential areas," National Safe Kids Campaign, October, 2003.

861. By David Wann, "Waste Makes Haste," *AlterNet*, June 16, 2003, http://www.alternet.org/story.html?StoryID=16173.

862. Deborah Tannen, "Hey, Did You Catch That? Why They're Talking as Fast as They Can," *Washington Post*, January 5, 2003.

863. Sue Shellenbarger, "Females Rate As Better Multitaskers; With Humans, the Debate Rages On," *Wall Street Journal*, 2003, page D1.

864. Tom W. Smith, "American Sexual Behavior: Trends, Socio-Demographic Differences, and Risk Behavior," National Opinion Research Center, GSS Topical Report No. 25, Table 10, March, 2006. Adult sex frequency, 59.6 per year. The Kinsey Report pegs the length of typical intercourse at 15 minutes, including foreplay.

865. Jean-Paul Sartre, *Wall (Intimacy): And Other Stories*, New Directions Publishing, 1972.

866. Simon Baron-Cohen, "The extreme male brain theory of autism," *Trends in Cognitive Science*, 2002; 6:248–254.

867. June Price Tangney and Ronda L. Dearing, *Shame and Guilt*, New York: Guilford Press, 2004, page 154.

868. Simon Baron-Cohen, Svetlana Lutchmaya and Rebecca Knickmeyer, *Prenatal Testosterone in Mind: Amniotic Fluid Studies*, Cambridge: MIT Press, 2004. James Randerson, "Too much testosterone blights social skills," *NewScientist*, May 12, 2004. Baron-Cohen notes that the fetal testosterone studies are small and require replication.

869. C. D. Good, I. Johnsrude, et al., "Cerebral asymmetry and the effects of sex and handedness on brain structure: a voxel-based morphometric analysis of 465 normal adult human brains," *Neuroimage*, September 2001; 14(3):685-700.

870. Harriet Hanlon, Robert Thatcher, and Marvin Cline, "Gender differences in the development of EEG coherence in normal children," *Developmental Neuropsychology*, 1999; 16(3):479-506.

871. Bernadette Pelissier and Nicole Jones, "A Review of Gender Differences Among Substance Abusers," *Crime & Delinquency*, July, 2005; 51(3):343-372.

872. Wendy J. Lynch, Megan E. Roth, Marilyn E. Carroll, "Biological basis of sex differences in drug abuse: preclinical and clinical studies," *Psychopharmacology*, September, 2002; 164:121-137. Men versus women for illegal drug use (7.7% versus 5.0%); tobacco use (35.2% versus 23.9%); alcohol use (53.6% versus 40.2%).

873. Munro CA, McCaul ME, Wong DF, Oswald LM, Zhou Y, Brasic J, Kuwabara H, Kumar A, Alexander M, Ye W, Wand GS., "Sex differences in striatal dopamine release in healthy adults," *Biological Psychiatry*, May 15, 2006; 59(10):966-74. Male response to amphetamines ranged from 50 to 200 percent greater in three of four regions of the striatum tested. Some of these gender differences can be explained by easier male access to illegal drugs.

874. Fumiko Hoeft, Christa L. Watson, Shelli R. Kesler, Keith E. Bettinger, Allan L. Reiss, "Gender differences in the mesocorticolimbic system during computer game-play," *Journal of Psychiatric Research*, March, 2008; 42(4):253-8. Right handed subjects only were participants in this experiment.

875. Haier, Richard J.; Jung, Rex E.; Yeo, Ronald A.; Head, Kevin; Alkire, Michael T., "The neuroanatomy of general intelligence: sex matters," *NeuroImage*, March, 2005; 25(1):320-27.

876. Ian W. Craig, Emma Harper and Caroline S. Loat, "The Genetic Basis for Sex Differences in Human Behaviour: Role of the Sex Chromosomes," *Annals of Human Genetics*, February, 2004; 68:269-84.

877. Luders, E.; Thompson, P.M.; Narr, K.L.; Toga, A.W.; Jancke, L.; Gaser, C., "A curvature-based approach to estimate local gyrification on the cortical surface," *NeuroImage*, February, 2006; 29(4):1224-1230.

878. Wheelwright S, Baron-Cohen S, Goldenfeld N, Delaney J, Fine D, Smith R, Weil L, Wakabayashi A., "Predicting Autism Spectrum Quotient (AQ) from the Systemizing

Quotient-Revised (SQ-R) and Empathy Quotient (EQ)," *Brain Research*, March 24, 2006; 1079(1):47-56. Simon Baron-Cohen, Rebecca C. Knickmeyer, Matthew K. Belmonte, "Sex Differences in the Brain: Implications for Explaining Autism," *Science*, November 4, 2005; 310(5749):819-823.

879. Micheal Phillips, Mark Lowe, Joseph T. Lurito, Mario Dzemidzic, and Vincent Matthews, "Temporal lobe activation demonstrates sex-based differences during passive listening," *Radiology*, July, 2001; 220:202-7. Image at: http://www.medicine.indiana.edu/news_ releases/archive_00/images/brainscans.jpg.

880. *This American Life*, National Public Radio, August 20, 2002.

881. Aleman A, Bronk E, Kessels RP, Koppeschaar HP, van Honk J., "A single administration of testosterone improves visuospatial ability in young women," *Psychoneuroendocrinology*, June, 2004; 29(5):612-7.

882. Cherrier MM, Rose AL, Higano C., "The effects of combined androgen blockade on cognitive function during the first cycle of intermittent androgen suppression in patients with prostate cancer," *Journal of Urology*, November, 2003; 170(5):1808-11.

883. Mazur, A.,& Booth, A. , "The biosociology of testosterone in men," in D. Franks & S. Smith (Eds.), *Mind, Brain, and Society: Toward a Neurosociology of Emotion*, 1999, Stamford, CT: JAI Press, Volume 5, pages 311-338.

884. Newman ML, Sellers JG, Josephs RA., "Testosterone, cognition, and social status," *Hormones and Behavior*, February, 2005; 47(2):205-11. John Coates and Joe Herbert, "Endogenous steroids and financial risk taking on a London trading floor," *Proceedings of the National Academy of Sciences*, U.S.A., April 22, 2008, 105(16):6167-72.

885. Jovanovic H, Lundberg J, Karlsson P, Cerin A, Saijo T, Varrone A, Halldin C, Nordström AL., "Sex differences in the serotonin 1A receptor and serotonin transporter binding in the human brain measured by PET," *Neuroimage*, February 1, 2008; 39(3):1408-19.

886. Michael McGuire, Fawzy Fawzy, James Spar & Alfonso Troisi, "Dysthymic Disorder, Regulation-Disregulation Theory, CNS Blood Flow, and CNS Metabolism," in Leon Sloman & Paul Gilbert (eds), *Subordination and Defeat: An Evolutionary Approach to Mood Disorders and Their Therapy*, Mahway, New Jersey: Lawrence Erlbaum Associates, 2000, pages 71-93.

887. J.B. Hamilton and G.E. Mestler , "Mortality and Survival: Comparison of Eunuchs with intact Men and Women in a Mentally Retarded Population," *Journal of Gerontology*, 1969; 24:395-411.

888. National Center for Health Statistics, "Table 27, Life expectancy at birth, at 65 years of age, and at 75 years of age, by race and sex: United States, selected years 1900–2004," February, 2007.

889. David R. Williams, "The Health of Men: Structured Inequalities and Opportunities," *American Journal of Public Health*, May, 2003, pages 724-731.

890. C. Edward Coffey; Joseph F. Lucke; Judith A. Saxton; Graham Ratcliff; Lori Jo Unitas; Brenda Billig; R. Nick Bryan, "Sex Differences in Brain Aging: A Quantitative Magnetic Resonance Imaging Study," *Arch Neurol*, February, 1998; 55:169-179.

891. Thomas J. Songer, report delivered at a U.S. Centers for Disease Control and Prevention meeting, May, 2003. From 1994 to 2000, there were 1,442 thunderstorm-related deaths in US: 70 percent of the victims were male.

892. National Center for Health Statistics, National Vital Statistics Report, "Deaths, percent of total deaths, and death rates for the 10 leading causes of death in selected age groups, by race and sex: United States, 2000, Table 1," 50(16), September 16, 2002.

893. Canetto, S. and Lester, D., "Gender and the primary prevention of suicide mortality," *Suicide and Life Threatening Behavior*, 1995; 25:58-69.

894. National Center for Health Statistics, "Table 46, Death rates for suicide, according to sex, race, Hispanic origin, and age: United States, selected years 1950–2004," February, 2007.

895. Glenn E. Weisfeld & Craig A. Wendorf, "The Involuntary Defeat Strategy and Discrete Emotions Theory," in Leon Sloman & Paul Gilbert (eds), *Subordination and Defeat: An*

Evolutionary Approach to Mood Disorders and Their Therapy, Mahway, New Jersey: Lawrence Erlbaum Associates, 2000, page 136.

896. David H. Skuse, "X-linked genes and mental functioning," *Human Molecular Genetics*, April 15, 2005; 14(1):R27-R32. Ian W. Craig, Emma Harper and Caroline S. Loat, "The Genetic Basis for Sex Differences in Human Behaviour: Role of the Sex Chromosomes," *Annals of Human Genetics*, February, 2004; 68:269-84.

897. Larry Hedges and Amy Nowell, "Sex Differences in Mental Test Scores, Variability, and Numbers of High-Scoring Individuals," *Science*, July 7, 1995; 269(5220):41-5. The authors conclude: "Except in tests of reading comprehension, perceptual speed, and associative memory, males typically outnumber females substantially among high-scoring individuals."

898. Helmuth Nyborg, "Sex-related differences in general intelligence g, brain size, and social status," *Personality & Individual Differences*, August, 2005; 39(3):497-509.

899. Charles Murray, *Human Accomplishment: The Pursuit of Excellence in the Arts and Sciences, 800 B.C. to 1950*, New York: HarperCollins, 2003, pages 266, 289.

900. Waverly Ding, Fiona Murray and Toby Stuart, "Gender differences in patenting in the academic life sciences," *Science*, August 4, 2006; 313(5787):665-7.

901. John Brockman, "Edge," January, 2007, http://edge.org/q2007/q07_index.html.

902. "The Gender Gap: Boys Lagging," *60 Minutes*, May 25, 2003.

903. Michelle Conlin, "The New Gender Gap: From kindergarten to grad school, boys are becoming the second sex," *Business Week*, May 26, 2003.

904. Christina Hoff Sommers, *The War Against Boys: How Misguided Feminism Is Harming Our Young Men*, New York: Simon & Schuster, 2000.

905. Ruth-Ellen Cohen, "UM Education Study Indicates Gender Gap," *Bangor Daily News*, June 9, 2003.

906. Michelle Galley, "Research: Boys to Men," *Education Week*, January 23, 2002.

907. *Science Daily*, "Mayo Clinic Study Finds Higher Incidence Rate Of Reading Disability Among Boys," November 15, 2001, http://www.sciencedaily.com/releases/2001/11/011115072452.htm.

908. Biederman J, Farina SV., "The Massachusetts General Hospital studies of gender influences on attention-deficit/hyperactivity disorder in youth and relatives," *Psychiatr Clin North Am.*, June, 2004; 27(2):225-32. I place the words "psychiatric disorder" in quotes because ADHD, in its less-than-debilitating forms, may be an advantage not recognized by schools, endowing creativity and rapid assimilation of novel stimuli.

909. Annysa Johnson, "State probing complaint of grading bias against boys," *Milwaukee Journal Sentinel*, April 27, 2003.

910. National Center for Education Statistics, "Digest of Education Statistics, 2005, Table 68, Selected characteristics of public school teachers: Selected years, spring 1961 through spring 2001."

911. Ruth-Ellen Cohen, "UM Education Study Indicates Gender Gap," *Bangor Daily News*, June 9, 2003; Linda Shaw, "Schools' gender-gap concern now is boys," *Seattle Times*, September 30, 2002; Emily Richmond, "District schools see drop in test scores," *Las Vegas Sun*, December 19, 2002.

912. National Center for Education Statistics, "The Nation's Report Card: 12th-Grade Reading and Mathematics 2005," February, 2007. 41 percent of girls scored proficient or above, boys 29 percent.

913. National Center for Education Statistics, "Trends in Educational Equity of Girls & Women, 2004," http://nces.ed.gov/pubs2005/equity/.

914. National Center for Education Statistics, "Digest of Education Statistics, 2007," June, 2007, Table 258. Degrees conferred by degree-granting institutions, by level of degree and sex of student: Selected years, 1869-70 through 2016-17, http://nces.ed.gov/programs/digest/d07/tables/dt07_258.asp. Years 2006-2017 are NCES projections.

915. "Doctorate Recipients from United States Universities: Summary Report 2005," Chicago: National Opinion Research Center, 2006, Table B-2b and B-2c.

916. Kuhn, Peter J. and Lozano, Fernando, "The Expanding Workweek? Understanding Trends in Long Work Hours Among U.S. Men, 1979-2004," December, 2005, NBER Working Paper No. W11895, http://www.econ.ucsb.edu/~pjkuhn/Research%20Papers/LongHours.pdf. Data is for other than self-employed men, aged 25-64, 1979-2004.

917. Jacob Hacker, Suzanne Mettler, Dianne Pinderhughes, Theda Skocpol, "Inequality and Public Policy," Task Force on Inequality and American Democracy, American Political Science Association, 2004, page 13, https://www.apsanet.org/imgtest/feedbackmemo.pdf.

918. U.S. Census Bureau, "Historical Income Tables – People: Full-Time, Year-Round Workers (All Races) by Median Earnings and Sex: 1960 to 2005," Table P-38, March 7, 2007, http://www.census.gov/hhes/www/income/histinc/p38ar.html.

919. U.S. Census Bureau, "Marital Status–People 18 Years Old and Over, by Total Money Income in 2005, Work Experience in 2005, Age, Race, Hispanic Origin, and Sex," August 29, 2006, http://pubdb3.census.gov/macro/032006/perinc/new02_040.htm, and http://pubdb3.census.gov/macro/032006/perinc/new02_064.htm. For never-married, full time workers aged 25-44, all races, median income for men was $31,926 and for women $31,866. This ratio slipped in 2006, with men at $33,071 and women at $31,972.

920. Bureau of Labor Statistics, "Women in the Labor Force, Table 25, Wives who earn more than their husbands, 1987-2005," September, 2007, http://www.bls.gov/cps/wlf-databook2007.htm. Anne Winkler, "Wives Who Outearn Their Husbands: A Transitory or Persistent Phenomenon for Couples?," *Demography*, August, 2005; 42(3):523-35.

921. Bureau of Labor Statistics, "Women in the Labor Force: A Databook," Table 11, Employed persons by detailed occupation and sex, 2006 annual averages, September, 2007.

922. Helen Fisher, *The First Sex: The Natural Talents of Women and How They Are Changing the World*, New York: Random House, 1999.

923. Warren and Tyagi, 2003, page 195, footnote 15.

924. Steven L. Nock, "When Married Spouses Are Equal," *Virginia Journal of Social Policy and the Law*, Fall 2001; 9:48-70.

925. James L. Starkey, "The Effects of a Wife's Earnings on Marital Dissolution: The Role of a Husband's Interpersonal Competence," *The Journal of Socio-Economics*, 1991; 20(2):125-54.

926. Andrew Hacker, *Mismatch: The Growing Gulf Between Women and Men*, 2003, New York: Scribner, page 28.

927. Hacker, 2003, page 47. Data for 2002. The remaining 44 percent received an average of $3,844 per year.

928. Hacker, 2003, pages 4, 43.

929. Hacker, 2003, pages 158-160. Among blacks, female advance is more pronounced with 192 black women graduating from college for every 100 black men. In the year 2000, black women college graduates are 66 percent of all black college graduates, 58 percent of black MBA's, 61 percent of law degree recipients, 61 percent of doctors, 57 percent of dentists and 61 percent of Ph.D.s. Black women are 53 percent of the black workforce and 60 percent of black managers and executives.

930. Hacker, 2003, page 84.

931. Bureau of Labor Statistics, civilian noninstitutional population, age 16-24, by race, sex, school enrollment and labor force status, 1985-2008, January-April + November-December averages. Data retrieved March, 2008. Indexed number is the percentage of the population not in school and not looking for work and does not include those unemployed, but looking for work. Thanks to Charles Murray for providing this chart concept via personal communication.

932. Michelle Conlin, "It's a Bart Simpson Culture" *Business Week*, May 26, 2003.

933. "Women Outnumber Men Among College Graduates," Morning Edition, NPR, May 17, 2005.

934. Burney J Le Boeuf and Richard S Peterson, "Social Status and Mating Activity in Elephant Seals," *Science*, January 3, 1969; 163(3862):91-93. Four percent of male elephant seals tracked off the California coast impregnated 85 percent of females.

935. McElligott, Alan G.; Mattiangeli, Valeria; Mattiello, Silvana; Verga, Marina; Reynolds, Catherine A.; Hayden, Thomas J., "Fighting Tactics of Fallow Bucks (Dama dama, Cervidae): Reducing the Risks of Serious Conflict," *Ethology*, September, 1998; 104(9):789-803.

936. http://en.wikipedia.org/wiki/Genghis_Khan.

937. Jack Weatherford, *Genghis Khan and the Making of the Modern World*, New York: Crown, 2004.

938. Tatiana Zerjal et al, "The Genetic Legacy of the Mongols," *American Journal of Human Genetics*, 72:717–721, 2003. George Vernadsky quoted in Steve Sailer, "Genes of history's greatest lover found?" *United Press International*, February 6, 2003.

939. Steven Goldberg, *Why Men Rule*, Chicago: Open Court Publishing, 1993.

940. David M. Buss, *The Evolution of Desire: Strategies of Human Mating*, New York: Basic Books, 1994.

941. Buss, D.M., Shackelford, T.K, & LeBlanc, G., "Number of Children Desired and Preferred Spousal Age Difference: Context-Specific Mate Preference Patterns Across 37 Cultures," *Evolution and Human Behavior*, September, 2000; 21(5):323-331.

942. Robecca Gardyn, "The Mating Game," *American Demographics*, July/August, 2002; 24(7):32-37.

943. Eric R. Bressler and Sigal Balshine, "The influence of humor on desirability," *Evolution and Human Behavior*, January, 2006; 27(1):29-39.

944. Moore FR, Cassidy C, Law Smith MJ, Perrett DI, "The effects of female control of resources on sex- differentiated mate preferences," *Evolution and Human Behavior*, May, 2006; 27(3):193-205.

945. Stroud, Laura R., Salovey, Peter, and Epel, Elissa S., "Sex differences in stress responses: social rejection versus achievement stress," *Biological Psychiatry*, August, 2002; 52(4):318-327.

946. Stroud, Laura R.; Niaura, Raymond S.; Stoney, Catherine M., "Sex Differences in Cardiovascular Reactivity to Physical Appearance and Performance Challenges," *International Journal of Behavioral Medicine*, September, 2001; 8(3):240-250.

947. FBI, "Crime in the United States, 2006," Table 42, September, 2007, http://www.fbi.gov/ucr/cius2006/data/table_42.html.

948. Anne Campbell, "Staying Alive: Evolution, Culture and Women's Intrasexual Aggression," *Behavioral and Brain Sciences*, April, 1999; 22(2):203-214.

949. United Nations Office on Drugs and Crime, Centre for International Crime Prevention, "Seventh United Nations Survey of Crime Trends and Operations of Criminal Justice Systems," data for the period 1998 – 2000. Roy Walmsley, "World Prison Population List, Sixth Edition," International Center for Prison Studies, February, 2005. Among 211 nations and territories.

950. Shankar Vedantam, Research Links Lead Exposure, Criminal Activity, *Washington Post*, July 8, 2007, page A2.

951. Mark Anderson et al, "School-Associated Violent Deaths in the United States," *Journal of the American Medical Association*, December 5, 2001; 286(21):2695-2702. Over the 1990s, where single-victim homicides in incidents of school violence decreased significantly, multi-victim Columbine-like incidents have increased from zero to 42 percent of all school homicides.

952. Data sources: Bryan Vossekuil, Robert A. Fein, Marisa Reddy, Randy Borum, William Modzeleski, "The Final Report and Findings of the Safe School Initiative: Implications for the Prevention of School Attacks in the United States," United States Secret Service and United State Department of Education, May 2002, http://www.secretservice.gov/ntac.shtml. Kenneth S. Trump, National School Safety and Security Services, "School-Related Deaths, School Shootings, & School Violence Incidents," 1999-2007, http://www.schoolsecurity.org/trends/school_violence.html. Trump has culled news reports for deaths "1) inside a school, on school property, on or immediately around (and associated with) a school bus, or in the immediate area (and

associated with) a K-12 elementary or secondary public, private, or parochial school; 2) on the way to or from a school for a school session; 3) while attending, or on the way to or from, a school-sponsored event; 4) as a clear result of school-related incidents/ conflicts, functions, activities, regardless of whether on or off actual school property." Using Trump's descriptions of each incident, I have selected those involving planning by students or student-aged persons in ongoing conflict with students for each calendar year. My selection criteria is roughly comparable to that used by Vossekuil, et al. My 1999 count (five) using Trump data is the same as Vossekuil's.

953. Peter R. Breggin, "Eric Harris was taking Luvox (a Prozac-like drug) at the time of the Littleton murders," April 30, 1999, http://www.breggin.com/luvox.html and http://www.breggin.com/harris.html. Dr. Breggin is the author of *Talking Back to Prozac.*

954. Alan Prendergast, "I'm Full of Hate and I Love It," *Denver Westword*, December 6, 2001, http://www.westword.com/issues/2001-12-06/news.html/1/index.html.

955. Miscellaneous investigative files on Columbine, *Boulder Daily Camera*, http://www.boulderdailycamera.com/shooting/report/p10401-10500.pdf. Harris' journal is posted by Dave Cullen, http://davecullen.com/columbine.htm. The substitution of asterisks for some letters in vulgar words is mine.

956. Dave Cullen, "These guys wanted to become cult heroes," *Salon.com*, November 11, 1999, http://www.salon.com/news/feature/1999/11/11/columbine/index.html; and Nancy Gibbs and Timothy Roche, "The Columbine Tapes," *Time Magazine*, December 20, 1999.

957. Matt Appuzzo, "Virginia Tech Shooter Was Picked on In School," *AP*, April 19, 2007.

958. I have altered the order of the sentences, but none of the words in Cho's videotape.

959. Bryan Vossekuil, Robert A. Fein, Marisa Reddy, Randy Borum, William Modzeleski, "The Final Report and Findings of the Safe School Initiative: Implications for the Prevention of School Attacks in the United States," United States Secret Service and United State Department of Education, May 2002, http://www.secretservice.gov/ntac.shtml. Leary, M. R., Kowalski, R. M., Smith, L., & Phillips, S., "Teasing, rejection, and violence: Case studies of the school shootings," *Aggressive Behavior*, 2003, 29: 202-214. In this smaller study of the fifteen school shooting incidents between 1995 and 2001 involving students killing or injuring their classmates, the perpetrators in twelve had been systematically teased, bullied and ostracized.

960. Arseneault L, Walsh E, Trzesniewski K, Newcombe R, Caspi A, Moffitt TE., "Bullying victimization uniquely contributes to adjustment problems in young children: a nationally representative cohort study," *Pediatrics*, July, 2006; 118(1):130-8. Results are at age seven after bullying during ages 5-7.

961. Michael Newton, author of the *Encyclopedia of Serial Killers*, personal communication, August 29, 2003.

962. Elliot Leyton, *Hunting Humans: The Rise of the Modern Multiple Murderer*, Toronto: McClelland & Stewart Ltd., 1995, 1986; and personal communication with the author.

963. Leyton, 1995, 1986, pages 220-243.

964. Shirley Lynn Scott, "What Makes Serial Killers Tick?" 2003, http://www.crimelibrary.com.

965. Tim Cahill, *Buried Dreams*, New York: Bantam Books, 1987.

966. Meloy, J. Reid; Hempel, Anthony G.; Gray, B. Thomas; Mohandie, Kris; Shiva, Andrew; Richards, Thomas C., "A comparative analysis of North American adolescent and adult mass murderers," *Behavioral Sciences & the Law*, May, 2004; 22(3):291-309. Mass murder is distinguished from serial killing, the former more impulsive, the latter more planned.

967. James Gilligan, *Violence: Our Deadly Epidemic and its Causes*, New York: G. P. Putnam's Sons, 1996, page 110.

968. Helen Morrison and Harold Goldberg, *My Life Among the Serial Killers*, New York: HarperCollins, 2004.

969. Jonathan Pincus, "The Neurological Contribution to Violence," University Seminar on Cognitive and Behavioral Neuroscience, Washington VA Hospital, December 12, 2002. Jonathan Pincus, *Base Instincts: What Makes Killers Kill?*, 2001, New York: W.W. Norton & Company.

970. Andreas Reif, Klaus-Peter Lesch, "Toward a molecular architecture of personality," *Behavioural Brain Research*, 2003; 139:1-20.

971. Kim-Cohen J., Caspi A., Taylor A., Williams B., Newcombe R., Craig IW., Moffitt TE., "MAOA, maltreatment, and gene-environment interaction predicting children's mental health: new evidence and a meta-analysis," *Molecular Psychiatry*, October, 2006; 11(10):903-13. Huang, Y. Y., Cate, S. P., Battistuzzi, C., Oquendo, M. A., Brent, D. & Mann, J. J., "An association between a functional polymorphism in the monoamine oxidase a gene promoter, impulsive traits and early abuse experiences," *Neuropsychopharmacology*, August, 2004; 29:1498-1505. Meyer-Lindenberg, A., Buckholtz, J. W., Kolachana, B., Hariri, A. R., Pezawas, L., Blasi, G., Wabnitz, A., Honea, R., Verchinski, B. & Callicott, J., et al., "Neural mechanisms of genetic risk for impulsivity and violence in humans," *Proceedings of the National Academy of Sciences*, USA, April 18, 2006; 103(16);6269–6274. The genetic variations reported here are associated more with impulsive, as contrasted with planned violence. Nelly Alia-Klein, Rita Z. Goldstein, Aarti Kriplani, Jean Logan, Dardo Tomasi, Benjamin Williams, Frank Telang, Elena Shumay, Anat Biegon, Ian W. Craig, Fritz Henn, Gene-Jack Wang, Nora D. Volkow, and Joanna S. Fowler, "Brain Monoamine Oxidase A Activity Predicts Trait Aggression," *The Journal of Neuroscience*, May 7, 2008; 28(19):5099-5104.

972. Robert D. Hare, *Without Conscience: The Disturbing World of the Psychopaths Among Us*, New York: Pocket Books, 1995.

973. Seto, M. E. & Barbaree, H. E., "Psychopathy, Treatment Behavior, and Sex Offender Recidivism," *Journal of Interpersonal Violence*, December, 1999; 14:1235-48.

974. Jonathan Kellerman, *Savage Spawn: Reflections on Violent Children*, New York: Ballantyne Books, 1999.

975. Robins, LN., "A 70-year history of conduct disorder: Variations in definition, prevalence, and correlates," in: Cohen P, Slomkowski C, Robins, LN, Eds., *Time, Place and Psychopathology*, Mahwah, New Jersey: Lawrence Erlbaum, 1999, pages 37-56.

976. Dr James Blair, author interview, November 22, 2004. R.J.R. Blair, et al., "Reduced sensitivity to others' fearful expressions in psychopathic individuals," *Personality and Individual Differences*, October, 2004; 37:1111-22.

977. R.J.R. Blair, "The roles of orbital frontal cortex in the modulation of antisocial behavior," *Brain and Cognition*, March 5, 2004; 55:198-208.

978. Pietro Pietrini, Mario Guazzelli, Gianpaolo Basso, Karen Jaffe, Jordan Grafman, "Neural Correlates of Imaginal Aggressive Behavior Assessed by Positron Emission Tomography in Healthy Subjects," *American Journal of Psychiatry*, 2000; 157:1772-81. Jordan Grafman, "Anger is a wind that blows out the light of the mind (old proverb)," *Molecular Psychiatry*, 2003; 8:131-132. Mah, L., Arnold, M.C., and Grafman, J., "Lesions of Prefrontal Cortex Impair Social Perception," *American Journal of Psychiatry*, 2004; 161(7):1247-1255. Adrian Raine, "Annotation: the role of prefrontal deficits, low autonomic arousal, and early health factors in the development of antisocial and aggressive behavior in children," *J Child Psychol Psychiatry*, May, 2002; 43(4):417-34.

979. James R. Blair, "Neurobiological basis of psychopathy," *British Journal of Psychiatry*, 2003; 182:5-7.

980. My very crude estimate: In 2006 there were 37.7 million American males under age 18; ten percent of boys are physically or sexually abused (see Chapter 7); one-third of males have the MAO-A-low gene. Thus, 1.4 million American boys are at high risk of becoming violent. Crosscheck: in 2006, there were 37.7 million boys; in 1990, before the disproportionate growth in drug crime, males had a 9.0 percent lifetime risk of imprisonment (the 2001 lifetime risk estimate is 11.3 percent); 32.8 percent of males first imprisoned had committed a violent offense (murder, rape, assault, or robbery). Thus roughly 1.1 million of today's boys are likely to be imprisoned at some time during their lives for committing a violent crime. Sources: U.S. Census Bureau, 2006 American Community Survey. Thomas P. Bonczar, "Special Report: Prevalence of Imprisonment in the U.S. Population, 1974-2001," Bureau of Justice Statistics, August, 2003,

http://www.ojp.usdoj.gov/bjs/pub/pdf/piusp01.pdf. Thomas P. Bonczar and Allen J. Beck, "Lifetime Likelihood of Going to State or Federal Prison," Bureau of Justice Statistics, March, 1997, http://www.ojp.usdoj.gov/bjs/pub/pdf/llgsfp.pdf.

981. Twenge JM, Zhang L, Catanese KR, Dolan-Pascoe B, Lyche LF, Baumeister RF., "Replenishing connectedness: reminders of social activity reduce aggression after social exclusion," *British Journal of Social Psychology*, March, 2007; 46(Part 1):205-24. Twenge JM, Baumeister RF, DeWall CN, Ciarocco NJ, Bartels JM., "Social exclusion decreases prosocial behavior," *Journal of Personality and Social Psychology*, January, 2007; 92(1):56-66.

982. Leo Braudy, *The Frenzy of Renown: Fame and Its History*, New York: Random House, 1986, [1997], page 562.

983. Henry Wadsworth Longfellow, *Driftwood; Table Talk*, 1857.

984. www.SorryWorks.net.

985. Yves Erwin Salomon, "Lil' Kim's Former Manager Headed To Jail," *Launch*, February 3, 2003, http://music.yahoo.com/read/news/12053708.

986. "Pat Grossmith, "Gentleman Bandit Hits Manchester West Side bank," *The Union Leader*, March 30, 2004, page B1.

987. "Thief thanks clerk before stealing diamond ring," *New Hampshire Union Leader*, December 24, 2007.

988. "Center Ossipee fire strikes home of family already hit by tragedy," *The Union Leader*, June 21, 2003. "NH heroes to be honored at annual awards gathering," *The Union Leader*, March 21, 2004.

989. Clare Ansberry, "The Tender Trap: Parents Devoted To a Disabled Child Confront Old Age," *The Wall Street Journal*, January 7, 2004, page A1. Gary Rotstein, "Caring for Tim: Autistic man finds new home at 50," *Pittsburgh Post-Gazette*, May 23, 2004, http://www.post-gazette.com/pg/04144/319496.stm.

990. The notion that anyone willing to train hard enough can be an Armstrong should face the fact Armstrong's ". . . heart is at least 20% larger than a normal person's, he produces one-third less lactic acid than do other top cyclists and delivers oxygen to his legs at a rate higher than all but maybe 100 of his fellow earthlings . . . When you add up the odds of all these things being consolidated in one body . . . [h]e's probably one in a billion." Source: Sam Walker, "The Lactic Acid Test: New Research on Sports Stars Reveals Biology Is Destiny," *The Wall Street Journal*, July 22, 2005, page W1.

991. Gregory E. Miller and Carsten Wrosch, "You've Gotta Know When to Fold 'Em: Goal Disengagement and Systemic Inflammation in Adolescence," *Psychological Science*, September, 2007; 18(9):773-7. Carsten Wrosch, Gregory E. Miller, Michael F. Scheier and Stephanie Brun de Pontet, "Giving Up on Unattainable Goals: Benefits for Health?" *Personality and Social Psychology Bulletin*, February, 2007; 33(2):251-265. See Figure 2 for the life satisfaction impact of low ability to abandon unattainable goals.

992. Dutton, J. E., Debebe, G., & Wrziesnewski, A., "The re-valuing of de-valued work: The importance of relationships for hospital cleaning staff," Paper presented at the Annual Meeting of the Academy of Management, August 1996, Cincinnati, OH.

993. Ed Diener, "Selected Publications," http://www.psych.uiuc.edu/~ediener/research/publictn. html. David G. Myers, *The Pursuit of Happiness*, Avon Books, 1993, digested by the author at http://www.davidmyers.org/happiness/research.html.Martin E.P.Seligman,*AuthenticHappiness*, New York: Free Press, New York, 2002. Information on behavior induction: Fredrickson, B. L., "Cultivating positive emotions to optimize health and well-being," *Prevention and Treatment*, 2000; 3, Article 1, http://journals.apa.org/prevention/volume3/pre0030001a.html.

994. Kasser, T. and Ryan, R.M., "Be careful what you wish for: Optimal functioning and the relative attainment of intrinsic and extrinsic goals," in P. Schmuck and K.M. Sheldon (eds), *Life Goals and Well-Being: Towards a Positive Psychology of Human Striving*, Geottingen, Germany: Hogrefe & Huber, 2001, pages 116-131.

995. Dr. Seligman's 245 question VIA Signature Strengths Survey is here: http://www.authentic happiness.sas.upenn.edu/questionnaires.aspx. For an academic treatise on this, see:

Peterson, C. and Seligman, M.E.P., *Character Strengths and Virtues: A Classification and Handbook*, Oxford University Press, 2004.

996. Mihaly Csikszentmihalyi, *Finding Flow: The Psychology of Engagement With Everyday Life*, New York: Basic Books, 1998.

997. Michael F. Steger, Todd B. Kashdan, and Shigehiro Oishi, "Being good by doing good: Daily eudaimonic activity and well-being," *Journal of Research in Personality*; March 31, 2007; 42(2008):22-42.

998. Elizabeth W. Dunn, Lara B. Aknin, Michael I. Norton, "Spending Money on Others Promotes Happiness," *Science*, March 21, 2008; 319(5870):1687-8.

999. Ed Diener and Martin E.P. Seligman, "Beyond Money: Toward an Economy of Well-Being," *Psychological Science in the Public Interest*, 2004; 5(1):1-31.

1000. Murray CJL, Lopez AD, eds., "The global burden of disease and injury series, volume 1: a comprehensive assessment of mortality and disability from diseases, injuries, and risk factors in 1990 and projected to 2020," Cambridge, MA: Harvard University Press, 1996.

1001. Ronald C. Kessler, Patricia Berglund, Olga Demler, Robert Jin, Kathleen R. Merikangas, Ellen E. Walters, "Lifetime Prevalence and Age-of-Onset Distributions of *DSM-IV* Disorders in the National Comorbidity Survey Replication," *Archives of General Psychiatry*, June, 2005; 62:593-602, Tables 3 and 4. The authors acknowledge risk of methodological error in their age cohort versus lifetime risk estimates, but are certain that prevalence of mental illness has increased for more recent generations.

1002. Philip S. Wang, Patricia Berglund, Mark Olfson, Harold A. Pincus, Kenneth B. Wells, and Ronald C. Kessler, "Failure and Delay in Initial Treatment Contact After First Onset of Mental Disorders in the National Comorbidity Survey Replication," *Archives of General Psychiatry*, 2005; 62:603-613. Philip S. Wang, Michael Lane, Mark Olfson, Harold A. Pincus, Kenneth B. Wells, and Ronald C. Kessler, "Twelve-Month Use of Mental Health Services in the United States: Results From the National Comorbidity Survey Replication," *Archives of General Psychiatry*, 2005; 62:629-640. See Table 4 for "minimally adequate" care data by disorder. "Minimally adequate treatment was defined based on available evidence-based guidelines as receiving either pharmacotherapy (≥2 months of an appropriate medication for the focal disorder plus ≥ 4 visits to any type of physician) or psychotherapy (≥ 8 visits with any HC or HS professional lasting an average of ≥ 30 minutes)."

1003. Ed Diener and Martin E.P. Seligman, "Beyond Money," *Psychological Science in the Public Interest*, May, 2004; 5(1):1-31; and, Seligman et al., 2001, pages 251, 293.

1004. National Alliance for the Mentally Ill, www.nami.org. I will carve out the following exception for the seriously violent, even if mental illness is the cause: provide evidence-proven treatment, but lock 'em up.

1005. IMS Health, Inc., "2007 Top Therapeutic Classes by U.S. Sales," and "2007 Top Therapeutic Classes by U.S. Dispensed Prescriptions," March 12, 2008. SSRIs constitute most, but not all of the sales of anti-depressants, IMS's reported class of drugs, meaning that the numbers I report may be high by as much as 20 percent.

1006. Richards JB, Papaioannou A, Adachi JD, Joseph L, Whitson HE, Prior JC, Goltzman D, "Effect of selective serotonin reuptake inhibitors on the risk of fracture," *Archives of Internal Medicine*, January 22, 2007; 167(2):188-94.

1007. Irving Kirsch, Brett J. Deacon, Tania B. Huedo-Medina, Alan Scoboria, Thomas J. Moore, Blair T. Johnson, "Initial Severity and Antidepressant Benefits: A Meta-Analysis of Data Submitted to the Food and Drug Administration," *PLoS Medicine*, February 26, 2008; 5(2):260-268.

1008. Raúl de la Fuente-Fernández, Thomas J. Ruth, Vesna Sossi, Michael Schulzer, Donald B. Calne, and A. Jon Stoessl, "Expectation and Dopamine Release: Mechanism of the Placebo Effect in Parkinson's Disease," *Science*, August 10, 2001; 293(5532):1164.

1009. Amy Dockser Marcus, "Two, Four, Six, Eight . . . This Pill Works Great!" *The Wall Street Journal*, October 28, 2003, page D1.

1010. Uriel Nitzan, Pesach Lichtenberg, "Questionnaire survey on use of placebo," *British Medical Journal*, October 23, 2004; 329(7472):944-6.

1011. Wager TD, Rilling JK, Smith EE, Sokolik A, Casey KL, Davidson RJ, Kosslyn SM, Rose RM, Cohen JD, "Placebo-induced changes in FMRI in the anticipation and experience of pain," *Science*, February, 20, 2004; 303(5661):1162-7.

1012. Zubieta, Jon-Kar; Bueller, Joshua A.; Jackson, Lisa R.; Scott, David J.; Yanjun Xu; Koeppe, Robert A.; Nichols, Thomas E.; Stohler, Christian S., "Placebo Effects Mediated by Endogenous Opioid Activity on μ-Opioid Receptors," *Journal of Neuroscience*, August 24, 2005; 25(34):7754-62.

1013. Waber RL, Shiv B, Carmon Z, Ariely D., "Commercial features of placebo and therapeutic efficacy," *Journal of the American Medical Association*, March 5, 2008; 299(9):1016-7.

1014. Decharms RC, Maeda F, Glover GH, Ludlow D, Pauly JM, Soneji D, Gabrieli JD, Mackey SC., "Control over brain activation and pain learned by using real-time functional MRI." *Proc Natl Acad Sci U S A.*, December 20, 2005; 102(51):18626-31. Real-time fMRI actually involves a signal delay of 3 to 5 seconds. Long-term effect of this brain training for pain relief is not yet known.

1015. Weintraub D, Siderowf AD, Potenza MN, Goveas J, Morales KH, Duda JE, Moberg PJ, Stern MB., "Association of dopamine agonist use with impulse control disorders in Parkinson disease," *Archives of Neurology*, July, 2006; 63(7):969-73.

1016. Samuel H. Barondes, *Better Than Prozac: Creating the Next Generation of Psychiatric Drugs*, London: Oxford University Press, 2003.

1017. Green-Sadan T, Kinor N, Roth-Deri I, Geffen-Aricha R, Schindler CJ, Yadid G., "Transplantation of glial cell line-derived neurotrophic factor-expressing cells into the striatum and nucleus accumbens attenuates acquisition of cocaine self-administration in rats," *Eur J Neurosci.*, October, 2003; 18(7):2093-8.

1018. Michael Kosfeld, Markus Heinrichs, Paul J. Zak, Urs Fischbacher & Ernst Fehr, "Oxytocin increases trust in humans," *Nature*, June 2, 2005; 435:673-6.

1019. Christen Brownlee, "Food Fix: Neurobiology highlights similarities between obesity and drug addiction," *ScienceNews*, September 3, 2005, page 156.

1020. Chris Baum, "Fourth case of leukaemia in the first SCID-X1 gene therapy trial, and the diversity of gene therapy," Commentary from the Board of the European Society of Gene and Cell Therapy, March, 2007.

1021. Jon Wolff, "Intravascular Delivery of Naked DNA for Muscular Dystrophy," paper presented at The American Society of Gene Therapy's 7th Annual Meeting, June, 2004. Tim WR Lee, David A Matthews and G Eric Blair, "Novel molecular approaches to cystic fibrosis gene therapy," *Biochemical Journal*, April 1, 2005; 387(1):1-15. The Wolff paper reports that, as of mid-2004, human trials were about to begin on a potentially safer means of delivering genetic payloads to target cells, already demonstrated in rats, dogs and monkeys. "Naked" genetic material in the animal experiments found its way into the intended target cells after simply being injected under high pressure into neighboring blood vessels. The Lee paper discusses the various experimental approaches to delivering corrective genetic material to cure cystic fibrosis.

1022. Baum, 2007. Gaspar, H Bobby; Parsley, Kathryn L.; Howe, Steven; King, Doug; Gilmour, Kimberly C; Sinclair, Joanna; Brouns, Gaby; Schmidt, Manfred; Von Kalle, Christof; Barington, Torben; Jakobsen, Marianne A; Christensen, Hans O; Al Ghonaium, Abdulaziz; White, Harry N; Smith, John L; Levinsky, Roland J; Ali, Robin R; Kinnon, Christine; Thrasher, Adrian J., "Gene therapy of X-linked severe combined immunodeficiency by use of a pseudotyped gammaretroviral vector," *Lancet*, December 18, 2004; 364(9452):2181-7.

1023. Neurologix received FDA approval to commence Phase two trials of its gene therapy procedure on March 27, 2008. I owned securities in this company as I wrote this.

1024. Thanos, Panayotis K.; Volkow, Nora D.; Freimuth, Paul; Umegaki, Hiroyuki; Ikari, Hiroyuki; Roth, George; Ingram, Donald K.; Hitzemann, Robert., "Overexpression of dopamine D2 receptors reduces alcohol self-administration.," *Journal of Neurochemistry*, September 9, 2001; 78(5):1094-1103.

1025. Lorena Lobos-González, Carlos Muñoz-Brauning and Amalia Sapag, "Ribozymes: towards gene therapy for alcoholism by silencing the mRNA for mitochondrial aldehyde dehydrogenase (ALDH2)," Abstract presented at ISBRA 2006 World Congress on Alcohol Research. Drew MR, Simpson EH, Kellendonk C, Herzberg WG, Lipatova O, Fairhurst S, Kandel ER, Malapani C, Balsam PD., "Transient overexpression of striatal D2 receptors impairs operant motivation and interval timing," *Journal of Neuroscience*, July 18, 2007; 27(29):7731-9. Kellendonk C, Simpson EH, Polan HJ, Malleret G, Vronskaya S, Winiger V, Moore H, Kandel ER., "Transient and selective overexpression of dopamine D2 receptors in the striatum causes persistent abnormalities in prefrontal cortex functioning," *Neuron*, February 16, 2006; 49(4):603-15.

1026. Vaishnav Krishnan, Ming-Hu Han, Danielle L. Graham, Olivier Berton, William Renthal, Scott J. Russo, Quincey LaPlant, Ami Graham, Michael Lutter, Diane C. Lagace, Subroto Ghose, Robin Reister, Paul Tannous, Thomas A. Green, Rachael L. Neve, Sumana Chakravarty, Arvind Kumar, Amelia J. Eisch, David W. Self, Francis S. Lee, Carol A. Tamminga, Donald C. Cooper, Howard K. Gershenfeld, and Eric J. Nestler, "Molecular Adaptations Underlying Susceptibility and Resistance to Social Defeat in Brain Reward Regions," *Cell*, October 19, 2007; 131:391-404. O. Berton, C. A. McClung, R. J. DiLeone, V. Krishnan, W. Renthal, S. J. Russo, D. Graham, N. M. Tsankova, C. A. Bolanos, M. Rios, L. M. Monteggia, D. W. Self, E. J. Nestler, "Essential role of BDNF in the mesolimbic dopamine pathway in social defeat stress," *Science*, February 10, 2006; 311:864-868.

1027. American Medical Association, Code of Ethics, E-2.11 Gene Therapy, June, 1996.

1028. Frederic Mery and Tadeusz Kawecki, "A fitness cost of learning ability in Drosophila melanogaster," *Proceedings of the Royal Society of London*, December 7, 2003; 270(1532):2465-9.

1029. William Carlezon, "Neurobiological Consequences of Early Developmental Exposure to Methylphenidate in Rats," Presented at the Annual Meeting of the American College of Neuropsychopharmacology, December 21, 2004. Bolanos CA, Barrot M, Berton O, Wallace-Black D, Nestler EJ., "Methylphenidate treatment during pre- and periadolescence alters behavioral responses to emotional stimuli at adulthood," *Biological Psychiatry*, December 15, 2003; 54(12):1317-29.

1030. Boyd Huppert, "The Girl Who Feels No Pain," *KARE 11 News*, March 2, 2004.

1031. Ian C. G. Weaver, Frances A. Champagne, Shelley E. Brown, Sergiy Dymov, Shakti Sharma, Michael J. Meaney, and Moshe Szyf, "Reversal of Maternal Programming of Stress Responses in Adult Offspring through Methyl Supplementation: Altering Epigenetic Marking Later in Life," *The Journal of Neuroscience*, November 23, 2005; 25(47):11045-11054.

1032. http://www.camh.net/Research/Areas_of_research/Epigenomics/index.html

1033. Bob Weinhold, "Epigenetics: the science of change," *Environmental Health Perspectives*, March, 2006; 114(3):A160-7.

1034. J.H. Snider, "The Citizen's Guide to the Airwaves," New America Foundation Spectrum Policy Program, July 1, 2003. Michael Calabrese, "The Future of Spectrum Policy and the FCC Spectrum Policy Task Force Report," Testimony Before the U.S. Senate Committee on Commerce, Science and Transportation, March 6, 2003, http://www.newamerica.net/Download_Docs/pdfs/Pub_File_1165_1.pdf. The 13 percent auctioned calculation is mine using FCC Auctions Summary, Completed Auctions through March 18, 2008, applying BEA's GDP price deflator to the proceeds of each auction, adding the total and comparing that to the $771 billion estimated spectrum value. Most auctioned spectrum is assumed to be given right to defacto free, perpetual renewal.

1035. Lake Snell Perry & Associates, 1999 poll.

1036. Sascha Meinrath, personal communication, March 23-24, 2008. Sascha D. Meinrath and Michael Calabrese, "Unlicensed Broadband Device Technologies: 'White Space Device' Operations on the TV Band and the Myth of Harmful Interference," New America Foundation, December, 2007. Ex Parte filing by Google counsel Richard S. Whitt, Esq. to the FCC, ET Docket 04-186, March 21, 2008. Even in the most broadcast-congested metro area, New York, as of 2009, thirty percent of the Channel 2-51 spectrum is not reserved or used for any purpose. Only about five percent of the desirable spectrum between 50 and 3000 MHz is now being used.

1037. OECD Broadband Statistics to December, 2006.

1038. KOCE-TV, "PBS #1 in Public Trust, Respect According To New Roper Poll," http://www.koce.org/press_trust.htm.

1039. New America Society, "The Decline of Broadcasters' Public Interest Obligations," March 29, 2004, http://www.newamerica.net/Download_Docs/pdfs/Pub_File_1518_1.pdf.

1040. The Center for Public Integrity, "Media Tracker," October, 2006, http://www.publicintegrity.org/telecom/search/list.aspx?act=members. Total reflects contributions to candidates and political parties from and lobbying on behalf of media, communications, computer and electronics companies over the period January 1, 1997 – June 30, 2006.

1041. Associated Press v. United States, 326 U.S. 1, 20 (1945).

1042. Ben H. Bagdikian, *The Media Monopoly, The New Communications Cartel*, Fifth Edition, 1997, Boston: Beacon Press, from the preface.

1043. John Dunbar, "Lawyer Says FCC Ordered Study Destroyed," *Associated Press*, September 14, 2006.

1044. Dennis R. Martin, "The Music of Murder," *ACJS Today*, November/December, 1993, http://www.axt.org.uk/HateMusic/Rappin.htm.

1045. Martin, 1993, source for information on Davidson's wife.

1046. Diane Herceg, letter to US Justice Department Commission on Pornography, September 10, 1985.

1047. Ronald B. Standler, "Infotorts," 2002, http://www.rbs2.com/infotort.htm#anchor999999.

1048. The Media Coalition, Inc. defends First Amendment litigation on behalf of media companies and maintains a website cataloguing related litigation at www.mediacoalition.org.

1049. American Amusement Machine Association vs. Kendrick, decided, March 23, 2001, http://www.ca7.uscourts.gov/op3.fwx?yr=00&num=3643&Submit1=Request+Opinion.

1050. Nicole C. Wong, "Law curbing sales of violent video games is blocked," *Mercury News*, December 23, 2005.

1051. Kevin W. Saunders, "Regulating Youth Access to Violent Video Games: Three Responses to First Amendment Concerns," *Law Review*, Michigan State University, 2003; 1(51):52-114, http://www.law.msu.edu/lawrev/2003-1/2-Saunders.pdf.Kevin W.Saunders,Testimonybeforethe United States Senate Committee on the Judiciary Subcommittee on the Constitution, Civil Rights, and Property Rights, March 29, 2006. It was only after the 1896 *Swearingen v. United States* case that the previously broad definition of obscenity was narrowed to apply only to depictions of sex.

1052. John Charles Kunich, "Natural Born Copycat Killers and the Law of Shock Torts," *Washington University Law Quarterly*, 2000; 78(4):1157-1270, http://law.wustl.edu/WULQ/78-4/1157Kunich.pdf.

1053. *Rice v. Paladin*, 128 F.3d 233 (4th Circuit, 1997).

1054. Rex Feral, *Hit Man: A Technical Manual for Independent Contractors*, Boulder, Colorado: Paladin Press, 1983. While the publisher settled the case by paying a multi-million dollar payment to the victims' family and ceased publishing the book, its complete text remains available online.

1055. F. Jay Dougherty, Rex S. Heinke, Frank J. Janecek, Jr., Zazi Pope, Rodney A. Smolla, "A Panel Discussion: Potential Liability Arising from the Dissemination of Violent Music," February 22, 2002, http://elr.lls.edu/issues/v22-issue2/media-liability-panel.pdf. Personal communication with author, September 9, 2003.

1056. Michael D. Green, D. Mical Freedman & Leon Gordis, "Reference Guide on Epidemiology," *Reference Manual on Scientific Evidence, 2nd Edition*, 2000, Federal Judicial Center, pages 374-379, http://www.fjc.gov/newweb/jnetweb.nsf. The FJC provides educational materials to help judges fulfill their evidentiary gate-keeping role in increasingly technical litigation. The FJC does not presuppose that evidence from the social sciences are inadmissible.

In fact, the chapter on use of epidemiological evidence to support causality is sound and eminently reasonable, suggesting that a causality determination is strengthened when cause and effect (exposure and injury) are linked in time, have a strong association, show stronger response when the exposure is increased and that the injury effect disappears when the exposure is eliminated, that results have been well replicated among multiple studies, that the causality is consistent with other science, that alternative explanations have been explored, that the injury is unique signature of the exposure. The Judicial Center says: "one or more factors may be absent even when a true causal relationship exists." Evidence linking media violence and real violence certainly fulfills this evidentiary screen. See Chapter 5 of this book.

1057. Personal communication, September, 2003.
1058. "Single-Sex Public Schools in the United States," National Association for Single Sex Education, February, 2005, http://www.singlesexschools.org/schools.html#Marshall. A listing of single-sex schools and their missions and opening dates is provided. Principal Wright's quote at http://www.singlesexschools.org/schools-schools.htm#08.
1059. U.S. Department of Education, National Center for Education Statistics, "Digest of Education Statistics, 2005, Table 68, Selected characteristics of public school teachers: Selected years, spring 1961 through spring 2001." National Center for Education Statistics, "Characteristics of Schools, Districts, Teachers, Principals, and School Libraries in the United States, 2003-04, Schools and Staffing Survey," April 2006, Table 19. Average age of school teachers and percentage distribution of teachers by sex, by school type and selected school characteristics: 2003-04, http://nces.ed.gov/pubs2006/2006313.pdf. U.S. Department of Education, National Center for Education Statistics, Schools and Staffing Survey (SASS), "Public Teacher Questionnaire," "Charter Teacher Questionnaire," and "Private Teacher Questionnaire," 1999-2000.
1060. *Portland Press Herald*, "The New Gender Gap," March, 2006, special series.
1061. Robert Frank, *Choosing the Right Pond: Human Behavior and the Quest for Status*, New York: Oxford University Press, 1985.
1062. Americans for Fair Taxation, www.FairTax.org.
1063. Ecological Footprint Quiz, http://www.myfootprint.org/
1064. June Price Tangney and Ronda L. Dearing, *Shame and Guilt*, Guilford Press, [2002], 2003, pages 2, 140-154. Tibbetts SG., "Self-conscious emotions and criminal offending," *Psychol Rep*, August, 2003; 93(1):101-26. Nathan Harris, "Reassessing the dimensionality of the moral emotions," *British Journal of Psychology*, November, 2003; 94(4):457-473. In Tangney's longitudinal study tracking guilt- and shame-prone fifth graders through early adulthood, the shame-prone were more likely to drop out, become involved in hard drugs and attempt suicide. The guilt-prone are less prone to depression and suicide than average. Guilt-prone fifth graders' higher rates of college attendance and community service and lower criminality are after statistically controlling for socio-economic status and fifth grade propensity to anger. Shame is more strongly heritable, guilt more influenced by environment. Tibbetts' study confirms that higher guilt-proneness is linked to reduced criminal activity. Harris' research confirms most of Tangney's research, but shows a more limited distinction between guilt and shame.
1065. Ernst Fehr and Urs Fischbacher, "Third-party punishment and social norms," *Evolution and Human Behavior*, 2004; 25:63–87. Up to about 60 percent of unaffected third parties punish violations of the cooperation norm. Tomasello, Michael; Carpenter, Malinda; Call, Josep; Behne, Tanya; Moll, Henrike, "Understanding and sharing intentions: The origins of cultural cognition," *Behavioral & Brain Sciences*, October, 2005; 28(5):675-691. Proposing a concept parallel to extended cooperation, Tomasello, et al peg the most unique human trait to be "shared intentionality," which results in our collective belief systems such as the institution of marriage or a religious faith.
1066. Joseph Henrich, Robert Boyd, Samuel Bowles, Colin Camerer, Ernst Fehr, Herbert Gintis, and Richard McElreath, "Cooperation, Reciprocity and Punishment in Fifteen Small-scale Societies," *American Economics Review*, May, 2001; 91(2): 73-78. J. Henrich, R. Boyd, S.

Bowles, C. Camerer, E. Fehr, H. Gintis, R. McElreath, M. Alvard, A. Barr, J. Ensminger, K. Hill, F. Gil-White, M. Gurven, F. Marlowe, J. Q. Patton, N. Smith, and D. Tracer, "'Economic Man' in Cross-cultural Perspective: Behavioral Experiments in 15 Small-scale Societies," *Behavioral and Brain Sciences*, December, 2005; 28(6):795-815. None of the 15 small societies displayed the "rational economic man" behavioral model, where individuals act according to only calculations of their self-interest.

1067. Henrich J, McElreath R, Barr A, Ensminger J, Barrett C, Bolyanatz A, Cardenas JC, Gurven M, Gwako E, Henrich N, Lesorogol C, Marlowe F, Tracer D, Ziker J., "Costly punishment across human societies," *Science*, June 23, 2006; 312(5781):1767-70.

1068. Yudhijit Bhattacharjee, "The Value of the Stick: Punishment Was a Driver of Altruism," *Science*, June 23, 2006; 312:1727.

1069. Robert Boyd, Herbert Gintis, Samuel Bowles, and Peter J. Richerson, "The evolution of altruistic punishment," *Proceedings of the National Academy of Sciences*, March 18, 2003; 100(6):3531-5. Ernst Fehr and Urs Fischbacher, "The nature of human altruism," *Nature*, October, 23, 2003; 425(6960):785-91.

1070. Benedikt Herrmann, Christian Thöni, and Simon Gächter, "Antisocial Punishment Across Societies," *Science*, March 7, 2008; 319:1362-7. See also supplementary tables S1 and S10. Information about the World Values Survey can be found in the next section of this chapter.

1071. DeQuervain, Dominique J.-F.; Fischbacher, Urs; Treyer, Valerie; Schellhammer, Melanie; Schnyder, Ulrich; Buck, Alfred; Fehr, Ernst, "The Neural Basis of Altruistic Punishment," *Science*, August, 27, 2004; 305(5688):1254-8. Ernst Fehr and Joseph Henrich, "Is Strong Reciprocity a Maladaptation? On the Evolutionary Foundations of Human Altruism," in P. Hammerstein (Ed.), *The Genetic and Cultural Evolution of Cooperation*, 2003, Cambridge, Mass: MIT Press, http://www.iew.unizh.ch/home/fehr/papers/IsStrongReciprocityaMaladaptation.pdf.

1072. Singer T, Seymour B, O'Doherty JP, Stephan KE, Dolan RJ, Frith CD, "Empathic neural responses are modulated by the perceived fairness of others," *Nature*, January 26, 2006; 439(7075):466-9.

1073. M. R. Delgado, H. M. Locke, V. A. Stenger and J. A. Fiez, "Dorsal striatum responses to reward and punishment: Effects of valence and magnitude manipulations," *Cognitive, Affective, & Behavioral Neuroscience*, 2003; 3(1):27-38. Rilling, James K.; Sanfey, Alan G.; Aronson, Jessica A.; Nystrom, Leigh E. and Cohen, Jonathan D, "Opposing Bold Responses to Reciprocated and Unreciprocated Altruism in Putative Reward Pathways," *Neuroreport*, 2004; 15(16):2539-243. This later study shows greater activation of the ventral striatum in response to mutual cooperation with a human than a computer partner.

1074. Ernst Fehr and Urs Fischbacher, "Social norms and human cooperation," *Trends in Cognitive Science*, April, 2004; 8(4):185-90. Ernst Fehr and Urs Fischbacher, "The nature of human altruism," *Nature*, October, 23, 2003; 425(6960):785-791.

1075. Keith Jensen, Josep Call, and Michael Tomasello, "Chimpanzees Are Rational Maximizers in an Ultimatum Game," *Science*, October 5, 2007; 318(5847):107-9. This experiment used a chimp version of the ultimatum game, which has been used repeatedly to show that humans will reject unfair offers, even if they wind up getting nothing as a result.

1076. Richard Dawkins, *River Out of Eden: A Darwinian View of Life*, New York: Basic Books, 1995, page 133.

1077. George H. Gallup Jr. and Byron R. Johnson, "New Index Tracks Spiritual State of the Union, Jan 28, 2003 http://www.gallup.com/poll/tb/religvalue/20030128.asp. Jeffrey M. Jones, "Wide Ideology Gap Evident in Religious Index," Gallup Poll, February 18, 2003, http://www.gallup.com/poll/tb/religValue/20030218.asp.

1078. Myers, D. G., "The funds, friends, and faith of happy people," *American Psychologist*, 2000; 55:56-67. Martin E.P. Seligman, *Authentic Happiness*, 2002, New York: Free Press, page 60.

1079. Charles Murray, *Human Accomplishment: The Pursuit of Excellence in the Arts and Sciences, 800 B.C. to 1950*, New York: HarperCollins, 2003, page 422.

1080. Ronald Inglehart and Wayne E. Baker, "Modernization, Cultural Change, and the Persistence of Traditional Values," *American Sociological Review*, February, 2000; 65:19-51. The cultural map of the world can be viewed at www.worldvaluessurvey.org.

1081. Miller JD, Scott EC, Okamoto S., "Public acceptance of evolution," *Science*, August 11, 2006; 313(5788):765-6.

1082. Michael Marmot, *The Status Syndrome: How Social Standing Affects Health and Longevity*, New York: Henry Holt, 2004 , pages 239-257.

1083. "The Sunday Times 100 Best Companies to Work For," *The Sunday Times*, March 7, 2004. Great Place To Work Institute, http://www.greatplacetowork.co.uk/best/list-uk-2007.htm, March, 2007. Gore rated number 15 in *Fortune's* 2008 ranking of best U.S. companies to work for.

1084. Bill Gore, "One Pioneer," *In Context*, #11, Autumn, 1985.

1085. Mark Van Vugt, Robert Hogan, and Robert B. Kaiser, "Leadership, Followership, and Evolution: Some Lessons From the Past," *American Psychologist*, April, 2008; 63(3):182–196.

1086. Perks retired from this job in April, 2007, just before I spoke with him.

1087. Franklin and two Jefferson quotes compiled by: J. David Gowdy, "Quotes on Liberty and Virtue," http://www.liberty1.org/virtue.htm.

1088. Encyclopedia Britannica Online, "George Washington: First Inaugural Address," April 30, 1789, http://www.britannica.com/eb/article?tocId=9116981.

1089. John Adams, Presidential address to the military, October 11, 1798, in Charles Francis Adams, ed., *The Works of John Adams—Second President of the United States*, Boston: Little, Brown, & Co., 1854, Volume IX, page 229.

PRISONERS
OF HISTORY

ALSO BY KEITH LOWE

Inferno: The Fiery Destruction of Hamburg 1943
Savage Continent: Europe in the Aftermath of World War II
The Fear and the Freedom: How the Second World War Changed Us

PRISONERS OF HISTORY

WHAT MONUMENTS TO WORLD WAR II TELL US ABOUT OUR HISTORY AND OURSELVES

KEITH LOWE

ST. MARTIN'S PRESS
NEW YORK

First published in the United States by St. Martin's Press, an imprint of St. Martin's Publishing Group

PRISONERS OF HISTORY. Copyright © 2020 by Keith Lowe. All rights reserved. Printed in the United States of America. For information, address St. Martin's Publishing Group, 120 Broadway, New York, NY 10271.

www.stmartins.com

Maps by Martin Brown

Library of Congress Cataloging-in-Publication Data

Names: Lowe, Keith, 1970– author.
Title: Prisoners of history : what monuments to World War II tell us about our history and
  ourselves / Keith Lowe.
Other titles: What monuments to World War II tell us about our history and ourselves
Description: New York : St. Martin's Press, 2020. | Includes bibliographical references.
Identifiers: LCCN 2020030034 | ISBN 9781250235022 (hardcover) | ISBN 9781250235046
  (ebook)
Subjects: LCSH: World War, 1939–1945—Monuments. | World War, 1939–1945—
  Historiography. | Memorialization—Case studies. | War Memorials—Political aspects. |
  World War, 1939–1945—Public opinion. | Collective memory—Case studies. | War and
  society—Case studies.
Classification: LCC D830 .L68 2020 | DDC 940.54/6—dc23
LC record available at https://lccn.loc.gov/2020030034

Our books may be purchased in bulk for promotional, educational, or business use. Please contact your local bookseller or the Macmillan Corporate and Premium Sales Department at 1-800-221-7945, extension 5442, or by email at MacmillanSpecialMarkets@macmillan.com.

Originally published in Great Britain by William Collins, an imprint of Harper Collins*Publishers*

First U.S. Edition: 2020

10 9 8 7 6 5 4 3 2 1

For Creo

Contents

Part III – Monsters

Part IV – Apocalypse

Part V – Rebirth

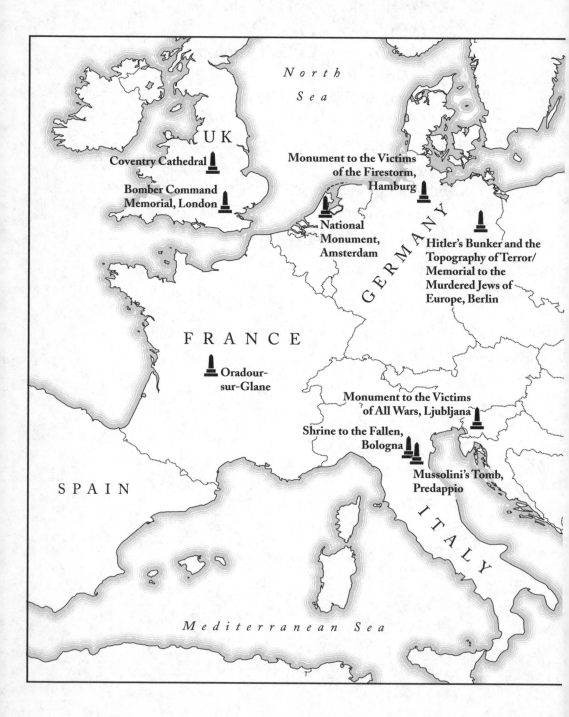

North Sea

UK

Coventry Cathedral

Bomber Command
Memorial, London

Monument to the Victims
of the Firestorm,
Hamburg

GERMANY

National
Monument,
Amsterdam

Hitler's Bunker and the
Topography of Terror/
Memorial to the
Murdered Jews of
Europe, Berlin

FRANCE

Oradour-
sur-Glane

Monument to the Victims
of All Wars, Ljubljana

Shrine to the Fallen,
Bologna

Mussolini's Tomb,
Predappio

SPAIN

ITALY

Mediterranean Sea

RUSSIA

LITHUANIA

Statue of Stalin, Grūtas Park

'Four Sleepers'
Monument, Warsaw

POLAND

Auschwitz

UKRAINE

'The Motherland Calls',
Volgograd

Monument for the Victims of
German Occupation, Budapest

HUNGARY

SYRIA

LEBANON

Mediterranean
Sea

Yad Vashem,
Jerusalem

JORDAN

ISRAEL

EGYPT

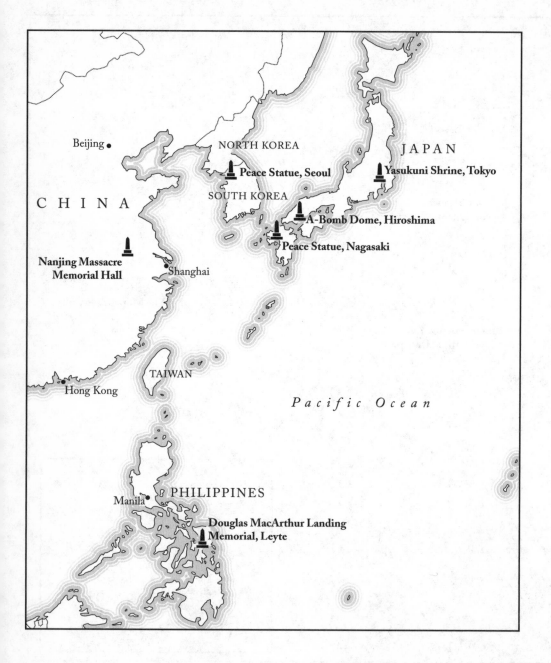

Beijing

CHINA

NORTH KOREA

Peace Statue, Seoul

SOUTH KOREA

JAPAN

Yasukuni Shrine, Tokyo

A-Bomb Dome, Hiroshima

Peace Statue, Nagasaki

Nanjing Massacre
Memorial Hall

Shanghai

TAIWAN

Hong Kong

Pacific Ocean

PHILIPPINES

Manila

Douglas MacArthur Landing
Memorial, Leyte

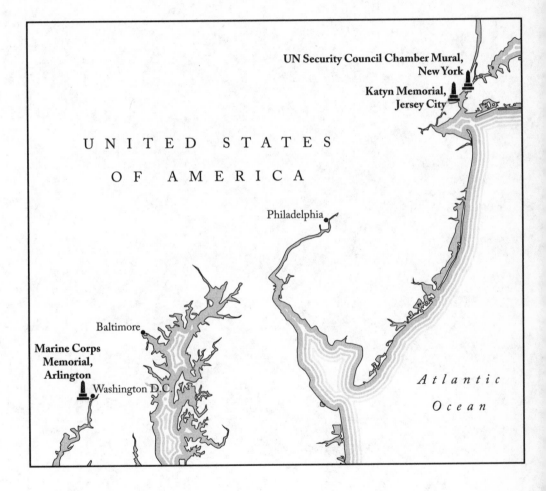

UN Security Council Chamber Mural,
New York

Katyn Memorial,
Jersey City

UNITED STATES

OF AMERICA

Philadelphia

Baltimore

Marine Corps
Memorial,
Arlington
Washington D.C.

Atlantic

Ocean

Introduction

In the summer of 2017, American state legislators began removing statues of Confederate heroes from the streets and squares outside public buildings. Nineteenth-century figures like Robert E. Lee and Jefferson Davis, who had fought for the right to keep black slaves, were no longer considered suitable role models for twenty-first-century Americans. And so they came down. All across America, to a chorus of protest and counter-protest, monument after monument was removed.

There was nothing unique about what happened in America: elsewhere, other monuments were also coming down. In 2015, after the removal of a statue of Cecil Rhodes from outside the University of Cape Town, there were calls for the elimination of all symbols of colonialism across South Africa. Soon the 'Rhodes Must Fall' campaign spread to other countries around the world, including the UK, Germany and Canada. In the same year, Islamic fundamentalists began destroying hundreds of ancient statues in Syria and Iraq on the grounds that they were idolatrous. Meanwhile, the national governments of Poland and Ukraine announced the wholesale removal of monuments to Communism. A wave of iconoclasm was sweeping the world.

I watched all this happening with great fascination, but also with a certain incredulity. When I was growing up in the 1970s and 1980s, such occurrences would have been unthinkable. Monuments everywhere were regarded merely as street furniture: they were convenient places to meet and hang out, but few people paid them much attention in themselves. Some were statues of forgotten old men, often with strange headgear and improbable moustaches; others were abstract shapes made of concrete or steel; but either way we did not really understand them. There was certainly no point in calling for their removal, because the majority of people did not care enough about them to make any kind of fuss. But in the past few years, objects that were once all but invisible have suddenly become the centre of attention. Something important seems to have changed.

At the same time as tearing down some of our old monuments, we continue to build new ones. In 2003, the toppling of Saddam Hussein's statue in central Baghdad became one of the defining images of the Iraq War. But within two years of the statue's destruction, a new monument had taken its place: a sculpture of an Iraqi family holding aloft the sun and the moon. For the artists who designed it, the monument represented Iraq's hopes for a new society characterised by peace and freedom – hopes that were almost immediately dashed in the face of renewed corruption, extremism and violence.

Similar changes are taking place all over the world. In America, statues of Robert E. Lee are gradually being replaced by monuments to Rosa Parks or Martin Luther King. In South Africa, the statues of Cecil Rhodes have come down, and monuments to Nelson Mandela have gone up. In eastern Europe, statues of Lenin and Marx make way for depictions of Thomas Masaryk, Józef Piłsudski and other nationalist heroes.

Some of our newest monuments are truly vast in scale,

especially in parts of Asia. At the end of 2018, for example, India unveiled a brand new statue of Sardar Vallabhbhai Patel, who was an important figure in the nation's independence movement during the 1930s and 1940s. Standing at 182 metres (almost 600 feet), it is now the tallest statue in the world. To create such gigantic structures, at such huge cost, implies an incredible level of self-confidence. These are not temporary structures: they have been designed to last hundreds of years. And yet who is to say that they will fare any better than the statues of Lenin or Rhodes or any of the other figures that once seemed so permanent?

It seems to me that several things are going on here at once. Monuments reflect our values, and every society deceives itself that its values are eternal: it is for this reason that we cast those values in stone and set them upon a pedestal. But when the world changes, our monuments – and the values that they represent – remain frozen in time. Today's world is changing at an unprecedented pace, and monuments erected decades or even centuries ago no longer represent the values we hold dear.

The debates currently taking place over our monuments are almost always about identity. In the days when the world was dominated by old white men, it made sense to raise statues in their honour; but in today's world of multiculturalism and greater gender equality, it is not surprising that people are beginning to ask questions. Where are all the statues of women? In a country like South Africa, with its majority black population, why should there be so many statues of white Europeans? In the USA, which has a population as diverse as any on the planet, why is there not more diversity on display in its public spaces?

But beneath these debates lies something even more funda-mental: we can't seem to make up our minds what role our communal history should play in our lives. On the one hand we see history as the solid foundation upon which our world has been built. We imagine it as a benign force, offering us opportunities to learn from the past and progress to our future. History is the very basis of our identity. But on the other hand we view it as a force that stultifies us, holding us hostage to centuries of outdated tradition. It leads us down the same old paths, to make the same mistakes again and again. When left unchallenged, history can ensnare us. It becomes a trap, from which escape seems impossible.

This is the paradox that lies at the heart of our society. Every generation longs to free itself from the tyranny of history; and yet every generation knows instinctively that without it they are nothing, because history and identity are so intertwined.

This book is about our monuments, and what they really tell us about our history and identity. I have picked twenty-five memorials from around the world which say something important about the societies that erected them. Some of these memorials are now massive tourist attractions: millions of people visit them every year. Each of them is controversial. Each tells a story. Some deliberately try to hide more than they reveal, but in doing so show us more about ourselves than they ever intended. What I most want to demonstrate is that none of these monuments is really about the past at all: rather, they are an expression of a history that is still alive today, and which continues to govern our lives whether we like it or not.

The monuments I have chosen are all dedicated to one period in our communal past: the Second World War. There are many reasons for this, but the most important is that, of all our memorials, these are the only ones that seem to have bucked the current trend of iconoclasm. In other words, these monuments continue to say something about who we are in a way that so many of our other monuments no longer do.

Very few war monuments have been torn down in recent years. In fact, quite the opposite has happened: we are building new war memorials at an unprecedented rate. This is not just the case in Europe and America, but also in Asian countries like the Philippines and China. Why should this be? It is not as if our war leaders were any less controversial than some of the figures whose statues have recently been taken down. British and French leaders were just as much champions of colonialism as Cecil Rhodes ever was; American leaders still presided over a racially segregated army; and men from all the Allied forces engaged in acts that would now be considered war crimes. Their attitudes towards women were not always enlightened either. One of our most famous images of the end of the war, *Life* magazine's iconic photograph of a sailor kissing a nurse in New York's Times Square, celebrates what we now know to be a sexual assault. Our collective memory of the Second World War seems to be able to skip over these issues in a way that our memory of other periods can't.

In order to get to the bottom of these questions, I have divided our Second World War monuments into five broad categories. In the first part of the book I will look at some of our most famous monuments to the heroes of the war. I will show how these are the most vulnerable of all our Second World War memorials, and the only ones that show any sign of being toppled or removed. Part II will explore our memorials to the martyrs of the war, and Part III will look at some of the memorial spaces that have been carved out for the war's main villains. The interplay between these three categories is as important as each category itself: the heroes cannot exist without the villains, and neither can the martyrs. In Part IV I will describe memorials to the apocalyptic destruction of the war; and in Part V I will describe some of those to the rebirth that came afterwards. These five categories reflect and reinforce one another. They have created a kind of mythological framework that protects them from the iconoclasm that has ripped through other parts of our collective memory.

I have tried to include a wide variety of monuments, if only to represent the sheer diversity of places that have been used to contain our memories of the past. So I will describe not only figurative statues and abstract sculptures, but also shrines, tombs, ruins, murals, parks and architectural features. Some of the monuments I have chosen were created in the immediate aftermath of the war, while others are much newer – indeed, some are still under construction as I write. Some have an intensely local meaning, while others are of national or even international significance. I have tried to include monuments from many different parts of the world – so, for example, I have included memorials in Israel, China and the Philippines as well as those in the UK, Russia and the USA.

There are great advantages in writing about a period that everyone understands – or, at least, thinks they understand. The Second World War affected every corner of the globe, and most nations around the world commemorate it in one way or another. It is a great cultural equaliser. And yet, as will quickly become apparent in this book, the war is remembered in vastly different ways in different nations. What better way is there to understand the differences between us and our neighbours than to be confronted by our conflicting views on something that we always thought was a shared experience?

Lastly, I have concentrated on Second World War monuments quite simply because of their quality. We sometimes tend to think of monuments as solid, grey, boring, but the sculptures in this book are some of the most dramatic and emotive pieces of public art anywhere in the world. Beneath all the granite and bronze is a mix of everything that makes us who we are – power, glory, bravery, fear, oppression, greatness, hope, love and loss.

We celebrate these and a thousand other qualities in the anticipation that they might free us from the tyranny of the past. And yet, through our desire to immortalise them in stone, they inevitably end up expressing the very forces that continue to keep us prisoners of our history.

Part I

Heroes

We live today in an age of scandal. Our media is so often dominated by stories of corruption among our politicians, our business and religious leaders, our sports stars and screen idols that sometimes it can feel difficult to believe in heroes any more.

It has not always been like this. According to popular memory at least, we once knew exactly who our heroes were. In 1945 we built monuments to the men and women who fought for us in the Second World War, and we continue to build such monuments even today. These monuments speak to us of a simpler time, when people knew right from wrong, and were willing to do their duty for the sake of a greater good.

But how accurate are these memories? Were our heroes really any stronger, braver, or more dutiful than we ourselves are? If we subjected them to the same scrutiny that our politicians and celebrities receive today, would we still be able to see them as heroes?

Our veneration of the Second World War generation says a great deal about how we view our history, and the hold that it still has over us today. In the following pages I will take a look at some of our monuments to heroism around the world, and ask what they say not only about the past, but also about today's values and ideals. I will also explore what happens when those values change over time. Can our heroes ever live up to our expectations? And what happens when our cosy memories of the past clash with a much colder historical reality?

1

Russia: 'The Motherland Calls', Volgograd

The Second World War was probably the greatest human catastrophe the world has ever seen. Historians have always struggled to find words that can convey even a glimpse of its total scale. We give endless statistics – more than 100 million soldiers mobilised, more than 60 million people killed, more than $1.6 trillion squandered – but such numbers are so large that they are meaningless to most of us.

Monuments, memorials and museums do not rely on statistics: they find other ways to suggest the scale of wartime events. A single well-chosen symbol can often hint at this far better than any words. For example, who can look at the mountain of shoes on display in the Holocaust museum at Auschwitz–Birkenau without imagining the host of corpses from which those shoes were stolen? Sometimes even a tiny object can bring to mind something gigantic. In the Hiroshima Peace Memorial Museum there is a display of clocks and watches that all stopped at the exact moment of the atomic blast. The atom bomb, they seem to say, was so great that it had the power to stop time.

But perhaps the most effective way that memorials convey

the vastness of wartime events is also the simplest: through their own sheer size. Many of the memorials in this book are larger than life. Some are truly gigantic. There is a simple rule of thumb that holds true for most of them: the bigger the event being commemorated, the bigger the monument.

This chapter tells the story of one of the largest of them all: the huge statue that stands on top of Mamayev Kurgan, in the city of Volgograd in Russia. Its size tells us a great deal – not only about the Second World War, but also about the Russian psyche, and the bonds that continue to hold it prisoner.

Mamayev Kurgan is not the site of a single monument, but of a complex of monuments, each more gigantic than the last. The first time I came here, I felt I was entering a realm of titans. At the foot of the hill stands a huge sculpture of a bare-chested man clutching a machine gun in one hand and a grenade in the other. He seems to rise out of the very rock, torso rippling, as tall as a three-storey building. Beyond him, on either side of the steps that lead to the summit, are relief sculptures of giant soldiers springing out of the ruined walls as if in the midst of battle. Farther up the hill is the gigantic figure of a grieving mother, more than twice the size of my house. She is hunched over the body of her dead son, sobbing into a large pool of water, called the 'Lake of Tears'.

The dozens of statues arranged in this park are all giants: not one of them is under six metres (20 feet) tall, and some of them depict heroes three or four times that size. And yet they are dwarfed by the single statue that rises above them all, on the summit of the hill. Here, overlooking the Volga, stands a colossal representation of Mother Russia beckoning to her children to come and fight for her. Her mouth is open in battle cry, her hair and dress fluttering in the wind; and in her right hand she holds a vast sword pointing up into the sky. From her feet to the tip of her sword she stands 85 metres (280 feet) high. She is nearly twice as tall, and forty times as heavy, as the Statue of Liberty in New York City. When she was first unveiled in 1967, she was the largest statue in the world.

This memorial, entitled 'The Motherland Calls!', is one of Russia's most iconic statues. It was the creation of Soviet sculptor Yevgeny Vuchetich, who spent years designing and building it. It contains around 2,500 metric tonnes of metal and 5,500 tonnes of concrete. The sword alone weighs 14 tonnes. So huge was the statue that Vuchetich was obliged to collaborate with a structural engineer, Nikolai Nikitin, to ensure that it did not collapse under its own weight. Holes had to be drilled into the sword to reduce the threat of the wind catching it and causing the whole structure to sway.

Were this monument in Italy or France it would appear absurdly grandiose, but here on the banks of the Volga, in the city that was once called Stalingrad, it feels quietly appropriate. The battle that took place here in 1942 dwarfs anything that happened in the West. It began with the greatest German bombardment of the war, and progressed with attacks and counterattacks by more than a dozen entire armies. Within the city itself, soldiers fought from street to street, and even from room to room, in a landscape of shattered houses. Over the course of five months around two million men lost their lives, their health or their liberty. The combined casualties of this one battle were greater than the casualties that Britain and America together suffered during the whole of the war.

As one stands on the summit of Mamayev Kurgan in the shadow of the gigantic statue of the Motherland, one can feel the weight of all this history. It is oppressive even for a foreigner. But for many Russians this place is sacred. The word 'Kurgan' in Russian means a tumulus or burial mound. The hill is an ancient site dedicated to a fourteenth-century warlord, but in the wake of the greatest battle of the greatest war in history, it carries a new symbolism. This place was one of the major battlegrounds of 1942, and an unknown number of soldiers and civilians are buried here. Even today, when walking on the hill, it is possible to find fragments of metal and bone buried in the soil. The Motherland statue stands, both figuratively and literally, upon a mountain of corpses.

The scale of the war in Russia is one reason why the monuments on Mamayev Kurgan are so huge, but it is not the only reason – in fact, it is not even the main reason. The statues of muscular heroes and weeping mothers might be huge, but it is the giantess on the summit of the hill that dominates them all. It is important to remember that this is a representation not of the war, but of the Motherland. Its message is simple: no matter how great the battle, and no matter how great the enemy, the Motherland is greater still. Her colossal size is supposed to be a comfort to the struggling soldiers and weeping mothers, a reminder that for all their sacrifice, they are at least a part of something powerful and magnificent. This is the true meaning of Mamayev Kurgan.

In the aftermath of the Second World War, the people of the Soviet Union had little to console them. Not only were they traumatised by loss, but they also faced an uncertain future. Russians did not benefit economically from the war as the Americans did: the violence had left their economy in ruins. Nor did Russians win any new freedoms: despite widespread hopes of a political thaw after 1945, Stalinist repression soon started up all over again. Life in Russia after the war was grim.

I can't help feeling that there must be a renewed sense of instability, or vulnerability, which is driving Russians to insist ever more stridently upon their wartime heroism. In other words, the monuments that they are erecting today have as much to do with the present as with the past.

Or perhaps this is simply about nation-building. Russia is not the country that it once was. It has lost an empire, and not yet found a new role for itself in the world. For many Russians, the building of war memorials serves as a reminder of the status that their country once had, and perhaps also gives a sense of hope that, one day soon, Russia might rise again. The bigger the monument, the greater the sense of pride – and the greater the nostalgia. The glorification of the war has become a central pillar of Vladimir Putin's programme to forge a new sense of national identity.

This too can be felt at Mamayev Kurgan. During the 1990s, when Russian power was crumbling, the Motherland statue also began to fall apart. Decaying pipes around the 'Lake of Tears' began to leak water into the hill around the statue, making the soil unstable. By the year 2000, deep cracks had begun to appear in the statue's shoulders. A few years later, reports emerged that it was listing 20 centimetres to one side. The cash-strapped Russian government kept promising to pay for reconstruction work, but the money never arrived. Nobody knew whether this official neglect was due to Russia's new-found poverty, or its new-found ambivalence towards its Soviet past.

In recent years, however, the monument has had a new lease of life. When I visited in 2018, the Motherland statue had just been repaired. The other monuments in downtown Volgograd had also been given a facelift, and the whole of the city's Victory Park was closed for refurbishment. In the

The only consolation offered to Russian and other Soviet people was that their country had proven itself at last to be a truly great nation. In 1945, the USSR possessed the largest army the world has ever seen. It dominated not only the vast Eurasian land mass, but also the Baltic and the Black Sea. The Second World War had not only restored the country's borders, but extended them, both to the west and to the east, and Soviet influence now stretched deep into the heart of Europe. Before the war, the Soviet Union had been a second-rate power, weakened by internal upheaval. After the war, it was a superpower.

The Motherland statue on Mamayev Kurgan was designed to be proof of all this. It was built in the 1960s, when the USSR was at the height of its strength. It stood as a warning to anyone who dared attack the Soviet Union, but also as a symbol of reassurance to the Soviet people. The giant, it declared, would always protect them.

For the Russian citizens who first stood on the summit of this hill with the Motherland statue at their backs, the vistas looked endless. Everything to the west of them for a thousand miles was Soviet territory. To the east they could travel through nine time zones without once leaving their country. Even the heavens seemed to belong to them: the first man in space was a Russian, and the first woman too. It is impossible to look up at the Motherland statue without also gazing beyond, to the endless skies above her.

Since those days, Russia has never stopped building war memorials. Many of them are on a similar scale to those in Volgograd. In 1974, for example, a statue 42 metres (138 feet) high of a Soviet soldier was erected in Murmansk, in memory of the men who died during the defence of Arctic Russia in July 1941. In the early 1980s, when Ukraine was still a part of the Soviet Union, a second Motherland statue was erected in Kiev. (Like the statue on Mamayev Kurgan, it was designed by Vuchetich. Including its plinth, it stands over 100 metres, or around 320 feet, tall.) And in 1985, in celebration of the fortieth anniversary of the end of the war, a 79-metre-high victory monument (around 260 feet tall) was erected in Riga, the capital of Soviet Latvia.

All these statues and monuments were meant to be symbols of power and confidence. But a generation after the Motherland statue in Volgograd was inaugurated, Soviet power began to waver. In the 1980s, Eastern Bloc countries like Poland and East Germany began to pull away from Soviet influence, culminating in the collapse of Communism in those countries in 1989. Then pieces of the Soviet Union itself began to break off: first Lithuania in March 1990, followed in quick succession by thirteen other states in the Baltic, eastern Europe, the Caucasus and central Asia. The giant was crumbling. The dissolution of the USSR was finally announced on 26 December 1991.

The sense of despair felt by many Russians during this period was palpable. Madeleine Albright, America's Secretary of State at the end of the 1990s, tells the story of meeting a Russian man who complained that 'We used to be a super-power, but now we're Bangladesh with missiles.' For decades, national greatness had been the only consolation for all the loss that men like him had suffered throughout the century. Now this too had been taken away.

In such an atmosphere, Russia's gargantuan war memorials began to look less like symbols of power, and more like Ozymandias in the famous poem by Shelley: relics of past glories, destined to be swallowed, slowly but surely, by the sands of time. But this did not stop the Russian authorities

from building them. On the contrary: Russia ha stopped celebrating the glories of the Second World 1995, for example, a brand new 'Museum of the Great War' was opened in Moscow. In front of it stands a mo that is even taller than the statue on Mamayev Ku fact, standing at 141.8 metres (or 465 feet) tall, it is th Second World War memorial anywhere in the world monuments followed. In April 2007, Belgorod, Ku Oryol were declared 'Cities of Military Glory' because role they had played during the war, and brand new c were erected in each location. The following Octob more cities were given the title, and five more obelisks e Within just another five years, more than forty cities Russia were honoured in the same way, with brand new ments springing up from Vyborg to Vladivostok.

Why do the Russians continue to commemorate th in this manner? More than seventy-five years have since the final days of the conflict. Is it not time to la rest?

There are a couple of possible explanations for the cou seemingly limitless addiction to massive Second World monuments. The first is that the trauma caused by the was so great that Russians simply cannot forget it. They compelled to tell the stories of the war again and agai the same way that individuals who have experienced tra often have flashbacks. These new memorials, each seemi bigger than the last, are Russia's way of coming to terms its past.

I'm sure that this is true, but it is also a little simplistic. example, it does not explain why the memorials are grow and replicating now more than ever. Is there something ab life in Russia today that triggers these concrete flashbac central square, which is named the 'Square of the Fallen Heroes', school children were practising their marching for a ceremony to honour the Stalingrad dead.

There is pride here, and sorrow, in equal measure. When you climb the hill today, you see people from all over Russia who have come to this place to pay their respects. Families bring children to teach them about the heroism of their great-grandfathers. Young women pose for photos in front of the Motherland statue, and carry red carnations to lay at the feet of the monuments. Military men come in full dress uniform, their medals clanking as they climb the steps.

None of these people can escape the history that has forged them, nor the longing for greatness that has been so integral to their nation's consciousness since 1945. For better or worse, they continue to live in the shadow of the great statue that stands on top of the hill.

The 'Four Sleepers' monument in 2010, before it was taken down

2

Russia and Poland: 'Four Sleepers' Monument, Warsaw

Every nation takes pride in its heroes. The monuments we create to those heroes have a special place in our hearts, because they are representative of all we hold dear: they show us at our very best, with all our most attractive qualities on display. But how we would like to think of ourselves is not always the same as how we really are. And neither is it the same as how we are viewed by others. Our monuments may look glorious to us, but to other people, with other values, they may look distinctly unheroic, even grotesque.

The Russian people are rightly proud of their Second World War heroes, but one does not have to travel far from Russia to find a very different narrative about the role played by that country during the conflict. In neighbouring states like Ukraine and Poland, the Russians are often regarded not as heroes but as colonisers. This narrative too is played out in the story of Europe's monuments. And one monument in particular shows how polarised our different versions of history have become.

* * *

The Monument to Brotherhood in Arms was built in 1945,
and erected in Warsaw at the end of that year. It was designed
by a Soviet army engineer, Major Alexander Nienko, but was
constructed by a group of Polish sculptors. It depicted three
larger-than-life soldiers on top of a six-metre plinth (around
20 foot), striding forward, weapons in hand. Standing at the
corners of the plinth were four further statues – two Soviet
soldiers and two Polish ones – their heads bowed in sombre
contemplation. As a result of wartime shortages, the original
statues were made of painted plaster; but two years later they
were replaced with bronze casts made from melted-down
German ammunition. On the plinth itself were inscribed the
words: 'Glory to the heroes of the Soviet Army, comrades in
arms, who gave their lives for the freedom and independence
of the Polish nation'.

This monument was meant to depict a new era of friendship
between Poland and the Soviet Union. The two countries had
shared an extremely difficult history, stretching right back
into Tsarist times. They had actually begun the war on opposite sides: the USSR had initially allied itself with Hitler, and
had taken part in the invasion of Poland in 1939. But two
years later, when the Nazis had turned against them, the
Soviets had sought to build a new relationship with the Poles.
They released Polish prisoners and exiles, and allowed them
to reform an army. As a consequence, some 200,000 Polish
troops fought alongside their former enemies in 1945. The
liberation of Warsaw was carried out by Polish soldiers and
Soviet soldiers fighting together.

The Monument to Brotherhood in Arms therefore fulfilled
several functions at once. It was an acknowledgement of the
genuine debt that Poland owed to the Soviets: had it not been
for the sacrifices of the Red Army, Poland would not even

have existed in 1945. It promoted hopes for the future: if Poland and the USSR could collaborate in wartime, then why not in peacetime too? And, of course, it was a work of political propaganda. The soldiers who stand on the top of the plinth are Soviets, with the Polish soldiers below them: from now on, as far as the Soviets were concerned, that would be the correct hierarchy.

This was the first monument to be built in Warsaw after the war, but it was soon followed by others. All over the country, similar memorials began to appear. There were sculptures celebrating Polish-Soviet friendship, obelisks commemorating their joint victory over the Nazis, plaques dedicated to their common war dead, tombs, cemeteries, everlasting flames. According to a list drawn up in 1994, around 570 monuments dedicated to fallen Soviet soldiers were built across Poland in the aftermath of the war. This was all part of an official drive to build on the wartime collaboration between Poland and the USSR and forge a new, Communist future together.

Unfortunately, none of these memorials inspired anything like the love and devotion that similar memorials did in the USSR. Since they celebrated the exploits and sacrifices of foreign people, they were not monuments in which Poles themselves could take much personal pride – at most they were monuments to gratitude and friendship. But when that gratitude ran dry and that friendship turned sour, the monuments began to take on an altogether darker meaning.

Most Poles knew very well where they stood in any partnership with the USSR. They saw these symbols of power and glory and began to suspect that it was not only the Nazis who had been ground beneath the wheels of Soviet greatness. Soon they began to take out their frustrations on those symbols.

Soviet monuments were often vandalised, defaced, and covered with nationalist graffiti. They were given derogatory nicknames based on popular memories of the way that Soviet soldiers had behaved during the liberation: names like 'the looters' memorial' or 'the tomb of the unknown rapist'. The Monument to Brotherhood in Arms in Warsaw was no exception. People joked that the statues at each corner were not hanging their heads in mourning, but because they had fallen asleep on duty. Thereafter, the memorial was popularly known as *Czterech Śpiących*, or 'The Four Sleepers'.*

Over the next forty years, the monument continued to stand on its plinth in Warsaw's Praga district. It was occasionally used as a site of remembrance for the war or as a venue for celebrating the more general victory of Communism in Europe. On the thirty-fifth anniversary of the October Revolution, for example, the Warsaw Philharmonic played here, while officials laid flowers at the foot of the monument.

But in 1989, everything changed. During that extraordinary year, Communist governments across eastern Europe began to collapse. The Berlin Wall was breached, dictatorships were toppled, and Soviet monuments everywhere were torn down. For a while the world's newspapers regularly carried photographs of statues falling: Romania's Petru Groza, Albania's Enver Hoxha, Poland's Bolesław Bierut and, all over Europe, Lenin after Lenin after Lenin.

---

* This nickname is more radical than it at first appears. According to popular memory, the Soviet Red Army could have liberated Warsaw as early as 1944, when the local population launched an uprising against the Nazi occupiers. Instead, the Soviets waited until the uprising had been crushed, thereby eliminating any future resistance to their own regime, before finally crossing the Vistula to liberate the shattered city. In other words, they 'slept' while Warsaw burned.

Remarkably, the 'Four Sleepers' monument in Warsaw survived these years unscathed. In 1992 the local authority briefly considered dismantling it; but the idea caused such disagreement – especially when one of the artists who had helped to create it, Stefan Momot, stood up in a meeting to defend it – that the proposal was eventually dropped.

Fifteen years later, however, another attempt was made to remove it, this time on practical grounds. Transport experts were considering the creation of a new tram stop on the exact location of the monument as part of a city-wide transport improvement plan. The tram idea was eventually abandoned, but four years later another transport plan insisted that the 'Four Sleepers' had to be moved to make way for a new underground station. The authorities promised that it would be put back just as soon as the construction of the station was finished. So, in 2011, it was taken down and transported to a conservation workshop in Michałowice.

This, it appeared, was exactly the opportunity that opponents of the memorial had been waiting for. Members of the Law and Justice Party, a right-wing populist movement, were especially vocal. They argued that the monument should never be allowed back to the square, on the grounds that it glorified a foreign power that had subjugated Poland for more than forty years. They called the 'Four Sleepers' a monument to shame, which painted the Polish people as passive bystanders in a Soviet story. It, and all monuments like it, was an insult to Poland, and a falsification of Polish history.

Other figures joined in with the vilification of the monument. Various historians and former dissidents pointed out that the 'Four Sleepers' stood at the centre of a district that had been filled with institutions of state repression. The Warsaw Office of Public Security, a provincial detention centre, the headquarters of the NKVD and a city prison had all stood within 100 metres (328 feet) of the monument. 'In each of these places "the enemies of the state" . . . were interrogated and tortured,' wrote Dr Andrzej Zawistowski of the Polish Institute for National Remembrance. For such people, the monument represented not only the prison of history, but *actual* prisons, where real people had been persecuted.

And yet many others were willing to defend the monument. Socialist politicians argued that the memorial did not glorify Stalinism at all, or commemorate the Soviet leaders who repressed Poland, but merely the ordinary foot-soldiers, who were often conscripted into the Red Army by force. Ageing veterans pointed out that 600,000 of these 'Sachas and Vanyas' had died on Polish soil, and that Polish soldiers were also represented on the monument.

The controversy raged for four years, and involved countless articles in the press, petitions, media debates, demonstrations and acts of vandalism. In 2013, the local authority carried out an opinion poll about whether the monument should stay or go. The results seemed quite emphatic: only 8 per cent wanted the monument to be destroyed, and 12 per cent wanted it moved to a far-off location, but 72 per cent wanted it to be put back in the square. Opponents countered that the sample size had been less than a thousand, and that most people only wanted to keep the monument because it was something they had grown used to. If Poland was to look to the future it needed to free itself from this toxic history.

In the end, it was the nationalist faction that won out. In 2015, the city council announced that it would not return the 'Four Sleepers' monument to Wileński Square after all. Three years later, it was announced that it had been donated

The only consolation offered to Russian and other Soviet people was that their country had proven itself at last to be a truly great nation. In 1945, the USSR possessed the largest army the world has ever seen. It dominated not only the vast Eurasian land mass, but also the Baltic and the Black Sea. The Second World War had not only restored the country's borders, but extended them, both to the west and to the east, and Soviet influence now stretched deep into the heart of Europe. Before the war, the Soviet Union had been a second-rate power, weakened by internal upheaval. After the war, it was a superpower.

The Motherland statue on Mamayev Kurgan was designed to be proof of all this. It was built in the 1960s, when the USSR was at the height of its strength. It stood as a warning to anyone who dared attack the Soviet Union, but also as a symbol of reassurance to the Soviet people. The giant, it declared, would always protect them.

For the Russian citizens who first stood on the summit of this hill with the Motherland statue at their backs, the vistas looked endless. Everything to the west of them for a thousand miles was Soviet territory. To the east they could travel through nine time zones without once leaving their country. Even the heavens seemed to belong to them: the first man in space was a Russian, and the first woman too. It is impossible to look up at the Motherland statue without also gazing beyond, to the endless skies above her.

Since those days, Russia has never stopped building war memorials. Many of them are on a similar scale to those in Volgograd. In 1974, for example, a statue 42 metres (138 feet) high of a Soviet soldier was erected in Murmansk, in memory of the men who died during the defence of Arctic Russia in July 1941. In the early 1980s, when Ukraine was still a part

of the Soviet Union, a second Motherland statue was erected
in Kiev. (Like the statue on Mamayev Kurgan, it was designed
by Vuchetich. Including its plinth, it stands over 100 metres,
or around 320 feet, tall.) And in 1985, in celebration of the
fortieth anniversary of the end of the war, a 79-metre-high
victory monument (around 260 feet tall) was erected in Riga,
the capital of Soviet Latvia.

All these statues and monuments were meant to be
symbols of power and confidence. But a generation after the
Motherland statue in Volgograd was inaugurated, Soviet
power began to waver. In the 1980s, Eastern Bloc countries
like Poland and East Germany began to pull away from
Soviet influence, culminating in the collapse of Communism
in those countries in 1989. Then pieces of the Soviet Union
itself began to break off: first Lithuania in March 1990,
followed in quick succession by thirteen other states in the
Baltic, eastern Europe, the Caucasus and central Asia. The
giant was crumbling. The dissolution of the USSR was finally
announced on 26 December 1991.

The sense of despair felt by many Russians during this
period was palpable. Madeleine Albright, America's Secretary
of State at the end of the 1990s, tells the story of meeting a
Russian man who complained that 'We used to be a superpower, but now we're Bangladesh with missiles.' For decades,
national greatness had been the only consolation for all the
loss that men like him had suffered throughout the century.
Now this too had been taken away.

In such an atmosphere, Russia's gargantuan war memorials
began to look less like symbols of power, and more like
Ozymandias in the famous poem by Shelley: relics of past
glories, destined to be swallowed, slowly but surely, by the
sands of time. But this did not stop the Russian authorities

from building them. On the contrary: Russia has never stopped celebrating the glories of the Second World War. In 1995, for example, a brand new 'Museum of the Great Patriotic War' was opened in Moscow. In front of it stands a monument that is even taller than the statue on Mamayev Kurgan: in fact, standing at 141.8 metres (or 465 feet) tall, it is the tallest Second World War memorial anywhere in the world. Other monuments followed. In April 2007, Belgorod, Kursk and Oryol were declared 'Cities of Military Glory' because of the role they had played during the war, and brand new obelisks were erected in each location. The following October, five more cities were given the title, and five more obelisks erected. Within just another five years, more than forty cities across Russia were honoured in the same way, with brand new monuments springing up from Vyborg to Vladivostok.

Why do the Russians continue to commemorate the war in this manner? More than seventy-five years have passed since the final days of the conflict. Is it not time to lay it to rest?

There are a couple of possible explanations for the country's seemingly limitless addiction to massive Second World War monuments. The first is that the trauma caused by the war was so great that Russians simply cannot forget it. They feel compelled to tell the stories of the war again and again, in the same way that individuals who have experienced trauma often have flashbacks. These new memorials, each seemingly bigger than the last, are Russia's way of coming to terms with its past.

I'm sure that this is true, but it is also a little simplistic. For example, it does not explain why the memorials are growing and replicating now more than ever. Is there something about life in Russia today that triggers these concrete flashbacks?

I can't help feeling that there must be a renewed sense of instability, or vulnerability, which is driving Russians to insist ever more stridently upon their wartime heroism. In other words, the monuments that they are erecting today have as much to do with the present as with the past.

Or perhaps this is simply about nation-building. Russia is not the country that it once was. It has lost an empire, and not yet found a new role for itself in the world. For many Russians, the building of war memorials serves as a reminder of the status that their country once had, and perhaps also gives a sense of hope that, one day soon, Russia might rise again. The bigger the monument, the greater the sense of pride – and the greater the nostalgia. The glorification of the war has become a central pillar of Vladimir Putin's programme to forge a new sense of national identity.

This too can be felt at Mamayev Kurgan. During the 1990s, when Russian power was crumbling, the Motherland statue also began to fall apart. Decaying pipes around the 'Lake of Tears' began to leak water into the hill around the statue, making the soil unstable. By the year 2000, deep cracks had begun to appear in the statue's shoulders. A few years later, reports emerged that it was listing 20 centimetres to one side. The cash-strapped Russian government kept promising to pay for reconstruction work, but the money never arrived. Nobody knew whether this official neglect was due to Russia's new-found poverty, or its new-found ambivalence towards its Soviet past.

In recent years, however, the monument has had a new lease of life. When I visited in 2018, the Motherland statue had just been repaired. The other monuments in downtown Volgograd had also been given a facelift, and the whole of the city's Victory Park was closed for refurbishment. In the to a new Museum of Polish History in the north of the city. According to museum staff, it will finally be on display in 2021 – some ten years after it was removed from its original site.

What is a hero? What is a hero for? Russians see the deconstruction of their war heroes as a personal affront, but heroes are much more than mere representations of actual people; they are also representations of ideas. If you no longer agree with the ideas, then perhaps the heroes must come down.

For Russians, statues like the 'Four Sleepers' represent bravery, liberation, brotherhood – and, of course, greatness. But for Poles and other eastern Europeans, they represent something entirely different: subjugation, humiliation, repression. The truth is that they represent both sets of ideas at the same time, but the emotions surrounding these monuments are so strong that many people are simply not willing to entertain such ambiguity.

The 'Four Sleepers' monument is a single casualty in a war over the memory of 1945 that has swept across Poland in recent years. Dozens of Soviet war monuments were pulled down or destroyed in the exuberant atmosphere of 1989, and dozens more were removed by local councils in the years that followed. In 2017, the national government finally embarked on an official programme to remove those that remained. This went against an agreement made in 1994 between Russia and Poland to respect one another's 'places of memory'. But the Polish government, which by now was dominated by the populist Law and Justice Party, stated that all they were really doing was removing the symbols of foreign power from their towns and cities: they promised not to touch any memorials that marked genuine burial places.

It is not only Poland that has embarked on such a programme. In 2015, for example, the Ukrainian government also passed a law aimed at the complete de-Sovietisation of the country. It included the removal of all Communist symbols and statues of Communist figures, and the renaming of thousands of streets, towns and villages. This was carried out quite quickly. By 2018, the director of the Ukrainian Institute of National Remembrance, Volodymyr Vyatrovych, was able to announce that the de-Communisation of the nation had been achieved.

Similar controversies have hit Soviet war memorials all over eastern and central Europe. The Monument to the Heroes of the Red Army in Vienna is regularly vandalised. The Monument to the Soviet Army in Sofia has repeatedly been daubed with paint – sometimes in jest, but more often in protest over recent actions by the Russian government. The Victory Monument in Riga was bombed in 1997 by a far-right Latvian nationalist group, and since then veterans of the Second World War have repeatedly called for it to be taken down. In Estonia, in 2007, the Bronze Soldier memorial to the 'liberators of Tallinn' was removed from the city centre and relocated in the military cemetery a few kilometres away, sparking two days of protest by Tallinn's ethnic Russian minority.

Many people across eastern Europe regard this iconoclasm as the only way to free their countries from the burden of their Communist past. Given all that they have suffered, this is quite understandable; but, as any psychologist will tell you, history is not so easily escaped. As will become apparent, these people seem to be deconstructing one prison only to build themselves another.

In the meantime, most ordinary Russians struggle to

understand why they should be so hated in eastern Europe. They see the dismantling of monuments to their war heroes as a personal affront. But since they no longer rule in eastern Europe, there is nothing they can do about it.

3

USA: Marine Corps Memorial, Arlington, Virginia

If Russia's monumental heroes reflect that nation's longing for greatness, what of the other post-war superpower? How do Americans tend to view their heroes?

In my working life, I often travel to different parts of the world giving lectures about the Second World War. In one particular lecture I talk about America's mythology of heroism. It is a subject that fascinates me because, to a European like me, it seems so extreme. Americans sometimes seem to regard their war heroes as if they were not human at all, but figures from legend, or even saints. President Reagan spoke of them as a Christian army, impelled by faith and blessed by God. President Clinton called them 'freedom's warriors', who had immortalised themselves by fighting 'the forces of darkness'. TV journalist Tom Brokaw famously proclaimed them 'the greatest generation any society has ever produced'. How can any real-life soldier or veteran possibly live up to such expectations?

I have noticed that reactions to my lecture differ depending on where I deliver it. Whenever I'm in America, my audience tends to listen respectfully in silence: some of them agree with me, and some of them don't. But when I give this lecture anywhere in Europe, the audience tends to snigger. At one point, when I quote at length from a speech given by Bill Clinton to commemorate the fiftieth anniversary of VE Day, they sometimes laugh out loud. American rhetoric, to many Europeans, sounds ridiculous.

It is always nice to get a laugh when you're speaking; but there is something about this particular laughter that worries me. Europeans often make fun of America's insular view of the world, but they themselves are often equally ignorant of America. They don't mean to be disrespectful; they simply can't quite believe that anyone is serious when they speak about their war veterans in this way. But Americans are deadly serious. In the American consciousness, the role that their soldiers played during the Second World War has come to represent everything that is best about their country.

This gulf in understanding between Europeans and Americans is immediately apparent as soon as one looks at their war memorials. America makes monuments to its heroes; Europe much more often makes monuments to its victims. American monuments are triumphant; European ones are melancholy. American monuments are idealistic, while European ones – occasionally, at least – are more likely to be morally ambiguous.

If America does not understand Europe, it is because America never suffered as Europe or Asia did. The vast majority of Americans only ever experienced the war through the images brought home by film units and war photographers, which did not always give the most truthful or complete picture of what was taking place. Some of the most famous American monuments to the war are based on these photographs, and it is no wonder that they portray a rather idealistic view.

If Europe does not understand America, however, it is for very different reasons. Europeans have failed to grasp the fact that American depth of feeling about the war comes not from a sense of history, but from a sense of identity. The war is nothing but a screen upon which they have projected much deeper ideas and emotions that are right at the heart of the American psyche. In other words, when public figures in America wax lyrical about the war, they aren't really talking about the war at all. This, as we shall see, is obvious as soon as one takes a closer look at their war memorials.

One of the best-loved monuments to American heroism during the Second World War is the Marine Corps memorial in Arlington, Virginia. It stands at the very heart of American power, not far from the Pentagon building, with an unrestricted view across the Potomac River to the Lincoln Memorial, the Washington Monument and the US Capitol. It is undeniably one of the most important monuments in the country.

Strictly speaking, this isn't a Second World War memorial at all – it is a memorial to *all* the marines who have fallen since the formation of the corps in 1775. But it was built in the immediate aftermath of the Second World War, and paid for by donations from marines who had served during that war. Furthermore, it is based on one of the most iconic images from 1945 – Joe Rosenthal's photograph of the moment when a group of marines raised a flag on Mount Suribachi during the battle for the island of Iwo Jima.

The memorial depicts six soldiers, their weapons slung over their shoulders, standing on a patch of jagged, unforgiving ground. Like all the statues we have seen so far they are colossal – more than five times taller than an average man.

The figure at the front of the group leans forward, his body almost horizontal, using all his weight to drive a gigantic flagpole into the ground. Those behind him are hunched together, trying also to lend their weight to the task. At the back of the group, one of the marines stretches upwards, his fingers not quite reaching the pole. Beneath them, on the black granite plinth, are Fleet Admiral Chester Nimitz's words summing up the performance of the Marines at Iwo Jima, 'Uncommon valor was a common virtue'.

Like all good memorials, this one tells a story. However, it is a story with many layers, and to understand it properly, one needs to go right back to the beginning of the conflict.

America's war began on 7 December 1941 when the Japanese launched their notorious attack on the US Pacific Fleet at Pearl Harbor. This remains one of the defining events of American history. For ninety minutes, hundreds of Japanese planes bombed American ships, airfields and port facilities, killing more than 2,400 people and wounding almost 1,200 more. Twenty-one ships were sunk, and 188 military aircraft destroyed. The attack came as a complete surprise, because the US Secretary of State did not receive a declaration of war until after it had begun. The sense of shock that this produced in American society is impossible to overstate. Its only recent parallel has been the terrorist attacks of 9/11.

The logic behind this military strike was simple. Japan wanted to take control of the whole Pacific region, and knew that in order to do so they would have to discourage America from stepping in. The Japanese leadership did not think that America had the stomach for a long war in the Pacific, and were willing to gamble that a quick, decisive victory would force them to negotiate a settlement. In other words, Pearl

Harbor was not supposed to start a war with America; it was supposed to prevent one.

Anyone with even a cursory knowledge of US history could have told them that this was a risky strategy. America *never* gives up without a fight. Once they had recovered from their initial surprise, the American military responded with ruthless determination. Over the next three and a half years it clawed its way, step by step, back across the Pacific Ocean. It fought huge naval battles in the Coral Sea and at Midway; it launched submarine strikes against Japanese supply lines; it liberated one island group after another.

The Marines were often at the forefront of the action. The battles they fought to secure Guadalcanal, Tarawa, the Marshall Islands, the Mariana Islands and Palau were some of the most brutal of the whole war. At this time, Japanese soldiers were considered notorious for their viciousness and their refusal to surrender, and inflicted terrible casualties on the less experienced Americans. Before long, the US Marines began repaying them in kind, taking few prisoners, and occasionally massacring them after they had been disarmed. Reports and photographs of atrocities by either side rarely made it back home to America, because US censors wished to spare the public both the anguish and the shame of what was really going on.

Eventually, US forces advanced all the way to the shores of Japan. The first island they reached was Iwo Jima. After four days of savage fighting, a group of marines managed to fight their way to the top of Mount Suribachi, the highest point of the island. To signal that they had reached the summit, they attached a US flag to a length of piping and raised it. Later that day, a second group of marines brought a larger flag up to replace it, and war photographer Joe Rosenthal was there to capture the moment for posterity.

It is this second flag-raising that the Marine Corps Memorial immortalises in bronze. The sculpture is a study in determination. The effort required to plant the flag is plain to see: each one of the six figures appears to be straining every sinew. They are the personification of American grit. The sculpture is also a study in unity: these Americans are all working together in harmony, their hands placed along the same pole, their legs bent in parallel with one another. It is a study in violence – more so, perhaps, than any other American monument to the war. No Japanese soldiers are being killed here, but the force with which the six men are driving the flag into hostile foreign ground is at least suggestive of something darker, which the US censor never allowed the American people to see.

Most of all, however, this is a study in vengeance. The story that begins with Pearl Harbor ends with American troops raising their flag on Japanese soil. In this sense, it is as stark a warning as the statue of the Motherland in Volgograd: this is what happens to anyone who dares attack America.

All these qualities would have been keenly felt by those who stood before the memorial when it was first unveiled in November 1954. Three of the men depicted in the sculpture were present at the inauguration ceremony, as were the mothers of the other three, who had been killed shortly after Joe Rosenthal's iconic photograph was taken. They and the 5,000 other attendees, many of whom had direct experience of the Pacific War, would have had good cause to nurture some of the darker emotions inspired by the monument.

But vengeance and grim determination are not qualities that explain the reverence with which the majority of Americans regard this monument. The thousands of people who come each week to pay their respects, or to watch one of the sunset parades that are performed in front of the monument during the summer months, are not here to celebrate violence. There is clearly something else going on.

To understand this, one must move one's gaze from the figures at the front of the monument to those at the back. These men are not driving a spike into the soil, they are reaching their hands up, as if to heaven. Above them flies the US flag. The figure right at the back is trying to touch the flagpole, his outstretched fingers not quite reaching it. The effect is reminiscent of Michelangelo's famous painting of Adam stretching his hand towards God in the Sistine Chapel in Rome.

Felix de Weldon, the artist who sculpted the memorial, explained the image in a speech at the inauguration in 1954. 'The hands of these men reaching out,' he said, are 'groping for that which may be beyond one's means to attain, needing assistance from the power above, that power which we all need in time of adversity, and without whose guidance our efforts might well be fruitless.' This divine guidance is symbolised by the flag above them, which de Weldon called 'the emblem of our unity, our power, our thoughts and purpose as a nation'.

In other words, the real subject of the sculpture is not the US Marines at all, nor the victory over the Japanese, nor anything else to do with the Second World War. It is the flag which gives the monument its real meaning. This symbol, with its fusion of God and nation, is the real reason why the memorial is so well loved in America.

If there is a gulf of understanding between Europeans and Americans over the memory of the Second World War, then this is one of the issues that lies at the heart of it. Europe and

America learned very different lessons from the war. In the 1930s Europe was exposed to all the dangers of flag-waving. In the violent years that followed it experienced firsthand what happens when fanatical nationalism is allowed to get out of control. As a consequence, flags today are symbols that must be treated with great care. In post-war, post-colonial Europe, anyone who shows excessive passion towards their national flag is generally treated with suspicion. The idea of a monument glorifying the planting of a national flag on foreign soil would be absolutely unthinkable.

In the USA, by contrast, flags are everywhere: outside court-rooms, outside schools and government buildings, in public parks, outside people's homes, on their cars, adorning their clothes. The national anthem, which is nothing less than a hymn to the flag, is sung before every NFL football game; and the pledge of allegiance to the flag is recited by every child from the moment they are old enough to attend school. This has been the case since long before the Second World War; but the war cemented the holy bond between Americans and their flag.

What Europeans fail to understand is that, to most Americans, the flag means much more than mere nationhood. It is a symbol of virtues they believe to be universal: hope, freedom, justice and democracy. Between 1941 and 1945, Americans watched the progress of their flag across Europe and the Pacific, saw liberation spreading in its wake, and knew that they were doing something remarkable. After the war they were magnanimous to those they had defeated, nursing their economies back to health, and quickly handing them back their independence. This is the final meaning of the Iwo Jima memorial: when an American soldier plants a flag on foreign soil it is not an act of domination, but of liberation.

Americans understand this instinctively. That is why, since 1945, America has paraded its flag so proudly in Korea, Vietnam, Grenada, Somalia and Afghanistan. It is why, during the liberation of Baghdad in 2003, a modern marine climbed the statue of Saddam Hussein in Firdos Square and wrapped a US flag around his face. Americans believe passionately in the values they promote, which are no different from the values for which they fought the Second World War.

Unfortunately, other parts of the world see things rather differently. As we shall see next, however glorious an American flag seems when flown in the USA, it begins to look very different when planted on foreign soil.

4

USA and the Philippines: Douglas MacArthur Landing Memorial, Leyte

Just as the Soviets had monuments erected in their honour in other countries after the war, so too did the Americans. There are several in western Europe, most famously in Normandy near the beaches where the Allies landed on D-Day. There are also several in the Pacific, in places like Guadalcanal and Papua New Guinea, which saw some of the most vicious fighting of the war.

Unlike the Soviets, however, the Americans did not impose their own visions of glory upon the nations that they liberated. They did not seize positions on hill tops and in town squares, so that their monuments would dominate the urban land-scape. On the whole, they confined their memorials to the cemeteries where US servicemen lay buried. As a conse-quence, American monuments have never aroused the same animosity that monuments to the Soviets have: what nation could possibly object to their liberators paying quiet tribute to their dead?

Every now and then, however, a different kind of monument to American heroism is raised on foreign soil, and things suddenly become much more controversial.

One such monument can be found in the municipality of Palo, on the coast of Leyte in the Philippines. It consists of seven statues, standing in a pool of water near the shore. They are larger-than-life representations of the American officers and aides who led the liberation of the country from the Japanese in 1944. Among them is the Filipino president of the time, Sergio Osmeña – but he is not the main figure. Standing front and centre, taller than all the others, is the Supreme Commander of the Allied Forces for the South West Pacific Area, General Douglas MacArthur. He stands upright, chest out, shoulders back, as he strides purposefully towards the shore. His eyes are hidden behind dark glasses, but it is clear that his gaze is fixed on the land he is liberating.

The Douglas MacArthur Landing Memorial is based on a photograph that was taken on this very coastline in 1944 when its liberators first waded ashore. Like most monuments devoted to American soldiers, it represents a variety of heroic virtues: perseverance, bravery, goodness, redemption, victory. Unlike most other monuments, however, it locates those virtues not in a generic hero or American everyman, but in a real-life historical figure. And not just any figure: Douglas MacArthur was one of the most controversial generals of the war.

Had the Americans themselves erected this memorial, it would have raised a few eyebrows. But the fact that it was commissioned and paid for by the Filipino government is even more interesting. No other monument says more than this one about the fallibility of American heroes, or how they are viewed by the nations they liberated.

* * *

'I have returned': Gaetano Faillace's famous photograph of
MacArthur striding ashore at Leyte in 1944

Douglas MacArthur was a towering figure in the history of
both the Philippines and the US Army. His father was military
governor of the islands during their first days as a US colony,
and MacArthur himself served there several times, first as a
junior officer and later as commander. In the mid-1930s he
was appointed field marshal of the Philippine Army – the first
and only American ever to have held this rank. But what
would make him truly famous, and indeed infamous, was the
role that he played here and in other parts of Asia during and
after the Second World War.

MacArthur's war began on the morning of 8 December
1941, when the Japanese attacked the Philippines just a few
hours after they had struck Pearl Harbor. MacArthur, who
had only recently been put in charge of all US Army forces
in the Far East, was taken completely by surprise. Most of his
planes were destroyed on the ground before they even had a

chance to take off. Soon his coastal defences on Luzon were also overwhelmed, and his troops were forced to fall back in disarray.

They retreated to the Bataan peninsula, a mountainous stretch of jungle just across the bay from Manila, where they hoped to hold out until help arrived from the US Navy. But that help never came. For three and a half months MacArthur's men fought a series of desperate skirmishes against the Japanese with barely enough food and supplies to sustain them. Eventually they could hold out no longer. At the beginning of April 1942, around 80,000 starving men gave themselves up to the Japanese. Over the next two weeks at least 5,000 would die on an infamous 'death march' to internment camps in the north of the island. Thousands more were to die in squalid conditions as they waited out the rest of the war in captivity.

MacArthur himself escaped this fate at the last minute. Under the cover of night, he and a few key staff boarded a handful of patrol torpedo boats on the island of Corregidor and fled south to Mindanao. From here they caught one of the last flights out of the Philippines to safety in Australia.

Almost as soon as he arrived on Australian soil, MacArthur announced his determination to redeem himself. 'I shall return,' he told reporters on the station platform while he was changing trains at Terowie in South Australia. Over the next two and a half years he devoted himself to fulfilling this promise. Building up a force of eighteen American divisions, he fought desperate battles in Papua New Guinea and the Admiralty Islands. Gradually he clawed his way north towards the Philippines.

His return was just as dramatic as his escape. On 20 October 1944, backed up by the power of the US Seventh

Fleet, MacArthur began landing 200,000 men on the island of Leyte. While the battle was still raging, MacArthur himself boarded one of the landing boats and headed towards the shore. When it hit ground a few yards from the shoreline, he and his staff stepped down into the water and waded through the surf. The sound of small arms fire could be heard all around them, but MacArthur continued to walk fearlessly up onto the beach.

In the following days, a photograph of him striding through the waves would make front pages all over the world, accompanied by gushing articles which sang his praises to the skies. 'The successful Philippines invasion is more than a great military victory, it is a personal triumph for MacArthur,' announced one Australian newspaper. 'With a crusader's zeal and singleness of purpose rarely encountered, he concentrated everything into redeeming his pledge to the Filipino nation and to the haggard, battleworn Americans overrun on Bataan and Corregidor.'

MacArthur himself seemed to sense the huge historical importance of the moment. After he had waded ashore, he made his way to a radio and broadcast an extraordinary speech full of religious imagery. 'To the people of the Philippines,' he announced, 'I have returned . . . The hour of your redemption is here . . . Rally to me! . . . The guidance of divine God points the way. Follow in His name to the Holy Grail of righteous victory!'

This is the story told by the memorial that stands on the beach today. It depicts an American hero: compassionate but tough, determined not to give up on a desperate cause, unafraid to get his hands dirty, or his shoes wet, in the pursuit of liberating his people. Symbolically speaking, MacArthur *is* America. He is shown here bestowing upon the Philippines the most precious gift that America had to offer – the gift of freedom. But he is more than America, too: he is a father returning to save his children, a shepherd returning to save his flock. Looking at the memorial today, there is more than a touch of the Messiah about the way that he and his disciples stand in their pool of water: they appear to be walking on top of the water rather than wading through it. Behind them is nothing but sea and sky: it is as if they have descended not from a landing craft but from heaven itself.

Most memorials endow a kind of mythical power to the events of the past – that's the whole point of them. But imbuing a real historical figure with such qualities is a dangerous game. No man can possibly live up to such ideals, let alone a man as flamboyantly flawed as Douglas MacArthur.

There are other ways of telling the story which are not nearly so flattering to MacArthur. Many historians believe that his leadership, particularly at the beginning of the war, was greatly overrated. Why were his men not prepared for an attack? Why was their retreat to Bataan such a shambles? And why did he take such credit for the return to the Philippines, when it was only the victories of commanders in other branches of the military – particularly the US Navy – that made it possible?

Far from being the selfless, moral paragon of contemporary news stories, MacArthur is often accused of carelessness towards his men. At the beginning of the war, while his troops were starving on Bataan, he set up his command post on the well-stocked and well-fortified island of Corregidor. Records show that he only visited his beleaguered men on the main-land once. Embittered by his absence, they began calling him 'Dugout Doug', and composed disparaging songs about him, sung to the tune of 'The Battle Hymn of the Republic':

Dugout Doug, come out from hiding
Dugout Doug, come out from hiding
Give to Franklin the glad tidings
That his troops go starving on!

The care he took of civilian lives was not always exemplary either. During the landings at Palo he ruthlessly shelled the coastline, regardless of the civilians who lived there: it was only thanks to an American spy called Charles Parsons that local residents evacuated the area before the bombardment began. Later on in the campaign, MacArthur's forces bombarded Manila so comprehensively that by the end there was little left to liberate: around 100,000 Filipinos are thought to have been killed, and the historic heart of the city was reduced to rubble. When viewed from this perspective, MacArthur's record is not nearly as admirable as it at first appears.

If MacArthur was an exceptional military leader, he was also a highly narcissistic one. It was not mere chance that made the photograph of MacArthur wading ashore so famous: he himself gave it a helping hand. The picture was taken by his personal photographer, Gaetano Faillace, and promoted by his personal team of public relations officers. This team was notorious for stretching the truth in order to make the general look good. They often pretended that MacArthur was at the front with his men when he was actually hundreds of miles away in the comfort of Australia. They gave him credit for other people's successes, much to the chagrin of the US Navy, the Marine Corps, and even his own subordinates. According to George Kenny, MacArthur's air force chief, 'unless a news release painted the General with a halo and seated him on the highest pedestal in the universe, it should be killed.'

After his death, questions also began to arise about

MacArthur's moral character. In a groundbreaking article in the *Pacific Historical Review*, historian Carol Petillo revealed that the general had accepted a mysterious payment from the pre-war president of the Philippines, Manuel Quezon, of half a million dollars. The payment was made in the desperate days of early 1942, when Filipino leaders like Quezon were scrambling to escape falling into the hands of the Japanese. MacArthur had already told Washington that he was not willing to rescue Quezon; but after he received the money, Quezon was indeed evacuated. Most historians would stop short of suggesting that the money was a bribe to get MacArthur to change his mind; but all agree that there is something distasteful about an American leader accepting such a huge sum of money during the darkest days of the war, when his own men, just a few miles away on the Bataan peninsula, were starving.

Once one knows all this about Douglas MacArthur, is it possible to look at the memorial in the same way? The monument was supposed to celebrate the virtues of bravery, perseverance and morality, but what if it inadvertently celebrated a different set of qualities – vanity, arrogance and corruption? And what if these qualities also ended up being identified, via MacArthur, with America?

It is unlikely that the artist who created the monument asked himself any of these questions. Filipino sculptor Anastacio Caedo was commissioned to build the memorial in the mid-1970s, when memories of the war were still strong in the Philippines and MacArthur was still universally held in high regard. MacArthur was always the central figure in the monument. By his own admission, Caedo did not know the identity of all the men he was sculpting – he was simply trying to make a three-dimensional image of Faillace's famous photograph.

Caedo wanted to make the sculptures out of bronze, but there was not enough time or funds to get them ready for the inauguration. He therefore cast them in reinforced concrete and painted them with metallic olive-drab paint. (Today's bronze statues are a later replacement.) The unveiling was to take place in October 1977, but first there were political hurdles to negotiate. The president's wife, Imelda Marcos, ordered major changes to the memorial at the last moment. Caedo's sculpture included a giant landing craft as a backdrop to the seven statues, exactly as the wartime photographs showed; but the First Lady ordered the backdrop torn down, saying that the monument 'should honour men, not barges'. Caedo, who had spent eight months building this element of the memorial, reportedly burst into tears when it was dismantled.

It was not only Imelda Marcos who took a direct interest in the memorial. Her husband, President Ferdinand Marcos, was also heavily involved both in the planning of the monument and in the celebration of it when it was unveiled. In a speech at the inauguration, he made it clear what the memorial was supposed to symbolise: 'Let this Landing Memorial . . . be a tribute to the American fighting men who crossed the vast Pacific in fulfilment of a promise to return,' he said. Furthermore, 'Let it be a renewal of the Filipino people's bond of friendship with the people of the United States of America.'

Other public figures of the time expressed similar sentiments. The Filipino foreign minister, Carlos Romulo, emphasised how important the memory of MacArthur was for Filipino–American relations. 'We owe him a debt of gratitude that we cannot forget,' he said in an interview in 1981. 'His name is revered and idolised in the Philippines.'

There was a certain amount of national self-interest in

making such statements. During the 1970s, the Philippines was in thrall to American investment, American financial and military aid, and American credit. The country was moreover home to dozens of American military bases, from which US troops dominated the western Pacific and the South China Sea. In such an atmosphere, it certainly made sense to pay tribute to 'American fighting men' like MacArthur. Corrupt Filipino officials also had darker reasons to sing America's praises. Many of them, starting with President Marcos himself, were making a fortune out of bribes from American businesses, or from skimming development aid as it entered the country. The occasional grand gesture towards the USA was probably considered a sound investment.

However, alongside such cynical motivations, there was also a great deal of sincerity. Corrupt or not, Marcos and his administration did not impose the memorial upon his nation: it was always backed by popular sentiment. And probably personal sentiment too: it is impossible to escape the suspicion that government leaders had their own private reasons for wanting to see MacArthur honoured in this way. President Marcos had served under the general during the war, and claimed to have been personally decorated by him (although such claims later turned out to be more than a little exaggerated). Marcos was every bit as narcissistic as MacArthur, and repeatedly tried to wrap himself in the general's reflected glory. His wife, Imelda, also had a personal interest in the memorial: she had grown up in Leyte, very close to where the landings took place, and had witnessed the liberation first hand. Carlos Romulo, meanwhile, was even closer to MacArthur; so close, in fact, that he himself appears in the monument (he is the helmeted figure standing at the back of the group).

In commissioning this memorial, interfering in its design, and celebrating it so wholeheartedly, those at the centre of government were not only honouring an important moment in Filipino history; nor were they merely acknowledging an important military, political and economic alliance. They were also dramatising one of the most important moments in their own lives.

* * *

Times change. When I first visited the Philippines in 1990, a fresh wind had already begun to blow. Marcos had gone, ousted by a popular uprising in 1986; his government had been revealed as one of the most fantastically corrupt and violent regimes of the post-war era; and a new, democratic government under Cory Aquino had begun investigating his crimes. The whole country was struggling to come to terms with its immediate past.

At the same time, resentment of American power was running high, particularly regarding the presence of American military bases on the islands. US soldiers were no longer regarded as heroes, but as a humiliating imposition upon a sovereign nation. The Filipino press often carried stories about the exploitation of women around the huge air force and naval bases at Angeles City and Subic Bay. The national conversation was all about taking back control from a giant, neo-colonial power.

Anti-Americanism also found its way into academic circles. Several historians, among them the renowned Renato Constantino, had begun to challenge the popular view of the liberation at the end of the Second World War. They claimed that the Philippines had not needed rescuing by outsiders, and that the Filipino resistance had been on the verge of defeating the Japanese on their own. MacArthur was no longer the unequivocal hero he had once been: in some quarters he was regarded as a symbol of continued American imperialism, stepping ashore in Leyte not to liberate the Philippines, but to reclaim it.

Over the following years, successive governments decided to try to commemorate a much more Filipino-focused view of history. New monuments were built, most notably a Filipino Heroes Memorial (inaugurated in 1992) and a monument to the victims of the liberation of Manila (in 1995). In more recent years memorials have even been built to the Hukbalahap – a wartime guerrilla movement that fought against not only the Japanese but also the return of the Americans.

If the Philippines were to follow the same pattern as other countries, the next step would be clear: there would be calls on politicians to shake off their colonial history and tear down the memorial to MacArthur. In one or two other Asian countries something similar has already happened. In South Korea, for example, where MacArthur was long revered as the commander who turned the tide of the Korean War, his statue in Incheon has been the focus of repeated demonstrations against American influence in the country. In 2005, riots broke out around the statue, with protesters calling for it to be torn down.

So far, however, the Filipino people have stopped short of such moves, at least as far as the MacArthur Landing Memorial is concerned. The authorities still treat this monument with great care and respect. When one of the seven statues (that of Carlos Romulo) was toppled by a typhoon in 2013, it was immediately repaired by the government and restored to its position. War veterans and their families continue to visit the memorial every year on 20 October, accompanied by dignitaries from Manila, Washington, Canberra and Tokyo. Down on the beach there are regular re-enactments of the battle, and the nearby city of Tacloban holds an annual Liberation Day parade.

Despite all his faults, and the long-running arguments between historians, MacArthur is still a hero in the Philippines – if only for the single moment when he stepped upon the shore of Leyte. Today the statues in Palo representing him and his aides are a little tarnished by weather and corrosion. They have been soiled by the birds that occasionally land on them. But they stand nevertheless, their eyes focused on the Philippine shore, their faces still a picture of grim determination.

5

UK: Bomber Command Memorial, London

The USSR and the USA were not the only major victors of the Second World War: Britain also belonged to this elite club of heroes. Of the so-called 'Big Three', Britain was the only one to have been engaged in the war right from the very start. It therefore holds a special place in Allied history.

Britain's capital, London, was for many years the epicentre of the Allied war effort. As a consequence, it has become home to dozens of different war memorials devoted to all manner of people and nationalities. There are monuments to the civilians who died in the Blitz, to the city's firefighters, its railway workers and its air raid wardens. There are large installations dedicated to the Canadian soldiers who fought for Britain, to the Australians, to the New Zealanders and to the soldiers from India and the rest of the British Empire. Every branch of the military seems to have its own monument here, from fighter pilots and tank crews to Gurkhas and Chindits. There are statues of generals, admirals and air marshals. There is even a memorial to the animals that served during the war.

However, one monument in London stands out among all

the others. The RAF Bomber Command Memorial in Green Park is one of London's newest: it was only inaugurated in 2012, long after almost all the others were built. It is also by far the largest Second World War memorial in the city: over 8 metres (26 feet) high and 80 metres (262 feet) long, it is probably twice as big as its nearest rival. But what really makes the memorial unique is its design. Unlike London's other war monuments, which all stand out in the open, this one is semi-enclosed. It conceals its message inside an elaborate structure of Doric columns and classical balustrades: it looks more like a Greek temple than a war memorial. Inside, taking the place of Mars or Apollo, are the statues of seven airmen, standing in a group as though they have just returned from a mission. It is quite clear from their size, their stance, and the way that each of them gazes confidently into the distance that these men are supposed to be heroes. As you enter the temple-like structure, you are forced to look up at them as if they were objects of worship. Above their heads, the roof is open, so that nothing stands between them and heaven. If ever there were a temple to British heroism, this surely is it.

The Bomber Command Memorial is one of the most important monuments in London, but it is also one of the most problematic. Despite the heroic pose of the statues within, it is not at all clear *why* these men should be considered heroes. Unlike so many other statues devoted to the war, they are not raising a flag, or wielding a sword, or stepping onto a beach to liberate a nation. In fact, they are not in any kind of dynamic pose at all: they are just standing there. On the wall, carved deep into the stone, is an inscription telling us that 55,573 similar men were killed during the war. But this does not explain their heroic stance either: dying in large numbers like this implies some kind of victimhood, not heroism. On the opposite wall is a quote from Winston Churchill, claiming that 'the bombers alone provide the means of victory'. But how? And why? What exactly did these men do to win our adulation?

To understand what this memorial is commemorating, you need to know something about the bomber war, and the leading role that Britain took in this type of combat during the Second World War. But to understand why it looks as it does, why it is so much bigger than every other British war memorial, and what it is really trying to say, you need to understand the political atmosphere in the UK at the beginning of the twenty-first century, and the forces that led to the building of the monument in the first place.

Britain's bomber war is one of the most controversial episodes in the country's recent history. It began with the best of intentions. The British government made a solemn promise to spare civilians wherever possible, and only sent its bombers to strike specific military installations. But bombing specific targets in those days meant getting in close and bombing in broad daylight. In such circumstances the slow bomber planes were easy targets for flak guns and fighter planes: casualties among British aircrews were catastrophic.

So the Royal Air Force changed tactics. It began bombing at night instead, and from higher altitudes. This kept British planes and crews safer, but it also made their bombing far less accurate. According to a government report in 1942, only one in three British bombs landed within *five miles* of its target.

Far from being Churchill's 'means of victory', therefore, bombing was turning out to be a costly failure. The RAF seemed to be faced with two alternatives, both of them equally hopeless. They could attack in daylight and be shot down, or they could attack by night and miss their targets.

It was at this point that a new commander-in-chief took charge at Bomber Command – a brusque, uncompromising leader named Arthur Harris. It was Harris who championed the idea of a different kind of bombing: to forget about picking out individual military targets, and simply bomb entire cities instead. There was a certain brutal logic to this. If bombing were to work then it would have to be acknowledged as the blunt instrument that it was. By bombing large areas, the RAF could destroy not only the factories and installations that were supplying Germany with arms, but also the homes of the workers who staffed those factories. Killing the workers themselves was part of the plan: in a total war, factory workers were considered a target just as legitimate as the soldiers they supplied.

But Harris went further. By devastating entire cities, he believed that he could break not only the German economy, but also the will of the German people to continue fighting at all. According to this reasoning, shops, restaurants, schools and hospitals were legitimate targets. The purpose was to drive Germany to despair. Thus, ordinary civilians were no longer collateral damage – they had themselves become targets.

Harris knew that he was crossing a moral line, but believed that the ends justified the means: if he could bring an early end to the war, he reasoned, then his brutal policy might end up saving more lives than it took. He was quite open about this, and wanted to enlist the support of the British people. The only reason he did not explain his strategy publicly was that the government prevented him from doing so. Churchill and his cabinet wholeheartedly endorsed the strategy; but they wanted to keep up the pretence that Bomber Command's targets were always strictly military.

Unfortunately German morale never collapsed as Harris hoped it would. The war dragged on, and city after city in Germany was devastated. According to military historian Richard Overy, some 600,000 civilians were killed beneath Allied bombs, not only in Germany, but also in those countries that the Allies were liberating. It was a horrific death toll, outnumbering the British victims of German bombs by almost ten to one. At the time, however, the British public did not seem to care too much. Every successful bombing was reported in the newspapers with triumphant glee. Bomber crews went on publicity tours of British factories, and the stories they told the workers were invariably greeted with cheers. The loss of German civilian life was deemed a price worth paying.

Towards the end of the war, however, the atmosphere suddenly changed. The turning point was the bombing of Dresden in February 1945. During a press conference after the raid, a senior officer let slip that it had been conducted partly to destroy 'what is left of German morale'. In the following days, stories began to appear claiming that the British were conducting 'terror bombing'. Questions were asked in the House of Commons. After the American press got hold of the story, the Royal Air Force was put under considerable international pressure to explain its actions.

It was not long before the British establishment turned its back on the men of Bomber Command. Churchill drafted a memo to his chiefs of staff berating them for indulging in 'acts of terror and wanton destruction' (although he toned down his rhetoric in the final version of the memo). The hypocrisy of this memo is really quite something. Churchill had always known what strategy Harris was following, but had never before expressed much concern about it. After the Allied victory in May 1945, Churchill praised every branch of the armed forces in his victory speech – but made almost no mention of Britain's bombers. In his bestselling memoirs, published after the war, Churchill omitted the bombing of Dresden. It was as if he hoped that the episode could be erased from public memory simply by not talking about it.

Naturally, the men who flew the bombers were quite disoriented by this sudden change of heart. As the official historian of the bomber war, Noble Frankland, put it, 'Most people were very pleased with Bomber Command during the war and until it was virtually won; then they turned around and said it wasn't a very nice way to wage war.'

The indignation this caused over the following years cannot be overestimated. I have known and interviewed dozens of British bomber crew, and most of them have spoken bitterly about the way they were shunned by the establishment after 1945. Many were upset that they were never granted their own specific medal, but instead had to make do with a more generic campaign medal that was granted to everyone in the air force. They saw this as yet another way in which their contribution to the war was being discreetly brushed under the carpet. Worse still was the way that they were treated by the general public. During the war, a bomber crewman who walked into a pub in uniform would rarely have to buy his own drinks; but after 1945 he would have to think twice before admitting to what he'd done during the war. In the 1960s especially, when a new generation was questioning the actions of its parents, students sometimes mocked the claims of bomber veterans that they were 'only following orders'. Right-wing historians like David Irving also drew deliberate, if dubious, parallels between Nazi atrocities and the actions of the RAF. The men of Bomber Command, once heroes, were suddenly being treated as villains.

Eventually this backlash against veterans of the air war fizzled out, and a more nuanced view began to take hold. In the late 1970s, historians like Martin Middlebrook and Max Hastings led the way in rehabilitating the men of Bomber Command in the minds of the public. Since then there have been dozens and dozens of popular histories by authors like Robin Neillands, Mel Rolfe and Kevin Wilson. In the years when I used to work in military publishing I collaborated with many of these authors, and indeed commissioned some of their books myself.

In the 1990s and 2000s a succession of British TV dramas and documentaries about the bomber war brought this nuanced view of history into the mainstream. Viewers of the BBC drama *Bomber Harris*, or the Channel 4 documentary *Reaping the Whirlwind*, were invited to put themselves in the shoes of the airmen before making moral judgements. Gradually the British public was learning to come to terms with an uncomfortable history.

Sensing that the public was ready to support them, the Bomber Command Association began in 2009 to campaign for a memorial. They were granted their wish three years later, in the summer of 2012, when the Bomber Command Memorial was finally inaugurated.

Had this been all there was to the story, the Bomber Command Memorial would not have been nearly as interesting, or as problematic, as it is today. It might have ended up resembling some of the memorials to the bomber war in other parts of Britain and Germany. For example, it could have been a monument to reconciliation, like Coventry Cathedral's 'Cross of

Nails' (see Chapter 24). It might have been an anti-war sculpture, like the Dammtordamm monument in central Hamburg.
At the very least, it might have made a nod to the dark moral
choices that Britain was forced to make because of the war.
But then a new wave of popular sentiment swept over the
issue, making any such nuance almost impossible.

The problems began when the newspapers started to
become involved. The Bomber Command Memorial was to
be built with private funding, so three daily newspapers – the
Telegraph, the *Mail* and the *Express* – ran campaigns to raise
money. Since these are all newspapers of the political right,
the memorial was largely supported by right-wing donors,
particularly Lord Ashcroft, the former deputy chairman of
the Conservative Party, who contributed £1 million. The political left, by contrast, were scarcely invited to have a say – and
nor, to their shame, did they particularly seem to want one.
Thus, what should have been a project that brought people
together from across the political spectrum ended up being
a highly partisan *cause célèbre*.

In order to drum up support for the memorial, the three
newspapers, especially the *Daily Mail*, began to publish highly
emotive stories about how the men of Bomber Command had
been snubbed. Articles began to appear calling them 'Forgotten
Heroes', or 'the black sheep of the British popular memory of
the Second World War' – despite the fact that they were neither
forgotten, nor any longer regarded as 'black sheep'. Online
rumours began to spread suggesting that the local council was
blocking the construction of a memorial because its planners
were ashamed of Britain's bomber crews, or that Germany was
putting pressure on the British government to veto the project
– stories that had little foundation in truth.

When historians insisted that there should be at least some

mention of the controversial aspects of bombing, they were derided as milksops with no sense of national pride. Columnists claimed that the men of Bomber Command were under attack once again, this time by the forces of political correctness. (In the end, the builders of the memorial did agree to add an inscription mentioning 'those of all nations who lost their lives in the bombing of 1939–1945'. But it was in an awkward position, high up near the roof, and obscured from view by the statue. It was quite obviously an afterthought.)

I watched this happening with a certain amusement, but also with growing incredulity, because I knew from years of research that the vast majority of what was being said was complete nonsense. I was particularly struck by the way that the veterans of Bomber Command were portrayed. The British press always labelled them 'heroes', but in fact were depicting them as victims. None of the men I had interviewed over the years felt nearly as sorry for themselves as the newspapers seemed to feel for them. On the whole they had been sensible men, who had long since come to terms with the way they had fought the war and were generally satisfied with the way that British society had belatedly come to accept them. So where was all this indignation coming from?

The truth is that the Bomber Command Memorial, like all the monuments in this book, says at least as much about the society that erected it as it does about the people it supposedly commemorates. There is nothing modern or contemporary about it, like so many of the other recent memorials that stand nearby: this is a monument to nostalgia. Its classical columns and balustrades evoke a bygone era when Britain was still a great colonial power. The architect, Liam O'Connor, made much of the fact that the style of the memorial echoed the façades of the houses opposite – houses that were built at the height of Britain's imperial splendour. Its size and prominence are the result of a deliberate attempt to create something physically impressive, just as Britain once used to do in the days of Admiral Nelson and Queen Victoria.

The statues, too, are an exercise in nostalgia. Their stance and attitude evoke the stoic heroes of British war films of the 1950s – films like *Reach for the Sky* and *The Dam Busters*. These are heroes who don't have to be seen doing anything dramatic: the drama is all beneath their strong, silent surface. We do not make heroes like this any more.

British people still speak of the Second World War as their 'finest hour', but deep down they also understand that it was the end of something. The Second World War cost Britain its empire, its prestige, and its pre-eminent place in the world economy. After 1945, it was no longer the workshop of the world; and it was never again able to dictate world events as it had done during the previous two centuries. Britain was left virtually bankrupt by the war, and was forced for years to rely on financial aid from the USA. No wonder the British feel indignant, snubbed, cheated by history. No wonder they can't quite make up their minds whether they are heroes or victims.

This has been one of the major themes of post-war life in Britain, and one that the nation still has not come to terms with. During the war itself, officials were already joking that the USA, the USSR and Great Britain were not really the Big Three, but the Big Two and a Half. In the 1960s, the former American Secretary of State Dean Acheson famously said that 'Great Britain has lost an empire and not yet found a role'. The nation regained some of its pride in the 1980s and 1990s, during the age of Thatcherism and 'Cool Britannia', but at the start of the twenty-first century it once again feels itself in the shadow of others: the USA, China, the European Union.

This is the true meaning of the Bomber Command Memorial, with its heroes staring out between Doric columns like prisoners in a cage. They are a group of heroes who appear to have nothing heroic to do. They have finished their mission, but have been cheated of their glory, and now they merely stand there, gazing across London's Green Park, waiting stoically to see what new disappointments might be looming on the horizon.

6

Italy: Shrine to the Fallen, Bologna

The themes on display at London's Bomber Command Memorial are part of a much greater pattern that is evident not only in the UK but all over the world. In the twenty-first century, every nation likes to believe itself a nation of heroes; but deep down, most nations are beginning to think of themselves as victims.

This process has been decades in the making. In the immediate aftermath of the Second World War, heroism was still in great demand. But in the years since then, many nations have come to realise that heroism comes with responsibilities. For example, the USA, the one undisputed winner of the war, has found itself obliged to act as the world's policeman ever since. Britain too felt obliged to keep the world's peace after 1945, despite the fact that it could no longer afford to do so.

There are other dangers, too. Heroes always run the risk of being exposed as the flawed human beings they really are; and, once exposed, they can quickly fall from grace – much as the old Soviet heroes have recently fallen from grace in eastern Europe. In an effort to stave off this trend, some nations have resorted to defending their Second World War

heroes with a manic vigour. One need only look at the way
that the USA mythologises its 'greatest generation', or that
Britain continuously mythologises the figure of Winston
Churchill, to see how much work it takes to maintain hero
status.

Other nations, however, have given up portraying themselves as heroes altogether. Instead they have increasingly
begun to choose another motif for their memorials, equally
powerful, and equally pure – that of martyrdom. This is a
much easier identity to maintain. It allows a nation to keep
the moral high ground without having to shoulder any of the
work or responsibility for maintaining peace; and it is an easy
way to deflect criticism. In the next part of the book I will
discuss the growth of victimhood as a national motif, which
comes with its own drawbacks and dangers.

First, however, I want to explore one final monument to
heroism, which shows a very different side of what it is to be
a hero.

The Shrine to the Fallen in Bologna, Italy, is a much more
intimate memorial than any I have described so far. Based on
the simplest of ideas, it consists of some 2,000 portraits and
names of local resistance fighters attached to the wall of the
municipal building in Piazza del Nettuno, right in the centre
of the city. This was the site where captured partisans were
publicly executed during the war. Since 1945 it has become
a commemorative site not only for those who died here, but
also for those who died fighting the Nazis and Italian Fascists
all over the region.

Unlike any of the other monuments in this book, this one
was not erected by the state, or by a museum, or by any other
kind of remembrance organisation. It was not planned in

advance, but born in a spontaneous burst of emotion. It was put together by local people to commemorate the lives and deaths of those they had known and loved. It highlights something about the war that does not come across in most larger, state-sponsored memorials: the Second World War was not only a titanic conflict between giant armies on the battlefield, it was also an intensely local war fought in the hills and the forests, and on the streets of towns far behind the front lines. The war had a different flavour in Italy from that of Poland or France; and it had a different flavour in Bologna from that of Naples or Milan. The Shrine to the Fallen was not constructed to express national virtues or ambitions; it was simply an expression of local pride, and local loss. It is reminiscent of something that we all do privately in our living rooms at home – display the portraits of those we most love. This is who we are, it says. These people are family.

The war in Italy was much more complicated than it was in other parts of Europe. Italy had begun the war as an ally of Germany, but ended up being occupied by German forces when it tried to change sides in 1943. After the Allies invaded the south, the Germans set up a puppet government under Benito Mussolini in the north, and the country was effectively split in two. In the midst of this upheaval, a resistance movement grew up. All kinds of groups joined the partisans, but the driving force behind it was the Italian Communist Party, which sought not only to liberate the nation from the Germans, but also to overthrow the Fascists who had ruled Italy since the 1920s, and to institute widespread social change in the process.

As a major centre of the Resistance, Bologna suffered more than most places in Italy. In the last year of the war, the region was awash with intrigue and violence. In nearby Marzabotto, an entire village was massacred by the Waffen-SS in reprisal for local resistance activity – at least 770 men, women and children were shot in cold blood, or burned to death in their houses. Within Bologna city centre there were more than forty different public shootings, involving around 140 men and women. Piazza del Nettuno was a favourite spot for both the Nazis and the Italian Fascists to carry out these executions. Between July 1944 and the end of the war at least eighteen people were shot here. Their bodies were left on display as a warning to the local population; and to drive the point home, a sarcastic notice was placed on the wall proclaiming it a 'place of refreshment for partisans'.

However, if such violence was supposed to deter people from joining the Resistance, it did not work. By the end of the war the Bolognese people had had enough. On 19 April they rose up in insurrection, and within two days had taken control of the city. According to official figures, by this time more than 14,000 local people were actively fighting for the partisans, of which more than 2,200 were women. Bologna was in the vanguard of a nationwide movement: a few days later, on 25 April, insurrection spread to all parts of northern Italy.

As the Germans and their Fascist puppets fled the city, the people of Bologna were at last able to mourn their losses publicly. The families of those who had been executed returned to Piazza del Nettuno and set up a shrine to their loved ones. Someone pushed an old green table against the wall, upon which people could place little mementos, flowers and framed photographs of those who had died. An Italian flag was hung on the wall, and more photographs were pinned to it.

In the coming days, this shrine grew and grew. Within a couple of months there were hundreds of photographs spreading for 20 metres along the wall. It quickly became not only a place of mourning for those who had been killed on this spot, but also a place of respect for all those who had died in the name of freedom. There were photographs and tributes to all kinds of people: teenage boys executed for resistance activities, women in their sixties who had died heroically in combat, men in their prime who had died in training accidents or had been tortured to death by the authorities. The full range of the partisan experience was represented here.

It was not long before the new city authorities decided that the shrine should become a permanent feature affixed to the medieval wall of the Palazzo d'Accursio. In 1955 the paper photographs were taken down and replaced with weatherproof tiles, each one displaying the name or portrait of a single man or woman. Today there are more than two thousand tiles on that wall, along with sixteen larger tiles reproducing photos of the time. It is an enduring reminder of the suffering and bravery of the people of Bologna.

As the saying goes, everything is political. The Shrine to the Fallen may have begun as a simple symbol of mourning; but there was always more to it than that. It was inevitable that it would include some political overtones; after all, it had been built to commemorate those who had died for their beliefs. Political themes were therefore present in the shrine from the beginning, and would continue to characterise it over the following decades.

The liberation of Bologna in April 1945 was a chaotic and violent event. According to Edward Reep, an American war artist who witnessed the liberation of the city, one of the first acts to take place in Piazza del Nettuno in April 1945 was not one of mourning at all, but one of vengeance. Before the shrine was first set up, a Fascist collaborator was shot here: his fresh blood was still visible on the wall. In other words, the political violence that had characterised the war years was not quite over; it was just that the boot was now on the other foot. In the long aftermath of the war, similar violence would continue to rear its head from time to time all over Italy.

The original shrine in 1945

According to Reep, political symbols were incorporated into the shrine even while it was first taking shape:

Within minutes, an Italian flag was hung on the wall, above and to the left of the blood stain . . . The House of Savoy emblem had been ripped away from the white central panel of the flag; pinned in its place was a stiff black ribbon of mourning. This became a dual gesture: it signified the end of the monarchy and Fascism, and it became a memorial to those who had given their lives in the long struggle for liberation.

It was upon this flag that mourners first pinned their photographs.*

In the following years, the Shrine became one of many monuments in Bologna dedicated to the partisans. In 1946, a bronze statue of Mussolini on horseback was melted down to create two new statues of Italian Resistance fighters: they can be seen today at Porta Lame, north-west of the city centre. In 1959, an Ossuary to the Fallen Partisans was built in Certosa Cemetery by architect Piero Bottoni, and in the 1970s two more monuments were built: one in Villa Spada, and another at Sabbiuno, just south of the city. In addition, several streets and piazzas were renamed after the war. For example, the piazza named after King Umberto I became 'Piazza of the Martyrs of 1943–1945'.

All this was part of a deliberate attempt not only to demonstrate the city's moral and social rebirth after the war, but also to redefine its very identity. Monarchist and Fascist symbols were torn down, and symbols of the Resistance were put up in their place. If Bologna was to be a city of heroes, they were not to be the old, elitist heroes. From now on it would be workers and students who were celebrated – ordinary people, with faces like those on display in Piazza del Nettuno.

Under the gaze of all those dead heroes, the people of Bologna were more or less obliged to follow the future laid out for them by the memory of their wartime struggles. In

---

* In 1946, Reep painted a prize-winning picture of this shrine, which launched his career as an artist. Today it is part of the permanent collection of Washington, DC's National Museum of American Art.

the first post-war municipal elections, held in March 1946, they elected a member of the Resistance as their mayor. Giuseppe Dozza would lead the city council for the next twenty years; and his party, the Italian Communist Party, would remain the major force in Bolognese politics for most of the rest of the century.

In the 1970s and 1980s the city once again came under attack. During the *anni di piombo* – the 'years of lead' – the whole of Italy became embroiled in political violence. Many other cities suffered terrorist attacks at the hands of the Communist 'Red Brigades'; but Bologna came under assault from neo-Fascists. In 1980, a bomb was set off at the main railway station, killing eighty-five people and injuring some two hundred more. Two smaller-scale attacks also happened in 1974 and 1984, killing a dozen or so people each time. The reason was clear: Bologna had been targeted because it was a left-wing city.

To commemorate these attacks, a new plaque was put up in Piazza del Nettuno close to the Shrine, listing the names of the dead. Unwittingly, however, the new plaque marked a subtle shift in the city's memorial landscape. The original Shrine to the Fallen had never given the impression of a people that felt sorry for themselves, despite the terrible atrocities they had suffered during the war. The wording above it states clearly, in large metal letters, that the wartime partisans were heroes who had died in a just cause: 'for liberty and justice, for honour and the independence of the fatherland'. The wording on the new plaque, however, carried no such message. Here, the dead were simply 'victims of Fascist terrorism'. They had not died in a cause. There was no semblance of heroism. When the two memorials are taken together, the lines between heroism and victimhood no longer seem so clear-cut. The senseless violence of the 1980s is reflected back in time to the equally senseless violence of the war years, and even the partisans begin to look less like heroes and more like martyrs.

In recent years, there have been even greater shifts in the city's identity. The old certainties of Bolognese political life have long since broken down: Communism died here, just as it did all over Europe, with the end of the Cold War. Since the turn of the century there has been little continuity between the city's wartime past and its present: largely speaking, the Communists have given way to the more moderate Social Democrats. The tides of globalisation are also visible, not only in the university, which has always welcomed students from all over Italy and the world, but also in the general population. More than 10 per cent of the people living in Bologna today come from other countries, and that percentage is growing all the time.

In such a world, the 2,000 portraits on Piazza del Nettuno no longer have the power that they once did. They are obviously from a bygone era. Their faces look stiff, formal – nothing like the smiling selfies that today's generations routinely post on social media. Why should these old portraits be relevant any more? Why should today's city be held prisoner to *their* history, and *their* ideas?

And yet they still dominate the wall of this medieval piazza. Local politicians making their way to and from the town hall must walk past them every day. Students who gather on the steps of the public library sit in their shadow. Like the photographs of long-dead aunts and uncles in countless homes across Bologna, they gaze down on the inhabitants of this left-wing city, silently reminding them of who they are, and where they have come from.

Coda: The End of Heroism

Heroes are like rainbows: they can only really be appreciated from a distance. As soon as we get too close, the very qualities that make them shine tend to disappear.

None of the monuments I have described so far reflect the nuances of historical reality. The greatness of the Russian Motherland was always built on shaky foundations. America's devotion to its flag, while glorious to Americans themselves, always looked a little dubious to everyone else. Britain needed its famous stiff upper lip not only to win the war but also to weather the disappointments that would follow. And resistance movements – not only in Bologna, but all over Europe and Asia – usually did far more dying than they ever did resisting. But none of this really matters, because these monuments were never meant to express historical reality. They are representations of our mythological idea of what it means to be a hero, that's all. They are as much expressions of identity as they are of history.

In some ways our monuments to our Second World War heroes seem quite timeless. The values they express – strength, stoicism, brotherhood, virtue – are no different from the values that all societies have held dear since ancient times. But in other ways they seem hopelessly dated: indeed, some of them, like the Bomber Command Memorial in London, already looked old-fashioned from the moment they were first unveiled. It is no coincidence that all the monuments I have mentioned in this section are conventional statues, or photographs, or statues based on photographs. This is the way that heroes are generally commemorated throughout the world. Compared to some of the monuments I will describe later, they are rather unadventurous.

Heroes represent our ideals. They must be brave but gentle, steadfast but flexible, strong but tolerant; they must always be virtuous, always be flawless, always be ready to spring into action; and as our communal champions they must represent all of us, all the time. No individual can possibly live up to such expectations. Neither can any group.

And yet some nations have been bequeathed these responsibilities by history. As the undisputed victor of the Second World War, America has been called upon to act the hero ever since. To a lesser degree, the UK and France have also felt obliged to take a leading role in international affairs, particularly when it comes to their former colonies. Even Russia sometimes feels obliged to live up to its status as a great power. The efforts of these nations are not always appreciated, and unsurprisingly so: no modern-day international policeman can ever live up to the Second World War ideal.

Times change. Values, even timeless values, go in and out of fashion: who today celebrates qualities like stubbornness, inflexibility, or the willingness to endure silently? Inevitably some of the heroes we used to revere seem faintly tragic, or even slightly ridiculous, to modern sensibilities. Communities also change. Our heroes are supposed to represent who we think we are, or at least who we would like to imagine ourselves to be, but when we begin to adopt new political outlooks, or when our communities absorb people of different classes, religions or ethnicities, it becomes hard to identify with the old heroes any longer.

All this highlights a strange paradox: our heroes, who in our minds seem so strong and indestructible, are actually the most vulnerable figures in the historical pantheon. It does not take much to knock them from their pedestals.

There are other, more robust motifs. As I have already hinted, many groups are now much more likely to portray themselves as martyrs than as heroes. In most cases, the groups in question have little choice in the matter: we are all prisoners of our history, and these are the roles that the tragic events of the past have bequeathed them. Nevertheless, as will become clear, martyrdom turns out to be a much stronger identity than heroism ever was. Heroes come and go. But a martyr is for ever.

Part II

Martyrs

In 1945, every nation believed itself a nation of heroes. However, there is no escaping the fact that in most places the Second World War was not glorious – it was brutal. Whole populations had been bombed, starved, enslaved and humiliated. Millions had died in the most unheroic of settings – not on the battlefield, but in their homes, in gas chambers, or cowering in bomb shelters. Hundreds of thousands of women had been raped. Hundreds of thousands of children had been orphaned. These people were not heroes: they were victims.

Memorials to the victims of the war are some of the most important remembrance sites we have. Most of them have been created for very good reasons. Suffering must be acknowledged. A well-designed memorial can provide a place for people to mourn what they have lost, and remember those who have died. It can bring a divided nation together in its common grief. And it can allow a humiliated population at least some space to forgive themselves: not everyone can be a hero, particularly when they have been rendered powerless by massive forces beyond their control.

However, there is a darker side to such memorials that is rarely confronted. On the one hand they offer us the chance to acknowledge our painful past and rise above it; on the other hand they invite us to wallow in that past until our souls are enchained by it. They can allow us to take ownership of our suffering and thereby control it; or they can allow us to give in to our suffering, abandon all responsibility, and look around for someone else to blame. Remembering the past like this can lead us to dangerous places. Rather than inspiring unity, it can promote division. Rather than bringing us peace, it can rouse us to anger.

There has been a shift in our memorial culture in recent decades. Where once we used to erect monuments to our Second World War heroes, nowadays we much more readily erect monuments to victims and martyrs. There are straight-forward political reasons for this. Martyrs, like heroes, inspire loyalty. But while a nation of heroes is obliged to take respon-sibility for its place in the world, a nation of martyrs is free to be as selfish as it wishes. Martyrs cannot be criticised. Their faults must always be forgiven. Their past suffering is like a perpetual 'Get out of jail free' card, absolving them of all sins.

Unfortunately, this apparent freedom is something of an illusion. As will become apparent in the following chapters, there are costs as well as benefits to such ways of thinking. Nations that view themselves as martyrs are in thrall to their history just like everyone else.

7

Netherlands: National Monument, Amsterdam

The people of the Netherlands suffered greatly during the Second World War. In 1940, their country was invaded by a massive, unstoppable force which inflicted massive damage, particularly in cities like Rotterdam, which was flattened by bombing. For the next five years they suffered the full consequences of Nazi occupation: the stripping of their sovereignty, the rounding up of Jews and other 'undesirables', the exploitation of the Dutch people and the brutal repression of dissent. When resistance activity increased towards the end of the war, the Nazis retaliated by cutting off all shipments of food and fuel to the west of the country. A famine quickly descended: around 18,000 people are thought to have died in what soon became known as the 'Hunger Winter', and hundreds of thousands more were left severely malnourished. By the time the country was finally liberated in May 1945, the Netherlands was on its knees.

In the aftermath of this terrible conflict, the new Dutch government commissioned the building of a monument to ensure that the people never forgot the humiliation and suffering they had been forced to endure. From the very beginning the National Monument was intended to be the most important in the country. It was to be built in the historic heart of Amsterdam, in Dam Square. Its central motif was to be Dutch martyrdom.

The first component of the memorial was built as early as 1946. It was a curved wall, in which were a series of niches, each containing an urn. Each urn was filled with soil taken from a site where Dutch people had been tortured and executed. Originally there were eleven urns in all – one from each province – making this a truly national monument. A few years later a twelfth urn was added containing soil from the Dutch East Indies (present-day Indonesia), in recognition of the suffering that Dutch citizens had also experienced at the hands of the Japanese.

A few years later, a stone pillar was built in front of this curved wall. It was 22 metres (72 feet) tall, and adorned with sculptures created by John Rädecker, one of the Netherlands' most prominent artists. Rädecker's design says a great deal about how the Dutch saw themselves in the aftermath of the war. The main image, which sits on the front of the pillar, consists of four men in chains, one of whom has his arms outstretched like a crucified Christ figure. On either side of this sculpture stand two statues representing the resistance: a bearded figure on the left, who embodies the resistance of the intellectuals, and a muscular figure on the right who represents the workers' resistance. By their feet sit three howling dogs, symbolising fidelity. Above the central image stands a woman holding a child, symbolising the new life that was possible after the end of the war. Above her head is a wreath, symbolising victory. Finally, on the back of the column is a series of doves ascending to heaven, symbolising peace.

The National Monument in 1958, two years after it was first built

The memorial therefore offers several messages at once. The Dutch resisted oppression. They were unified in their suffering. They were faithful to an ideal. And in the end their suffering paid off: they were rewarded with victory, peace, and the opportunity for rebirth.

All in all, it is a very well thought out monument. Its central images are mostly religious in nature. The doves are reminiscent of the Christian symbol for the Holy Spirit; the woman and child are like classical images of the Madonna; and, most importantly, the Christ-like figure represents the martyrdom of the people – tortured, enchained and sacrificed, in the faith that the end of the war would bring them resurrection. It is impossible for a Christian to stand before this monument without feeling the same kind of religious awe that he or she might feel in a church. It is a transcendent vision of the Netherlands during the war: it is the nation as Messiah.

There is just one problem. Not everyone in the Netherlands was Christian, even in 1945. And not everyone who was persecuted by the Nazis died on Dutch soil. By portraying the nation in this way, the monument excludes a variety of groups who do not fit into Rädecker's definition of what it was to be Dutch. The most important of these groups was the one sector of the population that suffered most: the Jews.

If you are looking for a figure to represent martyrdom during the Second World War, there is no better place to start than with Europe's Jews. In the Netherlands they made up only 1.5 per cent of the population; and yet, by the end of the war, they accounted for half of all Dutch casualties. Jews were singled out like no other group in the country. They were hunted down mercilessly, hounded onto trains and sent east to concentration camps. Here, they were either murdered on arrival or slowly worked to death. Around 110,000 were deported in this way. Only about 5,000 ever returned.

Today it seems obvious that any monument to remember the dead should not only include such people, but give them pride of place. So why does the Dutch National Monument ignore them? Were they deliberately excluded? Was it merely an unfortunate oversight? Or was something else going on?

To get an idea of how this might have been allowed to happen, it is worth considering the stories of some of those 5,000 Holocaust survivors who returned to the Netherlands in 1945. At the end of the twentieth century, Dutch historian Dienke Hondius interviewed dozens of these people about their experience of returning home, and found that their stories were broadly similar. Almost all of them felt ignored in 1945. Almost all felt a pressure not to talk about what they had suffered. Worst of all, many found themselves the target of a perverse and misplaced kind of envy. 'You were lucky,' one Jewish survivor was told by an acquaintance in 1945. 'We suffered such hunger!' Another was denied an advance from his employer on the grounds that in Auschwitz, 'You had a roof over your head and food the whole time!'

A charitable excuse for such insensitivity is that it was largely born of ignorance. Unlike in eastern Europe, where the Holocaust took place right under the noses of the people, in the Netherlands there was only ever a vague understanding of what had happened to Jews after they had been deported. Many Dutch people did not acknowledge Jewish suffering because they were scarcely aware of it. It is quite possible that this ignorance extends to the National Monument, whose creators simply did not think to include Jewish suffering as a separate category to be represented.

There are, of course, darker possibilities. Anti-Semitism was prevalent in the Netherlands even before the war, but years of Nazi propaganda were bound to have had some effect on the nation and its people. If no one bothered to think about what had happened to Jews during the war, it was partly because they were not interested. It is conceivable that one of the reasons why Jews were left off the National Monument was because they were not considered worthy. At an unconscious level at least, perhaps they were not really considered Dutch at all.

However, contemporary documents point to another, more political explanation for why the experience of Jews was overlooked. In 1945 there was a great push to bring a divided nation back together. A myth grew up that the Dutch people had suffered as one – a single people, united in their martyrdom. This is the central message of the National

Monument, with its Christian images and its samples of earth taken from atrocity sites in each of the Dutch provinces. Such a myth suited almost everyone, from former collaborators who wanted a chance to be brought back into the fold, to an exhausted public that was eager to put the war behind them.

Unfortunately, however, the Jews did not fit into this comfortable myth – indeed, any acknowledgement of what had happened to them automatically made a mockery of it. Deep down, everyone knew that Jews had been singled out during the war, and that they had suffered in quite a different way from everyone else. Not only that, but they felt ashamed at their failure to come to the Jews' aid. Rather than acknowledge these uncomfortable truths, it was much easier simply to ignore the issue altogether. And so, at a national level at least, Dutch Jews suddenly became invisible.

Whatever the reasons for their exclusion from the National Monument, there was little that Jews in the Netherlands could do about it. Even in Amsterdam, which had once been a thriving Jewish centre, there were now so few Jews left that they were in no position to make much of a fuss. On the whole, they simply kept their heads down and tried to rebuild their lives in silence. After all they had been through, most Jews were unwilling to draw attention to themselves. They were resigned to being invisible.

It was years before the fate of the Jews was properly acknowledged in the Netherlands, but eventually things did change. It began with the publication of Anne Frank's diary in 1947. This Jewish teenager had been forced into hiding, along with her family, for more than two years. They lived in the back rooms of the building where Anne's father had his business, accessed through a secret doorway hidden behind a bookcase.

The family was finally discovered in August 1944, and deported to concentration camps in Germany and occupied Poland. Anne Frank died in Belsen at the beginning of 1945, but her diary survived, and would go on to be an international bestseller.

If Amsterdam's living Jews were silenced and sidelined after the war, this book at least gave them some kind of voice. In the late 1950s, Anne's father, Otto Frank, the only member of his family to survive, purchased the house where they had hidden during the war and converted it into a museum. It opened in 1960 and has gradually grown in importance ever since. Today it attracts more than a million visitors each year, and is one of the most visited museums in the country.

Other commemorations of the Jewish experience of the war eventually followed. In 1962, a new monument to Jewish victims was opened up at the Hollandsche Schouwburg, a former theatre in Amsterdam that had been used as a deportation centre during the war. A memorial wall was erected, listing the surnames of the 104,000 Dutch Jews who had been killed. The inscription on the wall makes it clear that these were not people who had 'died for the Fatherland', but who had been taken away to be murdered. They were not heroes, but victims.

In 1977, a monument to the Jews who had died at Auschwitz was built at the Ooster cemetery. Later, in 1993, this was moved to the Wertheimpark in the Jewish Quarter, and greatly enlarged. It consists of a series of broken mirrors, laid over an urn containing ashes taken from Auschwitz concentration camp. Consciously or otherwise, it makes up for the lack of any similar urn built into the memorial wall of the National Monument in Dam Square.

The commemoration of Jewish suffering in Amsterdam continues in our own century. Since the mid-2000s,

'Stolpersteine' have become a feature of dozens of Amsterdam streets, as they have in many other cities across Europe. These are small brass cobbles, placed in the ground outside the former homes of Jews who were deported during the Holocaust. They are engraved with the names of the Jews who once lived here, the date of their arrest, and their ultimate fate. Today there are more than four hundred of these across Amsterdam.

Finally, as recently as 2016, a National Holocaust Museum opened in Amsterdam, also in the former Jewish Quarter. The suffering that once went ignored here is now commemorated more than any other.

No memorial exists in isolation. In the aftermath of the war, the Dutch government built a single monument that they believed would express the unifying qualities of Dutch suffering during the Second World War. They failed. But in the years since then, Amsterdam has made up for its exclusions and oversights. Today the city has a rich memorial culture that includes many of the victims ignored in the immediate aftermath of the war. For example, Amsterdam was the first city in the world to build a public monument to the gypsies persecuted by the Nazis during the war. Unveiled in 1978, it stands in the Museumplein. Amsterdam was also the first city to build a 'Homomonument' in 1987: a memorial to those persecuted by the Nazis because of their sexuality.

When you stand before the National Monument in Dam Square today, it is worth remembering that this important memorial, with its dramatic Christian imagery, is just the headline: the rest of Amsterdam contains a network of subtexts. The city, like many other cities in Europe, is indeed a city of martyrs; but those martyrs come in a variety of shapes and sizes.

Wu Weishan's sculpture of a mother and dead child at the entrance
of the Nanjing Massacre Memorial Hall

8

China: Nanjing Massacre Memorial Hall

When did the Second World War begin? The answer to this question depends very much on whom you ask. For Americans, the war began in December 1941, with the bombing of Pearl Harbor. For Europeans it began earlier, in September 1939, with Hitler's invasion of Poland. But for the Chinese the beginning came earlier still, in July 1937, when Japanese and Chinese troops first exchanged fire at the Marco Polo Bridge, just outside Peking (modern Beijing). Unlike earlier incidents, which had usually ended in an embarrassing Chinese capitulation, this one prompted Chiang Kai-shek, the Chinese nationalist leader, to launch a full-scale attack against Japanese troops elsewhere in the country. So began more than eight years of conflict that would cost millions of lives and leave much of eastern China in ruins.

Today, Chinese memories of the war are dominated by what happened in these opening few months. This was the period in which several of the greatest battles took place, and in which Chinese troops inflicted the greatest damage on Japan: there are many tales of heroism for the Chinese to feel pride in. Chiang committed all his best resources at the beginning of the war, in the hope that he might at least give the Japanese a bloody nose, and perhaps even draw the support of the international community on his side. However, at this stage of the war his troops were no match for Japan's strength and technical superiority, and it was not long before this heroic Chinese story gave way to tragedy.

One episode in particular stands out. In November 1937, just a few months after the conflict had begun, Chinese forces were driven back to their capital city, Nanking (modern Nanjing). At the beginning of December, the Japanese began to surround the city. After fierce fighting around the city walls, Chiang decided to abandon his position. Tens of thousands of Chinese troops were forced to escape across the Yangtze River. Those who could not flee fought on, or surrendered, only to be slaughtered in a series of mass executions along the river bank. Others tried to hide among the general population by putting on civilian clothing, but they were ruthlessly hunted down by Japanese troops, who conducted inspections of all the men they came across. Anyone deemed to have a 'military posture' was pulled out of the crowd, as were men with calloused hands or shoe sores; and anyone with strap marks on their shoulders was assumed to have recently been carrying a military backpack or a rifle. Naturally there were plenty of ordinary civilians who fell foul of such inspections, and who were taken off to their deaths.

Neither did the massacres end with those suspected of being military men. In the aftermath of the battle, Japanese troops lost all discipline and fell to sacking the city. Women of all ages were raped and then murdered, as were children and even infants. There are numerous eyewitness accounts of pregnant women being bayoneted and slit open, and photographic evidence to back up those accounts. Some Japanese soldiers even took their own photographs – not as evidence, but as souvenirs.

Unsurprisingly, the city quickly descended into chaos. In desperation, civilians began streaming into the city's international zone in the hope that they might find some protection among Nanking's European residents. A small group of twenty or so schoolteachers and missionaries did what they could to help. They negotiated with the Japanese to allow them to set up a 'Safety Zone' for refugees. When Japanese troops came looking for women, they stood between the soldiers and their prey. There is no question that the Japanese were more cautious around the Europeans – they did not want to provoke any kind of incident with the West at this stage. Nevertheless, atrocities continued even in the international Safety Zone for several weeks after the defeat of the city. The testimonies of neutral Europeans, who were able to take photographs and even cine film of the massacres, provide some of the most compelling evidence of the atrocities that took place.

It is not known precisely how many people were murdered during those tragic weeks in December 1937 and January 1938, but it is certainly in the tens if not hundreds of thousands. According to the war crimes tribunal held after the war, around 200,000 were massacred, and at least 20,000 women raped. The official Chinese figure today is 300,000 dead. Some Japanese scholars dispute the higher figures, but nobody – or at least, nobody with any academic credibility – denies that the massacre took place. What has come to be known as the 'Rape of Nanking' was one of the most shameful episodes in the history of the war in China.

* * *

The Chinese institution that leads the way in commemorating these events is called the 'Memorial Hall of the Victims in Nanjing Massacre by Japanese Invaders'. It is truly huge. The site consists of a museum, two mass graves, an academic institute, a series of memorial squares and a peace park. There are dozens of memorial statues and sculptures here, some of them quite epic in scale: the tallest is some 30 metres (98 feet) high, and the longest is 30 metres long. In all, the memorial site occupies more than 28,000 square metres of land, close to the heart of the city. It attracts a remarkable eight million visitors every year.

The first sight that greets you, even before you have entered the complex, is the statue of a mother in torn clothing, carrying the limp body of her dead child. Her head is thrown back in anguish, her mouth a silent wail. The statue, which was sculpted by Chinese artist Wu Weishan, is at least 10 metres (32 feet) tall, and dominates the entrance to the site on Nanjing's busy Shuiximen Street. There is something visceral about the anguish expressed in the sculpture. The despairing slump of the woman's shoulders, the vulnerability of her long, exposed neck, and the lifelessness of her child, which she no longer has the energy to hold up – all this is a statement about what awaits you inside the memorial site.

Once you have followed the crowds past this statue, you come to a series of other statues by the same artist, depicting refugees fleeing the city in 1937. Their faces are contorted in terror. Some of the sculptures show figures dragging or carrying wounded or dying loved ones. Some show corpses of women or children.

There are gruesome statues all around the site. In one place, a giant arm bends out of the ground, its hand clutching life-lessly at the stones that surround it. Nearby a huge severed head lies beside a wall pocked with bullet holes. A stone cross 16 metres (52 feet) high looms over one of the memorial squares, like a tombstone, marked with the dates of the massacre. A statue of a lonely mother stands in a field of stones, searching for the bodies of her dead family. Elsewhere there is a bronze pavement, marked with the cast footprints of 222 witnesses to the massacre.

Everything about the place screams victimhood. To drive the point home, the official number of victims appears several times in metre-high letters. Inside the museum this number – 300,000 – is cast in bronze and lit from above in an otherwise darkened room. In the memorial square it is written in eleven different languages on a granite wall. It is carved in stone on one of the memorial's giant staircases; and it is written in black paint across the side of one of the many sculptures. It is repeated like a mantra throughout the memorial site, as if daring anyone to challenge its authority.

As with all such numbers, there is an element of deception going on here. The figure of 300,000 is high enough to be horrifying, round enough to be memorable, and low enough to be plausible – but in reality, nobody knows how many people were slaughtered in Nanjing at the end of 1937. For the Chinese, the number 300,000 is a symbol in which they can invest emotional energy, while allowing them some respite from contemplating the distressing reality of the individual details of murder and mutilation. For the Japanese, particularly for right-wing deniers of the massacre, the number conveniently gives them something to argue with. How exactly was this number reached? Does it include military as well as civilian casualties? Does it include people from the surrounding region, or only those from Nanjing's city centre? How can so many people possibly have been killed

This iconic number is reproduced repeatedly across the memorial site

when the official population of Nanjing at the time was only around 190,000 – or were refugees also included in the head count? All these questions are valid, but they also provide a useful distraction from the horror of what Japanese soldiers actually did.

At the centre of the memorial site is a museum which contains over a thousand relics and photographs of the massacre. The most important part of the museum contains graphic photographic evidence of the atrocity. There is a picture of a nineteen-year-old pregnant woman who had been raped and stabbed thirty times in the face, belly and thighs – miraculously she lived to tell the tale, but she lost her baby. There are relics and remains found at the sites of mass graves around the city. There is even a mass grave right here, inside the museum: a dark pit containing twenty-three skeletons that was discovered during the construction of the building's extension in 2007.

In a separate building beyond the museum is a second mass grave site containing the remains of 208 corpses. After seeing their skeletons, visitors are invited to a meditation hall, where they can contemplate the full horror of the things they have just seen and meditate on the names of some of the hundreds of victims that are recorded here.

The overall experience of visiting this place is quite overwhelming, even for foreigners with no personal connection to Nanjing. For those who call the city home, and for those whose parents or grandparents were caught up in these events, it must be close to unbearable. The museum designers obviously understood this, and have done their best to ease visitors out of the disturbing sights they have just witnessed. After coming through the darkness of the mass grave sites and the meditation hall, visitors emerge into a bright and beautiful 'Peace Garden' surrounded by mature trees which sway in the breeze, masking the sound of the traffic outside. A long pool lined with yellow flowers reflects the colours of the sky; and at the far end of the garden a statue of the goddess of peace rises above the city.

Nevertheless, it is difficult to leave this place without an acute sense of trauma. It is not the statue of peace that one remembers when one returns home, but the statue of the bereaved mother at the entrance to the museum, whose silent scream seems like a metaphor for the anguish of an entire city.

The first time I visited the Nanjing Memorial Hall was in April 2019. I had been invited to Nanjing by its curator, Zhang Jianjun, who wanted me to present some of my work to his colleagues. While I was there he offered to show me around with the help of one of his tour guides.

Whenever I meet a Chinese scholar of twentieth-century

history, the question I ask them is this: why did it take China forty years to get around to commemorating the events of the Second World War? It was not until the 1980s that any public memory projects really took off. The Nanjing Memorial Hall is a perfect example: it was not opened until 1985. What took them so long?

Over the years, some of the answers I have received to this question have been quite prosaic. A few historians have told me baldly that China had quite enough to deal with during those four decades, including a civil war, the Korean War, the Great Leap Forward and the Cultural Revolution: there was simply no time or energy to revisit the events of the Second World War with any degree of thought. Others have brushed my question aside with the observation that China is not so different from many western countries: few of the world's great Holocaust museums and memorials existed before the 1980s either. It takes time for any nation to come to terms with past traumas.

Some of the scholars I met in Nanjing took a more political view of my question: they told me that while the Chinese Communist Party was so focused on class war, memories of a nationalist war against Japan were not considered politically useful or interesting. Chairman Mao is reputed to have thanked the Japanese for invading China because ultimately it helped him to seize control of the country. It was not until after Mao's death that it became possible to revisit the traumas of 1937; and it was only in the 1980s that Communist leaders realised the potential of Chinese wartime suffering as a motif that might be used to bring greater unity to the nation.

When I asked Zhang Jianjun why he believed there had been such a delay in commemorating the events of 1937, the answer he gave me was not entirely unexpected, but was nevertheless disturbing. Before 1982, he explained, there was no appetite for reopening old wounds. But in that year, according to Zhang, the Japanese Ministry of Education committed a seemingly wilful act of provocation: they altered their school history textbooks in order to downplay Japanese responsibility for the war. 'People here would like to forget these unhappy past events,' he told me. 'Personally, I think that if the Japanese government had never revised their textbooks denying the massacre, we probably would never have had a memorial museum, because it would not have been necessary.'

Zhang's remarks, although true in spirit, gloss over a more nuanced history. There was indeed a huge international controversy about Japanese school textbooks in 1982, but it was based on a misunderstanding: the revisions Zhang referred to never exactly took place. He was absolutely right that Japanese textbooks tended to play down the invasion, but in the 1980s this was not a new phenomenon. The more egregious revisions and omissions had largely taken place decades earlier: the typical Japanese textbook of the 1950s and 1960s barely mentioned the massacre in Nanjing, and only ever in the blandest of terms. To put it simply, in 1982 no real revisions took place because there was nothing much to revise.

What the Chinese authorities were reacting to in 1982 was not the mainstream Japanese point of view, which was in fact beginning to change in favour of the Chinese, but rather the *backlash* against that point of view. As Zhang pointed out to me, right-wing nationalists in Japan became much more vocal in the 1980s, and a few of them were also very violent. They sent death threats to those who spoke about Japanese guilt, and occasionally even acted upon such threats. But the reason for their violence was that they had so demonstrably lost the argument about Japan's wartime history. By the end of that decade, the overwhelming majority of Japanese academic thinking had rejected right-wing rhetoric and accepted Japan's collective guilt for the war: and indeed, since then, almost all Japan's history textbooks have been revised to *include* the Nanjing Massacre.

The Nanjing Memorial Hall therefore seems to have been created out of several impulses at once. First, it fulfilled an academic need for greater understanding – and public documentation – of an important moment in Chinese history. Second, it provided a much-needed public acknowledgement of a trauma that had scarred a whole community. Lastly, however, it also played a political role in a new rivalry between Japan and China that began to emerge in the 1980s, and which was being expressed through the symbolism of the Second World War. For better or worse, the Nanjing Memorial Hall has become an aspect of that rivalry, as Japan and China compete over memories of their collective past.

In the past three decades there has been an explosion of historical consciousness in China, particularly in the public memory of the Second World War. The Nanjing Massacre has been at the heart of this revolution: it has become a national symbol of Chinese martyrdom. Thousands of books have been written about the atrocity over the last thirty years, and thousands of films, TV dramas and documentaries have been made. Today, Chinese TV companies make some two hundred programmes a year dramatising the 1937–45 war, the vast majority of which use the Nanjing Massacre as their central motif. The reason why the Nanjing Memorial Hall is so huge – and the reason why it sees such a phenomenal number of visitors each year – is that it is not merely a local institution, but a national one. Nanjing stands for all the atrocities that took place during the war, no matter where in China they occurred. Since 2014 the anniversary of the Nanjing Massacre has been a national holiday.

In Japan, by contrast, the pace of change has been much slower and more erratic. Some members of the general public, particularly those on the political right, have been reluctant to acknowledge the darker facts of their history. They do not generally deny that war crimes occurred, but they have begun to question whether the scale of those crimes was as great as the Chinese claim they were. They have also become extremely suspicious of Chinese motives for continually bringing up the past. As some Japanese politicians point out, there have been many Japanese apologies over the years – from individuals, from institutions and from the government itself – and yet the Chinese never seem to be satisfied. In recent years, right-wing revisionism has begun to gain ground again, especially on social media. The Nanjing Memorial Hall has been accused, quite unfairly, of being an institution whose only function is to point an admonishing finger directly at Japan.

Herein lies one of the great problems of our times. The only way that the Chinese sense of martyrdom can ever be assuaged is through apology, followed by apology, followed by apology – and each apology must be absolutely unequivocal. Germany has managed to do this with its neighbours in Europe; why can't Japan follow suit? But at the moment this is not something that even mainstream Japan, let alone Japan's right wing, is prepared to do.

In the absence of any such unconditional surrender from Japan, feelings in China are only likely to grow stronger. This is simply human nature: victims cannot overcome their past when those who wronged them insist on calling their most traumatic memories into question. All they can do is to reaffirm their own stories more loudly and more vehemently. The louder the Chinese shout, the more defensive the Japanese become. Along the way, objective history is increasingly smothered by a seemingly endless cycle of accusation and denial.

Given the poisonous history between these two countries, it would be easy to become gloomy about their future relations; but in fact there is also cause for hope, especially at a local level. The Nanjing Memorial Hall carries out a huge amount of reconciliation work with partners in Japan; and thousands of Japanese people come here each year to pay their respects. Relations between the curators of this institution and their counterparts in Japan are generally very good.

There is evidence of this spirit of cooperation elsewhere too. During my visit to Nanjing, I happened to meet a local historian – a quiet, thoughtful man named Liu Xiaoping, whose knowledge of his home city was truly encyclopaedic. Liu offered to show me another memorial to the massacre, off the beaten track, next to a main road by the river. This was the site where 9,800 Chinese soldiers were executed during the massacre. In 1985 a memorial stone was placed here to mark the site, along with an abstract tripod sculpture, topped with a carved stone wreath of flowers.

Today the monument is well-tended, with neatly cropped hedges that screen it slightly from the busy road; but thirty years ago, soon after it was erected, it fell into disrepair. Local people paid little attention to it, and used the site to dump rubbish.

According to Liu, the reason why it is so well looked after today is that a group of Japanese tourists came here to pay their respects and express their remorse. They were so shocked to discover the state it was in that they alerted the local government, which stepped in to tidy the place up. It was Japanese concern that rescued this place, and the Chinese local officials worked together with them to make sure that the memory of the massacre was respected here.

Neither the Chinese nor the Japanese will ever escape the history of what happened in Nanjing at the end of 1937. But it is small gestures like these that provide the best hope for making that history seem just a little more bearable.

The original Peace Statue sits outside the Japanese embassy in Seoul, but dozens of duplicates, like this one, stand in parks and cities all over the country

9

South Korea:
Peace Statue, Seoul

If the relationship between China and Japan is occasionally strained, then that between South Korea and Japan sometimes appears even worse. Korea was a Japanese colony between 1910 and 1945, and was ruthlessly exploited by the colonisers, especially during the Second World War. Today, however, South Korean politicians often use the past as a weapon to attack contemporary Japan. In recent years, claim and counter-claim between the two countries have degenerated into another seemingly endless cycle of finger-pointing.

At the centre of this storm of mutual indignation stand two monuments. In Japan, much nationalist sentiment about the war years is focused on the Yasukuni Shrine – a place that arouses nothing but outrage in South Korea. (I shall discuss the various controversies around this institution later, in Chapter 14.) For Koreans, meanwhile, painful memories of the past are expressed in the form of a bronze statue in down-town Seoul – a statue that many Japanese people, especially on the political right, have come to hate.

At first sight it is difficult to see what could possibly be offensive about the Peace Statue. It is a bronze sculpture of a young woman – little more than a girl, really – sitting on a chair with her hands clenched. She is wearing a traditional Korean dress. On her shoulder is a little bird, representing peace and freedom. She stares straight ahead of her, with an impassive but determined expression on her face. Beside her is a second, empty chair: an invitation to sit beside her, perhaps, or else a symbol of another, missing, person.

On the face of it, there should be nothing controversial about this statue at all. The girl does not appear particularly angry or upset; she is not scowling, or gesturing in any way that could be considered offensive. Even the title of the monument seems quite benign: what could possibly be wrong with a 'Peace Statue'?

It is only when one knows who this girl represents that one begins to understand why she provokes such emotion. She is in fact a depiction of a 'comfort woman' – the Japanese euphemism for a prostitute who serviced Japanese soldiers during the war. Between 1937 and 1945, tens of thousands of Korean women were tricked into becoming 'comfort women'. They were often promised good jobs in factories far from home, before being abducted and held in brothels as sex slaves. Rather than cracking down on such trafficking, the Japanese authorities turned a blind eye. Indeed, according to some accounts at least, the Japanese military not only colluded in this vast system of sexual slavery, but may even have set it up deliberately.

What makes this statue so controversial is that it sits on the pavement directly opposite the Japanese embassy in Seoul. The girl's face may not show any signs of anger or hurt, but she is staring directly at the diplomatic mission, and her clenched fists speak volumes. Koreans call it a 'Peace Statue', but it is quite clearly much, much more than that.

* * *

There has always been a very strong undercurrent of anti-Japanese sentiment in Korea. Before the twentieth century, the country had frequently been in conflict with its neighbour, often having to rely on China or Russia to provide a counterbalance to Japanese power. After 1905, however, when Japan had defeated the last of its regional rivals, Korea fell entirely within the Japanese sphere of influence. The country was formally annexed into the Japanese empire in 1910; and thus began thirty-five years of colonial exploitation.

The zenith of this exploitation came during the Second World War, when Japanese rule began to intrude on all aspects of Korean life. Between 1939 and 1945, some 200,000 Korean men were drafted into the Japanese Imperial Army, and at least a further 1.5 million were conscripted to work in Japanese factories. Women were also forced into all kinds of work for the Japanese. According to a proclamation in 1941, all Korean women between the ages of 14 and 25 were obliged to give up thirty days of work for the government each year – a system that seemed only to encourage the abuse of young girls. By the end of the war women of all ages were being forcibly drafted by the Japanese for much longer periods. A proportion of these women never made it to the factories, but were kidnapped and imprisoned in Japanese military brothels.

Unfortunately, the end of the Second World War did not bring an end to Korea's troubles. Unlike the people of neighbouring China, or of other colonial countries like Indonesia and Vietnam, Koreans never had the satisfaction of taking part in their own liberation. The Japanese ruled right up to the last moments of the war, at which point they were replaced by other outsiders: the Russians in the north and the Americans in the south. Koreans themselves seemed to have little control over their own destiny.

In the years that followed, two opposing systems were imposed upon Korea, each of them equally brutal, and each sponsored by a different superpower. In the north, the Soviets installed the Communist dictator Kim Il-sung, whose dynasty has ruled there ever since. In the south, the Americans sponsored a series of brutal military dictatorships that lasted until the 1980s. Conflict between the two systems erupted violently in 1950 with the onset of the Korean War, which went on to claim the lives of at least 1.2 million people. Despite the bloodshed nothing was resolved, and to this day Korea is split in two.

None of these later tragedies can be laid at Japan's door; however, as is frequently pointed out, they would never have happened were it not for the way that Japan had first subjugated Korea, and then involved the country in the Second World War.

Soon there were other reasons for Koreans to be resentful. In the 1950s, 1960s and 1970s, while Korea was still reeling from its recent upheavals, its neighbour saw unprecedented economic growth. Soon Japan was once again the undisputed powerhouse of the region, not only provoking a great deal of envy, but reviving unpleasant memories from the past.

Alongside economic power came political power. In 1965, Japan offered the South Korean government around $800 million in grants and loans as compensation for its brutal rule before and during the Second World War. In return it asked for a normalisation of relations, and the end of any future claims on Japan. South Korea's military dictatorship had no mandate from the people to sign such a treaty, but under pressure from the USA it did so anyway. In the coming weeks a series of anti-Japanese demonstrations burst onto the streets of Seoul.

For many South Koreans, their country's renewed subservience to Japan and the USA was symbolised by a huge new
sex industry catering mostly to Japanese tourists and American
servicemen. It seemed that Korean women – and by extension
Korea itself – had not yet managed to shake off foreign
exploitation.

Given such a history, it seems obvious today that the image
of the 'comfort woman' was set to become something of a
national symbol in South Korea. This image of a woman who
had been dominated, raped and enslaved by outsiders – but
who had nevertheless managed somehow to maintain her
dignity – is a perfect metaphor for Korean suffering in the
twentieth century. All these things are expressed by the Peace
Statue in Seoul.

But I am getting ahead of myself: at the beginning of the
1980s nothing was quite so obvious. In fact, until the end of
that decade very few people in South Korea had ever heard
of 'comfort women'. Few of the women themselves had ever
dared to tell their stories, for fear of the humiliation it would
bring upon their families. Neither did the South Korean
authorities ever encourage them to come forward. The whole
issue was hidden away under a pall of shame.

The silence was not broken until 1988, after the country
had started down the path towards democratic reform. That
year, a Korean Church group organised an academic conference on sex tourism, where a scholar named Yun Chung-ok
presented her research about how Korean women had been
treated during the Second World War. Her paper caused something of a sensation. In the ensuing media storm, the Korean
and Japanese governments were suddenly inundated with
requests for more information.

In Japan, unfortunately, the initial reaction was to deny everything. In 1990, the Japanese government claimed that the comfort woman system had never been the work of the government or the military, only of private entrepreneurs.

Then a former comfort woman named Kim Hak-sun stepped forward to tell her story, and the issue suddenly became much more real. Kim was first raped in 1941 at the age of seventeen, after being abducted by a Japanese soldier. She had been travelling in Beijing with her foster father, trying to find work, when the two of them were arrested and separated from one another. For the next four months she was imprisoned in a military brothel, before she escaped with a Korean travelling salesman, whom she later married.

In the following months and years, hundreds of other women from all over Asia came forward to tell similar stories. Some of them, like the Filipina Lola Rosa, were imprisoned in brothels as a punishment for resistance activities. Others, like the white Dutch expatriate Jan Ruff O'Herne, were kept almost as military trophies for groups of Japanese officers. But the vast majority were ordinary peasants, factory workers or schoolgirls who were either abducted by soldiers or enticed away from their families by unscrupulous middlemen. Their stories are uniformly horrific. The Korean Council for Women Drafted for Military Sexual Slavery, an NGO based in Seoul, has gathered dozens of testimonies involving not only repeated rape but also other extremes of physical violence. Similar organisations in China, Indonesia and the Philippines have also gathered such stories. Later these issues were brought up by the United Nations Commission on Human Rights, and an investigation was carried out by the Geneva International Commission of Jurists.

The findings of all these groups, as well as those of Japanese academics, were unequivocal: the Japanese military might not have formally conscripted Korean women as sex slaves, but they had certainly planned, built and operated a network of brothels where Korean women had been imprisoned. Furthermore, it was clear that key figures at the very top of the army had been aware that many of these women were being recruited against their will.

As these facts gradually became known in South Korea at the beginning of the 1990s, they caused widespread outrage. In Seoul, local activists decided to take their outrage onto the streets. When the Japanese prime minister, Kiichi Miyazawa, visited the country in January 1992, a demonstration was organised outside the Japanese embassy, where protesters held up banners demanding an unequivocal, legal apology.

Before long, such demonstrations became a weekly occurrence, with crowds gathering outside the embassy every Wednesday at noon. These demonstrations were held each week for more than twenty-five years – in fact, at the time of writing they are still being held. Whenever possible, a group of old ladies, the former 'comfort women' themselves, takes pride of place, sitting at the front of the demonstration. These women have been hailed as living symbols of Korea's national victimhood. Collectively, they are known as the people's 'grandmothers'.

It was in this context that the Peace Statue was erected. In 2011, the organisers of the Wednesday demonstrations wanted to commemorate the upcoming anniversary of their protest: 14 December that year would mark their 1,000th demonstration in front of the Japanese embassy. They commissioned a pair of artists, a married couple named Kim Seo-kyung and Kim Eun-sung, to create a memorial to be placed on the site

where the demonstrators gathered. At first it was thought that
they might design a simple memorial stone with some kind
of inscription on it, but when the Japanese government began
to protest at such an object being placed outside its embassy,
the artists reacted by proposing something more prominent:
a statue.

Had the statue been erected in a different location – outside
a church, perhaps, or a government building, or at the site of
a former military brothel – it might have had a gentler
meaning. As an expression of victimhood, it might have given
Koreans a place to mourn, to reflect on their troubled past,
and to heal old wounds. It might even have helped in the
process that its sculptors say they wish to promote – the search
for some kind of peace. But from the very beginning the
statue was intended for *this* site only. As a consequence it can
never be considered simply as an expression of victimhood
or a symbol of peace. It is also the embodiment of a highly
emotional protest directed against Japan.

The problem with a bronze statue, or for that matter a stone
plaque, is that it implies a kind of permanence. Unlike a
protest, even a weekly protest that continues for years, a
memorial does not go home on Wednesday evening, or gradually disperse over time. It stays on the pavement outside the
embassy twenty-four hours a day. It states a single, seemingly
eternal truth, regardless of any political concessions that might
be made by either side: South Korea will always be the victim,
and Japan will always be the perpetrator.

The Japanese argue that this is unfair. They say that they
have repeatedly made financial reparations, and have repeatedly apologised for the wrongs that were done to Korea before
and during the war. This is undeniably true. In the mid-1990s
the Japanese government helped to establish the Asian

Women's Fund, an organisation devoted to publicising the 'comfort woman' issue and compensating the victims with 'atonement money'. Around the same time the Japanese prime minister, Tomiichi Murayama, expressed his apologies several times, not only during state visits to South Korea but also in individual letters to the victims themselves. Subsequent Japanese prime ministers have done likewise. Even Shinzo Abe, who is known for his right-wing nationalist views, went out of his way in December 2015 to express his 'most sincere apologies and remorse to all the women who underwent immeasurable and painful experiences and suffered incurable physical and psychological wounds as comfort women'.

As Korean protesters point out, however, this is not quite the whole story. They argue that some of the Japanese apologies have been half-hearted at best, and are often drowned out by loud and offensive denials by Japanese nationalists in the media. Yes, money was paid to former victims of the 'comfort woman' system via the Asian Women's Fund, but it should have been paid directly by the Japanese government itself. Taking this indirect path was just another example of the Japanese government trying to wriggle out of its legal responsibilities. A new fund, set up more directly by the Japanese government in 2015, has also been rejected.

The crux of the matter is that, while the Japanese seem willing to accept moral responsibility for the past, they have never yet accepted direct, legal responsibility. This is what South Korean activists crave more than anything else. They want an official admission that the Japanese government deliberately planned to enslave Korean women, set up a system to do so, and knew from start to finish exactly what they were doing.

Unfortunately, without conclusive documentary evidence

to prove precisely that, this is not something that the Japanese are prepared to do.

In the meantime, the Peace Statue will continue to sit in the street in downtown Seoul, staring at the Japanese embassy in silent accusation. Since 2011 it has become a permanent feature of the city.

Today other cities have also taken up the cry. According to the artists, there are now dozens of other identical statues in parks and cities all over South Korea. In 2018, one of these statues was erected outside the Japanese consulate in Busan, in direct imitation of the protest in Seoul. Not only that, but they have also started to appear in other countries as well, including the USA, Canada, Australia and Germany.

This is martyrdom as a weapon. South Korea's victims know that they have the moral high ground, and that continued protest – perhaps even perpetual protest – is the best way to make sure that their stories are heard.

The women who were repeatedly raped between 1937 and 1945 will never be able to escape their history. The best they can hope for is that, through monuments like the Peace Statue, Japan will never be able to escape it either.

10

USA and Poland: Katyn Memorial, Jersey City

In Jersey City, overlooking the Hudson River, stands one of the most dramatic Second World War memorials in the world. Ten metres (32 feet) high, standing on a granite plinth, is a bronze statue of a bound-and-gagged soldier being stabbed through the back with a bayonet. He appears to be in the throes of death. His body is arched in pain, and his face is tilted up towards heaven. The point of the bayonet emerges through the left side of his chest, exactly where his heart is.

The memorial commemorates an atrocity committed in 1940 by the Soviet secret police: the massacre of thousands of Polish officers in the Russian forest of Katyn. Ever since it was first installed in 1991, it has divided local opinion. Some residents complain that it is ugly and vulgar, and that its depiction of violent death is simply too graphic. But others have always defended it as darkly beautiful. The feelings of discomfort it provokes, they say, are exactly the emotions that a good war memorial should inspire.

In May 2018, however, the statue suddenly became the centre of a quarrel that went far beyond local sensibilities. It began when the mayor of Jersey City, Steven Fulop, announced plans to move the monument to a different place nearby. The area was being redeveloped, and the spot was earmarked as the location of a new, riverside public park. The statue had to be moved to make way for this new development.

A group of Polish Americans immediately protested against the move, and launched a lawsuit against the city council: it was their memorial, and they did not feel properly consulted. They were backed up by other local residents, who opposed the redevelopment plan more generally.

Within days, the issue had escalated into a full-blown international incident. The Polish ambassador to the USA complained on social media about the monument's relocation. Politicians in Poland accused Jersey City of disrespecting Polish heroes, and condemned their plans as 'really scandalous'. Mayor Fulop hit back by accusing one of these politicians of being a 'known anti-Semite' and 'holocaust denier', prompting the politician in question to take legal action. Soon, tempers were flaring all round. The developer tasked with renovating the area denounced the monument as 'gruesome'; the artist who designed it called the developer a 'schmuck'.

For neutral observers, this unseemly spectacle raises all kinds of questions. Why were local people so quick to take offence, when all that seemed to be happening was that the memorial was being moved from one prominent place to another, just a few hundred metres away? Why all the fuss now, more than seventy years after the Second World War was over? And most importantly, what was this statue doing in New Jersey in the first place? The events it commemorates involved no US citizens, and took place 4,500 miles away from US soil. So why was it even there?

So many different themes demand attention here, both local

and international, that it is difficult to know where to start. But the element that binds them together into such an insoluble tangle is history. There could be no better demonstration of how impossible it is to escape our history, especially when that history involves an element of victimhood.

It is worth taking a moment to consider what exactly the memorial commemorates, because, like many memorials, this one is not quite as straightforward as it seems.

At the very beginning of the Second World War, while Poland was defending itself from the German invasion, it was attacked again, this time by the Soviets, from the rear. In other words, it was 'stabbed in the back'.

Within a few weeks, the country was split down the middle: the Nazis ruled in the west, the Soviets in the east. The Soviet occupiers were just as cruel as the Nazis. Between September 1939 and March 1940, their secret police arrested hundreds of thousands of people. This included anyone who might pose a future threat to their rule: Polish landowners, businessmen, priests, lawyers, teachers and other members of the intelligentsia. The majority were deported to Siberia and Kazakhstan, and abandoned there to fend for themselves. Tens of thousands starved to death. These events are commemorated on the back of the plinth by a bronze relief depicting a woman and three children, barefoot and dressed in rags. Above them are the words '1939 Siberia', and below a description of the series of betrayals carried out by the Soviet Union which led to their banishment.

While these people were being deported, other groups suffered a much more gruesome fate. Polish soldiers and policemen were often simply executed. The most notorious killing grounds were in the Russian forest of Katyn, where several thousand Polish army officers were murdered and piled into mass graves. These terrible events are quite literally at the heart of the monument: buried within its granite base is soil taken from the forest where the atrocities were committed.

During the rest of the war, Poland was to suffer a series of other 'stabs in the back'. For example, at the Big Three conference at Yalta, at the beginning of 1945, Stalin demanded a large area of eastern Poland to be incorporated into the Soviet Union. In return, Poland would be compensated with new land taken from defeated Germany. The deal was struck in the absence of any consultation with the Poles themselves, and its consequences were huge. After the war, around 1.2 million Poles were forcibly expelled from the eastern regions of Poland and sent west. Over a million more who had been abroad in 1945 suddenly found themselves without a homeland to return to. They included hundreds of thousands of Polish soldiers and airmen who had spent the war fighting for the Allies, and slave labourers liberated from German factories and work camps. These people felt betrayed not only by the Soviets who had taken their lands, but by the British and Americans who had stood by and let it happen.

The final insult came with the Soviet subjugation of Poland in 1945. Despite promises that the Polish people would be free to choose their own form of government, the Soviets imposed a puppet administration. For the next forty-four years, Poland would be a vassal state, serving the interests of the Soviet Union. Free elections would not take place again until the fall of Communism in 1989.

The memorial in Jersey City commemorates all these events. While it is ostensibly dedicated to the Katyn massacres, the word 'Katyn' has itself become a symbol of every betrayal that the Poles were forced to suffer during the second half of the twentieth century. The soldier who is being bayoneted upon his plinth represents much more than the thousands of Polish officers killed at Katyn in 1940. He represents Poland itself, in all its tragic martyrdom.

It is tempting to leave the analysis here: the monument is a national symbol, representing national suffering. But to the people who built it, it is much more than that. It is intimately bound up not only with Polish history, but also with the local history of Jersey City, and the personal history of those who came here in the aftermath of the war.

In 1945, there were more political refugees from Poland than from any other European country. Of the 200,000 or so who ended up in the USA, around 10,000 settled in New Jersey, where there was already a thriving community of Polish immigrants. They found jobs, built new lives for themselves, learned to speak English and embraced American life. But they never forgot their heritage. Many joined Polish-American cultural and political groups, such as the Polish American Congress and the Polish Roman Catholic Union of America. For immigrants whose lives had been so fractured by the Second World War, such organisations offered them the chance to forge a new identity for themselves. They helped them learn to be both Polish *and* American.

In the early 1980s a group of Polish veterans gathered to discuss ways of commemorating the various tragedies they had lived through, particularly the massacre at Katyn. The group included men like Walter Sosulski and Ryszard Winowski, who had fought with the western Allies in Italy; and Stanisław Paszul, who had not only fought with the Polish resistance against the Nazis but had also spent many years in

Soviet gulags in Siberia. They got together with other Polish Americans and tried to come up with ideas for a memorial in the heart of their community.

In 1986 they formed a non-profit corporation devoted to raising money. They hired sculptor Andrzej Pitynski to design something dramatic, and worthy of the strength of emotion they felt. After lobbying the city council for permission to display their memorial in public, they were eventually granted a spot in Exchange Place, a riverside location with a view across the Hudson towards Manhattan. The Katyn Memorial was finally inaugurated in June 1991.

Jersey City was a very different place in those days. It was still a largely working-class city, whose residents worked in the many local factories, freight terminals and warehouses that lined the Hudson. This was reflected in the group that had championed the memorial, which included not only journalists and teachers but also carpenters and foundry workers.

In the following years, however, new businesses began to move here in search of cheaper real estate than they could find across the river in Manhattan. New residents quickly followed: yuppies, hipsters and white-collar workers in the financial industries. These people could not understand why there should be such a graphic representation of violent death at the centre of their community. Gentrification began to sweep the city, driving up prices and driving out many of the older, blue-collar residents. The redevelopment of Exchange Place, where the Katyn Memorial is situated, was just the latest instance of this gentrification. An important element of the protest against moving the memorial was nothing to do with Polish identity or memories of the Second World War, but about local identity and memories of a community that was fast disappearing.

There are markers of this very local identity on the memorial itself. In 2001, when two airliners were flown into the Twin Towers in Manhattan, visitors to the Katyn Memorial had an unrestricted view of the unfolding disaster across the river. Three years later, a plaque was added to the base of the memorial commemorating 9/11. It shows a relief sculpture, in bronze, of the New York City skyline, with smoke billowing from the twin towers of the stricken World Trade Center. 'Never forget!' reads the inscription beneath it. 'Pray for all the innocent victims and heroes who died in the terrorist attack on America, September 11, 2001.'

What does this plaque have to do with Katyn, or Poland, or the Second World War? The answer is, absolutely nothing. But it has everything to do with local memories of yet another 'stab in the back'.

International history, national history, local history, personal history – each of these layers of history is represented in this one memorial. And each layer is suffused with trauma and deep feelings of suffering and betrayal. The Katyn monument is one of the most emotionally charged memorials in the world. Is it any wonder, then, that Steven Fulop's surprise announcement that the monument would be moved away from Exchange Place – purely for the sake of commercial redevelopment – was greeted with such defensive outrage?

In the days after the announcement was made, debates about it took place in the local and national newspapers, on social media, in the city council, on Polish radio, and between Polish and American diplomats. At the centre of this storm of emotion stood the local Polish-American community, many of whom felt betrayed all over again. What had seemed like a minor detail to councillors – the movement of a memorial from one prominent location to another – affected Polish Americans in ways they could not possibly fathom. These survivors of the war knew what it was to be uprooted and moved against their will. The decision to move their memorial without consulting them was just another reminder of a deeply traumatic history.

Across the Atlantic, in Poland, there was a much better understanding of the emotions involved, but even here they did not quite get the full picture. Poland embraced the Katyn Memorial as a symbol of Polish identity, when in fact it was something slightly different – it was a symbol of *Polish–American* identity. It commemorates a specific kind of loss, and a specific kind of martyrdom, unique to those Poles who were forced into exile after 1945.

It is no coincidence that the Katyn Memorial in Jersey City is much more graphic, and much more dramatic, than any of the numerous Katyn memorials that exist in Poland itself. The people who built it had lost not only friends and family, but also their homeland and their sense of belonging. Some of them never saw Poland again after 1945. Their very Polishness was therefore defined by this memorial in a way that other people, even other Poles, could never truly understand.

Finally, there was a local dimension to the controversy that could only be fully appreciated by Jersey City residents. The city's old-timers already felt betrayed by their council, whose gentrification drive appeared to be putting the needs of newcomers and big businesses above their own. To such people, the Katyn Memorial was the symbol of a local identity that, ironically, was itself being stabbed in the back.

Even some council members were swept up in these emotions. One city councillor, Rich Boggiano, was particularly vocal about leaving the memorial where it was. 'I'm sick and tired of all these new people coming here,' he told the local newspaper, 'wanting to change everything about Jersey City.'

Once people get riled up, it is difficult to calm them down again. The city council tried to rectify their mistake and started to consult local Polish-American community leaders, but it was too late. They promised to move the monument just one block south, to the foot of York Street, but indignant protesters refused to negotiate. Anyone who argued in favour of the move was shouted down. When the president of the Katyn Memorial Committee said at a press conference that he was willing to accept the council's offer, he was booed. When the Polish ambassador tried to pour oil on troubled waters, and offered his support, Councillor Boggiano called him a 'piece of shit'. The Polish president himself gave the relocation his blessing, but was immediately denounced by local protesters as a traitor to their cause: in May 2018, when he made a personal visit to the memorial, he was greeted there by demonstrators with cries of 'Shame!'

The forces that fuelled this maelstrom of protest were memory and martyrdom – which in the minds of the protesters combined to form a single entity called 'history'. At council planning meetings they accused the city of trying to 'erase history'. At their public demonstrations they unfurled huge banners which read 'Respect Our History'. This history was more important to them than progress, or harmony, or compromise, or anything else; and any threat to it was regarded as a threat to their very identity.

Eventually, after several heated meetings, two petitions and the scheduling of a public referendum, the city council backed down. The subject of the monument had simply become too toxic, and threatened to disrupt too much other business. In

December 2018, seven months after the controversy had begun, the council voted unanimously to leave the statue where it was, 'in perpetuity'.

There are different ways of viewing this story, depending on your political point of view. You might see it as a victory for the common citizen, standing up fearlessly against the combined forces of power and money. Or you might see it as a defeat for the forces of progress, held to ransom by a hysterical mob. Either way, it demonstrates one fundamental truth: in the day-to-day running of our communities, we are all prisoners of our history. When we forget that truth, or try to ignore it, it inevitably comes back to bite us.

For the protesters who won this battle, their memorial now has yet another meaning, and one that speaks not of suffering but of empowerment. For once, the martyr has come out on top. The psychological consequences of their victory are potentially profound. Today, the people of Jersey City are able to identify themselves not only with the blindfolded soldier but also, on a symbolic level at least, with the invisible hands that hold the rifle and its bayonet.

In the words of one resident, posted on a local internet forum: 'I love that memorial. Welcome to Jersey City. Don't fuck with us.'

A NÉMET MEGSZÁLLÁS ÁLDOZATAINAK EMLÉKMŰVE

11

Hungary: Monument for the Victims of German Occupation, Budapest

One of the problems with the Peace Statue in Seoul is the way that it focuses all the blame for what happened to Korea's 'comfort women' upon Japan. Of course, the Japanese military will always bear ultimate responsibility; but there were many others who contributed to this tragedy. According to their own accounts, Korean women were often abducted not by Japanese soldiers but by Korean collaborators or middlemen. After the war, the shame these women suffered was perpetuated by their own society. And the financial reparations that they might have received from the Japanese government in 1965 were actually pocketed by the Korean government to pay for public infrastructure projects. None of these things are expressed in the Peace Statue. It's always much easier for a nation to blame outsiders than to look at itself.

That is one of the problems with figurative monuments and memorials: they often simplify history too much. In the pursuit of a single, dramatic story about our past, they can obscure other, more nuanced stories. Furthermore, this obfuscation is sometimes more than an accident. Cynical politicians occasionally erect monuments that seem

deliberately designed to whitewash the past, and the motif
of the martyr is often their main tool. Martyrs have moral
power. Martyrs are untouchable. In the twenty-first century,
almost every nation wants to portray itself as a martyr.

Europe's most controversial memorial in this regard is probably Budapest's Monument for the Victims of the German
Occupation. It was erected in 2014 by Hungary's Fidesz
government to commemorate the moment when, seventy
years earlier, the German army seized control of the country.
During the German occupation, hundreds of thousands of
Hungarians were killed. Either they were deported to concentration camps, or they died on the battlefield while fighting
under German leadership. This monument is supposed to
stand in memory of all those who died.

The design consists of two main figures arranged before a
classical colonnade. In the foreground is the archangel Gabriel,
a symbol of Hungary, standing with his arms outstretched.
One of his wings has been broken off, leaving only the fluttering end of his body cloth to suggest where it once was. His
face shows an expression of serene suffering, and his eyes are
shut. In his hand is a golden orb topped with a double cross
– another symbol of Hungary – which he is holding up rather
carelessly, seemingly oblivious of the fact that it is about to
be snatched from his grasp.

Above him, swooping down from the top of the colonnade,
is the second figure in the allegory: an eagle representing
Germany. In contrast to the serene and innocent angel below
him, everything about this eagle is aggressive. Its outstretched
talons are sharp; its feathers are nothing like the soft feathers
of Gabriel's wings – they are more like blades. Around its
ankle is a metal ring with the date on it: 1944.

The message of the sculpture is not difficult to work out. Serene, peaceful Hungary is being attacked by a ruthless and aggressive Germany. Hungary is being portrayed as an innocent victim – a wounded angel. Germany, and only Germany, is guilty of violence.

There have been so many objections to this monument, from so many different people, that once again it is difficult to know where to begin. Architects, planners and political geographers criticised its location, which they said was unsuitable for a national monument. It stands on a narrow strip of land at the southern edge of Budapest's Szabadság Tér (Liberty Square), with a narrow road running directly in front of it, making it difficult to see and impossible to approach. Artists criticised its aesthetics, which they said were an uneasy mix of Viennese baroque and social-realist kitsch. Prize-winning sculptor György Jovánovics called it a 'messy nightmare'.

But the main objections concerned its flawed symbolism. Nobody denied that March 1944 was indeed a tragic moment for Hungary, but they certainly questioned the way that the monument was portraying the event. Was Hungary such an innocent angel at the time? And was Germany the only aggressor? Did not other events that happened around this time tell a very different, and much more uncomfortable story?

Even before the monument was built, a group of prominent Hungarian historians wrote an open letter to their government complaining that its symbolism was 'based on a falsification of history'. They were joined by a variety of politicians, international organisations and local Jewish groups who also issued open letters in the press saying similar things. There were protests on the international stage too. Diplomats in the USA and Israel expressed outrage at the proposed monument, and a group of American senators wrote a collective letter to the

Hungarian government urging them to consult representatives of the Jewish community before going ahead with their design. In the European Parliament the monument quickly became the subject of furious debate.

As all these groups pointed out, the history of the occupation was much more controversial than the monument suggested. They wanted to remind the Hungarian government that, far from being a victim of Germany, Hungary had actually spent most of the war as its ally. The German occupation had only taken place in 1944 because Hitler had wanted to prevent the possibility of the Hungarians making a separate peace with the Allies, and in the event it had not been a particularly violent affair. In fact the Germans arrived unopposed, and took over with no bloodshed at all. Resistance to German rule was virtually non-existent.

The real victims of the German occupation were not to become apparent until later. Contrary to the impression given by this memorial, the vast majority of victims were not Hungarians in general, but quite specifically Hungarian Jews. One of the first German administrators to arrive in Budapest on 19 March, the very day of the occupation, was Adolf Eichmann, the main architect of the Holocaust. Within four months he and his team had organised the deportation of 438,000 Jews to Auschwitz. According to Holocaust historian Saul Friedländer, 90 per cent of these Jews – some 394,000 people in total – were exterminated upon arrival. Later on, some 20,000 Roma people were also taken off to be murdered, along with a small number of 'degenerates' and political prisoners.

Contrary to the impression given by the monument, the Germans were not the sole perpetrators of these crimes. It is true that the Holocaust did not begin in Hungary until after the German occupation, but it would never have taken place so quickly had Hungarians not willingly collaborated. In truth, the groundwork for the Holocaust had already been laid years before. The first anti-Semitic laws were introduced in Hungary as early as 1920, when Miklós Horthy's government imposed strict legal limits on the number of Jewish students allowed in universities. From 1938 onwards a series of other anti-Semitic laws followed. Hungarian Jews were defined, labelled and registered. They were officially excluded from jobs in government, and their opportunities in the media and in the legal and medical professions were tightly restricted. They were denied the right to vote. From 1941 they were forbidden from marrying non-Jews or having sexual relations with them. Even after the occupation it was not the Germans who rounded Jews up, beat them, packed them onto trains and then shared out their property: all these things were done by Hungarian policemen and local government officials.

Soon, Hungarian fascists also joined in more directly with the killing. In October 1944, after Horthy was finally forced from office, the Germans installed a Hungarian fascist as prime minister. Ferenc Szálasy was the leader of the Arrow Cross Party, a popular far-right group that advocated an even more violent form of anti-Semitism. Within a month of taking power, Szálasi's followers were rounding up Jews and shooting them on the banks of the River Danube. The worst atrocities occurred just a few hundred metres away from the site of today's Monument to the Victims of the German Occupation, where between 10,000 and 15,000 were murdered and thrown into the river. (There is, incidentally, another memorial here, the Shoes on the Danube Bank – sixty pairs of empty shoes lined up by the water's edge to represent some of the people who were killed.)

In the light of all this, how could the monument's creators possibly justify the portrayal of Hungary as an innocent victim – a wounded angel, whose only sin was not to have seen the occupation coming? How could they justify grouping the victims of the Holocaust together with other so-called victims of the German occupation, including politicians who until 1944 had willingly collaborated with the Nazis?

Other objections to the monument had less to do with history than they did with contemporary politics. No sooner had its construction been announced than people began to ask why it was necessary at all. There had been no great popular campaign to erect a memorial to the victims of the occupation. Why was the government so keen to erect one now? And why the hurry?

The monument was first approved in a government decree on 31 December 2013, but officials originally wanted it to be commissioned, constructed and inaugurated in time for the seventieth anniversary of the occupation on 19 March – a mere eleven weeks later. Critics claimed that the real reason for this impossible deadline was not the anniversary at all, but the upcoming general election at the beginning of April. The ruling party at the time – Viktor Orbán's Fidesz Party – already had an unassailable majority in the parliament, which everyone expected to continue after the election. Nevertheless, Fidesz had long been under pressure from the radical right-wing Jobbik party, which already commanded nearly 17 per cent of the popular vote. The creation of a monument to Hungarian martyrdom was exactly the sort of populist gesture that might lure some of these voters over to Fidesz.

There were also serious questions about how the monument

had been commissioned. Over the previous few years, Orbán's government had been repeatedly accused of authoritarianism by other politicians and campaigners, and the monument seemed to be a perfect case in point. It had never been discussed or debated in parliament. It had not been presented to Hungarian experts, and there was certainly no consultation with the public. Neither was the contract for building the memorial put out to tender: a construction company had simply been appointed. Nor was there any kind of competition to find a suitable artist: the minister in charge had simply handed the project to Péter Párkányi Raab, a sculptor who had been a favourite of the Fidesz Party for years. Párkányi Raab came up with a design within a few days, and it was rapidly approved by a committee consisting of just five people. In other words, the whole project was the result of a top-down decision, rushed through by government decree, and imposed on the Budapest cityscape without any public scrutiny.

In such a context, it is hardly surprising that people began to protest. At first the objections came in the form of private letters to the government and open letters published in the press. The strength of public feeling over the issue seems to have taken the Fidesz government completely by surprise, and for a while in March 2014 they called a temporary halt to construction of the monument. But it was not long before they changed their minds. Two days after their victory in the election that April, they decided to press ahead regardless.

Frustrated by the government's refusal to engage with anyone's concerns, a group of artists and civic activists decided to take matters into their own hands. Since they seemed unable to influence what the official monument looked like, they decided to do the next best thing and build one of their own. Unlike the official memorial, theirs would not be made from stone and metal, but would consist of photographs, hand-written stories and personal relics from 1944, all of which were to be donated by members of the general public. They set up a Facebook group, and invited people to bring along 'symbols of their souls'. They specifically asked people not only to bring emblems of their personal victimhood, but also symbols of repentance, of forgiveness for the past.

Before long, the group had gathered hundreds of such items, which they arranged in front of the construction site. There were prayer books, shoes, pairs of spectacles and battered old suitcases. There were yellow stars made of cloth, of the sort that Jews were forced to wear during the war. Hundreds of people brought small stones, as they might to a Jewish grave, some of them inscribed with the names and details of individuals deported to Auschwitz. Others brought flowers, plants and candles.

The organisers called their counter-monument a 'Living Memorial', because of the way that it changed and evolved from day to day. At the centre of their display sat two white chairs, facing one another. These were supposed to symbolise the invitation to sit down and discuss the past, and the way that it was being portrayed in the present – exactly the sort of conversations that had been missing during the commissioning of the official monument. True to this symbolism, the group began to organise formal public discussions at the site. Artists and critics gave talks about different monuments around the world, and compared them to the monument being built in Budapest. Poetry slams took place in the open air beside the memorial. Holocaust survivors and their relatives were invited to share their memories;

20 July 2014: the day the monument was first erected. The 'counter-monument' lies before it, on the ground and attached to the railings, along with a banner reading 'Falsification of history is the moral equivalent of well-poisoning'

and commemorations were held for the victims of the Roma genocide.

By the time the government contractors were completing the official monument, the unofficial counter-monument was already well established. It consisted of hundreds of items, spread along more than 30 metres of roadside. Hundreds, possibly even thousands of local people had already come to visit it.

The final elements of Fidesz's grandiose sculpture were winched into place during the night of 20 July 2014, but by that point the government already seemed to be losing interest in the project. Their monument has never been formally inaugurated, and no official government events have ever taken place at the site. It has been on the receiving end of so much criticism, not only in Hungary but around the world, that it was difficult to keep standing up to defend it. Calls to have the monument pulled down continue to this day. In 2018, the leader of the Socialist Party pledged to take the monument down if he was elected; and one or two candidates from other parties followed suit.

The 'Living Memorial' by contrast seems to have gone from strength to strength. It continues to grow and evolve even today; and various groups and activists still hold regular events here. The range of topics debated on the chairs beside the memorial has expanded: this is now a forum not only to debate Hungarian history, but also to explore a range of contemporary social, political and artistic issues. But the heart of it remains the slightly chaotic collection of personal relics and photographs that line the pavement opposite the arch-angel Gabriel, which has become something of a local tourist attraction.

The history of the Second World War is still a deeply painful and controversial subject in Hungary. The period of the German occupation in 1944–5 was a particularly dark episode: it was a time when a deeply flawed government was obliged to make a series of impossible political and moral choices while being increasingly powerless. There is not a great deal for Hungarians to feel proud of here.

As my friend Áron Máthé at Hungary's Committee of National Remembrance once pointed out to me, 'It is not possible to build a nation on a sense of guilt.' When the Fidesz government commissioned the Monument to the Victims of the German Occupation, it was attempting to paper over the complications of Hungary's troubled history and find common ground. There might have been some cynical intent in all this, but I have no doubt that there were many good intentions behind it too.

However, if a nation can't be built on a sense of guilt, neither can it be built on the falsification of its history. It is not good enough merely to proclaim yourself a martyr: the facts also need to stack up. Neither is it good enough to appropriate someone else's victimhood and proclaim it as your own: that is not something that the real victims will ever be prepared to stand for. The Monument to the Victims of the German Occupation was originally conceived as a symbol of national martyrdom – but today, in part because of the 'Living Memorial' that stands opposite, it has become little more than a symbol of national hypocrisy.

The events of 2014 in Budapest demonstrate two fundamental truths about monuments. The first is that it doesn't matter if you construct a monument with a specific message in mind: it is impossible to predict how it will be used and interpreted by the public once it is up.

The second is that if you build a monument in an attempt to rewrite history, it won't work. One way or another, history always catches up with you in the end.

The gatehouse of Auschwitz–Birkenau, from inside the camp

12

Poland: Auschwitz

Of all the many victims of the Second World War, there was probably no single group that suffered more than the Jews. Between 1939 and 1945 around two-thirds of Europe's Jews were exterminated. Almost six million people were killed all over the continent, but particularly in the eastern European 'Bloodlands' of Poland, Lithuania, Belarus and Ukraine.

Today there are hundreds of memorials marking their places of execution, but none is more famous than the museum and memorial at Oświęcim in Poland. Before 1939 very few people outside Poland had ever heard of this small town; but during the German occupation it was renamed Auschwitz, and it became home to one of the largest concentration camps in history. As a consequence, the word 'Auschwitz' has since become a byword for horror and suffering. Today, it is perhaps the world's best-known symbol of victimhood.

Auschwitz was not a single concentration camp, but a complex of camps. At its peak it was spread over forty separate sites, mostly centred around factories and farms, where prisoners of many different nationalities and religions were forced to work in abject conditions as slave labour. From 1942, however, Auschwitz also began to be used for a second purpose: it became a centre for the mass murder of Europe's Jews.

When most people think of Auschwitz today, they are thinking about the two main camps: Auschwitz I and Auschwitz II (otherwise known as Birkenau). The original camp at Auschwitz I was established in 1940 on the site of an old army barracks. In the beginning it was used as a jail for Polish political prisoners, but as time went on it also began to serve as a concentration camp for Russian prisoners of war, Jews, gypsies and a dozen other ethnic groups and nationalities. There was a summary court here, administration blocks, workshops and warehouses where the prisoners were expected to work.

The camp first became a centre for mass killing towards the end of 1941. Until that summer, the Nazis had generally carried out mass executions by shooting – not so much in concentration camps as in forests, fields, quarries and other remote places across eastern Europe. However, shooting large numbers of people was time-consuming, inefficient, and stressful for the executioners. So the Nazis began to look for other ways of killing.

In Auschwitz, SS prison guards discovered that groups of prisoners could be killed much more efficiently by grouping them together in a single room and gassing them with Zyklon B, the powerful insecticide that was used to fumigate the prisoners' clothing. The first experiments were carried out on Russian and Polish prisoners, in the basement cells of Block 11, the prison block. However, since the place was difficult to ventilate, and a long way from the camp crematorium, another block was converted to be used specifically for this purpose. Auschwitz now had its first gas chamber.

As the war progressed, the camp expanded rapidly. To relieve the congestion, a second camp was built on the site of a nearby village called Brzezinka – or Birkenau, as the Germans called it. This was originally conceived as a camp for holding Soviet prisoners of war, but when the Nazis began transporting huge numbers of Jews here in 1942 they realised that it could also double up as a place to exterminate their racial enemies. So they converted two remote farmhouses into gas chambers, and constructed a series of purpose-built crematoria, with gas chambers attached. Any Jews who could not be exploited as slave labourers were simply brought here and murdered.

Over time, the Nazis honed the execution process into a model of efficiency. Transports of Jews were unloaded from trains that came directly to the camp, and were sorted into groups on the platform. Those deemed fit for work were funnelled off to live in the camp's vastly overcrowded barracks: they would spend the following months being exploited as slaves until they were too weak to continue. Those considered economically worthless – children, pregnant mothers, the elderly, the weak – were relieved of their possessions, stripped, shaved, gassed and cremated. It was like a production line in a factory. Between 1942 and 1944 over a million people were killed here. At its peak, in the summer of 1944, Auschwitz–Birkenau was capable of processing thousands of bodies each day.

Auschwitz remained in operation until the end of 1944, when the advance of the Soviet Red Army meant that the camp had to be evacuated. When the Nazis finally left in January 1945, they tried to destroy the evidence of what they had done. The inmates were force-marched to other concentration camps closer to Germany. Documents were removed or destroyed, warehouses were torched, gas chambers and crematoria were dismantled or blown up. In their hurry to retreat, however, the camp guards left plenty of physical evidence behind, particularly in the original camp of Auschwitz I, which remained largely intact. They also failed to kill all the witnesses to their crimes. Unlike some of the other killing centres for Jews, Auschwitz was never exclusively a death camp, but also served as a work camp for slave labour. As a consequence, thousands of labourers who survived the war were able to bear witness to the terrible sights they had seen there.

In the decades since then, countless people have come forward with evidence of the atrocities that were carried out at this notorious place. In 1947, the post-war Polish author-ities decided to preserve what was left of the site for future generations. Auschwitz I was made into a museum, curated by people who had themselves been imprisoned there during the war. Nearby Auschwitz II, which by this time had been largely dismantled, was preserved as a memorial site.

Today, the two sites combined have come to represent the Holocaust as a whole. They became a UNESCO World Heritage Site in 1979, and are now considered among the most important symbols of martyrdom anywhere in the world.

Visitors who come to Oświęcim today can see for themselves the evidence of what happened here. Along the way they can experience a tiny slice of that horror. They can pass beneath the notorious wrought-iron gates at Auschwitz I, upon which the famous lie was written – *Arbeit macht frei* ('work makes you free'). In the museum they can see a mountain of shoes stolen from those who were about to be killed. There are rooms full of personal possessions taken from the victims –

battered suitcases, spectacles, children's toys and clothes, shaving brushes, kitchen utensils. There are more sinister displays too – a vault full of human hair, a vast heap of prosthetic limbs, a pile of empty Zyklon B canisters. Visitors can enter the punishment block, where prisoners were beaten and tortured, and where the first experiments with mass murder took place. They can stand beside the wall where prisoners were shot. And, most disturbingly of all, they can enter a reconstruction of one of the gas chambers and stand in the very place where thousands of people were killed.

At nearby Auschwitz II–Birkenau, you can continue your tour by visiting the epicentre of the Nazi system of organised murder. You can walk along the infamous railway track that brought more than a million Jews to their doom. You can stand on the very ramp where the selections took place. You can gaze through the barbed wire at the rows and rows of chimneys, sticking straight out of the ground like admonishing fingers, which are the only remains of the hundreds of barrack huts that used to house tens of thousands of human beings. The scale of the place is truly immense. It is the size of a small city – more than 80 hectares of ground devoted to negation and death.

It is impossible to enter the site without feeling the weight of history bearing down upon you. The moral crime that was committed concerns not only Jews, or Slavs, or Gypsies, or any of the other groups who were murdered here: it makes victims of us all. It is an affront to humanity itself: indeed, it is because of places like this that a new legal term was created after the war, 'crimes against humanity'.

These things are expressed so well at Auschwitz that the site has attracted visitors in ever greater numbers. But such success has itself brought problems. In recent years Auschwitz has begun to drown under the sheer number of visitors it receives. Before 2007, the site received less than a million visitors each year; today that number has more than doubled. Every day, particularly in summer, bus after bus of visitors arrives, and thousands of people are funnelled through the gates to the museum. There is now not nearly so much time to stand and absorb the horror of the place. Tour guides rush their groups through at a steady pace because they have to make room for the groups pressing them from behind. Ironically, such phenomenal success threatens to undermine everything that the museum is supposed to represent.

It is safe to say that not everyone approaches the site in the spirit of sombre contemplation that it deserves. Hundreds of school groups come here as part of their education, predominantly from Poland – but also from Israel, Germany, the UK and other countries – and not all of them treat the place with the appropriate solemnity. Teenagers will be teenagers, after all: they are more concerned with living life than with lingering so long in the presence of death.

There are few places to buy food here, so visitors sometimes bring picnics to enjoy in the car park, or in the shade of one of the birch trees that surround the site. It's not an unreasonable thing to do. The journey from Krakow to Oświęcim takes at least an hour and a half each way, and people need to eat. Nevertheless, I can't help wondering if there is something disrespectful about enjoying a good meal in a place where so many people starved to death. Last time I was here I watched a group of men relaxing in the sun near the entrance to Auschwitz I, drinking cans of beer.

Such occurrences seem to me to be a part of something greater that has happened here. Auschwitz today finds itself on people's holiday itineraries alongside palaces, art galleries, water parks and beer festivals. As many people come here each year as visit the Uffizi in Florence. Even the memorial site itself boasts that it is now by far the most popular museum in Poland. If Auschwitz is a prisoner to its history, it is also a prisoner to tourism.

There are other concerns about the popularity of Auschwitz. In past years, the memorial site was still mostly the domain of scholars, and Holocaust historians, and people trying to find out about where their own family members had died. In such circumstances, it was much easier to embrace a wide range of stories from those who had suffered here. No two stories were ever quite the same: the range of experience was vast.

Today there is much less time for visitors to take in the intricacies of life in the camp. The differences between the various categories of prisoners get lost. It is harder to appreciate how different life could be if one was in the camp orchestra, or the camp choir, or the hospital, or the medical experimentation units, or the *Sonderkommando* – Jews forced to work around the gas chambers and the crematoria clearing away the dead bodies. Visitors who rush through can only ever get the basic facts of what happened, and inevitably a standardised version of the story emerges: arrival, selection, death. Isn't the reduction of so much human experience to such a narrow narrative in itself dehumanising?

There are many other ways in which the story could be told, ways which only emerge if you are able to linger here a little longer. Jews were never merely victims during the Holocaust: many were also heroes. There were many places in eastern Europe where Jews stood up for themselves and fought back, and Auschwitz was no different. Jews resisted the Nazis in Auschwitz in various ways, ranging from simple acts of human kindness to violent confrontation with the camp guards; in 1944 the *Sonderkommando* staged a major rebellion. In the 1950s, these were the kinds of stories that many Jews themselves preferred to tell. They did not want to be portrayed merely as the passive victims of an inhuman system: such a thought was far too painful.

Among the heroes there were also those who were not quite so pure and innocent as today's accepted version of the story suggests. Some Jewish leaders collaborated in the deportation of Jews to Auschwitz. Some bought time for themselves and their families by feeding others to the monster first. At Auschwitz there were plenty of inmates who collaborated with camp guards and informed on their fellow Jews for the sake of a crust of bread. These people must be mentioned not to blame them in any way, but rather to emphasise their human fallibility. Regardless of what the Nazis always said, there was never anything particularly special about the Jews. There was and is no archetype here. Jews are just as human as everyone else.

When one drills right down into the individual experiences of the Holocaust, one can find the most surprising stories, rendered all the more poignant by their contrast with the standardised version that we have all come to know. For example, in his memoir of the Holocaust, historian Otto Dov Kulka remembers afternoons at Auschwitz when he would gaze up at the blue sky and feel overwhelmed by its beauty. Despite all that happened to him here, these are happy memories; but he was always forced to ask himself whether it was morally permissible to have happy memories of this place.

Such individual moments are lost when we are forced to

rush through the displays of the Auschwitz museum. For the sake of efficiency, today's museum administrators are obliged to push greater and greater numbers of people through their system. Surely this too evokes disturbing echoes of the past.

Auschwitz has become such a globally recognised symbol that it is now stamped upon our collective memory in a way that no other memorial site can rival. In a world of victims, this is the undisputed capital city. This too brings problems, because, unfortunately, alongside status comes envy.

There have always been plenty of people who can see the moral power of a place like Auschwitz, and who want to acquire some of that power for themselves. The first group who tried to claim ownership of Auschwitz after the war were the Polish Communists. When the first commemorative plaques were put up at Birkenau, there was no mention of Jews: the plaques referred instead to the '4 million people' who had 'suffered and died here at the hands of Nazi murderers'. Tour guides at the museum also used to speak only of 'victims' and 'people', with no mention of their ethnic or religious origins. In a Communist narrative of the war, the specific fate of the Jews was irrelevant. Instead, the concentration camp was portrayed as a place where ordinary Poles, along with their brothers and sisters from other countries, had been exploited until every drop of economic worth had been squeezed from their bodies. Auschwitz was the ultimate symbol of capitalist exploitation.

In the 1970s, Polish Catholics also tried to appropriate the site as their own. It was certainly true that tens of thousands of Catholics died here. One of them, a Franciscan friar named Father Maximilian Kolbe, was even canonised as a saint because of the way he had volunteered to take the place of a stranger who had been sentenced to death. In 1972 Cardinal Karol Wojtyla, the future Pope John Paul II, held a major Catholic service here in honour of Father Kolbe. Wojtyla returned seven years later, after being elected Pope, to give another, even bigger service. A cross was erected on the ramp where Jews had once been selected for life or death, and the Pope proclaimed Auschwitz to be 'the Golgotha of our time'. In 1984, a group of Carmelite nuns went further still, and established a convent right beside the perimeter fence at Auschwitz I. Many Jews were profoundly uncomfortable about the fact that they were being forced to compete with Catholics over whose stories should be given greater prominence, and which religious symbols – if any – should be allowed to go on display. Here, in the place where Jews had been exterminated, the very Jewishness of their experience was being taken from them. It was not until the mid-1990s that the Catholic Church finally backed off. Most of the crosses erected around the site were taken down, and the convent was moved elsewhere.

Today Auschwitz is universally recognised as a place predominantly of Jewish suffering, just as it should be. Once again, the balance of historical truth has won out in the end.

But that does not mean that the controversies are at an end. In recent years people have begun to question Auschwitz's pre-eminent status among the world's monuments to the Second World War. Why should this place be more important than the Nanjing Memorial Hall? Why should the suffering of the Jews be considered substantially worse than the suffering of Korea's comfort women?

The argument goes well beyond the Second World War. What about the million or so Armenians massacred by Turkish soldiers earlier in the century? What about the six million or so Ukrainians starved to death by Stalin in the 1930s? What about all those who died in the killing fields of Cambodia in the 1970s, or in the Rwandan and Yugoslavian genocides of the 1990s? When there are so many other victims in the world, why should we continue to regard the Holocaust as special?

These questions come up again and again in our international institutions, and there is no satisfactory answer to them. It is fruitless to weigh the traumas of one victim against those of another: suffering cannot be measured out like grains of rice. The memorials I have described over the past six chapters represent only a tiny proportion of the world's monuments to victimhood. Great or small, each and every one deserves recognition.

And yet, for better or worse, there remains something unique about Auschwitz. During my research for this book I visited mass graves, killing sites and victims' memorials all over the world, but Auschwitz feels different from all of them.

First there is its sheer scale: it's difficult to think of another site where so many people were killed in such a concentrated area. Auschwitz–Birkenau is huge, close to 900,000 square metres in total. And yet every square metre represents at least one victim.

Then there is the unique character of the atrocity that unfolded here. It was not born of military frenzy, like the Rape of Nanjing; nor merely out of political expediency, like the shooting of Polish officers in the forest of Katyn. The main method of killing here was not particularly bloodthirsty compared to what happened in other places – in fact, quite the opposite: the distinguishing feature of Auschwitz was not its passion, but its coldness. It is the impersonal, machine-like indifference of this kind of murder that makes it so unbearable to contemplate.

This is perhaps one of the reasons why the Jewish victims of the Holocaust have become such a symbol for our age. They were not only prey to men with guns; they were also fodder for a vast political and industrial system that had reduced them to mere units to be processed and eliminated. In this sense, they were the victims not only of war, but of modernity. If you can bear to follow this thread to its logical conclusion, it leads to all kinds of other victims in other times and places, from the slave trade in the eighteenth century to the sex trade in the twenty-first century. The victims of the Holocaust are representative of a much greater phenomenon that has never entirely gone away.

In 2005, the United Nations recognised the universal nature of this symbolism by instituting an International Holocaust Remembrance Day. This is now observed every year on 27 January – the anniversary of the liberation of Auschwitz. According to UN thinking, the victims of the Holocaust are not only Jewish victims – they are archetypal victims. They represent humanity as a whole, in all its precariousness.

I would love to believe that this is also in part why Auschwitz itself is such a global symbol. It would be heartening to think that more than two million people come here each year simply to pay their respects to a universal victim, and pledge to make sure that the suffering those victims endured never happens again. But I know that this is not quite true. Because the atmosphere that pervades the site is not only one of sadness and mourning, but also one of dread. This is another thing that makes Auschwitz unique. It is impossible to walk around the site without feeling the presence of some gigantic evil, at once both repellent and beguiling.

Many people come here because they want to experience this presence, and remind themselves of what it feels like to be alive. This is one of the reasons why so many Jews come each spring to walk from Auschwitz I to Birkenau in a demonstration called the March of the Living. There can be nothing more life-affirming than to visit such a place of death and stand right at its heart, vibrantly and defiantly alive.

But I suspect that there are also darker motivations for wanting to experience the presence of such evil. Who among us is not impressed by the power of death, particularly death on such a gigantic scale? Is there not a part of us that secretly longs to appropriate just a sliver of that power for ourselves?

Every year people are caught stealing buttons or fragments of cloth from the museum site at Auschwitz, which they intend to take home as souvenirs. In 2010 a Swedish neo-fascist went so far as to steal the famous wrought-iron sign above the Auschwitz gates, intending to sell it to a collector of ghoulish memorabilia. His crime made headlines all over the world, but I can't help wondering if the meaning behind it was all that different from what every visitor does when he or she comes here. We all take photos. I myself have hundreds of photos of Auschwitz in my collection. What could I possibly want with such souvenirs?

If Auschwitz makes victims of us all, then it also makes monsters of us all. By coming here, we necessarily implicate ourselves in both sides of this sickening story. In other words, Auschwitz is not only a memorial to the victims of the Holocaust, but also a memorial to its perpetrators. And that, as I shall explore next, is a much more disturbing thought altogether.

Part III

Monsters

What makes a monster? By all accounts, the devil can be quite charming when he needs to be. Men like Hitler and Stalin did not win power only through force: they were also charismatic, eloquent, and able to mesmerise millions through the power of their rhetoric. They certainly did not see themselves as evildoers, but as men of action. According to their own warped logic they were simply trying to take back control from the sinister global forces – capitalists, imperialists, Jews – that they believed had made victims of their people. The reality of what they were doing, however, was the demonising of these groups and the fuelling of genocidal hatred.

Rather disturbingly, many of the qualities of a monster are the same ones we look for in our heroes and martyrs: strength, cunning, determination and an unwavering devotion to their cause. But in a true hero or martyr, these qualities stand beside other virtues, such as compassion, mercy, and a willingness to stand up for the rule of law and the universal norms of morality. A monster has contempt for such things. During the 1930s and 1940s, powerful fanatics pursued their aims with an utter disregard for the rights, the dignity and the lives of millions. They killed without thought or conscience. They treated human beings like objects to be used and then discarded; indeed, they often treated them not as humans at all, but as vermin to be exterminated. In such men, obsessive devotion to a cause is not a quality to be admired. It has become a sickness, one which cloaks all their actions in the same dark atmosphere that is so palpable in the grounds of Auschwitz–Birkenau.

* * *

Nobody deliberately sets out to make a monument to a monster. Some of the monuments in this part of the book were created when their subjects were still considered heroes, and only began to look dubious in later years, after the crimes of their subjects became more widely understood. Some of them became monuments almost by mistake, simply because of the attitudes of those who come to visit them. Some are barely monuments at all: they include shrines, tombs and other sites of memory that have become associated with the darker aspects of the war. By including them in this book I hope to widen our understanding of what constitutes a monument in the first place.

Is it ever right to visit such locations? Should they be shunned, or even erased – just as the men they call to mind tried to erase their own enemies? Can we ever escape these symbols, or are we bound forever to remain prisoners of their memory?

Of all the monuments described in this book, these are the most problematic. They throw up moral dilemmas that are impossible to solve. But by confronting these dilemmas I hope we can at least learn valuable lessons about what happens when the qualities we so admire in our heroes and martyrs are taken to extremes.

13

Slovenia: Monument to the Victims of All Wars, Ljubljana

In the centre of Slovenia's capital city, Ljubljana, stands one of the most interesting and problematic memorials I have ever come across. Unlike all the other monuments discussed so far, this one does not try to lock up the nation's past in a figurative image. There are no statues, no portrayals of people frozen in action. In fact, the memorial is entirely abstract. But this does not make it any less controversial.

The Monument to the Victims of All Wars consists of two giant slabs of stone, set in an open-sided courtyard. The slabs stand close together but do not touch; they are parallel, and yet slightly askew from one another. One monolith is almost square, some 12 metres (39 feet) high and 12 metres wide; the other is narrower, rectangular, and made of much thicker blocks. However, their differences are greatly outweighed by their similarities: they are built from exactly the same stone; beneath the ground they share the same foundations; and though they are of different shapes, they are exactly the same height, weight and volume. They are like a pair of perpetually warring siblings, always independent, always in opposition, and yet inextricably linked to each other.

Unlike some other memorials, this one is not designed to grab the attention. The last time I visited it, in November 2018, I stood and watched it for a couple of hours, and in all that time not one person stopped to look up at it. Nobody waited for their friends on the wedge-shaped step that forms its southern edge. Nobody lingered in the shade of the great stone slabs to eat a sandwich. The memorial dominates one side of Congress Square, right in the heart of the city; but it seems to be impregnated with a quality that repels attention.

This is no accident. Politically speaking, invisibility is one of the monument's greatest strengths. When one considers what might have stood here instead, and the dark history that still grips at the heart of Slovenian nationhood, it is easy to understand why this particular design was chosen.

I was fortunate enough to be present at the birth of this monument. In May 2015 I was invited to the Slovenian parliament to witness the unveiling of the design. I sat in a large chamber along with a selection of journalists and politicians, and watched the president, Borut Pahor, make a speech. A scale model of the monument sat in the centre of the room. Afterwards we were all invited to take a closer look, have a glass of wine and shake hands with the designers.

In my naiveté, I thought that the reception would be a fairly jolly affair; but in fact it was not jolly at all. There was something quite uncomfortable about it that I, as an outsider, did not entirely understand. When I spoke to some of the MPs at the reception, none of them seemed very pleased with the design of the monument. It was too bland, they said. It was not *satisfying* as a memorial. It didn't say anything about heroes or villains, or the victims of the war. None of them could fully explain what they didn't like about it, or what they might have preferred instead. Nevertheless, most of them seemed to feel the same.

It was at this point that a Slovenian historian who was also present took me to one side. Mitja Ferenc, a professor from the University of Ljubljana, was the man who had invited me to the event in the first place. After talking to me for a while, he said something along the lines of, 'Let me show you why nobody likes this design. Let me take you to a place that explains why we can only ever have bland, abstract memorials here.'

So we left the parliament. We got in his car and drove out of the city – me, Ferenc, a journalist friend and my publisher. We travelled east, through Slovenia's beautiful countryside. To our left were rolling hills, with the Alps shining white in the distance; to our right was the River Sava.

After an hour or two we turned off the main road and travelled up a narrow track through the forest. Eventually we came to a place called Huda Jama – a lonely spot by the side of a mountain. Here, built into the cliff, was a giant concrete doorway with an iron door. We stopped the car and got out.

The place had once been a coal mine, Ferenc explained, but it had been sealed up ever since 1945. In the last days of the war, when the German army was fleeing Yugoslavia, the partisans under General Tito had rounded up tens of thousands of fascist collaborators and massacred them. This mine was one of dozens of mass graves all over Slovenia. Around 2,500 people had been brought here, where they had been forced to strip and were then shot and thrown down mine shafts. Mitja Ferenc knew all about this particular site because he had been in charge of the government team that had exhumed it a few years earlier.

Ferenc called up the caretaker, who came and unlocked the

gate for us. First we walked down a long tunnel, deep into the mountainside – some 400 metres into the darkness. At one point Ferenc stopped and pointed to a hollow in the tunnel wall. 'This is where we found the first body,' he said. Someone had apparently survived the massacre and had been trying to tunnel his way out. He had ripped up a fragment of metal from the railway line and had been using it to dig. Unfortunately for him, Tito's men had been extraordinarily thorough: they had plugged the tunnel not only with tons of earth and rubble, but also with a series of brick and concrete walls. This lone survivor had come up against the first concrete barrier and had been forced to give up. This was where he had died, alone in the darkness.

We carried on walking. Soon we came to a mine shaft. Ferenc made me climb down a ladder to the bottom of the pit and stand where the bodies had been thrown. 'They filled this shaft to the top with corpses,' he called down to me. 'We pulled out 346 bodies – there are probably another 1,500 people still down there, beneath your feet.'

It was a uniquely disturbing feeling, standing at the bottom of that pit. It crossed my mind that Ferenc and the others could quite easily abandon me here, switch the lights off and lock the door, and no one would have known. I quickly climbed back up the ladder.

Next Ferenc took me deeper into the tunnel, where another 432 bodies had been found. Once again, he explained what had happened here. First, the men had been made to undress – Ferenc and his team had found a heap of their clothes and shoes in the tunnel. Then they had been forced to lie flat on the tunnel floor, where they had been shot in the back of the head. The next group had then been told to lie down on top of their bodies so that they too could be shot. Then the next group, and the next, until the bodies were stacked eight high.

I hardly had time to take this in before Ferenc took me to another section of the tunnel, where there was another metal door. He unlocked it and led me inside. 'Here they are,' he said.

Before me were hundreds and hundreds of plastic crates, stacked on shelves along the tunnel. Sticking out of the crates were bones and skulls and bits of human hair.

'We wanted to give them a proper burial,' Ferenc told me, 'but none of our politicians was willing to do it.' These people had been victims of the Communists; but since they had themselves been fascists, nobody wanted to make a shrine to them. It was difficult to know how to remember them at all. So in the end the authorities had simply locked the doors and tried to forget about them. According to Ferenc, in the previous seven years, only a handful of people had bothered to come and see this place for themselves – a couple of journalists, the US ambassador, and now me. It remained a guilty memory: everybody knew it was here, but nobody wanted to acknowledge it.*

That night, in my hotel room, I found it difficult to sleep. It wasn't the image of all those dead bodies stacked up in crates that kept me awake. I have spent years researching war atrocities, and was well acquainted with the general story of what had happened at sites like this in the former Yugoslavia. What really disturbed me was the thought of the lone man who had survived the massacre and tried to dig his way out. I could not stop imagining what it must have been like for him, stepping out of the pit in the darkness, finding a chunk of metal, and desperately trying to scratch his way through

---

*   Since I visited Huda Jama, the Slovenian government have interred the bones. They were buried in October 2017 at Dobrava memorial park near Maribor.

the earth and rubble. There was something heroic about it. But in the end, this man had not been a hero but just another victim. And perhaps worse than merely a victim: after all, he had himself been a fascist collaborator, and a soldier – perhaps he too had taken part in his own atrocities. I just couldn't work out how to feel about him.

This was precisely why Mitja Ferenc had taken me to Huda Jama. I realised now that the discomfort I was feeling was not so different from the discomfort I had sensed in that room full of politicians: how can one possibly remember a past like this *without* feeling uncomfortable? I also began to understand the antipathy expressed by some of those politicians about the proposed design for their monument to the war. What did this bland, abstract memorial say about the horrors I had just witnessed? How can one accept a monument built out of clean white stone when the reality is much more squalid, hidden at the bottom of a dark pit in the Slovenian hills?

For anyone who has studied the war in Yugoslavia, this kind of moral confusion is quite normal. British and American historians often characterise the Second World War as a relatively simple conflict between the Allies on the one hand and the Axis on the other – but in Yugoslavia things were never so simple. The country had only existed since 1918, when it was constructed out of the ruins of the First World War. It lay across the fault lines between the remnants of three great nineteenth-century powers – Russia, Austria-Hungary and the Ottoman Empire. It was therefore the meeting point of three great religions – Christian Orthodoxy, Catholicism and Islam (or indeed four, if one includes the small Jewish minority that was all but wiped out by the war). More than half a dozen large national and ethnic minorities

lived here, all of whom had nursed petty rivalries and jeal-
ousies for generations. When the Germans and Italians
invaded in 1941, all these tensions were unleashed at once.

It did not take long before the whole country had descended
into chaos. Croats began massacring Serbs in the name of
Catholicism; Serbs began torching Muslim villages in Bosnia
and Hungarian villages in Vojvodina; monarchist Chetniks
began fighting pitched battles against Communist Partisans.
In order to hide their crimes, militias sometimes deliberately
wore the uniforms of their rivals, so it is not always easy for
historians to work out who was massacring whom. Presiding
over this soup of violent conflicts were the German, Italian
and other occupiers of the country, who not only committed
their own war crimes but also encouraged in-fighting between
the different groups.

After years of war, the various groups began to coalesce
into two main camps. On the one hand there was the German
army and its collaborators from each of the different ethnic
groups in Yugoslavia: the Croatian Ustasha and its militias,
the Slovenian Home Guard, the Serbia Volunteer Corps, and
so on. These ultra-nationalist groups never trusted one
another – but they each collaborated with the Germans, and
as long as the Germans were in control, they were all effectively fighting on the same side.

Opposing them was the resistance. By 1945, Tito's
Communist Partisans had already defeated the other main
resistance groups and assimilated most of their members. This
group was no longer the amateurish force it had been in 1941,
but a full-blown army of some 800,000 men. It also had the
backing of both London and Moscow, and so was relatively
well equipped. Unlike the Slovenian or Croatian fascists, Tito
had no intention of allowing separate nations to set themselves

up after the war. His mantra, and the phrase he used in all his speeches at the end of the war, was 'brotherhood and unity'. He wanted to restore a single country called Yugoslavia which would encompass all the different nationalities, united under Communist rule.

Given everything that had happened before, the final showdown between these two groups was always going to have an apocalyptic flavour. In the dying days of the war, when it became obvious that the Partisans were going to win, the German army and its various fascist collaborators fled northwards. Their aim was to retreat to Austria where the British were waiting for them. If they could surrender to the British Army, they reasoned, they might be treated with a modicum of mercy. They knew that they would receive no mercy from Tito.

The first Slovenian troops fought their way through to Austria on 14 May, almost a week after the German army and its auxiliaries were supposed to have surrendered. They gave themselves up to the British in the town of Klagenfurt, just across the Austrian border. A day or so later, the first Croatian units also fought their way through to Austrian border, near the town of Bleiburg.

Unfortunately, the British had no intention of giving these troops and refugees asylum. They did not have the resources to look after so many people, and they were more interested in keeping good relations with Tito, whose massive army was already encroaching on British territory. And so British troops either turned them away at the border, or disarmed them and handed them back to the Partisans.

What happened next was no less than a bloodbath. Most of the atrocities committed over the following weeks occurred in the Yugoslavian Republic of Slovenia, which lay on the border with Austria. In the fields and forests near Maribor, some 15,000 Croatian fascists were lined up along an anti-tank trench and shot. At Kočevje Rog, and further west near the border with Italy, thousands of Slovenians and Croatians were thrown into deep ravines, whose sides were then blown up with dynamite to cover the bodies. And at Huda Jama, which I visited in 2015, thousands more were murdered and hidden away in the tunnels and mine shafts.

It is tempting to characterise these massacres as hot-blooded vengeance for the violence unleashed upon Yugoslavia by the Germans and their fascist collaborators, but the evidence suggests that this was not just about revenge. The men who died in the mine at Huda Jama are a good example: they were not killed in the heat of battle, but were kept for three weeks in a prisoner-of-war camp before being taken off to be executed. During this time, the officers were separated from the rank and file, and long-serving members of the Slovenian Home Guard were separated from those who had only been drafted in the dying days of the war. This implies not merely an element of selection but a great deal of organisation. The massacres were obviously taking place on orders from above, and quite possibly from the very top.

The reality is that the massacres were carried out for cynical, political motives. Killing all these people solved a lot of problems – at least in the short term. Tito wanted to create a unified, Communist Yugoslavia after the war. It would be much easier to do so without tens of thousands of ultra-nationalist Croats and Slovenians undermining his idea of 'brotherhood and unity'.

Years later Tito's right-hand man, Milovan Djilas, looked back on the days of May 1945 and admitted that the massacres had been carried out for purely practical reasons. 'Yugoslavia was in a state of chaos and destruction,' he told a British interviewer in 1979. 'There was hardly any civil administration. There were no properly constituted courts. There was no way in which the cases of 20–30,000 people could have been reliably investigated. So the easy way out was to have them all shot, and have done with the problem.'

This was the bloody foundation upon which Tito's new Yugoslavia was built. Over the next forty-five years or so, an uneasy peace settled across the country. While Tito lived, nobody dared question his vision of brotherhood and unity – but in truth, the spectre of darker, nationalist sentiments never entirely went away. After Tito's death in 1980, an unhealthy rivalry between different republics and ethnic groups started up again. Conflict finally erupted at the beginning of the 1990s, when Yugoslavia descended once more into bloody civil war.

Slovenia was the first republic formally to break away from the Yugoslavian federation in 1991. It escaped the worst of the violence that engulfed Serbia, Croatia, Bosnia and Kosovo; nevertheless, tensions between Slovenia's former Communists, its new democrats, and hard-line nationalists remained high. Meanwhile, the terrible things that were taking place in other parts of the region reawakened painful memories of the past.

The idea of a monument to the events of the war was first mooted in the Slovenian parliament in 2009. From the beginning, it was conceived as a way to promote reconciliation between groups of different political persuasions, whose memories of the past clashed so painfully with one another.

In 2013 a competition was held, and thirty-nine proposals were received. The winning design, by a group of architects headed by Rok Žnidaršič, was the one that I saw unveiled in 2015. The monument was finally built two years later, and inaugurated on 13 June 2017.

The very blandness of the memorial is probably its greatest selling point. It has been designed to be sensitive – in other words, to offend no one, to avoid resurrecting the destructive passions of the war. If it says nothing about heroes, or martyrs, or perpetrators, then this is a deliberate choice. Even its title is purposely vague: despite the fact that everyone knows it to be a Second World War memorial, it is dedicated to the victims of *all* wars.

Most monuments are designed to stimulate and direct national memories; this one, by contrast, seems designed to disperse them. What struck me when I first saw it is that there is nothing for either one's eyes or one's mind to grab hold of. There are no figures, no carvings, no details of any sort. There are just a couple of smooth, empty walls. Its blankness is like a sheet thrown over a crime scene: it hides away something that is simply too painful for most people to look at.

If you can bear to look beyond this, however, and peel away the other layers of obfuscation that cloak the monument, you will see that it poses some very difficult questions. The most important of these is the most fundamental: what does the monument really *say*?

The official line, promoted by both the architects who built the memorial and the president who championed it, is that it symbolises the Slovenian people and the ideas by which they live: they may be opposed to one another, but they are made of the same material, and built on the same foundations. It is supposed to be a gesture of reconciliation. But if we follow this line to its logical conclusion, it leads us to a dangerous place. If each of these giant slabs of stone represents a different side of the people, what *are* the two opposing sides? The state against the people? The military against the civilian? Left against right?

Since this is a war memorial, and it is focused mainly on the Second World War, only one interpretation makes any sense. The two main blocs that faced one another here in 1945 were the fascists on one side (with their local collaborators, such as the Slovenian Home Guard) and the Communist Partisans on the other. In other words, the two blocks of stone don't represent the majority of Slovenians at all, but the extremes.

In order to genuinely represent the Slovenian people during the war, something should have been placed between the two blocks – the victim, oppressed from both sides by two vast and pitiless ideologies. Of course, visitors to the monument can, if they wish, put *themselves* in this position. Today, when you stand between the monoliths you can feel the weight of them on either side, and the sensation is quite claustrophobic. But if you stand back and look at the blocks from any distance, they say nothing about victimhood at all. All you can see is the monoliths themselves – fascism and Communism. An installation supposedly dedicated to the victims has inadvertently become a monument to the perpetrators.

This is certainly the conclusion that some people in Ljubljana have come to. In the summer after I first visited, vandals attacked the site where the monument was due to be built. In mid-July it was spray-painted with swastikas. A week later Communist red stars were put up. Two months after that, chunks of slaughtered pigs were strewn across the site, along with printed notices reading 'Death to Fascism' and 'Freedom for the people'. One piece of graffiti seemed to say it all: '*Nehajte že se igrat partizane in domobrane*' – 'Stop playing Partisans and Home Guards'.

Few politicians or city administrators paid much attention to such protests. Some expressed outrage at the vandalism, others expressed concern, and President Borut Pahor, as always, tried to pour oil on troubled waters. But nobody was willing to tackle the fundamental problem that lay beneath the attacks, or ask the questions that still needed to be asked. What did the nation need to remember and what should it try to forget? Was it acceptable to acknowledge the presence of war criminals among the victims? What was the memorial's purpose: was it to heal wounds, or merely to acknowledge them? And, most important of all, how could Slovenia free itself from the darkest chapters of its history? Such questions were lost in the fog of emotion and denial, of calculation and compromise, that makes up Slovenian politics.

Today, the monument seems to have been swallowed up in a bubble of invisibility. It has already become a familiar part of the urban landscape – everyone knows it is there, but few give it any thought. Since its inauguration in July 2017 it has largely been left alone – not only by political activists, but by people in general. Hundreds walk past it every morning and every evening on their way to and from work, but none of them ever look up. Why should they? The monument represents a painful aspect of their history. Who wants to interrupt their day with uncomfortable thoughts about Communism or fascism or victimhood? And so they hurry on. At the very most they might shoot it a sideways glance, noticing but not noticing, remembering but not remembering.

14

Japan: Yasukuni Shrine, Tokyo

It is not only in Slovenia that the line between heroes, martyrs and monsters has become blurred. Many nations, including my own, shy away from looking too closely at some of their past deeds. This is simply human nature. Whenever it feels too difficult to draw a clear line between our guilty actions and our innocent ones, or when it risks making us too uncomfortable, every nation will take shelter in the grey areas between right and wrong.

Those grey areas are not there by chance. They provide a very useful function in society: they allow us to move towards the idea that we have done wrong, without forcing us to fully acknowledge our guilt. They are, in effect, a cushion which softens our fall.

Take for example the legacy of British colonialism. British people know, deep down, that the subjugation and exploitation of other nations was morally indefensible; but they salve their conscience with the thought that the empire also brought one or two benefits to Britain's colonies, such as the railways, and cricket, and western-style education. 'Perhaps we did wrong,' they can tell themselves, 'but we weren't *monsters*.'

Some nations do not have that luxury. In 1945, Japan and Germany were defeated so comprehensively that they had no opportunity to construct their own narrative about the crimes they had committed during the war. At the Nuremberg and Tokyo trials, those crimes were laid bare for all to see. They included some of the worst possible violations of humanity: mass enslavement, mass rape, mass murder, genocide. Both regimes routinely worked their prisoners to death. Both conducted medical experiments on live human beings. There was no hiding from the fact that the people who committed these crimes *did* behave like monsters.

What does this do to a country? How do you come to terms with the idea that you belong to a nation of perpetrators? In such a context is it possible to mourn your dead? How can you honour military sacrifice without also excusing military crime?

These are the questions that faced Japan in the years after 1945, and have plagued it ever since. How to remember the war has become one of the most problematic issues in Japanese society. Some organisations have tackled the matter head on: they have embraced Japan's guilt, tried to make amends, apologised. But one institution in particular has chosen a different path: that of denial. The Yasukuni Shrine in Tokyo has never accepted the version of history that every other nation accepts. It rejects the verdicts of the war crimes trials; indeed, it seems to reject any distinction at all between the innocent and the guilty. It has repeatedly tried to muddy the waters around the subject in an artificial attempt to recreate those moral grey areas that other nations are allowed to enjoy.

Unfortunately, things have not quite worked out like that. History is a prison that cannot be escaped. By trying to wriggle out of the country's responsibilities towards the past, the priests in charge of the Yasukuni Shrine have only succeeded in angering all of Japan's near neighbours, who have now begun to view it not as a place of mourning and respect, but rather as a sanctuary for monsters.

There are so many misconceptions about the Yasukuni Shrine, particularly in the West, that it is important to clear some of them up at the outset. First, the shrine is not devoted exclusively to those who died in the Second World War, as some people assume, but to all Japanese soldiers who have sacrificed their lives on the battlefield since the Meiji Restoration in 1868. Tens of thousands of souls were already enshrined here long before 1937: those who had died in the Russo-Japanese war of 1904–5, for example, or in the First World War, or in various wars against the Chinese, the Taiwanese or the Koreans. If the Second World War seems to dominate, it is only because that war was of a different order of magnitude. As a consequence of the Second World War, the number of souls enshrined here increased by a factor of *seventeen*. Today there are more than 2,466,000 names listed in the symbolic registry of deities; 94 per cent belong to people who died between 1937 and 1945.

Unlike most of the other places described in this book, the Yasukuni Shrine is not a memorial or a monument; strictly speaking it is a holy site, more akin to a church or a temple. Ordinary Japanese people come here to pay their respects to their ancestors, much as Americans might honour their fathers at Arlington Cemetery, or British people might honour their grandfathers at the Thiepval memorial in France. However, no one is buried here. Rather, the souls of the dead are enshrined here: their names and other details are hand-written on rolls of paper, which are stored in a repository behind the main sanctuary of the shrine. Visitors who wish to pay their respects will stand before the shrine, bow deeply, clap their hands twice in order to draw the attention of the deities, and pray.

For the casual tourist passing through, it must be difficult to see why there is so much fuss about this place. The atmosphere that presides is one not of drama or conflict, but of tranquillity, beauty and harmony. As you enter the site from the east, you walk down a long, paved boulevard lined with mature trees. There are exquisitely carved stone lions, and monoliths decorated with carved inscriptions. There is a statue of the founder of the Japanese army, standing on a pillar, a little like Nelson's Column in London. Through the main gate to the shrine are dozens of cherry trees, which burst into a spectacular display of blooms every April. Beyond the shrine is a shady walkway through a series of monuments, and a sacred pond garden, whose mirror-like surface is broken only by the occasional rise of one of the giant koi carp that swim within it.

On the face of it, there is nothing offensive about this place. Every nation must mourn its war dead, and Japan is no different. It is only right that Japanese people should be allowed to honour the memory of those who died for a greater cause, regardless of whether or not that cause eventually proved to be misguided. Their sacrifice must be acknowledged, and this haven of peace in an otherwise overwhelming city seems like a fitting place to do so.

If this were the only message of the Yasukuni Shrine, there would be no controversy. Unfortunately, however, other messages hidden among the pines and cherry trees are not nearly so straightforward.

Take, for example, the many monuments that scatter the

site. Few people would have a problem with the memorials dedicated to war widows, or animals, or patrol boat crews, or even the one to kamikaze pilots. But tucked away behind the shrine is a memorial to the Kenpeitai – the military police that terrorised civilians not only in the countries conquered by Japan, but also within Japan itself. There is a vast and undisputed literature listing the human rights abuses that were carried out by this much-feared organisa- tion. It was responsible for operating prison camps where hundreds of thousands of civilians and prisoners of war were worked and starved to death. It was responsible for running military brothels, where tens of thousands of women were forced into a life of sexual slavery. It was responsible for rooting out and terrorising Japanese citizens who expressed any kind of anti-war sentiments. Its closest equivalents in the West would be the Nazi SS or the Soviet NKVD. Why on earth, then, is it memorialised with such respect here?

More prominent is another memorial, which stands out in the open, closer to the shrine – it is a monument to Dr Radhabinod Pal, a judge in the Tokyo war crimes trials in 1946. Pal was the only one of eleven judges to insist that all the Japanese defendants should have been found not guilty. He had some important and valid points to make about victor's justice, and also about judging Japan's leaders harshly for acts that the Allies had themselves committed. Nevertheless, all the other judges agreed, more or less, that the Japanese leadership should be held accountable for the war. Furthermore, the Japanese government itself accepted the judgements of the war crimes tribunals when it signed the San Francisco Treaty in 1951. To erect a memorial to Pal, while ignoring the judgement of the vast majority, is not only a distortion of history, but it also sends out a strong political message: what the shrine authorities are effectively saying is that Japan did no wrong, and needs to take no responsibility for its actions.

To muddy the waters still further, there is also a war museum on the site, whose entrance lies just 30 or 40 metres (approximately 115 feet) from the shrine itself. I spent several hours in this museum, determined to view it with an open mind, but by the time I left I felt utterly sickened. The museum blamed the Chinese for Japan's invasion of China. It blamed the Americans for Japan's attack on Pearl Harbor. It suggested that the only reason Japan invaded south-east Asia was out of a selfless desire to liberate Asian people from European rule, rather than an entirely selfish desire to colonise these places for itself. I have spent much of my career trying to coax Europeans to face up to the terrible things that they have done in the past, including some of the crimes committed in the name of colonialism, but the scale of denial in this museum was beyond anything I'd ever come across before. There was not a glimmer of acceptance that Japan might have been even partly responsible for the war.

Perhaps even worse than these historical distortions were the museum's omissions. In the lobby of the museum stands a locomotive that was used on the infamous Burma railway. I have personally spoken to prisoners of war who were almost starved to death as they built this railway: around 100,000 people are supposed to have died during its construction. After the war was over, more than a hundred Japanese military officials were tried for their brutality during the project, and thirty-two of them were sentenced to death. *None* of these facts are mentioned in the display. As far as the museum is concerned, this is simply a locomotive – a symbol of modernity – proudly built by a Japanese company, Nippon Sharyo Ltd.

This was just one omission among many. The Rape of Nanking (or the 'Nanking incident', as it is euphemistically called here) was portrayed as a straightforward operation that involved the killing of no civilians, only Chinese soldiers hiding in civilian clothes. There was no mention of comfort women. There were no medical experiments on Chinese civilians, no torture of dissenters, no starvation of people in Indonesia, no massacre of women and children in Manila. These events are well known all over the world, and have been repeatedly proven – not only by foreign historians, but by Japanese ones. But they are entirely absent from the museum.

All these issues are problematic, but they are not the main reason why the Yasukuni Shrine has become so controversial. They do not explain why a Chinese man tried to set fire to the gates of the shrine in 2011. They do not explain why a South Korean man threw a bottle of paint thinners into the main hall in 2013, or why another set off a bomb in 2015. Those attacks were not directed at the museum, or the monuments, but at something far more fundamental: the shrine itself, and the very souls who are housed here.

The Yasukuni Shrine is hated by Japan's neighbours because it is not merely an institution that honours ordinary Japanese soldiers who died while doing their duty: since the late 1950s, it has also been an institution that openly and explicitly honours the souls of convicted war criminals.

The problem began in 1959. Until this point, convicted war criminals had always been excluded from the shrine. However, the families of some war criminals had long been lobbying for the enshrinement of their relatives, and they eventually succeeded in enlisting the support of the Ministry of Health and Welfare. In 1956, the ministry began passing on the names of Class B and C war criminals to the Yasukuni Shrine, and three years later the enshrinement of their souls began.

Between April 1959 and October 1967, some 984 Class B and C war criminals were enshrined. These were men who had been personally involved in the mass killing, exploitation and torture of prisoners and innocent civilians around Asia. The process took place quietly, without fanfare, partly in order to avoid any kind of public backlash, but also to avoid any accusations of a merging of religious and governmental affairs – something that was banned under the new Japanese constitution. It seems that the shrine did not even seek permission from the families of those they enshrined, some of whom were deeply ashamed of what their relatives had done, and did not want them to be given such an honour.

In 1969, the Ministry of Health and Welfare and the Yasukuni Shrine also agreed on a plan to enshrine fourteen of Japan's Class A war criminals. These were not men who had personally conducted atrocities, but rather the top brass: those who had masterminded and initiated an aggressive war. From the very beginning, the plan to enshrine these people was ideologically driven. Several members of the ministry and priests at the shrine were themselves ex-military men, and had never accepted the verdicts of the Tokyo trials. The process was stalled for a few years by the head priest, Tsukuba Fujimaro, but after his death his successor, Matsudaira Nagayoshi, proceeded quickly. In a secret ceremony on 17 October 1978, he enshrined all fourteen Class A criminals.

None of these steps was necessary. In the 1960s and 1970s there were far more people in Japan who opposed the enshrinements than there were those who supported them.

Unsurprisingly so: these people had broken all codes of morality and had brought shame upon Japan. The reason why so much secrecy surrounded the events is that the Yasukuni Shrine wanted to avoid provoking public opinion against them.

It appears that the emperor did not approve the enshrine-ment either. Between 1945 and 1975, he visited the Yasukuni Shrine eight times, but after the Class A war criminals were enshrined he never visited again. After he died, his son followed suit, and has never visited the shrine.

Japan's prime ministers, however, have not been quite so diplomatic. In August 1985, Prime Minister Yasuhiro Nakasone paid his respects at the shrine, as part of the fortieth anni-versary commemoration of the end of the war. His visit, which implied a level of official approval for the shrine and everything it had done, caused a storm of criticism from the Chinese for the first time. In 2001, Prime Minister Junichiro Koizumi, who was running for the presidency of the Liberal Democratic Party, made a campaign pledge to visit the shrine every year regardless of the criticism it would cause. He claimed to be visiting in a private capacity, but the fact that he made it a campaign pledge speaks otherwise. Once again, his visits caused outrage in China and South Korea. In 2013 Prime Minister Shinzo Abe also paid his respects at the shrine, despite knowing that it would only cause further damage to international relations.

It is difficult to know what can be done to salvage the situ-ation now. Some people have suggested 'de-enshrining' the spirits of Japan's war criminals or moving them to another location – but the priests at the shrine insist that this is impossible for theological reasons. What they forget to mention is that it would also go against the political ethos pursued by the shrine authorities ever since the 1950s. It suits the priests to have the guilty mixed up with the innocent, just as it suits them to allow monuments to the secret police to remain on their grounds, along with a museum full of misdirection and denial. It is all part of the same attempt to muddy the waters regarding Japan's responsibility for the Second World War.

Supporters of the shrine point out that British and American institutions are often guilty of similar evasions and moral equivocations, particularly regarding their bombing campaigns and their colonial record in south-east Asia. They also point the finger at China, which is much happier to cry foul on Japanese war crimes than it is to own up to its own questionable human rights record. They have a point. Why should Japan be held to a different standard from everyone else? But there is a qualitative difference that these people are failing to take into account. Western nations have at least been moving in the right direction: their denials are generally becoming weaker as, year by year, they swallow just a little more of their pride and admit to greater responsibility. The Yasukuni Shrine is moving in the opposite direction, increasing their denial rather than diminishing it.

Along the way, it has caused a great deal of distress, not only to the families of those who died at Japanese hands during the war, but also to the Japanese people. Had it not been for the actions of the authorities at the shrine, Japanese families would have been able to come here in peace, without ever having to think about the actions of war criminals. They might have been able to pay their respects to their ancestors without being harangued by ultra-nationalists waving banners or shouting at them through loudspeakers, and without having to worry about the possibility of an arson attack or a bomb.

The ordinary Japanese people who come here already had to shoulder the burden of history. Now, because of this toxic power play, every act of worship has also become a political act that threatens to poison the future as much as the past.

15

Italy: Mussolini's Tomb, Predappio

It is 28 April 2018, and a long procession is making its way out of the village of Predappio in central Italy. There are several hundred people here, almost all of them dressed in black, as if for a funeral. They walk slowly, solemnly, along the Viale della Libertà in the direction of the church of San Cassiano and its cemetery. Many wear strange black hats – sometimes a fez, sometimes a beret, sometimes even an old-fashioned military helmet adorned with black feathers. Some carry Italian flags decorated with eagles; others carry banners bearing the names of military organisations and marching bands. One holds a placard reading *Gli hanno sparato, ma non sono riusciti a ucciderlo* ('They shot him, but they didn't manage to kill him').

Anyone unacquainted with Italy and its history would be forgiven for thinking that the participants were here to attend the burial of a recent murder victim, but in fact they were here to commemorate a man who had died seventy-three years earlier. Benito Mussolini, the wartime dictator of Fascist Italy, was born in this village, and is also buried here. His body lies in the family crypt, and these people have come to honour his memory. They do this three times a year – on the anniversaries of his birth (29 July) and death (28 April), and on the anniversary of the day he and his followers marched on Rome to seize power (28 October).

There is something slightly spooky about the gathering. Very few people here are from the village itself, whose inhabitants generally frown upon the processions. Their black shirts are reminiscent of the uniforms worn by Mussolini's notorious Fascist militia, as are some of the slogans on their banners: *Onore e fedeltà* ('Honour and loyalty'), for example, or *Boia chi molla* ('Death to cowards'). The symbols they carry all come from a bygone era: eagles, daggers, Celtic crosses; and everywhere the symbol of the fasces – a bundle of sticks tied together with an axe. These symbols, still taboo, are carried openly and brazenly.

But most unnerving of all is the quasi-religious atmosphere that pervades. Italy is a country where processions like this happen every year in every village – but they usually take place in honour of the Madonna, or of a local saint. Today they are taking place in honour of a man that most of the world considers a monster. These people are making a pilgrimage not to the tomb of a Catholic saint or apostle, but to that of a Fascist dictator.

When the procession arrives at the cemetery, Edda Negri Mussolini stands on the steps to make a short speech. 'We are here to commemorate my grandfather,' she says, 'to pay our respects in this sacred place.' It is not entirely clear that she regards the place as sacred because it is attached to a church, or because Mussolini is buried here.

If the Yasukuni Shrine is guilty of blurring the line between the guilty and the innocent, the shrine to Mussolini blurs nothing. It is abundantly clear what this place represents, and there is no apology about it.

*   *   *

Mussolini did not spring from nowhere. In the early 1920s he was just one of many people promising to bring an end to the months of turmoil and civil unrest that had followed the First World War. The difference between Mussolini and most of his rivals was that he was not afraid to use violence to achieve his aims. His followers broke up strikes and demonstrations, and mercilessly hunted down Communist leaders and trade union representatives. Such methods proved so effective that he quickly won a great deal of support from business owners, military leaders and Italian aristocrats.

Unfortunately, Mussolini did not stop with breaking workers' strikes. In October 1922, 30,000 of his followers marched on Rome and demanded the resignation of the prime minister. Fearing further violence, the king simply handed power to Mussolini. In the following years, he and his followers used this power to terrorise his political rivals, assassinate those who stood in his way, remove the rights of the people to choose any other leader, and set up a police state. Mussolini provided the template for other fascist dictators like Hitler and Franco. Among his other faults, therefore, he is guilty of paving the way for years of ethnic cleansing, political violence and eventually a world war.

Mussolini repeatedly stated that his aim was to return Italy to its ancient imperial splendour through war and conquest. In 1923 he invaded Corfu, and refused to withdraw his troops until Greece paid a ransom. In 1935 he invaded Ethiopia, and gave his commanders written instructions to use poison gas on civilian populations, kill all prisoners and 'systematically conduct a politics of terror and extermination on the rebels and the complicit population' – all of which were war crimes, even at the time. In 1937 he sent thousands of troops to Spain to 'terrorise Valencia and Barcelona' for Franco. In 1939 he invaded Albania, and in 1940 he tried to invade Greece and Egypt. All this was done in complete independence of Hitler. His support of Nazi Germany in its even more murderous campaigns was merely the icing on the cake.

There are dozens of myths about Mussolini that survive to this day. The first is that he was not racist, on the grounds that his regime did not pursue Jews in the same way that the Nazis did. Anyone who has studied the ethnic cleansing of Libya in the 1920s and 1930s might take issue with that. Mussolini himself instructed the governor of Libya, Pietro Badoglio, to make intermarriage between Italians and Libyans a crime, for fear that the Italian race might become polluted with foreign blood. Though he repeatedly claimed that he bore no ill-will towards Jews or Muslims, his actions spoke louder than his words. In 1938, when he was at the height of his powers, he introduced race laws to Italy that were little different from Hitler's Nuremberg Laws.

Another dictum has it that, whatever his faults, Mussolini at least made the trains run on time – as if institutional violence and the loss of personal freedom were a price worth paying for getting to work promptly. Like many other tales that are told about him, this myth is the result of Mussolini's own propaganda. One needs only read the travel diaries of journalists in the 1930s to see that Italian trains remained pretty awful during the dictator's reign. According to the American journalist Bergen Evans, who worked as a courier in Italy in 1930, it was not just a matter of a few trains: '*most* Italian trains,' he wrote, 'were not on schedule – or near it'. When it came to public infrastructure projects, Mussolini was no more successful than many other European leaders, even those who did not feel the need to strip their populations of their rights.

It was the Second World War that caused Mussolini's downfall. As defeat followed defeat in the middle of the war, his popularity among his own people began to wane. By 1943, even his own government were getting tired of him. In July that year, the Grand Council voted to strip him of his dictatorial powers: he was arrested and held in a luxury resort in Abruzzo while his successor, Pietro Badoglio, made peace overtures towards the Allies.

Mussolini was famously rescued that autumn, not by his own people, but by German special forces. It was the Germans, too, who set him up again as their puppet leader in the north of the country. Italy's far right nationalists choose to forget this fact: between 1943 and 1945 Mussolini did not fight for Italy, but for Germany.

Now, at last, the viciousness that Mussolini had sanctioned against Ethiopians and Libyans was turned upon his own people. With German help, he organised the executions of some of the government members who had turned against him, including his own son-in-law, Count Ciano. With German help, his followers brutally suppressed any hint of resistance among the Italian population. Many of the portraits displayed in Bologna's Piazza del Nettuno (see Chapter 6) are of people tortured and executed not by Germans, but by their fellow Italians.

Some of the most notorious German atrocities were carried out with enthusiastic Italian collaboration. In Sant'Anna di Stazzema, for example, around 560 villagers were massacred in reprisal for resistance activity in the area. The victims included old people, pregnant women and around 100 children. It was the German SS who were responsible; but they were helped by the Italian XXXVI Black Brigade. It is worth noting that each of the Black Brigades was named after a prominent Fascist leader: this particular unit bore the name 'Benito Mussolini'.

This is the man who is honoured three times a year with processions in Predappio. The cruelty that gripped northern Italy in the last two years of the war was a direct consequence of his ultra-nationalist ideology, his glorification of brute force, and his utter disregard of the rule of law – qualities celebrated every time one of his modern-day disciples lays a wreath at his tomb.

Mussolini eventually reaped what he had sown. In the spring of 1945, German control of northern Italy collapsed under Allied pressure, and a widespread insurrection against Fascist rule broke out. Mussolini was captured by partisans as he tried to flee the country. He and his mistress, Clara Petacci, were executed by the side of the road, and their bodies were taken back to Milan and dumped in Piazzale Loreto – a site deliberately chosen because fifteen partisans had been executed here by Fascists the previous year.

The bodies soon attracted a large crowd, some of whom exercised their disgust by kicking and beating them. One woman tried to shove a dead mouse in Mussolini's mouth; others put a hunk of cheap, low-grade black bread in his hands, as if to say that he was now as poor and contemptible as he had made them. Another woman reportedly fired a gun into his body several times – once for each of her dead sons. In the end, it was the partisans themselves who stepped in to spare the bodies further indignity. To carry on displaying them to the crowd, as proof that the Fascist leader was indeed dead, the bodies were suspended by their feet from the roof of a petrol station. Clara Petacci's skirt was tied round her legs to preserve her modesty. Photographs were taken, and appeared in newspapers all over the country.

What happened next is both bizarre and quite gruesome. Mussolini was buried in an unmarked grave in a Milanese cemetery, but about a year later was dug up by a journalist named Domenico Leccisi and two other former Fascists. For several months his body was moved from place to place, before the authorities finally traced it to a monastery outside Pavia, where it had been concealed by two Franciscan monks.

Had the body been cremated, or disposed of at sea, then perhaps that might have been the end of the matter, but instead the authorities dithered. For over ten years the body was hidden at another monastery, in the small town of Cerro Maggiore, while a succession of governments tried to work out what to do with it. Eventually, in 1957, newly appointed Prime Minister Adone Zoli agreed to give the body back to the Mussolini family and allow it to be interred in the family crypt in Predappio. It is probably no coincidence that the minority Christian Democratic government led by Zoli was embarrassingly dependent on neo-Fascist votes.

Mussolini was finally reinterred on 1 September 1957, in a stone sarcophagus decorated with Fascist symbols. Above the sarcophagus, a larger-than-life white marble bust of Mussolini sits in an alcove, with carved stone fasces on either side. The whole space is lit from above, as if the light of God is shining down upon him.

In the years since, the town of Predappio has become something of a pilgrimage site for neo-Fascists the world over. The house where Mussolini was born has long been a tourist destination. In the centre of town are souvenir shops which sell everything from T-shirts and keyrings with Fascist slogans on them, to swastika flags and life-sized busts of *Il Duce*

194 PRISONERS OF HISTORY

himself. Technically, these shops are breaking the law – ever since 1952 it has been illegal to glorify the 'exponents, principles, facts and methods' of Fascism – but the authorities here simply turn a blind eye. Prosecuting shop owners for peddling the trinkets of far right nostalgia is simply not seen as a priority.

For most neo-Fascist visitors, however, the spiritual heart of the place has always been Mussolini's tomb. Over the years the site has become a real object of worship. According to the Italian newspaper *Il Giornale*, it sees up to 200,000 visitors each year, many of whom seem to have formed a cult-like attachment to Mussolini. 'This place is our Bethlehem,' one visitor told a reporter for the *Washington Post* in 2018, before confessing that he visits Predappio several times a year 'to pay thanks for what he did for the world'. He is not the only one who seems to regard Mussolini as a kind of religious or mythical saviour. The visitors' book, which lies on an altar in front of the tomb, contains several messages exhorting the former dictator to 'rise again and save Italy'.

The sense of history here is so potent as to be almost palpable. It is impossible to enter the crypt where Mussolini is interred without feeling chills down your spine. And yet, in an academic sense, there is no proper history here at all. There is no weighing up of Mussolini's legacy; no documentation balancing his achievements against his crimes; no mention of the overwhelming evidence against him as a war criminal. This is a shrine, not a museum: local memories of this Fascist dictator have not been curated, but simply left to the shameless nostalgia of his apologists.

When I last visited in 2018, the town authorities were planning to fill the void by building a proper museum in the heart of town. They insisted that this was the only way to reclaim their town from those who were misusing it. Predappio is a prisoner of its history, whether it likes it or not: its only sensible course of action is to embrace that history and take charge of it. A proper museum, they hope, might at least attract tourists who are interested in what *really* happened in Italy's past, rather than mere worshippers of a Mussolini personality cult.

Critics of the plan, however, were worried that building a Mussolini museum might simply entrench the town's reputation, and make it an even more attractive destination for neo-Fascists. A handful of historians have opposed the project. While I was there, the president of the National Association of Italian Partisans, Carla Nespolo, also voiced her concern that any Predappio museum would simply become another 'place of pilgrimage for Fascists'. There are no easy answers to this problem.

Many people in Predappio wish that Mussolini's body had never been discovered. They say that if it had remained in its unmarked grave, far away, then they might have been spared the neo-Fascist processions that have made their town notorious throughout Italy. But there is no guarantee that the absence of Mussolini's body would have been any better, either for Predappio or for Italy as a whole. The problem with absence is that it can itself become a kind of presence. Or, to put it another way, a corpse that is nowhere is everywhere.

In the next chapter I will take a look at a country that has never discovered where the body of its fascist dictator is buried. Germany's treatment of its wartime past is, in many ways, a model of good practice. Its bans on Nazi symbols and the glorification of Hitler are strictly enforced. There is nothing in Germany that resembles a shrine to Hitler in the same way that Predappio has become a shrine to Mussolini, and the idea of any site tolerating quasi-religious processions every year in Hitler's honour is unthinkable.

But this does not mean that Germans can sleep easy in their beds. Their history is just as inescapable as Italy's. If not more so – because in parts of Germany, particularly in Berlin, history is everywhere you turn.

The noticeboard at the site of Hitler's bunker

The Topography of Terror

16

Germany: Hitler's Bunker and the Topography of Terror, Berlin

Adolf Hitler has no tomb. In the last days of the war, when Berlin was surrounded and under constant bombardment, Hitler retreated to the bunker beneath the gardens of the Reich Chancellery. Since it was obvious that his reign was over, this man – who has come to be known as the greatest monster of the twentieth century – decided to take his own life. It seems that his decision was made partly to deny anyone else the satisfaction of killing him, but mostly so that he could control what happened to his body. He had heard what had happened to Mussolini's corpse in Milan and didn't want to be subjected to the same indignities.

So, on 30 April, two days after the death of Mussolini, Hitler shot himself. His long-term mistress, now wife, Eva Braun, committed suicide at the same time by biting on a cyanide capsule. Then, in accordance with Hitler's written instructions, their bodies were carried to a bomb crater outside, doused with petrol, and burned. After the bodies had been consumed, the crater was covered over with earth and rubble.

When Berlin fell to the Soviets a few days later, a team of SMERSH counter-intelligence agents went in search of Hitler's body. They found his and Eva Braun's remains in their shallow grave, along with those of Hitler's propaganda minister Josef Goebbels and his wife (who had killed themselves and their children shortly after their leader's suicide). Their bodies were taken away to be examined, and Hitler was soon identified by his dental records.

The Soviet authorities were then presented with a problem: what should they do with the bodies? At first they buried them in a forest in Brandenburg, but this was considered insufficiently secure. So a few months later they were exhumed and moved to a SMERSH facility in Magdeburg. In 1970, to put an end to any possibility of Hitler's burial site becoming a shrine, all the bodies were exhumed one final time: they were thoroughly burned and crushed, and the ashes were dumped into a nearby river to be flushed away to the sea.

Without a body, there could be no tomb; but there remained the worry that Hitler's bunker might become a shrine instead. After all, this was the place where he had committed suicide, which gave it a kind of totemic power. The last thing the Soviets wanted was for it to become a symbol around which neo-Nazis could regroup.

Accordingly, they went about destroying the site as comprehensively as they had destroyed Hitler's body. This was no easy task. The bunker had been built to withstand the biggest bombs in the Allied arsenal. Its ceiling was made of reinforced concrete 3.5 metres (11.5 feet) thick, and its walls were even thicker. When Red Army pioneers tried to blow the place up in 1947, they succeeded in destroying the entrance and the ventilation towers, and many of the interior walls, but the main structure remained largely intact.

In 1959 they tried again. Further blasts were carried out,

the entrances were filled in, and a mound of earth was piled over the top of the reinforced concrete. But various tunnels still existed, and the East German secret police were able to open the bunker up again in 1967 to photograph it.

In the 1980s, the East Berlin authorities decided to remove all outward signs of what lay beneath the ground. They erected an apartment complex on the site of the old Reich Chancellery: while they were digging the foundations, they also removed the concrete roof of the bunker and filled the entire structure with gravel, sand and other debris. The area was levelled and a car park planned on top of it. As far as the eye could see, all traces of the bunker had gone.

There is still no shrine here, even today. There is no museum, or tourist recreation of Hitler's bunker. There is not even a plaque or a stone to mark where the bunker once stood, just a rather shabby information board at the side of the road with some dry text in German and English describing the history of the building.

I have been to this place, but only once, and only for ten minutes. This was not out of any scruples about 'paying homage' to Hitler, but because there is really nothing to see. That's exactly as it is intended to be: it is not a place to visit if you want to feel chills down your spine, or to daydream about the Führer and his legacy. There isn't even a bench to sit down on.

And yet there is still something slightly disturbing about the place. The attempt to erase all traces of Hitler in this way is reminiscent of some of the totalitarian actions carried out by the Nazis themselves: the annihilation of Lidice, for example, or the razing of Warsaw. Perhaps this is appropriate. Nevertheless, it feels like an exercise in denial. Berlin might like to pretend that this place is just an ordinary block of flats with an ordinary car park in front of it, but it is not, and never can be. Hitler's bunker will always be there, just beneath the surface.

In the aftermath of the war there was a tremendous desire in Germany for the nation to put the past behind it. Germans began to call 1945 'Year Zero', as if the war had swept away everything that had gone before and the whole country had been given the opportunity to start again from the beginning. A purge of sorts took place. Nazi officials were arrested and replaced. Nazi laws were repealed. Nazi symbols were banned, statues of Hitler were taken down and streets were renamed. The embarrassments of the past were hastily buried, and the whole country tried to focus its attention on the future.

Hitler's bunker was not the only historically significant building to be destroyed after the war. Nearby, on Wilhelmstrasse and Prinz Albrecht Strasse, stood the headquarters of the SS, the Reich Security Main Office and the other major organs of state terror. These buildings had been notorious during the Nazi era, particularly the Gestapo headquarters at No. 8 Prinz Albrecht Strasse, where 'enemies of the state' had been inter-rogated and tortured. Despite some bomb damage, there is no reason why this building could not have been rebuilt after the war. Instead, parts of it were pulled down in the early 1950s, and the rest was finally blown up in 1956. No attempt was made to commemorate what had once stood here.

Had it not been for the Cold War, it is quite possible that the place might have ended up much the same as Hitler's bunker – the site of a nondescript post-war apartment block. But in 1961 the Berlin Wall was built right through this area, and the ground was left vacant.

By the 1980s, the atmosphere in West Berlin had changed considerably. There was a new desire to confront the past, to acknowledge its inescapable shadow and to commemorate it. When plans were drawn up to build a new street through the site where the Gestapo headquarters had once stood, a group of western architects and civil rights organisations protested. Instead the site was partially excavated. A series of information boards were erected, explaining what had once existed here. It was opened to the public in 1987 as part of Berlin's 750th anniversary celebrations, and eventually given a new name, the 'Topography of Terror'.

After the reunification of Germany in 1990, the Berlin parliament decided to make this into a permanent memorial site. There were a couple of false starts, but at the beginning of the new century a research centre was erected on the ground where the Gestapo headquarters had once stood. Since 2010 a permanent exhibition has been on display, documenting the crimes of the Nazi state. It is now one of the most popular remembrance sites in Berlin, attracting around 1.3 million visitors each year.

And yet, at the heart of the project there is still a feeling of absence. It is a much more positive absence than that of Hitler's bunker, but an absence nevertheless: 'Look what Germany once was,' it says; but also, 'This is not what we are today.' To drive the point home, the rest of the site has been left deliberately and ostentatiously empty. Where once stood the offices devoted to terrorising the people, there is now a field of rubble. Nothing is allowed to grow here. There is not a single plant or blade of grass: it is completely barren. This is the legacy of Nazism: death, emptiness, nothingness.

* * *

These two places – Hitler's bunker and the Topography of Terror – are excellent metaphors for the legacy of Nazism in Germany today.

The first is an attempt to free Germany from its history. The Soviet authorities in East Berlin thought they could bury the past, just as they had buried Hitler's bunker. In the West, too, there was a strong belief that if Germans simply focused their energies on building a new, brighter future, then the shame of their recent past could be put behind them. But no matter how well they thought it was buried, their history was always just beneath the surface.

Ever since then a new scandal has hit the newspapers every couple of years, in which the past breaks through the shallow topsoil. Sometimes a German police chief, or company boss, or Nobel Prize winner is revealed to have had a Nazi past. Sometimes historians weigh in, as they did in the 1980s, to say that the Nazis were not so bad, or that their crimes originated elsewhere, or that only a few people were ever genuinely guilty. Or, as is happening today, a new political group starts up, espousing racist or nationalistic views that everyone thought were long dead. And each time this happens the whole nation is shocked, because it has told itself that the monsters of the past have been vanquished. It seems that every generation must learn the hard way that history is not merely what happened to another people in another time, but still has an irresistible power over us today.

The second site, the Topography of Terror, comes at history from the opposite direction: it is an attempt to defeat the past by confronting it head on. Here, the crimes of Nazism are put under the spotlight to be examined in forensic detail. Denial is almost impossible. Like a frightened animal on the memorial site's vast field of rubble, the past lies entirely exposed, and there is nowhere for it to hide.

The Topography of Terror is not the only such location in Berlin. There are dozens of similar sites, all within a short walking distance: the Holocaust Memorial (see Chapter 19), the Jewish Museum, the memorial to murdered Sinti and Roma, the memorial to persecuted homosexuals, the Neue Wache memorial, the book-burning memorial in Bebelplatz, the memorial to the German resistance, the 'Stolpersteine' placed in the ground outside the houses of Jews who were taken away – the list goes on. Almost every building on Wilhelmstrasse has an information board outside it explaining its history and how it was used during the Second World War. Sometimes it seems as if the whole of central Berlin is an open air museum dedicated to its troubled wartime and Cold War past.

This overwhelming wealth of information, and the sense of universal guilt that comes with it, can feel stifling even to outsiders. When I first brought my children to see Berlin, their initial enthusiasm for the city's history was gradually crushed beneath the sheer weight of depressing detail: they felt compelled to turn away and concentrate their efforts on Berlin's more contemporary delights. If this is the way that English teenagers experience Germany's history, how must German teenagers feel, who are obliged to live with that history every day?

And yet, what is the alternative? Either we acknowledge our history or we don't: there is nothing we can do to change it.

Germans, just like everyone else, switch between these two positions – acknowledgement and denial – depending on their own shifting circumstances and the political atmosphere of the times in which they live. When they are feeling brave, they will face up to their history. They will grimly admit that most institutions, most corporations, most buildings and most families have some kind of Nazi past; and they will gird their loins for the perennial battle to prevent that past from reasserting itself in the present day. There is a little piece of Hitler, they will say, in everything we do; and we forget this at our peril.

But every now and then the uncompromising bleakness of the past will be too much for them, and they will turn away. They begin to look for excuses that will free them of their historic burden. On such occasions the omnipresence of Hitler becomes a kind of comfort. If all the evils of National Socialism can be gathered together and placed at Hitler's door, if this one monster can shoulder all the responsibility for the past, then everyone else is free to breathe once more. In this way, Hitler has become a kind of dark Messiah, whose evil presence absolves the rest of society of guilt for the sins of the past.

It is perhaps for this reason that the image of Hitler, though purged from German society in 1945, is still so prevalent in the country today. He appears in bestselling books by Joachim Fest or Volker Ullrich, and in history documentaries by Guido Knopp or Ullrich Kasten. He appears in award-winning movies such as Oliver Hirschbiegel's *Downfall*, which recreates the scenes in Hitler's bunker more vividly than any tourist attraction could ever manage. He appears in debates between journalists and between politicians. And in all internet discussions, according to Godwin's Law, it is only a matter of time before his memory is invoked by one party or the other.

I sometimes wonder what the victorious Allies of 1945 would have made of all this. When they tore down the statues and busts of Hitler, and changed the name of the streets and squares named after him, they must have imagined that they had dispensed with this monstrous warmonger for good. When they watched the people hurriedly destroying the portraits of Hitler that used to hang on their walls, and burning their copies of the once omnipresent *Mein Kampf*, they must have hoped that Germans would be too ashamed ever to invoke his memory again. The comprehensive annihilation of his body was supposed to symbolise all this and mark a definitive ending.

And yet today, in the twenty-first century, Hitler's memory seems to be stronger than ever. All it takes to bring him back to life is an outstretched arm, or a sketch of a slanting fringe above a black toothbrush moustache. In 2012, when Timur Vermes published his fantastically successful novel *Er ist wieder da* ('He's Back Again' or 'Look Who's Back'), there was no need to explain who 'He' was. The central message of the book, that his presence is still alive and thriving in Germany, is one that seemed to resonate with almost everyone.

This is something that does not come across at the site of Hitler's bunker or at the Topography of Terror. The sense of absence promoted by both sites is, at best, only half true.

Hitler has no tomb, but he doesn't need one. Even without a physical body, or a shrine in his honour, his memory continues to live alongside us whether we like it or not.

17

Lithuania: Statue of Stalin, Grūtas Park

No matter how much we might wish to, there is no escaping the monsters of our past. We might try to ignore them, or bury them, but sooner or later they always burrow their way back up to the surface. We might be tempted to rehabilitate them or excuse them; but that only makes us complicit in their crimes. Or we might try to annihilate them; but then their absence itself becomes a sort of presence. As the memorials described in the last few chapters demonstrate, monsters will always remain, whether we like it or not.

There is one final course open to us: ridicule. If we cannot escape our history, perhaps we can thumb our noses at it.

I recently attended a conference on public memorials, and one of the questions that came up was about the name of a lecture hall in London dedicated to Francis Galton. Some delegates insisted that, since Galton is the father of eugenics, the name of the hall should be changed immediately. Others insisted that Galton should not be judged by today's standards, and that the name should be retained. Others still sought a compromise: the name might stay, but some plaque or display should be added outlining the toxic side of Galton's legacy. The debate was quite heated, and very earnest on all sides.

Afterwards, in private, one delegate told me about a piece of graffiti that she had once seen scrawled beneath a statue of Galton: it read, simply, 'What a nob'. She suggested, somewhat tongue-in-cheek, that the building be renamed the Francis Galton 'What a Nob' Lecture Hall.

This is not the place to debate whether or not Francis Galton deserves to be vilified. My point is that there are all kinds of ways to protest against those we regard as monsters without tearing down their memorials. Ridicule is perhaps our most important weapon.

Before I move on to some of the more apocalyptic visions bequeathed us by the Second World War, I want to describe a place that has become one of my favourite memorial sites in all of Europe. Grūtas Park in Lithuania contains a collection of monuments dedicated to some of the greatest monsters of the twentieth century, including a statue of Joseph Stalin. It is a bizarre place, which breaks almost all the rules followed by conventional museums and monuments. What makes it work – perhaps the *only* thing that makes it work – is the way that it ridicules its subjects. Somehow this memorial park has stumbled upon an innovative way to acknowledge some of the darkest corners of our history.

Lithuania has had a very troubled past. Like several of its Baltic neighbours, it began the twentieth century as part of Russia, and only gained its independence in the chaotic aftermath of the First World War. Twenty years later, at the beginning of the Second World War, it was invaded by Soviet troops all over again. Then came the Nazis, followed once more by the Soviets three years later; and with each new invasion came new brutality.

In 1945 the country was swallowed whole into the Soviet Union. Anyone who refused to accept the nation's new Stalinist rulers was arrested, deported to Siberia, imprisoned or executed. Lithuania suffered terribly over the coming years. According to the Museum of Genocide Victims in Vilnius, around 300,000 Lithuanians were sent to Soviet gulags in the 1940s and 1950s. Between a third and a half of these people never came back.

Given such a history, it is not surprising that the symbols of Soviet power are regarded with universal horror in Lithuania. When the country finally regained its independence in 1990, almost all the monuments to Lenin and other Communist figures were torn down. Countless statues were decapitated, cut into pieces with blow-torches or crushed into rubble. Some were even dynamited. In an attempt to save some of these sculptures for posterity, the new Lithuanian government carted many of them away for storage in state-owned warehouses and salvage yards; but since no one had much love for them they simply sat there, for years, gathering dust.

Storing monuments costs money. In 1998, the government decided to spare itself the expense by loaning out forty or so of the best-known statues. A competition was announced, and proposals started to come in from municipal museums, such as the KGB Museum in Vilnius. But it was not clear that the government would save much money this way: most of the proposals insisted that they would require state funding to put the monuments on display.

There was one bid, however, that did not ask for any state funding at all. An entrepreneur named Viliumas Malinauskas

offered to display the monuments in a specially constructed
sculpture park, which he promised to build on his own land
near Druskininkai, in the south of the country. He would pay
all the transport and maintenance costs out of his own pocket.
He would even pay the restoration costs. He asked for nothing
but the statues. He was duly awarded the contract.

This was where the controversy began. Malinauskas was
not a historian, an art critic or a museum professional – or
indeed anyone who had any background in this kind of work.
In fact he was a former wrestling champion who made his
living as a mushroom farmer: he now has a multi-million-
dollar business exporting his mushrooms all over the world.
Some of his proposals for the sculpture park were quite bizarre.
He wanted to build a special railway line, so that tourists from
Vilnius could be brought here on cattle trucks, as if they were
being deported to a Soviet-era gulag. He wanted to hire actors
who would pretend to be soldiers, herding the tourists onto
the trains. For the full gulag experience, Grūtas Park itself
would be surrounded by barbed wire and guard towers, and
the monuments would be displayed as if they were part of a
Siberian prison camp. Unsurprisingly, critics began to call
Malinauskas's project a 'Stalin theme park'.

It did not take long for the complaints to come rolling in.
Local politicians opposed the building of the park. National
politicians opposed the building of the rail line. A petition
drawn up denouncing the whole idea of his sculpture park
was signed by Catholic Church officials, national NGOs,
prominent academics, art professors and over a million other
people around the world. 'This part of history is full of
suffering,' said one member of parliament, Juozas Galdikas,
in 2000. 'It should not be used for show business.'

There were other controversies too. One of the statues due

to go on display was that of a schoolteacher called Ona
Sukackienė, a local martyr said to have been killed by Lithuanian
'bandits' (the term that the Soviets always used to describe
partisans and freedom fighters). In 1975 a statue had been
erected in her honour in the nearby town of Lazdijai. After
independence, however, the newly opened archives revealed
that she had actually been killed in a staged attack by the KGB.
Her two sons wanted the monument to be destroyed, and were
appalled that it was going to be displayed in Grūtas Park as a
tourist attraction. In a letter to parliament they wrote, 'Nobody
asked our permission when they created the monument.
Nobody asked us when it was taken down. And now nobody
is asking our permission for it to be re-established.'

Perhaps the strongest voice of opposition came from
former victims of the regime. More than thirty groups
of former partisans and political prisoners banded together
to protest about the sculptures going on display. They accused
Malinauskas of trying to profit from their misery, and
described the statues as 'monsters from a horror film'. Some
of them even went on hunger strike. 'Imagine yourself as a
resident in a small village,' said one former independence
fighter named Leonas Kerosierius, 'and someone came and
attacked your village, killed your brother and raped your
daughter. Would you allow your neighbour to build a park
for these executioners and rapists, or make money off these
crimes?'

MPs pushed for a vote in parliament to take back the statues
and keep them in state hands, and the resolution was accepted
by a majority. But their victory was short-lived, because it
was overturned by the constitutional court: Malinauskas had
won the government contract fair and square, and parliament
had no right to take it away from him simply on a matter of

taste. The most they could do was create a government watchdog to oversee the construction of the sculpture park.

The controversy quickly became international news. It featured not only in newspapers throughout the Baltic countries, but also in other parts of Europe. It even made the newspapers in America, parts of Asia and Australia. 'Miss the Soviet Era? Come to Stalin World' ran the headline in the *Sydney Morning Herald*.

Grūtas Park officially opened to the public in 2001, and immediately proved a hit with visitors from all over Lithuania and beyond. Even before the official opening it had already seen around 100,000 visitors. Since then it has added to its collection and become a well-established tourist destination.

I first came here on a sunny September afternoon in 2018. From the moment I arrived, it was plain to me that this was unlike any of the other memorial sites I've visited. Malinauskas's original vision of a bespoke railway line with cattle trucks for tourists was never given the go-ahead, but he has still placed a train carriage at the entrance of the park, as if it is just arriving at a gulag. Beyond the train carriage is a barbed-wire enclosure overlooked by guard towers. The towers are manned by mannequins in Soviet army uniforms, but there is no attempt to make the soldiers look realistic: they are obviously shop dummies. And what are they guarding? Beneath them, in the enclosure, is a row of plinths, displaying several huge busts of Lenin and other prominent Communists. The message is fairly clear: today it is not Lithuanian dissidents who have been sent to the gulag, but the architects of the gulag themselves. To add to their humiliation, they share this enclosure with half a dozen llamas.

The atmosphere only gets weirder once you enter the park.

One of the first places you come to after paying your entrance fee is a children's play area with brightly painted swings and slides. It is surrounded by engines, armoured cars, pieces of artillery and a huge monument to the Soviet wartime partisans. On the day I was there, the children did not seem to discriminate much between the sculptures, the guns and the slides – they were happy to climb on everything. The jolly atmosphere was enhanced by rousing Soviet-era anthems, blaring from nearby loudspeakers.

This place can't seem to make up its mind whether it is a museum or a toddlers' day out. On one side is a handful of huts, built in the style of gulag barracks, housing a nostalgic array of Soviet posters, flags and copies of *Tiesa*, the old Communist Party newspaper. On another side is a zoo, containing baboons, emus and a rather shabby, depressed-looking brown bear. Dozens of species of birds sing to you from aviaries as you pass by.

However, the real attraction lies beyond, in the forest. A wooden walkway takes you on a journey through pines and birch trees to a procession of socialist realist art. There are allegorical representations of Mother Russia, and stained-glass windows depicting soldiers and workers and farmers. There are statues of Lenin, busts of Felix Dzerzhinsky, and depictions of Lithuanian Communist leaders like Vincas Mickievičius-Kapsukas and Karolis Didžiulis, all displayed among the trees as if they had sprouted here like one of the proprietor's mushrooms.

At the time I visited there were eighty-six monuments in the park, some of them enormous. There was a bronze bust of Marx 4 metres in height (13 feet), and a statue of Lenin 6 metres high (19 feet) that once stood in the main square of Vilnius. There was a representation of a Lithuanian 'Mother'

8 metres high (26 feet) and weighing around 12 metric tonnes: she used to stand beside a highway until someone tried to blow her up shortly after independence. While visitors contemplate the sculptures they are never far away from one of the Disney-style guard towers, an ominous stretch of barbed wire, or a loudspeaker blaring out Soviet propaganda.

People still occasionally call this place 'Stalin World', but in fact there is only one full-size statue of Stalin in the whole park. I found him just beyond the zoo, peeping out between the trees like some fairy-tale troll. (The comparison to a fairy tale is not random: in a nearby glade, closer to the children's playground, is a set of sculptures representing Snow White and the seven dwarves. The difference between folk tale and reality is not always scrupulously delineated here.)

This particular statue used to stand outside a station in Vilnius, until it was taken down in 1960. It is one of hundreds of Stalin statues, some of them truly vast, that used to adorn streets and squares all over eastern and central Europe. After Stalin's death in 1953, however, even the Soviets began to recognise him as a monster. In the following years he was universally denounced and discredited. Statues of him everywhere were taken down and destroyed. This is one of the very few survivors.

It is easy to see why so many people became upset when the park's creation was first announced. Many dissidents had spent their lives struggling against the Soviet system. In 1991 they had torn down these icons of Soviet power with great joy: it must have been deeply painful to see them so lovingly restored and put back on their pedestals, regardless of the setting.

The resurrection of Stalin's statue was perhaps the most

painful of all. This man had been responsible for tens of millions of deaths across eastern Europe, and for the enslavement of hundreds of thousands of Lithuanians. He had not been on public display for decades. And yet here he was, standing in a sunny glade, waiting for tourists to come and take selfies with him. Critics pointed to a worrying trend in contemporary Russia for the rehabilitation of Stalin's memory, with brand new memorials to him being raised in Pskov, Lipetsk, Novosibirsk and several other places. What if the trend were to spread to Lithuania and beyond? What if Grūtas Park, too, were to become a twenty-first-century shrine to this monstrous dictator?

Had this statue, and all the others, been given to another bidder, perhaps there would have been less controversy. Europos Parkas, in Vilnius, wanted to exhibit the statues purely as works of art alongside a range of avant-garde creations by artists from all over the world. Here, perhaps, the aesthetic qualities of a Stalin statue might have been divorced from its political meaning.

The KGB Museum in Vilnius also applied for the contract. It would have displayed the monuments in its main hall and courtyard. Had Stalin's statue been placed here, it would have been seen alongside an extensive exhibition dedicated to his crimes. Many of those who protested against Grūtas Park wanted the KGB Museum to win the bid precisely because it would have put the benign-looking statues of figures like Stalin in a much, much grimmer context.

But there is something about the way that Grūtas Park displays its statues that is enormously refreshing. Seeing Stalin with a squirrel on his head takes away some of the nightmarish power he continues to exercise over us from beyond the grave. When birds are nesting in Lenin's fingers, and children are climbing over the guns that were once aimed at Lithuanian partisans, these symbols of state power no longer seem as frightening as they once did.

This seems to be exactly what Viliumas Malinauskas is trying to achieve. In an interview with the *Guardian* in 2000, the proprietor was unapologetic about his peculiar approach to Lithuania's troubled history. 'People can come here and joke about the sculptures,' he said. 'And that will mean Lithuania is no longer afraid of Communism.'

Grūtas Park is bizarre mix of playground, zoo and atrocity museum. It trivialises the past in the most appalling ways, especially with its Disneyfied guard towers and barbed wire. Some of the displays in its barrack-style huts are more nostalgic than critical of the regime, and its commercial exploitation of Lithuania's painful past is questionable to say the least: I managed to buy myself a Stalin mug and a Stalin key ring in the gift shop on my way out. In fact, so many aspects of Grūtas Park could be considered offensive that I hardly know where to start; and yet somehow, through its sheer banality, it comes closer to freeing us from our history than any of the more serious and thoughtful monuments that have been so carefully produced in other parts of Europe.

The magic ingredient is ridicule. I'm not sure how much this was ever intended by the park's founder and owner, and how much is just a function of a ridiculous set-up. Nevertheless, it is there, and it is a powerful antidote to the atmosphere of fear that plagued this country for so many years.

Josef Stalin, eh? What a nob.

Coda: The Value of Monsters

There is no good way to commemorate the criminals of the Second World War. If we portray them as devils, we give them far more power over us than they deserve. If we ridicule them, we risk making light of a history that is unbearably painful for huge numbers of people. If we try to be nuanced, if we portray the undoubted historical reality that such criminals were mere human beings, and probably not so different from ourselves, then we lose all moral power. Any memorial that acknowledges their humanity opens the door to apologists whose only wish is to rehabilitate our war criminals, deny their crimes, and pretend that they were never monsters but merely misunderstood heroes.

Our solution to the problem is, generally speaking, to avoid commemorating them at all. Commemoration of any sort is an honour, and such men deserve no place in our public spaces. But this too has consequences. The memory of figures like Hitler and Stalin has been dispersed throughout society: they continue to exercise a hold over our imagination even when they are not present. This has profoundly affected our memorial landscape. Our memory of our Second World War criminals is much more widespread than we ever give it credit for.

It is our memory of these people – these monsters – that makes the monuments to our heroes and martyrs possible. When we honour figures like Churchill or Douglas MacArthur, we are also remembering the evils that they faced and fought. When we mourn our dead and our damaged, we are also remembering the monsters who victimised them. Our heroes become more heroic, and our martyrs more tragic, because of the contrast with these monsters. Without the monsters, they would not be nearly so revered.

I began this book with a look at the numerous monuments around the world that have been taken down in recent years. Why, I asked, should our Second World War monuments have been comparatively immune to this wave of iconoclasm?

The answer lies partly not in what these monuments represent, but in what they oppose. The reason why Winston Churchill is still revered as a hero is not because of his grit and determination, but because he was the man who stood up to Hitler. Had his adversary been less monstrous, we might be more inclined to remember Churchill's many, many faults – his pompous grandiosity, for example, his permanent drunkenness, or his Victorian attitudes towards race and empire. It was Hitler who made Churchill.

What is true of our heroes is also true of our martyrs. The victims of any war will always be mourned; but what makes the victims of this war so tragic – what transforms them into symbols of such purity and innocence – is the nature of the people who persecuted them. It is one thing for a Korean woman to be raped in wartime; quite another for her to be consumed by a system of organised sexual slavery. The death of a Polish officer in battle is not the same as the wholesale massacre of Polish officers after they have surrendered. The reason why these victims hold such an important place in our communal memory is not only the fact that they suffered, but because they suffered at the hands of such monsters.

This highlights another important fact about our Second World War monuments: our memories of our heroes, martyrs and monsters do not stand alone, they reinforce one another. The monuments we have created to these people are part of a much bigger memorial framework. This is not just history, but mythology. We have built a story not only of war and suffering, but also of an epic struggle between the forces of good and the forces of evil.

This is precisely what our monuments are for. They transform the ordinary, everyday stories into timeless archetypes that tell us important truths about the human condition.

In the next part I shall explore another category of Second World War monuments that also taps into our need to express our memories in mythological terms. Only this time it is not the people who fought the war that are being transformed into legendary figures – but the war itself.

Part IV

Apocalypse

If the Second World War was a titanic struggle between good and evil, then we can be rightly satisfied that, in the end, good won. But at what cost?

In America, the war is generally remembered as a glorious event – one that transformed the nation into a global super-power and a champion of peace and democracy around the world. In Britain, too, it is often remembered in the words of Winston Churchill as 'our finest hour'. But in other parts of the world very different memories take priority. The whole-sale destruction of cities like Manila, Warsaw, Tokyo or Berlin allowed little scope for glorification. Instead the war is remembered as uniquely destructive: a twentieth-century Armageddon.

In the following chapters I will describe some of the world's most moving monuments to the devastation caused by monsters and heroes alike. They each have the same motto, which is in some cases literally inscribed on the monuments themselves: 'Never Again'.

18

France: Oradour-sur-Glane

In west-central France, about 20 kilometres (around 12 miles) north-west of Limoges, there is a village unlike any other in Europe. From a distance it looks like a typical French village, nestling among the trees and fields, but as you come closer you discover that none of the houses have roofs. There are no doors on the buildings, and the windows are empty spaces through which the wind blows freely. Nothing moves in the streets. The only vehicle is a decaying old car which lies abandoned near the empty market place: from its make and model, it looks as if it was parked here three-quarters of a century ago and has not been moved since. At the western end of the village, not far from the abandoned post office and the vacant town hall, is a tram station; but from the rusted state of the tracks that run down the centre of the main street, it is quite clear that no tram has passed through here in decades.

This was obviously once a busy place, thronging with rural life. All the houses and shop fronts along the main street have plaques on them bearing the names and professions of people who once lived and worked here. If you put your head through any of the windows you can still see small indications of their lives: the remains of an old bicycle, pots and pans hanging on the wall, a rusting sewing machine sitting on a window sill.

The whole village has the atmosphere of having been abandoned in a hurry, as if in response to a natural disaster: it is like a modern-day Pompeii. In a way, that is exactly what happened, although there was nothing natural about the disaster that engulfed this place. A clue to what occurred lies in the abandoned church at the south-eastern end of the village. Beside the altar lie the charred remains of a baby carriage. Behind it, the stone wall is pockmarked with bullet holes.

Life in the small market town of Oradour-sur-Glane came to an end quite suddenly on the afternoon of 10 June 1944. It was a Saturday, and the place was busy with people going about their daily business. Some of the local men had taken time out from their tasks in the farms and fields – Saturday was the day when their tobacco rations were distributed. It was also a school day. Parents from the surrounding hamlets had made a particular effort to get their children to school today, because a medical check had been scheduled for that afternoon.

The calm of this perfectly ordinary day was shattered at around 2 p.m., when a regiment from the infamous 'Das Reich' division of the Waffen-SS suddenly drove into town. Unbeknownst to the residents of Oradour, the soldiers were in a vengeful mood. In the wake of the Normandy landings there had been a sudden surge in resistance activity all over France, particularly in this region: the Germans had come to take reprisals.

Soldiers quickly surrounded the town, and then went from house to house, summoning everyone to gather in the market place. Thinking that they were simply going to have their identity papers checked, most of Oradour's residents willingly complied. A few young men hid in basements or attics, afraid that the Germans might be here to round them up as forced labourers. One schoolchild, eight-year-old Roger Godfrin, fled through the back door of his school and ran towards the river. He was the only schoolchild in Oradour that afternoon who would survive.

Once everyone was assembled, the SS troops separated the women and children from the men and herded them off to the church. Then a German officer stepped forward to address the remaining men. Speaking through an interpreter, he told them that he knew there was a cache of arms in the town, and demanded that all those who owned firearms should step forward. When no one responded, he turned to the mayor and instructed him to select hostages from among the town's men. The mayor refused, offering up himself and his sons as hostages instead. After a brief pause and more discussion, the officer appeared to change his mind about taking hostages and announced instead that he was going to search the town. The men were divided into six groups and taken off to various barns and garages around the market place.

What happened next would transform the village of Oradour-sur-Glane for ever. As the men were herded into the barns, the soldiers were already setting up machine guns outside. At a signal from their officer, they opened fire. Within a few moments more than two hundred villagers had been shot. Various German soldiers then stepped forward to finish off what they had started: they walked among the bodies killing anyone they found still alive, before covering them with straw and fuel and setting fire to both the bodies and the buildings that held them.

The only people to survive the massacre were six young men in one of the larger groups, who had fallen to the floor during the initial round of firing and had been buried beneath the bodies of fifty-six others. As smoke and flames filled the barn where they lay, they crawled out from underneath their dead friends and neighbours and scrambled out of a small back door. Five men managed somehow to slip to safety through the back gardens of the town; the sixth was spotted by one of the German soldiers and shot.

After all the men were dead, the SS turned their attention to the town's women and children, who were still huddling, terrified, in the church. At around 5 p.m., two soldiers entered the church. Placing a large chest on the altar, they laid out a long fuse, lit it, and shut the door. After a huge explosion filled the church with smoke and noise, the soldiers threw open the doors and sprayed the surviving women and children with gunfire. They then piled up church pews around the bodies and set fire to them. The only woman to survive was forty-seven-year-old Marguerite Rouffanche, who had hidden behind the sacristy while the soldiers were firing. When the church was alight she found a stool and climbed up to one of the windows blown out by the blast. As she dropped to the ground, a woman and her baby who tried to follow were shot with machine guns.

Over the next few hours, SS troops combed the rest of the town pillaging the houses and shops, shooting anyone they found, and systematically setting everything on fire. Anyone who emerged from the smoke was immediately shot. Several bodies were thrown down a well.

By the time they had finished, the Waffen-SS had burned down 123 houses, 4 schools, 22 stores, 26 workshops, 19 garages, 40 barns, 35 agricultural sheds, 58 hangars and the tram station. These are the ruins that stand in the deserted town of Oradour-sur-Glane today. Piled up among the ruins, both individually and in large groups, were the bodies of 642 people.

Oradour-sur-Glane was just one village of many in France that suffered such atrocities towards the end of the German occupation. Eleven days after Oradour was put to the torch, Mouleydier in the Dordogne suffered a similar fate, albeit without quite so many deaths. A month later the same happened to the town of Dortan near the border with Switzerland; and a month after that SS troops surrounded the village of Maillé in the Touraine and massacred 124 men, women and children with machine guns and hand grenades. One of the most gruesome massacres occurred in the town of Tulle, around 100 kilometres from Oradour, where a German garrison had come under attack from members of the resistance. In reprisal, the Waffen-SS seized ninety-nine men from the town and hanged them from the balconies, trees and bridges all along the main street.

Other nations have similar tales to tell. In Czechoslovakia, the village of Lidice was literally levelled in reprisal for the assassination of Reinhard Heydrich in nearby Prague. Its menfolk were massacred and its women and children imprisoned or taken away to be murdered elsewhere. In Norway the coastal village of Telavåg was razed in reprisal for the killing of two German Gestapo officers. In Italy 770 people were massacred in Marzabotto in reprisal for local resistance activity. In Greece, the infamous massacre of more than 200 civilians in the village of Distomo took place on 10 June 1944, exactly the same day as that at Oradour-sur-Glane. Perhaps the worst destruction took place in Warsaw, the capital of

Poland, which was systematically destroyed by German soldiers at the end of 1944. They went from house to house with explosives and flame throwers, trying to wipe the entire city from the face of the earth.

Some of these places were rebuilt after the war, as local people tried to move on and put the past behind them. Oradour-sur-Glane is unique in that the entire town has been preserved as a ruin, exactly as it was on the day after the massacre.

The decision to turn the ruins of Oradour into a national monument was made very early on. In October 1944, just four months after the town had been burned down, various local notables were already making plans. They were aware that Oradour symbolised something of enormous importance, not only to the local community but to the whole of France. Their view was endorsed by President Charles de Gaulle when he visited the village in March 1945. 'Oradour is the symbol of what happened to the country itself,' he said in a short speech. 'A place like this remains something shared by all. Never again; a similar thing must never happen anywhere in France.'

In the following months the ruins would indeed become an official monument – but a monument to what? In the victorious atmosphere of 1945, it was tempting to portray them as a monument to the Resistance – after all, it had been destroyed in reprisal for Resistance activity in the area. Newspapers like *Ce Soir* often listed the people of Oradour alongside a litany of Resistance heroes, and others spoke proudly of the village's 'halo of glory'. But this begged uncomfortable questions: if the Resistance were indeed so active in this backwater area of France, do they not bear at least some of the responsibility for the reprisals that took place here?

Others wanted to emphasise the purity and innocence of those who had died in the village, especially the children. Many of the survivors have always denied that there was any real Resistance activity in Oradour in 1944 – there was no need to resist, since none of them had ever seen a German soldier anywhere near the village until that tragic day in June. For these people the village was, and will always be, a pure symbol of French martyrdom.

Then there were those who saw Oradour as a monument to the evil inflicted upon France by a nation of monsters. For Pierre Masfrand, the driving force behind the creation of the monument, its purpose was to 'symbolise heinous Nazi barbarism'. According to Pierre Pacquet, the architect charged with conserving the ruins in 1945, Oradour was a 'sacred place', devoted not only to the victims but to 'the savagery of the German race'.

In the following years, however, this comforting story of French martyrdom and German atrocity turned out not to be quite as clear cut as everyone wanted to believe. When a war crimes trial was held in 1953, German citizens were not the only people to appear. Fourteen of the twenty-one men who stood in the dock were from Alsace, a border region of France. Alsace had been annexed to Germany during the war, and its young men had been conscripted into the German army, most of them unwillingly. Nevertheless, these men – these *French* men – had been in Oradour, and had taken part in the massacre. Their trial was a painful reminder of the divisions within France itself, and of the painful legacy of French collaboration with the Nazis during the war.

In the end the ruins of Oradour-sur-Glane did not become a simple memorial to heroes, or to martyrs, or to monsters, because they were reminiscent of all these things at once.

More than anything else, they became a symbol of negation. The apocalypse that took place here in June 1944 was merely the tip of something much bigger: the old France – a nation untainted by collaboration, sure of its strength, its purity and its virtue – had effectively ceased to exist.

We are all prisoners of our history in one way or another, but Oradour-sur-Glane is more of a prisoner than most. Each place I have mentioned so far in this book has been trapped in a vision of its past. Some have been trying to live up to an ideal of past greatness; others have been struggling to come to terms with past suffering or atone for past sins; and in each case, the history of the Second World War threatens to poison both the present and the future. But Oradour has no present and no future: the entire village has been frozen at the exact moment of its destruction. It exists in a state of perpetual apocalypse.

Unlike Oradour, other places in Europe refused to be bowed by the devastation they faced. All the hundreds of European cities that were reduced to rubble by bombardment have since been rebuilt: from Glasgow to Odessa, from Leningrad to Marseille, they are now thriving once again. The centre of Warsaw has been lovingly reconstructed so that it now looks almost identical to the city as it was before the war. The centre of Dresden has likewise been reconstructed. But not Oradour. This devastated French village acknowledges what none of these other places is prepared to face: a whole world was destroyed in the Second World War, and no amount of reconstruction can ever bring it back.

Nobody understands this better than the survivors of the massacre themselves. After the war, many of them settled in a brand new town that was built next door to the old one and given the same name. Living here was inevitably both a comfort and a curse. On the one hand, being within sight of the ruins made it easier to mourn; on the other hand, the old town cast a constant shadow over the new one.

For years, mourning was strictly enforced, especially during the month of June. For example, when a new hotel opened in the town in 1952, its owner wanted to host a ball to celebrate – but a group of families came with rifles to stop the ball going ahead: celebrations like this were not to be permitted in a town so devoted to mourning. In her excellent book about the legacy of Oradour, *Martyred Village*, Sarah Farmer describes how gloomy it was for local teenagers to grow up in a town where they were only ever allowed to wear dark colours. The anniversary was always a particularly sombre time. It was not until 1988 that the association of the families of the martyrs lifted its blanket ban on June weddings.

Even today the memory of what happened in June 1944 makes it hard for residents of Oradour to move on. This is particularly the case for the survivors of the massacre itself. 'It's always difficult for me to come here,' said Robert Hébras, one of the men who survived the mass shooting in the barn by falling beneath the bodies of his neighbours, in an interview in 2013. 'I relive my village in my head,' he said, 'hear its old sounds, put faces to the ruins.'

But the old village of his memories no longer exists. The ruins are all that is left.

19

Germany: Memorial to the Murdered Jews of Europe, Berlin

What if the apocalypse were not something that affected the entire community of a nation, but just one strand of that community? What if it were a very selective kind of apocalypse?

Like the national monument at Oradour-sur-Glane, most memorials devoted to the apocalyptic destruction of the war highlight its random, indiscriminate nature: the violence claimed everyone and everything, without distinction. But the genocide of the Jews was different. There was nothing indiscriminate about it at all: it targeted a specific group of people, plucking them out of their communities and concentrating them in large groups, far from home, so that they could be killed more efficiently. In some places whole villages were wiped out. In other places it might have been just a handful of people – few enough for non-Jews to be able to tell themselves that nothing much out of the ordinary had happened. But make no mistake, the Holocaust was completely extraordinary. Collectively it added up to a wartime catastrophe far greater than any other: a true apocalypse.

Today there are monuments to this archetypal genocide all over the world, but perhaps the most important is in central

Berlin. There is nothing modest or retiring about the Memorial to the Murdered Jews of Europe. It is easily the biggest single, purpose-built monument in this book. Covering an area of 19,000 square metres, it is one hundred times the size of the Marine Corps memorial in Washington, DC, and twenty times as big as the site of the Bomber Command Memorial in London. Even America's National World War II Memorial is less than half its size.

The huge chunk of land that the monument occupies is not some obscure field in rural Germany: it stands right in the centre of Berlin, less than two minutes' walk from the Brandenburg Gate. The monetary value of the land runs into hundreds of millions of euros. The historical value is perhaps greater still. During the Second World War the site was surrounded by the offices and ministries where the war in general, and the Holocaust in particular, was planned. Goebbels' bunker lies directly beneath. During the Cold War it lay in the no-man's-land between Communist East Berlin and democratic West Berlin – indeed, the only reason why it was still vacant at the end of the twentieth century was that the Berlin Wall itself had run right through it. For decades, the area lay not only at the centre of Berlin, but at the centre of world events.

To sacrifice such a large and important piece of land shows how determined Germany is to atone for its past sins. It is supposed to be the mother of all grand gestures – a national act of contrition. But ever since it was first inaugurated in May 2005 I have always thought that there is something not quite right about the memorial. Like many of the other monuments in this book, it is not entirely honest about its intentions.

* * *

The Memorial to the Murdered Jews of Europe was designed at the end of the 1990s by the American architect Peter Eisenman. It consists of 2,711 rectangular concrete blocks, laid out in a grid pattern across the whole of the site. Each block is identical in width and length, but they are all of slightly different heights: those at the edges are less than a metre high, while those in the middle are much taller – some are almost 5 metres (16 feet) high.

The designer himself gave no specific meaning to the blocks except to say that they represented the dehumanisation that occurs when a rigid system is imposed upon the landscape without compromise. There is no significance in the number of blocks, and the blocks themselves do not represent anything. In fact, there is nothing symbolic in the memorial at all.

From the edge of the memorial, the play of light and shadow on the vast field of cuboid blocks is quite beautiful. It looks like some huge, satisfyingly geometrical pattern. Many people have commented that, from the outside at least, the memorial resembles a giant field of rectangular tombstones. Eisenman strenuously denies that this was ever his intention. He deliberately added no names or symbols to any of the blocks, as one would in a graveyard. Nevertheless, this was also my own reaction to the memorial when I first saw it: it looks as if this important location in central Berlin has been turned into a vast, symbolic cemetery for Europe's Jews.

When you walk into the memorial, however, and wander among the blocks, a different perspective emerges. As the ground dips down and the blocks become taller, you become immersed inside a series of claustrophobic concrete canyons, with only distant glimpses of the trees and buildings beyond. It can be quite disorienting. Being surrounded on all sides by identical concrete surfaces gives you the feeling of being inside some kind of maze: you turn down one avenue, then another and another, but they all look the same, and very soon you lose all understanding of where you are. Whenever I come here with anyone I always lose them within moments. Sometimes we don't find one another again until half an hour later on the opposite side of the memorial.

There are disturbing echoes here. The barrenness, the claustrophobia and the shadowy light inside the memorial all hint at some dark experience in our communal memory. But since that memory is never explicitly spelled out, it is worth reminding ourselves for a moment exactly what happened to the Jews during the war in Europe, and how their genocide was finally revealed to the world.

The Holocaust was not dreamed up halfway through the Second World War; it was implicit from the very moment that Germany began to view the existence of the Jews as a problem. Even before the war began, the Nazis had singled out Jews, isolated them and removed them from public life. After the invasion of Poland, when Germany found itself in control of the largest population of Jews anywhere in the world, the 'problem' became much greater. To isolate Jews more effectively, they were forced into ghettos. There was much talk of removing them from Europe altogether, to Siberia perhaps, or to Madagascar. But since this was always impossible, there was only ever one logical, final solution: they should all be killed.

The first large-scale massacres took place soon after the invasion of the Soviet Union in 1941. The massacre at Oradour looks insignificant by comparison. At Babi Yar, a deep ravine in central Ukraine, some 33,000 Jews from nearby Kiev were shot in an orgy of killing that lasted two days. There were so many bodies that their killers had to dynamite the sides of the ravine in order to bury them all.

In the following year, the *Einsatzgruppen* (SS death squads) murdered over a million Jews across eastern Europe, mostly in mass shootings. Canyons and quarries were filled with bodies. Vast fields and entire forests became mass graveyards. Eventually the Nazis set up specialised extermination centres at places like Treblinka, Sobibor, Belzec and Auschwitz, where the slaughter could be industrialised. By the end of the war they had murdered almost six million Jews, and caused hundreds of thousands more to flee their homelands.

Though the Allies had received reports of what was happening across Europe, the extent of the genocide was not revealed until the Allied armies began to take back territory from the Germans. As the Red Army advanced into Ukraine and Poland they discovered village after village whose population had been utterly wiped out. The Soviet journalist Vasily Grossman described his anguish as he passed through these empty communities. 'There are no Jews in the Ukraine,' he wrote in *Einikeit*, the journal of the Soviet Union's Jewish Anti-Fascist Committee:

Nowhere – Poltava, Kharkov, Kremenchug, Borispol, Yagutin – in none of the cities, hundreds of towns, or thousands of villages will you see the black, tear-filled eyes of little girls; you will not hear the pained voice of an old woman; you will not see the dark face of a hungry baby. All is silence. Everything is still. A whole people has been brutally murdered.

When the Red Army overran Majdanek concentration camp in July 1944 they discovered the first of a series of vast warehouses filled with hundreds of thousands of pairs of shoes stolen from the dead. At Treblinka, which they reached shortly afterwards, they captured former camp guards, who described it as a 'hell' where 900,000 Jews had been roasted in furnaces 'reminiscent of gigantic volcanoes'. The largest death camp, at Auschwitz, was discovered six months later.

In western Europe, the British and Americans soon began to uncover similar scenes at other concentration camps. War crimes investigators who entered Buchenwald, Dachau, Mauthausen and Bergen-Belsen found the same scenes of atrocity repeated again and again. When I interviewed one of these investigators, Ben Ferencz, in 2016, he told me that it was the sheer repetition that was hardest to take. 'They were all basically similar,' he said; 'dead bodies strewn across the camp grounds, piles of skin and bones, cadavers piled up like cordwood before the burning crematoria, helpless skeletons with diarrhoea, dysentery, typhus, TB, pneumonia, and other ailments, retching in their louse-ridden bunks or on the ground with only their pathetic eyes pleading for help.'

These scenes were caught on camera and played on news-reels in cinemas all over the world. In western Europe especially, they have formed our collective memories of 1945 as a vision of hell. But for Jewish communities all over the continent, this was more than mere hell – it seemed like the end of the world. Centuries of Jewish tradition, learning and craftsmanship had been snuffed out in an instant. Yiddish, the unique language of the Jews in eastern Europe, was all but dead. An entire culture, it seemed, had been eradicated.

The statistics at the end of the war do not make happy reading. Of 140,000 Dutch Jews, only around 20,000 survived the war: in most areas of the Netherlands, this effectively brought an end to more than eight hundred years of Jewish history. In Greece only 12,000 Jews were left in 1945: a culture that had survived here for over two thousand years was now on the brink of total extinction. And in Poland and Ukraine, once home to the world's largest community of Jews, there was nothing but a wasteland. Three million Polish Jews were killed during the Holocaust. The vast majority of those who survived fled the country in the following years – partly because they no longer felt safe, but partly because there was nothing left to stay for. Everything they had known before the war was gone.

The story told by one Jew speaks volumes. Eleven-year-old Celina Lieberman was the only member of her family to survive. In Ukraine in 1942 she was taken in by a Christian woman who promised to protect her. She quickly grew used to attending church like a good Catholic; but every now and then, in private, she would pray to her Jewish god. Years later, when interviewed by the Holocaust Education Centre in Vancouver, she confessed that this was her way of apologising to all the other Jews who had died. 'I was fourteen at the end of the war,' she said, 'and believed that I was the only surviving Jew left on earth.'

The Memorial to the Murdered Jews of Europe is supposed to commemorate this apocalypse. The rigid sense of order in the field of concrete blocks is intended to call to mind the rigidity of the Nazi system. The feeling of alienation we experience when we enter this field is supposed to remind us of the feeling of isolation that Jews like Celina Lieberman experienced at the end of the war.

I visit the memorial whenever I am in Berlin; however,

while I appreciate this remarkable space I can't help feeling that there is something distinctly odd about it. If it is supposed to be a memorial to Jews, it certainly does a good job of hiding the fact. Nothing here calls to mind the mass shootings at Babi Yar or the gas chambers at Auschwitz. There are no urns containing ash or earth from Holocaust sites. Neither is there any sense of nostalgia or lamentation for the Jewish worlds that were lost. (According to the designer, this is quite deliberate: nostalgia was the one emotion he insisted he was trying to avoid.) There are no symbols of Judaism here, nor of individual Jews, nor of the regime that organised their genocide. In fact, there is not even a sign bearing the title of the memorial. When I first brought my twelve-year-old daughter here she had no idea what the place was. Her first thought was that it must be some kind of gigantic playground: she was about to climb up onto one of the blocks and begin leaping from one to the next, and was mortified when I explained to her why this was inappropriate.

So what's really going on here? Why does this memorial seemingly not invite us to *remember* anything specific at all? And if it is supposed to be a memorial to *Jews*, why does it fail to make any reference to those Jews?

According to Peter Eisenman, there is a certain logic behind his design. Traditional monuments often take a single view of history and try to freeze it forever in stone – and this is precisely what Eisenman was trying to avoid. 'The enormity and horror of the Holocaust are such that any attempt to represent it by traditional means is inevitably inadequate,' he explained in his original proposal. 'In this monument there is no goal, no end, no working one's way in or out.' By making his memorial entirely abstract, and

Is this a cemetery? Or a playground? Without guidance from its designer, visitors to the memorial are free to interpret it as they choose

leaving absolutely everything open to interpretation, he wanted to allow visitors space for their own memories to arise spontaneously. Eisenman doesn't want to tell you what to remember. That is up to you.

It's a noble sentiment, but in the real world it runs into one problem after another. To begin with, is it really possible to create a monument that people can experience without preconceptions? Anyone familiar with the events of the Holocaust will come here with certain images already in mind. And anyone familiar with the language of memorials will immediately see parallels with other similar places they have seen: perhaps this is why so many visitors to Berlin instinctively liken this particular monument to a vast graveyard. I myself could not help noticing similarities between this memorial and one in the nearby Jewish Museum, called the 'Garden of Exile', which also consists of tall concrete blocks on a sloping ground. There is no such thing as a completely abstract monument – knowingly or not, viewers will always impose upon it the language of commemoration that they have picked up from other, less esoteric places.

For those who know little about monuments, and even less about the Holocaust, there is the opposite problem. Since there are no symbols and no signposts, this landscape of boxes could mean virtually anything. Perhaps the concrete blocks are a comment on environmental issues. Perhaps the grid-like pattern is symbolic of our grid-like modern cities, and the alienation we feel when we walk down into it is symbolic of social isolation. Or perhaps it is not alienating at all. Perhaps it is somewhere joyous, like a place to play hide-and-seek or a gigantic children's playground. Without any direction from the designer, any of these things could be true: who is to say that it is a monument about the Holocaust?

The first people to point out these problems were the German government, who were not entirely comfortable with Eisenman's abstractions. They were quite clear about the kind of monument they expected in this prime location in the centre of the capital: it should honour the dead, and keep alive 'the memory of these inconceivable events in German history'. When they voted on whether or not to approve the monument, they specified that their main motive was to 'admonish all future generations never again to violate human rights . . . and to resist all forms of dictatorship and regimes based on violence'.

It was not enough for the monument to imply rigidity and uncompromising order – what the government required was good, hard facts about the evils of Nazism. They therefore insisted that Eisenman's abstract monument should have an information centre next to it, with a permanent exhibition about the events of the Holocaust.

At first Eisenman fought hard against this idea. What was the point of building an abstract monument, designed to set the mind free, if he then attached an information centre which told visitors exactly what to remember and how to feel about it? In the end, however, he was forced to back down. An information centre was indeed built in a kind of underground bunker beneath the memorial. It contains a chronology of the genocide, an exhibition detailing the stories of fifteen individual families, and a 'Room of Names', where the details of all those known to have been murdered are read out, one by one, in a cycle that lasts over six and a half years. The only consolation for the designer was that he was allowed to keep the entrance to the centre inconspicuous. (Indeed, it was so inconspicuous that when a survey was carried out shortly after the memorial's opening in 2005, many respondents claimed that they had failed to notice that there was a museum here at all.)

The next group to criticise the monument was Germany's Jewish population, along with Jews from other countries. As a symbol of the apocalypse, they complained, it was wholly inadequate. There was nothing here to remind them of the world that had been destroyed or the suffering that they had been forced to endure. The monument, they said, had nothing to do with them: it was a monument for Germans, not Jews. Stephan Kramer, Secretary-General of the Central Council of Jews in Germany, was particularly vocal: 'We did not ask for it. We do not need it.' Other critics claimed that the monument was nothing more than an ostentatious display of German virtue, an attempt by Germany to 'wash its hands clean' of the past.

That sounds harsh, but when one considers the other memorials that surround this one – memorials that I have already described in Chapter 16 – it is hard to deny that they have a point. The real intention of most Second World War

memorials in Berlin is to remind us not that the Jews are all
gone, but that the Nazis are all gone. That is something to be
celebrated, for sure. But perhaps not in *this* memorial, which
is supposed to commemorate something quite different, and
much, much darker.

There are a couple of lessons to be learned from the controversy that surrounded Peter Eisenman's memorial. The first
is that, regardless of the benefits of abstract design, some areas
of history are simply too sensitive to leave open to interpretation. Societies develop rituals for a reason, and the rituals
around death are particularly sacred. What else is a memorial,
if not a ritual cast in stone?

A certain language about the Holocaust has developed over
the decades. All the major Holocaust museums across the
world tend to follow the same basic patterns in the way they
narrate their history; and memorials to the Holocaust have
likewise developed certain conventions. They often carry the
names of villages, towns or national communities that were
wiped out. They often include statistics regarding the number
of Jews killed. They often contain earth or ashes taken from
Auschwitz or other main killing sites; and they are almost
always inscribed with Jewish symbols, such as stars or meno-
rahs. There are lots of obelisks and monoliths, lots of off-kilter
walls and floors, and lots of images of barbed wire, or cattle
trucks, or chimneys. Over the years, Jews have become
familiar with such symbols. Sometimes they can seem inescapable and quite stifling – but at least there is a certain
comfort in the ritual of them. So when Peter Eisenman
dropped them all from his memorial, it is not surprising that
so many people hated the idea.

Germans, meanwhile, are also prisoners of this history,

although the emphasis is not on crimes suffered, but on crimes committed. German children go on school trips to former concentration camps to learn about the sins of their grandfathers and great-grandfathers. There are memorials everywhere, from the brass cobbles that mark the pavements outside the houses of Jews who were taken away, to plaques and statues devoted to larger, more communal crimes. Berlin's Memorial to the Murdered Jews of Europe is just one item in a whole landscape of guilt. As I shall show in the next chapter, in Germany, even those Second World War memorials that have nothing to do with the Holocaust are nevertheless tainted by it. Whether they like it or not, Germans and Jews cannot escape this history, and they cannot escape each other. The Holocaust has bound them together in an endless embrace.

It is a link that not even the most abstract of memorials could ever break.

20

Germany: Monument to the Victims of the Firestorm, Hamburg

One of the monuments that has most fascinated me over the years stands in Ohlsdorf Cemetery, in the German city of Hamburg. Unlike most of the monuments in this book, it is not particularly controversial; but it has a strange, other-worldly beauty that I find utterly compelling. Of every memorial I have visited over the past twenty years, this is the one that draws me back again and again; and each time I see it I find new layers of meaning.

I first came across this place in 2005, while I was researching a book about the Allied bombing raids on the city. I had just spent a week interviewing survivors and combing through eyewitness testimonies in various local history archives. The effort of struggling through endless documents in German, which I do not speak at all fluently, had been exhausting, and some of the stories I had uncovered were quite harrowing; so I had come to the cemetery to give myself a break. This was where most of the victims of the bombing were buried, and it seemed an apt place to gather my thoughts.

The monument to the bombing victims stands at the centre of four huge communal graves at the eastern end of the cemetery. One can only approach it by walking past the mass graves, which hold the bodies of 36,918 people. At regular intervals an oak beam stretches across each grave, marked with the name of an entire suburb that was destroyed in the bombing. Rothenburgsort, Veddel, Horn, Hamm, Hammerbook . . . eighteen districts of Hamburg are named here.

From a distance the monument itself looks like a mausoleum – rectangular, austere, made from large blocks of solid sandstone. As you come closer, however, you can see that it has no roof: it is, in fact, just four stone walls enclosing a paved courtyard. A wrought-iron gate in the front wall invites you to step up and peer inside. Through the gateway you can see a sculpture set into one of the internal walls: it is a scene from Greek mythology of the god Charon ferrying the souls of the dead to the underworld.

This sculpture forms the most important element of the monument. It is entitled *Fahrt über den Styx* ('Journey over the Styx'). What first struck me about the sculpture when I finally came face to face with it that April afternoon was how extraordinarily emotionless it seemed. All week long I had been uncovering stories of astonishing violence and terror – but there was nothing of that here. The characters on the boat looked sorrowful, but there was no suggestion of the fear that the victims must have experienced at the moment of their death; nor of the pain and anguish suffered by those left behind in a shattered city. It seemed to me that this was a memorial designed to soothe, not to evoke.

Aside from Charon, the deathly boatman, there are four other sets of characters here. On the prow of the boat is an old man: he is the only one who faces his destination, apparently resigned to his fate. Behind him is a sombre-looking mother, comforting a child who is too frightened to behold the reality of what is happening. Next is a young couple, holding one another for support; and at the stern, next to Charon himself, is a man in his prime.

Each character is very stylised, and it is clear that they represent not real people but archetypes. In other words, there is a figure representing every kind of individual who died in the bombing. Anyone coming to the cemetery to mourn a loved one would be able to find a representation of him or her in the sculpture.

For mourners this might be comforting, but there is also something terribly bleak about the idea. The old man in the sculpture does not represent a single old man but thousands of old men. The mother represents not one but thousands of mothers. An entire community was destroyed in 1943: the young and the old, men and women, the married and the single – all gone.

As I stood at the gates to the memorial, the stories of witnesses to the bombing still ringing in my ears, I suddenly understood the scale of what was being depicted here. It is not a group of individuals that is being ferried to the under-world by Charon, but the whole of Hamburg. This sculpture is not merely a portrayal of death and mourning; it is a portrayal of Armageddon.

What happened in Hamburg at the end of July 1943 was unlike anything the world had ever experienced before. Military theorists had long been speculating about the destruction of major cities through bombing, but this was the first time that it was ever carried out on a large scale. It remains, even today, the most destructive set of bombing raids in European history.

Operation Gomorrah, as it was aptly called, was a combined

attack by the British and American air forces: the Royal Air
Force bombed Hamburg by night, and the US Army Air Force
attacked specific targets in the Hamburg docks by day. During
the course of just a week and a half, they dropped 9,785 metric
tonnes of bombs on the city. That is equivalent to almost a
quarter of the bombs dropped on the *whole* of Britain during
the *whole* of the Blitz.

One of these attacks in particular was to become infamous.
On the night of 27 July, 722 RAF bombers appeared over the
city and dropped their bombs in a concentrated mass over
the working-class suburbs to the east of the city centre. The
majority of these bombs were incendiaries. Within minutes,
tens of thousands of fires had been started. The fires quickly
joined up to create a single conflagration more than four
square miles in area.

What happened next was so horrific that even those who
were used to dealing with large fires struggled to understand
it. It seems that the fire was so intense that it set off a kind
of chain reaction. As superheated air rose rapidly above the
city, more air was sucked in from the surrounding areas to
fill the vacuum. This air brought fresh oxygen, which in turn
made the fires burn even more fiercely. As the fire became
hotter and hotter, the winds became stronger and stronger,
until the whole city was like a furnace with a hurricane-force
wind blowing through it. A new phenomenon had been born:
the 'firestorm'.

According to the chronological record kept by the chief
engineer at the main fire station that night, the Hamburg
firestorm took hold even before the bombing itself had
finished. Within an hour the hurricane was so powerful that
firemen emerging from the station could only crawl on their
hands and knees against the force of the wind. Those who

made it out into the street were helpless against the wind and the blaze, and many were forced to abandon their vehicles to take cover in bomb craters.

One fireman reported seeing 'No smoke on the streets, only flames and flying sparks as thick as a snowstorm'. Other eyewitnesses also claimed that the hurricane was 'a blizzard of sparks', which set fire to people's hair and clothes as they tried to flee. Many survived only by throwing themselves into the canals, or by struggling on towards the open space of the city's parks. There are countless eyewitness accounts of people bursting into flames as they ran, of children being sucked into the fire by the wind, and of people fleeing across roads, becoming stuck in the boiling asphalt which had turned to liquid in the intense heat, and dying 'like flies in the hot wax of a candle'. Those who stayed in their basements and shelters were often no better off. According to a report by the Hamburg chief of police, those who were too afraid to run for it often baked to death, or died from smoke inhalation and carbon monoxide poisoning.

It is impossible to tell precisely how many people died during the catastrophe, but the best estimates from the various police reports, census data and post-war bombing surveys suggest that more than 30,000 people succumbed on this one night alone, and between 37,000 and 45,000 in total during the sequence of raids. In just ten days, the entire eastern quarter of the city had been utterly destroyed, and much of the western quarter too. Roughly 61 per cent of Hamburg's total living accommodation – more than 40,000 residential buildings in total – had been obliterated. In the following days, around a million refugees fled the city. To all intents and purposes, Hamburg had ceased to exist.

Those who ventured back into the city in the following

months described a scene of utter devastation. One eyewitness said she saw nothing but 'Ruins everywhere, as far as the eye could see. Debris on the streets, collapsed house fronts, far-flung stones on kerbs, charred trees and devastated gardens . . . One was without words.' The novelist Hans Erich Nossack was so alienated by the ruins that he found it difficult to believe he was in Hamburg at all. 'What surrounded us did not remind us in any way of what was lost,' he wrote. 'It had nothing to do with it. It was something else, it was strangeness itself, it was the essentially not possible.' He entitled his memoir of the destruction *Der Untergang* – 'The End' – as if what he were witnessing was the apocalypse itself.

Given the sheer scale of what happened in Hamburg, one would expect it to be commemorated in an impressive way, with memorials as large and ambitious as those in Berlin, Hiroshima and Oradour-sur-Glane. But there is no 'Peace Park' here, no gigantic monument taking up several blocks of the city centre. For decades nothing existed but this small, taciturn sculpture in a quiet corner of the cemetery, which hides itself inside an enclosed courtyard, almost as if it is ashamed.

It is worth remembering that no monument at all existed here until nine years after the firestorm devastated the city. The Nazis did not build one in 1943 because they were already hopelessly overstretched; and besides, they had little incentive to draw attention to how badly they were losing the war. When the British took over the city in 1945, they did not build a monument either: again, resources were scarce, and they were not keen to encourage local people to dwell on the traumas of the past (especially since the British themselves bore much of the responsibility for those traumas). The

Ohlsdorf memorial was only planned after 1949, when democratic power was finally handed back to local people. But the Germans, too, were desperate to look forward, not back. Nobody wanted a huge, grandiose memorial. The past was something that almost everyone wanted to forget.

It is difficult for people today to fully appreciate the sense of shame that engulfed Germany in the aftermath of the war. The apocalypse that overcame the country was not only physical but spiritual. Germans were ashamed of losing the war; they were ashamed of having to grovel at the feet of those who had defeated them; but more than anything else they were ashamed of what the Nazis had done in their name. They knew that, as far as other nations were concerned, they were now pariahs.

Worse still, they were pariahs in their own eyes. In the aftermath of the war, the German people were forced to question almost every aspect of their society. All their institutions had been revealed to be corrupt and exploitative – not only the government, which was rotten to the core, but also the army, the judiciary, big business and even the medical profession, which, during the Nuremberg trials, had been implicated in the crimes of the Holocaust. Nazism seemed to have left its taint on everything. Even the mass graves at Ohlsdorf had been dug and filled by forced labourers from the local concentration camps. Nothing seemed sacred any more, not even the burial of the dead.

There are traces of this sense of shame in the memorial itself. I have always been curious as to why this monument expresses nothing of the outrage that I have seen in so many other memorials around the world. There is no sense of martyrdom here, as there is in places like Oradour or Hiroshima. There is no indignation, as expressed by the Katyn

Memorial in New Jersey or the 'comfort woman' statue in Seoul. The characters depicted are not protesting in any way: they seem to be going willingly to their deaths. Is this not quite a chilling thought?

Perhaps there is a silent acknowledgement here that the violence and destruction suffered at the end of the war was simply the price that Germany had to pay for its crimes; perhaps there is even a suggestion that, since the violence ultimately led to the defeat of the Nazis, it was a price *worth* paying. The artist who created the memorial, Gerhard Marcks, was himself fervently anti-Nazi. Before the war he had been blacklisted for opposing the regime, and his sculptures had been declared 'degenerate art'. Perhaps this was his way of showing the people of Hamburg that, according to some kind of divine justice, they had only reaped what they had sown.

This was certainly the main message at the inauguration ceremony for the monument in August 1952. In a speech to the assembled crowd, the first post-war mayor of Hamburg, Max Brauer, asked the mourners to take a good long look at themselves. 'Have the courage to see the real reason for the deaths of your fathers, mothers, brothers and sisters!' he said. 'They did not have to be sacrificed. It was only because they put themselves in the hands of violent criminals that violence overcame our families and our peaceful cities.'

With this in mind, it is worth taking one last look at the monument in Ohlsdorf cemetery. In later years it was criticised for not openly condemning the Nazis and their crimes. Subsequent memorials to the firestorm have certainly been much more explicit. The ruined Nikolaikirche in central Hamburg, which was converted into a memorial space in the 1970s and 1980s, now has a sculpture in its grounds dedicated to the victims of a nearby concentration camp. And the monument to the firestorm victims in Hamburger Strasse, in the north-eastern suburb of Barmbek, has the words 'Never again Fascism' and 'Never again war' carved into its base. But anyone who thinks that these sentiments are not expressed in the Ohlsdorf monument needs to look again.

Gerhard Marcks's sculpture shows a series of archetypal characters on the way to the underworld. Each is emblematic of a particular virtue: the old man represents wisdom, the woman represents motherhood and femininity, the young couple represents love and loyalty. In other times, these virtues might have been considered sacred, but during the war they too had been twisted into the service of the regime. Wisdom had been replaced by propaganda. Mothers had been conscripted to churn out soldiers for the Reich. Even concepts like loyalty had been co-opted and exploited. The disturbing implication is that these virtues, so tainted by the past, have now lost their sacred qualities: the underworld is the best place for them.

Perhaps the most fascinating character in this respect is the one that sits towards the back of Charon's boat: the man in his prime. Of all the virtues worshipped in Nazi Germany during the war, those represented in this figure – strength, virility, power – were the most cherished. And yet he does not stand like the other passengers; instead, he sits with his head in his hands, as if in utter despair. This is what has become of the martial glory of the war years. He, like the Thousand Year Reich that the German people were promised, is on his way to oblivion.

The apocalypse took everything from the people of Hamburg. It killed their families and their friends. It destroyed their homes and businesses, and devastated their city. But worse than this, it took away their pride in who they were.

If the monument that stands in Ohlsdorf cemetery is only a modest one, it is because the people of Hamburg did not want anything bigger. They were tired of the past and its troubles.

In this they were not so different from the people of Dresden and Berlin, of Hiroshima and Nagasaki, or of countless other people in cities all over the world that had been affected by the war. After all the years of destruction and death, they were no longer interested in building monuments to the apocalypse. They were more interested in building something to celebrate the possibilities of the future.

A-Bomb Dome, Hiroshima

21

Japan: A-Bomb Dome, Hiroshima, and Peace Statue, Nagasaki

In the immediate aftermath of the war, the urge to mourn had to compete everywhere with the urge to forget. Some places, like Hamburg, tried to move on from the war as quickly as possible. Others, like Oradour, found the process of coming to terms with the past almost impossibly painful. But there are one or two locations, like Hiroshima and Nagasaki, that seem to have embraced the devastation that they experienced, and tried to use it as an opportunity for change.

Of all the cataclysms described in this book, none was quite so apocalyptic or so total as the one that struck Japan at the beginning of August 1945. The hot blast that ripped through the city of Hiroshima on 6 August was unlike anything the world had ever seen. It was the result of a single explosion, about 600 metres (nearly 2000 feet) above the city centre. Within moments, 90 per cent of the city was obliterated, and tens of thousands of people lay dead. The destruction was so complete, and so sudden, that witnesses had no rational way of explaining it. 'I thought it might have been something which had nothing to do with the war,' wrote novelist Ota Yoko, who survived the bombing, 'the collapse of the earth, which it was said would take place at the end of the world'. Other survivors said that 'it felt like the sun had fallen from the sky', or that they had suddenly been transported to a parallel world, 'the world of the dead'.

Three days later, at 11.02 a.m. on 9 August, a second atomic explosion destroyed Nagasaki. Once again, witnesses had no way of understanding what was happening to them. At the university hospital, doctors cowered in their shattered building, asking one another if the sun had just exploded. One of their colleagues, Nurse Hashimoto, described walking through the streets outside and seeing naked bodies lying everywhere surrounded by large trees torn up by the roots: for a while, she said, she truly believed that she was 'the only person left alive in the whole world'.

Unlike any of the other events I have described so far, these intimations of Armageddon were not confined to those who directly experienced the violence: they rapidly spread all around the world. People everywhere began to speculate about what future wars might look like if such weapons ever became widely available. 'One forgets the effect on Japan . . .' wrote the *New York Herald Tribune* directly after the Hiroshima bombing, 'as one senses the foundations of one's own universe trembling.' According to *Time* magazine, the war itself had suddenly shrunk to 'minor significance'; compared to the revelation of atomic power, the prospect of victory was nothing but 'the shout of a child in the street'. The French philosopher Jean-Paul Sartre called the atom bomb 'the negation of man'; while Albert Einstein considered the new situation 'the most terrible danger in which man has ever found himself'. All of a sudden, annihilation was not merely something that might strike a single village or a single people. Compared to other apocalyptic events, the devastation of

Hiroshima and Nagasaki had implications for the future of mankind as a whole.

How on earth does one commemorate events like this? In the immediate aftermath of the explosions, the Japanese people did not even try. Individual grave stones were erected by some survivors to mark where their relatives had died. In Nagasaki a single monolith was placed in the rubble to mark the hypo-centre – the spot directly beneath where the bomb had exploded. But otherwise very little was done. Both cities, still reeling under the shock, were simply too busy trying to survive.

In the absence of any formal memorial, the ruins themselves began to take on a special meaning. In Hiroshima, where virtually every building had been swept away by the blast, the charred remains of the Hiroshima Prefecture Industrial Promotion Hall became symbolic of the apocalypse that had so suddenly engulfed the city. Its dome, now reduced to a skeleton, was the tallest structure for miles around – everything around it was just ash.

Both cities struggled for years to get back on their feet. It was not until 1949, when the Japanese Diet passed specific laws allowing for their reconstruction, that the people of Hiroshima and Nagasaki were able to think properly about how to commemorate what they had been through.

In Hiroshima, a new plan was drawn up which included a significant memorial space in the former Nakajima district, once the commercial heart of the city. There was to be a museum devoted to the history of the bombing; a 'peace park' for the quiet contemplation of the apocalypse that had taken place; and monuments to the destruction, to the dead, and to hopes of rebirth. A design competition was held, and of the 145 proposals submitted, the city chose one by the modernist architect Kenzo Tange.

From the very beginning, the ruins of the Industrial Promotion Hall – now known as the 'A-Bomb Dome' – were central to Tange's design. His Peace Memorial Park was deliberately constructed with a museum at one end, the A-Bomb Dome at the other, and an arch-shaped Cenotaph in between. Wherever you stand on the central axis that links these three points, the A-Bomb Dome is always ahead of you. Furthermore, if you stand before the Cenotaph to pray for the dead, as the city's representatives do each August in their annual Peace Ceremony, you automatically find yourself gazing directly through its arch towards the A-Bomb Dome, which forms the main focal point of the memorial space.

As Japanese designers and historians often point out, the overall effect is similar to that in a Shinto shrine. The main entrance at the south end of the Peace Memorial Park is through the museum, which is built on pillars or pilotis: you pass beneath it, just as you would pass beneath a shrine's ceremonial gateway. The central path through the park is like a shrine's ceremonial path. It leads up to the Cenotaph, which is like the oratory, or *haiden,* where worshippers come to pray. Beyond this, the A-Bomb Dome stands like a shrine's most sacred building, the *honden.* By building the park in this way, Tange elevated the A-Bomb Dome from a mere ruin to an object of sacred significance: it is as if the souls of all of Hiroshima's 140,000 atomic bomb victims are enshrined here.

Even for those who know nothing of Shinto architecture, there is something darkly compelling about this building. While the rest of central Hiroshima has been redesigned and rebuilt from scratch, the dome alone remains to remind us of the city that used to exist before the apocalypse. That it survived at all seems something of a miracle. It is just 160 metres (525 feet) from the hypocentre, and therefore received the full force of the blast. Like the relics preserved in the museum – the melted watches and the charred children's tricycles – the building is forever marked by the divine force that obliterated so much else.

For twenty years after the war, many of the city's residents wanted the A-Bomb Dome torn down. Its presence was a constant reminder of the horror they had suffered and now wished to put behind them. But school children in the city's Paper Crane Club repeatedly petitioned the city council to make the ruins into an official memorial, and in 1966 they got their way: the council voted unanimously to preserve the ruins 'forever'. Contributions began to pour in to pay for the reinforcement work, which was completed the following year.

Thirty years later, in 1996, the dome was declared a UNESCO World Heritage Site. It has become a place of pilgrimage for people from all over the world: over a million tourists come here each year. While the vast majority only pause beside the ruins for a few moments in order to take photos and selfies, there is still an air of almost religious solemnity here. Most people seem to have taken on board the primary message of the monument, written on a plaque at the front of the ruin, that it stands as a 'lesson for mankind'.

In Nagasaki, commemoration of the bomb that destroyed the city has taken a different form. In the months directly after the war, the ruins were just as symbolic as those in Hiroshima, and perhaps even more so. Urakami Cathedral, like Hiroshima's A-Bomb Dome, was very close to the hypocentre, and was extremely badly damaged. To Nagasaki's Christian population the ruins began to seem symbolic of the huge sacrifice that the city had been made to suffer. However, unlike the A-Bomb Dome, the cathedral was rebuilt after the war, and only a few small fragments of the ruined original were preserved. Instead, the city invested its emotional energy in a new, purpose-built monument – the Peace Statue.

The statue stands in its own space, separate from most of the city. Unlike in Hiroshima, the memorial landscape in Nagasaki is not in the central, downtown area, but in the suburb of Urakami, a few kilometres north of the main harbour. It is spread out across three different sites. First are the A-Bomb Museum and the Peace Memorial Hall, which stand next to one another, connected by a subterranean corridor. Second, a short walk away, is the A-bomb hypo-centre, now a small park scattered with various monuments and relics. Further away still, and out of sight of the other two places, is the Peace Park. It is here, at the northern end of the park, that the Peace Statue stands.

This is easily Nagasaki's most important monument to the bombing. At the base of the statue is a black marble vault containing the names of the atomic bomb victims. Just as Hiroshima's city representatives hold their Peace Ceremony in front of the Cenotaph facing the A-Bomb Dome, Nagasaki's representatives stand each year before this statue. Like the dome, it is, symbolically, a shrine to the dead.

The Peace Statue was designed by the sculptor Seibo Kitamura, and was inaugurated by the city of Nagasaki on the tenth anniversary of the bombing in August 1955. It shows a virile, god-like figure, 10 metres (32 feet) high, seated on a rock. One huge, muscular leg is folded beneath him in a symbol of quiet meditation, but the other leg is poised for action in case he is called to spring forward to assist humanity. With his right hand he points towards heaven, to the threat

Peace Statue, Nagasaki

of nuclear weapons. His outstretched left hand, however, symbolises tranquillity and world peace. His eyes are closed 'in a solemn prayer for the victims of the war'. According to the artist, the statue is supposed to symbolise the desire for global harmony, and the turning away from war.

Far fewer tourists come here than visit the much larger and more central Peace Park in Hiroshima; but the same atmosphere of pious pilgrimage is evident. I first visited this place on a rainy Monday afternoon in March, and yet there were still dozens of visitors standing solemnly before the statue, umbrellas in hand. Some were speaking Chinese, others Korean, and still others English – this may not be a UNESCO World Heritage Site, but it nevertheless attracts visitors from all over the world.

It has to be said that among local residents the statue is not universally loved. One local language scholar has called it 'a clumsy approximation of a Greco-Roman deity', which thus pays tribute 'to the civilisation that deliberately dropped atomic bombs on two cities populated mostly by non-combatants'. Others have drawn attention to its Buddhist symbolism – hardly appropriate, they say, considering that the community most devastated by the bomb was Nagasaki's long-persecuted Christian minority. In an interview with the *Japan Times*, local historian Shigeyuki Anan pointed out that the statue was built at a time when the Japanese government should have had other priorities. 'It cost ¥40 million to build, at a time when there was no legal protection at all yet for *hibakusha* [atomic bomb survivors]'. All these people bemoan the fact that Nagasaki did not preserve the ruins of the Urakami Cathedral as the city's main memorial to the destruction.

According to the sculptor himself, however, such critics are missing the point. Seibo Kitamura deliberately fused eastern and western styles in order to evoke 'the qualities of both Buddha and God'. His intention was always to transcend the barriers of race and religion, and try to build a sense of harmony between the two cultures that had spent so many years fighting one another. He wanted to create a monument that would be more than simply a lament to what had been lost. 'After experiencing that nightmarish war, that blood-curdling carnage, that unendurable horror,' he wrote, 'who could walk away without praying for peace?'

Today, when visiting the various monuments in Hiroshima and Nagasaki, it is possible to pick out certain themes in the commemoration. The first and most important is exactly the theme that Kitamura highlighted: 'praying for peace' is the leitmotif that dominates the memorial landscape in both cities.

In Hiroshima, the A-Bomb Dome stands among dozens of other monuments, almost all of them dedicated to the idea of peace. For example, there is a Children's Peace Monument, a Peace Cairn, a Flame of Peace, a Peace Bell, a Peace Clock Tower and a Pond of Peace. There is even a statue directly representing a Prayer for Peace. Near the middle of the park is a Peace Memorial Hall containing the names, photographs and stories of atomic bomb victims. Beyond the Peace Memorial Museum is an installation called the Gates of Peace. In case the point has not been driven home strongly enough, the main road that connects the park to the rest of the city is called Peace Boulevard. The A-Bomb Dome presides over this landscape as a chilling example of what lies in store for any nation that abandons the path of peace.

In Nagasaki, meanwhile, the Peace Statue represents some-thing similar. It too stands inside a Peace Park, near a Peace Fountain, a Monument of Peace, a Maiden of Peace, several Cranes of Peace, and many other sculptures devoted to the concepts of peace, love, friendship and life.

All this is significant. Japan today still has one of the

strongest peace movements anywhere in the world – indeed, a commitment to peace is enshrined in the Japanese constitution. The experience of the war, and the phenomenal destruction it brought upon Japan, and especially upon Hiroshima and Nagasaki, taught it a lesson that it has never forgotten.

The second major theme that arises from the fate of the two cities is a message of victimhood. Hiroshima and Nagasaki unquestioningly mark out Japan as a victim rather than a perpetrator of the war. Nowadays the Japanese government and the Japanese newspapers routinely portray Japan as 'the only A-bombed nation', and they have been doing so since at least the 1970s. The A-Bomb Dome, especially, plays an important role in this sense of victimhood: it is the greatest symbol of Japan's atomic martyrdom.

The idea has angered many of Japan's former enemies because it automatically implies a kind of absolution for the whole country. Today Japanese people do not always take responsibility for their past, partly because they do not feel they need to: they regard Hiroshima and Nagasaki as proof that they have already paid the price.

It is easy to be indignant about this, but there is a rather more praiseworthy flip side to such an idea of victimhood: at least the memorials in Hiroshima and Nagasaki say nothing about blame.

The ruins of the A-Bomb Dome have not been preserved, as the ruins of Oradour have, to show the barbarism of the enemy. In fact, there is almost no mention of any enemy at all. The plaque in front of the A-Bomb Dome makes mention of the 'single bomb' that turned the city 'into ashes' – it says nothing of the American airmen who dropped that bomb. The nearby museum does exactly the same: it is dedicated to 'the horrors and the inhuman nature of nuclear weapons', not to any vilification of the American leaders who dared to use them.

Similarly, at Nagasaki's Peace Statue, the only enemies mentioned are 'the atomic bomb' and the abstract concept of 'war'. As you walk around the park, you will find no references to America, or President Truman, or the US Army Air Force. Furthermore, as Hiroko Okuda of Nanzan University has pointed out, the Japanese word for 'victim' used in Nagasaki commemorations is not *higaisha*, implying a victim who has suffered at the hands of another person, but *giseisha*, implying merely someone who suffers. It is almost as if the A-bomb was not perpetrated by an enemy at all, but was rather the result of some natural disaster, like an earthquake or a tsunami.

Thus Japan not only evades its own responsibility for the war, but allows its former enemies to evade their responsibilities too. This is not quite the same as forgiveness and reconciliation – nevertheless, it forms the basis of a new friendship that has served Japan and the USA well ever since 1945.

The final major theme on display at Hiroshima and Nagasaki is slightly more subtle. It involves the idea of national rebirth.

In Nagasaki's Peace Park, a short distance from the colossal Peace Statue, is a 'World Peace Symbols Zone'. This was established in 1978 by the city authorities, who invited donations of monuments from other nations around the world. There are sculptures here from several European countries, as well as from China, the Soviet Union, Argentina, Brazil, the USA, Australia, New Zealand and many others. If each sculpture represents a different nation, then that begs the question: what nation does the *main* Peace Statue represent? Is it possible that it doesn't symbolise international harmony after all, as its sculptor claimed? Does it perhaps represent Japan itself?

In the aftermath of the war, Japan knew that it had to change its ways, and do so rapidly. Less than two weeks after its historic surrender, before the Americans had even had the chance to occupy the country, the head of the Japanese government's Information Bureau was touting the experience of the atom bomb as the key to changing Japan's image in the world. In an article in one of Japan's national newspapers, *Asahi Shimbun*, he announced that the best way of showing 'repentance' was to wholeheartedly embrace the concept of peace. He suggested that by taking a lead role in a movement to prohibit the future use of nuclear weapons, the Japanese might be able to turn themselves from the 'losers of the war' into the 'winners of the peace'.

When I look at Nagasaki's colossal Peace Statue, I can't help remembering these words. It seems to me that this giant muscular figure does not in some ways represent 'peace' at all, but rather the might of the nation. Its obvious physical power seems to reflect the martial virtues that Japan had always strived for before and during the war. When the statue was inaugurated, the country was already on the path back to its former economic and national health. As the nation grew in strength during the 1950s and 1960s, statues like this were surely an effective way of reassuring Japan's neighbours that this new-found power was nothing to worry about. And perhaps not only Japan's neighbours, but also the people of Japan itself. As long as the nation's most iconic war monuments were devoted to the concept of peace, and not martial glory, there was no reason for Japan to be afraid of its own strength.

Even the A-Bomb Dome in Hiroshima flirts with this idea. The contrast between the ruins and the shiny new buildings that have risen out of the ashes has always been a part of the dome's emotional power. It is only by remembering how completely the city was destroyed that we can fully appreciate the miracle of Hiroshima's rebirth. The A-Bomb Dome is a measuring stick, which allows the people of Japan – and indeed the world – to see how far the nation has come in the years since 1945.

Hiroshima and Nagasaki will forever be tied to the events of August 1945. Rightly or wrongly, many people have come to regard them as the sacrifice that Japan had to make in order to bring an end to the war. Even some Japanese people occasionally refer to them this way. One of Nagasaki's most famous *hibakushas*, Takashi Nagai, called his city 'a whole-burnt offering on an altar of sacrifice, atoning for the sins of all the nations during World War II'.

The example of Hiroshima and Nagasaki has since served as a lesson to the rest of Japan – to modernise, to reinvent itself, and to embrace its former enemies. Like so many other places I have described so far, they have become prisoners of their history. But in the process, to a certain degree, they have also set their nation free.

Today, Hiroshima's A-Bomb Dome and Nagasaki's Peace Statue are symbols that resonate not only in Japan, but on the world stage. They represent a new danger that threatened the world for the first time after 1945 – the threat of nuclear war. But they also represent something more hopeful: a new age, and a new world order that was born out of the ashes of war. As such, perhaps they are not symbols of the apocalypse at all, but rather symbols of rebirth – not just on a national scale, but on an international one too.

This is the concept I will explore in the final part of this book.

Part V

Rebirth

The end of the Second World War in 1945 unleashed a wave of hope around the world. After years of conflict and destruction, the possibility of a lasting peace finally seemed within reach. The bombs would stop falling. The killing would stop. And the men and women who had devoted their lives to fighting would now be allowed to go home.

The atmosphere of hope inspired by the end of the hostilities was universal, and spread even to those parts that had suffered little or no violence during the war. The rhetoric of freedom, which had inspired the world to fight the forces of fascism, now inspired it to throw off other forms of oppression. In South America, for example, the years between 1945 and 1948 saw nations across the continent toppling their dictators at an unprecedented pace: a new age of democracy seemed to be dawning. Likewise, national leaders in Africa and Asia began to talk of a new era of self-determination: it was time for colonial peoples to throw off the yoke of imperialism and start governing their own affairs. In Europe, where the war had destroyed so much of the physical and institutional infrastructure, people everywhere saw the opportunity to build a kinder, fairer society, untainted by the old traditions that had led them to war in the first place: 1945 saw the birth of social security, social housing projects and health-care systems across the continent.

Some of our most moving Second World War monuments celebrate not the war itself, but the dawn of this new era of hope and peace. Many traditional monuments are worth mentioning. The Joy of Life Fountain in Rostock, Germany, and the Tree of Life Memorial in Birmingham in the UK both depict new life rising from the rubble of cities destroyed by bombing during the war. Numerous statues around the world depict wartime parents holding up babies – a symbol duplicated in real life by the baby boom that happened after the war ended. In the Hiroshima Peace Memorial Park, for example, there is a statue of a mother and her baby standing upon a crescent moon: the baby blows a trumpet to signify the beginning of a new, more peaceful era. Even some of the memorials dedicated to tragedy and destruction have room for a similar idea of rebirth. In the garden of the Nanjing Memorial Hall, for example, a goddess of peace stands upon a tall column. She too holds up a smiling child.

Such statues can be quite moving, but for the sake of variety I would like once again to widen our understanding of what constitutes a monument. In the last few chapters I will explore some of our less traditional memorial spaces. They include a painting, a balcony, a church and a hiking trail. Sometimes monuments can be all the more powerful for the fact that they appear to us in unexpected guises.

UN Security Council chamber, New York

22

United Nations: UN Security Council Chamber Mural, New York

In New York City stands one of the great icons of the post-war world – the United Nations headquarters. This complex of buildings was created by architects from every part of the globe, working in collaboration. It was built out of concrete, steel and glass – the materials of the new age. Like so many other buildings raised in the years after 1945, it was designed to be symbolic of everything that had been won during the war: freedom, hope, modernity, international cooperation and, most of all, rebirth.

If you walk around the UN headquarters today, you will find plenty of monumental works of art that represent the end of war and the birth of a new age of peace. There is a giant sculpture of a sword being beaten into a ploughshare, and another of a gun whose barrel has been tied in a knot. In front of the Secretariat building is a sculpture of St George slaying a dragon, entitled 'Good Defeats Evil': the dragon is made from pieces of scrapped nuclear missiles.

However, perhaps the most eloquent expression of what the UN is supposed to stand for is not in the architecture, or in the sculptures that litter the grounds, but in the decoration

of the most important room in the organisation. At the back of
the UN complex, in the Conference Building, is a large
chamber reserved for meetings of the UN's most powerful
organ, the Security Council. It is here that the world's leading
powers gather to discuss global peace and security. On the
wall above the circular debating table is a huge mural, some
9 metres (29 feet) wide and 5 metres (16 feet) high: it
completely dominates the room. It was painted by the
Norwegian artist Per Krohg in the aftermath of the Second
World War, and depicts a world coming back to life after years
of conflict. If you are looking for a single work of art that
sums up the United Nations and all it represents, then this
surely is it.

There are two parts to the mural. The lower part is painted
in dark, sombre colours, and shows a devastated landscape
full of shell holes and abandoned weapons. This world is very
much in the foreground. In the centre, curled around the
pillars of a subterranean bunker, a dragon plunges a sword
through its own body. On either side of this dying beast are
human figures in dire circumstances: some of them cower in
caves, others struggle to climb out of a dark abyss, others still
stagger, zombie-like, in chains.

The upper part of the painting depicts the world to which
all these figures are heading. This world is painted in bright
colours, and is full of happy, healthy-looking people in a
prosperous environment of order and plenty. Some of the
characters reach down to help those who are struggling up
from the lower region of the painting. On the left-hand side,
for example, a man has lowered a rope to a woman climbing
out of the abyss. On the right, an Asian man and a western
woman reach down to embrace some of the slaves in chains.

Everything about this brighter world speaks of freedom,

A close-up view of Per Krohg's mural

happiness and peace. On the left-hand side a woman throws open a pair of windows to let the light come flooding in. Closer to the centre, in a pair of rectangular panels, a community festival is going on: children of different races frolic, play drums and strew flowers, while their parents dance behind them in a line. One of the revellers holds up a UN flag. Along the top of the mural are scenes of peaceful activity: people on the left-hand side measure out grain, scientists on the right gaze through telescopes and microscopes, and between them are various artists, architects and musicians.

In the centre of the painting can be seen the figure of a phoenix rising from the chaos of the old, dying world beneath it. Behind this classical symbol of rebirth is an almond-shaped panel depicting the ideals that all nations are striving towards: a peaceful life of love and kindness. In Christian religious painting, particularly in church frescoes, the holiest images are always placed in a panel shaped exactly like this – it is called the 'mandorla'. For Per Krohg, who was very much influenced by Christian religious art, this is the most important part of his painting. It shows an idealised image of a loving family. A man and woman kneel together, surrounded by their children, clasping each other's arms in companionship. One child reaches down from a tree to hand a piece of fruit to his sister in a symbol of charity; while the youngest child reclines at his parents' feet, cradling a dove of peace.

These important, central images stand directly above the chair occupied by the president of the Security Council. They depict everything that the Council is supposed to be striving for: rebirth, charity, prosperity, brotherhood between peoples and, above all, peace.

As the Second World War entered its final stages in 1944 and 1945, these were the images that the whole world was crying out for. The creation of an organisation devoted to promoting world peace seemed to be an appropriate answer to all the years of hardship and violence. At a conference in Dumbarton Oaks in Washington, DC, representatives from Britain, China, the USA and the USSR hammered out a blueprint for exactly such an organisation. The spirit of their mission was probably best summed up by the head of the Chinese delegation, Dr Wellington Koo. 'The establishment of an effective international peace organisation,' he said, 'is the united hope and aspiration of all the freedom-loving peoples who have been making such heroic sacrifices in life, blood and toil. We owe it to them, as well as to humanity at large, to subordinate all other considerations to the achievement of our common object.'

Six months later, in April 1945, delegates from fifty nations gathered together in San Francisco in an attempt to bring this mission to fruition. Over the course of the next nine weeks they worked together to draft the United Nations' founding document, the UN Charter. Their success was greeted with universal enthusiasm. Newspapers across the world hailed it as 'a great historical act' (the *Gazette de Lausanne*), a 'great coalition for peace' (the *Times of India*), even a 'utopian garden' (*Straits Times*). 'Never before,' said the Nigerian campaigner Eyo Ita in the *West African Pilot*, 'has the human race seen a greater and better opportunity for a world community of free and equal peoples.'

Some of the most enthusiastic champions of the UN were from the one nation that had always previously tried to keep itself out of global affairs: the USA. American politicians from both parties seemed determined to outdo each other with their praise. Senator Tom Connally, a Democrat from Texas, called the UN Charter 'the most important document in the history of world statesmanship'. Republican Congressman Charles Eaton claimed it would lead to 'a golden age of freedom, justice, peace and social well-being'. The general public seemed to agree: in a Gallup poll taken in July 1945, those in favour of the United Nations Charter outnumbered those against by twenty to one. The whole world seemed to be imagining the same images that Per Krohg would soon be painting on the wall of the UN Security Council chamber.

It would be easy to dismiss all this as mere rhetoric, but in a world that was still being torn apart by war the prospect of future peace and harmony awoke deep longings to which it is difficult to do justice today. Some were almost religious in their intensity. One story, told by a French soldier, demonstrates exactly how desperate people were for an organisation like the United Nations. Jean Richardot was on the battlefield in northern France when he first heard about the UN. He was sheltering in a foxhole when a torn and muddy fragment of newspaper blew past. He grabbed it to distract himself from

288 PRISONERS OF HISTORY

his predicament. It carried a story about how the Allies were attempting to set up a new world organisation whose aim was 'to banish war forever from the face of the globe'. The news, he later confessed in his memoirs, 'had a tremendous impact on me – like a message sent by God. Right then and there I prayed for peace and the success of this great enterprise and, solemnly, in my foxhole, promised myself that I would do everything in my power to join this new organization if I came through the war alive.' After the war, true to his word, Richardot applied for a job at the UN. He was one of 20,000 applicants.

* * *

Unfortunately the UN was never quite able to live up to such ideals. Regardless of its aspirations, it simply is not set up in a way that promotes peace and harmony.

To begin with, the organisation was closely modelled on its predecessor, the pre-war League of Nations. Given that the League had been such an utter failure at preventing war in the 1930s, it was unclear why anyone believed that the UN would fare any better.

The most powerful organ of the UN was to be the one that would soon be meeting beneath Per Krohg's mural: the Security Council. This was effectively the heart and brains of the organisation. It was the only body with the power to make binding decisions that all member states were obliged to carry out. But it was not a council of equals. Five members were to have special privileges and responsibilities: Britain, China, France, the USA and the USSR. Unlike the other council members, the Big Five would not be elected to their seats every two years – they would have a permanent place at the table whether the rest of the world liked it or not. Furthermore, since the UN Charter states that all decisions of the Security Council must be unanimous, each of these five nations effectively had a permanent veto on any proposal they disagreed with.

In 1945, with the Second World War still raging, this made a certain amount of sense. These were the five nations that were doing most of the fighting in the war; and they were also the nations most likely to end up acting as the world's policemen once the war was over. It therefore seemed only fair that they should have a greater say than other nations in how their manpower and resources were to be deployed. However, structuring the Security Council like this also meant that power was entrenched in the hands of the very nations who were most capable of threatening world peace. As several smaller nations pointed out at the time, it was all very well to appoint the Big Five as policemen, but who was going to police the Big Five?

By the time Per Krohg's painting was unveiled in August 1952, the UN Security Council was already failing at its job. In the previous seven years it had presided over a catalogue of disappointments, largely because the veto powers of the Big Five had left it powerless to act. In the 1940s it had stood by as the Soviet Union enslaved much of eastern and central Europe. It had allowed France to reimpose colonial rule upon Algeria and Indochina, with disastrous consequences for both countries in the years to come. It had remained mute while Britain pursued its catastrophic policy of partition in India in 1947, and had likewise allowed the ethnic cleansing of Germans and other minorities from eastern Europe. The only time it had acted decisively was when it had intervened in the Korean War in 1950. But even this had not brought much cause for celebration: the war had been a bloodbath, and by the summer of 1952 it already looked as if it were going to end in stalemate.

Worst of all, the Security Council had proven powerless to end the increasingly bitter divide between the USA and the USSR.

The two superpowers disagreed on almost everything. By the time Per Krohg's painting was inaugurated, the Soviet Union had used its veto no fewer than forty-seven times, and the Security Council was virtually paralysed. A new Cold War had begun, fuelled by increasing paranoia on both sides, and backed up by nuclear weapons. (Nuclear proliferation was yet another dangerous development that the UN had failed to prevent.)

All this had taken place *before* Per Krohg painted his mural. If you look at the painting with this in mind, it begins to take on an entirely different meaning. It no longer seems like a depiction of the bright new world that was born out of the Second World War, because such a world demonstrably did not exist. Krohg himself never claimed it was a portrayal of the post-war world, saying only that he wanted to paint an ideal that lay somewhere in the future. '[T]he work of the UN and the Security Council [must] provide the seeds for a new and more valuable life,' he wrote; and, hopefully, his great mural would inspire them to strive towards this aim.

With this in mind, it seems painfully significant that the president of the Security Council always sits with his back to Krohg's painting. It is perhaps just as well, because the bright, harmonious world depicted in the top half of the picture is quite literally beyond the reach of anyone standing on the floor of the chamber. If the delegates were to look behind them, they would find themselves sitting among the forlorn figures at the bottom of the picture. In the summer of 1952, the foreground remained a place of darkness and struggle.

It is easy to be cynical about the United Nations from a distance; but cynicism is not something that the United Nations itself can afford. For the delegates who entered the gates of the organisation's headquarters in New York in the early 1950s, the expectations were huge, and the ensuing disappointments greater still. Such people needed ideals to strive for, otherwise where would they find the energy to keep up their endless struggle for compromise and consensus?

With this in mind, it is hardly surprising that idealism seems to be everywhere you look. Even for tourists coming here in the twenty-first century, the atmosphere of idealism is palpable. It is present in the art and the architecture. It is certainly present in Per Krohg's painting. It is hard to explain to someone who has never experienced the place for themselves, but there is an ambience of hope here every bit as tangible as that in the new Coventry Cathedral (see Chapter 24); and a feeling of earnestness at least as strong as that in Hiroshima Peace Memorial Park. But there is also a sense that, unlike those other places, here is a genuine chance for real change, if only the various delegates can muster the political will.

But if the United Nations is to make strides towards achieving world peace, then it must first make strides towards reforming itself. The first time I visited the UN Security Council chamber, what most struck me about it was how old-fashioned it looked. With its red leather chairs and dramatic lighting, the chamber itself looks like a time capsule left over from the 1950s. Krohg's painting, which dominates the eastern end of the room, looks hopelessly dated. It is not only a matter of the clothes, hats and hairstyles, which all belong to the 1940s and 1950s, but the bright colours themselves, which now look cartoonish. Some of the imagery also seems to belong to times gone by. For example, the clunky-looking telescope and microscope in the top right-hand corner no longer seem futuristic; and in an age dominated by social media, the old-fashioned idea of community portrayed here no longer feels quite real. If a complete overhaul of the chamber is out of the question, then surely at least some contemporary touches could be added to what is already there? A place of such symbolic importance needs to look relevant to our lives today.

The United Nations itself has also dated – and no organ more so than the one that sits in this particular chamber. The five great powers that still make up the core of the Security Council are no longer so powerful as they once were. Britain and France no longer command empires – they are today no greater than a dozen nations of similar size around the world. The Soviet Union is no more; and while Russia now holds the position that the USSR once held on the Security Council, it is a mere shadow of its predecessor. The only two nations that continue to dominate world affairs are the USA and China. In the meantime, nations that have grown in stature since 1945, such as Germany, Japan and India, have no greater say in UN affairs than do relative minnows like Liechtenstein or Micronesia.

Despite numerous attempts at reform, the Security Council has remained largely unchanged since its formation in 1945. Those who currently hold power are unwilling to relinquish it, regardless of their true position in global affairs; and no one can agree on whether, or how, to share power with the emerging world nations. Like Per Krohg's painting, it seems to be frozen in time.

In a curious way, therefore, the mural remains highly symbolic – although not, perhaps, in the way that Per Krohg intended it to be. The darkness of the foreground still feels unpleasantly close. The vision of Utopia in the background seems more out of reach than ever. And over it all hangs an atmosphere of paralysis that maintains us, like the characters inside the picture, as prisoners of history.

23

Israel: Balcony at Yad Vashem, Jerusalem

Not all monuments are statues or works of art. Not all monuments have plaques explaining what they represent. Sometimes our places of memory can come in surprising forms. A bridge, a gateway, a bunker, a ruin or a wall – even the simplest architectural feature can convey meaning, if viewed in the correct context.

This chapter is about exactly one such feature, the balcony at the end of the Holocaust museum at Yad Vashem in Jerusalem. Unlike every other architectural feature I have described so far, this one has never been the site of any particular historical event; indeed, it was only built in 2005. Despite this, it still carries a huge weight of historical meaning. It is a powerful symbol of rebirth – not only of a people, but of a political state – and as such it is as controversial as any of the other monuments in this book.

Yad Vashem is an unusual organisation. It was set up in 1953 after the Israeli Knesset voted unanimously to create a memorial site for the victims of the Holocaust. Over the following decades it developed in several different ways. It opened a

research institute, a library, a publishing house and an
International School for Holocaust Studies. It oversaw the
creation of a complex of memorials, which are dotted around
its grounds. And it opened a museum for the general public.
Today Yad Vashem is one of the world's foremost remembrance sites: in the words of Nobel Peace Prize laureate Elie
Wiesel, it is 'the heart and soul of Jewish memory'.

For the million or so people who visit each year, the
Holocaust History Museum is by far the most important
attraction. It was opened in 2005 to replace an older museum
dating back to the 1960s, and its architecture is one of its
most important elements. The museum building is a long,
narrow structure, shaped like a triangular prism, which slices
through Mount Herzl from one side to the other. Most of the
building is buried in the mountainside, but the two ends stick
out into the open air. One end is closed, like the box of a
Toblerone chocolate bar. But the other end holds a large, open
balcony which juts out over a forested valley below.

When you enter the museum, the balcony is one of the first
things you see. It stands at the very end of the dark, austere
walkway that forms the central axis of the museum: it is
literally the light at the end of a long tunnel. Your automatic
instinct is to head for this light, but you can't. The walkway
is blocked, repeatedly, by wires and trenches cut into the
concrete floor. There is no short cut to the balcony: it can
only be reached by zigzagging your way back and forth
through a series of dark rooms on either side of the central
walkway.

These rooms contain an increasingly harrowing history
of the attempted extermination of the Jews in Europe. The
exhibition starts with a poignant depiction of Jewish life
before the Holocaust, and proceeds through persecution,

imprisonment, massacre, ghettoisation, heroic resistance, and the horror of the concentration camps, to final liberation. Each time you cross the central walkway your eye is drawn towards the balcony at the end, but it remains out of reach.

The rooms grow progressively darker and more claustrophobic as you proceed. Videos, photos and information boards are all displayed against the grey, undecorated concrete of the museum walls. It is not until you are nearing the end of the exhibition, which shows the Jewish exodus from Europe towards Israel after the war, that the rooms open out again.

The final room is the Hall of Names: a circular vault where the biographical details of the millions of victims are stored.

It is only after you have left this final room that you are at last able to walk up a steep concrete slope towards the balcony at the end of the museum. As you step out through the doors into a flood of light, you are greeted with a panoramic view of the Judean hills. The effect is remarkably soothing. After the darkness, the concrete walls, the enclosed spaces and the terrible, terrible history, to stand here for a while looking at the sun shining on the trees below is an enormous relief.

The museum's architecture transforms it from an educational experience into a deeply emotional one. It takes you on a journey through the darkness and into the light, from the horrors of Europe to deliverance in Israel, out of apocalypse and into rebirth. The view from the balcony is the final exhibit in the museum. This is the reward that was granted to the survivors of the Holocaust as consolation for their suffering: the land of Israel, where they might at last find a safe home.

* * *

The message conveyed by the balcony is broadly similar to the message of Yad Vashem as a whole. The very existence of the memorial site is itself a symbol of rebirth and redemption. Yad Vashem was set up in 1953 by the Israeli government, but half of its initial funding came from the Conference on Jewish Material Claims against Germany. In other words, reparations payments from the former persecutor of the Jews were, aptly, used to create a permanent memorial to that persecution. The Claims Conference has continued to finance Yad Vashem ever since.

Yad Vashem was built on Mount Herzl, a site that was also highly symbolic. Unlike so many other places in and around Jerusalem, Mount Herzl is not associated with any aspect of ancient or biblical history. In other words, the location could not be placed within a long history of death and destruction, like Jerusalem's other Holocaust museum, the Chamber of the Holocaust: it was a fresh start. The founders of the memorial were effectively saying that this was where the historic persecution of the Jews would stop and finally be replaced with something new.

But that is not all. Mount Herzl is also a symbol of Israeli nationalism. It is named after Theodor Herzl, one of the founders of Zionism and the 'spiritual father of the Jewish State'. The body of Herzl himself was moved from his grave in Vienna and reinterred here in 1949. The hill is where Israel buries its national leaders, as well as its soldiers who have died in the line of duty. By the time Yad Vashem was instituted here, such traditions were already well established.

Today, Yad Vashem is intimately connected to the nearby sites belonging to the Israeli state. There is even a commemorative pathway joining them together. In case the message were not clear enough, a noticeboard spells it out explicitly.

The path, it states, links Yad Vashem to the national military cemetery, the national leaders' burial site and Herzl's grave: 'Passage along it is a symbolic voyage in time from catastrophe to rebirth. It represents the journey from the Diaspora to the homeland of the Jewish people, from exile and destruction to a life of endeavour and hope in the State of Israel.'

This is the official message that Israel preaches today. The Holocaust was a kind of apocalypse, but it was also the pathway to rebirth. Without the Holocaust, the state of Israel might never have come into being.

It is perhaps for this reason that visiting dignitaries to Israel are always given a tour of Yad Vashem before they embark upon official business. Foreign leaders first visit the Holocaust museum before laying a wreath in the nearby Hall of Remembrance. These visits are mandatory: according to one senior Israeli diplomat, Talya Lador-Fresher, any foreign leader who doesn't want to take part is politely told that they should not come to Israel at all. 'Yad Vashem is an important part of our history,' she told the *Times of Israel* in 2012. 'You cannot understand Israel, even today, without understanding the Holocaust.'

And so presidents and prime ministers from other countries are regularly taken to this long, prism-shaped building cut into the mountain outside Jerusalem. They must follow the route through the series of dark, claustrophobic rooms; and they must experience the relief of stepping out onto the balcony with its view of the Judean hills. They must see the history that Jews see. And they must feel it the way that Jews feel it. Yad Vashem, and its balcony, is an important diplomatic tool.

Like all nations, Israel is in thrall to its history. And like all nations, Israel strives hard to pay homage to the aspects of its history that illustrate a positive political message, and to avoid those that are not quite so attractive. It is what Israel ignores, and Yad Vashem omits, that makes this official message of redemption and rebirth so controversial.

First, it paints a rather rosy picture of the way that Holocaust survivors were treated when they arrived in Israel (or Palestine, as it was called until 1948) after the war. Many of the impoverished, bedraggled European Jews who disembarked from the ships at Haifa were given a chilly welcome by Palestinian-born Jews (or Sabras, as they had come to be known). Few Sabras properly understood quite how hopeless the situation in Europe had been during the war. Some regarded European Jews as weak and submissive people who had gone willingly 'like lambs to the slaughter'. As a consequence, while Holocaust survivors appreciated being given a new place to live away from Europe, they often did not feel at home here. It was not until the 1960s that Sabras and European Jews finally began to integrate more closely and accept one another more generally as brothers and sisters in the state of Israel.

Second, the idea that the new state of Israel was a safe haven for Jews is also hopelessly idealistic. At Yad Vashem, not far from the museum building, is a monument called the Memorial to the Last of Kin: it is dedicated to those Holocaust survivors who arrived in Israel as the final surviving members of their families, but who went on to die fighting for the new state. This indicates how dangerous Palestine was in the years immediately after the Second World War. In 1947, the country was already embroiled in a civil war between Jews and Arabs. The following year, when Israel declared its independence, it was invaded by several neighbouring states. If you had been able to stand on the balcony at Yad Vashem in 1948, the sight that greeted you would not have been one of peace and tranquillity at all. Israel was at war; and it would find itself at war again and again throughout the rest of the century.

The final point to make is perhaps the most controversial of all. The history on display at Yad Vashem is quite specifically *Jewish* history. Like national museums all over the world, it filters out the aspects of history that are not relevant to its immediate narrative. In this case, the most glaring silence involves the history of the Palestinian Arabs. I don't mean to criticise Yad Vashem for this: any museum must maintain its focus, and the purpose of this particular museum is to describe the horrors of the Holocaust, not the history of Arab–Jewish relations. Nevertheless, there is something faintly disingenuous about the way the architecture presents the land of Israel as a kind of divine gift to ease the suffering of the survivors of the Holocaust. Israel was not an empty land waiting to be colonised in 1948. Nor was it a kind of sanatorium, reserved for the rehabilitation of a traumatised people. It was a territory with a long and rich history of its own, much of which had nothing to do with Jews.

Jews undoubtedly have close spiritual and historical ties with this landscape, but in the 1940s that alone did not make it a Jewish land. Over the previous 1,500 years, the vast majority of the population had been Arab Palestinians, Bedouins and Christians. In all that time, the region had been ruled by a variety of Romans, Persians, Muslim caliphs, Mamluk sultans, Ottoman emperors and, since 1918, the British. Jews lived side by side with all these people over the centuries, but not in significant numbers. It was only towards the end of the nineteenth century, when immigrants started arriving from Europe, that the Jewish population began to grow once more. Successive waves of European Jews continued to move here in the 1920s and 1930s, often fleeing persecution elsewhere, but even by 1945 they made up less than a third of the population. Palestine was still an overwhelmingly Arab land.

In the early days of Zionist immigration Jews and Arabs generally lived side by side without too many problems. But inevitably there were Arabs who began to view the arrival of so many foreigners with resentment, particularly when they learned that Jews aimed not only to make this their homeland but eventually also to establish political control. In the early 1920s, riots broke out in Jerusalem and Jaffa and dozens of Jews were murdered. A few years later, after another riot, an Arab mob in Hebron massacred sixty-seven defenceless Jews, including women and children. A dangerous precedent had been set.

In retaliation, Jews set up their own militias. Most of these paramilitary groups were focused purely on protecting Jewish villages from attack, but some, including the infamous Irgun, were determined to be much more aggressive in their tactics. In retaliation for violence against Jews, they began terrorising Arab civilians. They targeted people in public locations such as buses, coffee shops and market places. On several occasions they threw hand grenades into Arab crowds in order to cause as much terror as possible. Another dangerous precedent had been set.

After the Second World War, tensions between the two sides increased still further; and both sides blamed the British for failing to bring the violence under control. Hardline Jewish organisations like the Irgun believed that the only way to properly protect themselves was to drive the British out of Palestine and take control of the country. They launched a series of terrorist attacks against the British, including the bombing of their headquarters in Jerusalem's King David

Hotel. Eventually, tired of mediating between the two sides, the British turned the problem over to the United Nations.

What happened next has been the subject of controversy ever since. When the UN voted to split Palestine into two parts – one for the Jews and one for the Arabs – Arab leaders refused to accept their decision. Attacks on Jews increased all over the country. In an effort to bring the matter to a close once and for all, Jewish troops simply seized the territory that they now regarded as their own, and drove away the Arabs who lived there. The only way to protect Jewish communities was to expel as many Arabs as possible – the innocent along with the guilty.

According to the official version of this violent chapter in Israel's early history, the Arabs were never formally expelled but fled of their own accord. But even the Jewish soldiers who took part in these operations acknowledge that Arabs were purposely driven away, and that an atmosphere of extreme violence encouraged them to go. Hundreds of villages were cleared in this way.

Inevitably there were atrocities. The most famous occurred in the village of Deir Yassin, not far from Jerusalem. In April 1948, just a month before Israel formally declared its independence, Jewish paramilitary forces entered the village and killed the majority of its inhabitants with guns and grenades. Once again, the Irgun played a central role in the action. At least a hundred people were massacred, including women and children. Just as the Hebron massacre of 1929 had become a symbol of Arab violence against Jews, so the Deir Yassin massacre would soon become a symbol of Jewish violence against Arabs.

A month later, the state of Israel was declared. After a brief but decisive war against its Arab neighbours, who tried to

destroy the new country even before it had a chance to establish itself, an uneasy peace descended. That uneasiness has
remained ever since.

None of this is mentioned in the exhibition at Yad Vashem.
And neither should it be: it is a subject for another institution,
not for a place dedicated to the memory of the Holocaust.
But foreign leaders who are brought to the museum for political reasons should remember that other stories about Israel's
past exist alongside the narrative presented here. The balcony
at the end of the exhibition, and its view over the Judean hills,
is not quite the happy ending that it seems.

Arabs have their own organisations devoted to ensuring
that the past is not forgotten. Many of them like to point out
that when one stands on the balcony at Yad Vashem and looks
north, one can see the hilltop where the village of Deir Yassin
used to stand.

To their great credit, certain Jewish organisations also strive
to remember this past. One of them, an organisation called
Deir Yassin Remembered, has this to say about Yad Vashem:

> The Holocaust museum is beautiful, and the message 'never
> to forget man's inhumanity to man' is timeless. The children's
> museum is particularly heart wrenching; in a dark room filled
> with candles and mirrors the names of Jewish children who
> perished in the Holocaust are read along with their places of
> birth. Even the most callous person is brought to tears. Upon
> exiting this portion of the museum a visitor is facing north
> and looking directly at Deir Yassin. There are no markers, no
> plaques, no memorials, and no mention from any tour guide.
> But for those who know what they are looking at, the irony
> is breathtaking.

Israelis cannot escape this history any more than they can escape the history of the events that took place during the Second World War. The rebirth of the Jewish people in Israel was indeed something tender and beautiful, but it was not nearly as straightforward as the iconic balcony at Yad Vashem implies. It was a messy, violent business, with winners and losers.

If Israelis really wish to come to terms with their past, they must remind themselves occasionally that for all the terrible power that the Holocaust still has over Israeli memory, it was not the only painful event that preceded the birth of their nation.

The ruins of Coventry Cathedral

24

UK: Coventry Cathedral
and the Cross of Nails

Of all the cities that were bombed in Britain during the Second World War, one has always stood out. Coventry is a city that became internationally famous after it was attacked in 1940: in symbolic terms, it is the closest that Britain has to Dresden in Germany or Hiroshima in Japan.

At the centre of Coventry stands a monument to this great tragedy. The ruins of Coventry Cathedral are probably the city's most famous landmark, and stand as a permanent reminder of the effects of the Second World War. The remains of red sandstone walls jut out of the ground like jagged teeth. Gothic windows stand empty, their ancient glass long since shattered or removed. The space once enclosed within the chancel, the nave and the aisles now lies open to the elements, with tufts of grass sprouting between the exposed flagstones of what used to be the church floor. Broken stumps of pillars form an avenue down the centre and, a little to one side, the remains of a stone staircase mark where the pulpit used to be before, like the rest of the church, it was burned down.

The site might have ended up being a symbol of terror and apocalypse, much like the ruins of Oradour-sur-Glane in

France. But in fact this is not its main message: other, more religious sentiments have won through instead. The ruins of Coventry Cathedral are a much richer and more hopeful monument than almost any other I have covered so far.

To understand how this transformation came about, one needs to look much more closely at the catastrophe that took place here during the war, and the dramatic impact it has made on Coventry's subsequent history.

The bombing that took place here on the night of 14 November 1940 was easily the most sustained raid carried out on Britain until this point in the war. It began soon after 7 p.m. and continued all night. By the time the last bombs landed some ten hours later, more than four hundred German planes had dropped over 500 tonnes of explosives and incendiaries on the city. A fraction of the quantity later dropped on cities like Hamburg and Dresden, it was nevertheless an enormous amount by the standards of the time.

The bombers were guided to their target by a revolutionary system of radar beams, but by all accounts the majority of them did not need it: within a short time the city was burning so brightly that it was visible for miles around. 'I have never seen such a concentration of fire during a raid, not even on London,' claimed Günter Unger, one of the German pilots who flew that night. 'Usually in our target cities the area of fires was dispersed, but not this time. There was no chance of missing the target.'

The Germans had good reason to bomb Coventry: the city contained some of the biggest and most important industrial complexes in the country. There were factories that produced aircraft engines, armoured cars, barrage balloons, electrical equipment, machine tools, VHF radios and many other items essential for the British war effort. But this was not the only reason to bomb the city. According to German propaganda, the bombing was carried out in retaliation for an earlier British raid on Munich. In other words, it was simply the latest victim in a cycle of reprisal and counter-reprisal that had been going on ever since the bomber war began.

Several of Coventry's factories were badly damaged by the German bombs, including the Triumph motor manufacturers and the General Electric Company's cable works, which were completely devastated. But alongside these military targets, thousands of civilian buildings were also destroyed. The Coventry City Library burned down, as did a brand new department store, a school and a hospital. Scores of shops, public buildings and offices were destroyed, along with 2,500 civilian houses. Another 20,000 houses were so badly damaged that they were considered uninhabitable.

Amid all this destruction stood the cathedral. The provost, Richard Howard, did his best to save it from the fires. He and three other volunteers braved the terror of the night in order to watch for incendiaries – but in the event, the bombs fell so thick and fast that the four of them were quickly overwhelmed. The fire brigade arrived after the fires had already taken hold, but when the water mains gave out even they were unable to save the building. In the end, firefighters and clergy alike were forced to stand and watch as the cathedral, along with the rest of the centre of Coventry, burned to the ground.

In the days that followed, the propaganda machines of both sides tried to make use of these events. The Nazis quickly proclaimed their bombing raid as a symbol of strength. The city, said one radio broadcast, had been 'smashed completely'. Another broadcast claimed that Coventry's factories had been damaged so badly that they would never work again: 'This was a total, not partial, destruction of Coventry.' Hitler's propaganda machine even coined a new word – *coventrieren*, 'to Coventrate' – with the implication that this was an act they could repeat again and again at will. It suggested that Britain would do well to capitulate sooner or later, because Germany was bound to win in the end.

The British newspapers, meanwhile, used Coventry as a potent emblem of Nazi brutality. In an editorial dated 16 November, *The Times* called Coventry 'A Martyred City' – a description that would define Coventry for the rest of the war. Almost every newspaper carried photographs of the ruined cathedral – partly because they were much more emotive than any picture of a ruined factory, but also because they made the German raid seem much more illegitimate and barbaric.

When these images made their way across the Atlantic, they became a useful tool in the recruitment of US support for Britain. A report in the *New York Herald Tribune* was typical: 'The gaunt ruins of St Michael's Cathedral, Coventry, stare from the photos,' it declared, 'the voiceless symbol of the insane, the unfathomable barbarity, which had been released on Western civilisation. No means of defense which the United States can place in British hands should be withheld.'

The pictures also made a rallying cry for those in Britain who wanted revenge. The front page of the *Sunday Express* on 17 November spoke volumes. It too showed a photograph of the ruined cathedral; and above it, running across the width of the paper, the headline read, 'Please God, you will avenge what was done to us that night'.

Both sides were attempting to use Coventry as a symbol of their respective causes. However, alongside the wartime propaganda, other voices were calling for a very different kind of symbolism. In Coventry itself, some of the city's most influential people appealed instead to a more spiritual set of values based on Christian tradition.

On the morning after the bombing, provost Richard Howard made a solemn declaration to his congregation. 'The cathedral will rise again,' he said, 'will be rebuilt, and it will be as great a pride to future generations as it has been to generations in the past.' To laymen this might have sounded like a straightforward statement of defiance: despite the destruction of his cathedral, he was refusing to admit defeat. However, there was more to it than that. Howard was expressing a vision of the doctrine that is central to Christianity: the resurrection. He was using the cathedral as a metaphor for Christ himself. It too would rise again from the dead.

Six weeks later, Provost Howard went a step further. In a Christmas message to the nation, broadcast by radio from the ruins of the cathedral, he spelt out his vision of what the future should look like. 'What we want to tell the world is this: that with Christ born again in our hearts today, we are trying, hard as it may be, to banish all thoughts of revenge . . . We are going to try to make a kinder, simpler, a more Christ-Child-like sort of world in the days beyond this strife.'

Many others in Coventry followed Howard's lead. In the weeks after the bombing, the cathedral's stonemason, Jock Forbes, gathered together some of the larger stones among the rubble and constructed a makeshift altar, so that services could continue to be held in the ruined church. He then picked up two charred oak roof beams and bound them together in the shape of a cross. This charred cross has been preserved, and remains on display inside the church to this day.

Meanwhile, a local priest named Arthur Wales made

another cross out of three medieval roof nails that he scavenged from the rubble. At first he tied them together with wire, but later he had them welded and plated. This 'Cross of Nails' was set upon the altar. It has been a potent symbol ever since of the cathedral and all it stands for.

Finally, after the war, the words 'Father Forgive' were inscribed on the stonework of the sanctuary. The words can still be seen today, written on the wall in gold lettering.

Unfortunately, in 1940 the world was not yet ready for this message of forgiveness. There was still a war to be won. Over the following months the bombing only intensified: Coventry ultimately proved to be just one target in a long list of British cities that were heavily damaged in the Blitz. In return, the RAF conducted devastating raids on Lübeck, Rostock, Cologne, Hamburg, Dresden, and a hundred other German towns and cities. The Second World War left cities all over Europe in ruins.

It was not until 1945, when the war finally came to an end, that anyone could seriously put their minds to rebuilding. In many places it took years just to clear the debris away. The rubble in Coventry Cathedral itself, for example, was not cleared until 1947, almost seven years after its destruction.

All over Europe, debates took place about how rebuilding should be carried out. Many people simply wanted their cities to be returned to the way they had been before the war; but there were others who saw the destruction as an opportunity to build something new, better, and more in tune with the needs of the post-war era. One of those people was Donald Gibson, Coventry's town planner. Gibson famously called the bombing 'a blessing in disguise': the Germans had 'cleared out the core of the city,' he said, 'and now we can start anew'.

In the years to come, Coventry would be regarded as a trail-blazer for modern city planning in Britain. It would be the first British city to make its town centre entirely car free: instead of driving into town, motorists would leave their cars in new, specially built parking garages and navigate their way around the shops on foot. With Gibson's new city plan, the old, historic streets, damaged and destroyed by the war, were swept away and replaced by a modern shopping centre with wide avenues and plazas free of noise and pollution.

Soon the city began to adopt a new symbol: the phoenix. When the 'Levelling Stone' was ceremonially laid in the centre of Coventry in 1946 to mark the start of the city's reconstruction, it was carved with an image of a phoenix. Phoenixes were added to the city's coat of arms, and to the logo of the city's Lanchester Polytechnic, now Coventry University. At the beginning of the 1960s, local artist George Wagstaffe was commissioned to erect a statue of a phoenix in the centre of Market Way. Today the mythical bird appears all over the city.

Perhaps the greatest phoenix of all was the cathedral itself. There had been plans to rebuild the historic building ever since Provost Howard made his famous declaration on the morning after the bombing, but progress had been slow because of a shortage of resources during and after the war.

Arguments raged back and forth about how the cathedral should be reconstructed, but eventually the decision was made to hold an open competition. In 1950 architects from all over the country were invited to submit plans. According to their brief, there was no reason to keep most of the ruins of the old cathedral – just the surviving tower and spire. Consequently, the vast majority of entrants envisaged either incorporating the ruins into a new building, or sweeping them away entirely.

The winning entry, by Basil Spence, was one of the few

designs that left the ruins of the old building as they were. Spence's idea was to build a brand new cathedral alongside the ruins, with a gigantic porch linking the two spaces together. The idea was, in his words, to build something 'that stood for the triumph of the resurrection' – in other words, to give concrete form to the religious image of Christ rising from the dead. In more secular terms, he was expressing the same as the city planners were doing elsewhere – the city of Coventry rising like a phoenix from the ashes.

And so the building of the new cathedral went ahead. The foundation stone was laid by Queen Elizabeth II in 1956. The building was completed six years later, a modernist master-piece of red sandstone, polished marble, reinforced concrete and a blaze of stained-glass windows. To this day, the original 'Cross of Nails' stands upon the high altar as a permanent reminder of the destruction of 1940, and of the resurrection that has been taking place ever since.

The new cathedral stands beside the ruins of the old.
They are linked by a huge, concrete porch

While the planning and rebuilding was taking place, Provost Howard also went about trying to live up to his wartime promise to try to create a kinder, 'more Christ-Child-like sort of world'. Now that the war was over, he was at last free to pursue his vision of forgiveness and reconciliation between nations. As early as 1946, he conducted a service in which the Bishop of Hamburg also took part via radio link. The following year he established a strong link with Kiel in northern Germany, and sent a 'Cross of Nails' to the city as a symbol of reconciliation. In the following months, more crosses were sent to Dresden, Berlin and several other German cities that had suffered from British bombing.

Over the years, Howard and his successors built up a community of fellow sufferers with ruined and rebuilt churches throughout Germany. These included the Kaiser Wilhelm Memorial Church in Berlin, which, much like Coventry Cathedral, was preserved as a ruin with a new, modernist church built alongside it. It also included the ruins of the Nikolaikirche in Hamburg, which has been preserved as a memorial to the firestorm; and St Katherine's church in the same city, which was rebuilt. And, perhaps most significantly of all, it included the Frauenkirche in Dresden. The Frauenkirche and Coventry Cathedral regularly hold exchange visits, especially on the anniversaries of each other's bombing raids.

Today, the idea of reconciliation is at the core of everything that Coventry Cathedral does. As one walks around the ruins of the old cathedral, it is not the symbols of destruction that dominate, but those of rebirth and reconciliation. In the north-west corner is a sculpture donated by the Frauenkirche in Dresden, which represents the survivors of bombing. Near it is another statue entitled 'Reconciliation', which is one of an identical pair – the other is in Hiroshima's Peace Memorial Park. The information board at the south side of the nave briefly describes the destruction of 1940 before giving a much lengthier description of the cathedral's reconciliation work around the world. Since 1945 the cathedral has formed links with more than 180 likeminded organisations in every continent, devoted to the idea of reconciliation between peoples. In recognition of its origins in Coventry, this worldwide partnership is called the 'Community of the Cross of Nails'.

Coventry as a city has embraced the same work. It officially styles itself the 'City of Peace and Reconciliation', and has been twinned with many other martyred cities around the world, including several already mentioned in this book: Volgograd, Warsaw, Dresden and Hiroshima. Its main theatre is named the Belgrade Theatre in honour of the Yugoslavian city destroyed by German bombers in 1941. It has streets named after the village of Lidice, which was razed to the ground by the Nazis in 1942; and the German town of Meschede, destroyed by the US Army Air Force in 1945.

I would love to be able to write that, through its reconciliation work, Coventry has managed to transcend the tragedies of the past – but of course things are never quite so simple. History is a prison from which no one escapes.

No matter how many symbols of reconciliation and rebirth are dotted around the ruins of Coventry Cathedral, it is still the ruins themselves that speak most eloquently. If the new cathedral next door is a symbol of the resurrection, then the ruins represent pure destruction. Their jagged outline against the sky is a permanent reminder of Coventry's martyrdom in November 1940.

Coventry today is Britain's closest equivalent to Dresden in Germany, or Hiroshima in Japan, and it is still regularly mentioned in the same breath as these other cities. This is not because the destruction that took place here was anywhere near as bad – 40 times as many people died in the bombing of Dresden, and around 250 times as many eventually died in Hiroshima. However, Coventry happened first, and thus was the harbinger of the devastation that was to come. In the British and American popular imagination, the destruction of Coventry and its famous cathedral has become a microcosm of the whole bombing war.

The resurrection that took place in this city is also partly a myth. Coventry's rebirth was never quite as glorious as the brochures and postcards of the 1950s and 1960s promised. The city centre boomed during those years, but in later decades began to look tired and grey. It was partially regenerated in the 1990s, and is undergoing a further round of regeneration even as I write. But no amount of modern planning will ever adequately replace the picturesque medieval city that was destroyed by both the German bombers and the British town planners of the 1930s, 1940s and 1950s. The ruins of the cathedral are a reminder of exactly what was lost.

The city is no longer the prosperous place that it was during the boom years of the mid-twentieth century. The dozens of factories that once attracted the ire of the Luftwaffe are long gone, much as they are across Britain. In recent decades Coventry has become a symbol of Britain's industrial decline. In the 1980s it had one of the highest unemployment rates in the country, and even today unemployment is far higher than the UK average. No matter how often the city's civic and religious institutions champion the idea of rebirth, there is still a feeling that the Second World War took a toll on the city, and that the post-war European consensus has let the people of Coventry down. This disillusionment was reflected in the 2016 Brexit referendum, when the majority of Coventry's voters elected to leave the European Union.

When you stand among the ruins of the old cathedral, it is difficult not to see these things as well as the story of rebirth towards which the church authorities so eagerly point you. The history of destruction necessarily precedes the history of reconciliation.

Like so many other places covered in this book, Coventry and its cathedral will always be defined by its Second World War history. Nevertheless, it has come closer than most to

Cross of Nails

rising above that history. The city continues to dream of rebirth, no matter how elusive that may be. The cathedral continues to pursue its work of reconciliation, both locally and in the wider world, regardless of its endless challenges.

Its people continue to do this, as they have done for more than eighty years, by harnessing the emotive power of the monument that still stands at the heart of their community: the cathedral ruins that remain one of the most richly complex monuments in the world today.

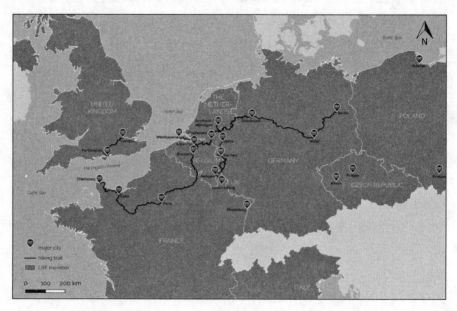

Liberation Route Europe's international hiking trail

25

European Union:
Liberation Route Europe

Monuments come in all shapes and sizes. During the course of this book I have explored the meanings and motivations behind a wide variety of memorials – not only conventional statues but also abstract sculptures, murals, architectural features, museums and memorial parks, ruined buildings and ruined villages, concentration camps, cemeteries, tombs and shrines. All these have become repositories for our memories of the Second World War. They are used to transmit those memories across the generations, so that even when there are no longer any veterans of the war left alive, we will continue to remember what they witnessed during the most tragic and dramatic events of the last century.

The final monument I would like to describe is different once again. It is a hiking trail that stretches for 2,000 kilometres (1240 miles) and spans several countries, following the route that the western Allies took during the liberation of Europe in 1944–5. As a transnational monument, it is by far the biggest memorial in this book. It is also the newest – in fact, at the time of writing, it does not yet even exist. It is due to be inaugurated in May 2020, the same month as the

seventy-fifth anniversary of Germany's surrender and the end
of the war in Europe.

The Liberation Route Europe bills itself as a hiking trail,
but in fact it is a memory trail linking the main sites of the
liberation of western Europe. It begins in London at the
Churchill War Rooms, where the idea for an invasion of
Europe was first discussed; and it ends in Berlin, where Nazism
finally reached its bitter end. Along the way it travels through
Normandy, Paris, Brussels, Arnhem and the sites of the Battle
of the Bulge, before crossing into Germany. Strictly speaking
it is not one route, but several, with numerous branches that
reach out into other places where major battles took place.

Those who walk the trail will be following in the footsteps
of the vast armies that fought their way through the continent
in 1944–5. Their journey will therefore be a kind of homage
to the memory of another, much tougher journey that took
place so many decades ago. The route takes in hundreds of
sites of memory along the way. Travellers will be able to visit
the major memorials, cemeteries and museums that are scattered along the route. They will walk on the very battlefields
where tens of thousands sacrificed their lives. And, all the
while, they will accumulate stories not only of the profound
events that took place in each location, but also of many of
the individuals who took part.

Among the most important aspects of the trail will be the
website and mobile app that accompany it, so that even in
the remotest sections of the route, its followers will be able
to download stories and descriptions of the events that took
place exactly where they are standing. In other words, this is
a monument that exists as much in the digital, virtual world
as it does in the physical world.

According to Rémi Praud, the director of Liberation Route

Europe, the organisation that created the hiking trail, the digital aspect of the project is essential. 'This is a new way of doing things,' he told me. 'You don't have any transnational monuments like this one, with different locations and so on . . . We want to make it a bit more modern, a bit more appealing for young generations and all types of audience, like hikers, tourists, families – not just the people that come to commemorations every year.'

For those who have no time to walk the entire route, the journey will be available online. However, the real emotional power of the trail lies in the experience of visiting the physical locations of the war's historic events.

To signify that this is a walking trail with a single message and purpose that brings together all these stories and events, the route will be signposted by waymarkers built to a common design. Specially devised by the architect Daniel Libeskind, they each consist of a spiral of metal and concrete, enclosing a sharp, triangular fin called a 'vector'. Some will be placed on the ground and others mounted on walls; and at major points along the way there will be larger versions, forming monuments in their own right.

The message of these vectors is clear. The smaller versions consist of sharp metal spikes. The larger, monumental versions are like a blade rising out of the ground and both large and small will point at Berlin. There is an inherent sense of threat in these sharp metal objects. But there is also a singleness of purpose: they all point one way. The armies that passed along the route in 1944–5 were not on a pleasure trip: they were driving a spearhead through the continent towards the heart of the beast that had terrorised the people of Europe for years.

In June 2019 I interviewed Daniel Libeskind about the

Hypothetical design for a 'Vector' monument at Normandy, one of
the key points on the Liberation Route hiking trail

meaning behind his vectors, and what they were supposed to
represent. He told me that their blade-like appearance was an
important aspect of the design: 'Yes, it has a sharpness, definitely, that's part of it, because it's cutting through all the evils
of history towards something good.' But more important was
the fact that all the markers point the same way. 'They are all
of different sizes; and they play different roles . . . but all of
them are united in revealing the *direction* of the liberation.'

In some ways the most interesting stretch of the route is
the journey through Germany. Were this a nationalist monument, like so many of the other memorials I have described
so far, Germany might be portrayed as the monster, and
Germans as the enemy. But this is a transnational monument
that passes through Germany for over 600 kilometres (372
miles) and includes Germany in its narrative of liberation. In
other words, Germany had to be liberated from Nazism along
with every other country involved in the war.

The purpose of this monument is to portray the liberation

as the key moment of the twentieth century. This was the one event that finally brought an end to the terror and violence, and signified the rebirth of the whole of western Europe, including Germany, into a new era of peace and prosperity.

Like all the monuments in this book, the Liberation Route Europe says as much about the world we live in today as it does about history. There is a political message – or, at least, a political point of view – behind the walking trail that stands beside its historical message.

I first came across Liberation Route Europe as an organisation in 2014, when they asked me to make a speech at an event they had organised at the European Parliament in Brussels. They were launching a new Europe-wide exhibition, whose purpose was to describe the liberation not from any one national point of view, but from a multinational perspective. One of the other people who gave a speech at the launch was Martin Schultz, who was then president of the European Parliament. Schultz was, and still is, one of the most active supporters of Liberation Route Europe.

Since 2014, the organisation has grown and flourished. It has forged links with scores of museums, memorials and tourist sites all over the continent, and has turned itself into a kind of umbrella group, helping those museums and memorials to communicate and interact with one another. The hiking trail is a culmination of that work: it is a physical path that links all the various institutions and sites of memory together. The trail from London to Berlin is just the first stage in a project that is likely to take many more years, and which one day will involve many other walking trails from northern, eastern and central Europe, likewise culminating in Berlin.

It is no coincidence that the European Parliament should want to endorse such an organisation, or that the former president of that Parliament should be one of its greatest champions. In April 2019 the European Council also formally endorsed the Liberation Route Europe by certifying it as an official European Cultural Route. The trail espouses many of the fundamental values that these institutions regard as sacred. It is a physical link between different countries in Europe. And it tells a narrative of freedom, of the triumph of democracy and, above all, of the importance of unity. It is the European Union in microcosm.

The EU has always mythologised the Second World War as the fire in which it was forged. The founding fathers of the EU were people with first-hand experience of the misery and chaos created by the war, and who saw the creation of what Churchill called 'a kind of United States of Europe' as the only long-term remedy. This is also the spirit that infuses the Liberation Route. The history that it commemorates is very much one of international cooperation. It speaks of a time when the western Allies arrived on the beaches of Normandy not to liberate individual countries, but the continent as a whole. The liberation, it reminds us, was not carried out by a single national force, but by an alliance of Americans, Brits, Canadians, Poles, Czechs, the forces of the Free French, and a dozen other nationalities. It was the very model of international cooperation.

According to Daniel Libeskind, this is the true message behind the Liberation Route. 'The aftermath of the liberation created a new sense of Europe, and a new sense of what it meant to *be* in Europe . . . The unity of an outlook of human beings towards peace and towards the past – and also looking hopefully towards the future – brought a new notion of what freedom means. That, at the core, is what this route means. It's not just looking backward at what happened, but at what was the gift that Europe received as a result of this conflict.'

One of the purposes of any monument is not simply to commemorate the events of the past, but to transform them into myth. In my conversations with Rémi Praud and Daniel Libeskind they both referred to the route as a 'pilgrimage'; Libeskind even compared his vectors to the kind of primeval route markers that Odysseus might have encountered on the road during ancient times. The Liberation Route is an attempt to create a mythological space somewhere between history and memory, where people walking the trail can begin to feel part of something much greater than their immediate environment. One does not need to walk the entire trail in order to feel an emotional connection to the vast undertaking that ended up in the liberation of Europe.

This is a message of hope and redemption that is difficult to resist: it is the happy ending to the war that makes all the suffering and heroism worthwhile. The only problem with this kind of mythology is that it must compete with other mythologies created by national or local groups, who are more interested in commemorating the things that make them unique than those that they have in common. A community that was once involved in a local triumph over the Nazis may not wish to share that glory with the wider Allied world. A community that has suffered may not wish to put aside its martyrdom for the sake of a greater story of redemption and rebirth.

The inauguration of the Liberation Route in 2020 coincides with a period of unprecedented tension between these two competing visions of the past. The success of this monumental hiking trail, much like that of the European Union itself, will depend on its ability to navigate the stormy waters that lie between the internationalist values that have sustained the continent ever since 1945, and the nationalist narratives that were also a part of the war, and which are still an important part of our heritage today.

The reason why I am optimistic about the future of this particular monument is that its sheer scale gives it the chance to pay homage to both visions of history at once. Indeed, it is big enough to incorporate all the ideas I have explored in this book. The trail passes through sites of heroism as well as sites of martyrdom and unforgivable atrocity. It encompasses stories of local triumph and national glory within its overall narrative of continental liberation. More than any other monument in this book, it has the potential for nuance and variety.

But, most of all, it has chained itself to a solid foundation of historical fact. Its long odyssey through a year of conflict and 2,000 kilometres of territory – mythological though it is – is anchored at every point along its route to the historic events that took place in each location.

The creators of the Liberation Route have realised that, if it is to survive in the long term, they had no other choice but to create it in this way. The old monuments, carved in metal and stone, are often torn down because they lose their relevance to later generations. History changes, and if monuments do not keep pace with that change they sometimes have to go.

Perhaps the best way to avoid future waves of iconoclasm is to embrace nuance, and cling as closely as possible to historical facts. Because monuments, just like peoples, will always be prisoners of history.

Conclusion

We live in an era when people question the symbols of the past with increasing frequency. Monuments representing ideas that are no longer palatable to us, or which seem too outdated or outlandish for modern sensibilities, are often taken down. I have watched the removal of some of these monuments in recent years – in the USA, in South Africa and in eastern Europe – and I must confess that, while I understand the intense emotions that the monuments can sometimes spark, and indeed share some of those emotions myself, I can't help mourning their loss when they're gone. Our monuments are valuable historical documents: they speak eloquently about the values of our ancestors, both good and bad. They are curiosities with the power to inspire and provoke all kinds of debate. They are often also great works of art, of astonishing craftsmanship and imagination. To tear all this down for the sake of contemporary politics seems like a great shame.

Monuments can indeed exert an oppressive power over our public spaces; but I hope I have shown that there are other ways to deal with the problem without tearing them down altogether. We can create counter-monuments, as the people of Budapest have done in protest at their government-sponsored symbols of Hungarian victimhood. We can build new monuments around the offending one, as they have in Amsterdam, where the National Monument now represents just one layer in a rich and nuanced memorial landscape. If worst comes to worst, we can move objectionable monuments to museums and sculpture parks, so that future generations can at least come to marvel at their artistic merit, even while they disagree with their politics. Should we really come to loathe our monuments, then we can always recast them as objects of ridicule. Nothing undermines the gravitas of a statue so well as putting it in an enclosure with a herd of llamas.

Tearing monuments down does not solve our history; it simply drives that history underground. While a monument still stands, it will always need to be confronted, discussed. In this way, our monuments hold us to account. They are objects that make sure we never forget our debt to history – or our enslavement to it.

So far, most of the monuments we have raised to the memory of the Second World War seem to have resisted this wave of iconoclasm. Unlike certain monuments to other eras, our Second World War memorials are still largely revered. This is in part because the war is still relatively recent – it's difficult to justify tearing down a monument when some of the people honoured by it are still alive.

On the whole, however, our war memorials have survived because they continue to say something important about who we are – or, at least, who we would like to believe ourselves to be. They speak to our present-day longings as much as to our memory of the past. They answer a need that is not being met by the contemporary world.

I have described five different categories of war monuments in this book, and each of them remains important to us in different ways. Our heroes offer up a vision of loyalty, bravery or moral fortitude that seems to be in short supply in our day-to-day lives: this is how we wish we could be. Our martyrs offer us something equally valuable: they remind us of the past sacrifices and traumas that have both scarred us and made us who we are. Our monsters remind us of everything we most reject in society, and that we were once willing to defend ourselves against, to the death. Our visions of Armageddon remind us of the vast destruction we once suffered; and our visions of rebirth celebrate our efforts to re-establish order after the chaos of the war.

None of these categories exists in isolation. Another major reason why our war monuments have proven more robust than those of other eras is that these five categories of memory not only support one another, but amplify one another. The idea of Armageddon provides the perfect backdrop for our folk memories of the war as a titanic struggle for the soul of mankind. Our heroes are made more heroic by the image of absolute evil against which they were fighting; and our monsters are made more monstrous by the innocence of the martyrs that they tortured. Tying all these images together is the final idea: our belief in a new world, born from the ashes of the old. This is the prize given to our heroes and martyrs. It's what ennobles their sacrifices and makes the suffering seem worthwhile. Without the resurrection, what was the point of all the heroism?

These five ideas form the mythological framework that underpins our collective memory of the Second World War. At a local level they allow us to mourn past traumas without becoming overwhelmed by them, because the forces that once victimised us were at least defeated and replaced with some-thing new. At a national level they allow us to take pride in our communal values, which led us, eventually, to victory. And at an international level they have given us faith in our new, international institutions, and inspired hope for a future free from the scourge of war. These ideas form the bedrock upon which our international system is built.

But just because this mythological framework has been so robust until now, that does not mean that it will remain so in the future. The cracks are already beginning to show. In eastern Europe, monuments to the heroes of the war have already started to come down: it is easy to dismiss the heroism of the USSR when its soldiers came not only as liberators, but as conquerors. Attitudes to the other great Allies of 1945 are also beginning to change. The British and the Americans no longer command the gratitude or respect that they once did: other nations now prefer to raise monuments to their own home-grown heroes. The day might come when memorials to American heroes – men like Douglas MacArthur, who had great flaws as well as great qualities – are also forced to come down.

All kinds of political changes also threaten our monuments to the heroes of the Second World War. Some of these monuments were raised by people holding a particular political point of view. The Bomber Command Memorial in London, for example, was raised with overwhelming support from the political right; while the Shrine to the Fallen in Bologna was erected by those on the left. If the political atmosphere were to change substantially in either place, such monuments might one day be seen as a problem. Furthermore, since monuments like the Bomber Command Memorial were raised without adequately addressing the controversies of the past, there is every possibility that they will one day fall foul of those controversies again.

As with our heroes, so too with our martyrs and our monsters. I have written at length about how our monuments to people regarded as monsters have almost all been taken down. This has created a vacuum in our public memory which has been filled with something much more nebulous and difficult to destroy. Nevertheless, our inclination to erase any monument to fascism and Stalinism persists. We might never be able to destroy the spirit behind such monuments, but we can at least try to prevent that spirit from ever finding a physical home.

At first glance, monuments to our Second World War martyrs seem much more robust: what government or institution would ever dare take down a memorial to national suffering? But even these monuments are not immune to the pressures of an ever-changing world. The ruins of Oradour-sur-Glane cannot be preserved forever exactly as they were in 1945 – at some point they will either crumble, or will have to be reinforced, or even rebuilt. The Katyn Memorial in Jersey City was saved from relocation in 2018, but who is to say that the commercial pressures that threatened it might not one day become irresistible?

Much like our monuments to heroes, our monuments to martyrs can be vulnerable to political considerations. For example, the 'comfort woman' statue in Seoul was raised partly as a symbol of anti-Japanese sentiment; as such, the Japanese have been calling for its removal ever since. Should their diplomatic efforts prove fruitful, or should a new era of friendship ever break out between the two nations, it is conceivable that the statue might one day have to come down. In Budapest, where Hungary's status as a victim of the Germans is hotly contested, there has always been a strong and vocal opposition to its monument to national martyrdom.

Perhaps most vulnerable of all are our monuments to the rebirth in 1945. Here, the greatest threat is disillusionment. The brave new world that seemed within reach after the Second World War never quite materialised in the way that people all around the world hoped it would. Whatever happened to the haven of safety and security for Jews promised by Yad Vashem? What happened to the vision of world peace and harmony promised by Per Krohg's mural in the UN Security Council chamber; or to the vision of reconciliation promised by Coventry Cathedral's 'Cross of Nails'? Why should we commemorate a rebirth that never really happened? Most of these monuments are fairly inoffensive and seem unlikely to be torn down; but even if they remain, there is no guarantee that people will continue to come and see them.

Once again, changes in the political atmosphere can also pose a threat to such monuments, even those that might seem relatively innocuous. Some of them were raised by international institutions, such as the United Nations or the European Union, and this might also prove to be their undoing. Nationalists have always been suspicious of such institutions. In Europe, especially, nationalist politicians have come to regard the EU as a threat to their own sovereignty. It is for this reason that the continent's first transnational war monument, the Liberation Route Europe, tries to avoid any overt connection to the one institution that most supports and endorses it. Instead, it is at pains to incorporate nationalist stories into its wider message of cooperation and unity. Any monument that fails to do likewise will always be vulnerable to nationalist sentiment.

* * *

Despite these threats, however, our Second World War memorials continue to multiply. Almost a third of the monuments described in this book were created after the year 2000, and more are inaugurated every year. Our fascination with the war seems to be growing, not diminishing.

As I write, several new memorials are being planned in Britain alone. A major new Holocaust memorial and museum is scheduled to open in central London in 2021, right next to the Houses of Parliament. There are also campaigns to raise monuments in Liverpool (to the seamen who died during the war in the Atlantic), in Staffordshire (to Caribbean military personnel who fought in the war), and again in London (to the Sikhs who fought for Britain during the war). Other monuments are also being raised in other countries. For example, a major Holocaust memorial is due to be built in Croatia's capital, Zagreb; and in Germany a campaign is under way for a new memorial to the Polish victims of the war in Berlin.

If history is the basis of our identity, then *this* history seems to define us more than any other. The Second World War is the screen upon which we like to project all our national sentiments. Our monuments are the images on that screen.

What will become of these monuments in future years is anyone's guess. We build them out of granite and bronze because we hope that they will last for ever. But in reality it is only the monuments that have the capacity to change with the times that will survive, because history, and memory, have a habit of developing in the most unpredictable ways.

Bibliography

Most of the information in this book was gleaned from visits to the monuments themselves and the museums and information centres associated with them.

For the present day controversies surrounding these monuments, I consulted a wide variety of newspapers and websites too numerous to list here. For example, the 2018 protests about the Katyn memorial in Jersey City made headlines in various national American and Polish newspapers, was covered in more detail by the Jersey Journal and its website www.nj.com, and with great passion and humour on the local community website, http://jclist.com. Likewise, the saga of the 'Four Sleepers' monument in Warsaw was described by newspapers in both Poland and Russia, particularly in Warsaw's *Gazeta Wyborcza*. The controversies over Budapest's Monument to the Victims of German Occupation were covered extensively in the international press, but the development of its counter-monument, the 'Living Memorial', can be traced in real time on its Facebook page, https://facebook.com/groups/elevenemlekmu.

The bibliography below, therefore, lists only works with substantial material on the monuments in this book, or which readers might find useful for further general reading.

Journal articles and dissertations

Chin, Sharon; Franke, Fabian & Halpern, Sheri, 'A Self-Serving Admission of Guilt: An Examination of the Intentions and Effects of Germany's Memorial to the Murdered Jews of Europe', available online: https://www.humanityinaction. org/knowledgebase/225-a-self-serving-admission-of-guilt-an-examination-of-the-intentions-and-effects-of-germany-s-memorial-to-the-murdered-jews-of-europe

Clark, Benjamin, 'Memory in Ruins: Remembering War in the Ruins of Coventry Cathedral' M.A. dissertation (21 September 2015), Bartlett School of Architecture, University College London

Ellick, Adam B., 'A Home for the Vilified', *World Sculpture News* (Autumn 2001), pp.24-9

Glambek, Ingeborg, 'The Council Chambers in the UN Building in New York', *Scandinavian Journal of Design History*, vol. 15 (2005), pp.8–39

Kumagai, Naoko, 'The Background to the Japan–Republic of Korea Agreement: Compromises Concerning the Understanding of the Comfort Women Issue' in *Asia–Pacific Review*, vol.23, No.1 (2016), pp.65–99

Kim, Mikyoung, 'Memorializing Comfort Women: Memory and Human Rights in Korea–Japan Relations', in *Asian Politics and Policy*, Vol.6, No.1 (2014)

Okuda, Hiroko 'Remembering the atomic bombing of Hiroshima and Nagasaki: Collective memory of post-war Japan', *Acta Orientalia Vilnensia* Vol.12, No.1 (2011), pp.11–28

Petillo, Carol M., 'Douglas MacArthur and Manuel Quezon: A Note on an Imperial Bond', *Pacific Historical Review*, Vol. 48 No. 1, Feb., 1979

van Cant, Katrin, 'Historical Memory in Post-Communist Poland: Warsaw's Monuments after 1989', available on the University of Pittsburgh's Dept. of Slavic Languages website: https://www.pitt.edu/~slavic/sisc/SISC8/docs/vancant.pdf

Varga, Aniko, 'National Bodies: The "Comfort Women" Discourse and Its controversies in South Korea' in *Studies in Ethnicity and Nationalism* Vol.9 No.2 (2009)

Yoshinobu, Higurashi, 'Yasukuni and the Enshrinement of War Criminals', 11 August 2013; English translation 25 November 2013 available online: https://www.nippon.com/en/in-depth/a02404/

Yad Vashem quarterly, especially issues 31 (Fall 2003) and 37 (Spring 2005)

Useful Websites

https://www.4en5mei.nl

http://auschwitz.org/en

https://www.medprostor.si/en/projects/project-victims-of-all-wars-memorial

https://www.topographie.de

https://www.oradour.info

www.stiftung-denkmal.de

https://www.gedenkstaetten-in-hamburg.de

www.yadvashem.org

https://liberationroute.com

https://www.bibliotecasalaborsa.it

https://www.storiaememoriadibologna.it

http://parridigit.istitutoparri.eu

http://www.museodellaresistenzadibologna.it

http://www.straginazifasciste.it
http://www.comune.bologna.it
www.nj.com
https://facebook.com/groups/elevenemlekmu

General books on collective memory

Bevernage, Berber & Wouters, Nico (eds.), *Palgrave Handbook of State Sponsored History After 1945* (Palgrave Macmillan, 2018)

Halbwachs, Maurice, *On Collective Memory* (University of Chicago Press, 1992)

Mrozik, Agnieszka & Holubek, Stanislav (eds.), *Historical Memory of Central and East European Communism* (Routledge, 2018)

Nora, Pierre (ed.), *Realms of Memory: Rethinking the French Past* (Columbia University Press, 1996)

Winter, Jay, *War Beyond Words: Languages of Remembrance from the Great War to the Present* (Cambridge University Press, 2017)

Yang, Daqing & Mochizuki, Mike (eds), *Memory, Identity, and Commemorations of World War II: Anniversary Politics in Asia Pacific* (Lexington Books, 2018)

Books on aspects of the Second World War

Beevor, Antony, *The Second Word War* (Weidenfeld & Nicolson, 2012)

Buruma, Ian, *Wages of Guilt* (Farrar, Straus & Giroux, 1994)

Constantino, Renato & Constantino, Letizia R., *The Philippines: The Continuing Past* (Foundation for Nationalist Studies, 1978)

Dower, John W., *War Without Mercy: Race and Power in the Pacific War* (Pantheon, 1986)

—*Embracing Defeat: Japan in the Wake of World War II* (WW Norton, 2000)

Duggan, Christopher, *Fascist Voices: An Intimate History of Mussolini's Italy* (Bodley Head, 2012)

Farmer, Sarah, *Martyred Village* (University of California Press, 2000)

Friedländer, Saul, *The Years of Extermination: Nazi Germany and the Jews 1939–1945* (Weidenfeld & Nicolson, 2007)

Ham, Paul, *Hiroshima Nagasaki* (Doubleday, 2011)

Hastings, Max, *All Hell Let Loose* (HarperCollins, 2011)

Hibbert, Christopher, *Mussolini: The Rise and Fall of Il Duce* (Palgrave Macmillan, 2008)

Hondius, Dienke, *Return: Holocaust Survivors and Dutch Anti-Semitism* (Praeger, 2003)

Inman, Nick & Staines, Joe, *Travel the Liberation Route Europe* (Rough Guides, 2019)

Jager, Sheila Miyoshi, *Brothers at War: The Unending Conflict in Korea* (WW Norton, 2013)

Kennedy, Paul, *The Parliament of Man* (Allen Lane, 2006)

Kershaw, Ian, *Hitler 1936–1945: Nemesis* (Allen Lane, 2000)

Landstra, Menno & Spruijt, Desmond, *Het Nationaal Monument op de Dam* (Landstra & Spruijt, 1998)

Lowe, Keith, *Inferno: The Devastation of Hamburg, 1943* (Viking, 2006)

—*Savage Continent: Europe in the Aftermath of World War II* (Viking, 2012)

—*The Fear and the Freedom* (Viking, 2017)

MacArthur, Douglas, *A Soldier Speaks* (Praeger, 1965)

Manchester, William, *American Caesar: Douglas MacArthur 1880–1964* (Hutchinson, 1979)

Mazower, Mark, *The Balkans* (Weidenfeld & Nicolson, 2000)

McCallus, Joseph P., *The MacArthur Highway and Other Relics of American Empire in the Philippines* (Potomac Books, 2010)

Milza, Pierre, *Gli Ultimi Giorni di Mussolini* (Longanesi, 2011)

Morgan, Philip, *The Fall of Mussolini* (Oxford University Press, 2007)

Moseley, Ray, *Mussolini: The Last 600 Days* (Taylor Trade, 2004)

Pavlowitch, Stefan K., *Hitler's New Disorder: The Second World War in Yugoslavia* (Hurst & Co, 2008)

Reep, Edward, *A Combat Artist in World War II* (University Press of Kentucky, 1987)

Roberts, Andrew, *The Storm of War* (Allen Lane, 2009)

Taylor, Frederick, *Coventry* (Bloomsbury, 2015)

Tomasevich, Jozo, *War and Revolution in Yugoslavia* (Stanford University Press, 2001)

Vinogradov, V. K.; Pogonyi, J.F.; & Teptzov, N.V., Hitler's Death: Russia's Last Great Secret from the Files of the KGB (Chaucer Press, 2005)

Yoshiaki, Yoshimi, *Comfort Women* (Columbia University Press, 2002)

Xianwen, Zhang & Jianjun, Zhang (eds.), *Human Memory: Solid Evidence of the Nanjing Massacre* (Nanjing, 2017)

Acknowledgements

This book would not have been possible without the help and support of all the institutions mentioned in the text, whose dedicated and knowledgeable staff were uniformly helpful. A few people, however, went out of their way to help me and deserve my deepest gratitude: they include Enrico Cavalieri; Luca Pastore of Istituto Parri; Otelo Sangiorgi of Museo Risorgimento; Máthé Áron of the Committee of National Remembrance in Budapest; Rémi Praud of Liberation Route Europe; and architect Daniel Libeskind.

The hospitality I received on my various trips to China and Japan was truly incredible. I owe special thanks to my friend and translator, Hans Lu and my Chinese publisher, Dong Fengyun; and also to Zou Dehuai, Liu Xiaoping, Wang Hao and Tang Kai who showed me round Nanjing with seemingly endless patience. I am also extremely grateful to Xue Gang, deputy curator of the Private Museum of the Anti-Japanese War in Nanjing; and Zhang Jianjun, curator of the Nanjing Massacre Memorial Hall. Jarl and Tomoko Smidt-Olsen were extremely generous in putting me up during my travels; and my Japanese agents Atsushi Hori and Tsutomu Yawata also entertained me generously in Tokyo.

As always, I owe thanks to my brilliant agent of twenty years, Simon Trewin; my American agent Jay Mandel; and to my principal editors, Arabella Pike and Michael Flamini, who helped shape the book. I would also like to thank my copy-editor, Steve Gove, as well as Katy Archer, Jo Thompson and all at HarperCollins who contributed to making this book come to fruition.

But the greatest thanks must go to my wife, Liza, who is also my greatest friend and fiercest critic, and who had to put up with long absences while I travelled abroad in the name of research. Without her this book, and much else, would have fallen apart long ago.

Picture Acknowledgements

The majority of photographs in this book are from the author's personal collection. The remainder are reproduced from the following sources, with thanks:

Monument to Brotherhood in Arms, p.14 – Cezary Piwowarski/ Wikimedia Commons CC BY-SA 4.0

Marine Corps Memorial, p.24 – Idawriter/Wikimedia Commons CC BY-SA 3.0

Douglas MacArthur Landing Memorial, p.34 – Jelpads/ Wikimedia Commons CC BY-SA 4.0

'I have returned' – Gaetano Faillace/US Army Signal Corps (NARA ID 531424)

The original shrine, 1945, p.37 – Edo Ansaloni/Museo Memoriale della Libertà

National Monument in 1958, p.83 – Harry Pot/Anefo/ Nationaal Archief, Amsterdam

Peace Statue, South Korea, p.104 – Yun-Ho Lee/Wikimedia Commons CC0 1.0

Katyn Memorial, Jersey City, p.116 – Colin Knowles/ Wikimedia Commons CC BY-SA 2.0

METROPOLITAN CLUB
washington, d.c.